Make sure that this is the right book for your Excel version

This book is designed only for use with **Excel 2021 for Windows.**

In: Lesson 1-3: Check that your Excel version is up to date, you'll learn more about identifying your Excel version.

Why you should use this book to learn Excel 2021

- **Learning success is guaranteed.** For over twenty years, Smart Method® classroom courses have been used by large corporations, government departments and the armed forces to train their employees. This book has been constantly refined by observing which skills students find difficult to understand and then developing simpler ways of explaining them. This has made the book effective for students of all ages and abilities. We have never had a student who has failed to learn Excel after taking one of our courses.
- **It is the book of choice for teachers.** As well as catering for those wishing to learn Excel by self-study, Smart Method® books have long been the preferred choice for Excel teachers as they are designed to teach Excel and not as reference books. Books follow best-practice adult teaching methodology with clearly defined objectives for each learning session and an exercise to confirm skills transfer. With single, self-contained lessons, the books cater for any teaching or self-learning period (from minutes to hours).
- **Smart Method® books are #1 best sellers.** Every paper printed Smart Method® Excel book (and there have been 34 of them starting with Excel 2007) has been an Amazon #1 best seller in its category. This provides you with the confidence that you are using a best-of-breed resource to learn Excel.
- **No previous exposure to Excel is assumed.** You will repeatedly hear the same criticism of most Excel books: "you have to already know Excel to understand the book". This book is different. If you've never seen Excel before, and your only computer skill is using a web browser, you'll have absolutely no problems working through the lessons. No previous exposure to Excel is assumed and everything is explained clearly and in a simple way that absolutely any student, of any age or ability, can easily understand.
- **It focuses upon the everyday Excel skills used in the workplace.** This *Essential Skills* book will equip you with excellent Excel 2021 skills, good enough to impress any employer, but it doesn't confuse by attempting to teach skills that are not common in the workplace. Only users who have advanced requirements need progress to the *Expert Skills* book.
- **This book was written using the final release version of Excel 2021.** Many other books are written using pre-release beta versions of Excel 2021. Work on this book didn't begin until the final Oct 2021 release of Excel 2021. This means that even features added at the last minute are covered and the screen grabs should perfectly match what you see on your screen.

Learn Excel in just a few minutes each day (or in as little as one full day)

Excel is a huge and daunting application and you'll need to invest some time in learning the skills presented in this book. This will be time well spent as you'll have a hugely marketable skill for life. With 1.2 billion Excel users, it is hard to imagine any non-manual occupation today that doesn't require Excel skills.

This book makes it easy to learn at your own pace because of its unique presentational style. The book contains short self-contained lessons and each lesson only takes a few minutes to complete.

You can complete as many, or as few, lessons as you have the time and energy for each day. Many learners have developed Excel skills by setting aside just a few minutes each day to complete a single lesson. Others have worked through the entire book in a single day.

Every lesson is presented on two facing pages

> Pray this day, on one side of one sheet of paper, explain how the Royal Navy is prepared to meet the coming conflict.
> ***Winston Churchill, Letter to the Admiralty, Sep 1, 1939***

Winston Churchill was aware of the power of brevity. The discipline of condensing thoughts into one side of a single sheet of A4 paper resulted in the efficient transfer of information.

A tenet of our teaching system is that every lesson is presented on *two* facing sheets of A4. We've had to double Churchill's rule as they didn't have to contend with screen grabs in 1939! If we can't teach an essential concept in two pages of A4 we know that the subject matter needs to be broken into two smaller lessons.

How this book avoids wasting your time.

Over the years I have read many hundreds of computer text books and most of my time was wasted. The big problem with most books is that I must wade through thousands of words just to learn one important technique. If I don't read everything, I might miss that one essential insight.

Many presentational methods have been used in this book to help you to avoid reading about things you already know how to do, or things that are of little interest to you.

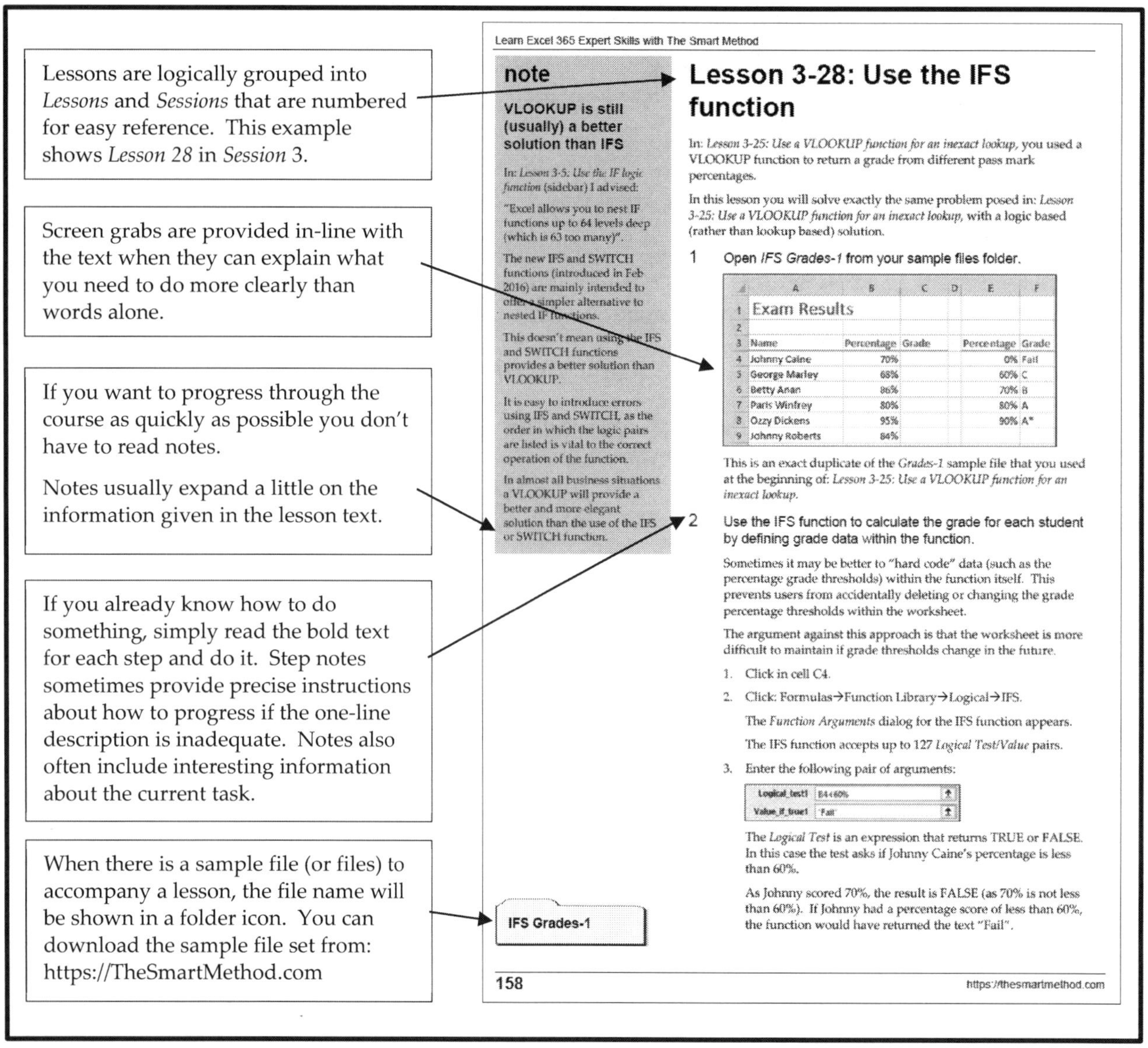

Learning by participation

> Tell me, and I will forget. Show me, and I may remember. Involve me, and I will understand.
>
> ***Confucius, Chinese teacher, editor, politician and philosopher (551-479 BC)***

Confucius would probably have agreed that the best way to teach IT skills is hands-on (actively) and not hands-off (passively). This is another of the principal tenets of The Smart Method® teaching method.

Research has backed up the assertion that you will learn more material, learn more quickly, and understand more of what you learn if you learn using active, rather than passive methods.

For this reason, pure theory pages are kept to an absolute minimum with most theory woven into the hands-on lessons, either within the text or in sidebars.

This echoes the teaching method used in Smart Method classroom courses where snippets of pertinent theory are woven into the lessons themselves so that interest and attention is maintained by hands-on involvement, but all necessary theory is still covered.

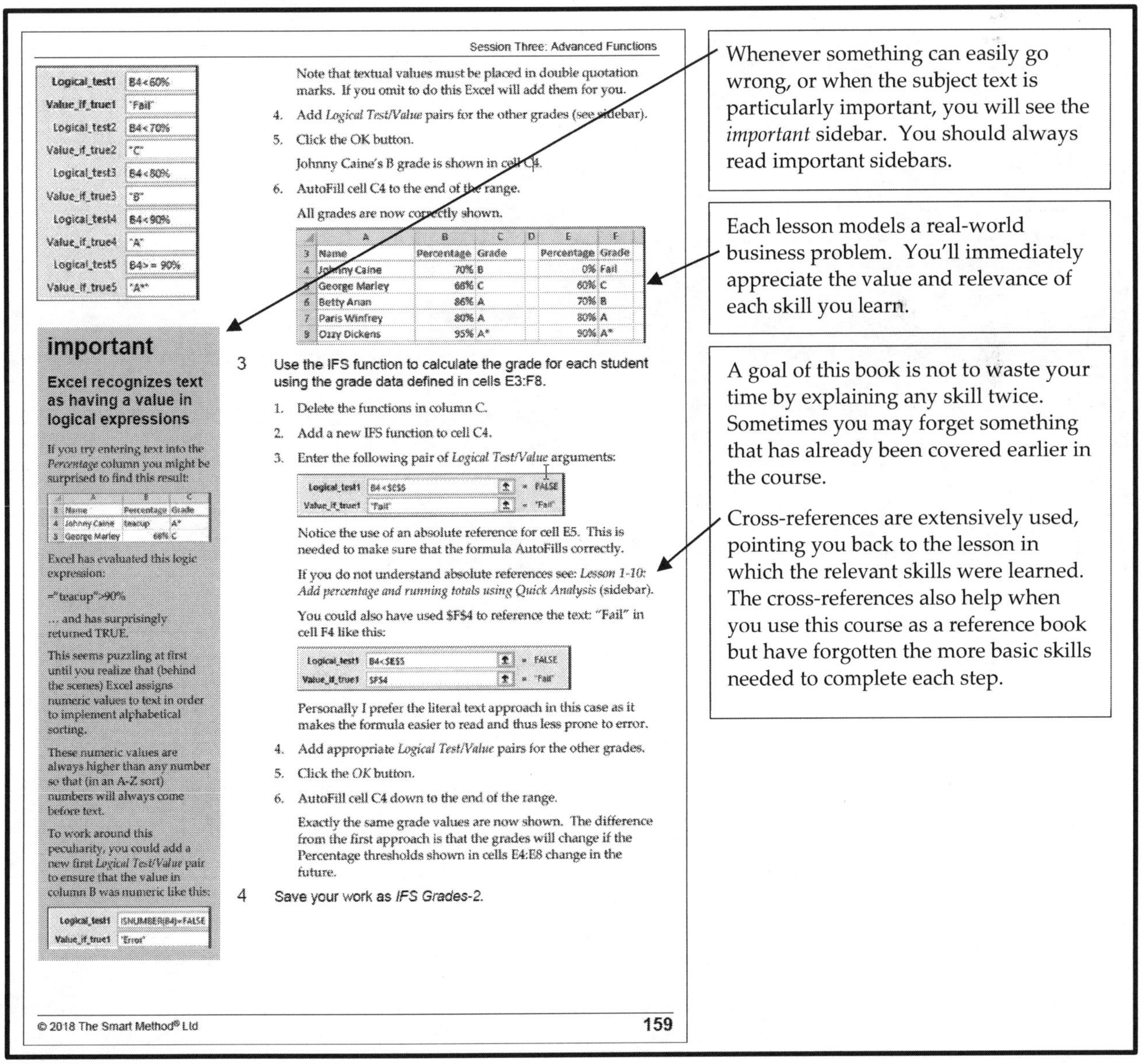

Session Three: Advanced Functions

Logical_test1	B4<60%
Value_if_true1	"Fail"
Logical_test2	B4<70%
Value_if_true2	"C"
Logical_test3	B4<80%
Value_if_true3	"B"
Logical_test4	B4<90%
Value_if_true4	"A"
Logical_test5	B4>=90%
Value_if_true5	"A*"

important

Excel recognizes text as having a value in logical expressions

If you try entering text into the *Percentage* column you might be surprised to find this result:

	A	B	C
3	Name	Percentage	Grade
4	Johnny Caine	teacup	A*
5	George Marley	68%	C

Excel has evaluated this logic expression:

="teacup">90%

... and has surprisingly returned TRUE.

This seems puzzling at first until you realize that (behind the scenes) Excel assigns numeric values to text in order to implement alphabetical sorting.

These numeric values are always higher than any number so that (in an A-Z sort) numbers will always come before text.

To work around this peculiarity, you could add a new first *Logical Test/Value* pair to ensure that the value in column B was numeric like this:

Logical_test1	ISNUMBER(B4)=FALSE
Value_if_true1	"Error"

Note that textual values must be placed in double quotation marks. If you omit to do this Excel will add them for you.

4. Add *Logical Test/Value* pairs for the other grades (see sidebar).
5. Click the OK button.

   Johnny Caine's B grade is shown in cell C4.
6. AutoFill cell C4 to the end of the range.

   All grades are now correctly shown.

	A	B	C	D	E	F
3	Name	Percentage	Grade		Percentage	Grade
4	Johnny Caine	70%	B		0%	Fail
5	George Marley	66%	C		60%	C
6	Betty Anan	86%	A		70%	B
7	Paris Winfrey	80%	A		80%	A
8	Ozzy Dickens	95%	A*		90%	A*

3 Use the IFS function to calculate the grade for each student using the grade data defined in cells E3:F8.

1. Delete the functions in column C.
2. Add a new IFS function to cell C4.
3. Enter the following pair of *Logical Test/Value* arguments:

Logical_test1	B4<$E$5	= FALSE
Value_if_true1	"Fail"	= "Fail"

Notice the use of an absolute reference for cell E5. This is needed to make sure that the formula AutoFills correctly.

If you do not understand absolute references see: *Lesson 1-10: Add percentage and running totals using Quick Analysis* (sidebar).

You could also have used $F$4 to reference the text: "Fail" in cell F4 like this:

Logical_test1	B4<$E$5	= FALSE
Value_if_true1	$F$4	= "Fail"

Personally I prefer the literal text approach in this case as it makes the formula easier to read and thus less prone to error.

4. Add appropriate *Logical Test/Value* pairs for the other grades.
5. Click the *OK* button.
6. AutoFill cell C4 down to the end of the range.

   Exactly the same grade values are now shown. The difference from the first approach is that the grades will change if the Percentage thresholds shown in cells E4:E8 change in the future.

4 Save your work as *IFS Grades-2*.

© 2018 The Smart Method® Ltd 159

Hardly anybody understands how to use <u>every</u> Excel feature

It is important to realize that Excel is probably the largest and most complex software application ever created. Hardly anybody understands how to use *every* Excel feature and for almost all business users, large parts of Excel's functionality wouldn't even be useful.

Many learners make the fundamental error of trying to learn from an Excel reference book that attempts to document (though not teach) *everything* that Excel can do. Of course, no single book could ever actually do this. (There are some advanced Excel features that easily justify an entire book of their own).

By the end of this *Essential Skills* book, you will have excellent Excel skills, good enough to impress any employer, and your Excel skills will be better than most office workers (even those with many years of experience). You'll be able to create beautifully laid-out worksheets. You'll also have mastered many advanced features that few Excel users understand such as absolute and relative cell references, visualizations, advanced charts, conditional formatting, date serial numbers, themes and cloud computing.

We also have a follow-on book that can advance your skills to expert-level

The *Expert Skills* book teaches Excel to an extremely high level of competence that is very rarely found in the workplace (even amongst top professionals).

At *Expert* level your skills will be greater and broader than almost all other Excel users and you will understand (and be able to use) absolutely every Excel feature. You'll have a complete mastery of skills that are often even a mystery to Excel power users.

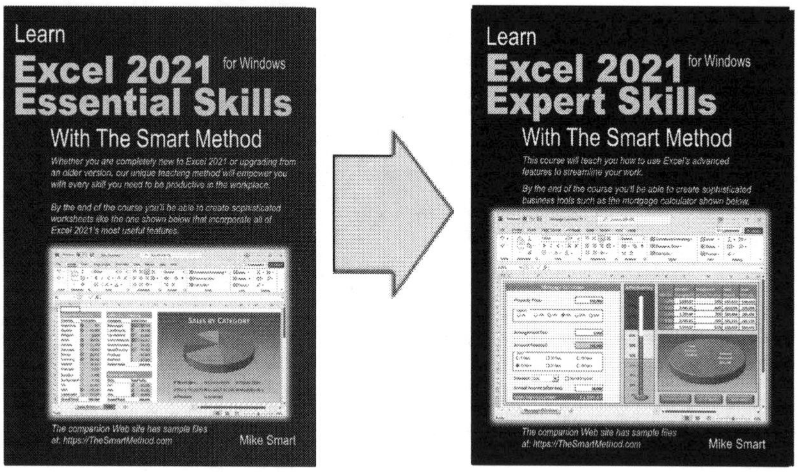

The full course outline for the *Expert Skills* book can be viewed on the <u>https://thesmartmethod.com</u> web site.

Learn Excel 2021 Essential Skills with The Smart Method

First Edition

Mike Smart

Learn Excel 2021 Essential Skills with The Smart Method®
First Edition

Published by:

Smart Method Enterprises Ltd
Kemp House
160 City Road
London
EC1V 2NX

The Smart Method® is a trading style of Smart Method Enterprises Ltd.

Tel: +44 (0)845 458 3282

E-mail: Use the contact page at https://thesmartmethod.com/contact
Web: https://thesmartmethod.com

International Standard Book Number (ISBN13): 978-1-909253-51-3

2 4 6 8 10 9 7 5 3 1

Contents

Session Five: Charts and Graphics 229

Session Six: Working with Multiple Worksheets and Workbooks 291

Introduction

Welcome to *Learn Excel 2021 Essential Skills with The Smart Method®*. This book has been designed to enable students to master Excel 2021 by self-study. The book is equally useful as courseware in order to deliver courses using The Smart Method® teaching system.

Smart Method publications are continually evolving as we discover better ways of explaining or teaching the concepts presented.

Feedback

At The Smart Method® we love feedback – both positive and negative. If you have any suggestions for improvements to future versions of this book, or if you find content or typographical errors, the author would always love to hear from you. You can make suggestions for improvements to this book using the online form at:

https://thesmartmethod.com/contact

Future editions of this book will always incorporate your feedback so that there are never any known errors at time of publication.

If you have any difficulty understanding or completing a lesson, or if you feel that anything could have been more clearly explained, we'd also love to hear from you. We've made hundreds of detail improvements to our books based upon reader's feedback and continue to chase the impossible goal of 100% perfection.

Downloading the sample files

In order to use this book, it is sometimes necessary to download free sample files from the Internet.

The process of downloading the free sample files will be explained later, in: *Lesson 1-8: Download the sample files.*

Problem resolution

If you encounter any problem using any aspect of the course, you can contact us using the online form at:

https://thesmartmethod.com/contact

We'll do everything possible to quickly resolve the problem.

Excel version and Region format settings used to write this book

This edition was written using the original release version of *Excel 2021* (version *2111),* released on Oct 5, 2021 running under the *Windows 11 operating system version 21H2.* You'll discover which version your computer is running later, in: *Lesson 1-3: Check that your Excel version is up to date.*

This book was written using English (United States) *Region format* settings. The English - US Region format uses the decimal separator for a period and a comma for the thousand's separator, producing formatted numbers such as 12,345.67. Dates are formatted as Month/Day/Year. If you are situated in a different region, it is possible to change your region format (in Windows settings) but there is no need to do so. Just be aware that some of the screen grabs in this book may be formatted differently to what you see on your screen.

Typographical Conventions Used in This Book

This guide consistently uses typographical conventions to differentiate parts of the text.

When you see this	Here's what it means
Click *Line Color* on the left-hand bar and then click *No line.*	Italics are used to refer to text that appears in a worksheet cell, an Excel dialog, on the Ribbon, or elsewhere within the Excel application. Italics may sometimes also be used for emphasis or distinction.
Click: Home→Font→Underline. 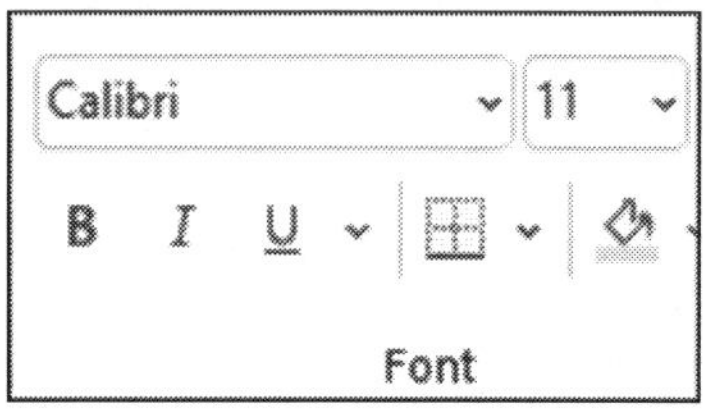 	Click on the Ribbon's *Home* tab and then look for the *Font* group. Click the *Underline* button within this group (that's the left-hand side of the button, not the drop-down arrow next to it). Don't worry if this doesn't make sense yet. You will cover the Ribbon in depth in session one.
Click: Home→Font→ Underline Drop Down→Double Underline. 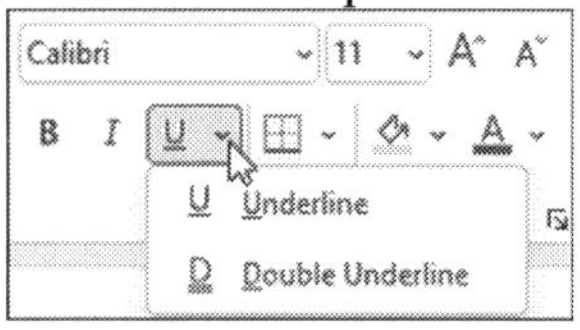 	Click on the Ribbon's *Home* tab and then look for the *Font* group. Click the drop-down arrow next to the Underline button (that's the right-hand side of the button) within this group and then choose *Double Underline* from the drop-down list.
Click: File→Options→ Advanced→General→ Edit Custom Lists→Import	This is a more involved example. 1. Click the *File* tab on the Ribbon, and then click the *Options* button towards the bottom of the left-hand pane. The *Excel Options* dialog appears. 2. Choose the *Advanced* list item in the left-hand pane and scroll down to the *General* group in the right-hand pane. 3. Click the *Edit Custom Lists…* button. Yet another dialog pops up. 4. Click the *Import* button.
Type: **European Sales** into the cell.	Whenever you are supposed to actually type something on the keyboard it is shown in bold faced text.
Press **<Ctrl>** + **<Z>**.	You should hold down the **Ctrl** key and then press the **Z** key.

When a lesson tells you to click a button, an image of the relevant button will often be shown either in the page margin or within the text itself.

note

An Excel worksheet can contain up to 16,585 columns and 1,048,476 rows.

If you want to read through the book as quickly as possible, you don't have to read notes.

Notes usually expand a little on the information given in the lesson text.

important

Do not click the *Delete* button at this point as to do so would erase the entire table.

Whenever something can easily go wrong, or when the subject text is particularly important, you will see the *important* sidebar.

You should always read important sidebars.

tip

Moving between tabs using the keyboard

You can also use the **<Ctrl>+<PgUp>** and **<Ctrl>+<PgDn>** keyboard shortcuts to cycle through all of the tabs in your workbook.

Tips add to the lesson text by showing you shortcuts or time-saving techniques relevant to the lesson.

The bold text at the top of the tip box enables you to establish whether the tip is appropriate to your needs without reading all of the text.

In this example if you are not interested in keyboard shortcuts you do not need to read any further.

anecdote

I ran an Excel course for a small company in London a couple of years ago...

Sometimes I add an anecdote gathered over the years from my Excel classes or from other areas of life.

If you simply want to learn Excel as quickly as possible you can ignore my anecdotes.

trivia

The feature that Excel uses to help you out with function calls first made an appearance in Visual Basic 5 back in 1996 …

Sometimes I indulge myself by adding a little piece of trivia in the context of the skill being taught.

Just like my anecdotes you can ignore these if you want to. They won't help you to learn Excel any better!

When there is a sample file (or files) to accompany a lesson, the file name will be shown in a folder icon. You can download the sample file from: *https://thesmartmethod.com.* Detailed instructions are given in: *Lesson 1-8: Download the sample files.*

How to use this course

This course utilizes some of the tried and tested techniques developed after teaching vast numbers of people to learn Excel during many years teaching Smart Method classroom courses.

In order to master Excel as quickly and efficiently as possible you should use the recommended learning method described below. If you do this there is absolutely no doubt that you will master the advanced Excel skills taught in this book.

Three important rules

#1 - Complete the course from beginning to end

It is always tempting to jump around the course completing lessons in a haphazard way.

We strongly suggest that you start at the beginning and complete lessons sequentially.

That's because each lesson builds upon skills learned in the previous lessons and one of our goals is not to waste your time by teaching the same skill twice. If you miss a skill by skipping a lesson, you'll find the later lessons more difficult, or even impossible to follow. This, in turn, may demoralize you and make you abandon the course.

#2 If possible, complete a session in one sitting

The book is arranged into *sessions* and *lessons*.

You can complete as many, or as few, lessons as you have the time and energy for each day. Many learners have developed Excel skills by setting aside just a few minutes each day to complete a single lesson.

If it is possible, the most effective way to learn is to lock yourself away, switch off your telephone, and complete a full session, without interruption, except for a 15-minute break each hour. The memory process is associative, and we've ensured that the lessons in each session are very closely coupled (contextually) with the others. By learning the whole session in one sitting, you'll store all that information in the same part of your memory and will find it easier to recall later.

The experience of being able to remember all of the words of a song as soon as somebody has got you "started" with the first line is an example of the memory's associative system of data storage.

#3 Rest at least every hour

In our classroom courses we have often observed a phenomenon that we call "running into a wall". This happens when a student becomes overloaded with new information to the point that they can no longer follow the simplest instruction. If you find this happening to you, you've studied for too long without a rest.

You should take a 15-minute break every hour (or more often if you begin to feel overwhelmed) and spend it relaxing rather than catching up with your e-mails. Ideally you should relax by lying down and closing your eyes. This allows your brain to use all its processing power to efficiently store and index the skills you've learned. We've found that this hugely improves retention of skills learned.

How to work through the lessons

At the end of each session, complete the session exercise

Keep attempting the exercise at the end of each session until you can complete it without having to refer to lessons in the session. Don't start the next session until you can complete the exercise from memory.

At the end of each session, review the objectives

The session objectives are stated at the beginning of each session.

Read each objective and ask yourself if you have truly mastered each skill. If you are not sure about any of the skills listed, review the relevant lesson(s) before moving on to the next session.

You will find it very frustrating if you move to a new session before you have truly mastered the skills covered in the previous session. This may demoralize you and make you abandon the course.

How to best use the incremental sample files

Many lessons in this course use a sample file that is incrementally improved during each lesson. At the end of each lesson an interim version is always saved. For example, a sample file called Sales-1 may provide the starting point to a sequence of three lessons. After each lesson, interim versions called Sales-2, Sales-3 and Sales-4 are saved by the student.

A complete set of sample files (including all incremental versions) are provided in the sample file set. This provides three important benefits:

- If you have difficulty with a lesson it is useful to be able to study the completed workbook (at the end of the lesson) by opening the finished version of the lesson's workbook.
- When you have completed the book, you will want to use it as a reference. The sample files allow you to work through any single lesson in isolation, as the workbook's state at the beginning of each lesson is always available.
- When teaching a class one student may corrupt their workbook by a series of errors (or by their computer crashing). It is possible to quickly and easily move the class on to the next lesson by instructing the student to open the next sample file in the set (instead of progressing with their own corrupted file or copying a file from another student).

The time you spend learning Excel is hugely worthwhile

If you persevere with this course there is no doubt that you will master Excel. A little time and effort are needed but the skills you'll acquire will be hugely valuable for the rest of your life. With 1.2 billion users worldwide, it is hard to imagine any organization of any size that does not value Excel skills.

Enjoy the course.

1

Session One: Setup and Basic Skills

A bad beginning makes a bad ending.

Euripides, Aegeus (484 BC - 406 BC).

Excel has hundreds of setup options. Before you can begin learning Excel it is important that your copy is properly configured. This session will show you how to correctly setup the user interface. You'll also ensure that you are updated to the latest Excel version.

You'll also learn the absolute basics you need before you can start to do useful work with Excel 2021.

In my classes I often teach professionals who have used Excel for over ten years and they *always* get some nugget of fantastically useful information from this session.

Session Objectives

By the end of this session, you will be able to:

- Start Excel and open a new blank workbook
- Check that your Excel version is up to date
- Change between the Simplified and Classic Ribbon
- Change between Touch Mode and Mouse Mode
- Change the Office Theme
- Maximize, minimize, re-size, move and close the Excel window
- Download the sample files and open/navigate a workbook
- Save a workbook to a local file
- Understand common file formats
- Pin a workbook and understand file organization
- View, move, add, rename, delete and navigate worksheet tabs
- Use the Versions feature to recover an unsaved Draft file
- Use the Versions feature to recover an earlier version of a workbook
- Use the Ribbon
- Understand Ribbon components
- Customize the Quick Access Toolbar and preview the printout
- Use the Mini Toolbar, Key Tips and keyboard shortcuts
- Understand views
- Hide and Show the Formula Bar and Ribbon
- Use the Tell Me help system
- Use other help features

Lesson 1-1: Start Excel and open a new blank workbook (Windows 10)

Excel 2021 will only run on the Windows 10 and Windows 11 operating systems. If you are using Windows 11 skip this lesson and move to: *Lesson 1-2: Start Excel and open a new blank workbook (Windows 11).*

1 Click the Start Button in the bottom left corner of the Windows 10 screen.

2 Drag the *Excel* tile to the top of the start menu (the start menu is on the right-hand side of the pop-up window).

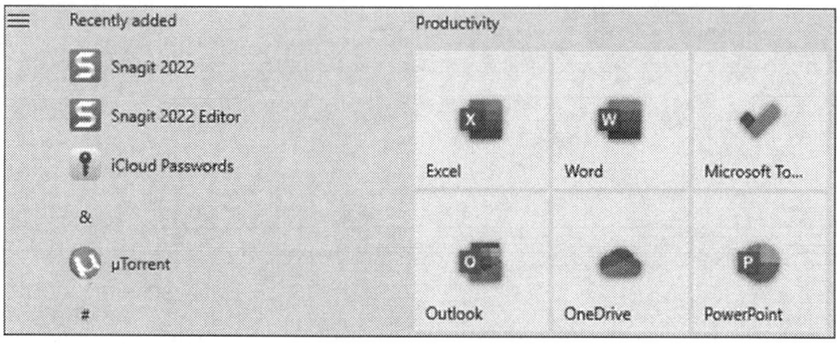

If you can't find the Excel tile, see sidebar for instructions on how to locate it.

You'll be using Excel a lot, so it makes sense to move the tile to the top of the Windows 10 start menu. You'll then be able to start Excel without having to search for the tile.

1. Point to the Excel tile.
2. Click and hold down the left mouse button.
3. With the left button held down, move your mouse towards the top of the start menu. The tile will move with the mouse cursor.
4. When you reach the top of the start menu, release the left mouse button.

   The Excel tile is now permanently positioned at the top of the Windows 10 start menu.

3 Left-click on the Excel tile to start Excel.

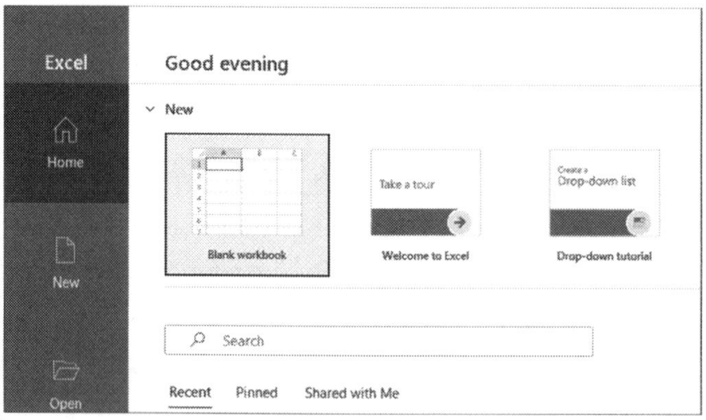

note

If you can't find the Excel tile in Windows 10

When you install Excel 365 on a Windows 10 computer a tile is automatically added to the Start Menu. If you can't find the tile proceed as follows:

1. Type: **Excel** into the Windows 10 search box at the bottom left of your screen.

You should then see the *Excel Desktop app* returned by the Windows 10 search. If you don't, Excel is not installed on this computer.

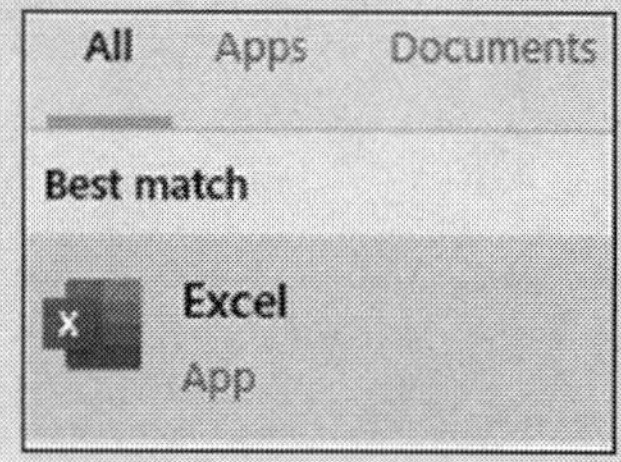

2. Right-click the Excel app icon and click: *Pin to Start* from the shortcut menu:

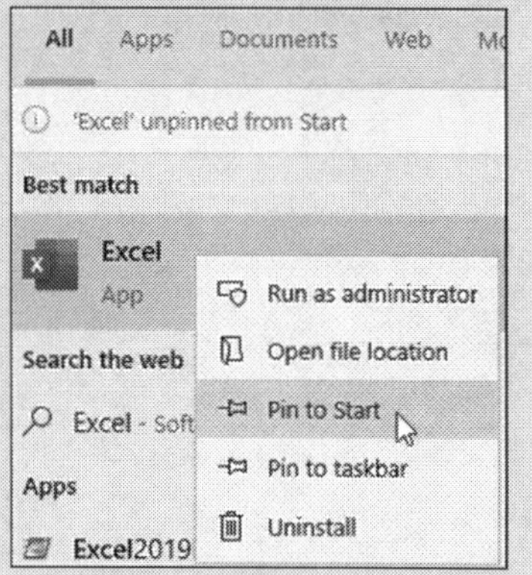

You will now be able to locate the Excel tile on the start menu (though you may have to scroll down to the bottom of the tile list to find it).

Now that Excel has started, Excel needs to know whether you want to create a new workbook, or whether you want to open a workbook that was created earlier.

4 Create a new blank workbook.

Left-click on the *Blank workbook* icon.

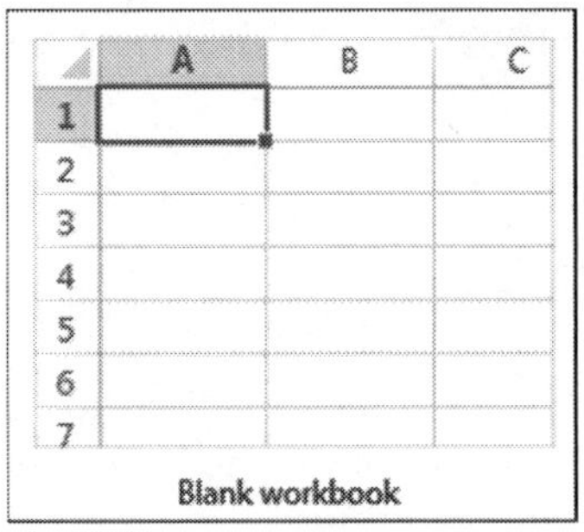

This icon represents a *template.*

When you click on the *Blank Workbook* icon you are telling Excel: "Create a new workbook using the *Blank workbook* template".

Excel provides many more templates (see sidebar) but the *Blank Workbook* template is the one you will use most of the time.

Note that, from now onwards, I will simply use the term "click" when I mean left-click (the mouse button you will use most of the time) and "right-click" only when you need to click the (less-used) right mouse button.

The Excel 2021 screen is displayed showing a blank workbook:

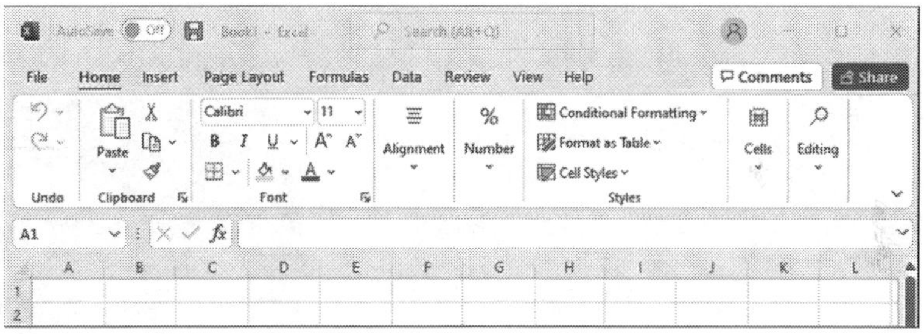

5 Leave the workbook open for the next lesson.

note

Templates

When you clicked on the *Blank Workbook* icon:

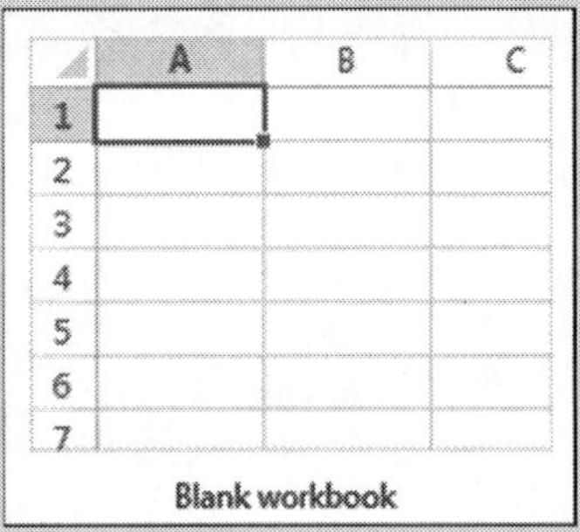

... you instructed Excel to create a new workbook using the *Blank Workbook* template.

If you had clicked the *New* icon on the left-hand menu bar or clicked the *More Templates* link you would have seen a gallery containing many more templates.

Templates are sample workbooks that you can adapt and modify for your own needs. They are designed to give you a "flying start" when creating your own workbooks.

Potential problems when using templates

Templates are not usually a good choice as it can take longer to adapt them to your true needs than to design from scratch

Many of Microsoft's templates have been created using some very advanced Excel skills and techniques. If you make use of them there's a danger that you may depend upon a workbook you don't understand and are unable to maintain.

In: *Lesson 3-16: Create a template,* you'll learn how to create your own custom templates.

Templates you create yourself are far more useful. Because you understand how they are built, you will be able to maintain them, and any workbook created from them.

Lesson 1-2: Start Excel and open a new blank workbook (Windows 11)

Excel 2021 only runs on the Windows 10 and Windows 11 operating systems. If you are using Windows 10 skip this lesson, the lesson content has already been covered in: *Lesson 1-1: Start Excel and open a new blank workbook (Windows 10).*

1 Add Excel to the taskbar.

The Windows 11 taskbar (the bar at the bottom of the screen) makes it easy to open applications you use regularly with a single mouse click.

Here's the taskbar on my own computer.

You can see that I use Google Chrome, Outlook, Word and Excel regularly so I have added them to the taskbar.

1. Click the Start button  in the bottom center section of the Windows 11 screen.

   You may already see the Excel icon in the *Pinned* pane.

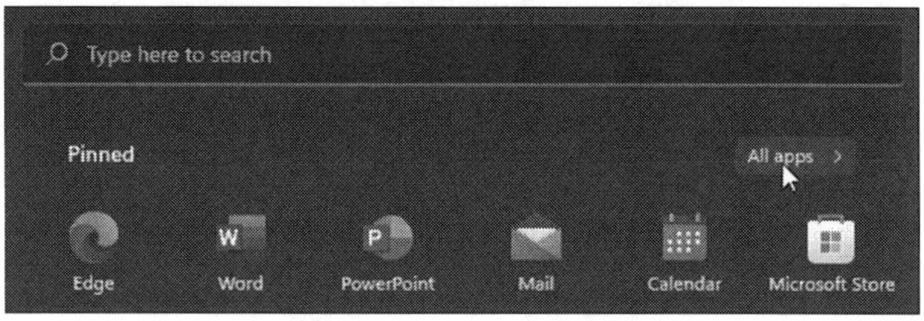

2. If you don't see it there click the *All Apps* button.

   You'll then see the Excel icon in the alphabetical listing (under E). If you don't see the Excel icon then Excel is not installed on your computer.

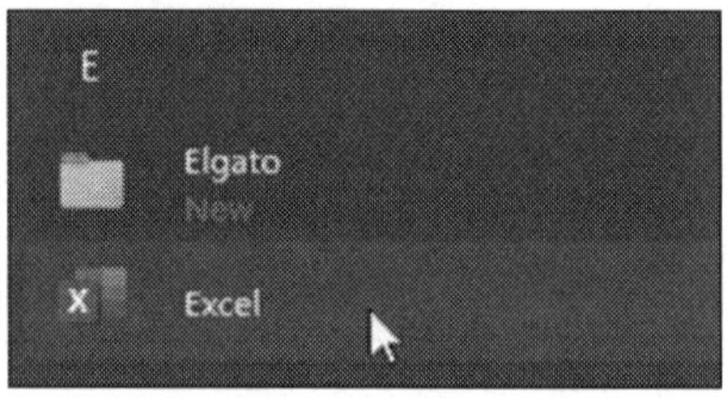

3. Right-click on the Excel icon.

   A pop-up menu appears.

note

Templates

When you clicked on the *Blank Workbook* icon:

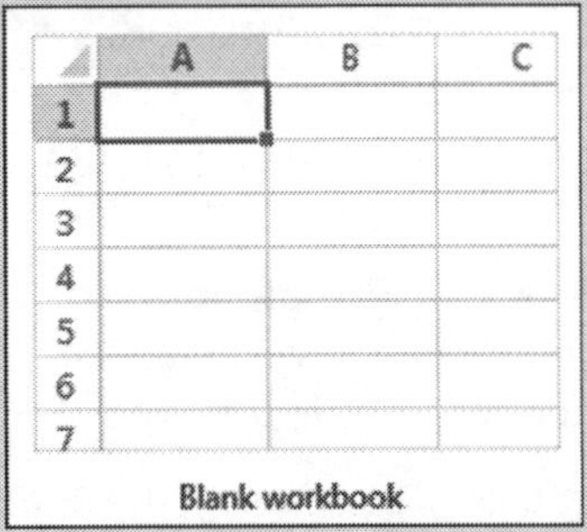

... you instructed Excel to create a new workbook using the *Blank Workbook* template.

If you had clicked the *New* icon on the left-hand menu bar or clicked the *More Templates* link you would have seen a gallery containing many more templates.

Templates are sample workbooks that you can adapt and modify for your own needs. They are designed to give you a "flying start" when creating your own workbooks.

Potential problems when using templates

Templates are not usually a good choice as it can take longer to adapt them to your true needs than to design from scratch

Many of Microsoft's templates have been created using some very advanced Excel skills and techniques. If you make use of them there's a danger that you may depend upon a workbook you don't understand and are unable to maintain.

In: *Lesson 3-16: Create a template*, you'll learn how to create your own custom templates.

Templates you create yourself are far more useful. Because you understand how they are built, you will be able to maintain them, and any workbook created from them.

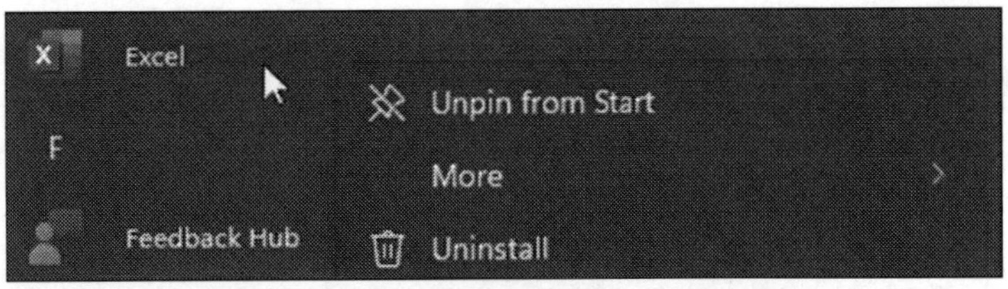

4. Hover the mouse cursor over the *More* option.
5. A pop-out menu appears.

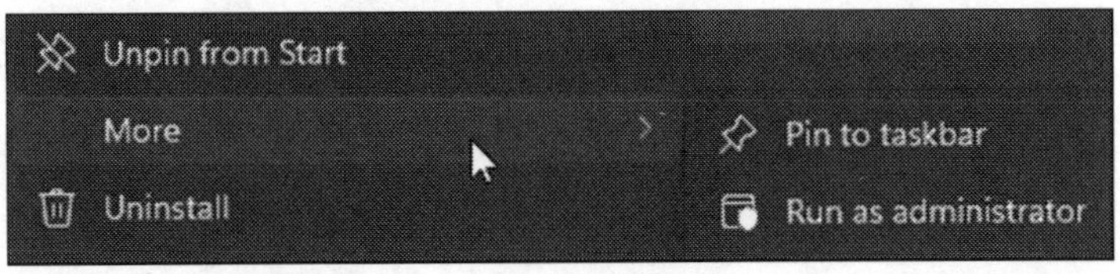

6. Left-click on the *Pin to taskbar* option.

   The Excel icon appears on the bottom taskbar.

2 Left-click on the Excel icon to start Excel.

Now that Excel has started, Excel needs to know whether you want to create a new workbook, or whether you want to open a workbook that was created earlier.

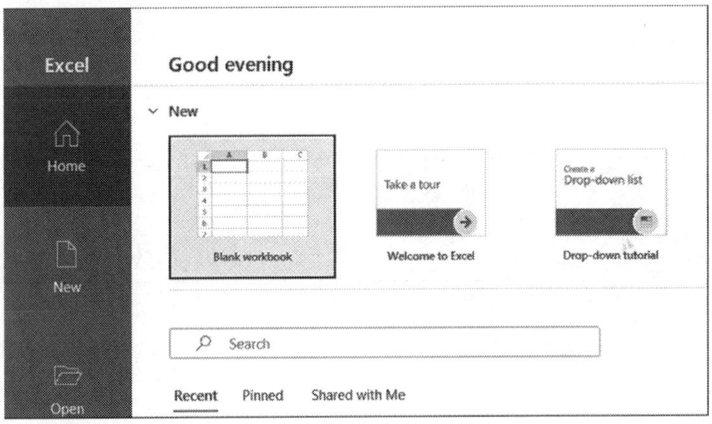

3 Create a new blank workbook.

Left-click on the *Blank workbook* icon.

This icon represents a *template*.

When you click on the *Blank Workbook* icon you are telling Excel: "Create a new workbook using the *Blank workbook* template".

Excel provides many more templates (see sidebar) but the *Blank Workbook* template is the one you will use most of the time.

Note that, from now onwards, I will simply use the term "click" when I mean left-click (the mouse button you will use most of the time) and "right-click" only when you need to click the (less-used) right mouse button.

The Excel 2021 screen is displayed showing a blank workbook:

4 Leave the workbook open for the next lesson.

important

Can I use this Excel 2021 book to learn Excel 365?

Microsoft release a new, updated version of Excel 365 every month. The new monthly version often includes new or improved features.

Microsoft can do this because Excel 365 is a subscription product, providing Microsoft with a constant income stream to finance constant improvements.

Excel 2021 is a "pay once" (also called "perpetual license") product that never has feature updates during its 5-year product life.

When Excel 2021 was first released (in October 2021) it was almost identical to the latest version of Excel 365. At that time, you'd have had no difficulty learning Excel 365 using this book.

As the years and months roll by, the differences between Excel 2021 and Excel 365 will become more significant. For this reason, Excel 365 users may see screen grabs in this book that differ from what they see on screen. Having said this, it shouldn't be too difficult to work around the differences.

New editions of our Excel 365 books are published when significant new features are added. The books are currently on their fifth edition (updated for the January 2021 release) but, by the time you read this book, there may have been later editions published.

New editions of this Excel 2021 book will never be needed as the features in Excel 2021 will always remain the same.

Lesson 1-3: Check that your Excel version is up to date

Automatic Updates

Normally Excel will look after updates without you having to do anything. By default, automatic updates are enabled. This means that updates are downloaded from the Internet and installed automatically.

It is possible that automatic updates have been switched off on your computer. In this case there is a danger that you may have an old, buggy, unsupported and out of date version of Excel 2021 installed.

This lesson will show you how to make sure that you are using the latest (most complete, and most reliable) version of Excel.

1 Start Excel and open a new blank workbook (if you have not already done this).

2 Make sure that automatic updates are enabled.

1. Click the *File* button  at the top-left of the screen.

   This takes you to *Backstage View*. Backstage View allows you to complete an enormous range of common tasks from a single window.

2. Click: *Account*  in the left-hand list.

   Your account details are displayed on screen. Notice the *Update Options* button displayed in the right-hand pane.

   If all is well, and automatic updates are switched on, you will see a button similar to this:

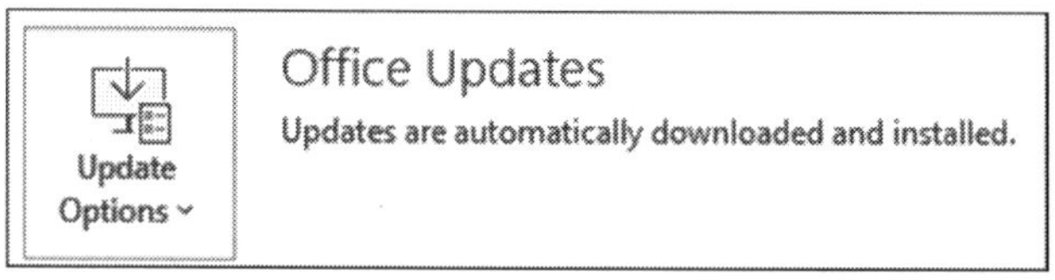

   If automatic updates have been switched off, you will see a similar button to this.

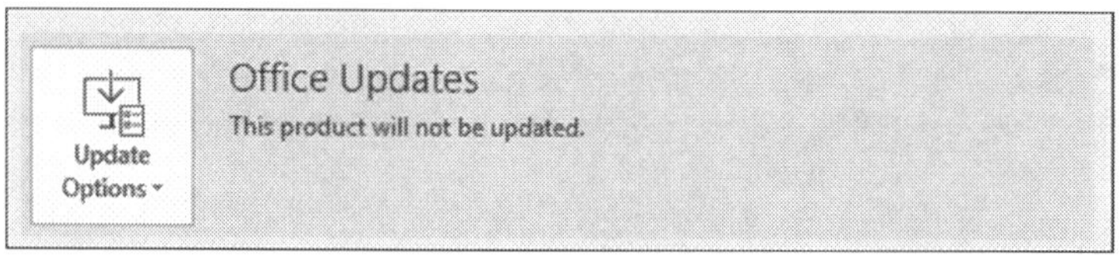

   In this case you will need to switch automatic updates on (see next step).

3 Switch on *automatic updates* if necessary.

Click: Update Options→Enable Updates.

note

Version number and Build

A new Excel version is usually released every month.

Each new version may add new features to Excel 365 (but these are not available to Excel 2021 users).

If bugs or security issues are found in a new version, Microsoft will fix them and publish a new *build* of the same version.

It is quite normal for there to be several new builds of each new version during the month that the new version is released.

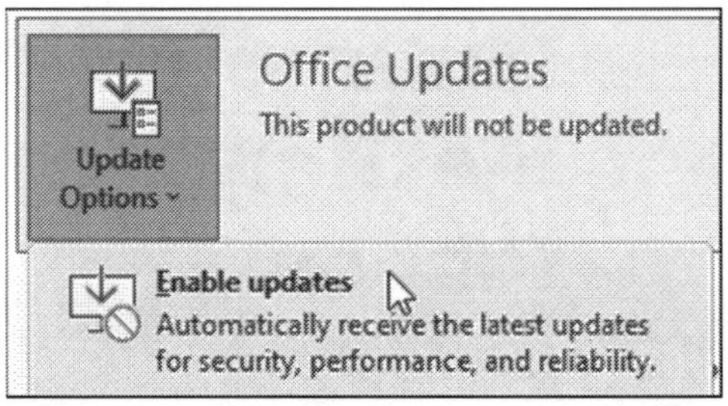

You may also see a second dialog asking if you want the app to make changes to your device. If you see this click the *Yes* button.

4 If there are updates waiting to install, apply them.

Sometimes Excel will download updates but will not install them automatically. In this case you will see an update button similar to the following:

If you see this type of button, you should apply the update.

Click: Update Options→Apply Updates.

You may be asked to confirm that you want to apply the update, and to close any open programs before applying the update.

5 Make sure that you are using Excel 2021.

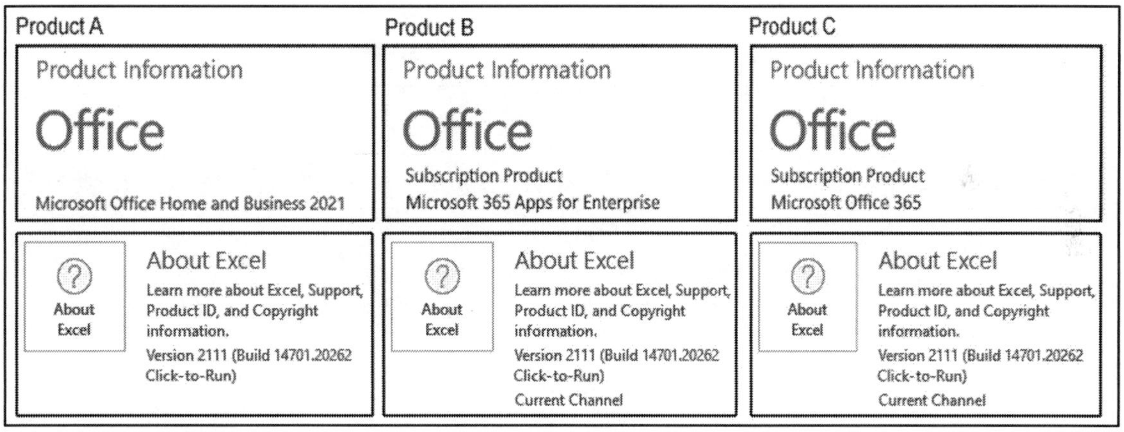

note

Excel 2021 users still receive security updates

Excel 2021 users still receive monthly version updates, but these only include security updates and bug fixes (not new features).

An Excel 2021 user running version 2111 will thus see fewer features than an Excel 365 user running the same Excel version.

Product information is also displayed. If you see the number: *2021* you are using Excel 2021 (the version that this book teaches). This is the case for *Product A* above.

If you see the number: *365* or the words: *Subscription Product*, you are using Excel 365. This is the case for products B and C above. If you are using Excel 365 see facing page sidebar.

Notice also the *Version and Build* (see sidebar for an explanation).

6 Click the *Back* button to leave *Backstage View* and return to the worksheet.

7 Click the *Close* button in the top-right corner of the Excel screen to close Excel.

Lesson 1-4: Change between the Simplified and Classic Ribbon

note

Simplified/Classic Ribbon are Office-wide settings

When you set Excel to work with the Simplified or Classic Ribbon, you'll find that all of your other Office applications (such as Word and PowerPoint) have inherited the same setting.

It isn't possible to set the Ribbon preference individually for each application.

Excel was originally designed to be used on home computers. Today Excel is sometimes used on mobile devices (such as an iPad or Smartphone).

Mobile devices have smaller screens than desktop computers.

For these reasons, Excel 2021 enables users to customize the user interface to make it more usable on mobile devices.

Most Excel commands are executed using a user interface component called the Ribbon. You'll learn how to use the Ribbon later in: *Lesson 1-16: Use the Ribbon.*

Depending upon the device you are using, you may see the *Simplified* or *Classic* Ribbon on your screen.

The Classic Ribbon

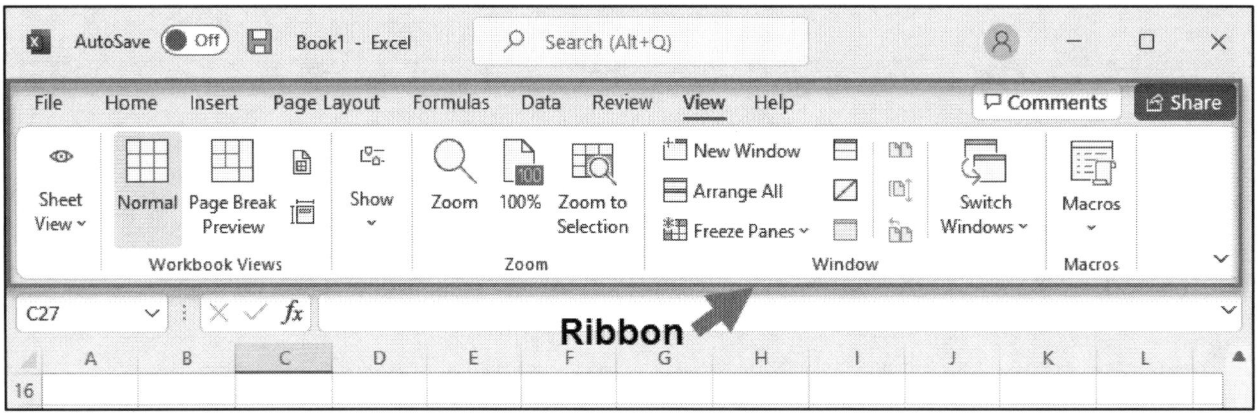

The Simplified Ribbon

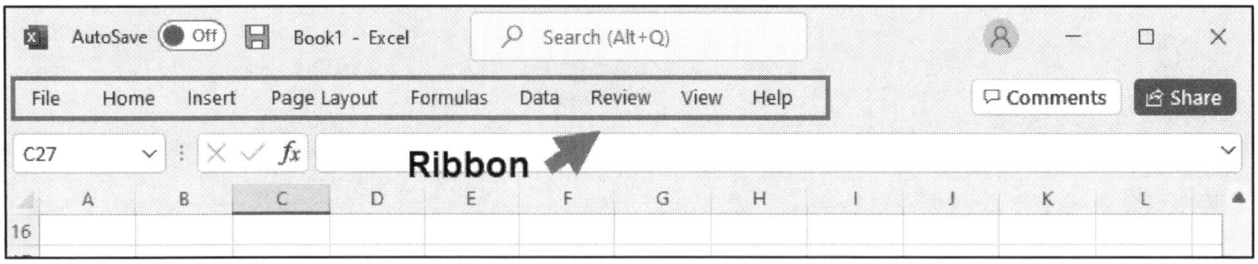

You can see that the *Simplified Ribbon* takes up far less space but doesn't include all of the commands and icons for each menu option.

1 Open Excel and open a new blank Excel workbook.

Excel attempts to automatically detect the type of device you are using. For this reason, you may see either the Simplified Ribbon or the Classic Ribbon on your screen.

2 Switch from the Classic Ribbon to the Simplified Ribbon.

1. When the Classic Ribbon is displayed you will see a small downward facing chevron on the bottom-right corner of the classic Ribbon.

   Click on the chevron to display the Ribbon Display Options.

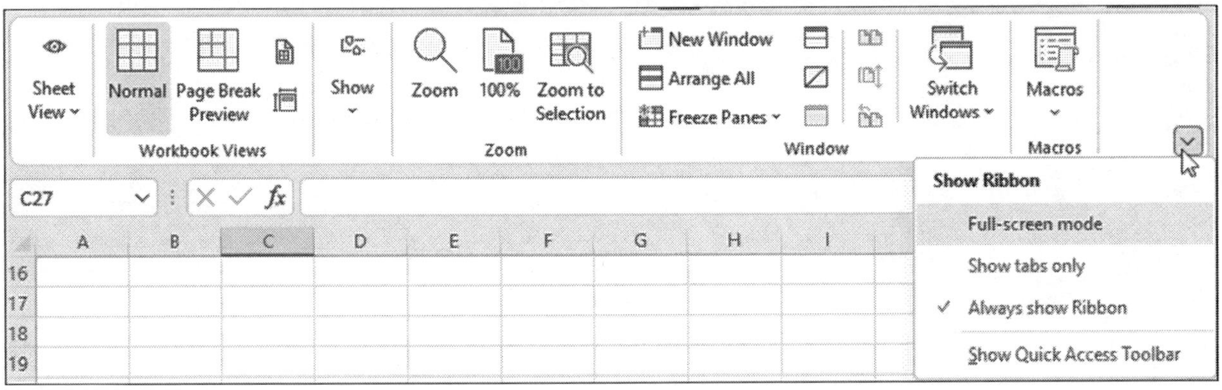

2. Click: *Show tabs only*.

   The Simplified Ribbon is displayed.

3 Switch from the Simplified Ribbon to the Classic Ribbon.

1. Click on any of the menu options shown on the Simplified Ribbon except the *File* option.

   The relevant Ribbon commands appear.

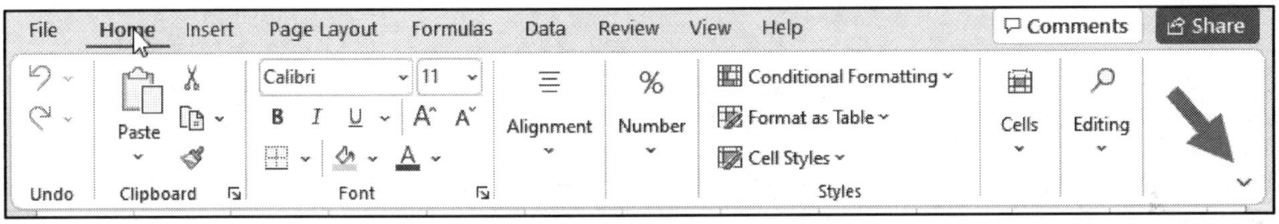

   Notice that you can now see the Ribbon Display Options chevron at the bottom right of the Ribbon.

2. Click on the chevron to display the Ribbon Display Options.

3. Click: *Always show Ribbon*.

   The Classic Ribbon is restored.

   All of the screen grabs in this book assume that you are working with the Classic Ribbon.

   Most Excel desktop users prefer to work with the Classic Ribbon as you can execute a command with one mouse click rather than two.

Lesson 1-5: Change between touch mode and mouse mode

Both Excel and Windows allow you to operate in one of two modes: Touch Mode and Mouse Mode. Excel tries to figure out which mode you want to use and then sets it for you automatically. This lesson will enable you to set the mode you prefer manually.

Touch Mode: In Touch Mode the icons are spaced further apart so that they are easier to tap with your finger.

Mouse Mode: This is the mode preferred by most Excel desktop users. In Mouse Mode the icons are displayed closer together. Unless you have a very large screen you will usually also see more icons on your screen when in Mouse Mode. This means that you can often execute a command with one click rather than two.

For this reason, it is usually more efficient to work with Excel in Mouse Mode (using a mouse to select commands) than to use Touch Mode (using your finger to select commands).

note

Touch mode and mouse mode are Office-wide settings

When you set Excel to work in touch mode or mouse mode, you'll find that all of your other Office applications (such as Word and PowerPoint) have inherited the same setting.

It isn't possible to set touch mode/mouse mode individually for each application.

1 Open Excel and open a new blank Excel workbook.

2 Enable the *Quick Access Toolbar.*

In Excel 2021 the Quick Access Toolbar is hidden by default.

Enable the Classic Ribbon if you have not already done so. You learned how to do this in: *Lesson 1-4: Change between the Simplified and Classic* Ribbon.

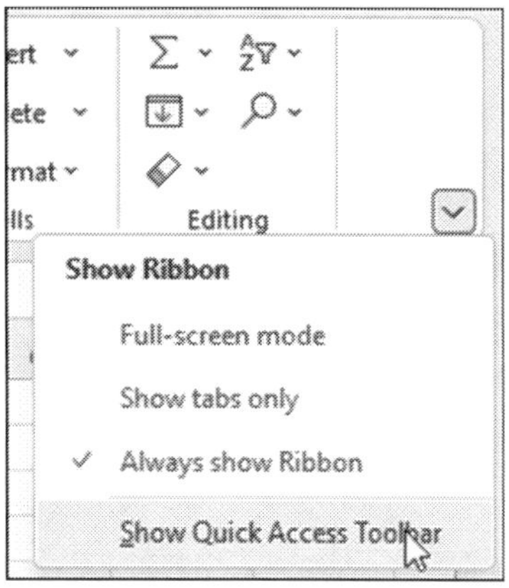

Click the Ribbon Display Options button (the small downward pointing chevron at the bottom-right of the Ribbon.

Click: *Show Quick Access Toolbar.*

Notice that a small icon has appeared beneath the left-hand side of the Ribbon.

This button enables you to customize the Quick Access Toolbar.

You'll learn a lot more about the Quick Access Toolbar later, in: *Lesson 1-18: Customize the Quick Access Toolbar and preview the printout.*

3 Enable the *Touch/Mouse Mode* button on the *Quick Access Toolbar.*

1. Click the *Customize Quick Access Toolbar* button.
2. Click: *Touch/Mouse Mode* from the drop-down menu.

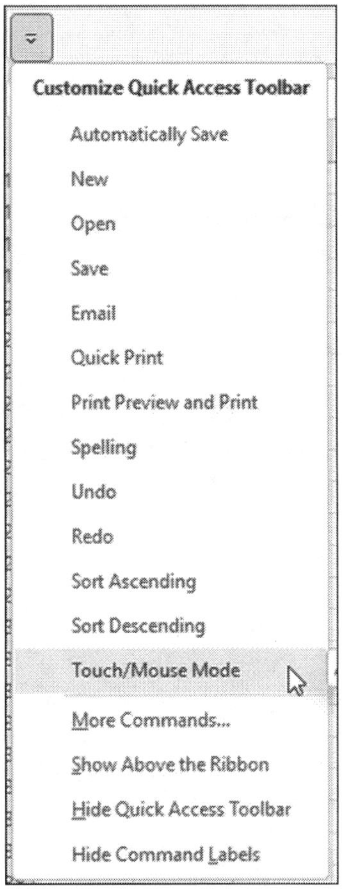

The *Touch/Mouse Mode* button is then added to the *Quick Access Toolbar*.

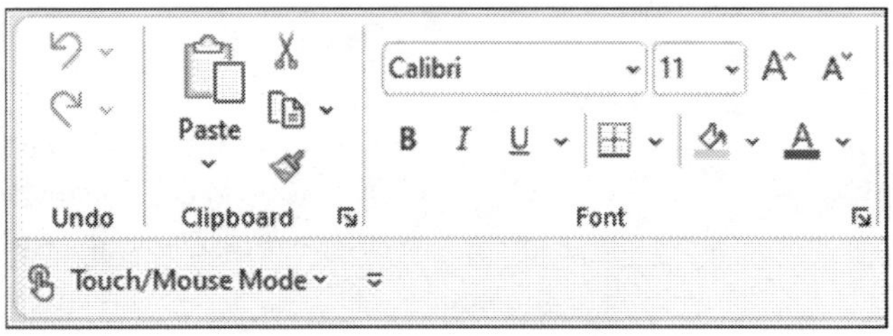

4 Set Excel to use *Touch Mode.*

If you are using a computer that has a touch screen, you may find that Excel is already using touch mode.

1. Click on the *Touch/Mouse Mode* button. Two options appear on the drop-down menu:

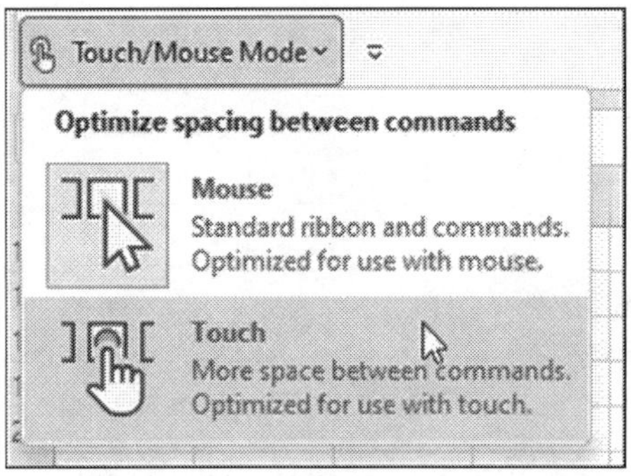

2. Click the Touch option.
3. Notice that fewer icons are now displayed. You are now using Excel in Touch Mode.

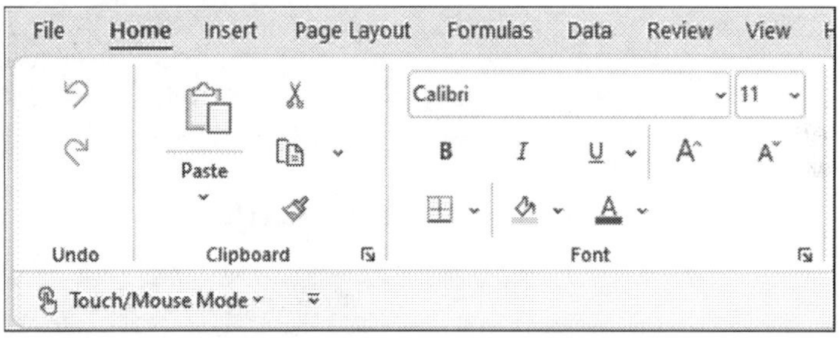

5 Set Excel to use *Mouse Mode.*

Now do the same thing but this time select *Mouse Mode.* Notice that the icons are now closer together.

Most of the screen grabs in this book were taken using *Mouse Mode.*

If you decide that you prefer *Touch Mode,* you'll still have no difficulty working through all of the lessons in this book.

anecdote

How touch mode baffled a Microsoft Surface user

One of my users had a Microsoft Surface tablet computer connected to a 32-inch monitor via a docking station.

He couldn't understand why his Ribbon was so difficult to work with when compared to the other users in the office.

Office had auto-detected his device and classed it as a mobile device with a touch screen. Office had then set itself to use Touch mode.

Without an understanding of Touch Mode and Mouse Mode he had found it impossible to correctly configure his computer for desktop use.

Lesson 1-6: Change the Office Theme

Excel allows you to change the colors of screen elements (such as the title bar and ribbon) by selecting a *theme*. There are four themes available: *Colorful, White, Dark Gray* and *Black.*

White

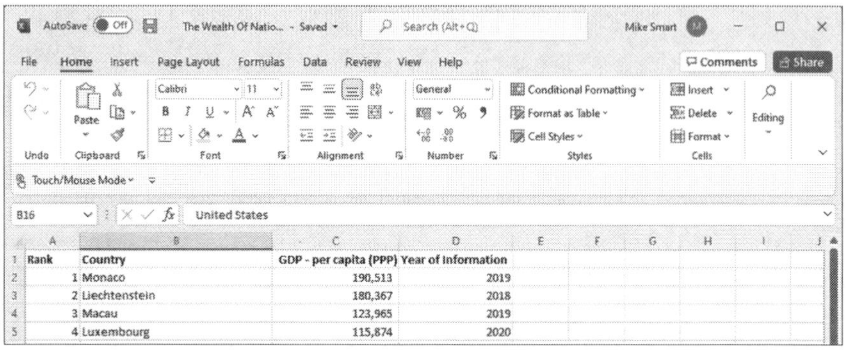

By default, Excel 2021 uses the theme that best complements the current Windows theme. This will be the White theme (assuming that the Windows theme has not been changed).

You may see a different theme if:

- You have changed the default Windows theme.
- You have upgraded from an earlier version of Office in which a different theme was selected.
- You have changed the theme on another computer that uses the same Windows account as this one.

Colorful

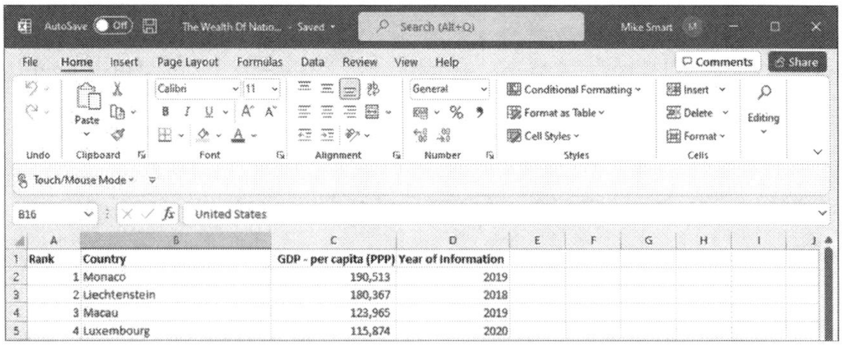

The *Colorful* theme was the default in Excel 2016 and Excel 2019.

This theme makes it clear which of the Office applications you are using as Word, Excel, PowerPoint, Outlook and other Office applications each have their own unique color for the Title Bar (the bar shown at the very top of the Excel window).

note

You can also personalize Excel by changing the background

Background customization can only be done if you are connected to the Internet and logged into a Microsoft Account. You'll learn more about Microsoft Accounts later, in: *Session Eight: Cloud Computing*.

If you are logged into your Microsoft Account, you will see an *Office Background* drop-down list (above the *Office Theme* setting) that enables backgrounds to be set:

When you choose a background a "tattoo" is added to the opening screen (when you first start Excel).

note

Themes and Backgrounds affect every Office application on all your devices

When you set a theme or background in Excel you are changing the theme and background for the entire Office suite.

This means that you will have a consistent experience when using other Office applications such as *Word* and *PowerPoint*.

In: *Session Eight: Cloud Computing*, you'll discover that Excel includes features that are useful for users with multiple devices (such as a work computer, home computer, laptop, tablet and smartphone).

If you are logged into a *Microsoft Account*, the theme you select will also magically change on all your devices.

note

Audio cues

If you enable *Audio Cues* a different sound will be played whenever you complete common Excel actions (such as cut and paste).

The idea is that you will subconsciously link sounds with actions so that when you make a mistake it will "sound wrong".

To enable Audio cues click:

File→Options→
Accessibility→
Feedback options→
Provide feedback with sound.

You are also able to choose between two different *Sound Schemes*.

Dark Gray and Black

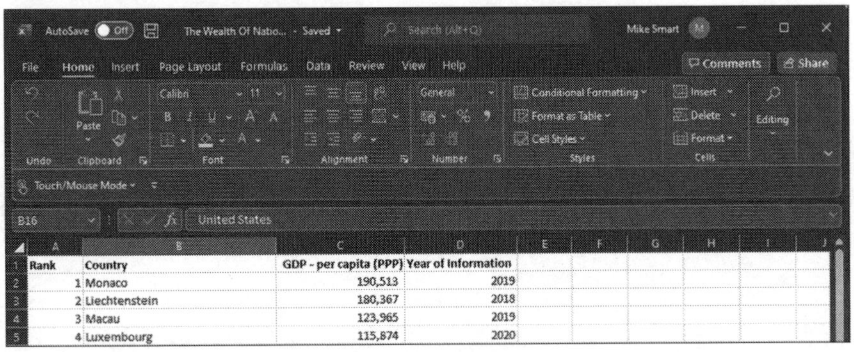

The *Dark Gray* and *Black* themes provide high contrast between different screen elements. It has been suggested that these themes would be particularly useful for users with impaired vision.

1 Open Excel and open a new blank Excel workbook.

2 Change the *Office Theme.*

1. Click the *File* button [File] at the top-left of the screen.
2. Click the *Options* button [Options] near the bottom of the left-hand menu bar.

   The *Excel Options* dialog box appears.

   In the *Personalize your copy of Microsoft Office* section, you'll see an *Office Theme* drop-down list. Click the drop-down arrow to see the different themes available.

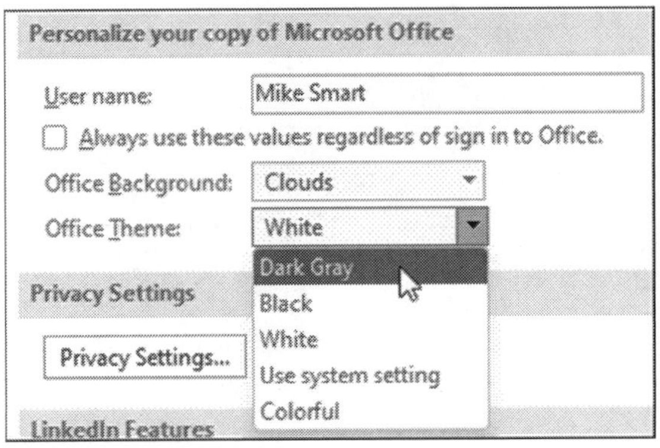

3. Click the *Dark Gray* theme.
4. Click *OK* to return to the Excel screen.

   Experiment with each theme until you discover the one you prefer.

   All of the screen grabs in this book were made using the *White* theme. If you choose a different theme the screen grabs in the book may look slightly different to what you see on your computer screen.

3 Close Excel.

Lesson 1-7: Maximize, minimize, re-size, move and close the Excel window

The main Excel window has a dazzling array of buttons, switches and other artifacts. By the end of this book, they will all make sense to you and you'll feel really comfortable with Excel.

For now, you'll explore the big picture by looking at how the Excel window can be sized and moved. The details will come later.

1 Open Excel.

2 Use the *Blank workbook* template to open a new blank workbook.

You learned how to do this in: *Lesson 1-1: Start Excel and open a new blank workbook.*

3 Understand the *Maximize, Minimize, Close* and *Restore Down* buttons

At the top right corner of the Excel window, you'll see three buttons.

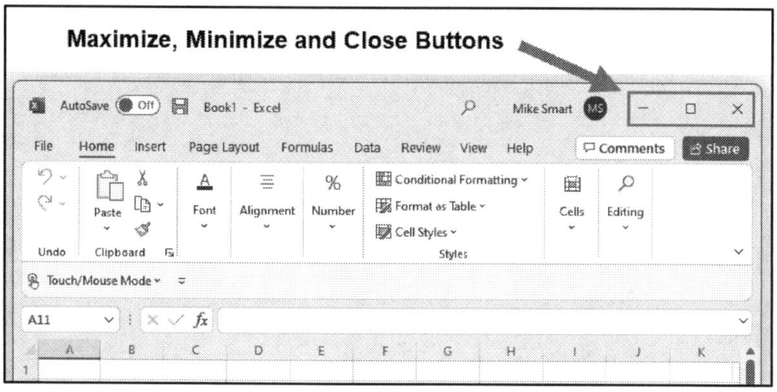

The buttons that you see will depend upon how the Excel window was left last time the application closed down. Normally the Excel screen is maximized to fill the screen and you'll see:

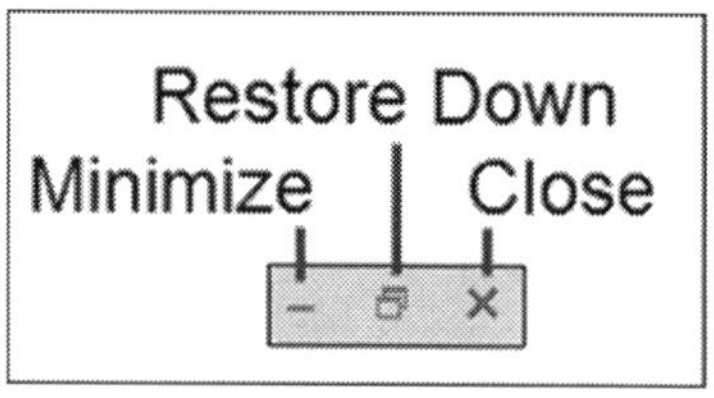

But if you had reduced the size of the Excel window so that it didn't fill the screen, you'd see this instead:

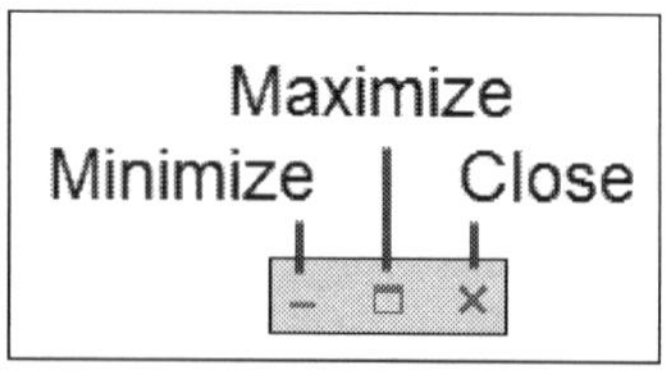

Try clicking the *Maximize, Minimize* and *Restore Down* buttons.

- *Maximize* makes the Excel window completely fill the screen.
- *Minimize* reduces Excel to a button on the bottom task bar.

Click this button again to restore the window to its previous size.

- *Restore Down* makes the Excel window smaller, allowing you to re-size the window.

4 Re-size the Excel window.

After clicking the *Restore Down* button you are able to re-size the Excel window. Hover over either the side of the window, or a corner of the window, with your mouse cursor. The cursor shape will change to a double-headed arrow.

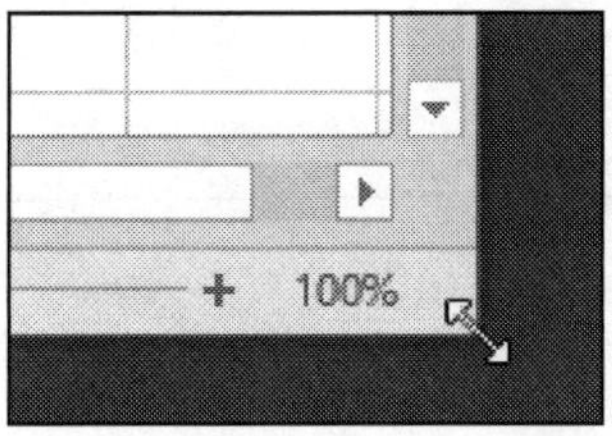

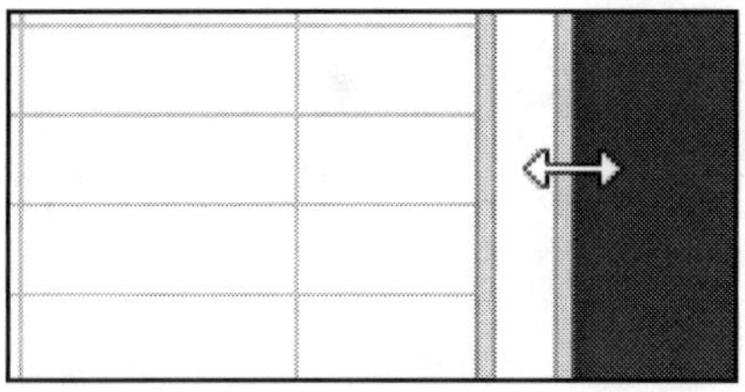

When you see either cursor shape, hold down the left mouse button and move the mouse (this is called *click and drag*) to re-size the window.

- Clicking and dragging a corner allows you to change both the height and width of the window.
- Clicking an edge allows you to change only one dimension.

5 Move the Excel window.

Click and drag the *Title Bar* (the bar at the very top of the window) to move the Excel window around the screen.

6 Close Excel.

Click on the *Close* button  at the top right of the Excel window.

This is the most common way to close Excel

It is also possible to close Excel by pressing the **<Alt>+<F4>** keys on your keyboard.

Excel often provides many ways to do exactly the same thing.

Lesson 1-8: Download the sample files

Many of the lessons in this book require the use of a sample file. The sample files for the book can be downloaded free from our web site.

You normally only have to download once but if you lose or otherwise corrupt the sample files you can download them again (as many times as you want) to start again with a fresh set of sample files.

Potential problems when downloading untrusted sample files

Protected View is a security feature that was first introduced in Excel 2010. It is designed to protect you from potential viruses by treating all files downloaded from the Internet as being suspicious.

Any workbooks that are downloaded from the Internet, or are sent by e-mail attachment, will open in *Protected View* by default.

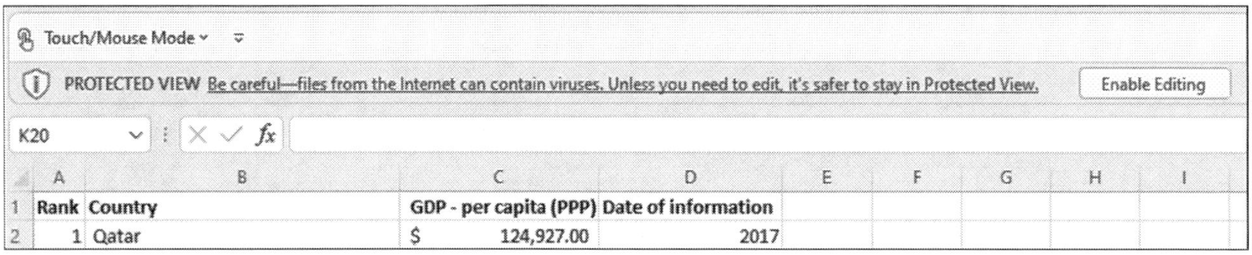

The user then has to click an *Enable Editing* button to use the file as normal.

Our sample files are available via a certified self-extracting .EXE file.

While some users may find it useful to be reminded about the origin of their files, others may find this feature annoying.

In order for Excel to trust the sample files they must be installed from an executable file (.exe file) that has a valid security certificate.

We provide the sample files as a digitally-signed self-extracting download and that is the easiest only way to install them onto your computer.

A single file is downloaded and run on your computer. All of the sample files are then installed into a folder on your computer called C:/Practice.

Our sample files are also available as a .ZIP file.

We also offer an alternative zip file download method (the link to this page is in the FAQ section at the bottom of the download web page).

note

Windows S Mode

The Windows 10 S operating system was discontinued in mid-2017 and replaced with "S Mode" (also available for Windows 2011).

Some new computers are sold with S mode enabled.

S mode locks Windows into a cut-down environment that only allows executable files to be purchased from the Windows store. That means that you cannot download the executable sample files when in S mode (you'll have to use the alternative zip file set instead).

Tech website Thurrott reported that 40% of users that had purchased a Windows 10 S computer have switched to Windows 10/11 Pro (this is a free upgrade).

important

Organizing your sample files folder

When you complete a lesson that involves a sample file that is changed, you will be instructed to save the file with a suffix.

By the time you've completed the course you'll have sample files such as:

Sales-1
Sales-2
Sales-3
Sales-4 ... etc

The first file is the sample file that you downloaded and the others (with the number suffix) are interim versions as you complete each lesson.

The sample file set includes the starting sample file and all interim versions.

The interim versions are provided for three reasons:

1. If your work-in-progress becomes unusable (for example after a system crash) you can continue without starting at the beginning again.

2. If a lesson doesn't seem to give the results described, you can view the example to get some clues about what has gone wrong.

3. When you have completed the course you will use this book as a reference. The interim versions allow you to work through any of the lessons in isolation if you need to remind yourself how to use a specific Excel feature.

It is a good idea to place the sample files in a different folder to your saved work. If you don't do this, you'll be over-writing the sample interim files (such as Sales-1, Sales-2 etc) with your own finished work.

The alternative zip file has been provided because some companies (or anti-virus products) block the download of executable files. You may also have to use the zip file option if you are using a (now discontinued) operating system called *Windows 10 S* that only allows executable files to be downloaded from the Windows store (see sidebar).

If you download using the zip file option, you'll have to click the *Enable Editing* button every time you open a sample file for the first time.

1 Download the sample files.

1. Open your web browser and type in the URL:

   https://thesmartmethod.com

2. Click the *Sample Files* link on the top right of the home page.

   Download the sample file set for *Excel 2021 Essential Skills.*

   If you have any difficulty downloading the sample files there is a FAQ section at the bottom of the page detailing the solutions to common problems.

   The file you have downloaded is named:

   Excel2021EssentialSkills.exe

3. Run the file (some browsers may call this *Open* the file or *Execute* the file).

   An unzip dialog will appear:

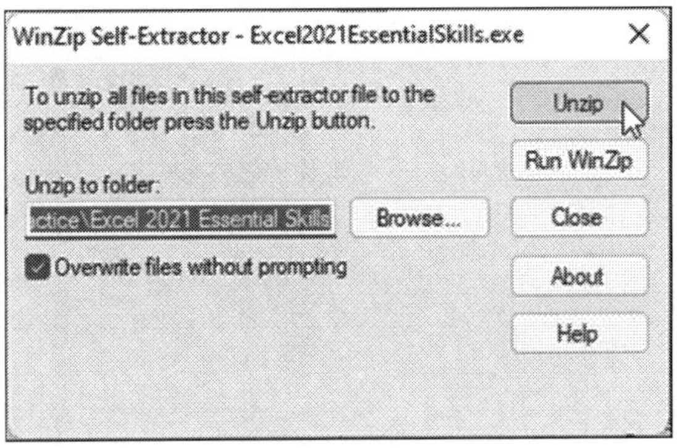

4. Click the *Unzip* button.

   The files will be unzipped and you'll see a success message.

   The files are (by default) installed into the directory:

   C:/Practice/Excel 2021 Essential Skills

Lesson 1-9: Open and navigate a workbook

Excel uses the analogy of a book that has many pages. In Excel terminology, the term: *Workbook* is used for the entire book and *Worksheet* for each of the pages. You'll learn about worksheets later in this session in: *Lesson 1-13: View, move, add, rename, delete and navigate worksheet tabs.*

1 Open the sample workbook: *The Wealth of Nations*.

1. Open Excel.
2. Click *Open* from the left-hand menu bar.
3. Click: *Browse* in the right-hand window.
4. Navigate to your sample files. If you downloaded using the recommended option and didn't change the normal file location, you will find these in the *C:/Practice* folder.
5. Open the *Excel 2021 Essential Skills* folder.
6. Open the *Session 1* folder.
7. Double click *The Wealth of Nations* to open the sample workbook.

2 Go to Cell ZZ3 using the Name Box.

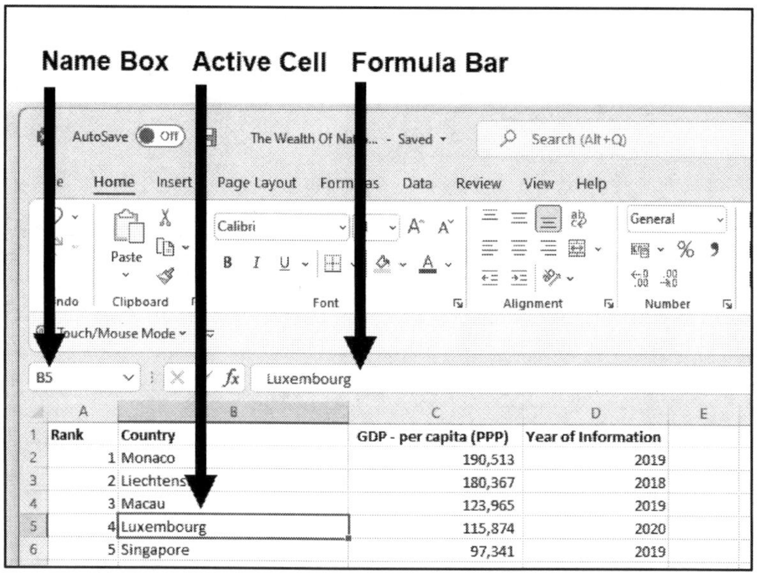

Excel uses the letter of the column and the number of the row to identify cells. This is called the *cell address*. In the above example, the cell address of the active cell is B5.

In Excel 2021 there are a little over a million rows and a little over sixteen thousand columns. You may wonder how it is possible to name these columns with only 26 letters in the alphabet.

When Excel runs out of letters it starts using two: X, Y, Z and then AA, AB, AC etc. But even two letters are not enough. When Excel reaches column ZZ it starts using three letters: ZX, ZY, ZZ and then AAA, AAB, AAC etc.

The Wealth of Nations

The currently selected cell is called the *Active Cell* and has a green line around it. The Active Cell's address is always displayed in the *Name Box* and its contents are displayed in the *Formula Bar*.

You can also use the *Name Box* to move to a specific cell.

To see this in action, type **ZZ3** into the *Name Box* and then press the **<Enter>** key. You are teleported to cell ZZ3:

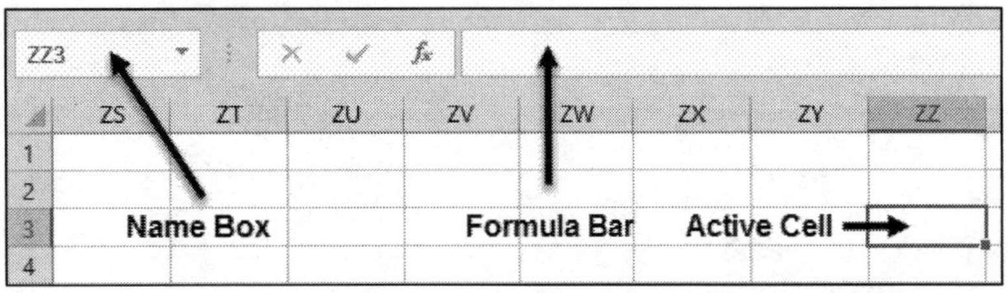

3 Return to cell A1 by pressing <Ctrl>+<Home>.

4 Go to the end of the worksheet by pressing <Ctrl>+<End>.

5 Use the scroll bars.

There are two scroll bars for the Excel window.

The vertical scroll bar runs from top to bottom of the window and allows you to quickly move up and down the worksheet.

The horizontal scroll bar is at the bottom right-hand side of the window and allows you to move to the left and right in wide worksheets. Here's how the scroll bars work:

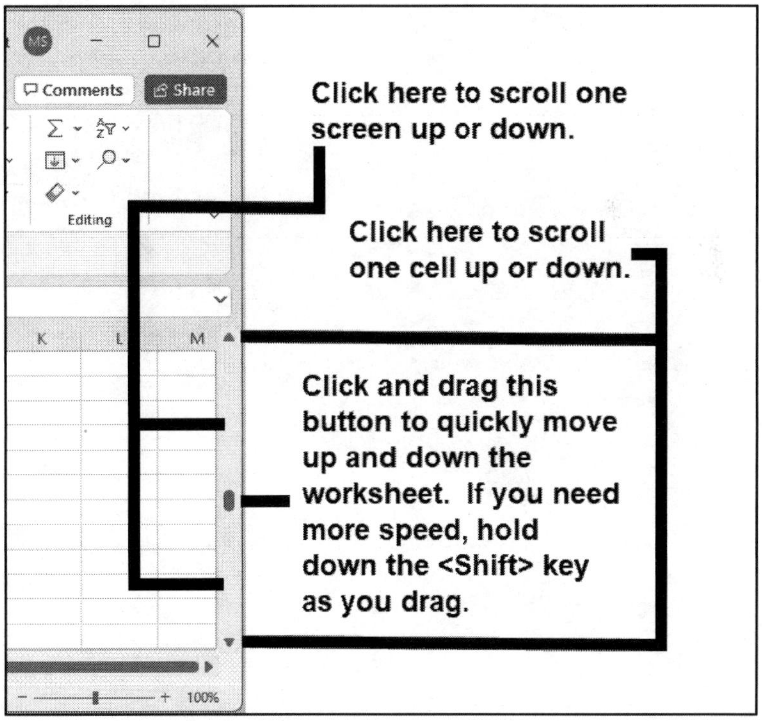

important

You may not be able to complete this lesson if the sample file is accessed from a OneDrive

A *OneDrive* is a virtual disk drive that is usually accessed via the Internet (see facing page sidebar).

When you save a file to a OneDrive it is automatically saved as you work. Notice the control to the left of the save button (on the Quick Access Toolbar).

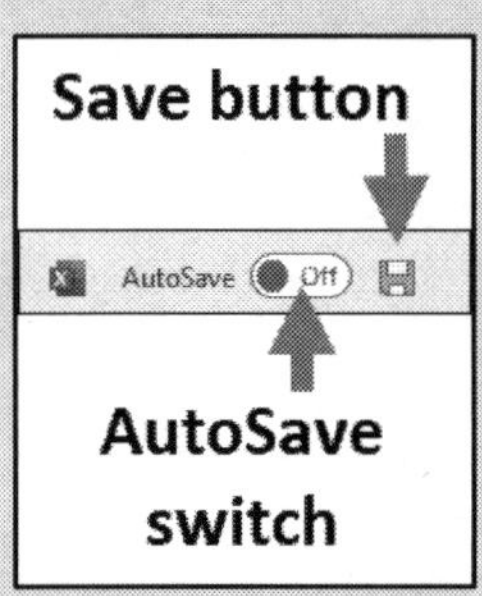

In the screen grab above the AutoSave switch is Off because the workbook I am using was not opened from a OneDrive.

When you open a workbook from a OneDrive you are able to control the AutoSave behaviour of the drive.

tip

You can also use the **<F12>** key to instantly display the *Save As* dialog.

tip

You can also use the **<Ctrl>+<S>** keyboard shortcut to save your work.

The Wealth of Nations

Lesson 1-10: Save a workbook to a local file

1 Open *The Wealth of Nations* from your sample files folder (if it isn't already open).

2 Save the workbook.

When you are editing a workbook that is saved on your local computer's hard drive, the changes that you make are only held in the computer's memory. If there is a power cut or your computer crashes, you may lose any work that has been done since the last save.

For this reason, you should get into the habit of regularly saving your work.

Even though you haven't changed this workbook, save it by clicking the *Save* button at the top left of the screen.

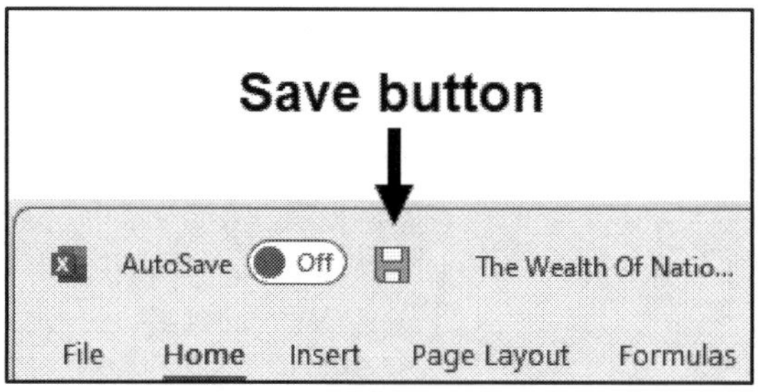

3 Save the workbook with a different name.

1. Click the *File* button.  at the top-left of the screen.

2. Click: *Save As*  in the left-hand list.

3. Click *Browse*  in the *Save As* menu.

The following dialog appears:

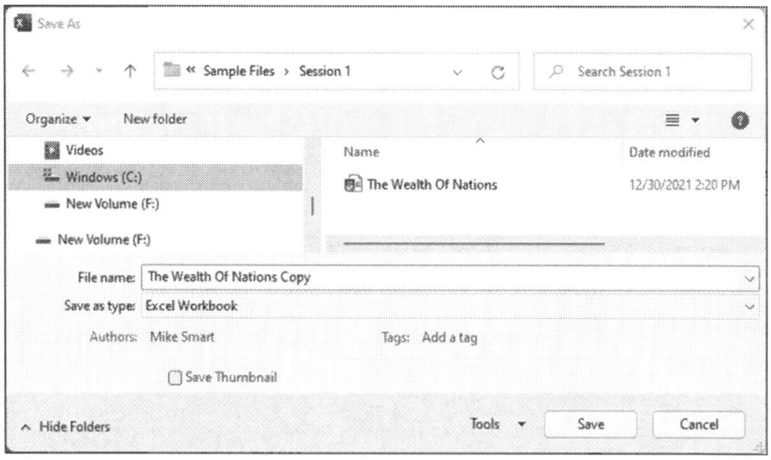

1. Click the drop-down arrow to the right of the *Save as type* drop-down list.

note

OneDrive and Cloud Computing

You may have noticed that the *Save As* dialog also has an option to save your workbook to a OneDrive:

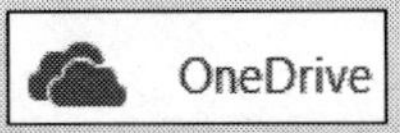

A OneDrive can be thought of as a "disk drive in the sky".

It is just like the C:\ drive on your computer but exists on a Microsoft server many miles away, accessed via the Internet.

The OneDrive can be very useful when you need to access your files from several different computers.

A OneDrive also provides an easier way to share files with others.

The OneDrive is part of a completely new way of working called *Cloud Computing*.

Because Cloud Computing is such an involved (and complex) subject I have devoted an entire session to it in: *Session Eight: Cloud Computing*.

I advise you not to jump ahead to the last session at this stage in your learning, as this session will be difficult to understand until you have completed the earlier sessions.

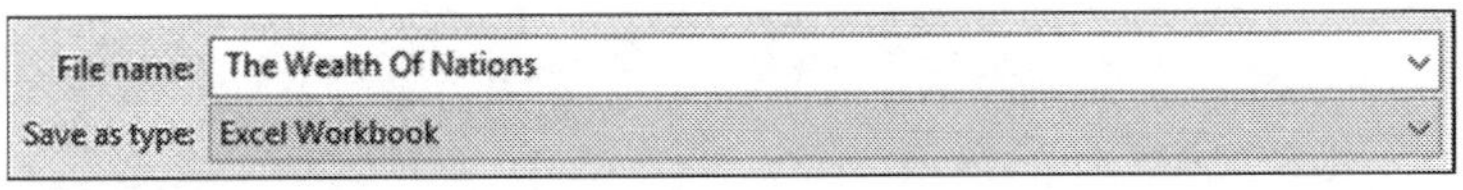

2. A list appears showing a large number of different file types:

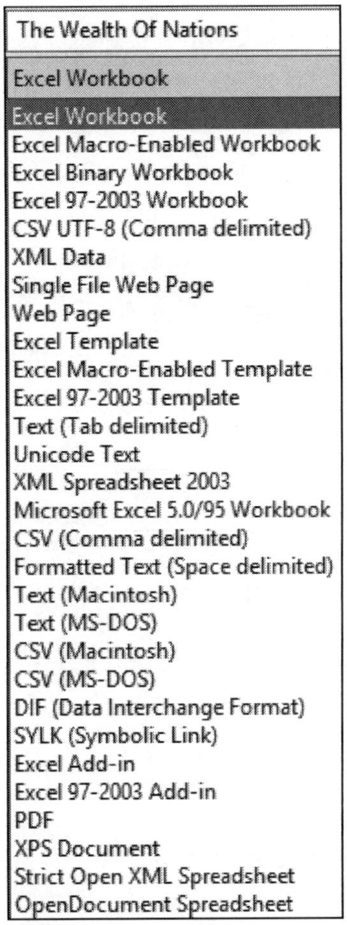

Most of the time you'll want to use the default format: *Excel Workbook* but there may be times when you'll need to save in one of the other formats. You'll learn about the most important formats (and when you should use them) in: *Lesson 1-11: Understand common file formats.* For now, you'll stay with the default: *Excel Workbook* format.

3. Click inside the *File name* box.
4. Type: **The Wealth of Nations Copy**

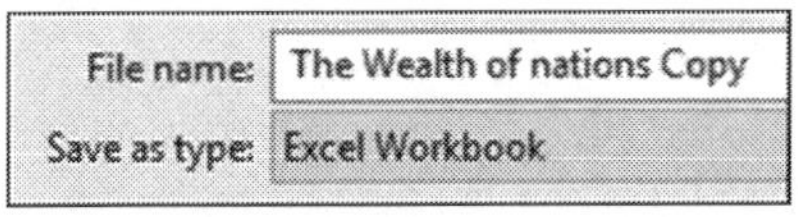

5. Click the *Save* button.

Notice that the name of the workbook in the title bar (at the top of the window) has now changed indicating that you are now viewing the new workbook that you have just saved.

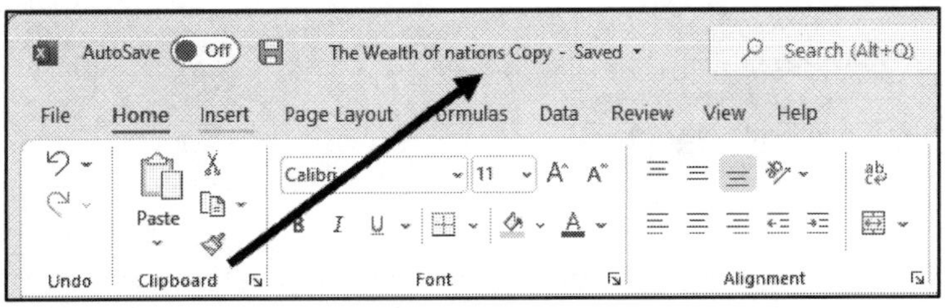

Lesson 1-11: Understand common file formats

1 Open a new blank workbook.

You learned how to do this in: *Lesson 1-1: Start Excel and open a new blank workbook.*

2 View the file formats supported by Excel.

1. Click the *File* button at the top-left of the screen.
2. Click: *Save As* in the left-hand list.
3. Click *Browse* in the *Save As* menu.

   The *Save As* dialog appears.
4. Click the drop-down arrow to the right of the *Save as type* list.

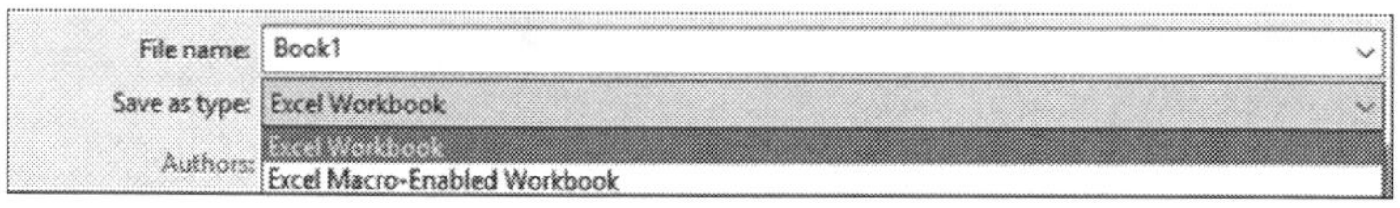

   A list appears showing all of the different file formats supported by Excel (see sidebar).

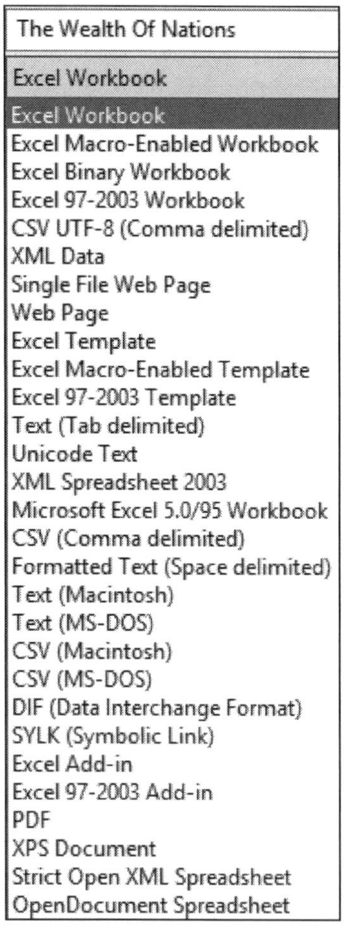

3 Understand the most important file formats.

Excel Workbook (the Open XML format)

Before Office 2007 was released, every program stored its information on the hard disk in a completely different way. These incompatible formats are called *binary formats*. This made it very difficult to write applications that could be used together.

All of this changed with a new format that was first introduced in Office 2007: *Office Open XML*.

In 2008 Office Open XML was ratified by the International Standards Organization as ISO/IEC 29500.

This published specification enables programmers to make other programs easily work with Excel workbook files.

Many Excel users will only use this format and it is the most usual way to save an Excel workbook.

Excel Binary Workbook

This is a binary alternative to Open XML.

Binary files generally result in smaller file sizes and open and save more quickly than Open XML.

You will only notice a speed (and file size) difference when working with very large worksheets. When working with small files you may even find that binary files take up more space than the Open XML format.

The *Excel Binary Workbook* format may also present a security threat as (just like the *Excel Macro-Enabled Workbook* format) it can contain macros that could infect your machine with a macro virus.

Excel Macro-Enabled Workbook

An Excel Macro-Enabled Workbook is a workbook that has program code (called VBA code) embedded within it. Macros (also called VBA program Code) are beyond the scope of this book but are covered in the *Learn Excel 2021 Expert Skills* book in this series.

While macro code is very powerful it can also be destructive as it is extremely simple to write damaging viruses within Excel macro code.

Versions of Excel before Excel 2007 could potentially allow a workbook to infect your machine with a macro virus because all Excel files could carry macros. Because the formats are now separate, it is easier to avoid opening potentially infected files.

Excel 97-2003 Workbook

This is the old binary format that allows users with very early versions of Excel to open your workbooks. Many features won't work in such old versions and if you've used those in your workbook, Excel will display a warning when you save telling you which features will be lost.

As Excel 2003 officially reached the end of its life in April 2014 it is unlikely that any business users will still use these obsolete versions.

PDF

If you need to send a worksheet to a user who does not own a copy of Excel, you can save it in PDF (Portable Document Format). This format was invented by Adobe and is also sometimes called *Adobe Acrobat* or simply *Acrobat*.

All major web browsers can open and display PDF files. In Windows 10 and 11, PDF files will, by default, open using the Edge browser. If you send a user a PDF file you can be confident that they will be able to read and print (but not change) the worksheet.

Other formats

As you can see, there are several other less commonly used formats supported by Excel 2021, but the above formats are the only ones you'll normally encounter. The most important thing to remember is that, unless there's a good reason to use a different format, you should always save documents in the default *Excel Workbook* format.

note

Sharing files using Cloud Computing features

Excel 2021 provides another way to share files with users that do not have any version of Excel installed upon their computer. This is done using Excel 2021's built in *Cloud Computing* features.

Cloud Computing also allows users to open (and even edit) Excel workbooks using devices such as iPads, Android pads, Apple Macs and Smartphones.

Because Cloud Computing is such an involved (and complex) subject I have devoted an entire session to it in: *Session Eight: Cloud Computing.*

Lesson 1-12: Pin a workbook and understand file organization

1 Close down and restart Excel.

2 Pin a workbook to the *Recent Workbooks* list.

Notice that there is a list of recently opened documents at the bottom of the main window.

You'll probably see the *Wealth of Nations* and *The Wealth of Nations Copy* workbooks that you opened earlier in this session in the list.

Notice that there is also a *Search* box that will enable you to quickly find a file that you've recently worked on.

1. Hover the mouse cursor over *The Wealth of nations*.

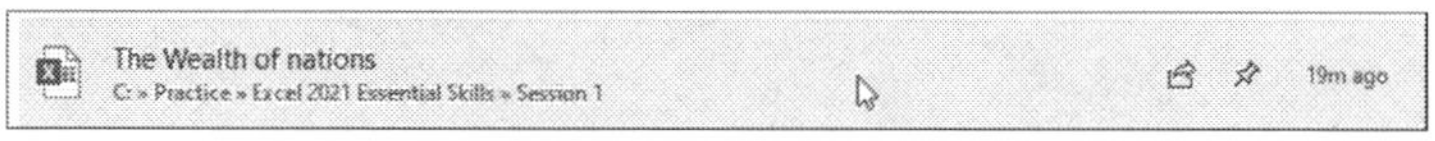

Notice that a pin icon  has appeared next to the workbook name.

When you hover the mouse cursor over the pin a tooltip is displayed saying: *Pin this item to the list.*

This can be a great time saver as it enables any workbook that you use a lot to always be at the top of the *Recent* list. You won't have to waste time looking for it on the hard drive.

2. Click the pin icon. The pin icon now appears next to the pinned item:

3. Click on *The Wealth of Nations* to open the workbook.

3 Understand file organization.

By default, Excel saves all workbooks into your *Documents* folder along with other Office documents (such as Word and PowerPoint files). This is clearly going to cause problems when you have a few hundred files.

tip

Reducing the number of items, or hiding items, in the recent workbooks or recent folders lists

Excel remembers the fifty most recently opened workbooks and folders.

As you open more documents the fiftieth oldest is removed from the *Recent* list unless you pin it.

If you'd like to reduce the number of workbooks or folders that Excel keeps track of, here's how it's done:

1. Click the *File* button at the top left of the screen.
2. Click the *Options* button at the bottom of the left-hand menu bar.
3. Choose *Advanced* from the left-hand menu bar.
4. Scroll down the right-hand list until you find the *Display* category. You'll see *Show this number of Recent Workbooks: 50* and *Show this number of unpinned Recent Folders: 50.*

5. Change the number to the number of recently opened workbooks/folders you'd prefer Excel to remember.

   If you set the value to zero, Excel will not show any entries in the list.

The Wealth of Nations

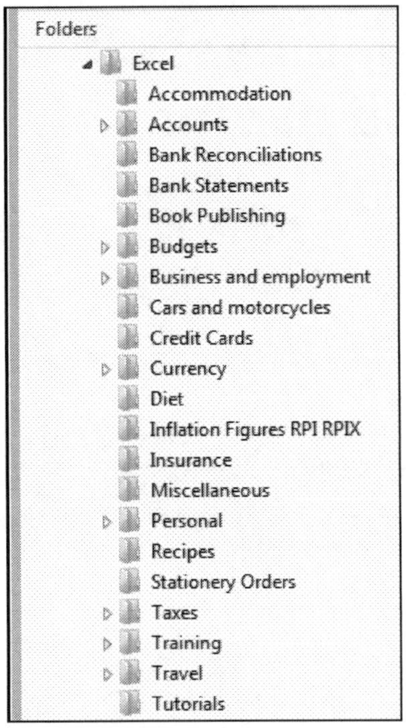

note

How do I create a subfolder?

The concept of folders, subfolders and files is a very fundamental Windows skill rather than an Excel skill.

If you do not have basic Windows skills (an understanding of how Windows organizes files) you would get good value from a Windows book.

Here's how you create a new subfolder:

1. Open the *Documents* folder.

2. Right-click in a blank area of the folder.

2. Click: New→Folder, from the shortcut menu.

A new folder will appear called *New Folder.*

3. You will now be able to type: **Excel** in order to name the folder.

If this doesn't work for you, right-click the new folder and select *Rename* from the shortcut menu. In Windows 11 you may have to click *Show more options* to select *Rename.*

It is better to organize yourself from the start by setting up an orderly filing system.

4 Create an *Excel* subfolder beneath your *Documents* folder.

I create a folder called *Excel* beneath the *Documents* folder. In this folder, I create subfolders to organize my work into categories. You can see a screen grab of my Excel folder in the sidebar (of course, your needs will be different to mine).

See sidebar if you don't know how to create a subfolder.

5 Set the default file location to point to the new *Excel* folder.

If you take my advice and create an Excel folder, you will waste a mouse click every time you open a file because Excel will take you to the *Documents* folder by default.

Here's how to reset the default file location to your new Excel folder:

1. Open Excel and click the *Blank workbook* template to open a new blank workbook.

2. Click the *File* button at the top left of the screen.

3. Click the *Options* button towards the bottom of the left-hand list.

   The *Excel Options* dialog appears.

4. Choose the *Save* category from the left-hand side of the dialog.

   During the remainder of the book, I'll explain the above three steps like this:

   Click: File→Options→Save.

5. Change the *Default local file location.*

   Type: **\Excel** after the end of the current *Default local file location.*

   You have to actually type this manually. Microsoft seem to have forgotten to add a browse button!

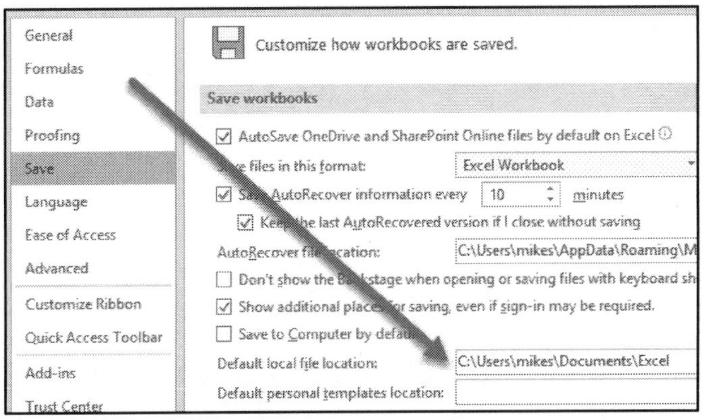

When you click File→Open→Browse in future you'll automatically be taken to your Excel folder ready to choose one of the subfolder categories you have created.

important

If your sample files are stored on a OneDrive, switch AutoSave off

Most learners will have the sample files installed onto their local hard drive (sample files are installed to *C:\Practice* by default).

Some users may have copied the sample files to their OneDrive. A OneDrive is a "cloud" drive meaning that it is located on a Microsoft server many miles away and accessed via the Internet.

When you purchased Office 2021 you were automatically allocated a 5Gb free OneDrive.

You'll learn more about OneDrive later in: *Session Eight: Cloud Computing.*

When files are located on your OneDrive the AutoSave feature is switched on by default. The AutoSave button (at the top left of the screen) then becomes enabled.

When AutoSave is On, every change you make is instantly updated to the OneDrive.

If you see this button at the top left of your screen, click the *On* button to switch AutoSave off before beginning this lesson.

You'll learn more about the AutoSave feature later in: *Lesson 8-8: Understand OneDrive AutoSave and Version History*

The Wealth of Nations

Lesson 1-13: View, move, add, rename, delete and navigate worksheet tabs

When you save an Excel file onto your hard disk, you save a single workbook containing one or more worksheets. You can add as many worksheets as you need to a workbook.

There are two types of worksheets. *Regular* worksheets contain cells. *Chart* sheets, as you would expect, each contain a single chart. You'll be exploring charts in depth in: *Session Five: Charts and Graphics.*

1 Open *The Wealth of Nations* from your sample files folder (if it isn't already open).

2 Move between worksheets.

Look at the tabs in the bottom left corner of your screen. Notice that this sample workbook contains three worksheets. Click on each tab in turn to view each worksheet.

3 Add a new worksheet and name it: **Population**

1. Click the *New Sheet* button (the circle with a plus sign inside it next to *Smartphones*).  A new tab appears named *Sheet1.*
2. Double-click the *Sheet1* tab.
3. Type the word **Population** followed by the **<Enter>** key.

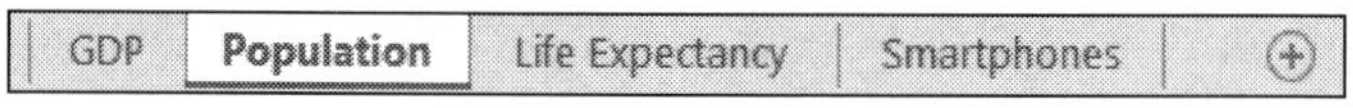

4 Move a worksheet's tab.

1. Click on the *Population* tab (you may have to do this twice).
2. Hold the mouse button down and drag to the left or right. As you drag you'll notice an icon of a page and a black arrow showing you where the tab will be placed.
3. Release the mouse button to move the tab to the location of your choice.

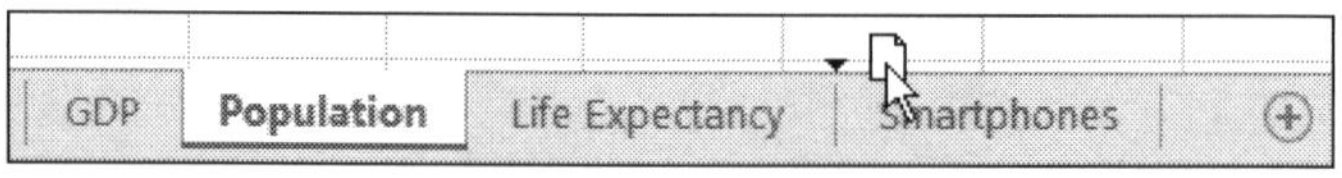

5 Understand the tab scroll buttons.

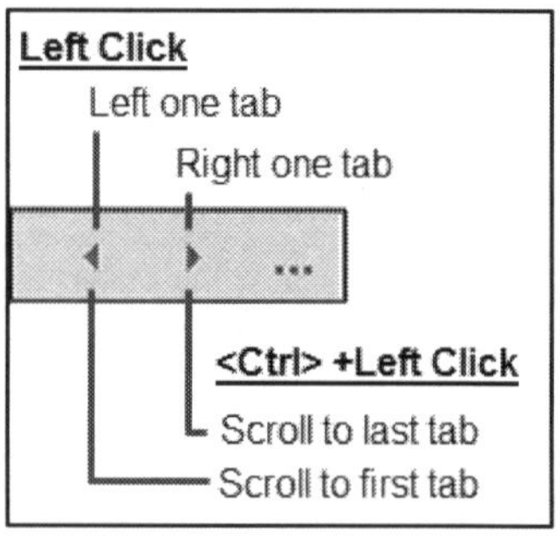

Because this workbook only has four tabs, there's no need to use the tab scroll buttons (in fact, they don't do anything and are grayed out when all tabs are visible).

When there are more tabs than will fit on the screen the *tab scroll buttons* are used to move between tabs.

6 Move between worksheets using the keyboard.

You can also move between worksheets using only the keyboard by pressing the **<Ctrl>+<PgUp>** and **<Ctrl>+<PgDn>** keyboard shortcuts to cycle through all the tabs in your workbook.

7 Change tab colors.

1. Right-click on any of the tabs and choose *Tab Color* from the shortcut menu.
2. Choose any color.

   It is best practice to choose a color from the top block of *Theme Colors* rather than one of the *Standard Colors.*

   You'll discover why later, in: *Lesson 4-9: Understand themes* and in: *Lesson 4-11: Add color and gradient effects to cells (sidebar).*
3. Repeat for the other tabs on the worksheet.

8 Delete a worksheet.

Right click on the *Population* tab and click *Delete* from the shortcut menu.

9 Delete several worksheets at the same time.

1. Hold down the **<Ctrl>** key.
2. Click each tab that you want to delete in turn. Don't select them all as it isn't possible to delete every worksheet in a workbook.
3. Right click any of the selected tabs and select *Delete* from the shortcut menu.
4. If prompted, click the *Delete* button to confirm that you want to delete the selected worksheets.

Don't worry about the missing tabs. You're going to close the workbook without saving, so you won't overwrite the original workbook.

10 Close the workbook without saving.

1. Click: File→Close.

   A dialog is displayed:

   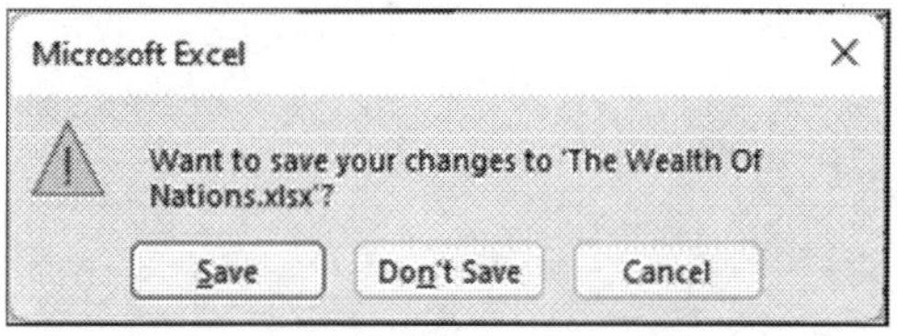

2. Click *Don't Save* so that you don't over-write the workbook.

   Because you haven't saved the workbook it will remain in its original state when you next open it.

note

The versions feature will not protect you from a hard drive failure

Carnegie Melon University conducted a study of 100,000 mechanical hard drives in 2007. They found that there's a probability of between 1 in 50 and 1 in 25 of a mechanical hard drive failing each year.

In an office of 100 workers (using mechanical hard drives) that means that between two and four unlucky workers will suffer a hard drive failure every year.

Solid state hard drives (SSD) tend to be more reliable than mechanical hard drives but will still eventually fail. For example, one very popular 250Gb SSD is only warrantied to remain reliable for the first 150 Terabytes written to it.

To insure against drive failure, you need to back up your data to a different hard drive (or other media).

If your computer is part of an office network, the normal solution is to save your files to a shared network drive. The IT department are then responsible for backing this up every night.

For home users (or small companies that only have one computer) you should back up all of your data to an external hard drive (or a memory stick if your files are not very large).

Cloud computing enables you to store or backup your files to a OneDrive (a virtual disk drive accessed via the Internet).

OneDrive has its own (better and more powerful) versions feature

You'll learn about the OneDrive versions feature later, in: *Lesson 8-8: Understand OneDrive AutoSave and Version History.*

Lesson 1-14: Use the Versions feature to recover an unsaved Draft file

This lesson refers to workbooks that are saved to a local hard drive (and not a OneDrive – see sidebar). OneDrive files have a different versions feature that you'll learn about later in: *Lesson 8-8: Understand OneDrive AutoSave and Version History.*

The Versions feature is fantastically useful as it solves two common problems that are as old as computing itself:

1. Your computer crashes, there's a power cut, or you close your work without saving, and then discover that you've lost all of your work since the last save.

2. You delete parts of your workbook and then save, only to realize that you deleted something important before saving. Because saving over-writes the old version of the file, you find that you've lost the deleted work forever.

Microsoft has a solution to both problems. The Versions feature works like this:

1. Every so often Excel saves a backup of your workbook (called a *Version*) for you. The default time interval for these automatic backups is every 10 minutes (but you can change this to any interval). You'll see the Versions feature at work in the next lesson: *Lesson 1-15: Use the Versions feature to recover an earlier version of a workbook.*

2. If you create a new workbook and then close it without saving, Excel will still keep the last automatic backup it made. Excel calls this a *Draft* version. Draft versions are automatically deleted after four days. The Draft feature is the subject of this lesson.

You'll need a watch or clock with a second hand for this lesson.

1 Open a new blank workbook.

You learned how to do this in: *Lesson 1-1: Start Excel and open a new blank workbook.*

2 Set the AutoSave interval to one minute and check that AutoSave features are enabled.

1. Click: File→Options→Save.
2. Change the *Save AutoRecover information every* box to 1 minute.
3. Make sure that the other options are set in the same way as in this screen grab (the two check boxes will already be checked unless another user has changed them):

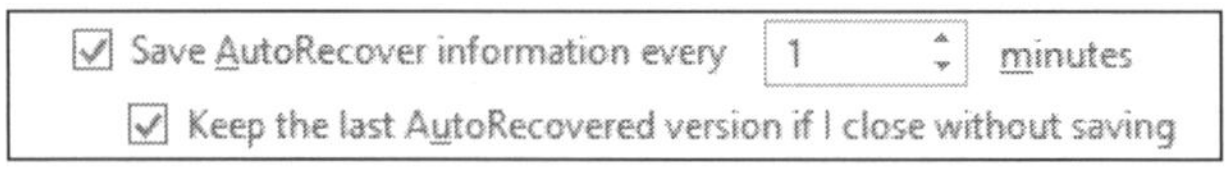

4. Click: *OK* and check the time on your clock or watch. The first AutoSave will happen one minute from now.

3 Type some text into cells A1 and A2.

anecdote

RAID arrays protect against hard drive failure

Loss of data has always been a concern for large organizations. It has been estimated that two to four percent of hard drives fail every year.

Many years ago, I implemented an EDMS (electronic document management system) for the world's largest car manufacturer. It would have been a disaster for them to lose even one hour's work, so I specified a special drive called a RAID Array (Redundant Array of Independent Disks) to store the documents.

The simplest RAID array consists of two hard drives and automatically writes all data to both drives (this is called mirroring). If one drive fails, the other will still have the data, meaning that any data loss is very unlikely.

RAID arrays don't stop workflow for even a moment. If a disk fails, the users don't even notice as data continues to be available from the other disk (or disks).

When the faulty disk drive is replaced, the files automatically restore themselves from the good disk (or disks) restoring the reliability of the array.

note

If you do not see the draft saved file

If your computer has many background processes running it is possible that the draft automatic save may take a lot longer than the one minute it should.

We've even had a report of nine minutes from one user).

1. Type the following into cells A1 and A2, pressing the **<Enter>** key after each line:

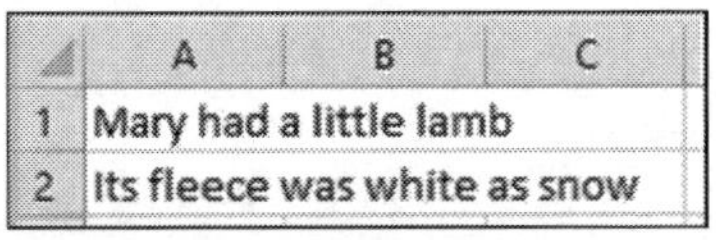

2. Wait for at least one minute. (After one-minute Excel will automatically save your workbook).

   After a little over a minute try to close the workbook. The following dialog should appear:

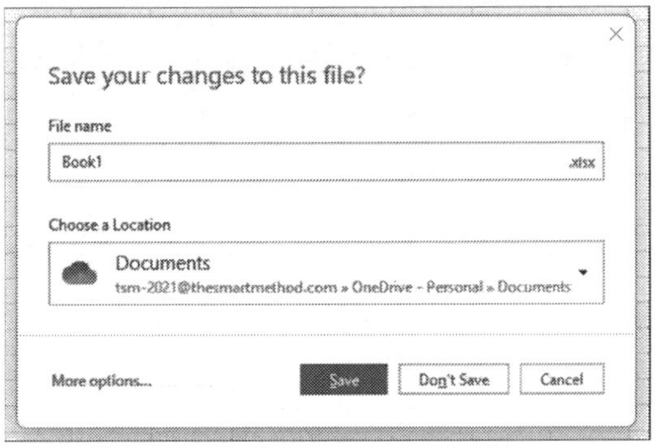

3. Click the *Don't Save* button.

   Even though you told Excel not to save, a draft copy has been secretly saved, just in case you made a mistake and may need the file later.

4 Recover the draft document.

1. Open Excel.
2. Click: *More Workbooks* at the bottom of the recent files list.

3. Click the *Recover Unsaved Workbooks* button.

   You'll find this at the bottom center of the screen (you may need to scroll down).

4. A dialog should appear showing the unsaved document that you were working on:

   If you don't see this dialog, see sidebar for more information.

5. Double-click the document to open it.

   The document is now shown on screen (even though you have never saved it).

6. Recover the unsaved file.

   Click the *Save As* button in the top information bar.

5 Save the file in your sample files folder with the name: *Mary*

Lesson 1-15: Use the Versions feature to recover an earlier version of a workbook

Excel's ability to automatically backup your document at a chosen time interval was explored in the previous lesson: *Lesson 1-14: Use the Versions feature to recover an unsaved Draft file.* This lesson will show you how to view the automatic backups and to revert to an earlier version if you've messed up the current version. You can even cut sections from older versions of a workbook and paste them into the current version.

You'll need a watch or clock with a second hand for this lesson.

1 Open *Mary* from your sample files folder (if it isn't already open).

This is the file that you saved in the last lesson.

2 Cause Excel to automatically save a different version of the workbook.

In the last lesson: *Lesson 1-14: Use the Versions feature to recover an unsaved Draft file*, you set the time interval for automatic backups to 1 minute. If you are not completing this course sequentially, you will need to go back to that lesson and make sure that this setting is set to 1 minute.

Add the following text to cells A4 and A5, pressing the **<Enter>** key after each line:

	A	B	C	D
1	Mary had a little lamb			
2	Its fleece was white as snow			
3				
4	and everywhere that Mary went			
5	The lamb was sure to go			
6				

Look at your watch or clock and wait for a little over one minute. Excel should have automatically saved a new version of the workbook.

3 Make sure that Excel has automatically saved the new version.

Some users have reported that Excel sometimes takes as long as ten minutes to automatically save a file (even when the AutoRecover interval is set to one minute). Here's how to check that AutoRecover has performed as it should:

1. Click the *File* button File at the top-left of the screen.
2. Click *Info* on the left-hand menu bar.

   You should see an AutoRecover file version alongside the *Manage Workbook* button.

important

This lesson does not apply to files saved to a OneDrive

This lesson refers to workbooks that are saved to a local hard drive and not a OneDrive.

OneDrive files have a different versions feature that you'll learn about later in: *Lesson 8-8: Understand OneDrive AutoSave and Version History.*

important

Version files don't stay around forever

As discussed in: *Lesson 1-14: Use the Versions feature to recover an unsaved Draft file*, draft versions of unsaved files are kept for four days.

But what about the regular *Version* backups that Excel makes? Obviously, Excel would fill up your hard drive with version files if it didn't have a mechanism for automatically deleting them.

Excel uses two rules when deciding whether version files are still useful.

1. While you are in the current editing session, version files are **never** deleted (even if you save the current version).

2. When you close the workbook **all version files are deleted** unless you close without saving. If you close without saving only the last version is retained (as a draft version).

Mary

If you don't see the AutoRecover version, click the *Back* button , wait another minute and then click File→Info again. Don't move on to the next step until it has appeared.

4 Further modify the file and then save it.

1. Click the Back button to return to the workbook. 
2. Add the following text to cells A7 and A8, pressing the **<Enter>** key after each line:

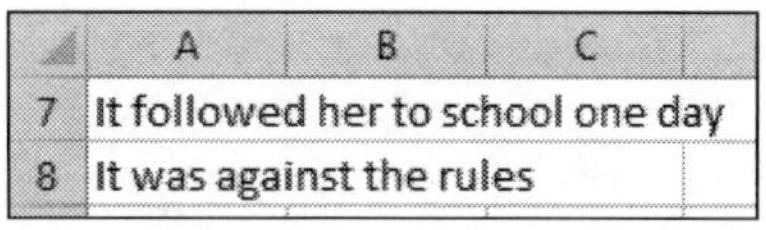

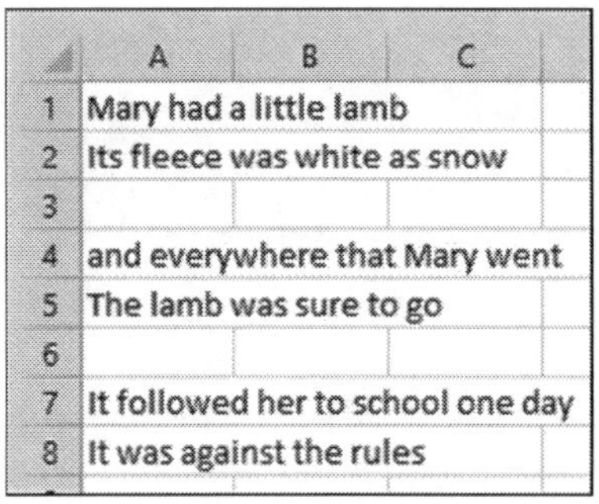

3. Save the workbook.

   You learned how to do this in: *Lesson 1-10: Save a workbook to a local file.*

5 View the earlier version that Excel automatically saved.

1. Click the *File* button  at the top left of the screen.
2. Click *Info* on the left-hand menu bar.
3. Click the earlier AutoSaved version.

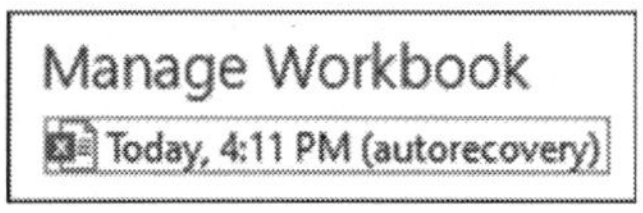

   The earlier version opens in a new Excel window.

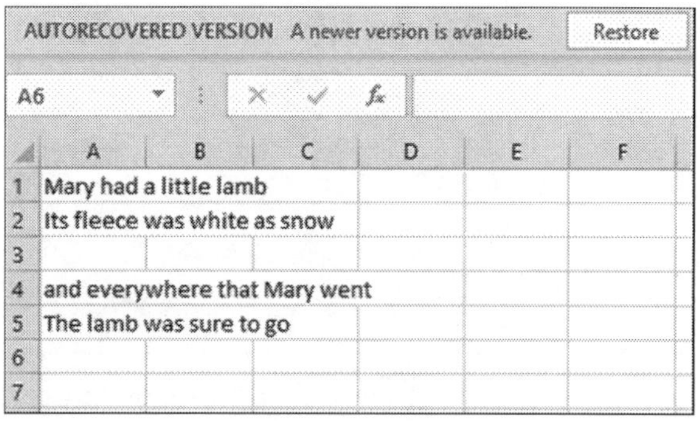

   Notice that Excel advises that there is a later version of your workbook available should you need to go back to the version that you have just replaced.

   Notice also that it would be possible to copy and paste sections from the older version into the newer version if you needed to do that.

6 Replace the current version of the workbook with the earlier AutoSaved version.

1. Click the *Restore* button on the top information bar.
2. Click the OK button to confirm.

7 Reset the AutoSave interval to 10 minutes.

You learned how to do this in: *Lesson 1-14: Use the Versions feature to recover an unsaved Draft file.*

note

The Versions feature isn't just for Excel

Microsoft has also included the Versions feature in Word and PowerPoint.

Now that you've learned how to use it in Excel, you should be able to figure out the small differences in the way it is implemented in the other Office applications.

important

The Ribbon shows more if you have a wider screen

When I work with Excel, I use a 32-inch monitor running at 2,560X1,440 pixels.

Excel uses all of the available screen space to display extended descriptions of each feature on the Ribbon.

For example, the *Styles* pane on the *Home* Ribbon shows ten buttons for common cell styles allowing them to be applied with a single click rather than two clicks.

Lesson 1-16: Use the Ribbon

The Ribbon provides fast access to hundreds of Excel features.

The sheer breadth of Excel features can seem overwhelming. This book will gently introduce all of the most important features, one at a time.

By the end of the book, you'll be really comfortable and productive with the Ribbon.

1 Start Excel and open a new blank workbook.

You learned how to do this in: *Lesson 1-1: Start Excel and open a new blank workbook.*

2 Use Ribbon tabs.

Each Ribbon tab has its own toolkit available to you. By far the most important tab is the *Home* tab which has buttons for all of the most common and useful features.

Click each tab in turn and view the buttons. The screen grab below has the *Home* tab selected. Don't worry if the buttons seem cryptic at the moment. Most of them will make complete sense by the end of this book. (And if you later go on to complete the *Expert Skills* course, Excel will have no mysteries left at all).

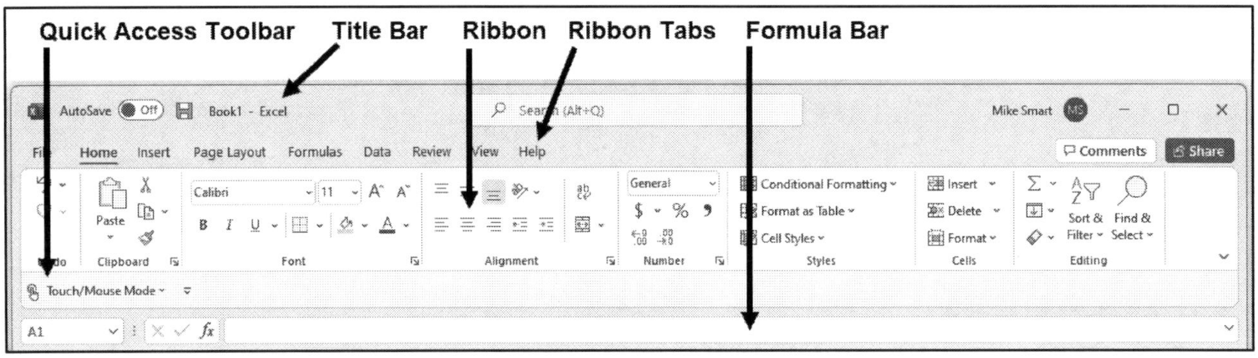

3 Type the word **Test** into any blank cell and then press the **<Enter>** key on the keyboard once.

Notice how the active cell moves to the cell beneath.

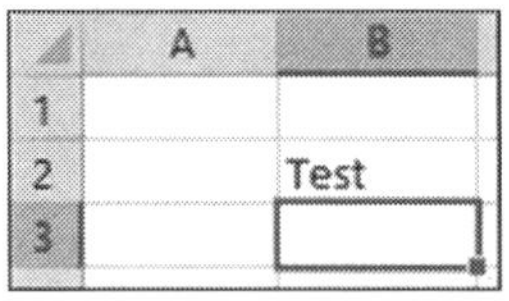

4 Make the cell with the word *Test* into the active cell.

Click once on the word *Test* or use the arrow keys on the keyboard to navigate back to the cell. Be very careful not to double-click, otherwise Excel will think that you want to edit the cell.

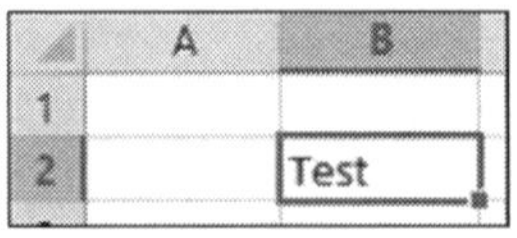

5 Click the *Home* tab on the Ribbon and focus upon the *Font* command group (it's the third panel from the left).

note

Contextual tabs

Sometimes Excel will show you even more tabs.

For example, in: *Session Five: Charts and Graphics*, you'll learn how to create charts.

When you click on a chart two new tabs called *Chart Design* and *Format* appear.

The new tabs provide access to a range of features relating to Charts.

important

If your Ribbon doesn't look like the illustrations in this book

The Ribbon will look different depending upon the size of your screen (see important sidebar on previous page).

Excel 2021 also allows you to customize the Ribbon.

Customizing the Ribbon is an expert-level skill covered in the *Expert Skills* book in this series.

If another user has customized the Ribbon using this feature, they may have rendered Excel unusable.

If you suspect this to be the case, you can put things back to normal like this:

1. Right-click in a blank area of the Ribbon.
2. Click: *Customize the Ribbon...* from the shortcut menu.
3. Click: Customizations→ Reset→ Reset all customizations.

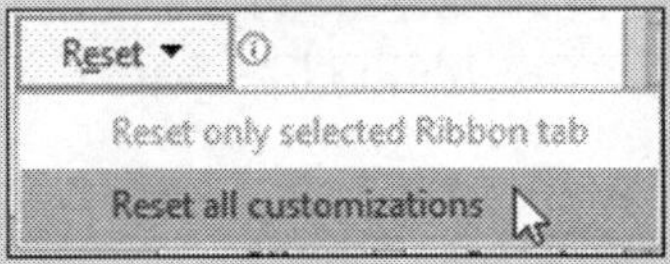

4. Click: Yes.

If you do this the Quick Access Toolbar and Touch/Mouse Mode button that you added in: *Lesson 1-5: Change between touch mode and mouse mode* will disappear.

You'll need to work through this lesson again to restore it.

Try clicking each of the buttons and you will see the word *Test* change to reflect your choices.

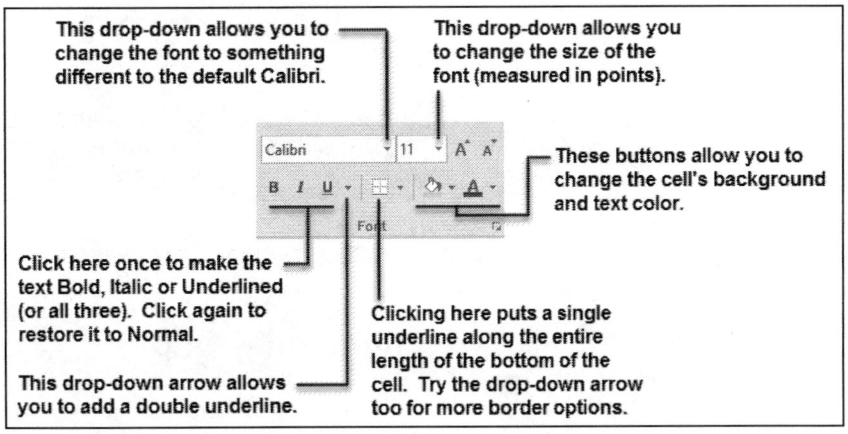

6 Minimize the Ribbon.

1. Double-click any of the Ribbon tabs except the *File* tab (for example the *Home* tab or the *Insert* tab).

   Notice how the Ribbon is now minimized in order to save screen space (though the *Formula Bar* is still visible).

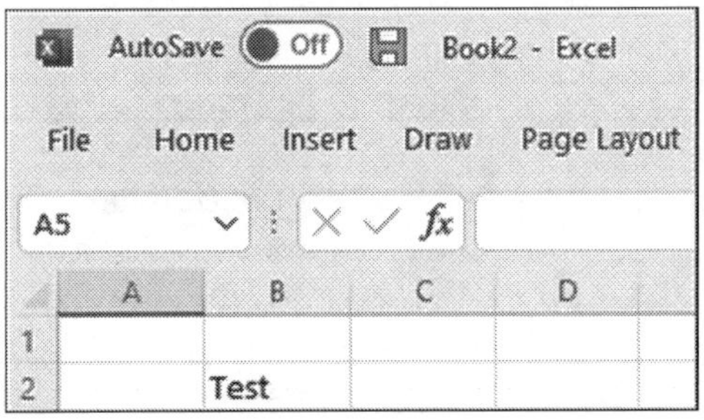

2. Click once on any tab, except the *File* tab, to temporarily bring the Ribbon back to full size.

   Notice that as soon as you click back onto the worksheet the Ribbon is minimized again.

7 Bring back the Ribbon.

Double-click on any tab except the *File* tab to permanently bring back the Ribbon.

8 Close Excel without saving changes.

1. Click: File→Close or click the cross in the top right corner.
2. When asked if you want to save your changes, click the *Don't Save* button.

Lesson 1-17: Understand Ribbon components

> The whole is more than the sum of its parts.
> ***Aristotle, Greek critic, philosopher, physicist & zoologist***
> ***(384 BC – 322 BC)***

The Ribbon is made up of several different controls.

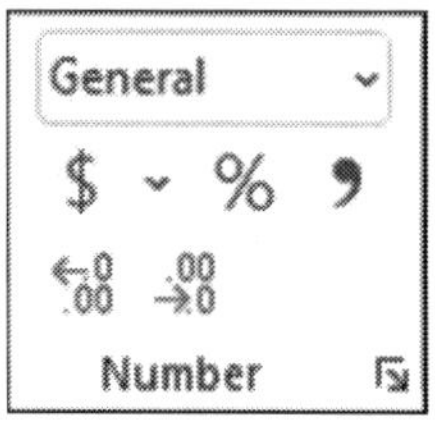

Command group

Similar actions are grouped into a cluster. For example, every control relating to numbers is clustered into the *Number* group.

Normal button

Simply executes a command when clicked. The *Bold* button on the *Home* tab is a good example.

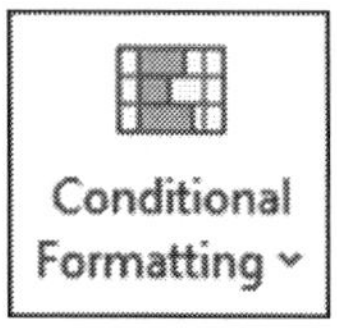

Menu button

This type of button has a little down-arrow underneath or next to it. Menu buttons display a *list, menu* or *rich menu* drop-down when clicked.

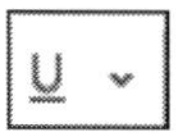

Split button

This button can be difficult to understand because *Split* buttons look almost the same as *Menu* buttons. When you hover the mouse cursor over a split button, the icon and drop-down arrow highlight separately as different "buttons within a button".

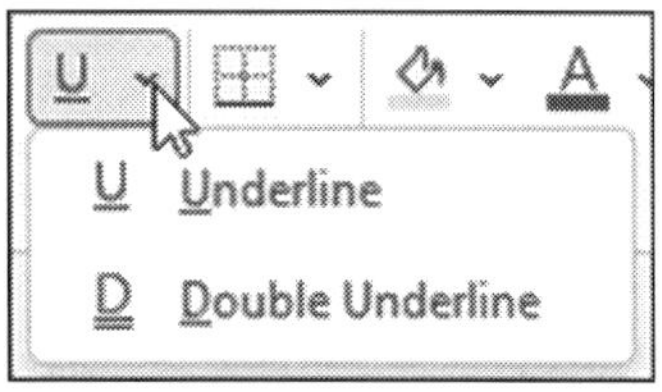

A good example is the *underline* button on the Home toolbar.

Clicking the icon part of a split button (the U) will perform the default action of the button (in this case a single underline). Clicking the arrow part of the button will display a drop-down list of further choices (in this case the choice between a single and double underline).

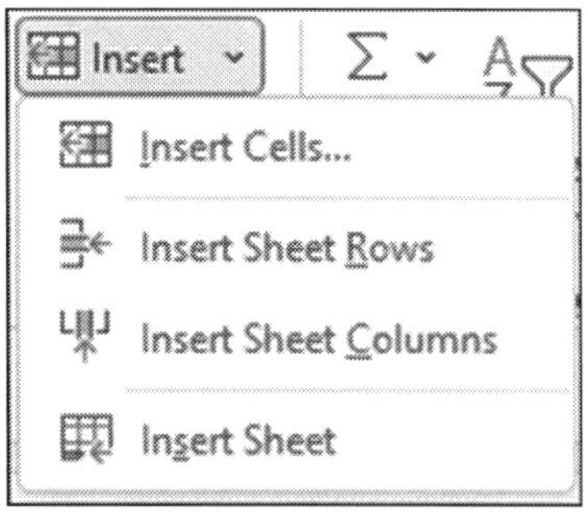

Drop-down list

I often shorten this to simply "Drop-Down" in this book. A drop-down is a simple menu listing several choices.

If you see an ellipsis (…) after a drop-down list item, this means that a dialog will be displayed after you click, offering further choices.

Rich menu

The rich menu is a drop-down list with added help text explaining what each item will do.

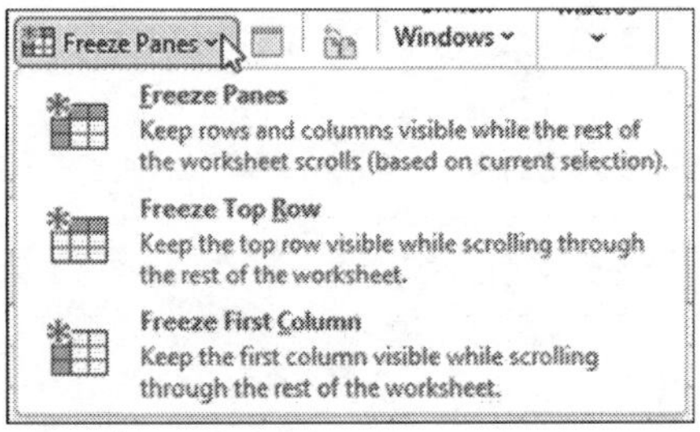

This rich menu can be found at:

View→Window→Freeze Panes

You'll find out what it is used for later in the book in: *Lesson 3-20: Freeze columns and rows.*

Drop-down gallery

This is a little like a drop-down list but has graphics to visually demonstrate the effect of each choice.

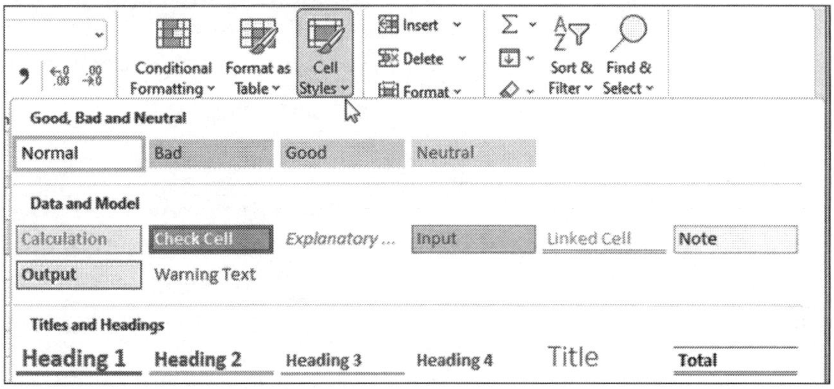

Check box

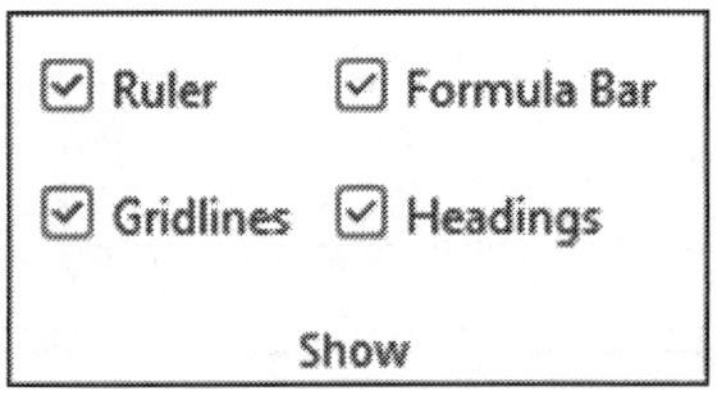

A little square box that you can click to switch an option on or off.

In this example (from the *Page Layout* Ribbon tab) you are able to switch the gridlines on and off for the screen display and/or the printout.

Dialog launcher

Dialog launchers appear on the bottom right-hand corner of some command groups. Dialogs offer more choices than it is possible for the Ribbon to express graphically.

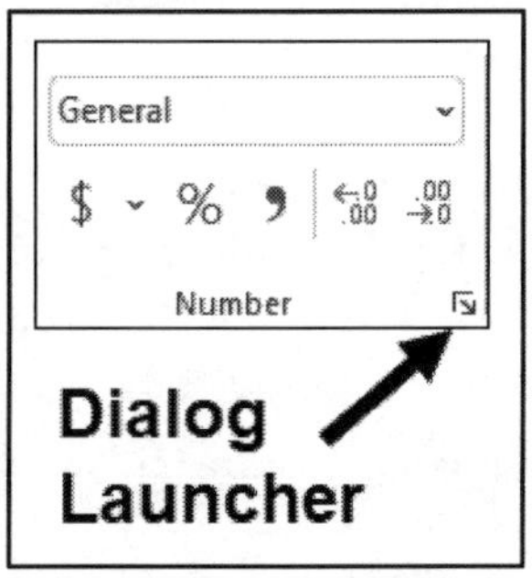

Lesson 1-18: Customize the Quick Access Toolbar and preview the printout

You added a Quick Access Toolbar to Excel in: *Lesson 1-5: Change between touch mode and mouse mode.*

In this lesson, you'll add some useful buttons to the *Quick Access Toolbar* to save a few clicks when accessing common commands.

1 Open *The Wealth of Nations* from your sample files folder.

2 Preview how the *Life Expectancy* worksheet will look when printed.

1. Click the *Life Expectancy* tab at the bottom of the worksheet.
2. Click: File→Print.

   Backstage View is displayed.

   Backstage view displays a large number of print-related features. A preview of how the page will look when it is printed is displayed on the right-hand side of the screen.
3. Click the *Next Page* and *Previous Page* buttons to move through the print preview.

   Notice there's a button to the bottom-left of the preview pane that allows you to cycle through each page:

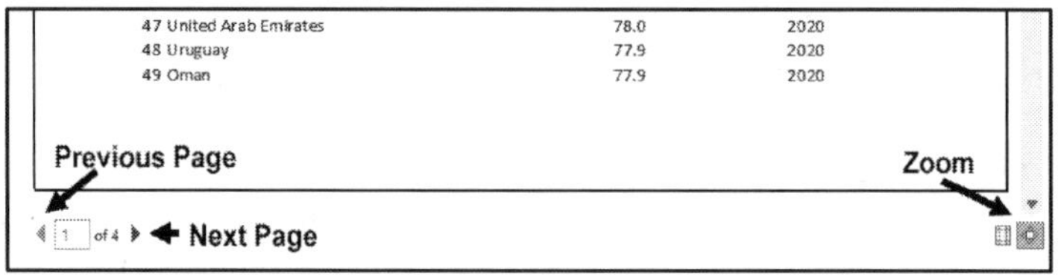

4. Use the *Zoom* button to magnify the page for a clearer view. (You may not notice much of a zoom if you have a large screen).
5. Click the *Back* button  at the top left of *Backstage View* to return to the workbook.

3 Add a *Print Preview* button to the Quick Access Toolbar.

The quick *Print Preview* offered by the *Backstage View* is a very useful feature and you'll probably use it a lot. Every time you use it, however, it is going to take two clicks of the mouse. Wouldn't it be better if you could show a print preview with just one click?

1. Click the *Customize Quick Access Toolbar* button (see sidebar).
2. Click the *Print Preview and Print* item in the drop-down list.

   A new button now appears on the Quick Access Toolbar. You are now able to *Print Preview* your work with a single click of the mouse.

Customize Quick Access Toolbar Button

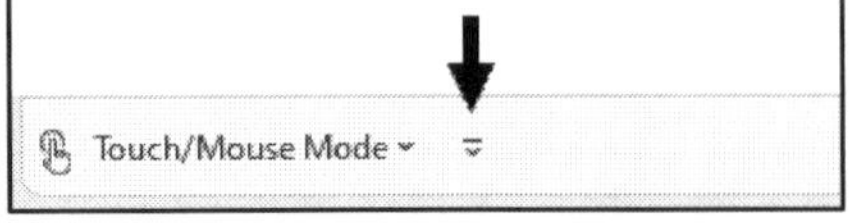

The Wealth of Nations

note

Some amazing "hidden" Excel features cannot be used at all without customizing the Quick Access Toolbar or the Ribbon

One of my favourite "hidden" features in Excel is its ability to read the workbook to me via its *Text to Voice* facility.

When I need to input lots of numbers from a sheet of paper and want to check them, I get Excel to read them to me as I tick each off my list. This is much faster than continuously looking first at the screen, then at the paper, for each entry.

This feature is covered in depth in the *Expert Skills* book in this series.

You can't use this feature at all unless you either add some custom buttons to the Quick Access Toolbar or customize the Ribbon.

tip

The Quick Access Toolbar is one of the keys to being really productive with Excel.

Always try to minimize the number of mouse clicks needed to do common tasks.

If you find yourself forever changing tabs to use a button, change two clicks into one by adding the button to the Quick Access Toolbar.

All of those extra clicks add up to a lot of time over the weeks and years.

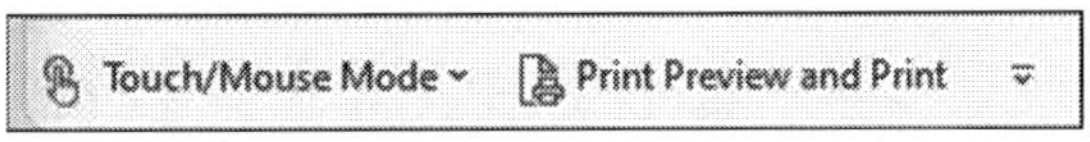

4 Add a *Font Color* button to the Quick Access Toolbar.

A *More Commands...* option is available when you click the *Customize Quick Access Toolbar* button. This enables you to add any of Excel's commands to the toolbar. But there's an easier way.

1. Click the *Home* tab on the Ribbon (if it isn't already selected).
2. Right-click on the *Font Color* button  in the *Font* group.

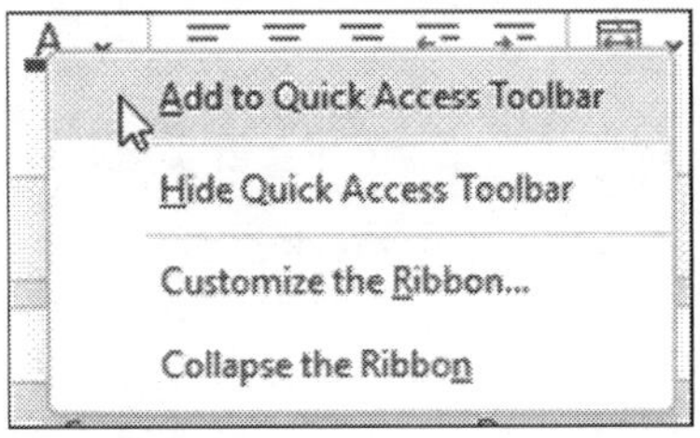

3. Click *Add to Quick Access Toolbar* from the shortcut menu.

   A *Font Color* button is added to the Quick Access Toolbar.

5 Remove a button from the Quick Access Toolbar.

1. Right-click on the *Font Color* button that you've just added to the Quick Access Toolbar. 
2. Click *Remove from Quick Access Toolbar* from the shortcut menu.

6 Add separators to make a heavily customized Quick Access Toolbar more readable.

When you add many items to the Quick Access Toolbar it is a good idea to use separators to split icons into logical groups.

1. Click the *Customize Quick Access Toolbar* button. 
2. Click *More Commands…* from the shortcut menu.
3. Click the  item at the top of the *Commands* list.

4. Click the Add>> button. 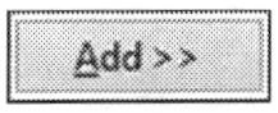

5. Use the up  and down  buttons to move the separator so that it appears between the *Touch/Mouse Mode* and *Print Preview and Print* commands.

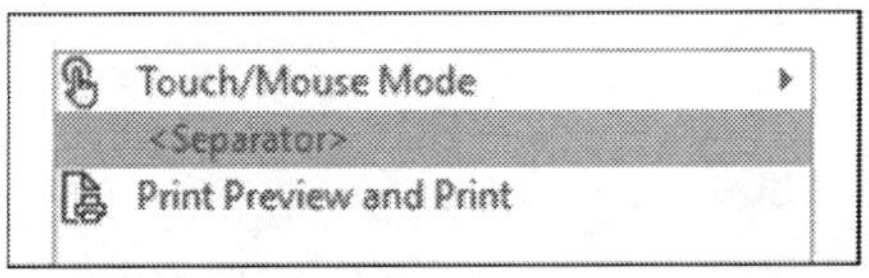

6. Click the OK button.

Lesson 1-19: Use the Mini Toolbar, Key Tips and keyboard shortcuts

1 Open *The Wealth of Nations* sample worksheet (if it isn't already open).

2 Select cell B2 (Monaco) on the GDP worksheet.

1. Click on the *GDP* tab.
2. Click on cell B2 (Monaco).

   Make sure that you only click once, otherwise Excel will think that you are trying to edit the cell.

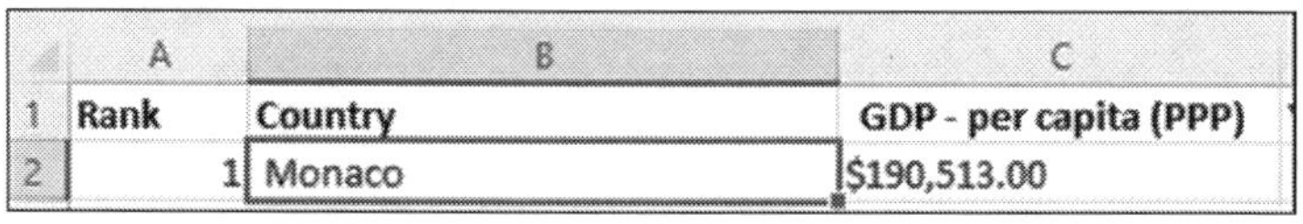

3 Make cell B2 (Monaco) bold, italicized and underlined.

1. Click: Home→Font→Bold.
2. Click: Home→Font→Italic.
3. Click: Home→Font→Underline.

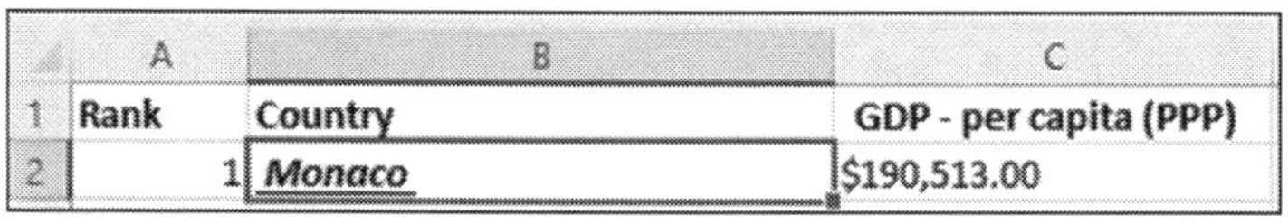

4 Display *Key Tips.*

Hold down the **<Alt>** key on the keyboard.

Notice how *Key Tips* are now displayed on the Ribbon and the Quick Access Toolbar:

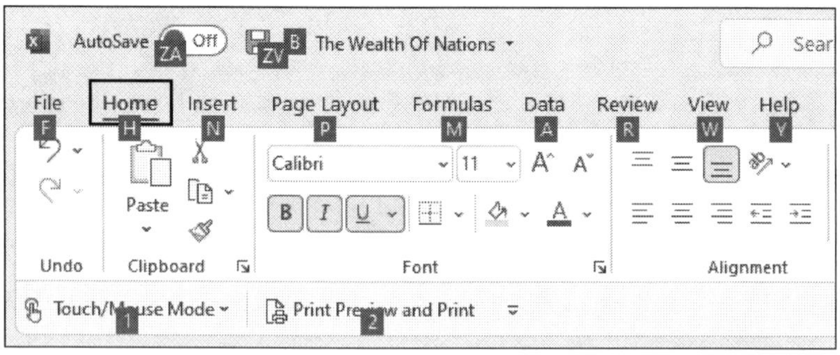

5 Use the *Key Tips* to show a print preview using only the keyboard.

The key tips reveal the key you need to press to simulate clicking any of the Ribbon and Quick Access Toolbar icons.

The print preview button will not be on the Quick Access Toolbar unless you added it during*: Lesson 1-18: Customize the Quick Access Toolbar and preview the printout.*

tip

Keyboard shortcuts are one of the secrets of maximizing productivity with Excel

Many years ago, I took my mouse and stuck it to the back of my monitor with sticky tape.

For a whole day, I struggled to work without it.

The first few hours weren't much fun, but after that my work became faster and faster. It became a challenge to figure out how to do things without the mouse.

You will be far more productive if you can get into the same habit.

These days, there are some things that you simply need the mouse for, and some things that are genuinely faster (or easier) with the mouse.

For many common tasks, however, you'll find it faster and more efficient to work with the keyboard.

The Wealth of Nations

Hold down the **<Alt>** key and press the relevant number to show a print preview (in the above example this is 2 but it may be different on your computer).

6 Click the *Back* button  to leave *Backstage View* and return to the worksheet.

7 Use the mouse to select the text *Monaco* in cell B2.

1. Double-click the cell containing the text.

   You can see the cursor flashing in the cell. This means that you have entered *Edit Mode,* enabling you to change the contents of the cell

2. Position the cursor just after the word *Monaco* and hold down the left mouse button.

3. Drag the mouse across the complete word until it is highlighted like this:

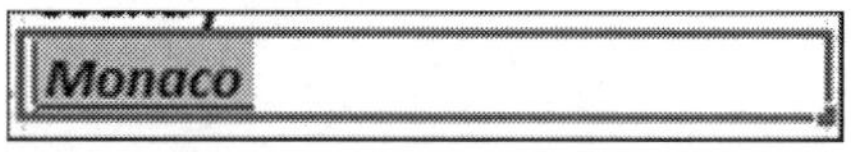

4. Release the mouse button but do not move it away from the text.

8 Observe the *Mini Toolbar.*

Provided you didn't move the mouse cursor away from cell B2 you will now see the mini toolbar above the cell:

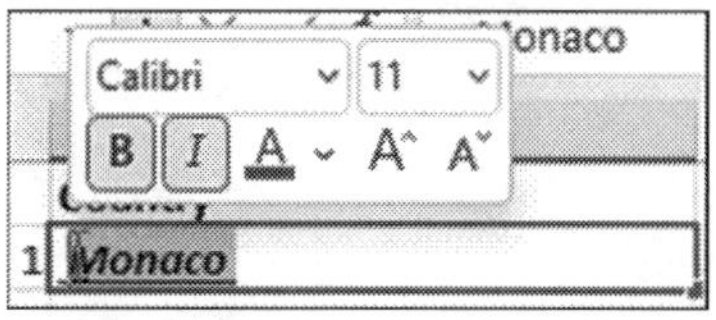

9 Use the *Mini Toolbar* to restore the text to non-bold and non-italic.

Click on the Bold  and Italic  buttons to remove the bold and italic attributes from the text.

10 Show a bigger Mini Toolbar with a right-click.

Right-click on the text *Singapore* in cell B6. Notice that, as well as the shortcut menu (see sidebar), you now get an even better Mini Toolbar with a few extra buttons.

11 Remove the underline from Monaco using a shortcut key.

1. Click once on the text *Monaco* in cell B2.

2. Press the **<Ctrl>+<U>** keys on the keyboard to remove the underline.

But how can you remember cryptic keyboard shortcuts like **<Ctrl>+<U>**? Fortunately, you don't have to. Hover the mouse over the underline button  (on the Home tab of the Ribbon) and you'll see the keyboard shortcut listed in the tooltip.

note

If you don't like the Mini Toolbar, you can switch it off

Personally, I really like the mini toolbar and wouldn't dream of switching it off but if you are used to an early version of Excel and find that it annoys you, here is how it's done:

1. Click:

   File→Options→General

2. In the *User Interface options* section, uncheck the *Show Mini Toolbar on selection* item.

3. Click the *OK* button.

note

The shortcut menu

If you right-click on a cell, a shortcut menu is displayed.

The shortcut menu doesn't display *everything* that you can do to a cell but Excel's best guesses at the *most likely* things you might want to do.

Because Excel is guessing at the actions you might want to take in the context of what you are doing, the *shortcut menu* is also sometimes referred to as the *contextual menu.*

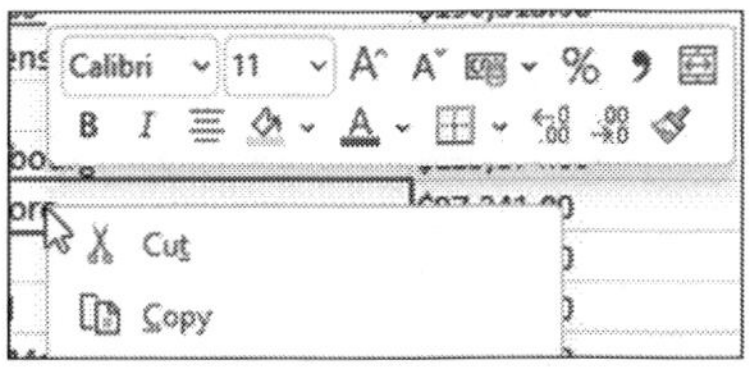

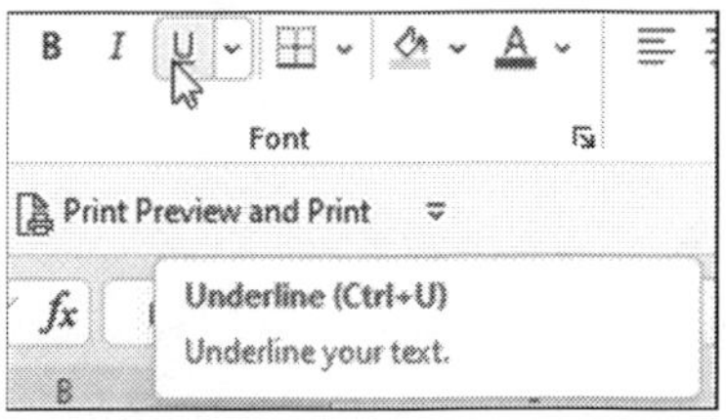

Lesson 1-20: Understand views

Views provide different ways to look at your worksheet.

Excel 2021 has three main views. They are:

View	Icon	What it is used for
Normal		This is the view you've been using until now. It's the view most users use all of the time when they are working with Excel.
Page Layout		This view allows you to see (almost) exactly what the printout will look like. Unlike running a *Print Preview,* you are able to edit cells just as you can in *Normal* view.
Page Break Preview		A page break indicates when the printer should advance onto a new sheet of paper. You'll use this view in: *Lesson 7-5: Insert, delete and preview page breaks* to make sure that the page breaks in the right place.

1 Open the *The Wealth of Nations* sample workbook (if it isn't already open).

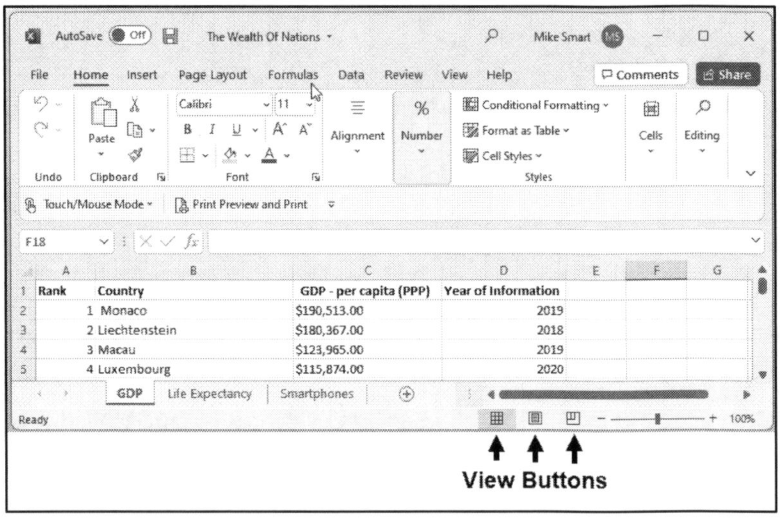

You can change views in two ways:

1. By clicking one of the View buttons at the bottom of the window (see above).
2. By clicking one of the buttons in the *Workbook Views* group on the Ribbon's *View* tab:

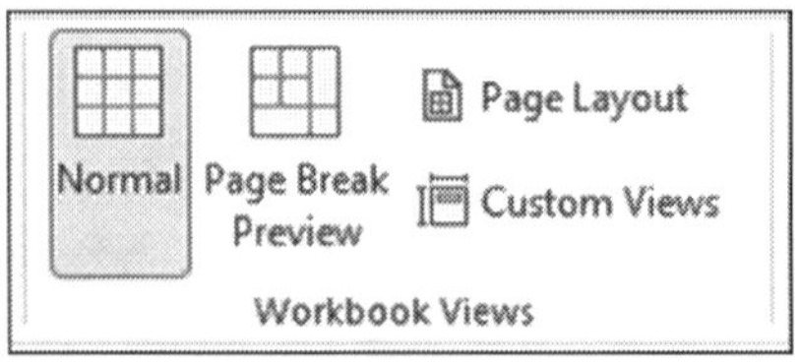

The Wealth of Nations

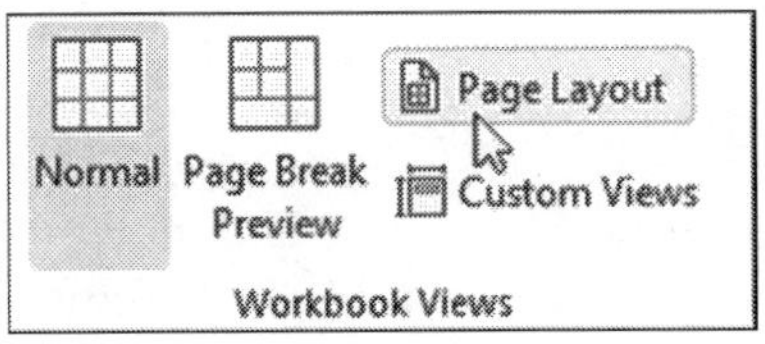

2 View the GDP worksheet in *Page Layout* view.

1. Click on the *GDP* tab to select it.
2. Click: View→Workbook Views→Page Layout.

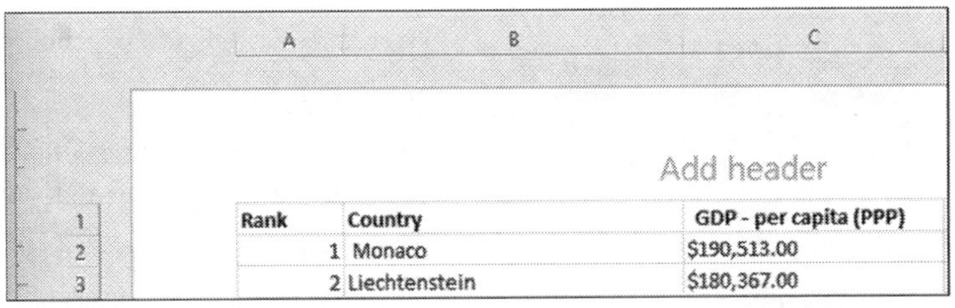

The worksheet is displayed in *Page Layout* view. You are able to see (almost) exactly what will be printed. Headers, footers and margins are all shown.

You are also able to edit the worksheet.

You may wonder why Excel users don't use *Page Layout* view all of the time when editing worksheets. While some users may prefer to do this, most will want to see the maximum amount of data possible on screen and so will prefer the *Normal* view.

3 Select Page Break Preview view.

Click: View→Workbook Views→Page Break Preview.

The worksheet is displayed in *Page Break Preview* view (you may also see a help dialog first).

This view shows each page with a watermark to indicate which sheet of paper it will be printed on:

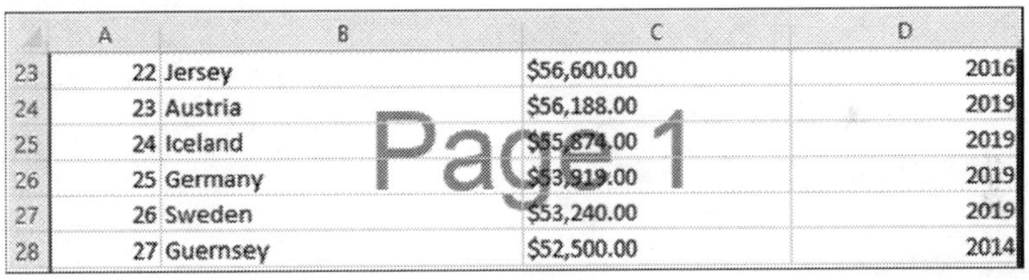

This view also shows the break between each page as a dotted line:

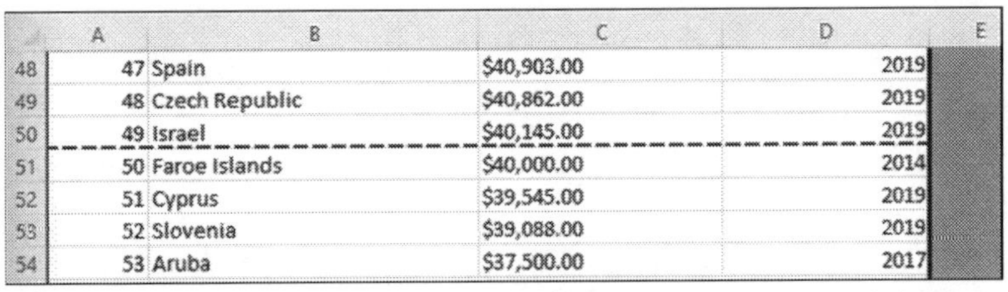

It is possible to click and drag the dotted line to change the place where the page breaks.

Adjusting page breaks using click and drag will be covered in depth later in*: Lesson 7-6: Adjust page breaks using Page Break Preview.*

4 Select *Normal* view.

Click: View→Workbook Views→Normal.

note

You need an Internet connection to use Excel 2021's help features

In previous versions of Excel, it was possible to access offline help when no Internet connection was available.

Support for offline help was dropped in 2016. If you have no Internet connection, you will not be able to access Excel's help features.

note

You can also use the **<Alt>+<Q>** shortcut keys to instantly move the cursor into the *Tell Me* help box.

note

The screen grabs shown in this lesson may differ from those you see on your screen

The Excel 2021 help system is delivered online. This means that Microsoft are able to constantly correct and update help topics.

For this reason, the information you see on your screen may differ from the screen grabs shown in this lesson.

The Wealth of Nations

Lesson 1-21: Use the Tell Me help system

The built-in Excel 2021 help feature is called: *Tell Me* help.

Tell Me help is novel because it not only provides information about Excel features but also enables you to execute Ribbon commands directly from inside the help system. This can be a huge time saver.

1. Open *The Wealth of Nations* from your sample files folder (if it isn't already open).

2. Click inside the *Search* box located on the title bar at the very top of the screen.

   When you click inside the *Search* box, a flashing cursor appears, and you can type a question.

3. Ask Excel how you can save a file.

   You learned how to save a file in: *Lesson 1-10: Save a workbook to a local file.* In that lesson, you clicked the *Save* button at the top-left of the screen.

   Imagine that you have forgotten how to save a file.

   Type your question into the box.

   You could ask Excel the question in several ways. You could use a plain English sentence, or you could just ask using a single word:

Excel displays a menu of choices.

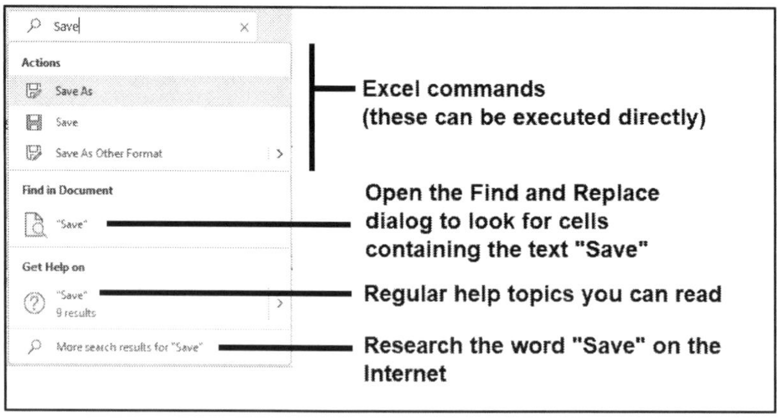

Notice that the list is delineated into three sections.

The first section provides a different way to execute commands.

The second section offers a different way to open the *Find and Replace* dialog (you'll learn about the *Find and Replace* dialog later, in: *Lesson 6-8: Use find and replace*).

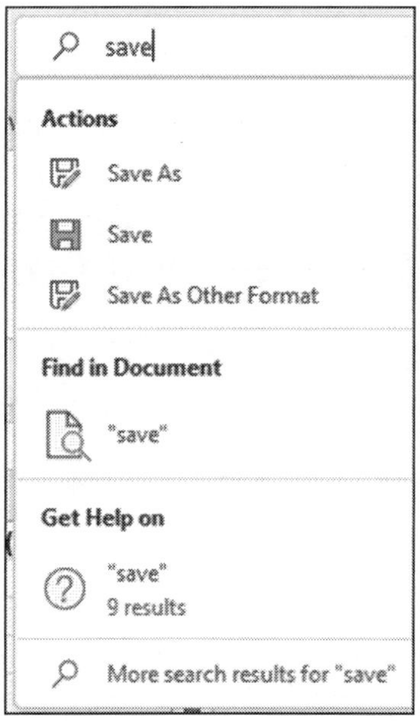

The last section gives access to the type of regular help topic that you are used to reading in traditional help systems, and also allows you to research the topic using a wider Internet search.

Note that the help features will only work if you are connected to the Internet (see sidebar).

4 Execute the *Save* command directly from *Tell Me* help.

Click the *Save* command at the top of the menu:

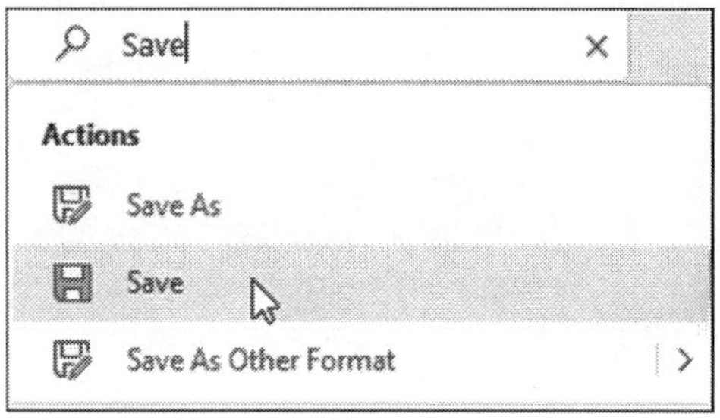

Tell Me help executes the command. The workbook is saved in the same way it would have been if you had clicked the *Save* button on the *Quick Access Toolbar.*

You can see how useful *Tell Me* help is when you can't remember where a command is situated on the Ribbon and want to execute the command as quickly as possible.

You can also see that it could be dangerous to execute commands that you don't understand.

5 Understand the other *Tell Me* help options.

Tell Me help also allows you to execute several other commands and to access regular help that you can read as a reference:

- *Save As.* You learned how to use the *Save As* command in: *Lesson 1-10: Save a workbook to a local file.*
- *Save As Other Format.* You learned about different file formats in: *Lesson 1-11: Understand common file formats.*

6 Read the Excel help topic relating to the Save command.

Click: *Get Help on "Save".*

Links to several topics from the Excel 2021 reference manual are shown. You can click on any of these links to read any of Microsoft's help topics about *Save* related features.

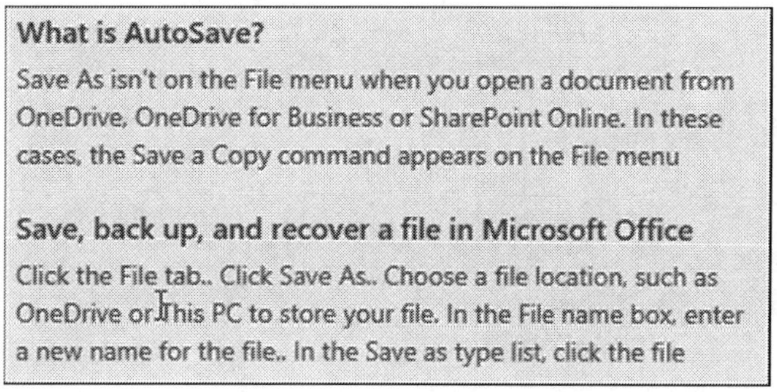

Lesson 1-22: Use other help features

You'll probably use *Tell Me* help (discussed in: *Lesson 1-21: Use the Tell Me help* system) most of the time as your help system of first choice.

You can also access the same help topics that are available in *Tell Me Help* directly from their associated Ribbon commands. This can be useful when exploring new and unfamiliar features you may discover on Excel's many Ribbon tabs.

Later, in: *Lesson 2-13: Create functions using Formula AutoComplete*, you'll learn how to access and use Excel's vast function library (that contains over 300 functions such as SUM and AVERAGE). You'll also learn how to access a special Excel help feature that documents the use of each function.

note

The screen grabs shown in this lesson may differ from those you see on your screen

The Excel 2021 help system is delivered online. This means that Microsoft can constantly correct and update help topics.

For this reason, the information you see on your screen may differ from the screen grabs shown in this lesson.

note

You can also open the Help task pane by pressing the **<F1>** key.

1 Access help using the *Help* task pane.

1. Click: Help→Help.

   A *Help* task pane appears at the right of the screen. You'll learn more about task panes later, in: *Lesson 3-7: Use the Multiple Item Clipboard.*

2. Type: **Save** into the text box at the top of the *Help* task pane:

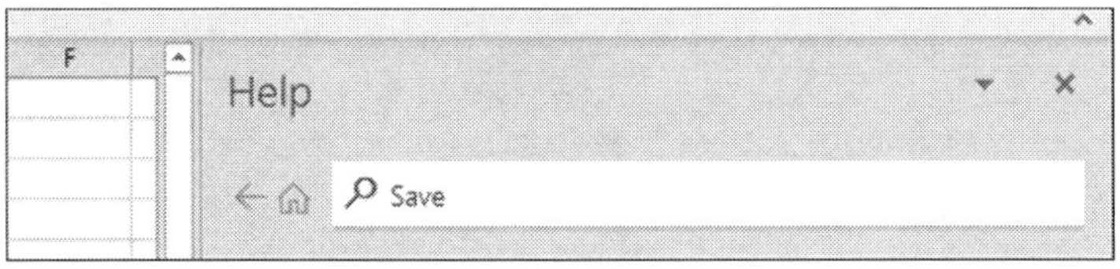

3. Click the magnifying glass icon or press the **<Enter>** key.

   A list of help topics relating to *Save* appears (see sidebar). Note that this list is served from the Internet and is constantly updated so may appear differently on your computer.

4. Click on any of the help topics displayed to read a detailed description.

2 Get help directly from the Ribbon.

1. Close the *Help* task pane by clicking the close button  in the top right corner of the Help pane.

2. Click the *Home* tab on the Ribbon and hover the mouse cursor over the drop-down arrow to the right of the word *General* in the *Number* group.

   If you keep the mouse still, after a short delay a screen tip pops up providing a short description of what the drop-down list is for:

note

Why can't you learn Excel using the Help system?

Excel's Help system is designed as a reference work and not as a structured tutorial.

Try reading the detailed help about any of the topics. You'll usually find that to make sense of the help topic you will already need to have learned to use Excel. This is because the writer assumes that you already know how to use Excel.

Many Excel books are also written in this way (as reference books).

This book is a structured *tutorial*. The book is carefully designed to teach Excel by building new skills upon existing skills so that each lesson is easy to understand.

Once you have learned Excel (using Smart Method tutorials) you will find Excel's reference topics easy to understand.

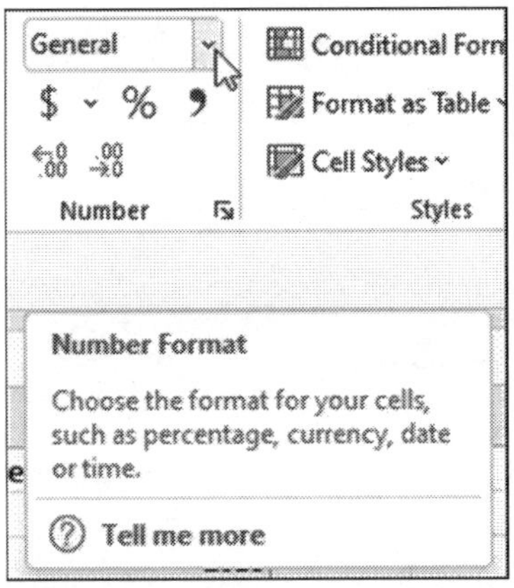

A *Tell me more* hyperlink is also provided offering more detailed help. This will only work if you are connected to the Internet.

3. Click the *Tell me more* hyperlink.

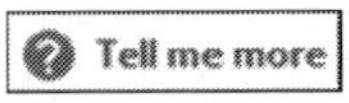

The *Help* task pane re-appears displaying a list of help topics relating to *Number Format* topics.

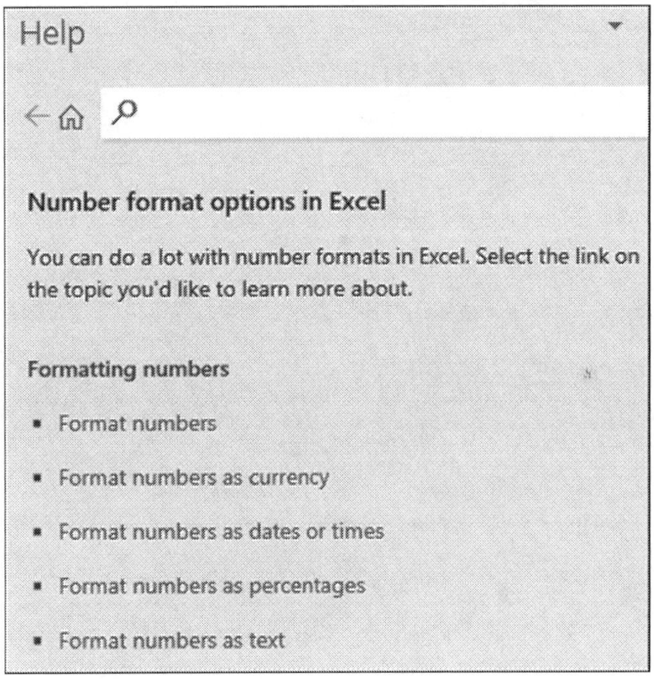

4. Click on any of the help topics displayed to read a detailed description.

Session 1: Exercise

In this exercise you'll try to remember the name of each of the Excel screen elements. The answers are on the next page, so you might want to recap by turning the page for a little revision before you start.

Keep trying until you are able to name each of the screen elements from memory. You'll be seeing this terminology used during the remainder of the book, so it's important that you can correctly identify each element.

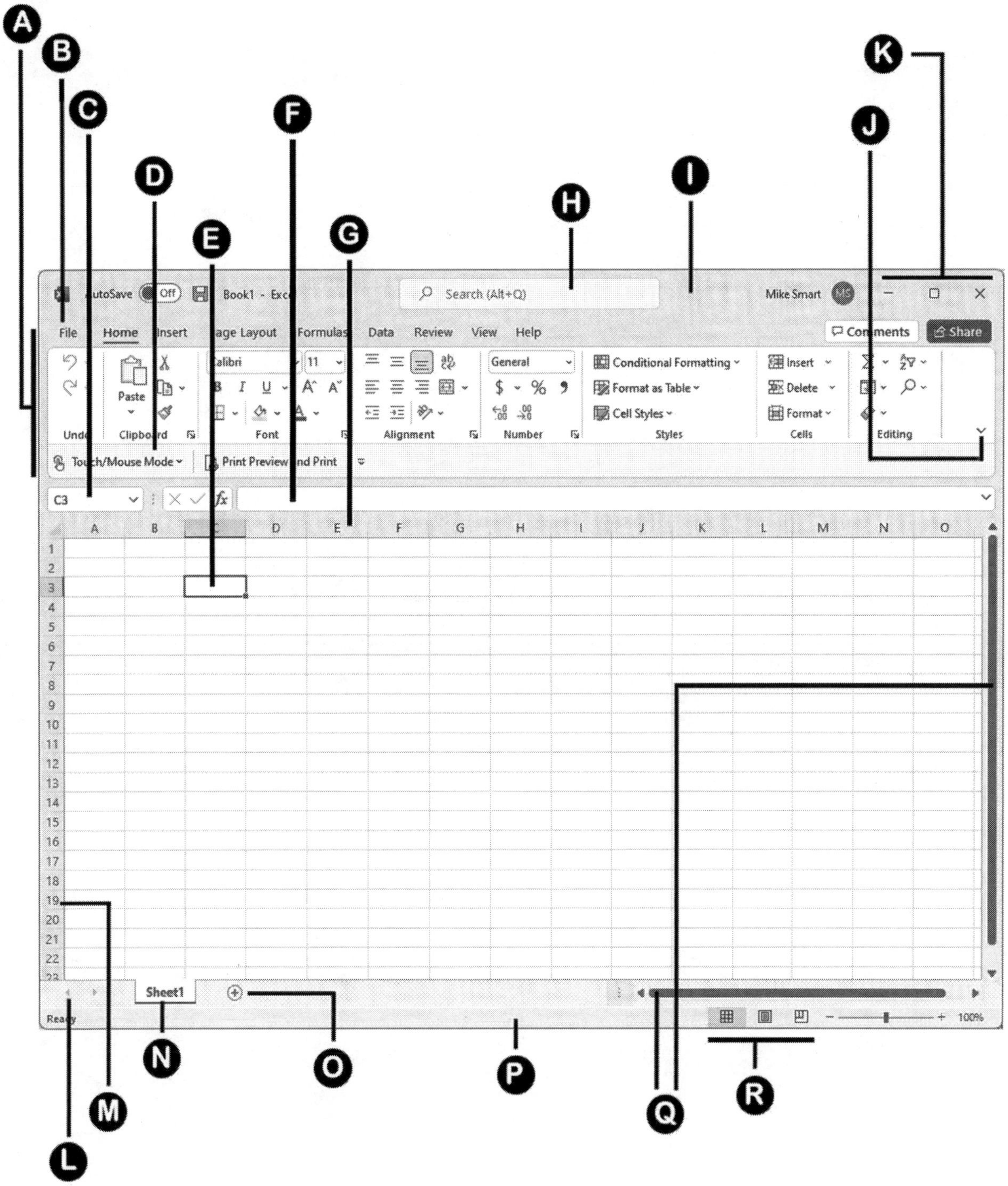

Session 1: Exercise answers

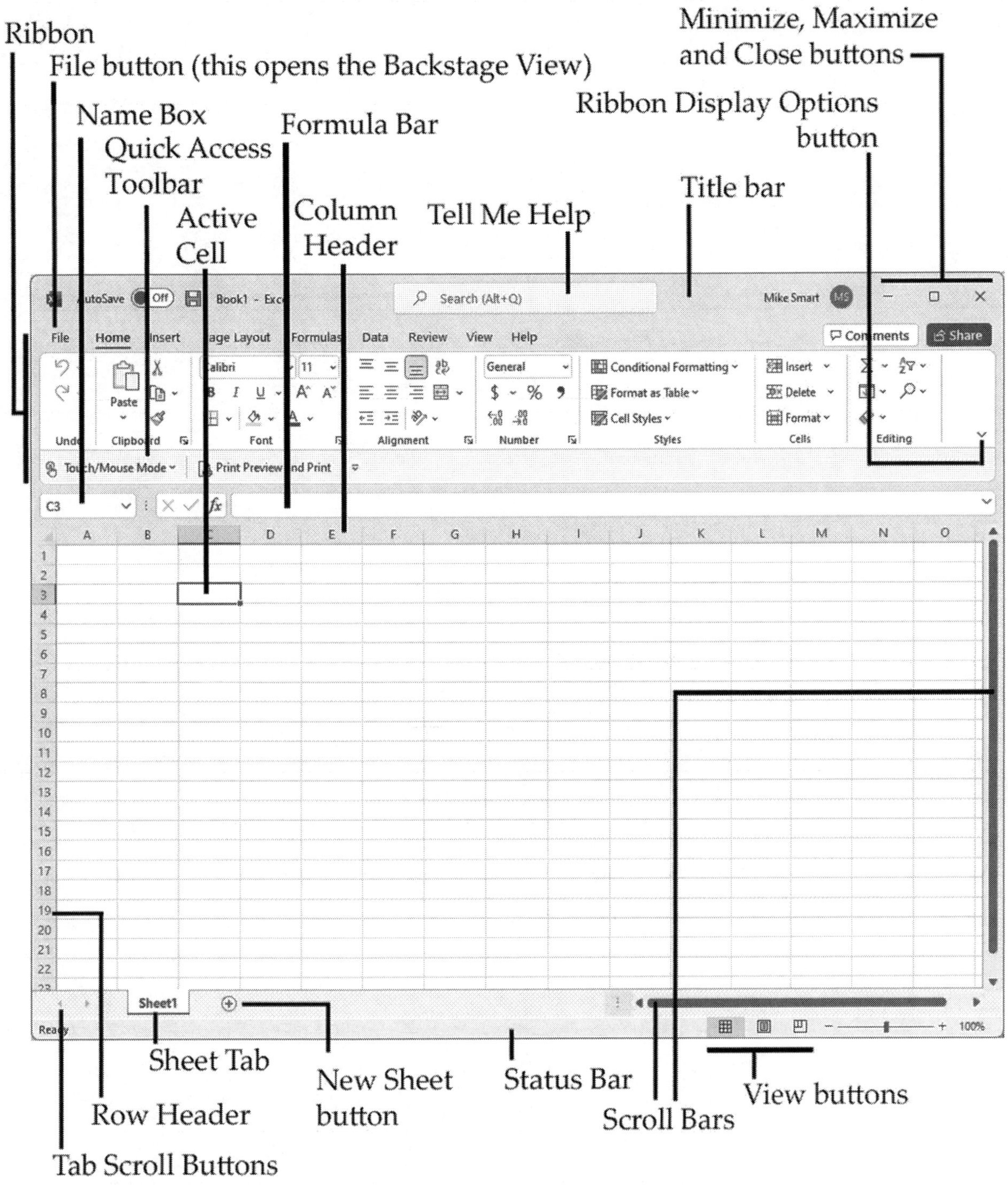

2

Session Two: Doing Useful Work with Excel

> Only those who have the patience to do simple things perfectly ever acquire the skill to do difficult things easily.
>
> ***Unknown author***

Now that you've mastered the basics, you are ready to do really useful work with this amazing tool. In this session, you will learn to use all of Excel's basic features properly. This will put you far ahead of anybody that hasn't been formally trained in Excel best practice.

Even after years of daily use, many users are unable to properly use Excel's fundamental features. They often reach their goal, but get there in a very inefficient way, simply because they were never taught how to do things correctly.

Session Objectives

By the end of this session, you will be able to:

- Enter text and numbers into a worksheet
- Create a new workbook and view two workbooks at the same time
- Use AutoSum to quickly calculate totals
- Select a range of cells and understand Smart Tags
- Enter data into a range and copy data across a range
- Select adjacent and non-adjacent rows and columns
- Select non-contiguous cell ranges and view summary information
- AutoSelect a range of cells
- Re-size rows and columns
- Use AutoSum to sum a non-contiguous range
- Use AutoSum to calculate average and maximum values
- Create your own formulas
- Create functions using Formula AutoComplete
- Use AutoFill for text and numeric series
- Use AutoFill to adjust formulas and use AutoFill options
- Speed up your AutoFills and create a custom fill series
- Understand linear and exponential series
- Use Flash Fill to split and concatenate text
- Analyze Data with the Ideas feature
- Use the zoom control
- Print out a worksheet

Lesson 2-1: Enter text and numbers into a worksheet

Excel beginners tend to reach for the mouse far too often. One of the keys to productivity with Excel is to avoid using the mouse when entering data. In this lesson, you'll quickly populate a worksheet without using the mouse at all.

1 Open *First Quarter Sales and Profit* from your sample files folder.

	A	B	C	D
1	Sales and Profit Report - First Quarter			
2				
3		Jan	Feb	Mar
4	New York	22,000	29,000	19,000
5	Los Angeles			
6	London			
7	Paris			
8	Munich			

2 Notice the difference between values and text.

Cells can contain values or text. Values can be numbers, dates or formulas (more on formulas later).

Excel usually does a great job of recognizing when there are values in a cell and when there is text. The giveaway is that text is always (by default) left aligned in the cell and values are right aligned.

Look at the numbers on this worksheet. Notice how they are all right aligned. This lets you know that Excel has correctly recognized them as values and will happily perform mathematical operations using them.

3 Save a value into a cell.

1. Type the value 42000 into cell B5. Notice that the mouse cursor is still flashing in the cell.

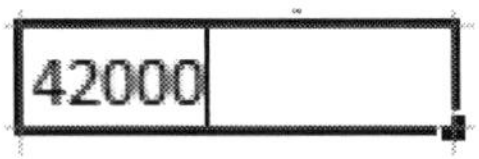

At this stage, the value has not been saved into the cell.

If you change your mind, you can still undo the value by pressing the **<ESC>** key at the top left of your keyboard or by clicking the *Cancel* button on the left-hand side of the Formula Bar.

2. Decide that you want to keep this value in the cell by either pressing the **<Enter>, <Tab>** or an **<Arrow>** key on the keyboard, or by clicking the *Enter* button on the left-hand side of the Formula Bar.

4 Enter a column of data without using the mouse.

When you enter data into a column, there's no need to use the mouse. Press the **<Enter>** key after each entry and the active cell

tip

Entering numbers as text

Sometimes you need Excel to recognize a number as text.

If you type an apostrophe (') before the number, Excel won't display the apostrophe but will format the cell as text. You'll notice that the number is then left justified to reflect this.

When a number is formatted as text you cannot perform any mathematical calculation with it.

You will learn a lot more about cell formatting later, in: *Session Four: Making Your Worksheets Look Professional.*

First Quarter Sales and Profit

moves to the cell beneath. Try this now with the following January sales data:

1. Type **18,000** into cell B6.
2. Press the **<Enter>** key to move to cell B7.
3. Do the same to enter the following values into the next two cells.

	A	B	C	D
3		Jan	Feb	Mar
4	New York	22,000	29,000	19,000
5	Los Angeles	42,000		
6	London	18,000		
7	Paris	35,000		
8	Munich	12,000		

5 Enter a row of data without using the mouse.

You can also enter a row of data without using the mouse.

1. Click in cell C5.
2. Type **39,000** and then press the **<Tab>** key on your keyboard.

   The **<Tab>** key is on the left-hand side of the keyboard above the **<Caps Lock>** key. Notice how pressing the **<Tab>** key saves the value into the cell and then moves one cell to the right.
3. Type **43,000** into cell D5 and press the **<Enter>** key.

   You magically move to cell C6, as Excel guesses that you probably want to begin entering data into the next row.

6 Complete the table without using the mouse.

By using the **<Tab>** or **<Enter>** key in the right places you should be able to complete the table now without using the mouse:

	A	B	C	D
3		Jan	Feb	Mar
4	New York	22,000	29,000	19,000
5	Los Angeles	42,000	39,000	43,000
6	London	18,000	20,000	22,000
7	Paris	35,000	26,000	31,000
8	Munich	12,000	15,000	13,000

7 Change the text in cell B3 to January.

1. Double-click cell B3. Notice that there is now a flashing cursor in the cell.

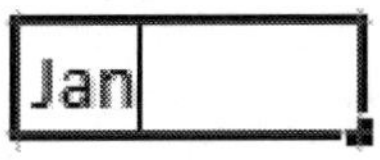

2. Type: **uary** on the keyboard to change Jan to January.
3. Press the **<Enter>** key.

8 Change the text in cell B3 back to **Jan** using the formula bar.

Click once in cell B3 and then change the text in the formula bar back to **Jan** (see sidebar).

9 Save your work as *First Quarter Sales and Profit-2.*

important

The many ways of entering numbers

Negative numbers

-123.56
(123.56)

Currency prefixes

Excel is quite happy for you to prefix a number with a currency symbol. The currency symbol it will accept depends upon how you defined the regional options in your operating system.

$123.56 (works in USA)
£123.56 (works in UK)

In: *Lesson 4-3: Format numbers using built-in number formats* you'll learn an easy method of setting $, £ and € currency prefixes whatever your locale.

Commas

12,234,567.78

Fractions

You must leave a space between a number and a fraction for this to work.

6 1/4
(six, space, one, /, four)

The above will appear on the worksheet as 6.25 after you enter it in this way.

0 1/4
(zero, space, one,/,four)

The above will appear on the worksheet as 0.25. The leading zero is needed to prevent Excel from assuming that you are entering a date.

Formula Bar

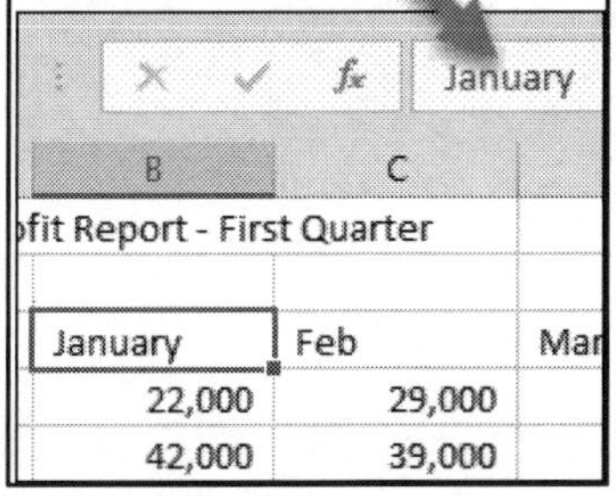

Lesson 2-2: Create a new workbook and view two workbooks at the same time

1 Create a new workbook by opening Excel.

1. Open Excel.
2. Click the *Blank workbook* template to create a new workbook.

   Excel helpfully creates a workbook, unimaginatively named *Book1*. If you already have a workbook open called *Book1*, the new workbook will be called *Book2...* and so on.

   Notice that *Book1 – Excel* is displayed on the *Title Bar*.

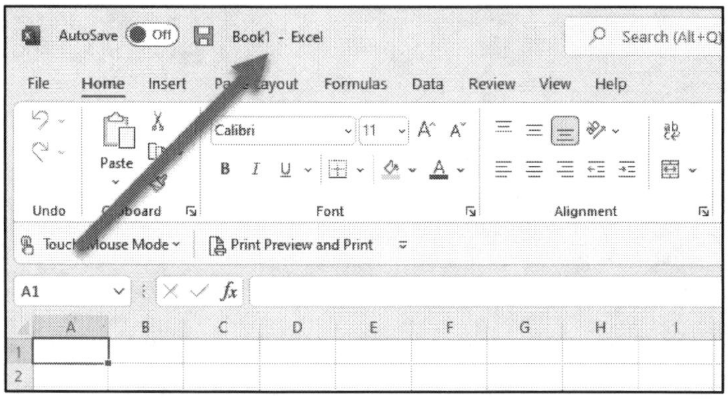

tip

Other ways of creating a new workbook

- Use the keyboard shortcut <Ctrl>+<N>.
- Add a button to the Quick Access Toolbar.

You learned how to add a button to the Quick Access Toolbar in: *Lesson 1-18: Customize the Quick Access Toolbar and preview the printout.*

2 Create another new workbook.

1. Click the *File* button  at the top left of the screen and click the *New* button in the left-hand menu.

   You are presented with a similar dialog to the one you saw when you started up Excel.

2. Click the *Blank workbook* template. A new blank workbook called *Book2* is displayed in the workbook window.

   You could be forgiven for thinking that nothing has happened but you can see that the *Title Bar* now says: *Book2 – Excel,* showing that you are looking at a different workbook.

3 Use the taskbar to move between workbooks.

You can see an Excel icon at the bottom of the screen (this area is called the Windows taskbar). Hover over this icon with your mouse. A gallery pops up showing two workbooks: *Book1* and *Book2*.

note

Finding a workbook when many are open

An alternative way to quickly find a workbook when many are open is to click:

View→Window→ Switch Windows

This presents you with a list of all open workbooks.

You can also use the **<Ctrl>+<Tab>** keyboard shortcut to cycle through all open workbooks.

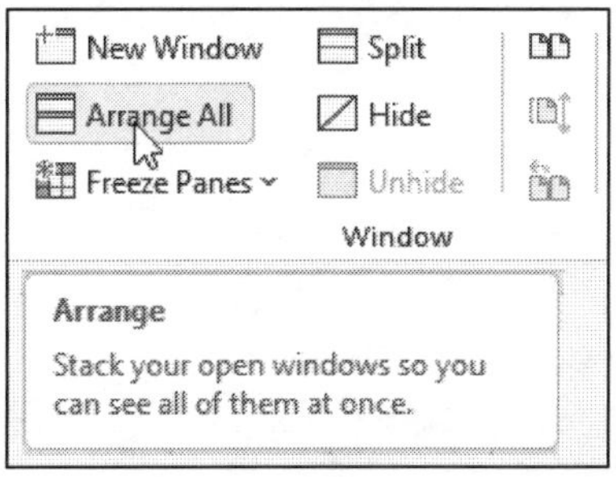

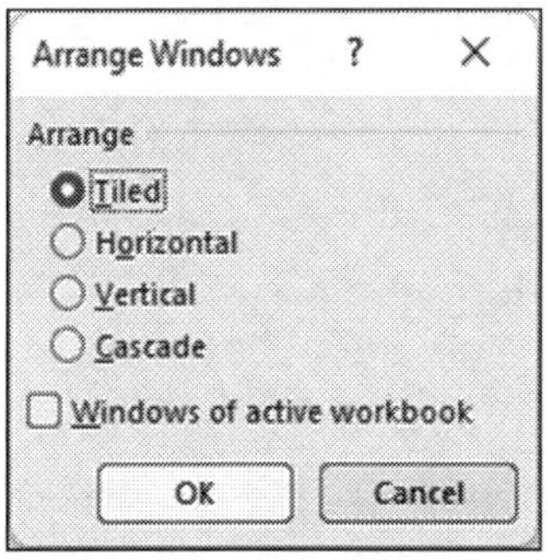

Hover the mouse cursor over each item in the pop-up gallery to display each workbook. The only difference you will see is the *Title Bar* changing from *Book1* to *Book2* because both workbooks are empty.

See sidebar for other methods of switching windows.

4 Display both *Book1* and *Book2* at the same time.

1. Make sure that the *Book1* and *Book2* workbooks are both visible on the screen (meaning that neither are minimized).
2. Click: View→Window→Arrange All.

   The *Arrange Windows* dialog is displayed.
3. Choose the *Horizontal* arrangement and click the OK button.

   Both workbooks are now shown, one above the other. Each window occupies exactly half of your screen:

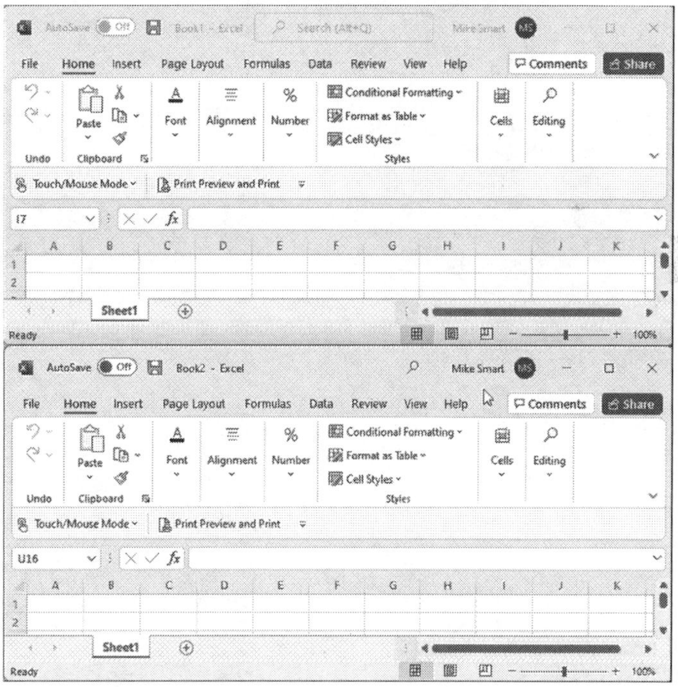

Notice that as you click each workbook window the *Title Bar* and the *Close/Minimize/Restore Down* buttons light up, to show that this is the active window.

5 Close *Book2* and maximize *Book1* to restore the display to a single workbook.

If you've forgotten how to do this, refer back to: *Lesson 1-7: Maximize, minimize, re-size, move and close the Excel window.*

Lesson 2-3: Use AutoSum to quickly calculate totals

Excel's *AutoSum* feature is a really useful and fast way to add the values in a range of cells together.

1 Open *First Quarter Sales and Profit-2* from your sample files folder.

2 In cell A9 type the word **Total** followed by the **<Tab>** key.

The active cell moves to the right and is now in cell B9:

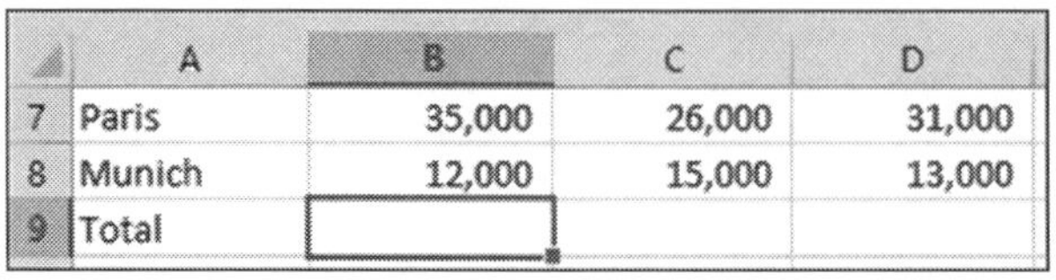

3 Click: Home→Editing→ Σ (this is the AutoSum button).

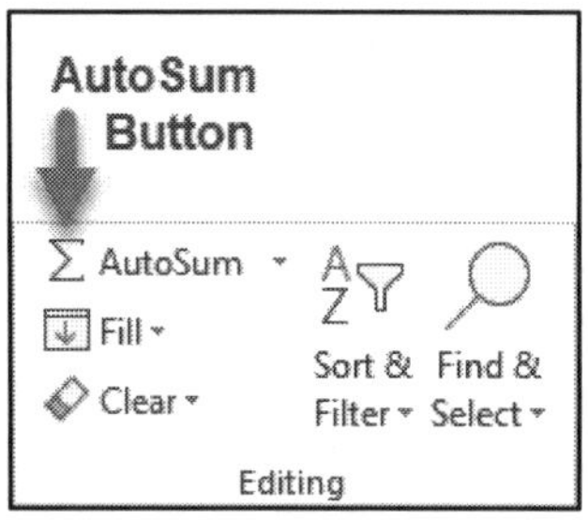

Something interesting has happened to the worksheet:

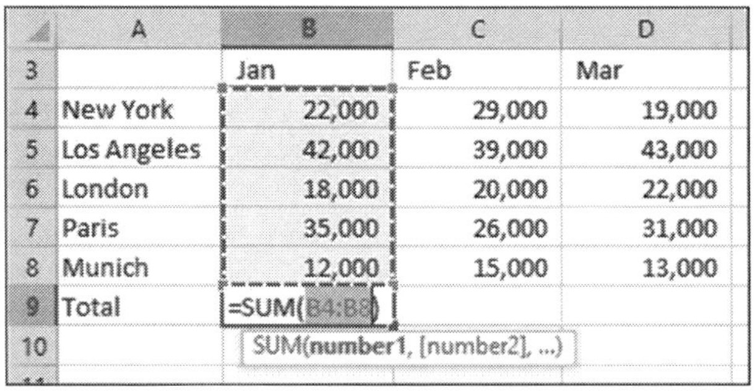

Excel has placed a *marquee* around the number range that AutoSum has guessed you want to work with. The dots that mark the boundary of the marquee are called the *marching ants.*

The marching ants surround all the numbers in the column above, up to the first blank cell or text cell (in this case, up to the word: Jan).

=SUM(B4:B8) is your first glimpse of an Excel *Formula.* Formulas always begin with an equal sign (=). This formula is using the SUM *function* to compute the Sum (or total) of the values in cells B4 to B8. You'll learn more about functions later, in: *Lesson 2-13: Create functions using Formula AutoComplete.*

4 Press the **<Enter>** key or click the AutoSum button Σ once more to display the total January sales:

anecdote

I ran an Excel course for a small company in London a few years ago.

The boss had sent his two office staff to learn a little more about Excel.

Before the course began, I asked the delegates how long they had been using Excel. They told me that they'd been using it for two years to do all of their office reports.

When I showed them AutoSum they gasped in delight. "This will save us hours" they told me.

I was curious how they had been doing their reports before.

Believe it or not, they had added up all of the figures in each column with a calculator and then manually typed the totals at the bottom of each column.

In this case the boss had given them Excel as he had heard it was a very good tool. Unfortunately, he had not initially seen the need to train the staff in its use.

With no training, it seemed quite logical to them to use it like a word processor and the boss had still been delighted that his staff were using such impressive technology.

First Quarter Sales and Profit-2

tip

Entering an AutoSum using only the keyboard

You can also execute an AutoSum using the keyboard shortcut:

<Alt>+<=>

note

You can also add an AutoSum formula using the Quick Analysis button

Later, in: *Lesson 2-4: Select a range of cells and understand Smart Tags*, you'll learn how to select a range of cells.

Whenever you select a range of cells, a *Quick Analysis* button appears just outside the bottom-right corner of the selected range.

Jan	Feb
22,000	
42,000	
18,000	
35,000	
12,000	

When you click the *Quick Analysis* button, the *Quick Analysis* dialog appears.

One of the menu options on this dialog is *Totals*.

The *Totals* dialog allows you to add an AutoSum beneath a selected range (in a similar way to the AutoSum button method described in this lesson).

	A	B	C	D
3		Jan	Feb	Mar
4	New York	22,000	29,000	19,000
5	Los Angeles	42,000	39,000	43,000
6	London	18,000	20,000	22,000
7	Paris	35,000	26,000	31,000
8	Munich	12,000	15,000	13,000
9	Total	129,000		

5 Type the word **Total** into cell E3 and press the **<Enter>** key once.

The active cell moves down one row and is now in cell E4.

	A	B	C	D	E
3		Jan	Feb	Mar	Total
4	New York	22,000	29,000	19,000	
5	Los Angeles	42,000	39,000	43,000	

6 Use AutoSum to calculate the total sales for New York.

1. Click: Home→Editing→AutoSum.

   This time AutoSum correctly guesses that you want to sum the values to the left of cell E4:

	B	C	D	E	F
3	Jan	Feb	Mar	Total	
4	22,000	29,000	19,000	=SUM(B4:D4)	
5	42,000	39,000	43,000	SUM(number1, [number2], ...)	

2. Press the **<Enter>** key or click the *AutoSum* button once more.

	A	B	C	D	E
1	Sales and Profit Report - First Quarter				
2					
3		Jan	Feb	Mar	Total
4	New York	22,000	29,000	19,000	70,000
5	Los Angeles	42,000	39,000	43,000	
6	London	18,000	20,000	22,000	
7	Paris	35,000	26,000	31,000	
8	Munich	12,000	15,000	13,000	
9	Total	129,000			

7 Save your work as *First Quarter Sales and Profit-3.*

Lesson 2-4: Select a range of cells and understand Smart Tags

1 Open *First Quarter Sales and Profit-3* from your sample files folder (if it isn't already open).

2 Observe the formula behind the value in cell B9.

Click once on cell B9 or move to it with the arrow keys on your keyboard.

Look at the *formula bar* at the top of the screen. Notice that the cell displays the *value* of a calculation and the formula bar shows the *formula* used to calculate the value:

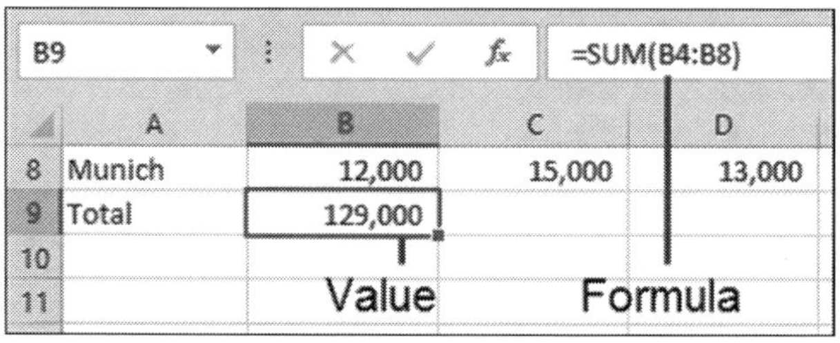

3 Delete the contents of cell B9.

Press the **<Delete>** key on your keyboard.

4 Change the word *Total* in cell A9 to: **USA Sales** and press the **<Tab>** key once.

The cursor moves to cell B9.

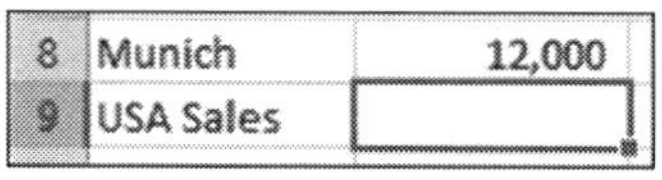

5 Select cells B4:B5 with your mouse.

When the mouse cursor is hovered over a selected cell there are three possible cursor shapes:

Cursor	What it does
	The white cross (Select) cursor appears when you hover over the center of the active cell. You can then click and drag to select a range of cells.
	The black cross (AutoFill) cursor appears when you hover over the bottom right-hand corner of the active cell. You'll be covering AutoFill later in this session.
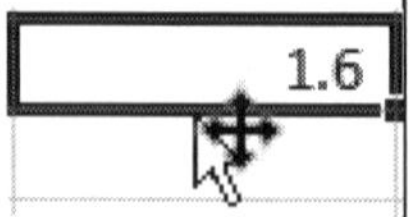	The four-headed arrow (Move) cursor appears when you hover over one of the edges of the active cell (but not the bottom right corner).

Beginners often have difficulty selecting cells and move or AutoFill them by mistake.

note

You can also delete cell contents using the mouse

Pressing the **<Delete>** key is the fastest way to delete cell contents.

You can also delete the contents of a cell using the mouse. To do this:

1. Right-click the cell.
2. Click *Clear Contents* from the shortcut menu.

note

Selecting cells with the keyboard

To select cells with the keyboard, hold down the **<Shift>** key and then use the **<Arrow>** keys to select the range needed.

First Quarter Sales and Profit-3

1. Click on cell B4 to make it the active cell.
2. Carefully position the mouse at the center of cell B4 so that you see the white cross (Select) cursor. When you see the white cross, hold down the left mouse button and drag down to cell B5.
3. Release the mouse button.

   You have now selected cells B4 and B5 (in Excel terminology you'd say that you have selected the *range* B4:B5).

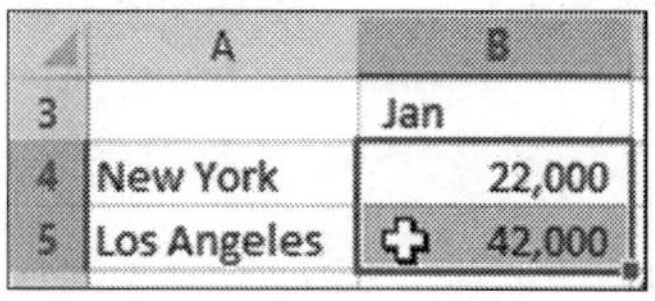

6 Display total USA sales in cell B9.

Because you have selected only the cells containing USA sales, (cells B4:B5), AutoSum can now be used to show the total value of the selected cells.

Click: Home→Editing→AutoSum. to display the total value of the selected cells.

USA sales are now shown in cell B9.

Notice the small green triangle at the top left of cell B9. This is Excel's way of saying: "I think you may have made a mistake".

7 Inspect a potential error using a Smart Tag.

1. Click once on cell B9 to make it the active cell.

   An exclamation mark icon appears. This is called a *Smart Tag*.

2. Hover the mouse cursor over the Smart Tag.

   A tip box pops up telling you what Excel thinks you may have done wrong (see below). Of course, in this case, everything is fine.

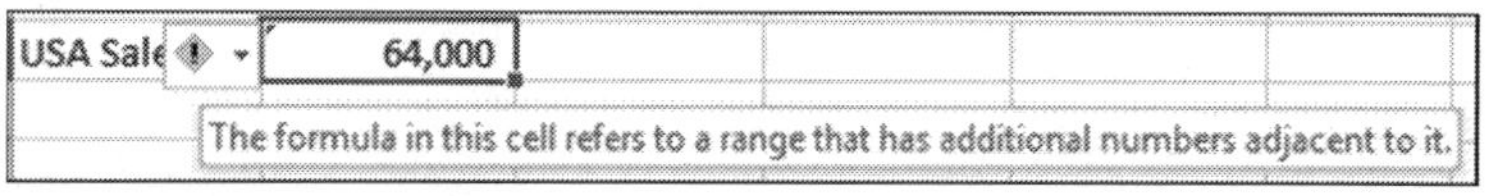

   The Smart Tag thinks that perhaps you didn't want to total just the USA sales but, in this case, the Smart Tag is wrong.

8 Examine the remedial actions suggested by the Smart Tag.

1. Hover the mouse cursor over the Smart Tag icon.
2. Click the drop-down arrow that appears next to it.

   A list of possible remedial actions is displayed. In this case you can choose *Ignore Error* to remove the green triangle from the corner of the cell.

9 Save your work as *First Quarter Sales and Profit-4.*

note

Selecting a large range of cells with the <Shift>-click technique

If you need to select a very large range of cells it is sometimes useful to use this technique:

1. Click the cell in the top left corner of the required range.
2. If necessary, use the scroll bars to make the bottom right corner of the required range visible.
3. Hold down the **<Shift>** key.
4. Click in the bottom right corner of the required range.

note

If you don't see a Smart Tag somebody may have switched this feature off

Smart Tags are enabled by default. It is possible that a user might have switched this useful feature off on your machine. Here's how to switch the Smart Tag feature back on:

1. Click:

File→Options→General→ Formulas→Error Checking

2. Make sure that the *Enable background error checking* checkbox is checked.

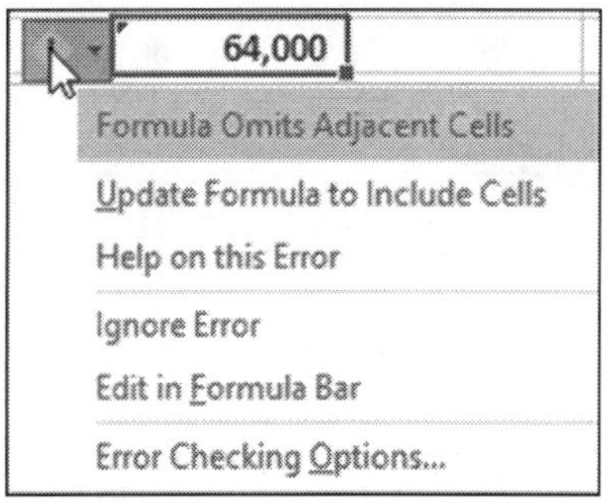

Lesson 2-5: Enter data into a range and copy data across a range

Now that you have mastered the technique of selecting cells, you can use it to speed up data entry.

When you select a range of cells prior to entering data, Excel knows that all data entered belongs in that range. Several key combinations are then available to greatly speed up data entry.

1 Open a new workbook and save it as *Data Range Test*.

2 Select cells B2:D4.

You learned how to do this in: *Lesson 2-4: Select a range of cells and understand Smart Tags.*

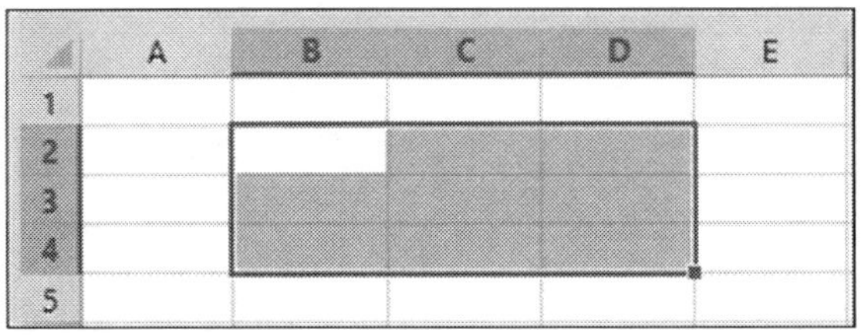

3 Type: **London**

The text appears in cell B2 (the top left cell in the range selected).

4 Press the **<Enter>** Key.

The cursor moves to cell B3 as it normally would.

5 Type: **Paris** followed by the **<Enter>** key.

The cursor moves to cell B4 as it normally would.

6 Type: **New York** followed by the **<Enter>** key.

This time something new happens. The cursor doesn't move to cell B5 as you might expect but jumps to cell C2 instead.

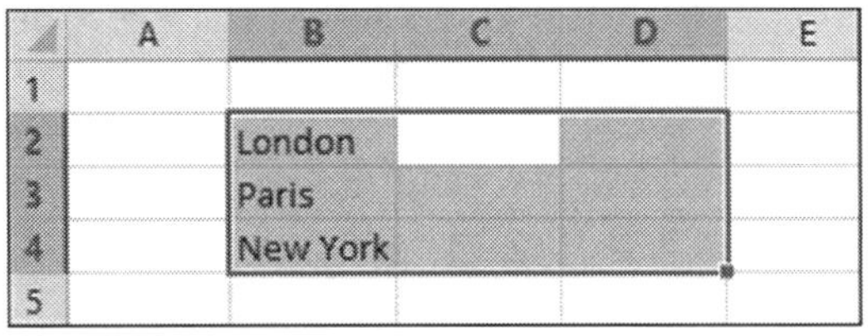

7 Type: **150,000** followed by the **<Enter>** key.

The value appears in cell C2 and Excel moves down the column again to cell C3.

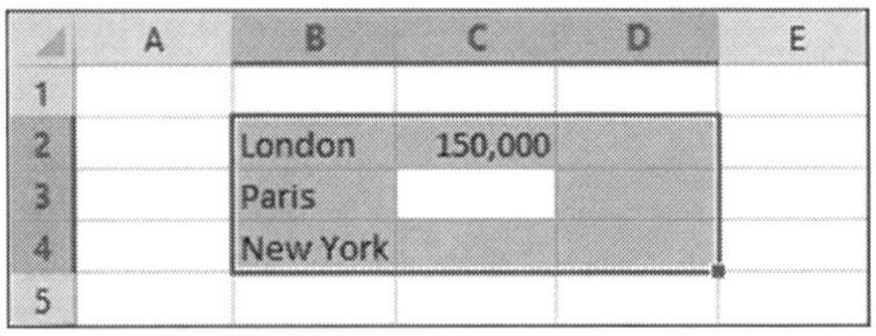

8 Press the **<Enter>** key without entering a value to leave cell C3 blank.

Excel moves down the column to cell C4.

9 Type **225,000** followed by the **<Enter>** key.

The cursor jumps to cell D2.

10 Press **<Shift>+<Enter>** twice to change your mind about leaving the value for Paris blank.

1. Press **<Shift>+<Enter>** to move backwards to the value for New York.
2. Press **<Shift>+<Enter>** a second time and you are back to the Paris cell.

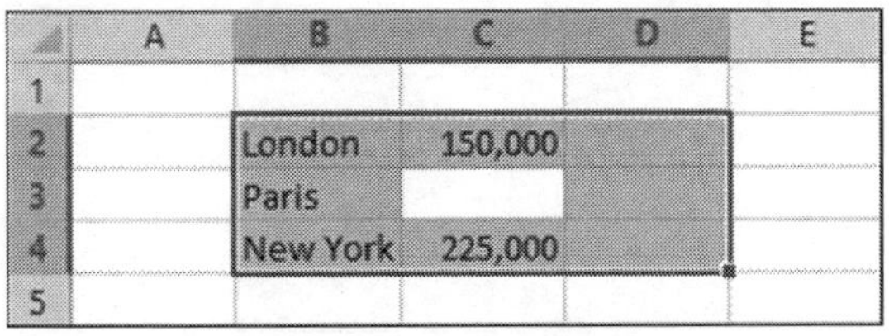

11 Type **180,000** followed by the **<Tab>** key.

<Tab> moves you across the range, to cell D3.

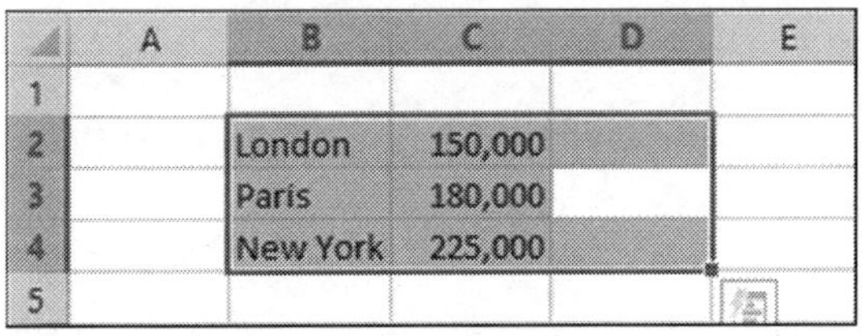

You can now appreciate how to use the technique of <Enter>, <Tab>, <Shift>+<Tab> and <Shift>+<Enter> to save a lot of time when entering a whole table of data.

12 Select cells D2:D4.

13 Type **50%** but don't press the <Enter> or <Tab> keys.

The challenge this time is to place the same value into cells D3 and D4 without having to type the value two more times.

14 Press **<Ctrl>+<Enter>**.

The value is replicated into the other cells in the selected range.

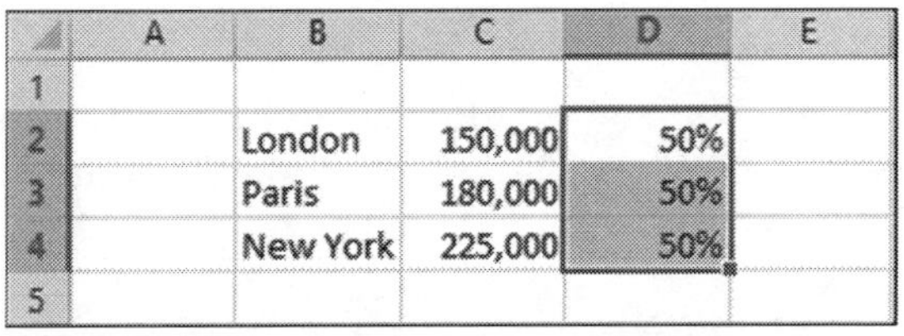

15 Click the *Save* button to save the *Data Range Test* workbook.

The *Save* button is at the top-left of your screen. 

Lesson 2-6: Select adjacent and non-adjacent rows and columns

1 Open *First Quarter Sales and Profit-4* from your sample files folder (if it isn't already open).

2 Select all of column A.

1. Hover the mouse cursor over the letter **A** at the top of the column. The column header lights up and the mouse cursor changes to a black down arrow:

2. Click to select the entire column. The column becomes slightly shaded and a green line surrounds all of the cells.

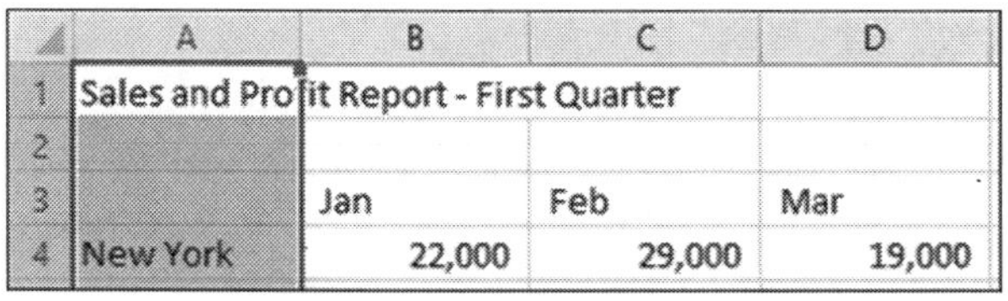

3 Bold face the contents of column A.

Click: Home→Font→Bold.

Because the whole of column A was selected, all of the cells in column A become bold faced.

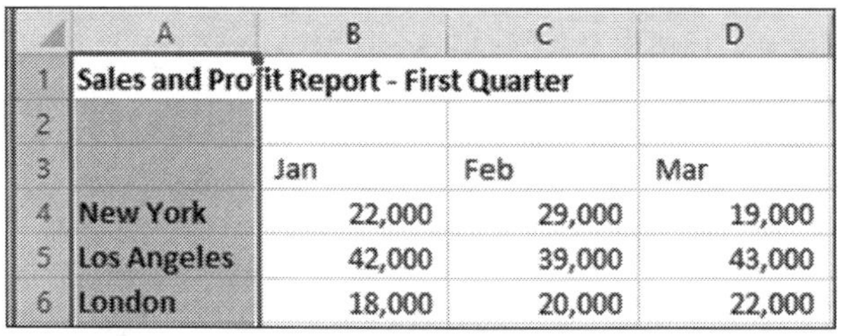

4 Click: Home→Font→Bold once more to change the cells in column A back to normal.

5 Select all of row 4.

1. Hover the mouse cursor over the number on the left-hand side of row 4. The number button lights up and the mouse cursor changes to a black arrow pointing across the row:

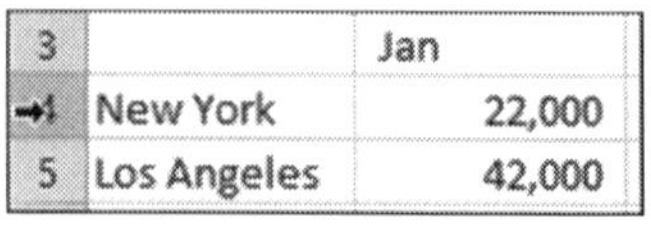

2. Click to select the row.

6 Select columns B and C.

First Quarter Sales and Profit-4

Hover the mouse cursor over the letter at the top of column B until you see the black down arrow. When you see the arrow, click and drag to the right to select columns B and C.

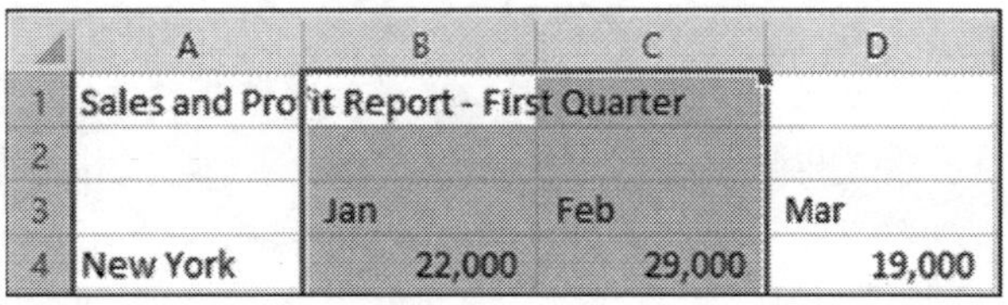

	A	B	C	D
1	Sales and Profit Report - First Quarter			
2				
3		Jan	Feb	Mar
4	New York	22,000	29,000	19,000

7 Select rows 6 and 7.

1. Hover over the number at the left of row 6 until you see the black arrow pointing across the row.
2. When you see the arrow, click and drag down to row 7 to select both rows.

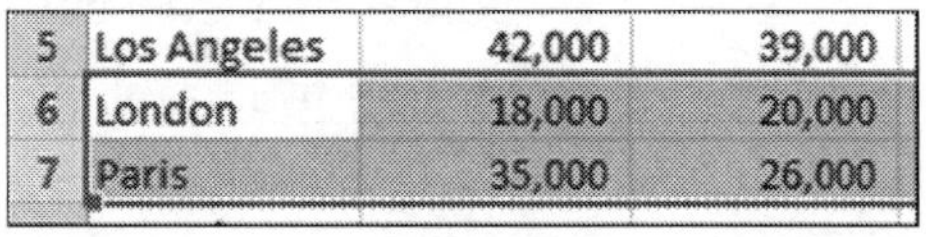

5	Los Angeles	42,000	39,000
6	London	18,000	20,000
7	Paris	35,000	26,000

8 Select columns A, B, C, D and E without dragging the mouse.

Sometimes you will need to select a large number of adjacent columns or rows. You could drag across them, but it is often easier to use the following technique:

1. Select column A.
2. Hold down the **<Shift>** key.
3. Select column E.

Columns A to E are selected.

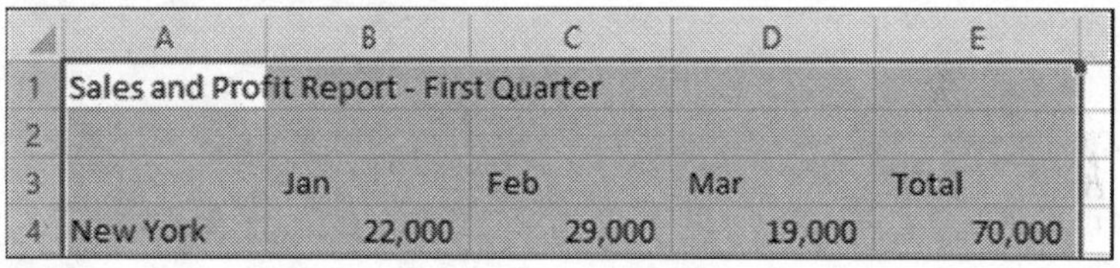

	A	B	C	D	E
1	Sales and Profit Report - First Quarter				
2					
3		Jan	Feb	Mar	Total
4	New York	22,000	29,000	19,000	70,000

9 Select rows 4 and 6.

Perhaps you need to perform an operation on two non-adjacent rows. To select rows 4 and 6 you need to:

1. Select row 4.
2. Hold down the **<Ctrl>** key on the keyboard.
3. Select row 6.

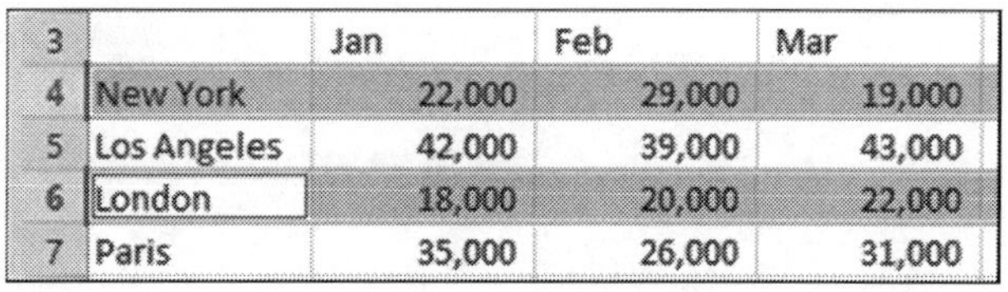

3		Jan	Feb	Mar
4	New York	22,000	29,000	19,000
5	Los Angeles	42,000	39,000	43,000
6	London	18,000	20,000	22,000
7	Paris	35,000	26,000	31,000

Lesson 2-7: Select non-contiguous cell ranges and view summary information

Non-contiguous is a very impressive word. It simply means a range of cells that is split across two or more blocks of cells in different parts of the worksheet.

Non-contiguous ranges can be selected using both the mouse and keyboard. The keyboard method may seem a little involved at first, but some users prefer it.

1 Open *First Quarter Sales and Profit-4* from your sample files folder (if it isn't already open).

2 Select the contiguous range B4:D8 with the keyboard.

When you need to select a contiguous range with the keyboard here's how it's done:

1. Use the arrow keys on the keyboard to navigate to cell B4.
2. Hold down the **<Shift>** key on the keyboard.
3. Still holding the **<Shift>** key down, use the arrow keys on the keyboard to navigate to cell D8.

The contiguous range B4:D8 is selected.

	A	B	C	D	E
1	Sales and Profit Report - First Quarter				
2					
3		Jan	Feb	Mar	Total
4	New York	22,000	29,000	19,000	70,000
5	Los Angeles	42,000	39,000	43,000	
6	London	18,000	20,000	22,000	
7	Paris	35,000	26,000	31,000	
8	Munich	12,000	15,000	13,000	
9	USA Sales	64,000			

3 Select the non-contiguous range B4:B8,D4:D8 using the mouse.

1. Select the range B4:B8 using the mouse.
2. Hold down the **<Ctrl>** key and select the range D4:D8 using the mouse.

The non-contiguous range B4:B8,D4:D8 is selected:

	A	B	C	D	E
3		Jan	Feb	Mar	Total
4	New York	22,000	29,000	19,000	70,000
5	Los Angeles	42,000	39,000	43,000	
6	London	18,000	20,000	22,000	
7	Paris	35,000	26,000	31,000	
8	Munich	12,000	15,000	13,000	
9	USA Sales	64,000			

important

You can also Deselect cells using Ctrl-Click

Excel 2019 added the ability to remove cells from a selection using **<Ctrl>+<Click>**.

Here's an example of how you can use this (fantastically useful) feature:

1. Use the mouse to select cells B4:B5.

	A	B
3		Jan
4	New York	22,000
5	Los Angeles	42,000
6	London	18,000

2. Hold down the **<Ctrl>** key and then use the mouse to select cells B6:B7.

The selected cells are added to the selection:

	A	B
3		Jan
4	New York	22,000
5	Los Angeles	42,000
6	London	18,000
7	Paris	35,000
8	Munich	12,000

3. Hold down the **<Ctrl>** key and then click on cell B4.

Cell B4 is removed from the selection:

	A	B
3		Jan
4	New York	22,000
5	Los Angeles	42,000
6	London	18,000
7	Paris	35,000
8	Munich	12,000

First Quarter Sales and Profit-4

4 **Select the same non-contiguous range with the keyboard.**

This is a little more involved than using the simple **<Shift>+<Arrow keys>** method used earlier.

Here's how it's done:

1. Use the arrow keys on the keyboard to navigate to cell B4.
2. Hold down the **<Shift>** key and then use the **<Down Arrow>** key to move down the column to cell B8.
3. Press: **<Shift>+<F8>** to enter *Add or Remove Selection* mode (see sidebar).
4. Use the arrow keys to navigate to cell D4.
5. Hold down the **<Shift>** key and then use the **<Down Arrow>** key to move down the column to cell D8.

The non-contiguous range B4:B8,D4:D8 is selected:

	A	B	C	D	E
3		Jan	Feb	Mar	Total
4	New York	22,000	29,000	19,000	70,000
5	Los Angeles	42,000	39,000	43,000	
6	London	18,000	20,000	22,000	
7	Paris	35,000	26,000	31,000	
8	Munich	12,000	15,000	13,000	
9	USA Sales	64,000			

5 **Obtain a total sales figure for January and March using the status bar.**

The status bar contains summary information for the currently selected range.

Look at the bottom right of your screen. You can see the average sales and total sales (sum of sales) for January and March:

Average: 25,700 Count: 10 Sum: 257,000

6 **View the maximum and minimum sales for January and March using the status bar.**

Right-click the status bar and click *Maximum* and *Minimum* on the shortcut menu.

✓	Average	25,700
✓	Count	10
	Numerical Count	
✓	Minimum	12,000
✓	Maximum	43,000
✓	Sum	257,000

The status bar now also displays maximum and minimum values.

Average: 25,700 Count: 10 Min: 12,000 Max: 43,000 Sum: 257,000

7 **Close the workbook without saving.**

Lesson 2-8: AutoSelect a range of cells

1 Open *Sales Report* from your sample files folder.

	A	B	C	D	E
1	Weekly Sales Report				
2					
3	Invoice No	Date	Customer	Country	Total
4	10918	Saturday, January 29, 2022	Bottom-Dollar Markets	Canada	1,700.81
5	10917	Saturday, January 29, 2022	Romero y tomillo	Spain	429.92
6	10926	Saturday, January 29, 2022	Ana Trujillo Emparedados y helados	Mexico	604.42
7	10929	Sunday, January 30, 2022	Frankenversand	Germany	1,380.33
8	10934	Sunday, January 30, 2022	Lehmanns Marktstand	Germany	587.50
9	10939	Sunday, January 30, 2022	Magazzini Alimentari Riuniti	Italy	749.05
10	10939	Sunday, January 30, 2022	Magazzini Alimentari Riuniti	Italy	749.05
11	10925	Monday, January 31, 2022	Hanari Carnes	Brazil	558.29
12	10944	Monday, January 31, 2022	Bottom-Dollar Markets	Canada	1,204.75
13	10923	Monday, January 31, 2022	La maison d'Asie	France	879.83
14	10937	Tuesday, February 1, 2022	Cactus Comidas para llevar	Argentina	757.64
15	10947	Tuesday, February 1, 2022	B's Beverages	UK	258.50
16	10933	Tuesday, February 1, 2022	Island Trading	UK	1,081.71
17	10938	Wednesday, February 2, 2022	QUICK-Stop	Germany	3,209.95
18	10949	Wednesday, February 2, 2022	Bottom-Dollar Markets	Canada	5,195.85
19	10945	Wednesday, February 2, 2022	Morgenstern Gesundkost	Germany	287.88
20					
21	This report excludes sales to Asia and South Africa.				

This report contains a single block of cells in the range A3 to E19.

When data is arranged in this way it is referred to as a *Range*.

You will often want to select a row or column of cells within a range, or even the entire range.

You can select ranges by using any of the techniques covered so far but this could be very time consuming if the range encompassed hundreds, or even thousands, of rows and columns.

In this lesson, you'll learn how to select range rows, range columns and entire ranges with a few clicks of the mouse.

2 Select all cells within the range to the right of cell A7.

1. Click in cell A7 to make it the active cell.
2. Hover over the right-hand border of cell A7 until you see the four-headed arrow cursor shape.

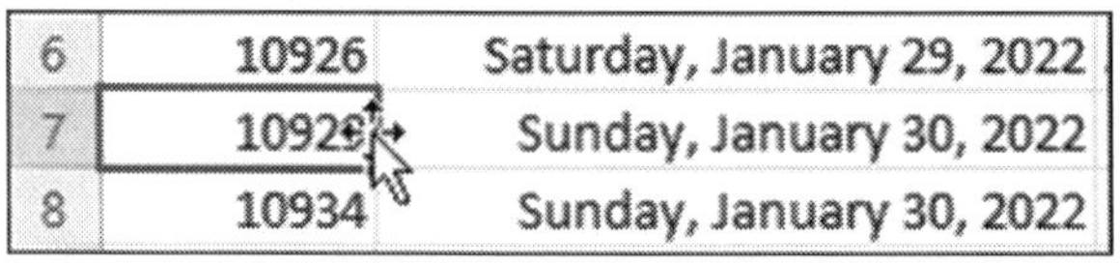

6	10926	Saturday, January 29, 2022
7	10929	Sunday, January 30, 2022
8	10934	Sunday, January 30, 2022

3. When you see this cursor shape, hold down the **<Shift>** key and double-click.

All cells to the right of A7, that are within the range, are selected.

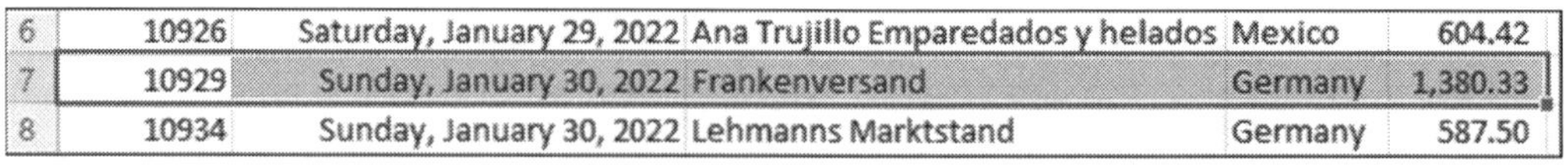

6	10926	Saturday, January 29, 2022	Ana Trujillo Emparedados y helados	Mexico	604.42
7	10929	Sunday, January 30, 2022	Frankenversand	Germany	1,380.33
8	10934	Sunday, January 30, 2022	Lehmanns Marktstand	Germany	587.50

3 Select all cells within the range except the header row.

1. Click in cell A4 to make it the active cell.
2. Hover over the right-hand border of cell A4 until you see the four-headed arrow cursor shape.

note

Why your dates may look different to those in the screen grabs

This book was written using the *English (United States) Region format* settings.

The *Region format* for *English (United States)* dates are:

Short Date

3/10/2021

Long Date

Thursday, March 10, 2021

If you are situated in a different country, your *Short Date* and *Long Date* Region formats may be in a different format that is more appropriate to your location.

While it is possible to change your *Region format* (in Windows settings) there is no need to do so to work through this book.

Just be aware that some of the screen grabs in this book will be formatted differently to what you see on your screen.

You'll learn more about date formats later, in: *Lesson 4-1: Format dates.*

Sales Report

note

Other ways to AutoSelect a range

Using the keyboard

Here's how you would select the entire range in the *Weekly Sales Report* (excluding the header row) using the keyboard method.

Make cell A4 the active cell by navigating to it with the **<Arrow>** keys.

1. Press: **<Ctrl>+<Shift>+<DownArrow>**

   Cells A4:A19 are selected.

2. Press: **<Ctrl>+<Shift>+<RightArrow>**

   The entire range (excluding the header row) is selected.

Using shortcut keys

The shortcut keys method is the fastest way to select the entire range *including* the header row.

1. Click anywhere inside the range.
2. Press: **<Ctrl>+<A>**

   The entire range (including the header row) is selected.

From the Ribbon

You can select the entire range including the header row (described as the *Current Region* in the dialog) using the Ribbon. This method is the least efficient way to select an entire range.

1. Make sure that the active cell is within the range.
2. Click:

   Home→Editing→
   Find & Select→
   Go To Special...

   The *Go To Special* dialog is displayed.

3. Click the *Current region* option button and then click the OK button.

The entire range (including the header row) is selected.

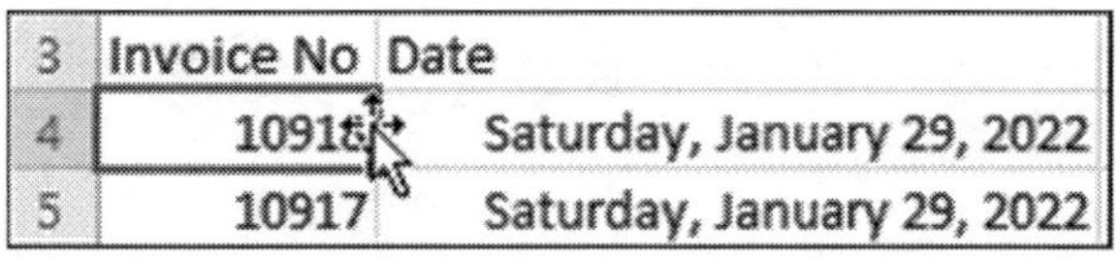

3	Invoice No	Date
4	10918	Saturday, January 29, 2022
5	10917	Saturday, January 29, 2022

3. When you see this cursor shape, hold down the **<Shift>** key and double-click.

   All cells to the right of cell A4, but within the range, are selected.

4. Hover over the bottom border of any selected cell until you see the four-headed arrow cursor shape.

Customer	Country
Bottom-Dollar Markets	Canada
Romero y tomillo	Spain

5. When you see this cursor shape, hold down the **<Shift>** key and double-click.

The entire range (except the header row) is selected.

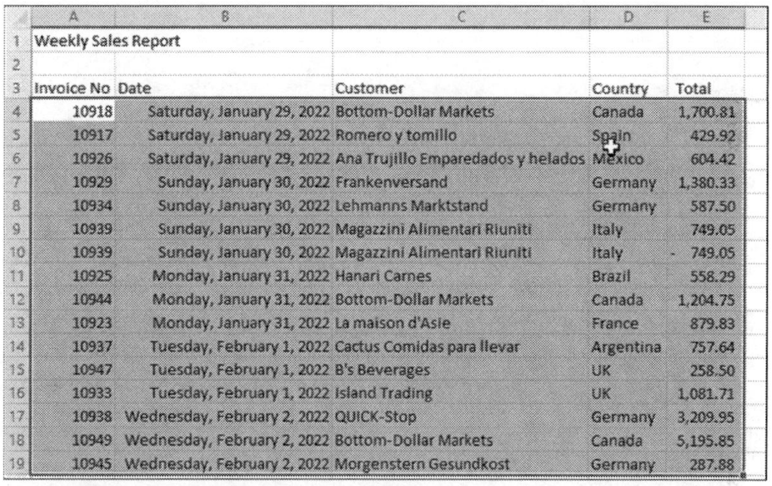

	A	B	C	D	E
1	Weekly Sales Report				
2					
3	Invoice No	Date	Customer	Country	Total
4	10918	Saturday, January 29, 2022	Bottom-Dollar Markets	Canada	1,700.81
5	10917	Saturday, January 29, 2022	Romero y tomillo	Spain	429.92
6	10926	Saturday, January 29, 2022	Ana Trujillo Emparedados y helados	Mexico	604.42
7	10929	Sunday, January 30, 2022	Frankenversand	Germany	1,380.33
8	10934	Sunday, January 30, 2022	Lehmanns Marktstand	Germany	587.50
9	10939	Sunday, January 30, 2022	Magazzini Alimentari Riuniti	Italy	749.05
10	10939	Sunday, January 30, 2022	Magazzini Alimentari Riuniti	Italy	749.05
11	10925	Monday, January 31, 2022	Hanari Carnes	Brazil	558.29
12	10944	Monday, January 31, 2022	Bottom-Dollar Markets	Canada	1,204.75
13	10923	Monday, January 31, 2022	La maison d'Asie	France	879.83
14	10937	Tuesday, February 1, 2022	Cactus Comidas para llevar	Argentina	757.64
15	10947	Tuesday, February 1, 2022	B's Beverages	UK	258.50
16	10933	Tuesday, February 1, 2022	Island Trading	UK	1,081.71
17	10938	Wednesday, February 2, 2022	QUICK-Stop	Germany	3,209.95
18	10949	Wednesday, February 2, 2022	Bottom-Dollar Markets	Canada	5,195.85
19	10945	Wednesday, February 2, 2022	Morgenstern Gesundkost	Germany	287.88

You can also use this technique to select cells (that are within the range) to the left of the active cell or above the active cell.

4 Close the workbook without saving.

Lesson 2-9: Re-size rows and columns

1 Open *First Quarter Sales and Profit-4* from your sample files folder.

Notice that columns B, C, D and E are far too wide for their contents. It would be useful to make them narrower to keep the worksheet compact.

2 Re-size column B so that it is just wide enough to contain the January sales figures.

1. Hover the mouse cursor over the line separating the letters B and C until you see the *re-size* cursor shape:

2. When you see the *re-size* cursor shape, keep the mouse still and then click and drag to the left. Column B will re-size as you drag. Make it narrower so that the values just fit in the column. Notice that the column width is displayed in characters and pixels (see sidebar) as you drag.

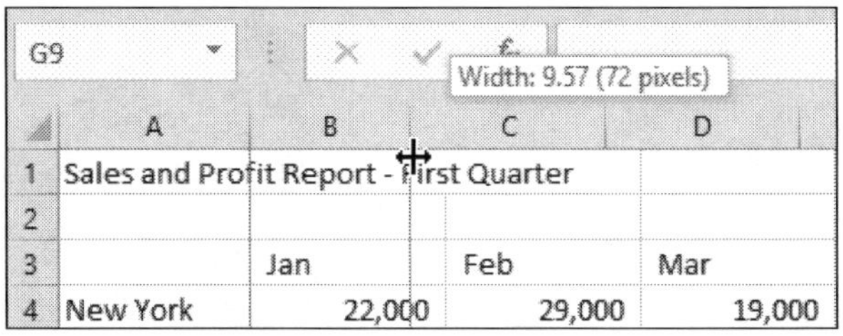

3 Re-size column B so that it is too narrow to contain the January sales figures.

Notice that when the column isn't wide enough to contain the contents, hash signs are shown instead of values (if you're used to hashes being called **pound signs** or **number signs** see the sidebar).

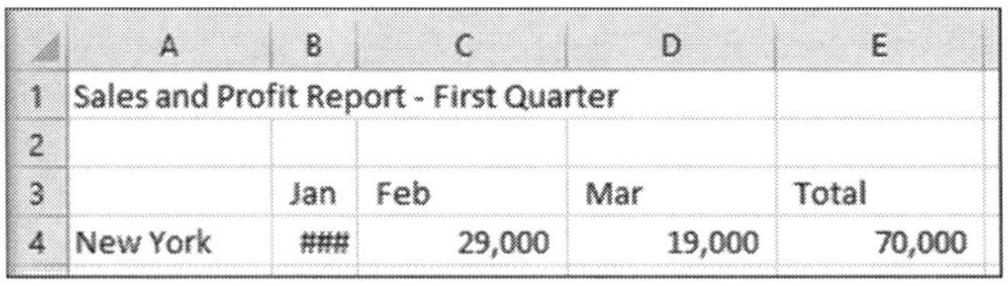

4 Automatically re-size column B so that it is a perfect fit for the widest cell in the column.

1. Hover over the line separating the letters B and C until you see the re-size cursor shape:

2. When you see this shape, double-click to automatically re-size column B.

5 Automatically re-size every column in the worksheet in one operation.

note

Why are you calling the pound sign a hash?

In the USA and Canada, the hash symbol is called the **pound sign** or the **number sign**.

In different USA/Canada regions the single symbol has different names because it can be used to denote a number (as in contestant #5) or as a weight (as in 3# of butter).

Throughout this book I will refer to the # as a *hash* because that is the term used in most other English-speaking countries.

note

Excel column widths are expressed in characters and pixels

In this lesson Excel displays the default column width as:

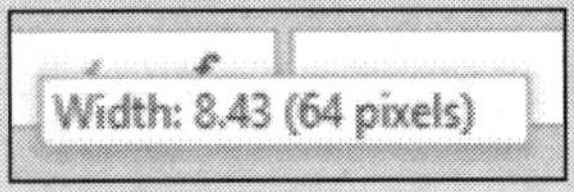

8.43 *characters* is Excel's default column size (meaning that 8.43 characters can be displayed in each cell using the default *Calibri* font and font size).

Pixels are the tiny dots that make up a computer display.

With 64 pixels to each column, a computer screen with a resolution of 1680X1050 (the normal resolution for a 22 inch display) should display about 1680/64=26.25 Excel columns.

Row heights are displayed in points (a point is approximately 1/72 inch or 0.035cm).

First Quarter Sales and Profit-4

note

Other ways to re-size rows and columns

You can also re-size rows and columns using the Ribbon.

Click: Home→Cells→Format.

A drop-down menu appears.

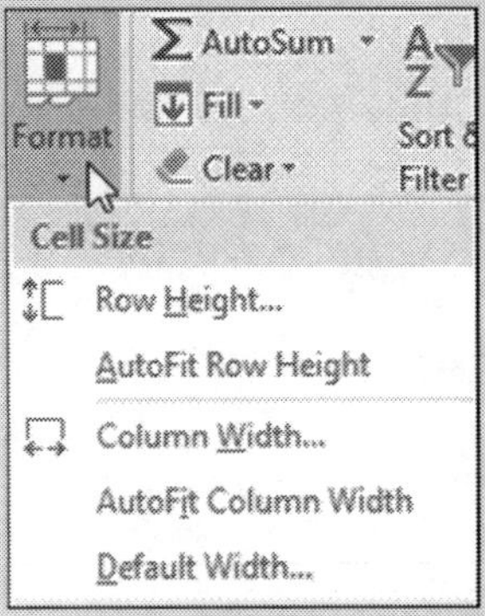

You can use the *Row Height* and *Column Width* options to set the selected row(s) or column(s) to a specific number of characters (for column widths) or points (for row height).

You can also use the *AutoFit Row Height* and *AutoFit Column Width* options to automatically re-size the selected cells in a row or column (you did this during the lesson).

Default Width… allows you to set a new width for all empty columns but will not affect columns that have already been manually resized.

note

Making several columns or rows the same size

Select the rows or columns that you want to resize and then click and drag the intersection of any of the selected rows or columns.

When the mouse button is released, this will make each of the selected rows or columns exactly the same height or width.

1. Select every cell in the worksheet by clicking the *Select All* button in the top left corner of the worksheet (you can also do this by clicking in any blank cell and then pressing **<Ctrl>+<A>**).

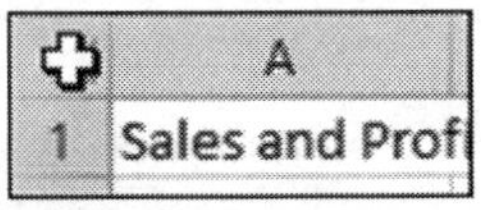

2. Hover over the intersection of any two columns until you see the re-size cursor shape and then double-click.

   Every column is now perfectly sized.

   Notice that AutoFit has done its job rather too well. Column A is now wide enough to accommodate all of the text in cell A1.

	A	B
1	Sales and Profit Report - First Quarter	

6 Automatically re-size column A so that it is only wide enough to contain the longest city name (Los Angeles).

1. Select cells A4:A9.
2. Click: Home→Cells→Format→AutoFit Column Width.

This time the column is automatically sized so that it is just wide enough to contain all of the text in the selected cells.

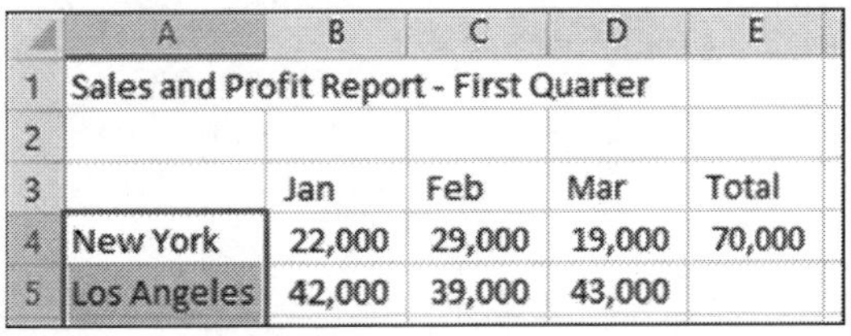

	A	B	C	D	E
1	Sales and Profit Report - First Quarter				
2					
3		Jan	Feb	Mar	Total
4	New York	22,000	29,000	19,000	70,000
5	Los Angeles	42,000	39,000	43,000	

Notice that the text in cell A1 has spilled over into the adjoining columns B, C, D and E. This always happens when a cell contains text and the adjacent cells are empty.

7 Manually re-size row 3 so that it is about twice as tall as the other rows.

Do this in the same way you re-sized the column but, this time, hover between the intersection of rows 3 and 4 until you see the re-size cursor shape, and then click and drag downwards.

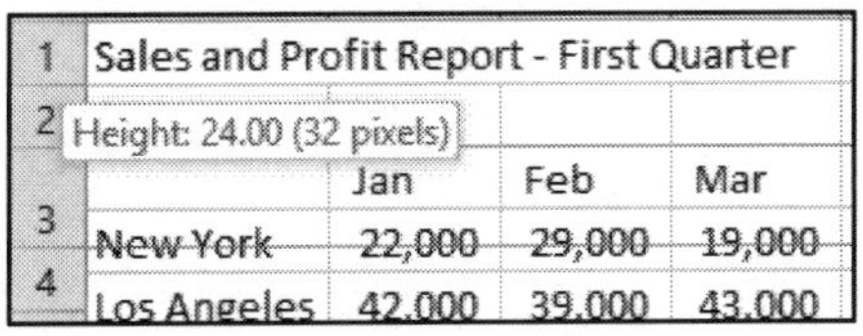

8 Auto-resize row 3 so that it is the same size as the other rows again.

1. Hover over the line separating the numbers 3 and 4 until you see the re-size cursor shape.
2. When you see this shape, double-click to automatically re-size row 3.

9 Close Excel without saving.

Lesson 2-10: Use AutoSum to sum a non-contiguous range

In: *Lesson 2-7: Select non-contiguous cell ranges and view summary information*, you learned how to view the sum of January and March sales using the status bar. But how can you put that value onto the worksheet?

Now that you have the hang of selecting non-contiguous ranges, you can use this skill in conjunction with your AutoSum skills to create a formula that will calculate the total of a non-contiguous range.

1 Open *First Quarter Sales and Profit*-4 from your sample files folder.

2 Enter the text: **Jan/Mar Sales** in cell A10 and press the <Tab> key.

The active cell moves to cell B10.

3 Re-size column A so that it is wide enough to contain the text.

1. Hover over the line separating the letters A and B until you see the re-size cursor shape:

2. When you see this shape, keep the mouse still and then click and drag to the right. Column A will re-size as you drag. Make it wider so that the words *Jan/Mar Sales* comfortably fit in the column:

	A	B	C	D
1	Sales and Profit Report - First Quarter			
2				
3		Jan	Feb	Mar
4	New York	22,000	29,000	19,000
5	Los Angeles	42,000	39,000	43,000
6	London	18,000	20,000	22,000
7	Paris	35,000	26,000	31,000
8	Munich	12,000	15,000	13,000
9	USA Sales	64,000		
10	Jan/Mar Sales			

4 Use AutoSum to calculate the total sales for January and March in cell B10.

1. Click in cell B10 to make it the active cell.

2. Click Home→Editing→Σ (the AutoSum button).

An AutoSum appears in cell B10, but it isn't the formula you need. AutoSum guesses that you simply want to repeat the value in the USA Sales cell.

8	Munich	12,000	15,000	13,000
9	USA Sales	64,000		
10	Jan/Mar Sales	=SUM(B9)		
11		SUM(**number1**, [number2], ...)		

First Quarter Sales and Profit-4

3. Select the range B4:B8 with the mouse and release the mouse button.

4. Hold down the **<Ctrl>** key and select the range D4:D8 with the mouse.

   Notice that the non-contiguous range *B4:B8,D4:D8* is shown in the AutoSum's formula:

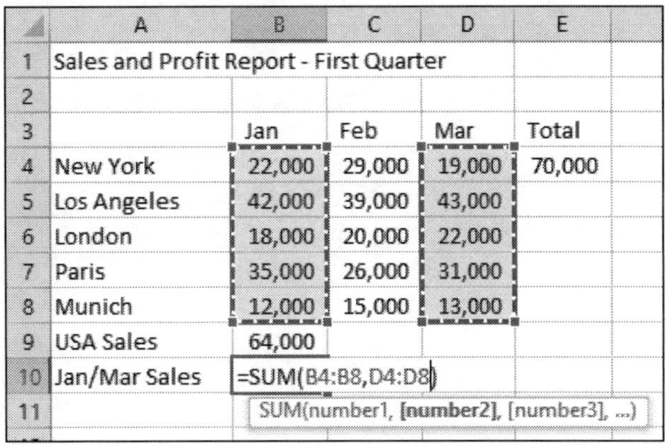

5. Press the **<Enter>** key or click the AutoSum button again to show the sales for January and March in cell B10.

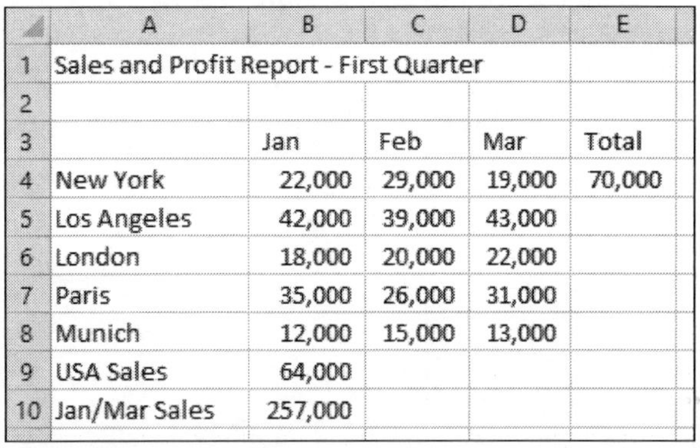

5 Save your work as *First Quarter Sales and Profit-5*.

Lesson 2-11: Use AutoSum to calculate average and maximum values

1 Open *First Quarter Sales and Profit-5* from your sample files folder (if it isn't already open).

2 Delete cells E3:E4.

Select cells E3 and E4 and press the **<Delete>** key on your keyboard.

3 Type the word: **Average** in cell E3 and press the **<Enter>** key.

The cursor moves to cell E4:

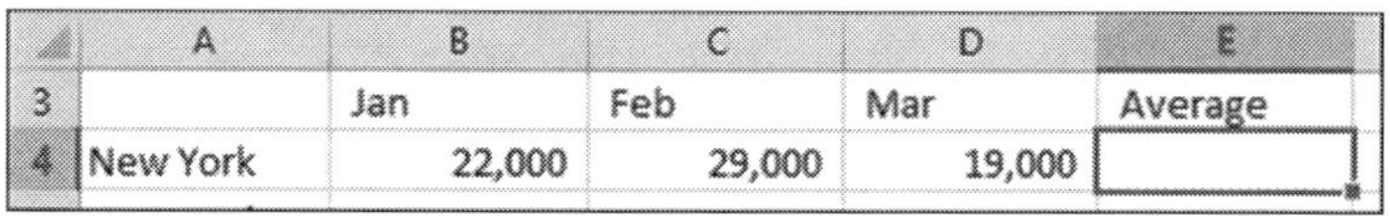

4 Use AutoSum to create a formula that will show the average New York sales in cell E4.

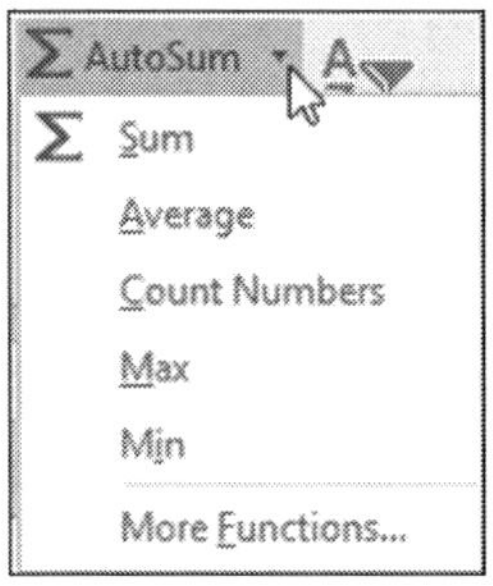

1. Click: Home→Editing→AutoSum→Drop-down arrow (see sidebar).

   A drop-down menu is displayed showing different ways in which AutoSum can operate upon a range of cells:

2. Click *Average*.

   Excel generates an AVERAGE function and inserts the cell range B4:D4. This is exactly what you want:

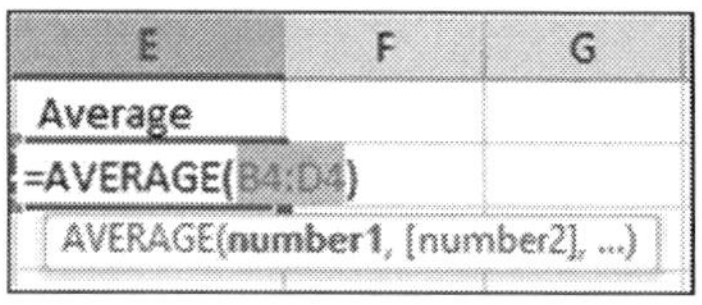

3. Press the **<Enter>** key or click the AutoSum button again to see the average sales for New York:

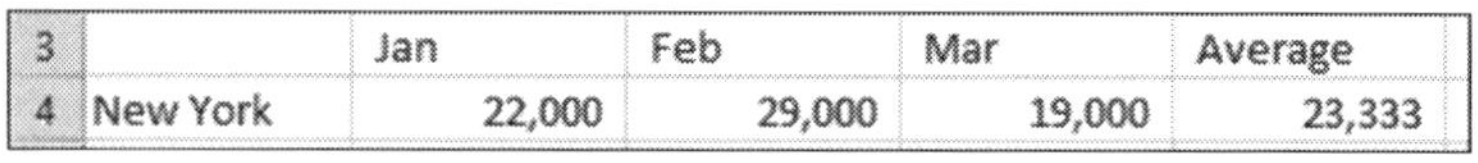

5 Type the word: **Maximum** into cell F3 and then press the **<Enter>** key.

6 Use AutoSum to create a formula in cell F4 that will show the Maximum New York Sales for this period.

1. Place an AutoSum in cell F4 but this time, choose *Max* from the drop-down menu.

   This time you have a small problem. AutoSum is including the average value (23,333) in the calculation.

First Quarter Sales and Profit-5

B	C	D	E	F
Jan	Feb	Mar	Average	Maximum
22,000	29,000	19,000	23,333	=MAX(B4:E4)

2. Select cells B4:D4 with the mouse.

3. Notice that the MAX function is now working with the (correct) range B4:D4.

	A	B	C	D	E	F
4	New York	22,000	29,000	19,000	23,333	=MAX(B4:D4)

4. Press the **<Enter>** key or click the AutoSum button Σ once more to see the maximum sales the New York office managed during the first quarter of the year:

3		Jan	Feb	Mar	Average	Maximum
4	New York	22,000	29,000	19,000	23,333	29,000

7 Change the words *USA Sales* in cell A9 back to: **Sales** and press the **<Tab>** key.

8 Press the **<F2>** key on the keyboard (or double-click cell B9) to bring back the marquee (shown as a blue box).

tip

Another way to bring back the blue box showing a range is to click the range in the *Formula Bar.*

9 Adjust the marquee using click and drag so that all offices are included in the Sales total.

Notice that there is a small blue spot on each corner of the range. These are called *sizing handles.*

1. Hover the mouse cursor over the bottom right (or bottom left) sizing handle until the cursor shape changes to a double-headed arrow. It is really important that you see the double-headed arrow and not the four-headed arrow or white cross.

4	New York	22,000
5	Los Angeles	42,000

2. When you see the double headed arrow click and drag with the mouse down to cell B8.

3. Release the mouse button.

4. Press the **<Enter>** key or click the AutoSum button Σ again.

	A	B
3		Jan
4	New York	22,000
5	Los Angeles	42,000
6	London	18,000
7	Paris	35,000
8	Munich	12,000
9	Sales	129,000
10	Jan/Mar Sales	257,000

10 Save your work as *First Quarter Sales and Profit-6.*

Lesson 2-12: Create your own formulas

The AutoSum tool is very useful for quickly inserting SUM, AVERAGE, COUNT, MAX and MIN formulas into cells. Many Excel users never get any further with their formulas than this.

In this session, you'll create your own formulas without the use of AutoSum.

1 Open *First Quarter Sales and Profit*-6 from your sample files folder (if it isn't already open).

2 Select cells A10:B10 and press the **<Delete>** key once.

The previous contents of cells A10:B10 are removed.

3 Type the word **Costs** into cell A11 and **Profit** into cell A12.

4 Type the value **83,000** into cell B11 and press the **<Enter>** key to move down to cell B12.

11	Costs	83,000
12	Profit	

5 Enter a formula into cell B12 to compute the profit made in January.

1. Type: **=B9-B11** into cell B12.
2. Press the **<Enter>** key.

The profit for January is displayed:

9	Sales	129,000
10		
11	Costs	83,000
12	Profit	46,000

6 Enter the formula again using the mouse to select cell references.

The method that you have just used to enter the formula works just fine, but it isn't best practice. Eventually you will make a mistake. For example, you could easily type =**B8-B11** resulting in an incorrect result.

To eliminate such errors, you should always select cell references visually rather than simply typing them in. You can visually select cells using either the mouse or the keyboard. First, you'll use the mouse method.

1. Click in cell B12 and press the **<Delete>** key on the keyboard to clear the old formula.
2. Press the equals <=> key on the keyboard.
3. Click once on the value 129,000 in cell B9.
4. Press the minus <-> key on the keyboard.
5. Click once on the value 83,000 in cell B11.

Important

Formulas automatically recalculate whenever any of the cells in the formula change.

For example: If you were to change the *Paris Jan* sales value in cell B7 to 45,000 (and then press the **<Enter>** key) this would cause the (total Jan) *Sales* value in cell B9 to re-calculate to 139,000.

Because the value in cell B9 has changed this would, in turn, cause the *Profit* value in cell B12 to recalculate to 56,000.

And because the value in cell B12 has changed this will cause the *10% Bonus* value to recalculate to 5,600.

First Quarter Sales and Profit-6

6. Press the **<Enter>** key on the keyboard.

If you followed the above steps carefully you will see that you have created the same formula but with a much lower possibility of making a mistake.

7 Enter the formula again using the visual keyboard technique.

The very best Excel experts hardly use the mouse. You waste valuable seconds every time you reach for the mouse.

Here's the expert technique of visual selection via keyboard:

1. Use the arrow keys to navigate to cell B12 and then press the **<Delete>** key on the keyboard to clear the old formula.
2. Press the **<=>** key on the keyboard.
3. Press the **<Up Arrow>** key three times to move to cell B9.
4. Press the **<->** key on the keyboard.
5. Press the **<Up Arrow>** key once to move to cell B11.
6. Press the **<Enter>** key on the keyboard.

8 Enter a formula that uses the multiplication operator to calculate a 10% bonus paid upon profits.

This employer is very generous and pays the staff ten percent of all profits as an incentive bonus.

1. In cell A13 type the words: **10% Bonus** and then press the **<Tab>** key on the keyboard to move to cell B13.

   The multiplication operator is not an X as you might expect but an asterisk (*). The other Excel operators are shown in the sidebar.

   You need to press **<Shift>+<8>** to enter an asterisk. If you are using a full size keyboard with a numeric keypad at the right-hand side you can also use the numeric keypad's **<*>** key.

   Whichever key you use you'll still see an asterisk in the formula.

2. Use either the *mouse selection* technique or the *visual keyboard* technique to enter the formula shown below into cell B13 and then press the **<Enter>** key to see how much bonus was earned:

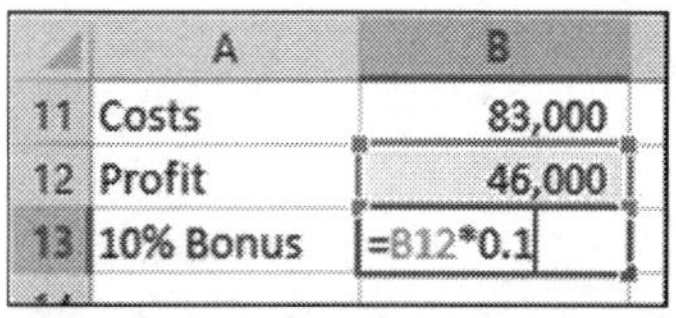

	A	B
11	Costs	83,000
12	Profit	46,000
13	10% Bonus	=B12*0.1

   Note that multiplying a value by 0.1 calculates ten percent of the value. You'll learn more about calculating percentages later, in: *Lesson 4-3: Format numbers using built-in number formats.*

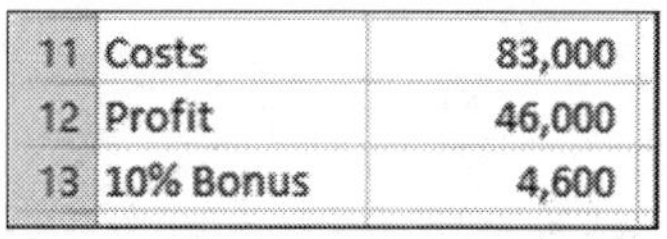

11	Costs	83,000
12	Profit	46,000
13	10% Bonus	4,600

9 Save your work as *First Quarter Sales and Profit-7.*

important

The Excel Operators

	Name	Example
+	Addition	1+2
-	Subtraction	7-5
*	Multiplication	6*3
/	Division	15/5
%	Percent	25%
^	Exponentiation	4^2

trivia

The feature that Excel uses to help you out with function calls first made an appearance in Visual Basic 5 back in 1996 and had the wonderful name: ***IntelliSense***. The Excel implementation is called *Formula AutoComplete.*

In 1996 I was working in Switzerland (as a programmer and analyst) developing a ski-school management application. I was extremely impressed by how easy *IntelliSense* made my job. I didn't have to remember hundreds of function names anymore.

I was even slightly worried that just about anybody could now program (but, of course, I was wrong).

Recently I was in London being driven by a Hackney cab driver (Hackney cab drivers know every shortcut and back street in London). He was worried that satellite navigation devices would now enable anybody to become a London cabbie.

Of course, he really had nothing to worry about either.

note

Excel automatically adds closing brackets to functions

If you type:

=SUM(B4:B5

... and then press the **<Enter>** or **<Tab>** key, Excel will automatically add the closing bracket for you resulting in:

=SUM(B4:B5)

First Quarter Sales and Profit-7

Lesson 2-13: Create functions using Formula AutoComplete

1 Open *First Quarter Sales and Profit*-7 from your sample files folder (if it isn't already open).

2 Type the words **USA Sales** into cell A15 and **European Sales** into cell A16.

3 If necessary, re-size column A so that it is wide enough for the words *European Sales* to fit within the column.

You learned how to do this in: *Lesson 2-9: Re-size rows and columns.*

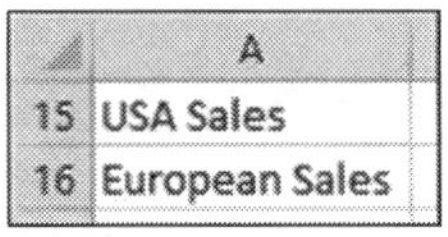

4 Click into cell B15 and type **=S** into the cell.

Something interesting happens:

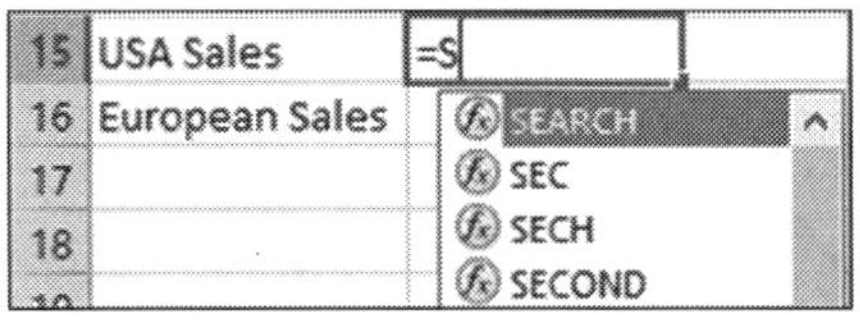

A list appears showing every function in the Excel function library beginning with S. This feature is called *Formula AutoComplete* (if AutoComplete didn't display as expected see the facing-page sidebar).

You've already encountered the SUM, AVERAGE and MAX functions provided by AutoSum.

You may be pleased (or dismayed) to know that there are over 500 functions in the current Excel 2021 function library. The good news is that most untrained Excel users only understand how to use the SUM and AVERAGE functions.

When you typed **=S** Excel listed all functions beginning with S.

5 Continue typing: **=SU**

Notice that the list now only shows functions beginning with SU and you can see the *SUM* function that you need three down in the list.

You could simply click on the SUM function with the mouse but let's work like an Excel pro and use the keyboard.

6 Press the **<Down Arrow>** key twice to move the cursor over the SUM function.

The SUM function now has a tip telling you what the function does:

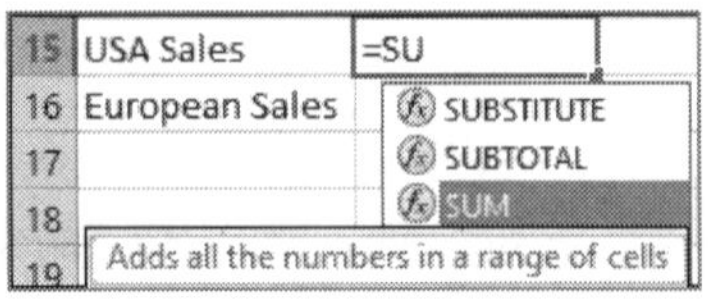

7 **Display Excel's help topic for the SUM function.**

The tip tells you a little about the SUM function but to get the full story press the **<F1>** key while SUM is still highlighted in the dropdown list.

The Excel help system opens showing detailed help for the SUM function.

Read the help text if you are interested and then close the help window.

Notice that Excel has now left you with only *=SU* in the cell.

8 **Complete the function by typing: M(**

Notice that a little box has appeared beneath the function. This box displays the *Syntax* of the SUM function (see sidebar for more information about the Syntax box).

9 **Select the cells that you need to sum (cells B4:B5) with the mouse or keyboard.**

If you want to be a real pro, you should select them with the keyboard. To do this:

1. Press the **<Up Arrow>** key repeatedly until you reach cell B4.
2. Hold down the **<Shift>** key and press the **<Down Arrow>** key once to select cells B4:B5.

10 **Type a closing bracket to complete the formula and then press the <Enter> key.**

The total USA sales are displayed in cell B15.

11 **Use the same technique to create a SUM function in cell B16 to show the total European sales (cells B6:B8).**

1. Click in cell B16.
2. Type **=SU**
3. Press the **<Down Arrow>** key twice to move the cursor over the SUM function.
4. Press the **<Tab>** key to automatically enter the SUM function into cell B16.
5. Select the range B6:B8.
6. Type the closing bracket (this isn't really necessary – see sidebar facing page).

   The formula should now be: **=SUM(B6:B8)**
7. Press the **<Enter>** key.

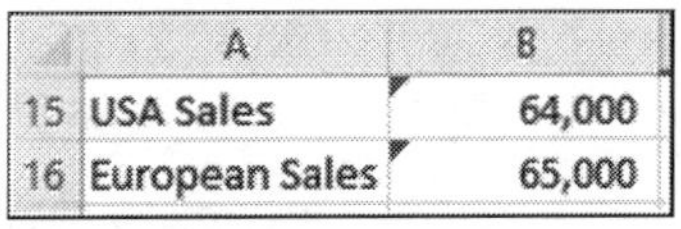

12 **Save your work as *First Quarter Sales and Profit-8.***

note

Enabling and disabling AutoComplete

As with so many other features, Microsoft allows you to turn this very useful feature off.

You'd never want to do this, but you may work on a machine that has had Formula AutoComplete switched off and you need to turn it on again.

Click:
File→Options→Formulas→ Working with formulas

...and make sure that the *Formula AutoComplete* box is checked.

note

The Syntax box

The Syntax box tells you which arguments (sometimes called parameters) the function needs.

The first argument has no square brackets meaning that you can't leave it out.

The second argument (shown in square brackets) is optional.

The third argument is an ellipsis (a row of three dots). This means that you could continue with more arguments such as [number3], [number4] etc.

For such a simple function as SUM the syntax box is hardly needed, but later in this course you'll encounter complex functions that require several arguments and then the syntax box will be invaluable.

Lesson 2-14: Use AutoFill for text and numeric series

1 Open *First Quarter Sales and Profit-8* from your sample files folder (if it isn't already open).

2 Delete the text **Feb** and **Mar** from cells C3:D3.

Select cells C3:D3 and then press the **<Delete>** key on your keyboard.

3 Make B3 the active cell.

Click once inside cell B3. Notice that there is a green border around the cell and a spot on the bottom right-hand corner. This is the AutoFill handle. If you don't see it, refer to the sidebar.

4 Hover over the AutoFill handle with your mouse until the cursor shape changes to a black cross.

Many of my students have great difficulty with this when they try it for the first time.

- You don't want the four-headed arrow:  – that would move the cell.
- You don't want the white cross:  – that would select the cell.
- You want the black cross:  – the AutoFill cursor.

5 When the black cross cursor is visible, hold down the mouse button and drag your mouse to the right to AutoFill the other months: **Feb** and **Mar**.

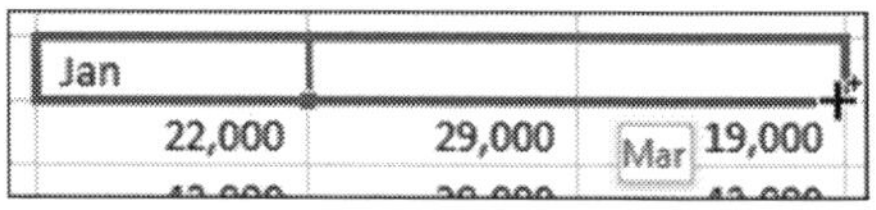

Notice the tip that appears as you drag, previewing the month that will appear in each cell.

When you release the mouse button, the name of each month appears in cells C3 and D3.

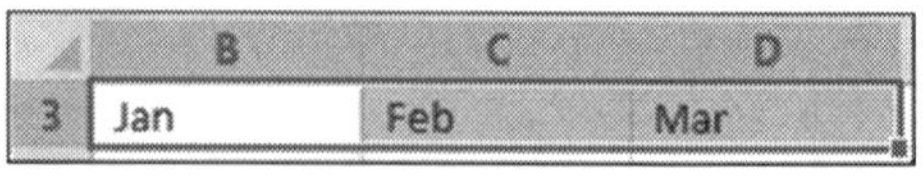

6 Type: **Monday** into cell A18 and AutoFill down to cell A24 to show the days of the week.

(If you are not using an English language version of Excel you will need to type **Monday** in your own language).

note

If you don't see the AutoFill handle somebody has disabled AutoFill

It's almost certain that AutoFill will be enabled on any computer that you work on. It is such a useful feature that you wouldn't want to disable it.

If you don't see the AutoFill handle (the black spot on the bottom right-hand corner of the active cell) it's because somebody has switched AutoFill off.

To bring it back click:

File→Options→Advanced

In the first section (*Editing Options*) check the box next to *Enable fill handle and cell drag-and-drop*.

First Quarter Sales and Profit-8

tip

You don't have to enter two numbers if you want to create a sequential numeric range.

If you simply type a number into a cell and then AutoFill while holding down the **<Ctrl>** key, you will automatically generate sequential numbers.

note

Why your numbers may display differently to those in the screen grabs

This book was written using the *English (United States) Region format* settings.

The *Region format* for *English (United States)* numbers uses the decimal separator for a period and a comma for the thousand's separator.

This displays formatted numbers such as 12,345.67.

If you are situated in a different country, your numbers may be formatted in a way that is more appropriate to your location. For example, the decimal separator in France, Germany and many other countries is a comma.

While it is possible to change your locale (in Windows settings) there is no need to do so to work through this book.

Just be aware that some of the screen grabs in this book will be formatted differently to what you see on your screen.

7 In cell B18 type the number **1** and in cell B19 type the number **2**.

8 Select cells B18 and B19.

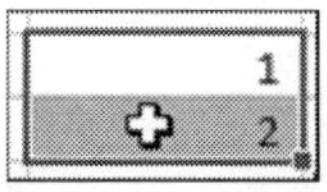

9 AutoFill down to cell B24 to create sequential numbers:

	A	B
18	Monday	1
19	Tuesday	2
20	Wednesday	3

10 In cell C18 type **9** and in cell C19 type **18**.

11 Select cells C18 and C19.

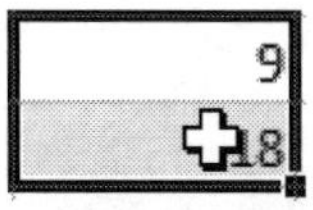

12 AutoFill down to cell C24 to create the nine times table.

	A	B	C
18	Monday	1	9
19	Tuesday	2	18
20	Wednesday	3	27

These are both examples of linear series. You'll learn more about linear series later, in: *Lesson 2-18: Understand linear and exponential series*

13 Use AutoFill to create sequential dates.

1. Type: **01-Jan-22** into cell D18.
2. Type: **02-Jan-22** into cell D19.
3. Select cells D18:D19.
4. AutoFill down to D24 to create sequential dates.

14 Use AutoFill to quickly copy text.

Sometimes you will want to duplicate the value from one cell into many others to the right of, left of, beneath, or above the active cell.

When a cell containing text is the active cell and it isn't defined as a *fill series* (the built-in fill series are days of the week and months of the year), AutoFill will simply duplicate the contents of the cell.

Type the text **Adjusted** into cell E18 and then AutoFill it down as far as cell E24. The same text is now shown in each of the cells:

	A	B	C	D	E
18	Monday	1	9	1-Jan-22	Adjusted
19	Tuesday	2	18	2-Jan-22	Adjusted
20	Wednesday	3	27	3-Jan-22	Adjusted
21	Thursday	4	36	4-Jan-22	Adjusted
22	Friday	5	45	5-Jan-22	Adjusted
23	Saturday	6	54	6-Jan-22	Adjusted
24	Sunday	7	63	7-Jan-22	Adjusted

15 Save your work as *First Quarter Sales and Profit-9*.

Lesson 2-15: Use AutoFill to adjust formulas

AutoFill can save you a lot of time when extending or copying text, number and date sequences.

In this lesson you'll discover that AutoFill is also able to adjust cell references within formulas.

1 Open *First Quarter Sales and Profit-9* from your sample files folder (if it isn't already open).

2 Consider the formula in cell B9.

Click onto cell B9 and view the formula displayed in the formula bar (the formula bar is at the top right of the screen grab below).

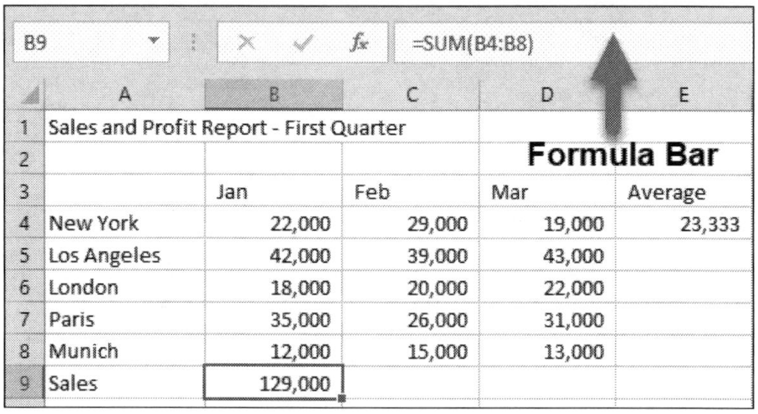

The formula is **=SUM(B4:B8)**. AutoSum created it for you in: *Lesson 2-3: Use AutoSum to quickly calculate totals*. The formula uses the SUM function to add together the values in the range B4:B8.

Think about the formula that would work in cell C9 (the total sales for February). It would be: **=SUM(C4:C8)**. Similarly the formula that would work in cell D9 (the total sales for March) would be **=SUM(D4:D8)**.

As you move to the right, all that is needed is to increment the letter for each cell reference in the formula and you'll get the right answer every time.

AutoFill understands this. When you AutoFill a cell containing a formula to the right, AutoFill automatically increments the letters in each cell reference.

Most of the time that is exactly what you want.

Later, in *Lesson 3-13: Understand absolute and relative cell references,* and *Lesson 3-14: Understand mixed cell references* you'll learn how to fine-tune the way in which AutoFill adjusts cell references. This will allow you to implement some more advanced AutoFill techniques.

3 AutoFill cell B9 to the right as far as cell D9.

You learned how to do this in: *Lesson 2-14: Use AutoFill for text and numeric series.*

First Quarter Sales and Profit-9

You may see a row of hashes in cell C9 and/or D9. This is because the value may be too wide to fit in the cell. If this is the case, AutoFit the column using the skills learned in: *Lesson 2-9: Re-size rows and columns.*

The correct answers for *Feb* and *Mar* sales are shown on the worksheet. Click on the *Feb* total cell (C9) and look at the formula in the formula bar.

C9 | =SUM(C4:C8)

	A	B	C	D
1	Sales and Profit Report - First Quarter			
2				
3		Jan	Feb	Mar
4	New York	22,000	29,000	19,000
5	Los Angeles	42,000	39,000	43,000
6	London	18,000	20,000	22,000
7	Paris	35,000	26,000	31,000
8	Munich	12,000	15,000	13,000
9	Sales	129,000	129,000	128,000

You can see that AutoFill has done its job perfectly, creating the sum of the values in cells C4:C8. Our five branches have sold exactly the same amount in both January and February, but a little less in March.

4 Consider the formula in cell E4.

Click onto cell E4 and view the formula displayed in the formula bar.

E4 | =AVERAGE(B4:D4)

	A	B	C	D	E
1	Sales and Profit Report - First Quarter				
2					
3		Jan	Feb	Mar	Average
4	New York	22,000	29,000	19,000	23,333
5	Los Angeles	42,000	39,000	43,000	
6	London	18,000	20,000	22,000	

The formula is **=AVERAGE(B4:D4)**. AutoSum created it for you in: *Lesson 2-11: Use AutoSum to calculate average and maximum values.*

Think about the formula that would work in cell E5 (the average sales for Los Angeles). It would be: **=AVERAGE(B5:D5)**. Similarly the formula that would work in cell E6 (the average sales for London) would be **=AVERAGE(B6:D6)**.

As you move downward, all that is needed is to increment the number for each cell reference in the formula. This is exactly what AutoFill will do.

E	F
Average	Maximum
23,333	29,000
41,333	43,000
20,000	22,000
30,667	35,000
13,333	15,000

5 AutoFill cell E4 down to E8 to see the average sales for each branch.

6 AutoFill cell F4 down to F8 to view the maximum sales for each branch.

7 Save your work as *First Quarter Sales and Profit-10.*

Lesson 2-16: Use AutoFill options

Sometimes AutoFill begins to misbehave and can even get in the way of efficient work by wrongly anticipating what you need.

1 Open *First Quarter Sales and Profit-10* from your sample files folder (If it isn't already open).

2 Populate cells F18 to F24 with sequential dates beginning with 1-Jan-22 using AutoFill.

1. In cell F18 type the date: **1-Jan-22**
2. AutoFill cell F18 down as far as cell F24.

   The cells are populated with sequential dates:

	A	B	C	D	E	F
18	Monday	1	9	1-Jan-22	Adjusted	1-Jan-22
19	Tuesday	2	18	2-Jan-22	Adjusted	2-Jan-22
20	Wednesday	3	27	3-Jan-22	Adjusted	3-Jan-22
21	Thursday	4	36	4-Jan-22	Adjusted	4-Jan-22
22	Friday	5	45	5-Jan-22	Adjusted	5-Jan-22
23	Saturday	6	54	6-Jan-22	Adjusted	6-Jan-22
24	Sunday	7	63	7-Jan-22	Adjusted	7-Jan-22

3 Populate cells G18 to G24 with the date *31-Mar-22* using the AutoFill Smart Tag.

1. In cell G18 type the date: **31-Mar-22**
2. AutoFill down as far as cell G24.

   At some time, you'll need to add transaction dates to a worksheet and will have four or five entries with the same date.

   AutoFill is perfect for eliminating the need to re-type the date for each transaction, but its insistence upon incrementing the date every time could be very frustrating.

   Fortunately, you can change the default behavior.

3. Click the Auto Fill Options Smart Tag  at the bottom right corner of the filled cells.

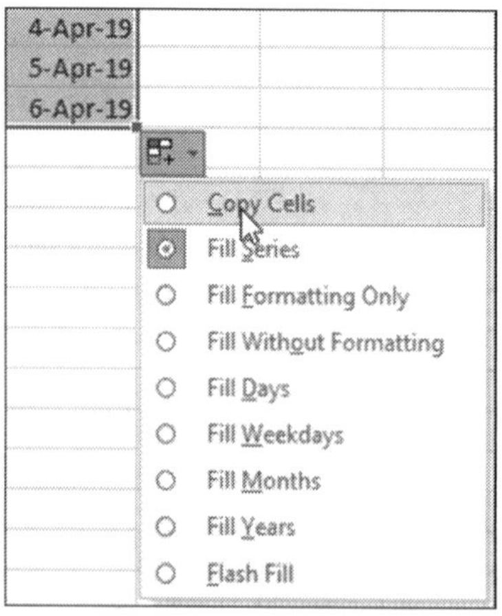

First Quarter Sales and Profit-10

4. Click *Copy Cells* to tell AutoFill not to increment the date.

4 Understand AutoFill options.

The *Fill Formatting* options will be covered later in: *Session Four: Making Your Worksheets Look Professional.*

Flash Fill will be introduced later in: *Lesson 2-19: Use automatic Flash Fill to split delimited text.* Here's what the other options will do:

Copy Cells	Fill Series	Fill Days	Fill Weekdays	Fill Months	Fill Years
This is what you just did. The first cell is copied to the other cells.	The default for dates that include the day. The date increments by one day at a time.	The date increments by one day at a time.	Because 1st April 2022 is a Friday the weekend days are omitted, and the series jumps from 1st April to 4th April.	Normally this would show the same day number for each month. In this example, there are only 30 days in three of the months so 30th is shown instead of 31st.	The same calendar day is shown for each subsequent year.
31-Mar-22 31-Mar-22 31-Mar-22 31-Mar-22 31-Mar-22 31-Mar-22 31-Mar-22	31-Mar-22 1-Apr-22 2-Apr-22 3-Apr-22 4-Apr-22 5-Apr-22 6-Apr-22	31-Mar-22 1-Apr-22 2-Apr-22 3-Apr-22 4-Apr-22 5-Apr-22 6-Apr-22	31-Mar-22 1-Apr-22 4-Apr-22 5-Apr-22 6-Apr-22 7-Apr-22 8-Apr-22	31-Mar-22 30-Apr-22 31-May-22 30-Jun-22 31-Jul-22 31-Aug-22 30-Sep-22	31-Mar-22 31-Mar-23 31-Mar-24 31-Mar-25 31-Mar-26 31-Mar-27 31-Mar-28

5 Populate cells G18 to G24 with sequential dates using a right-click AutoFill.

1. Click on cell G18 to make it the active cell.
2. AutoFill down to cell G24, but this time hold down the right mouse button (instead of the left).

   When you release the mouse button you are instantly presented with the AutoFill options (see sidebar).

   There are two new options here: *Linear Trend* and *Growth Trend.*

   You'll learn how these can be used later, in: *Lesson 2-18: Understand linear and exponential series.*

   This method is preferred to the Smart Tag method because it is faster (one click instead of two).
3. Click: *Fill Series* or *Fill Days.*

   In this example *Fill Series* and *Fill Days* produce exactly the same result.

6 Save your work as *First Quarter Sales and Profit-11.*

Lesson 2-17: Speed up your AutoFills and create a custom fill series

In this lesson, you're going to learn some advanced AutoFill techniques that will massively speed up your efficient use of the AutoFill feature.

1 Open *First Quarter Sales and Profit*-11 (if it isn't already open).

2 Delete the values in cells G18:G24.

3 Type the value: **31-Mar-22** into cell G18.

	A	B	C	D	E	F	G
18	Monday	1	9	1-Jan-22	Adjusted	1-Jan-22	31-Mar-22
19	Tuesday	2	18	2-Jan-22	Adjusted	2-Jan-22	
20	Wednesday	3	27	3-Jan-22	Adjusted	3-Jan-22	
21	Thursday	4	36	4-Jan-22	Adjusted	4-Jan-22	
22	Friday	5	45	5-Jan-22	Adjusted	5-Jan-22	
23	Saturday	6	54	6-Jan-22	Adjusted	6-Jan-22	
24	Sunday	7	63	7-Jan-22	Adjusted	7-Jan-22	

4 Use an AutoFill double-click to populate cells G19:G24 with sequential dates.

	F	G
17		
18	1-Jan-19	31-Mar-19
19	2-Jan-19	1-Apr-19
20	3-Jan-19	2-Apr-19
21	4-Jan-19	3-Apr-19
22	5-Jan-19	4-Apr-19
23	6-Jan-19	5-Apr-19
24	7-Jan-19	6-Apr-19

1. Click on cell G18 to select it.
2. Hover over the AutoFill handle (the black spot at the bottom right-hand corner of cell G18). When you are sure that you have the correct black cross cursor shape, double click to automatically fill down to the end of the range.

   Cells G19 to G24 are filled with sequential dates (as this is the default behavior of AutoFill).

5 Use *AutoFill <Ctrl>-Drag* to copy the value in cell G18 to cells G19:G24.

1. Delete all of the dates from cells G19:G24, leaving only the date *31-Mar-22* in cell G18.
2. Click in cell G18 to make it the active cell.
3. Hold down the **<Ctrl>** key and AutoFill cell G18 down as far as cell G24 by dragging the AutoFill handle down with the mouse.
4. Release the mouse button.

   Because you held the **<Ctrl>** key down, AutoFill copied the cell instead of creating a series of values.

	A	B	C	D	E	F	G
18	Monday	1	9	1-Jan-22	Adjusted	1-Jan-22	31-Mar-22
19	Tuesday	2	18	2-Jan-22	Adjusted	2-Jan-22	31-Mar-22
20	Wednesday	3	27	3-Jan-22	Adjusted	3-Jan-22	31-Mar-22
21	Thursday	4	36	4-Jan-22	Adjusted	4-Jan-22	31-Mar-22
22	Friday	5	45	5-Jan-22	Adjusted	5-Jan-22	31-Mar-22
23	Saturday	6	54	6-Jan-22	Adjusted	6-Jan-22	31-Mar-22
24	Sunday	7	63	7-Jan-22	Adjusted	7-Jan-22	31-Mar-22

First Quarter Sales and Profit-11

This is even faster than using the right-click method when you want to prevent the date (or a number) from incrementing.

6 Create a custom list containing the values: *North, South, East* and *West.*

1. Click: File→Options→Advanced.
2. Scroll down to the *General* category and click the *Edit Custom Lists...* button.

The *Custom Lists* dialog appears.

3. Click in the *List entries* window and add four custom list entries: **North, South, East** and **West** (pressing the **<Enter>** key after each entry).

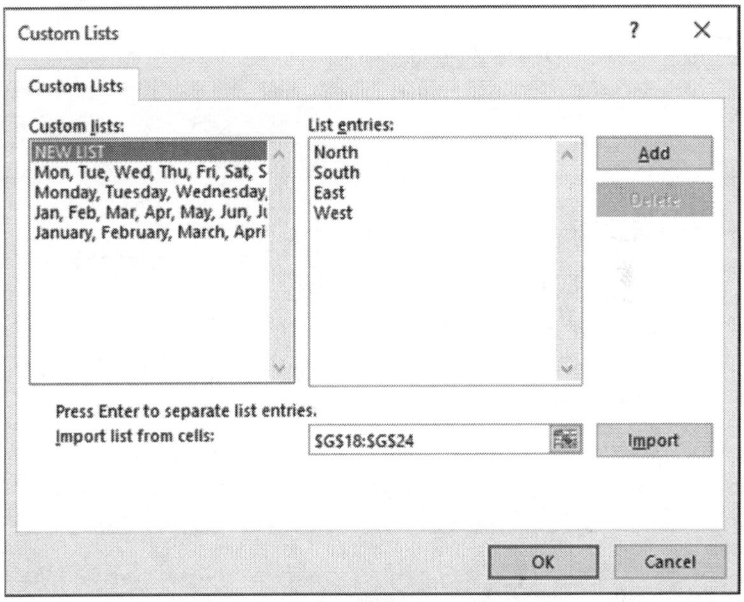

4. Click the OK button and OK again to close the dialogs.

7 Use the newly created custom list.

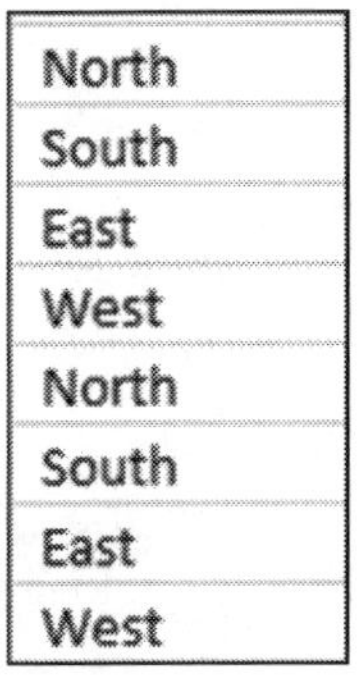

Type **North** in any cell and AutoFill down.

As you AutoFill, the custom list entries appear in the worksheet (see sidebar).

8 Delete the *North, South, East, West* cells from the worksheet.

9 Save your work as *First Quarter Sales and Profit-12.*

Lesson 2-18: Understand linear and exponential series

Linear series

In: *Lesson 2-14: Use AutoFill for text and numeric series*, you used AutoFill's *Fill Series* method to automatically create these numeric series:

	A	B	C
18	Monday	1	9
19	Tuesday	2	18
20	Wednesday	3	27

These are both examples of *Linear* series.

To create the linear series in column C you selected cells C18:C19 before AutoFilling down the column:

	A	B	C
18	Monday	1	9
19	Tuesday	2	18
20	Wednesday	3	
21	Thursday	4	

To calculate a linear series Excel first identifies the *step value*. The linear series in column C has a *step value* of nine (18-9=9).

When you use AutoFill's *Fill Series* method, Excel adds the *step value* to the *start value* (the number shown in the previous cell).

In the above example, if you AutoFill down to cell C20, the value shown in cell C20 will be 27. This is calculated by adding the *step value* of 9 to the *start value* of 18.

This is an example of a very simple linear series. Excel is also able to calculate a linear series even when the step values of the selected cells are not equal (see sidebar).

Exponential (or Growth) series

An exponential series is calculated by *multiplying* (rather than adding) the *start value* by the *step value*. This type of series is usually referred to as an *exponential* (rather than linear) series. Excel also uses the term *growth series* as a synonym for *exponential series* (see sidebar).

Here's an example:

- A truly excellent restaurant opens in town. On the first day they only have one customer, but the customer is so delighted by the food, service and value that the customer tells two friends.
- The next day the two friends eat there, and the restaurant has two diners.
- The two friends are also so pleased with their experience that they each tell two friends. On the third day the restaurant has four diners.

You can see that the restaurant owner might expect that this trend will continue and that each day the number of diners will double (in Excel's

important

A synonym is a word you use when you can't spell the other one.

Baltasar Gracián (Philsopher 1601-1658)

Excel uses different terminology in various menus, dialog boxes and task panes that mean the same thing (in the context of this lesson):

Series, *Forecast* and *Trend* mean the same thing.

Growth and *Exponential* also mean the same thing.

In this lesson I'll consistently use the terminology *Series* and *Exponential*.

note

Excel can calculate a linear series when the step values of cells are not equal

Excel calculates a linear series (AutoFill also calls this a *fill series*) using this formula:

Start Value + Step Value

Sometimes you may need to produce linear series values from a series of numbers that have different step values. For example, consider this range:

	A	B
2	Value	Step Value
3	1	
4	2.1	1.1
5	2.9	0.8
6	4.1	1.2

In this case Excel will use a more complex mathematical operation (called the *least-squares algorithm*) to determine the correct step value to use. In the above example, Excel would calculate a step value of 1.01.

Rabbit Population

terminology, the *step value* is 2). Eventually, of course, the restaurant will become full and the trend will have to end (in Excel's terminology the number of seats in the restaurant is the *stop value*).

In this lesson you will model this type of exponential series.

1 Open *Rabbit Population* from your sample files folder.

2 If the rabbit population of an island increases at the rate of 20% per month, use an exponential progression to calculate how a newly introduced community of 200 rabbits will grow in four years.

1. Type the value: **200** into cell B4 to set the rabbit population at the beginning of the period.
2. Type the value: **240** into cell B5 to set the rabbit population after one month.
3. Select the range B4:B5.
4. Hold down the right mouse button on the AutoFill handle at the bottom-right of the selected range and drag down to AutoFill to cell B51.

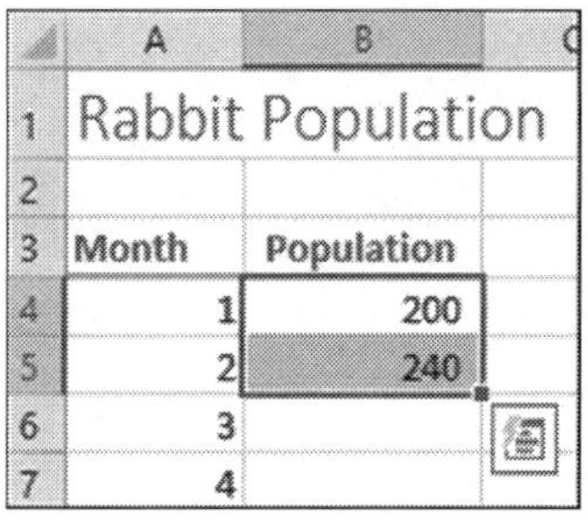

5. Click *Growth Trend* from the shortcut menu. Note that this is the shortcut menu's synonym for: *Exponential Series*.

After four years (48 months) the 200 rabbits will have grown to a population of a little over a million.

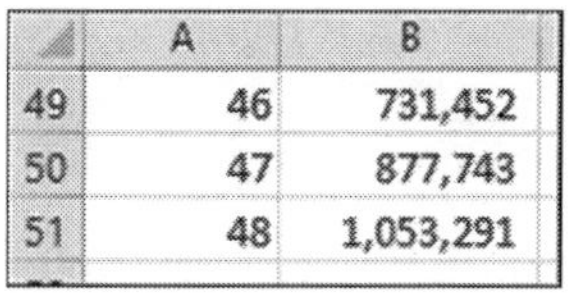

3 Save your work as *Rabbit Population-1.*

note

Here's how you could have used the Ribbon to complete this lesson:

1. Enter the value **200** into cell B4.

2. Select cells B4:B51.

3. Click: Home→Editing→Fill→Series…

The *Series* dialog appears.

4. Enter the following values into the *Series* dialog:

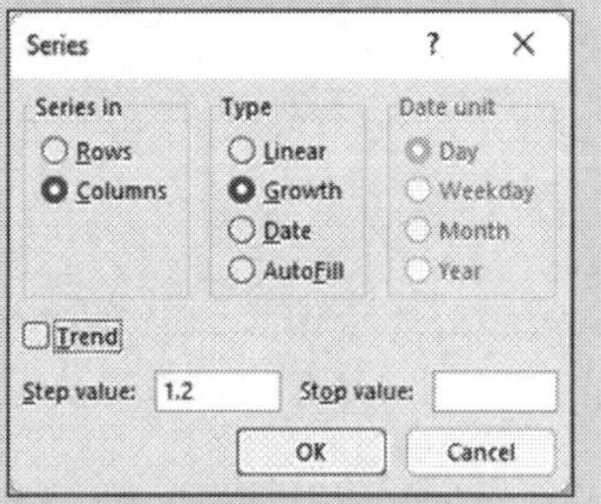

Note that the value: **1.2** is used because an exponential (growth) series multiplies each *start value* by the *step value.*

trivia

According to an old legend, the inventor of the game of chess presented his new game to a powerful king. The king was so pleased with the game that he offered the inventor any reasonable reward.

The inventor asked for one grain of rice for the first square on the chessboard, two for the second, four for the third… and so on for each of the 64 squares on the chessboard.

The king thought the inventor was foolish to ask for such a simple gift. Much later he found that there was not enough rice in the entire world to fulfil the inventor's request.

With the Excel skills you have learned in this lesson, you should easily be able to model the king's dilemma and discover exactly how many grains of rice would have been needed (about 18.5 quintillion).

Lesson 2-19: Use automatic Flash Fill to split delimited text

When you place data in cells it is useful to observe an important rule:

"Keep data atomic"

If you strictly observe this rule, you'll avoid an enormous number of potential problems.

The rule means that, in the same way that the atom is the smallest basic unit you can divide matter into, each worksheet cell should contain the smallest possible amount of data.

Here's a simple example to illustrate the concept:

	A	B
3	**Name**	
4	Jessica Sagan	
5	Stephen Bell	
6	John Jennings	

Imagine that you want to use the worksheet above to create a mail merge using Word. In this case you'd need the first names in a cell of their own. This would enable you to personalize the mail merge with an introduction such as: *Dear Jessica.*

If you had observed the *keep data atomic* rule, you would have split your data into multiple columns like this:

	B	C
3	**First Name**	**Last Name**
4	Jessica	Sagan
5	Stephen	Bell
6	John	Jennings

Excel has a wonderful feature called *Flash Fill.* This feature enables you to quickly and simply split delimited text (such as the above) into separate cells. The term *delimited text* means text that is split using a separator. In this case the separator is a space (see facing page sidebar).

Automatic Flash Fill will only work for very simple text splitting tasks such as the one described above. In the lessons that follow you'll learn more complex manual Flash Fill techniques that will enable you to perform some very advanced text splitting tasks.

1 Open *Employee Names-1* from your sample files folder.

2 Add column headings for *First Name* and *Last Name* in cells B3 and C3.

   1. Click in cell B3.
   2. Type: **First Name**
   3. Press the **<Tab>** key to move to cell C3.
   4. Type: **Last Name**
   5. Press the **<Tab>** key to save the value into the cell and move to cell D3.

note

If Flash Fill doesn't work for you, somebody has switched it off

It's almost certain that Flash Fill will be enabled on any computer that you work on. It is such a useful feature that you wouldn't want to disable it.

If Flash Fill doesn't work, there are two possible explanations:

1. You are using an earlier version of Excel. Flash Fill was only introduced in Excel 2013.

2. Somebody has switched Flash Fill off.

To switch it back on click:

File→Options→Advanced

In the first section (*Editing Options*) make sure that the *Automatically Flash Fill* check box is checked.

note

Help Flash Fill to work correctly by formatting header rows differently

You will notice that, in this lesson's sample file, I have bold-faced the header row:

	B	C
3	**First Name**	**Last Name**
4	Jessica	Sagan
5	Stephen	Bell
6	John	Jennings

When Flash Fill sees different formatting in the first row, it will treat this row (correctly) as a header row. Flash Fill then excludes the value in this row from its logic, providing more reliable results.

Employee Names-1

note

Limitations of automatic Flash Fill

Automatic Flash Fill always works perfectly when the source data column has the same type of *separators.*

In this lesson's example, space separators are used. The following example (using comma separators) would also work perfectly:

Sting, Musician
Kingdom Brunel, Engineer
Billie Jean King, Tennis Player

You can see that, without the commas, Flash Fill wouldn't know where the name ended, and the occupation began.

Sometimes you will need to extract data that does not have separators.

You'll discover how to solve this type of problem later, in: *Lesson 2-20: Use manual Flash Fill to split text.*

note

Use automatic Flash Fill to extract initials

You can often save a lot of space by showing initials instead of full names. Automatic Flash Fill is well suited to this task.

Try this (at the end of the lesson, after populating columns B and C with first and last names).

1. Type: **JS** (for Jessica Sagan) in cell D4.
2. Type **S** (Stephen Bell's first initial) into cell D5.
3. Press the **<Enter>** key to accept the Flash Fill.

	B	C	D
4	Jessica	Sagan	JS
5	Stephen	Bell	SB
6	John	Jennings	JJ

3 Bold face the text in cells B3 and C3 (if Excel has not done this for you automatically).

You learned how to do this in: *Lesson 1-19: Use the Mini Toolbar, Key Tips and keyboard shortcuts.*

	A	B	C
3	Name	First Name	Last Name

4 Use *Flash Fill* to extract the *First Name* values from column A into column B.

1. Type: **Jessica** into cell B4. Be careful to type it exactly as it is spelled in cell A4. Be careful not to leave any leading or trailing spaces.
2. Press the **<Enter>** key to move to cell B5.
3. Type: **S** (the first letter of *Stephen*) into cell B5.

   Notice that something interesting has happened. *Flash Fill* has figured out that you possibly want to extract all the first names from column A and has displayed them all as grayed out names in the cells below:

	A	B	C
3	Name	First Name	Last Name
4	Jessica Sagan	Jessica	
5	Stephen Bell	Stephen	
6	John Jennings	John	
7	Meryl Simpson	Meryl	
8	Alfred Hawking	Alfred	

4. Press the **<Enter>** key to instruct Flash Fill to enter all the remaining *First Name* values.

   All the first names appear in column B.

	A	B	C
3	Name	First Name	Last Name
4	Jessica Sagan	Jessica	
5	Stephen Bell	Stephen	
6	John Jennings	John	
7	Meryl Simpson	Meryl	
8	Alfred Hawking	Alfred	

   The status bar (at the bottom left of the screen) also confirms how many cells were changed:

   Ready   Flash Fill Changed Cells: 23

5 Use *Flash Fill* to extract the *Last Name* values from column A into column C.

Follow the same procedure that you used to extract the first names:

	A	B	C
3	Name	First Name	Last Name
4	Jessica Sagan	Jessica	Sagan
5	Stephen Bell	Stephen	Bell
6	John Jennings	John	Jennings
7	Meryl Simpson	Meryl	Simpson

6 Save your work as *Employee Names-2.*

Lesson 2-20: Use manual Flash Fill to split text

Here are two examples of international telephone numbers.

+44 (0)113-4960227 (a UK telephone number)
+356 (0)2138-3393 (a Maltese telephone number)

The *country code* (or international dialing code) is shown as a + symbol followed by one or more numbers. The *NDD* (National Direct Dialing prefix) is shown in brackets. This is the access code used to make a call within the relevant country but is omitted when calling from outside the country. The *Area Code* consists of the numbers after the closing bracket but before the hyphen.

In this lesson, you'll use *Manual Flash Fill* to split telephone numbers into the *Country Code, Area Code* and *Phone Number* like this:

	A	B	C	D	E
3	Company	Telephone	Country Code	Area Code	Phone Number
4	Books A Million	+44 (0)113-4960227	+44	113	4960227
5	Maltese Books	+356 (0)2138-3393	+356	2138	3393
6	Bargain Bookstore	+44 (0)115-4960498	+44	115	4960498

In early Excel versions you had to use some very complex formulas to split this type of text. With the *Flash Fill* feature, you can achieve the same result in seconds.

1 Open *Phone Book-1* from your sample files folder.

2 Extract the *Country Code* from the telephone number in column B and place it into column C.

If you were to type **+44** into cell C4, Excel would interpret it as a positive number and display the result as 44 (without the plus sign).

In order to signal to Excel that you want the plus sign to be displayed, you will need to indicate that +44 should be regarded as text rather than as a number.

You discovered the technique for doing this in: *Lesson 2-1: Enter text and numbers into a worksheet (sidebar).* If an apostrophe is placed before a number, Excel will regard it as text.

1. Type: **'+44** into cell C4 (an apostrophe followed by **+44**).
2. Press the **<Enter>** key.
3. Make sure that the active cell is in a cell within the range that will be Flash Filled (ie anywhere in the range C3:C18),
4. Flash Fill cells C5:C18.

   There are four different ways that you can invoke Flash Fill

   - Click: Home→Editing→Fill→Flash Fill.
   - Click: Data→Data Tools→Flash Fill.
   - Use the AutoFill handle (see sidebar).

note

You can also Flash Fill more quickly by using the AutoFill handle

The *AutoFill handle* is the small black dot on the bottom-right corner of the active cell (or range of cells).

In: *Lesson 2-16: Use AutoFill options,* you learned that if you right-click and drag the AutoFill handle you are presented with *AutoFill options*:

You can then use the *Flash Fill* item on the *AutoFill options* list to request a Flash Fill.

You'll find that this method is faster than using the Ribbon.

This method is also the preferred way to provide Flash Fill with more than one example result for more complex problems (you'll do this in: *Lesson 2-21: Use multiple example Flash Fill to concatenate text*).

Phone Book-1

note

The difference between Flash Fill and a formula-based solution

There are two ways to solve the problem posed in this lesson:

1. Use Flash Fill

This is the method used in this lesson. Flash Fill provides a fast and simple solution.

2. Use complex formulas

Only expert Excel users could construct the complex formulas required to split the telephone numbers contained in the sample file without the use of Flash Fill.

If you progress to the *Expert Skills* book in this series, you will complete a lesson that solves exactly the same problem presented in this lesson without Flash Fill.

Complex formulas are used instead, to provide a formula-based solution.

Advantage of a formula-based solution

The results of a Flash Fill do not automatically update when the source data changes.

This means that if you changed a telephone number in column B you would then need to Flash Fill three times to update columns C, D and E.

Formula results automatically update whenever the source cells change.

This means that if you changed a telephone number in the formula-based solution, the *Country Code, Area Code* and *Phone Number* would automatically update.

- Use the shortcut key: **<Ctrl>+<E>**

Whichever method you use, the country code is extracted into the remaining cells in column C.

	A	B	C
3	Company	Telephone	Country Code
4	Books A Million	+44 (0)113-4960227	+44
5	Maltese Books	+356 (0)2138-3393	+356
6	Bargain Bookstore	+44 (0)115-4960498	+44

Notice that Excel has placed a green triangle in the top-left corner of each cell. Excel thinks you may have made an error but, of course, the value is fine. If you want to remove the green triangles, use the method you learned in: *Lesson 2-4: Select a range of cells and understand Smart Tags.*

3 Extract the *Area Code* from the telephone number in column B and place it into column D.

Use the same method as you did for the country code. The first area code you need to type is: **'113**

Even though there is no plus sign, it is still useful to include the apostrophe as it will prevent Excel from re-formatting numbers (see next step for more on this).

4 Extract the *Phone Number* from the telephone number in column B and place it into column E.

Use the same method as you did for the country code. The first telephone number is: **'4960227**

In this case you must use a leading apostrophe to prevent Excel from re-formatting large numbers. For example, the telephone number: *20180948* would be displayed as *2E+07* if you didn't include the apostrophe.

The *Country Code, Area Code* and *Phone Number* are now extracted for every international telephone number:

	A	B	C	D	E
3	Company	Telephone	Country Code	Area Code	Phone Number
4	Books A Million	+44 (0)113-4960227	+44	113	4960227
5	Maltese Books	+356 (0)2138-3393	+356	2138	3393
6	Bargain Bookstore	+44 (0)115-4960498	+44	115	4960498

5 Save your work as *Phone Book-2.*

Lesson 2-21: Use multiple example Flash Fill to concatenate text

Understand concatenation

In: *Lesson 2-19: Use automatic Flash Fill to split delimited text,* you learned how to split text with this example:

	A	B	C
3	**Name**	**First Name**	**Last Name**
4	Jessica Sagan	Jessica	Sagan
5	Stephen Bell	Stephen	Bell

In the above example, the text: *Jessica Sagan* was split into two separate words: *Jessica* and *Sagan.*

Concatenation is exactly the opposite of splitting. The two separate words *Jessica* and *Sagan* can be concatenated to produce the single word: *Jessica Sagan.* This is an example of very simple concatenation.

In this lesson, you'll perform some very advanced concatenation using *Flash Fill.*

1 Open *Client Names-1* from your sample files folder.

This workbook contains a list of very inconsistently formatted client names:

	A	B	C	D
3	**Last**	**Middle**	**First**	
4	Sagan	Elizabeth	Jessica	
5	Bell	p	Stephen	
6	Jennings		John	

You want to clean up this data so that client names are consistently formatted like this:

	A	B	C	D
3	**Last**	**Middle**	**First**	**Formatted Name**
4	Sagan	Elizabeth	Jessica	Sagan, Jessica E.
5	Bell	p	Stephen	Bell, Stephen P.
6	jennings		John	Jennings, John
7	Simpson	Jane	Meryl	Simpson, Meryl J.
8	hawking		Alfred	Hawking, Alfred
9	Ashe	m	Lucille	Ashe, Lucille M.

For Flash Fill to automate this task you will need to tell Flash Fill what is needed by providing more than one example.

2 Type: **Formatted Name** into cell D3 and bold face the text.

(Excel will probably bold-face the text automatically).

It is important that the header text in row 3 is bold faced.

note

Flash Fill doesn't understand mathematics

Consider this problem:

	A	B
1	100	101
2	1120	1121
3	180	
4	149	

You could be forgiven for thinking that Flash Fill could populate cells B3 and B4 with the numbers 181 and 150. In order to produce this result Flash Fill would have to detect a mathematical relationship between the numbers in columns A and B.

Because Flash Fill doesn't understand mathematics, it will always see the problem as a textual one and will produce this result:

	A	B
1	100	101
2	1120	1121
3	180	181
4	149	141

Flash Fill has used the logic "replace the last character displayed in column A with 1" and not "Add one to the value displayed in column A".

Client Names-1

When Flash Fill sees different formatting in the first row, the row is assumed to be a header row. Flash Fill then excludes the value in the header row from its logic, providing more reliable results.

3 Provide a single example result in cell D4.

Type: **Sagan, Jessica E.** into cell D4.

4 Flash Fill cells D5:D9 based upon the example result in cell D4.

	A	B	C	D
3	Last	Middle	First	Formatted Name
4	Sagan	Elizabeth	Jessica	Sagan, Jessica E.
5	Bell	p	Stephen	Bell, Stephen T.
6	jennings		John	jennings, John O.
7	Simpson	Jane	Meryl	Simpson, Meryl E.
8	hawking		Alfred	hawking, Alfred L.
9	Ashe	m	Lucille	Ashe, Lucille U.

You learned how to do this in: *Lesson 2-20: Use manual Flash Fill to split text.*

Excel completes the task, but the results are not what you wanted (see sidebar).

With only one example, Flash Fill has completely misunderstood the requirement.

5 Provide two example results in cells D4 and D5.

1. Delete the names in cells D5:D9.
2. Provide another example of the correct result (in cell D5).

	A	B	C	D
3	Last	Middle	First	Formatted Name
4	Sagan	Elizabeth	Jessica	Sagan, Jessica E.
5	Bell	p	Stephen	Bell, Stephen P.
6	Jennings		John	

6 Flash Fill cells D6:D9 based upon the example results in cells D4 and D5.

1. Select cells D4:D9.
2. Click: Home→Editing→Fill→Flash Fill.

   This time Flash Fill has done a better job (see sidebar).

   Notice the two blank results (for *John Jennings* and *Alfred Hawking*).

   Flash Fill doesn't yet understand how to treat clients without a middle name. The blank spaces are Flash Fill's way of asking you for yet another example.

	A	B	C	D
3	Last	Middle	First	Formatted Name
4	Sagan	Elizabeth	Jessica	Sagan, Jessica E.
5	Bell	p	Stephen	Bell, Stephen P.
6	jennings		John	
7	Simpson	Jane	Meryl	Simpson, Meryl J.
8	hawking		Alfred	
9	Ashe	m	Lucille	Ashe, Lucille M.

7 Provide another example result in cell D6.

1. Type: **Jennings, John** into cell D6.
2. Press the **<Enter>** key.

   Usually, Flash Fill will instantly replace the value in cell D8. If it doesn't, you'll have to manually Flash Fill the entire list based upon the three examples provided. Do this by completing the following steps:

3. Select cells D4:D9.
4. Click: Home→Editing→Fill→Flash Fill.

   This time Flash Fill has completed the task successfully (see sidebar).

	A	B	C	D
3	Last	Middle	First	Formatted Name
4	Sagan	Elizabeth	Jessica	Sagan, Jessica E.
5	Bell	p	Stephen	Bell, Stephen P.
6	jennings		John	Jennings, John
7	Simpson	Jane	Meryl	Simpson, Meryl J.
8	hawking		Alfred	Hawking, Alfred
9	Ashe	m	Lucille	Ashe, Lucille M.

8 Save your work as *Client Names-2.*

Lesson 2-22: Use Flash Fill to solve common problems

Flash Fill is one of Excel's most useful features. It isn't possible to overstate how useful this tool is. I find myself using Flash Fill almost every day to solve a huge number of different problems.

This lesson gives examples of many everyday tasks that I have found can be quickly and simply completed using Flash Fill. I've also included all of the examples in the sample file: *Flash Fill Examples.*

In the following examples, Flash Fill filled the shaded cells.

Split text

Full Name	First Name	Last Name
Jessica Elizabeth Sagan	Jessica	Sagan
Stephen Bell	Stephen	Bell
John Paul Jennings	John	Jennings

Extract initials from names

Name	Initials
Jessica Elizabeth Sagan	JES
Stephen Bell	SB
John Paul Jennings	JPJ

Remove title from names

Full Name	Short Name
Miss Jessica Elizabeth Sagan	Jessica Sagan
Mr Stephen Bell	Stephen Bell
Mr John Paul Jennings	John Jennings

Add commas (a useful name format for alphabetical sorting)

Name	Sort Name
Jessica Elizabeth Sagan	Sagan, Jessica
Stephen Bell	Bell, Stephen
John Paul Jennings	Jennings, John

Concatenate text

First Name	Middle Name	Last Name	Full Name
Jessica	Elizabeth	Sagan	Jessica Elizabeth Sagan
Stephen		Bell	Stephen Bell
John	Paul	Jennings	John Paul Jennings

Flash Fill Examples

Concatenate text and insert extra text

First Name	Middle Name	Last Name	Full Name
Jessica	Elizabeth	Sagan	First Name: Jessica, Last Name: Sagan
Stephen		Bell	First Name: Stephen, Last Name: Bell
John	Paul	Jennings	First Name: John, Last Name: Jennings

Change capitalization

Mixed Case	Title Case
jessica elizabeth sagan	Jessica Elizabeth Sagan
stephen Bell	Stephen Bell
john Paul jennings	John Paul Jennings

Extract the day, month or year from a date

In all the date-based examples note that the *Date* column is formatted as a date. You will learn how to format cells as dates later in: *Lesson 4-1: Format dates.*

Date	Day	Date	Month	Date	Year
19th January 2013	19	19th January 2013	January	19th January 2013	2013
5th August 1967	5	5th August 1967	August	5th August 1967	1967
20th February 2022	20	20th February 2022	February	20th February 2022	2022

Extract the day/month from a date

Date	Day/Month
19th January 2013	19th January
5th August 1967	5th August
20th February 2022	20th February

Extract domain names from e-mail addresses

E-mail address	Domain
Mary@QuiteContrary.com	QuiteContrary.com
Humpty@Dumpty.com	Dumpty.com
Jack@Nimble.com	Nimble.com

Format telephone numbers

Name	Tel (unformatted)	Tel (formatted)
Books A Million	1134960227	(113) 496-0227
Bargain Bookstore	1154960498	(115) 496-0498
Books for Less	1164960593	(116) 496-0593

Lesson 2-23: Use the zoom control

Zooming is used to magnify or reduce the worksheet. If you have a lot of rows in a worksheet and have good eyes, you might want to zoom out sometimes to see more of the worksheet on one screen.

1 Open *First Quarter Sales and Profit-12* from your sample files folder.

2 Zoom in and out of the worksheet using the mouse wheel.

The fastest way to zoom a worksheet is by using the mouse.

Most mice these days have a wheel in the middle of the buttons. To zoom using this wheel hold down the **<Ctrl>** key on the keyboard and roll the wheel to zoom in and out.

3 Zoom in and out of a worksheet using the zoom control.

The zoom control is at the bottom right of your screen.

Click and drag on the zoom control slider to zoom in and out of your worksheet. You can also zoom by clicking the plus and minus buttons on either side of the Zoom control.

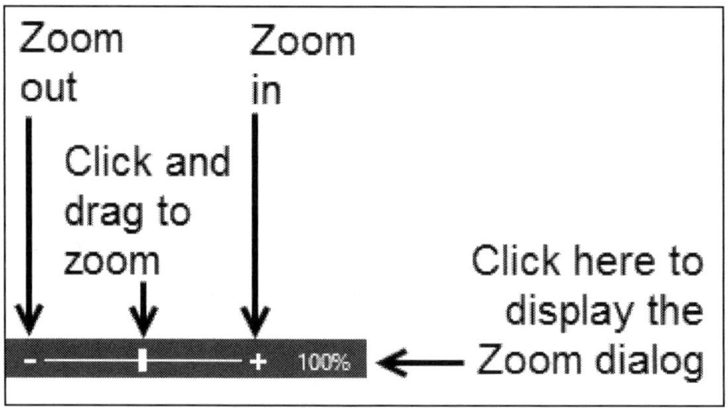

4 Use the Zoom dialog to make cells A3:D9 fill the screen.

1. Select cells A3:D9.

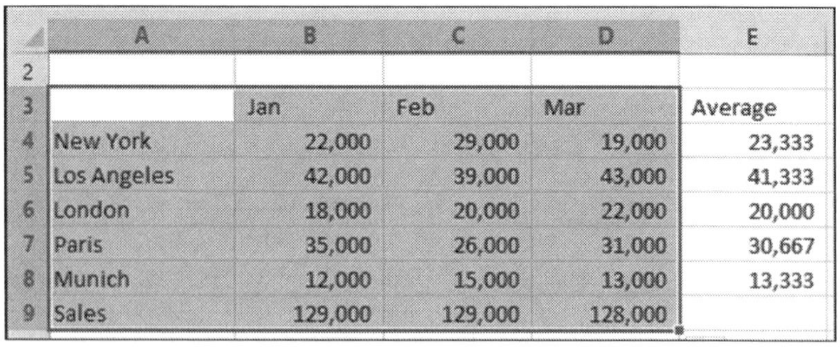

	A	B	C	D	E
2					
3		Jan	Feb	Mar	Average
4	New York	22,000	29,000	19,000	23,333
5	Los Angeles	42,000	39,000	43,000	41,333
6	London	18,000	20,000	22,000	20,000
7	Paris	35,000	26,000	31,000	30,667
8	Munich	12,000	15,000	13,000	13,333
9	Sales	129,000	129,000	128,000	

2. Click on the right-hand side of the zoom bar.

The *Zoom* dialog is displayed.

First Quarter Sales and Profit-12

3. Select the *Fit Selection* option button.

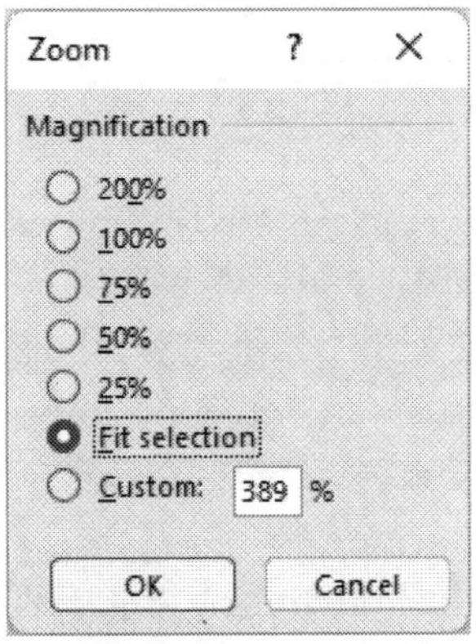

4. Click the OK button.

   The worksheet is zoomed so that the selected cells completely fill the screen.

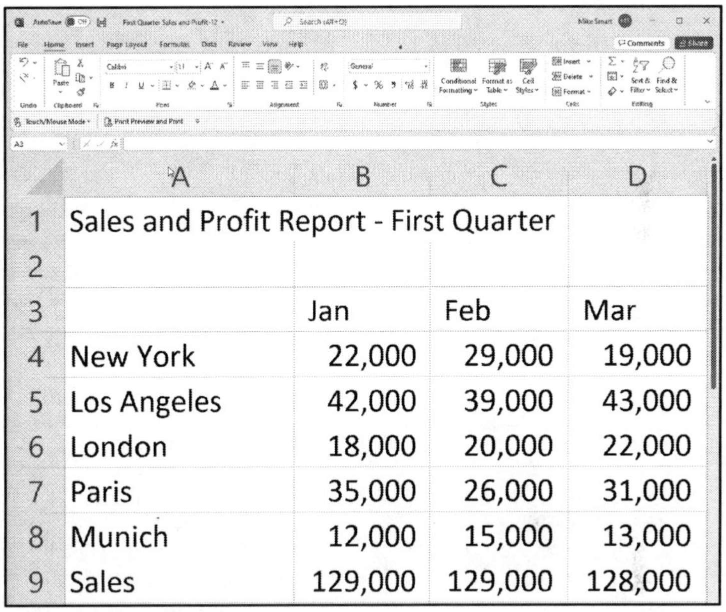

5 Zoom back to 100% using the Ribbon.

You'll probably find the zoom bar to be the quickest and most convenient way to zoom, but you can also zoom using the Ribbon.

Click: View→Zoom→100%.

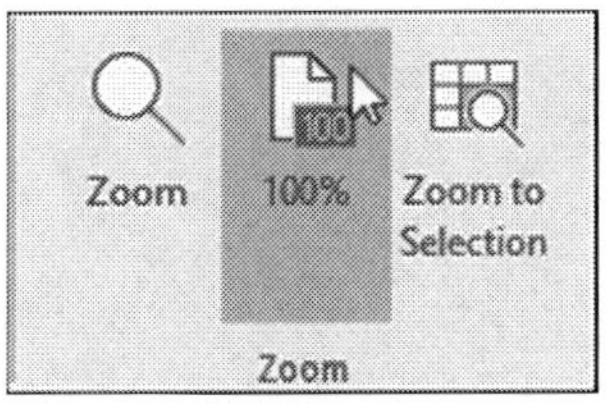

The screen is restored to normal size.

Lesson 2-24: Print out a worksheet

You aren't going to explore every option for preparing and printing a worksheet in this lesson. Printing is such a huge subject that this course devotes a whole session to it later, in: *Session Seven: Printing Your Work.*

This lesson only aims to teach you the bare minimum skills you need to put your work onto paper.

1 Open *First Quarter Sales and Profit-12* from your sample files folder (if it isn't already open).

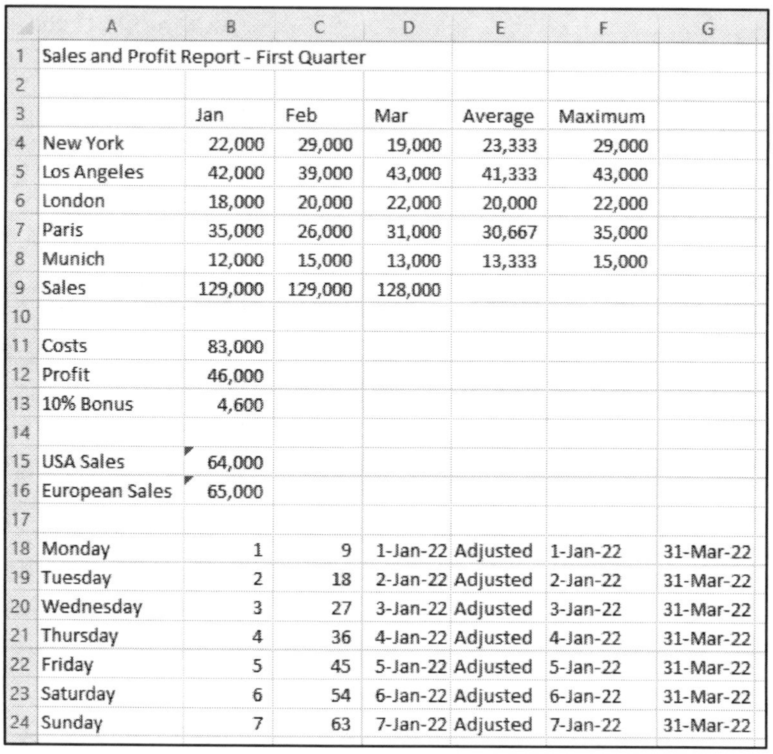

	A	B	C	D	E	F	G
1	Sales and Profit Report - First Quarter						
2							
3		Jan	Feb	Mar	Average	Maximum	
4	New York	22,000	29,000	19,000	23,333	29,000	
5	Los Angeles	42,000	39,000	43,000	41,333	43,000	
6	London	18,000	20,000	22,000	20,000	22,000	
7	Paris	35,000	26,000	31,000	30,667	35,000	
8	Munich	12,000	15,000	13,000	13,333	15,000	
9	Sales	129,000	129,000	128,000			
10							
11	Costs	83,000					
12	Profit	46,000					
13	10% Bonus	4,600					
14							
15	USA Sales	64,000					
16	European Sales	65,000					
17							
18	Monday	1	9	1-Jan-22	Adjusted	1-Jan-22	31-Mar-22
19	Tuesday	2	18	2-Jan-22	Adjusted	2-Jan-22	31-Mar-22
20	Wednesday	3	27	3-Jan-22	Adjusted	3-Jan-22	31-Mar-22
21	Thursday	4	36	4-Jan-22	Adjusted	4-Jan-22	31-Mar-22
22	Friday	5	45	5-Jan-22	Adjusted	5-Jan-22	31-Mar-22
23	Saturday	6	54	6-Jan-22	Adjusted	6-Jan-22	31-Mar-22
24	Sunday	7	63	7-Jan-22	Adjusted	7-Jan-22	31-Mar-22

2 Click File→Print.

Backstage View appears offering many preview and print options:

First Quarter Sales and Profit-12

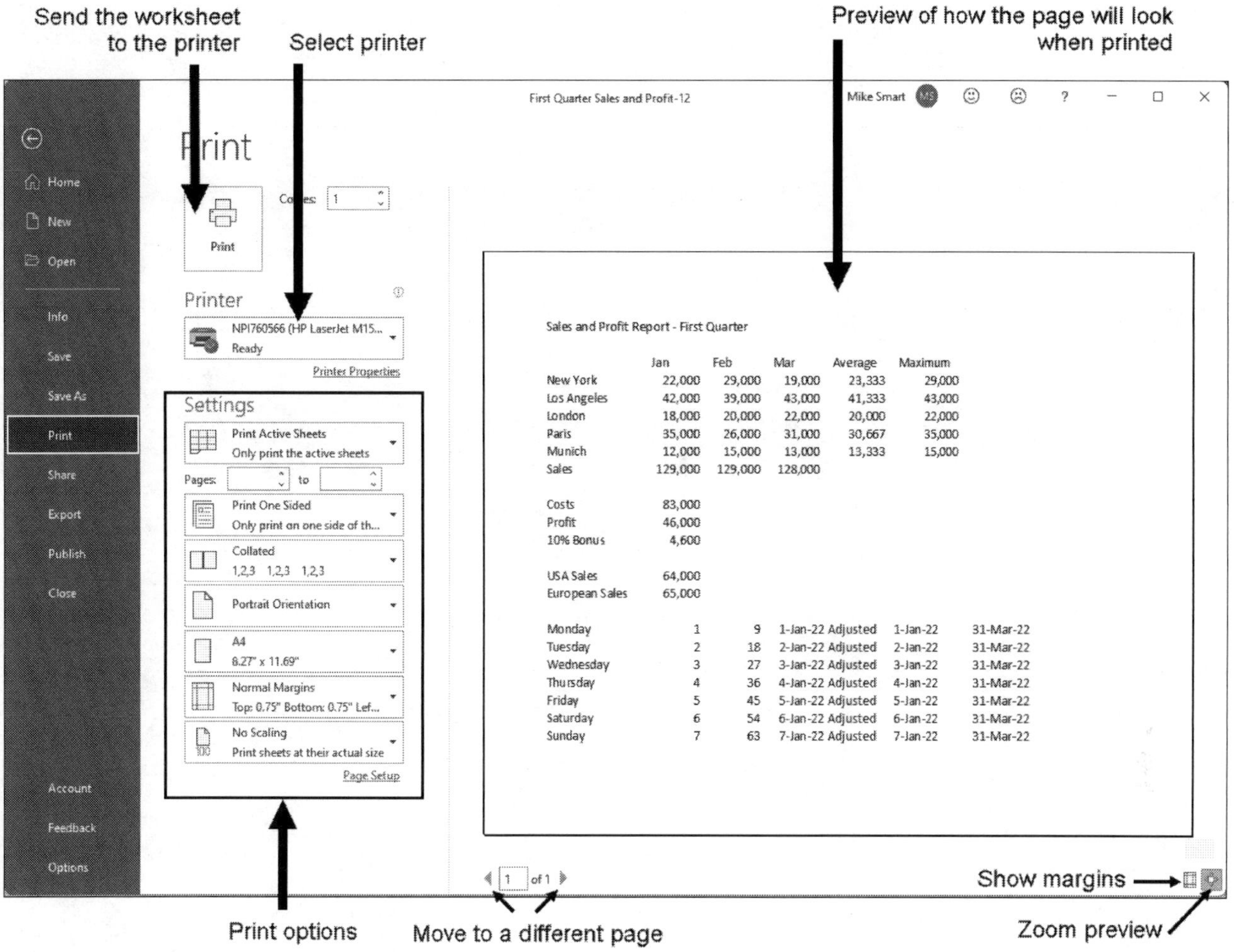

3 **Click on the zoom button**  **to see the zoom feature working.**

Each time you click on the button the page zooms in and out.

If you have a large screen, you may not see a lot of difference when you zoom.

4 **Print the worksheet.**

Click the *Print* button:

The page is printed on the selected printer.

Session 2: Exercise

1 Open a new blank workbook.

2 Use AutoFill to put the text: Jan, Feb, and Mar into cells A4:A6.

3 Using only the keyboard, add the following data:

	A	B	C	D	E
1	Profit Analysis				
2					
3		London	Paris	New York	Average
4	Jan	2,500	3,100	2,300	
5	Feb	2,200	2,700	2,600	
6	Mar	2,100	2,600	2,800	
7	Total				

4 Use AutoSum to compute London's total profit for Jan/Feb/Mar in cell B7.

5 Use AutoSum to calculate the average January profit in cell E4.

6 Use AutoFill to extend the London total in cell B7 to the Paris and New York totals in cells C7 and D7.

7 Use AutoFill to extend the January average profit in cell E4 to the February and March average profits in cells E5 and E6.

8 Select all of column A and all of column E (at the same time) and bold face the values in them.

9 Select row 3 and row 7 (at the same time) and bold face the values in them.

	A	B	C	D	E
1	**Profit Analysis**				
2					
3		**London**	**Paris**	**New York**	**Average**
4	**Jan**	2,500	3,100	2,300	**2,633**
5	**Feb**	2,200	2,700	2,600	**2,500**
6	**Mar**	2,100	2,600	2,800	**2,500**
7	**Total**	**6,800**	**8,400**	**7,700**	

10 Select cells B4:B6 and cells D4:D6 at the same time and then read the total (Sum) of London and New York sales for Jan, Feb and March from the summary information displayed on the status bar.

11 Select cells B4:D6 and zoom the selection so that these cells fill the screen.

12 Save your work as *Exercise2-End*.

Session 2: Exercise answers

These are the questions that students find the most difficult to answer:

Q 10	Q 8	Q 4	Q 2
1. Hover over the center of cell B4 so that you see the white cross cursor shape. 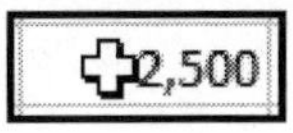 2. Click and drag down to cell B6. 3. Hold down the **<Ctrl>** key. 4. Hover over cell D4 until you see the white cross cursor shape. 5. Click and drag down to cell D6. 6. Look at the status bar at the bottom right of the screen. This was covered in: *Lesson 2-7: Select non-contiguous cell ranges and view summary information.*	1. Click on the column A header. 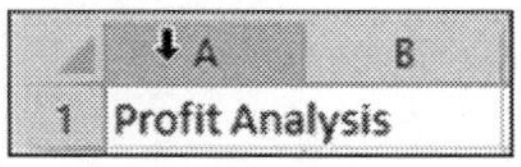 2. Hold down the **<Ctrl>** key. 3. Click on the column E header. 4. Click: Home→Font→Bold 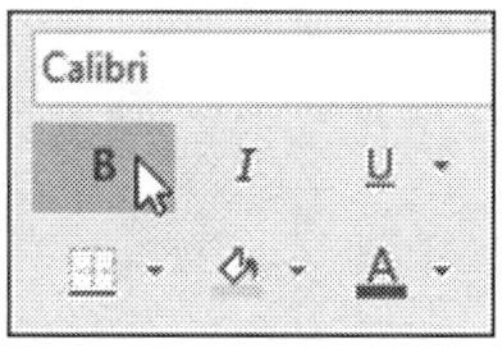 This was covered in: *Lesson 2-6: Select adjacent and non-adjacent rows and columns.*	1. Click in cell B7. 2. Click: Home→Editing→ AutoSum 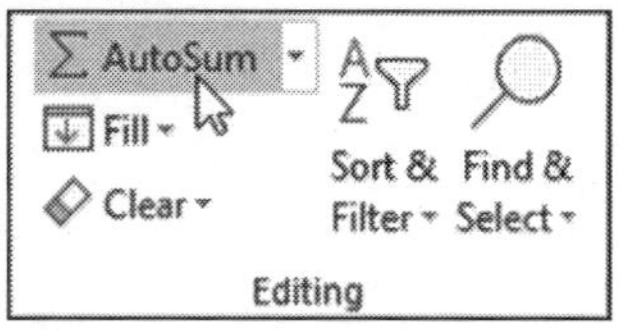 3. Either press the **<Enter>** key or click the AutoSum button again. This was covered in: *Lesson 2-3: Use AutoSum to quickly calculate totals.*	1. Type **Jan** into cell A4 and press the **<Enter>** key. 2. Click cell A4 once to make it the active cell. 3. Hover the mouse cursor over the bottom right corner of the cell until you see the black cross cursor shape.  4. Click and drag down to cell A6. This was covered in: *Lesson 2-14: Use AutoFill for text and numeric series.*

If you have difficulty with the other questions, here are the lessons that cover the relevant skills:

1 **Refer to: Lesson 1-1: Start Excel and open a new blank workbook.**

3 **Refer to: Lesson 2-1: Enter text and numbers into a worksheet.**

5 **Refer to: Lesson 2-3: Use AutoSum to quickly calculate totals.**

6 **Refer to: Lesson 2-15: Use AutoFill to adjust formulas.**

7 **Refer to: Lesson 2-15: Use AutoFill to adjust formulas.**

9 **Refer to: Lesson 2-6: Select adjacent and non-adjacent rows and columns.**

11 **Refer to: Lesson 2-23: Use the zoom control.**

12 **Refer to: Lesson 1-10: Save a workbook to a local file.**

3

Session Three: Taking Your Skills to the Next Level

One only gets to the top rung of the ladder by steadily climbing up one at a time, and suddenly all sorts of powers, all sorts of abilities which you thought never belonged to you – suddenly become within your own possibility.

Margaret Thatcher,
Prime Minister of the United Kingdom from 1979-1990

After mastering all the techniques covered in session two, you're already able to do useful work with the world's most powerful business tool, but of course, you're only on the first rung of a very long ladder.

While you are now able to do the simple things well, there are a few more insights you need to really get Excel working.

Most of the skills covered in this session will take your powers beyond those of casual Excel users.

Session Objectives

By the end of this session, you will be able to:

- Insert and delete rows and columns
- Use AutoComplete and fill data from adjacent cells
- Cut, copy and paste
- Cut, copy and paste using drag and drop
- Use Paste Values
- Increase/decrease decimal places displayed
- Transpose a range
- Use the Multiple Item Clipboard
- Use Undo and Redo
- Insert, View and Print cell notes and cell comments
- Understand absolute, relative and mixed cell references
- Understand templates and set the default custom template folder
- Create a template
- Use a template
- Add an Office Add-In to a workbook
- Freeze columns and rows
- Split the window into multiple panes
- Check spelling

Lesson 3-1: Insert and delete rows and columns

1 Open *The World's Fastest Cars* from your sample files folder.

	A	B	C	D	E	F	G
1	**The World's Fastest Cars**						
2							
3	**Make**	**Model**	**Top Speed (MPH)**	**0-60**	**BHP**	**Price (USD)**	**Country**
4	McLaren	720S	212	2.9	710	300,000	UK
5	Ferrari	812 Superfast	211	2.8	789	350,000	Italy
6	Ferrari	488 Pista	211	2.9	710	350,000	Italy
7	Aston Martin	DBS Superleggera	211	3.4	715	304,995	UK
8	McLaren	765 LT	205	2.8	755	368,000	UK
9	Porsche	911 Turbo S	205	2.6	640	203,500	Germany
10	Dodge	Challenger SRT Redeye	203	3.7	797	81,825	USA
11	Tesla	Model S Plaid	200	2.0	1020	123,740	USA
12	Cheverolet	Camero ZL1	198	3.7	650	65,895	USA
13	Mercedes	AMG E 63 S	196	3.3	603	107,350	Germany

A worksheet opens showing some of the fastest production cars in the world.

The list does not, however, show the true fastest production car in the world (in January 2022 this was the *Lamborghini Aventador Super Veloce* but there may be an even faster car by the time you read this book).

You need to insert a row above row 4 to add the Lamborghini to the list.

2 Insert a blank row above row 4.

Right-click the row header button 4 and click *Insert* from the shortcut menu.

3 Add the following data to the new row:

3	**Make**	**Model**	**Top Speed (MPH)**	**0-60**	**BHP**	**Price (USD)**	**Country**
4	Lamborghini	Aventador S	217	2.9	730	425,021	Italy
5	McLaren	720S	212	2.9	710	300,000	UK

4 If the text is bold faced restore it to normal.

You learned how to do this in: *Lesson 1-19: Use the Mini Toolbar, Key Tips and keyboard shortcuts.*

5 Add a column to the left of column A.

Adding columns is just like adding rows. Right-click on the column header A and then click *Insert* from the shortcut menu.

A blank column appears on the left-hand side of the worksheet:

	A	B	C	D	E	F	G	H
1		**The World's Fastest Cars**						
2								
3		**Make**	**Model**	**Top Speed (MPH)**	**0-60**	**BHP**	**Price (USD)**	**Country**
4		Lamborghini	Aventador S	217	2.9	730	425,021	Italy
5		McLaren	720S	212	2.9	710	300,000	UK
6		Ferrari	812 Superfast	211	2.8	789	350,000	Italy

6 Delete the newly inserted column A.

note

Other ways of inserting and deleting rows and columns

The right-click method, described in this lesson, is the fastest and most intuitive way to insert and delete rows and columns, but there are two additional methods.

To insert rows or columns:

1. Click: Home→Cells→Insert (drop down list)

2. Select: *Insert Sheet Rows* or *Insert Sheet Columns.*

OR

1. Press **<Ctrl>+<Shift>+<+>**

2. Select: *Entire Row* or *Entire Column.*

To delete rows or columns:

Click: Home→Cells→Delete (drop down list)

OR

Press **<Ctrl>+<->**

(and then select *Entire row* or *Entire column*).

The World's Fastest Cars

trivia

What is a production car?

In this lesson I've tried to define the world's fastest mass-produced cars.

In truth, the phrase "the world's fastest production car" is meaningless without defining what a production car really is.

For my list I've excluded cars that had a retail price of over $500,000 as such cars are only ever going to be sold in tiny quantities.

For example, the SSC Tuatara (often named as the world's fastest car) has production limited to 100 cars and a price tag of more than $2 Million.

Deleting a column is very similar to adding one. Right-click on the column header A but, this time, select *Delete* from the shortcut menu.

7 Insert four rows above row 3.

Nearly every Excel user does this by inserting a single row four times until they learn the correct technique.

1. Select rows 3, 4, 5 and 6. You learned how to do this in: *Lesson 2-6: Select adjacent and non-adjacent rows and columns.*
2. Right-click anywhere in the selected area.
3. Click *Insert* from the shortcut menu.

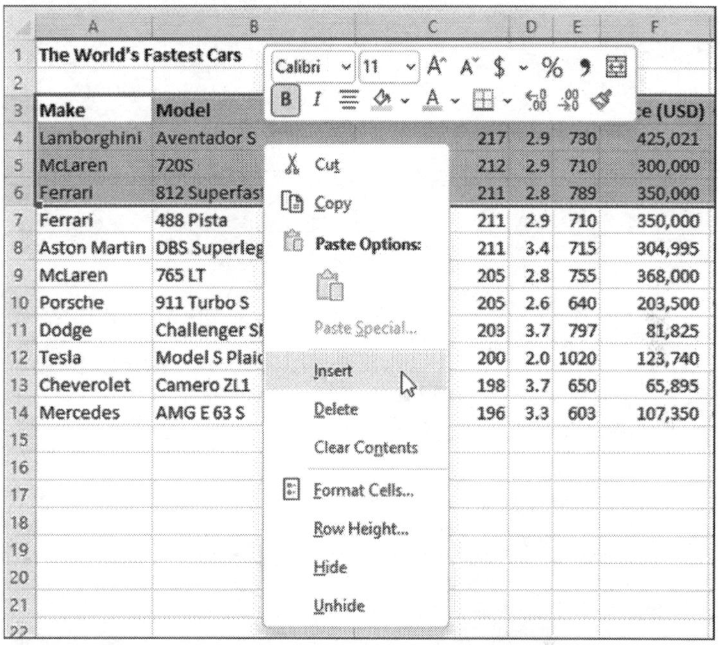

Four blank rows are inserted.

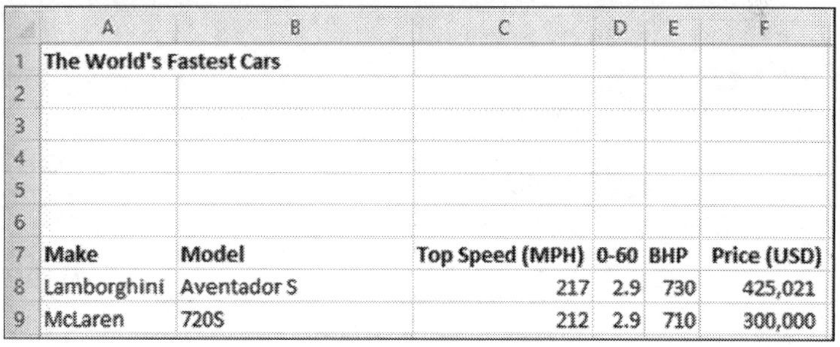

8 Delete the four newly inserted rows.

1. Select rows 3, 4, 5 and 6. You learned how to do this in: *Lesson 2-6: Select adjacent and non-adjacent rows and columns.*
2. Right-click anywhere in the selected area.
3. Click *Delete* from the shortcut menu.

9 Save your work as: *The World's Fastest Cars-2.*

Lesson 3-2: Use AutoComplete and fill data from adjacent cells

1 Open *The World's Fastest Cars-2* from your sample files folder (if it isn't already open).

	A	B	C	D	E	F	G
1	**The World's Fastest Cars**						
2							
3	**Make**	**Model**	**Top Speed (MPH)**	**0-60**	**BHP**	**Price (USD)**	**Country**
4	Lamborghini	Aventador S	217	2.9	730	425,021	Italy
5	McLaren	720S	212	2.9	710	300,000	UK
6	Ferrari	812 Superfast	211	2.8	789	350,000	Italy
7	Ferrari	488 Pista	211	2.9	710	350,000	Italy
8	Aston Martin	DBS Superleggera	211	3.4	715	304,995	UK
9	McLaren	765 LT	205	2.8	755	368,000	UK
10	Porsche	911 Turbo S	205	2.6	640	203,500	Germany
11	Dodge	Challenger SRT Redeye	203	3.7	797	81,825	USA
12	Tesla	Model S Plaid	200	2.0	1020	123,740	USA
13	Cheverolet	Camero ZL1	198	3.7	650	65,895	USA
14	Mercedes	AMG E 63 S	196	3.3	603	107,350	Germany

2 Type the letter **F** into cell A15.

Notice that Excel guesses that you want to type *Ferrari* into the cell. This is because the word Ferrari appears above it in the column.

If this doesn't happen, somebody has switched AutoComplete off. See the sidebar to find out how to switch it back on.

13	Cheverolet	Camero ZL1	198	3.7	650	65,895	USA
14	Mercedes	AMG E 63 S	196	3.3	603	107,350	Germany
15	Ferrari						

3 Press the **<Tab>** key to accept the guess.

4 Enter **Roma** for the model and then press the **<Tab>** key.

5 Enter **199** for the top speed and then press the **<Tab>** key.

	A	B	C	D	E	F	G
14	Mercedes	AMG E 63 S	196	3.3	603	107,350	Germany
15	Ferrari	Roma	199				

6 Use the *Fill* command to enter **3.3** into cell D15.

The Ferrari has the same 0-60 time as the Mercedes AMG. Instead of typing **3.3** into the cell you can use the *Fill* command.

1. Click in cell D15.
2. Click: Home→Editing→Fill→Down.

note

If AutoComplete doesn't work, somebody has switched it off

It's almost certain that AutoComplete will be enabled on any computer that you work on. It is such a useful feature that you'd never want to disable it.

If AutoComplete doesn't work for you it's because somebody has switched it off.

Bring it back like this:

Click: File→Options→ Advanced.

In the first section (*Editing Options*) check *Enable AutoComplete for cell values.*

The World's Fastest Cars-2

note

You can also Fill Down and Fill Right, using keyboard shortcuts

The following shortcut key combinations can be used for the *Fill Down* and *Fill Right* commands:

<Ctrl>+<D> Fill Down

<Ctrl>+<R> Fill Right

Unfortunately, there is no simple shortcut key combination for *Fill Up* or *Fill Left*.

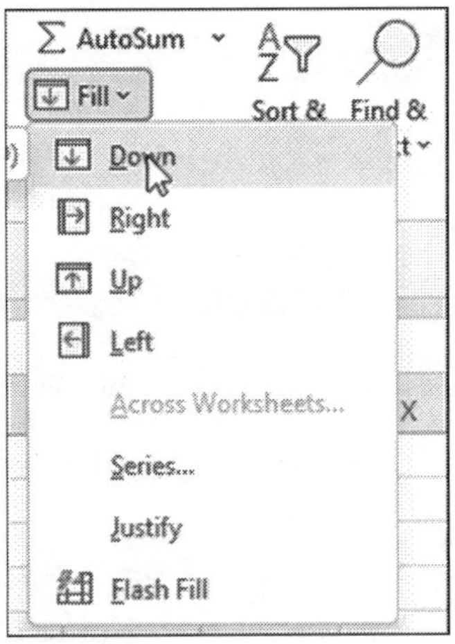

Notice that there are also *Right, Up* and *Left* options. These can be used to copy values from adjacent cells in any direction.

The *Across Worksheets…* option can only be used in conjunction with worksheet groups. You'll learn about worksheet groups later, in: *Lesson 6-7: Understand worksheet groups.*

7 Enter **612** for the BHP value and **245,000** for the price.

8 Right-click in G15 and choose *Pick From Drop-down List...* from the shortcut menu.

A drop-down list appears showing a list of all countries that currently exist in column G.

	A	B	C	D	E	F	G
1	**The World's Fastest Cars**						
2							
3	**Make**	**Model**	**Top Speed (MPH)**	**0-60**	**BHP**	**Price (USD)**	**Country**
4	Lamborghini	Aventador S	217	2.9	730	425,021	Italy
5	McLaren	720S	212	2.9	710	300,000	UK
6	Ferrari	812 Superfast	211	2.8	789	350,000	Italy
7	Ferrari	488 Pista	211	2.9	710	350,000	Italy
8	Aston Martin	DBS Superleggera	211	3.4	715	304,995	UK
9	McLaren	765 LT	205	2.8	755	368,000	UK
10	Porsche	911 Turbo S	205	2.6	640	203,500	Germany
11	Dodge	Challenger SRT Redeye	203	3.7	797	81,825	USA
12	Tesla	Model S Plaid	200	2.0	1020	123,740	USA
13	Cheverolet	Camero ZL1	198	3.7	650	65,895	USA
14	Mercedes	AMG E 63 S	196	3.3	603	107,350	Germany
15	Ferrari	Roma	199	3.3	612	245,000	
16							Germany
17							Italy UK
18							USA

9 Click *Italy* to enter the country.

10 Save your work as *The World's Fastest Cars-3.*

Lesson 3-3: Cut, copy and paste

trivia

The origins of cut and paste

The terms *Cut, Copy* and *Paste* remind us of the days when things weren't as easy as they are today.

Before the advent of computer technology, graphic artists would generate text for their work using a phototypesetting machine.

This machine used a photographic process to produce a strip of paper with high quality type printed upon it.

The layout artist would then cut the type into words or phrases and then paste it onto a sheet of paper.

When the work was finished it would be photographed to create a negative image ready to convert to a printing plate.

During the 1990's the layout business changed dramatically when graphic artists began to move to computer-based desktop publishing.

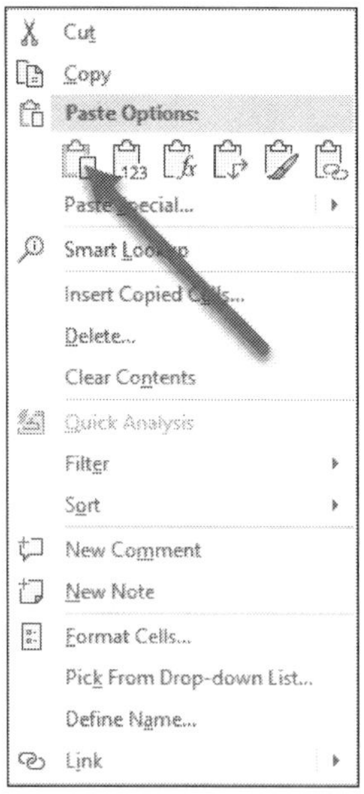

The World's Fastest Cars-3

1 Open *The World's Fastest Cars-3* from your sample files folder (if it isn't already open).

2 Click cell A1 to make it the active cell.

3 Copy the text from cell A1 to the clipboard.

The clipboard is a container for copied text and is common to all of Microsoft Office. When you ask Excel to copy, Excel takes the value in cell A1 (in this case text) and places a copy of it onto the clipboard. The existing contents of cell A1 remain unaltered.

The clipboard is useful because you can later paste the clipboard's contents back into the worksheet (or into any other Office document such as a PowerPoint presentation, Word document or Outlook e-mail).

There are three ways to copy but these two are the quickest:

EITHER

Right click cell A1 and select *Copy* from the shortcut menu.

OR

Press **<Ctrl>+<C>** on the keyboard.

The third (and slowest) method is to click:

Home→Clipboard→Copy

4 Click cell A17 to make it the active cell.

5 Paste the copied text into cell A17.

There are also three ways to paste but these two are the quickest:

EITHER

Right click cell A17 and then select: Paste Options→Paste  from the shortcut menu (see sidebar). The other paste options will be covered later in this lesson.

OR

Click cell A17 and then press **<Ctrl>+<V>** on the keyboard.

The third (and slowest) method is to click:

Home→Clipboard→Paste

The text appears in cell A17.

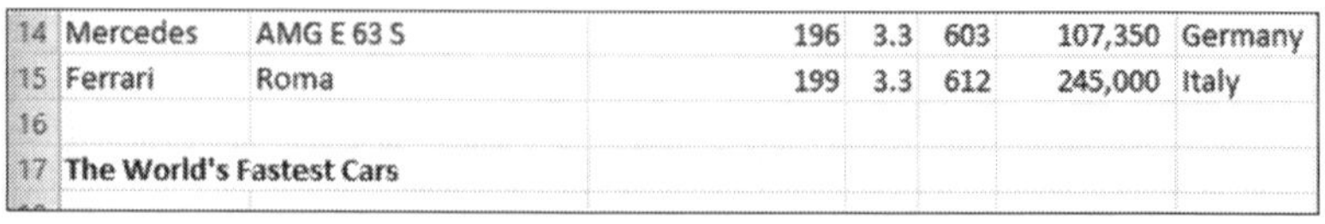

14	Mercedes	AMG E 63 S		196	3.3	603	107,350	Germany
15	Ferrari	Roma		199	3.3	612	245,000	Italy
16								
17	The World's Fastest Cars							

6 Edit the text in cell A17 to read: **The World's Fastest Italian Cars**

You learned how to do this in: *Lesson 2-1: Enter text and numbers into a worksheet.*

7 Select all of row 4 and copy it to the clipboard.

Selecting an entire row was covered in: *Lesson 2-6: Select adjacent and non-adjacent rows and columns.*

8 Select all of row 19 and paste into it.

The contents of row 4 are copied to row 19.

17	**The World's Fastest Italian Cars**				
18					
19	Lamborghini	Aventador S		217	2.9

9 Cut the text from the range A6:G7 to place it onto the clipboard.

When you cut text, the text is copied from the source cell(s) to the clipboard. If you then paste the text to a new location, the text is automatically deleted from the source cell(s).

1. Select the range A6 to G7.
2. Cut the range to place it onto the clipboard.

   There are three ways to cut but these two are the quickest:

   EITHER

   Right click inside the selected range and select *Cut* from the shortcut menu.

   OR

   Press **<Ctrl>+<X>**.

   The third (and slowest) method is to click:

   Home→Clipboard→Cut.

10 Click in cell A20 to make it the active cell.

11 Paste the cut range into the range beginning in cell A20.

The cut text appears with the top left-hand corner in cell A20.

5	McLaren	720S		212	2.9	710	300,000	UK
6								
7								
8	Aston Martin	DBS Superleggera		211	3.4	715	304,995	UK
9	McLaren	765 LT		205	2.8	755	368,000	UK
10	Porsche	911 Turbo S		205	2.6	640	203,500	Germany
11	Dodge	Challenger SRT Redeye		203	3.7	797	81,825	USA
12	Tesla	Model S Plaid		200	2.0	1020	123,740	USA
13	Cheverolet	Camero ZL1		198	3.7	650	65,895	USA
14	Mercedes	AMG E 63 S		196	3.3	603	107,350	Germany
15	Ferrari	Roma		199	3.3	612	245,000	Italy
16								
17	**The World's Fastest Italian Cars**							
18								
19	Lamborghini	Aventador S		217	2.9	730	425,021	Italy
20	Ferrari	812 Superfast		211	2.8	789	350,000	Italy
21	Ferrari	488 Pista		211	2.9	710	350,000	Italy
22								

12 Save your work as *The World's Fastest Cars-4.*

Lesson 3-4: Cut, copy and paste using drag and drop

1 Open *The World's Fastest Cars-4* from your sample files folder (if it isn't already open).

2 Move cells A20:G21 to cells A6:G7 using drag and drop.

1. Select cells A20:G21.
2. Hover the mouse cursor over the green border surrounding the range until you see the four-headed arrow cursor shape.

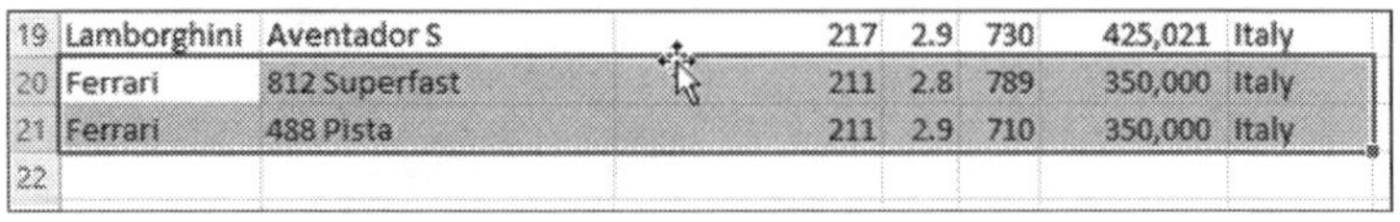

It is very important that you see the four-headed arrow and not the white cross or AutoFill cursor shape.

If you do not see a four-headed arrow somebody may have switched the drag and drop facility off. See sidebar for how to bring it back.

3. Click and drag the selected cells to their previous location (beginning at cell A6).

You will see a green outline showing where the cells will be dropped.

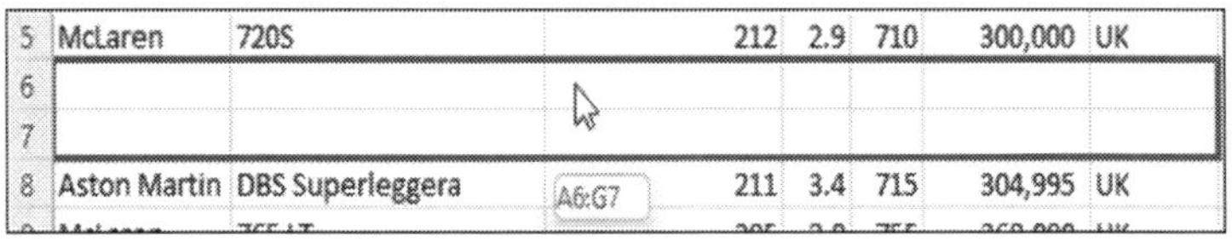

4. Release the mouse button.

The contents of the cells are moved back to A6:G7.

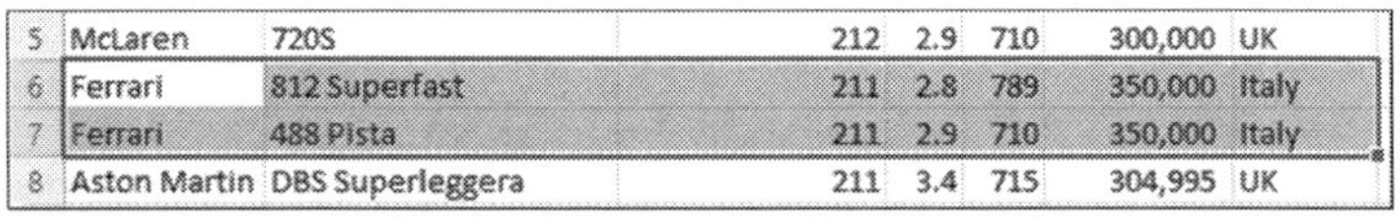

3 Copy cells A6:G7 to cells A20:G21 using right-click drag and drop.

1. Select cells A6:G7.
2. Hover the mouse cursor over the green border surrounding the range until you see the four-headed arrow cursor shape.
3. Right-click and drag the green rectangle to cells A20:G21.
4. Release the mouse button.

Several options are presented (see sidebar).

5. Click *Copy Here* from the shortcut menu.

This time the contents of the cells are copied rather than moved.

note

If drag and drop doesn't work somebody has switched it off

It's almost certain that drag and drop will be enabled on any computer that you work on. It is such a useful feature that you'd never want to disable it.

If drag and drop doesn't work for you it's because somebody has switched it off.

Bring it back like this:

1. Click: File→Options→Advanced.

2. In the first section (*Editing options*) check *Enable fill handle and cell drag and drop.*

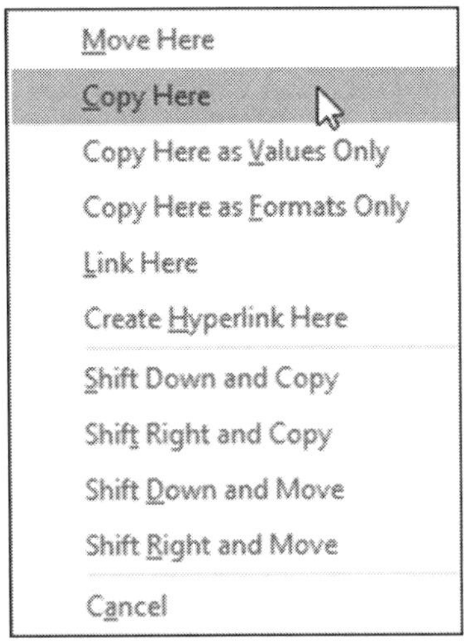

The World's Fastest Cars-4

note

Another way to copy cells via drag and drop

Hover over the border of the selected cells with the <Ctrl> key held down. You will see the mouse cursor shape change to a plus sign.

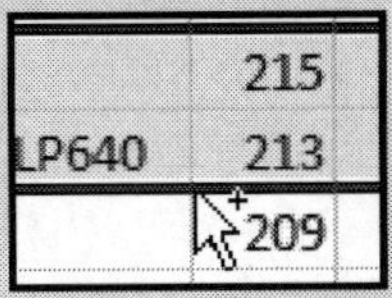

You can now drag and drop (holding the left mouse button down) to copy the cells to a new location.

17	The World's Fastest Italian Cars						
18							
19	Lamborghini	Aventador S	217	2.9	730	425,021	Italy
20	Ferrari	812 Superfast	211	2.8	789	350,000	Italy
21	Ferrari	488 Pista	211	2.9	710	350,000	Italy
22							

4 Copy the contents of row 15 to row 22 using right-click drag and drop.

17	The World's Fastest Italian Cars						
18							
19	Lamborghini	Aventador S	217	2.9	730	425,021	Italy
20	Ferrari	812 Superfast	211	2.8	789	350,000	Italy
21	Ferrari	488 Pista	211	2.9	710	350,000	Italy
22	Ferrari	Roma	199	3.3	612	245,000	Italy

5 Rename *Sheet1* to: ***World Cars***

You learned how to rename worksheet tabs in: *Lesson 1-13: View, move, add, rename, delete and navigate worksheet tabs.*

6 Add a new worksheet and name it: **Italian Cars**

You learned how to add new worksheets in: *Lesson 1-13: View, move, add, rename, delete and navigate worksheet tabs.*

7 Move cells A17:G22 from the *World Cars* worksheet to cells A1:G6 on the *Italian Cars* worksheet.

1. Select cells A17:G22 on the *World Cars* worksheet.
2. Cut the cells and paste them into cell A1 of the *Italian Cars* worksheet.

8 Insert one blank row above row 3 on the *Italian Cars* worksheet.

You learned how to do this in: *Lesson 3-1: Insert and delete rows and columns.*

9 Copy the titles from row 3 of the *World Cars* worksheet to row 3 of the *Italian Cars* worksheet.

10 Resize all columns on the *Italian Cars* worksheet so that they are wide enough to display their contents.

You learned how to do this in: *Lesson 2-9: Re-size rows and columns.*

	A	B	C	D	E	F	G
1	The World's Fastest Italian Cars						
2							
3	Make	Model	Top Spee	0-60	BHP	Price (US	Country
4	Lamborghini	Aventador S	217	2.9	730	425,021	Italy
5	Ferrari	812 Superfast	211	2.8	789	350,000	Italy
6	Ferrari	488 Pista	211	2.9	710	350,000	Italy
7	Ferrari	Roma	199	3.3	612	245,000	Italy

11 Save your work as *The World's Fastest Cars-5.*

Lesson 3-5: Use Paste Values and increase/decrease decimal places displayed

The World's Fastest Cars-5

1 Open *The World's Fastest Cars-5* from your sample files folder (if it isn't already open).

2 Select the *World Cars* worksheet and add a new column to the left of column D.

Right click on the column D header and click *Insert* from the shortcut menu.

3 Change the text in cell C3 from *Top Speed (MPH)* to: **MPH**

4 Type **KM/H** into cell D3.

5 Re-size column C so that it is just wide enough for its contents.

This skill was covered in: *Lesson 2-9: Re-size rows and columns.*

6 Given that one mile=1.609344 Km, enter a formula into cell D4 to convert MPH into KM/H.

This skill was covered in: *Lesson 2-12: Create your own formulas.*

The correct formula is: **=C4*1.609344**

7 Resize column D so that it is just wide enough to display its contents.

The Lamborghini's top speed is now displayed in Kilometers per hour.

	A	B	C	D	E	F
3	**Make**	**Model**	**MPH**	**KM/H**	**0-60**	**BHP**
4	Lamborghini	Aventador S	217	349.227648	2.9	730

8 AutoFill the formula in cell D4 down to the bottom of the list (cell D15).

This skill was covered in: *Lesson 2-15: Use AutoFill to adjust formulas.*

	A	B	C	D	E	F
3	**Make**	**Model**	**MPH**	**KM/H**	**0-60**	**BHP**
4	Lamborghini	Aventador S	217	349.227648	2.9	730
5	McLaren	720S	212	341.180928	2.9	710

9 Use the *Decrease Decimal* button to format the values in column D to display as whole numbers.

1. Select cells D4:D15.
2. Click the Home→Number→Decrease Decimal button six times.

10 Resize column D so that it is just wide enough to display its contents.

This skill was covered in: *Lesson 2-9: Re-size rows and columns.*

11 Copy cells D4:D15 to cells D17:D28 using copy and paste.

1. Select cells D4:D15.
2. Right-click anywhere in the selected range and then click *Copy* from the shortcut menu.
3. Right-click cell D17 and click: Paste Options→Paste from the shortcut menu.

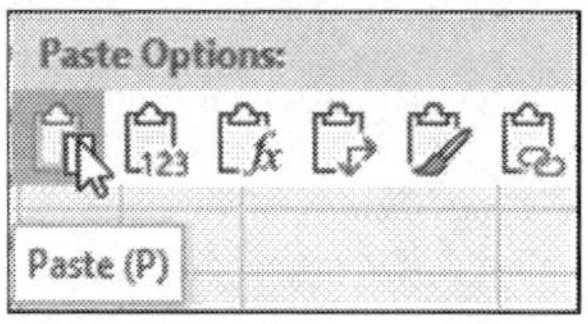

Unexpectedly, all of the values are pasted as zeros.

	A	B	C	D	E
16					
17				0	
18				0	

12 Inspect the formula in cell D17.

Click in cell D17 and look at the formula displayed in the Formula Bar at the top of the screen:

It is now clear why the value was correctly calculated as zero.

When you paste a formula, Excel will, by default, adjust the formula in the same way that it does when you AutoFill.

13 Undo the previous paste.

Click Home→Undo→Undo button. 

You are going to learn a lot more about the undo button later in: *Lesson 3-8: Use Undo and Redo.*

14 Paste again, this time using Paste Values.

Right-click in cell D17 and click: Paste Options→Values from the shortcut menu.

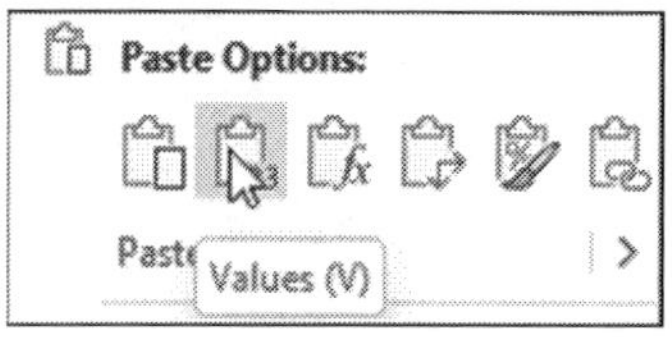

This time the values within the cells (rather than the formulas used to calculate the values) are pasted.

15	Ferrari	Roma	199	320	3.3	612
16						
17				349.2		
18				341.2		

15 Delete the values in cells D17:D28.

Select cells D17:D28 and press the **<Delete>** key.

16 Save your work as *The World's Fastest Cars-6.*

B	C	D	E
Model	MPH	KM/H	0-60
Aventador S	217	349	2.9
720S	212	341	2.9

note

Other ways to paste values

Using the Smart Tag

If you perform a regular *paste* and then suddenly realize that you really wanted to *paste values* you don't need to start again.

Notice that a Smart Tag is displayed at the bottom right corner of the pasted cells.

You can click the Smart Tag to change the paste to *Values.*

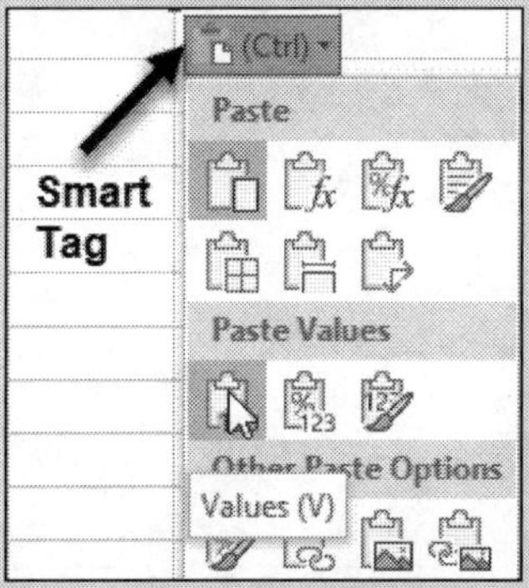

Using the Ribbon

If you click:

Home→Clipboard→Paste (drop-down arrow)

… you'll be presented with the same set of icons. You've only learned about the *Paste* and *Paste Values* options so far, but you'll encounter some of the others later in this course:

Lesson 3-6: Transpose a range

Paste Values is the most used special pasting option but there's another that is often very useful.

If a worksheet has many columns but few rows it may become impossible to print. In this case you may wish to reverse the arrangement so that the worksheet has many rows but few columns.

Transposing allows you to do this automatically.

1 Open *The World's Fastest Cars-6* from your sample files folder (if it isn't already open).

2 Add a new worksheet and name it: *Transposed.*

This skill was covered in: *Lesson 1-13: View, move, add, rename, delete and navigate worksheet tabs.*

3 Select and copy the range A3:H15 on the *World Cars* worksheet.

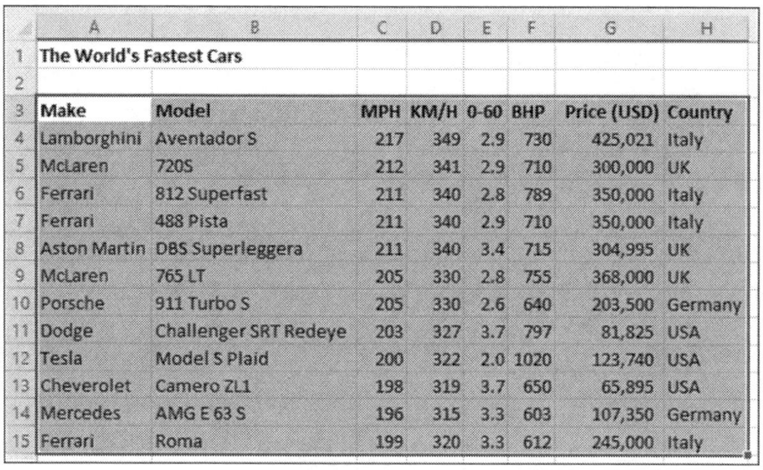

	A	B	C	D	E	F	G	H
1	The World's Fastest Cars							
2								
3	Make	Model	MPH	KM/H	0-60	BHP	Price (USD)	Country
4	Lamborghini	Aventador S	217	349	2.9	730	425,021	Italy
5	McLaren	720S	212	341	2.9	710	300,000	UK
6	Ferrari	812 Superfast	211	340	2.8	789	350,000	Italy
7	Ferrari	488 Pista	211	340	2.9	710	350,000	Italy
8	Aston Martin	DBS Superleggera	211	340	3.4	715	304,995	UK
9	McLaren	765 LT	205	330	2.8	755	368,000	UK
10	Porsche	911 Turbo S	205	330	2.6	640	203,500	Germany
11	Dodge	Challenger SRT Redeye	203	327	3.7	797	81,825	USA
12	Tesla	Model S Plaid	200	322	2.0	1020	123,740	USA
13	Cheverolet	Camero ZL1	198	319	3.7	650	65,895	USA
14	Mercedes	AMG E 63 S	196	315	3.3	603	107,350	Germany
15	Ferrari	Roma	199	320	3.3	612	245,000	Italy

4 Select cell A3 on the *Transposed* worksheet.

5 Click: Home→Clipboard→
Paste (drop down list)→Transpose.

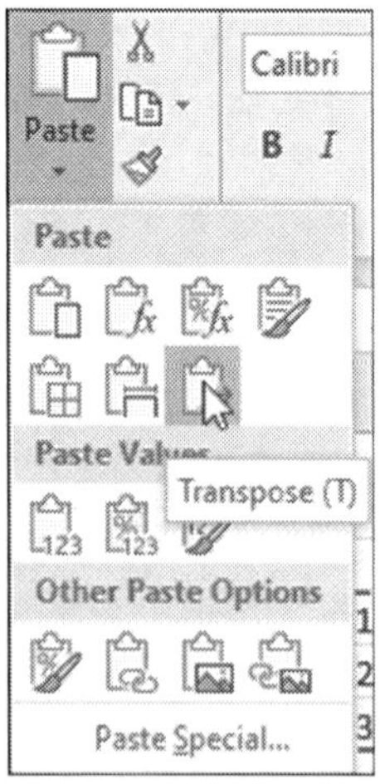

The cells are copied in a rather interesting way. The columns have now become rows and the rows have become columns.

The World's Fastest Cars-6

	A	B	C	D	E	F	G	H	I	J	K	L	M
1													
2													
3	**Make**	Lamborgh	McLaren	Ferrari	Ferrari	Aston Mai	McLaren	Porsche	Dodge	Tesla	Cheverole	Mercedes	Ferrari
4	**Model**	Aventado	720S	812 Super	488 Pista	DBS Supe	765 LT	911 Turbo	Challenge	Model S P	Camero Zl	AMG E 63	Roma
5	**MPH**	217	212	211	211	211	205	205	203	200	198	196	199
6	**KM/H**	349	341	340	340	340	330	330	327	322	319	315	320
7	**0-60**	2.9	2.9	2.8	2.9	3.4	2.8	2.6	3.7	2.0	3.7	3.3	3.3
8	**BHP**	730	710	789	710	715	755	640	797	1020	650	603	612
9	**Price (US**	425,021	300,000	350,000	350,000	304,995	368,000	203,500	81,825	123,740	65,895	107,350	245,000
10	**Country**	Italy	UK	Italy	Italy	UK	UK	Germany	USA	USA	USA	Germany	Italy

Notice also that the width of the columns has not been maintained.

You can see that several of the columns containing makes and models are not wide enough to fully display their contents.

6 Automatically size all columns in one operation.

You learned how to do this in: *Lesson 2-9: Re-size rows and columns.*

1. Select every cell in the workbook by clicking the *select all* button in the top left corner of the worksheet:

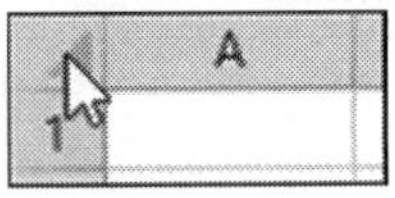

2. Hover the mouse cursor over the intersection of any two columns until you see the *re-size* cursor shape and then double-click.

3. Every column is now perfectly sized.

	A	B	C	D
1				
2				
3	**Make**	Lamborghini	McLaren	Ferrari
4	**Model**	Aventador S	720S	812 Superfast
5	**MPH**	217	212	211
6	**KM/H**	349	341	340
7	**0-60**	2.9	2.9	2.8
8	**BHP**	730	710	789
9	**Price (USD)**	425,021	300,000	350,000
10	**Country**	Italy	UK	Italy

7 Save your work as *The World's Fastest Cars-7.*

note

About task panes

Task panes are similar to dialogs but there are several important differences.

1. Task panes are modeless.

Windows dialogs (with very few exceptions) are *modal.*

This means that until you've dismissed a dialog (usually by clicking an *OK* or *Cancel* button) you can't do anything else.

If you click anywhere on the worksheet or Ribbon when a modal dialog is open, you'll just hear a "ding" noise.

Task panes are *modeless.*

This means that you can go on working and leave task panes happily sitting in the background.

2. Task panes can automatically update as you work.

Task panes can respond dynamically to any actions you take on the worksheet.

You can see this in action with the *Clipboard* task pane.

As you copy new items, they automatically update in the task pane.

3. Task panes can be re-sized and either docked to the left or right of the screen or floated.

If you click and drag the title bar of a task pane, you can "dock" the pane to the right or left of the screen. This means that the task pane snaps into place and is then re-sized with the Excel window.

If you drag a task pane to the centre of the screen it becomes a "floating" task pane and can be positioned anywhere.

The World's Fastest Cars-7

Lesson 3-7: Use the Multiple Item Clipboard

When you copy items from any non-Office Windows application, the selected item is copied to the *Windows Clipboard.* You are then able to paste this item into any other Windows application.

Office has its own clipboard that can contain up to 24 items.

Because all Office applications share the same *Office Clipboard,* it is possible to copy and paste up to 24 items between Excel, PowerPoint, Word, Access, Outlook and all other Office applications.

In this lesson, you'll use the *Office Clipboard* to add content to a new worksheet in the workbook. The new worksheet will contain details of the world's fastest *German* cars.

1 Open *The World's Fastest Cars-7* from your sample files folder (if it isn't already open).

2 Insert a new worksheet and name it: **German Cars**

You learned how to do this in: *Lesson 1-13: View, move, add, rename, delete and navigate worksheet tabs.*

3 Click: Home→Clipboard→Dialog Launcher.

This is your first experience of using a *dialog launcher* button. The dialog launcher button is situated on the bottom right-hand corner of some Ribbon command groups.

The *Clipboard* task pane is displayed (see sidebar for more on task panes).

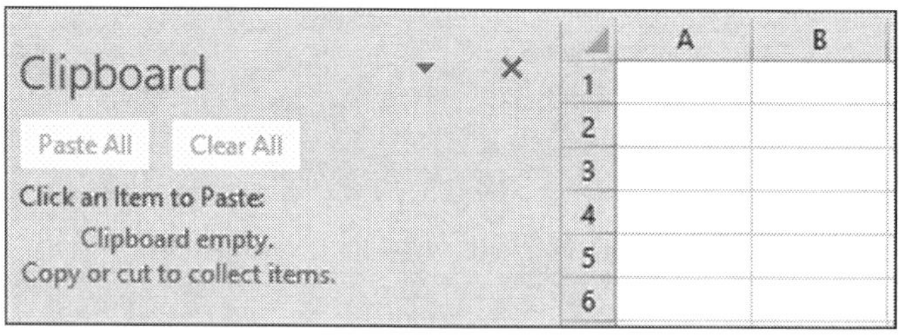

4 If any items are shown on the Clipboard click the *Clear All* button  to remove them.

5 Copy row 3 from the *World Cars* worksheet to the clipboard.

1. Click the *World Cars* worksheet tab to select it.
2. Right-click the row 3 row header and then click *Copy* from the shortcut menu.

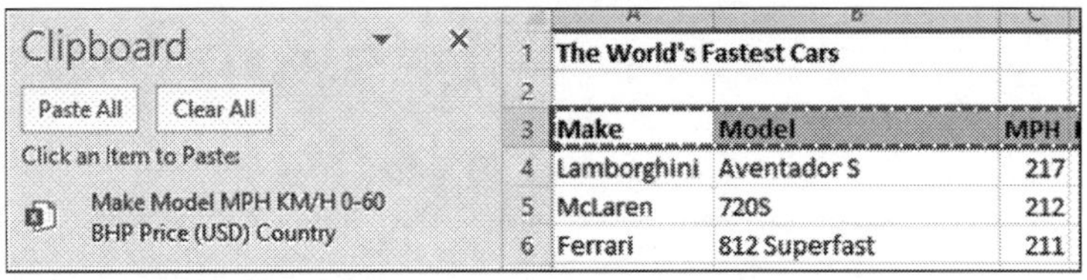

6 Copy row 10 from the *World Cars* worksheet to the clipboard.

7 Copy row 14 from the *World Cars* worksheet to the clipboard.

The header row, along with details for the two German cars, are now displayed on the clipboard task pane (see sidebar).

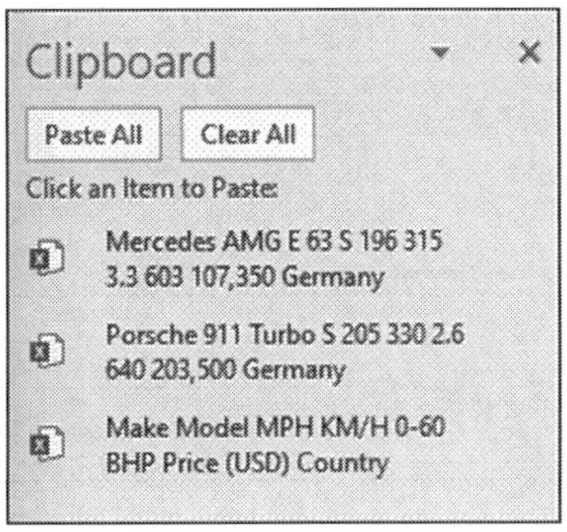

8 Click the *German Cars* worksheet tab.

The blank *German Cars* worksheet is displayed.

9 Type **The World's Fastest German Cars** into cell A1 and bold face the text.

10 Click cell A3 to make it the Active Cell.

11 Complete the worksheet with a single click by clicking the *Paste All* button on the Clipboard task pane.

It would be possible to achieve the same result by clicking once upon each of the three items on the Clipboard. Because you want the entire contents of the Clipboard, three clicks are saved by using the *Paste All* button.

When you click the *Paste All* button, all of the items on the clipboard should be pasted into adjacent rows.

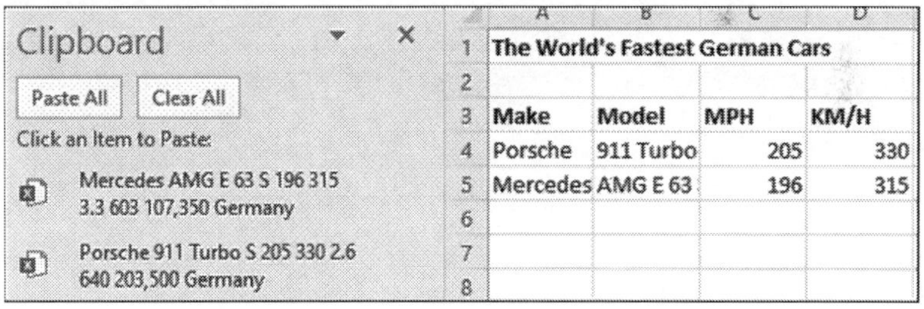

12 Automatically re-size all of the columns.

This skill was covered in: *Lesson 2-9: Re-size rows and columns.*

13 Close the clipboard task pane.

Click the *Close* button at the top right-hand corner of the clipboard task pane.

14 Save your work as *The World's Fastest Cars-8.*

Lesson 3-8: Use Undo and Redo

Excel's (fantastically useful) *Undo* feature enables you to reverse an action when you have made a mistake.

It is only possible to undo the previous 100 actions.

Sometimes you may undo an action and then change your mind. Redo will step through the operations in reverse, in effect "undoing the undo".

1 Close any workbooks that are open and then re-open Excel.

Excel keeps tabs on the last 100 actions taken. By closing and re-opening Excel, you'll clear the existing list of actions available for undo.

2 Open *The World's Fastest Cars-8* from your sample files folder and select the *World Cars* worksheet.

3 Type **UK Cars** into cell A17 and bold face the text.

4 Copy row 3 into row 19.

5 Copy row 5 into row 20.

6 Copy row 8 into row 21.

7 Copy row 9 into row 22.

The worksheet should now look like this:

	A	B	C	D	E	F	G	H
1	**The World's Fastest Cars**							
2								
3	**Make**	**Model**	**MPH**	**KM/H**	**0-60**	**BHP**	**Price (USD)**	**Country**
4	Lamborghini	Aventador S	217	349	2.9	730	425,021	Italy
5	McLaren	720S	212	341	2.9	710	300,000	UK
6	Ferrari	812 Superfast	211	340	2.8	789	350,000	Italy
7	Ferrari	488 Pista	211	340	2.9	710	350,000	Italy
8	Aston Martin	DBS Superleggera	211	340	3.4	715	304,995	UK
9	McLaren	765 LT	205	330	2.8	755	368,000	UK
10	Porsche	911 Turbo S	205	330	2.6	640	203,500	Germany
11	Dodge	Challenger SRT Redeye	203	327	3.7	797	81,825	USA
12	Tesla	Model S Plaid	200	322	2.0	1020	123,740	USA
13	Cheverolet	Camero ZL1	198	319	3.7	650	65,895	USA
14	Mercedes	AMG E 63 S	196	315	3.3	603	107,350	Germany
15	Ferrari	Roma	199	320	3.3	612	245,000	Italy
16								
17	**UK Cars**							
18								
19	**Make**	**Model**	**MPH**	**KM/H**	**0-60**	**BHP**	**Price (USD)**	**Country**
20	McLaren	720S	212	341	2.9	710	300,000	UK
21	Aston Martin	DBS Superleggera	211	340	3.4	715	304,995	UK
22	McLaren	765 LT	205	330	2.8	755	368,000	UK

8 Click the undo button on the Quick Access Toolbar.

The McLaren details disappear from row 21.

9 Click the redo button on the Quick Access Toolbar.

The McLaren details re-appear in row 21.

note

Using the keyboard to undo and redo

It is well worth remembering the undo keyboard shortcut:

<Ctrl>+<Z>

I use it all the time. It is also the undo shortcut for the other Office applications.

You'll use the Redo action far less, but for completeness it is:

<Ctrl>+<Y>

If you forget them, you'll see the keyboard shortcuts in the tooltip when you hover over the *Undo* and *Redo* buttons.

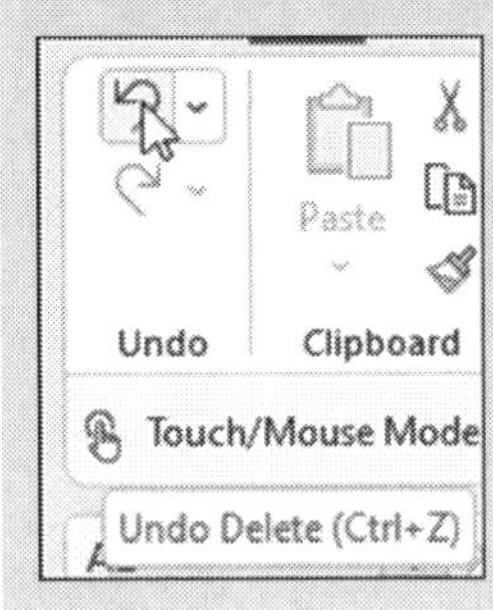

The World's Fastest Cars-8

10 Click the drop-down arrow to the right of the undo button on the Quick Access Toolbar.

A drop-down menu appears showing all of the actions that have taken place (or the previous 100 actions if more than 100 actions have taken place) since the workbook was opened.

11 Click the Bold action to *Undo 5 Actions*.

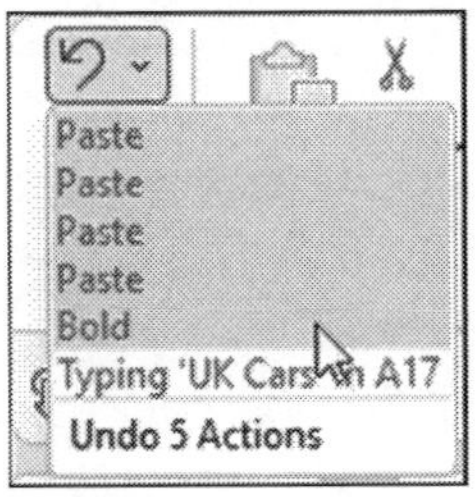

Only the text *UK Cars* remains on the worksheet and it is no longer bold faced.

14	Mercedes	AMG E 63 S	196	315
15	Ferrari	Roma	199	320
16				
17	UK Cars			
18				

12 Click the drop-down arrow to the right of the redo button on the Quick Access Toolbar.

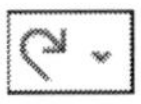

A drop-down menu appears showing all of the actions that have been undone and can be potentially re-done.

13 Click the last *Paste* action to *Redo 5 Actions*.

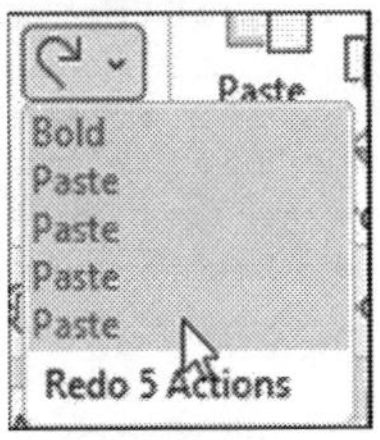

The worksheet reverts to its former state.

17	**UK Cars**							
18								
19	**Make**	**Model**	**MPH**	**KM/H**	**0-60**	**BHP**	**Price (USD)**	**Country**
20	McLaren	720S	212	341	2.9	710	300,000	UK
21	Aston Martin	DBS Superleggera	211	340	3.4	715	304,995	UK
22	McLaren	765 LT	205	330	2.8	755	368,000	UK

14 Delete rows 17 to 22.

15 Save your work as *The World's Fastest Cars-9*.

Lesson 3-9: Insert cell notes

1 Open *The World's Fastest Cars-9* from your sample files folder (if it isn't already open) and select the *World Cars* worksheet.

2 Using Microsoft Word (not Excel), open *Car Descriptions* from your sample files folder.

1. Open Microsoft Word.
2. Click: *Open* from the left-hand menu bar. 

3. Click *Browse* on the *Open* dialog. 

4. Navigate to *Car Descriptions* in your sample files folder.

3 Return to Excel without closing Word.

You will notice two buttons on the Windows task bar at the bottom of the screen:

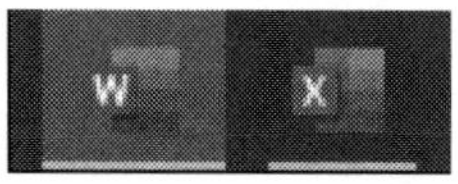

Click the button with the Excel logo to return to Excel.

4 Set up the name that will appear in the note box.

Whenever you enter a note, your name is added to the top.

This allows other users to identify the source of each note if you later distribute the workbook.

1. Click: File→Options→General.
2. In the category *Personalize your copy of Microsoft Office* type your name into the *User name* box.

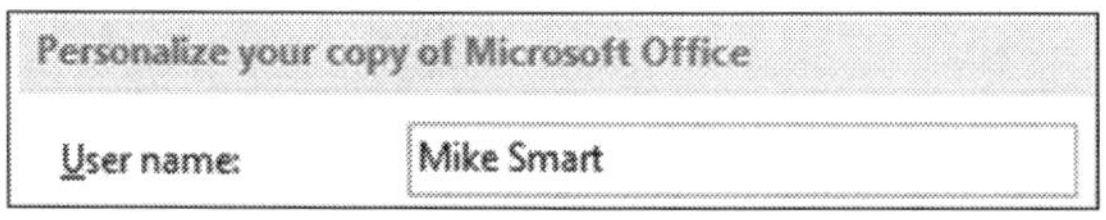

3. Click the OK button.

5 Copy the text for the Aston Martin DBS from the Word document.

1. Return to Word.
2. Click and drag across the Aston Martin DBS text with the mouse cursor.
3. Right-click within the selected text and click *Copy* from the shortcut menu.

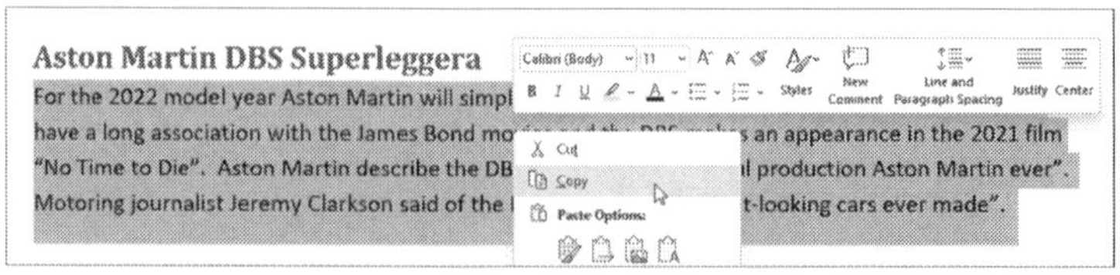

6 Add the note text to the Aston Martin DBS cell (cell B8).

note

Cell notes were formerly known as cell comments

A new feature has been added to Excel 2021 that allows users to associate threaded dialogs with an Excel cell.

This new feature is now known as *Comments*. This meant that the old *Comments* feature (described in this lesson) had to be re-named *Notes*.

You'll learn about the new Comments feature later in this session.

note

Excel uses your log in user name by default

If you don't set up your user name as described, Excel will use your Windows log-in user name instead.

This is the reason you'll often see cryptic user names (like JSmith93) in other people's worksheets.

note

Other ways to insert a note

Click: Review→Notes→Notes→New Note.

OR

Press: **<Shift>+<F2>**

Car Descriptions

The World's Fastest Cars-9

note

How to put a picture into a note box

Microsoft probably never intended that you put pictures into notes but there is a way to do this. Here's an example:

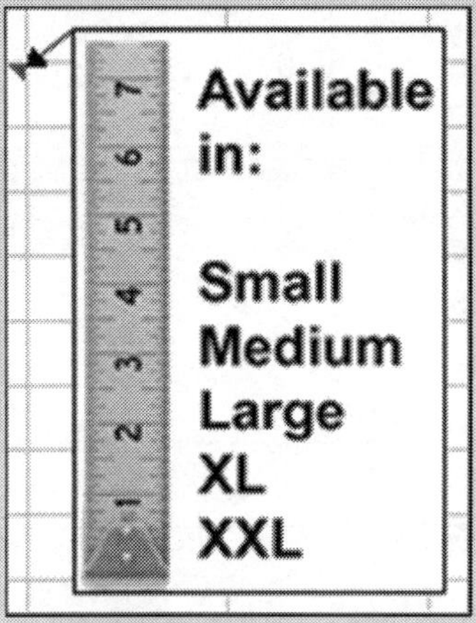

Here's the (rather long-winded) way in which you can do this:

1. Right-click into any cell and click: *New Note...* from the shortcut menu.

2. Remove any name text currently inside the cell.

3. Hover over the border of the comment until you see the four-headed arrow cursor shape.

4. Right-click and then click: *Format Comment...* from the shortcut menu.

5. Click the *Colors and Lines* tab and then the drop-down arrow next to Fill→Color.

6. Click: *Fill Effects...*

7. Click the *Picture* tab.

8. Click: *Select Picture...*

9. Click the *Browse...* button next to *From a file.*

10. Select the *SmallMediumLarge* graphic from your sample files folder (or any other picture).

11. Click *Insert, OK, OK* to close all of the dialogs.

12. Re-size the note to display the graphic correctly.

1. Return to Excel.

2. Right-click cell B12 and click *New Note* on the shortcut menu.

   A note box with your name at the top is shown next to cell B4.

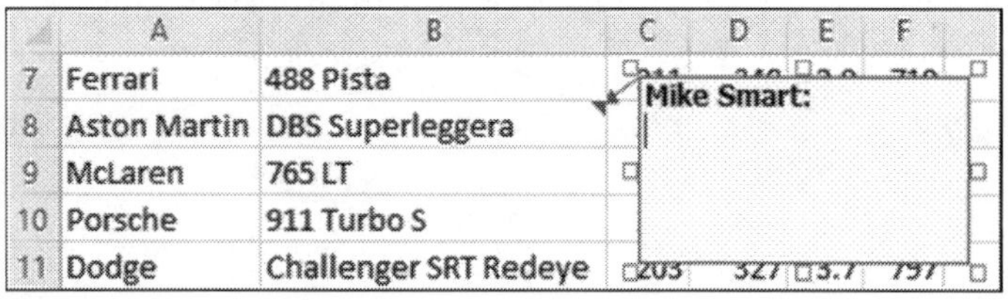

3. Paste into the note box.

   The text that you copied from the Word document appears in the box.

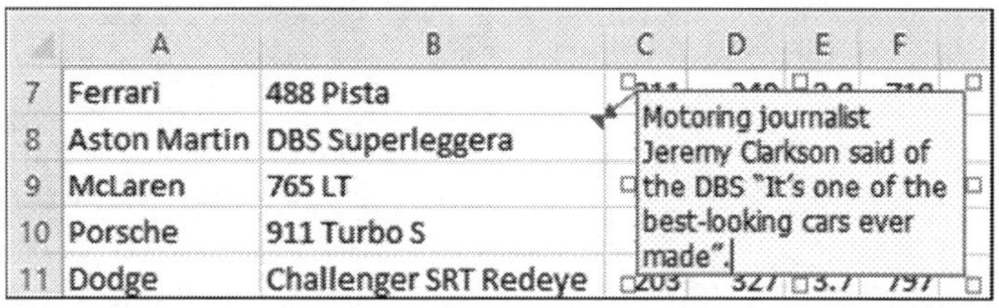

7 Use the sizing handles to enlarge the note box so that all text is visible.

1. If you do not see the sizing handles, right-click on cell B8 and select *Edit Note* from the shortcut menu.

   The sizing handles are the small white dots that appear on the corners and edges of a note box. When you hover over a sizing handle, the cursor shape changes to a double headed arrow.

2. Hover carefully over the bottom-right sizing handle until you see the double-headed arrow cursor shape.

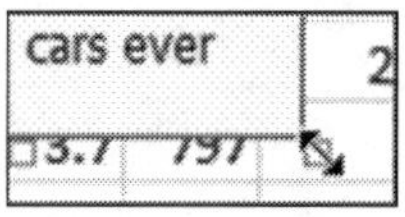

3. Click and drag the re-size handles to re-size the note box.

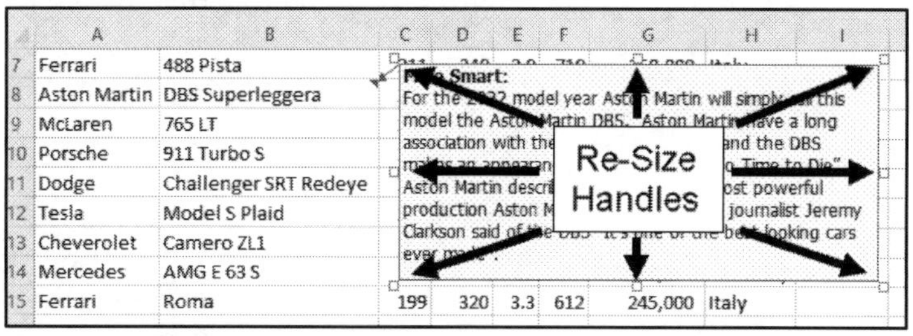

8 Click anywhere in the worksheet.

The note disappears but a small red triangle has appeared in the top right corner of the cell.

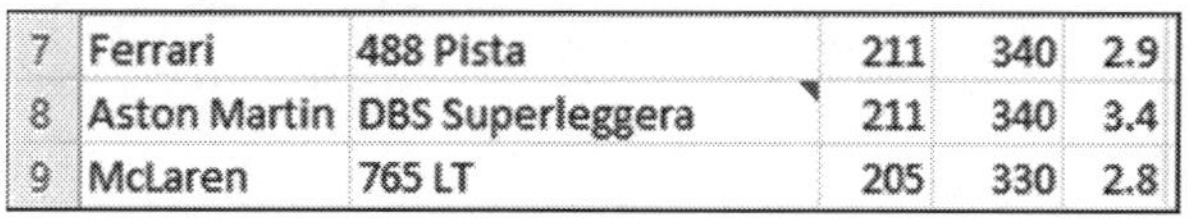

9 Add two more notes for the McLaren 765LT and Tesla Plaid.

10 Save your work as *The World's Fastest Cars-10.*

Lesson 3-10: View cell notes

1 Open *The World's Fastest Cars-10* from your sample files folder (if it isn't already open) and select the *World Cars* worksheet.

Cells with notes show a small red triangle in their top right-hand corner.

2 View the note behind a single cell.

Hover the mouse cursor over any of the cells with a red triangle. The cell note is displayed.

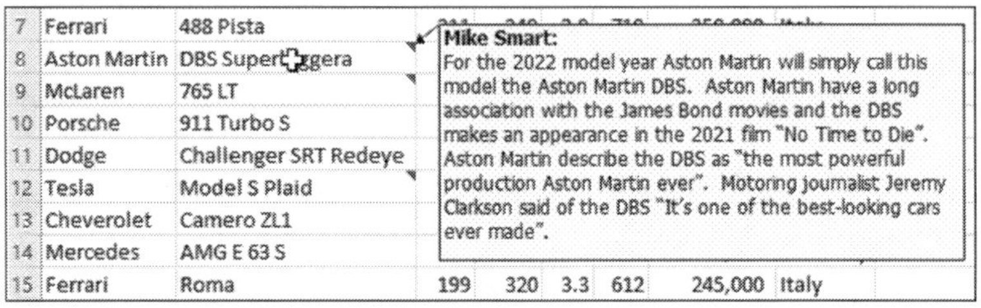

3 View all of the notes in a worksheet at the same time.

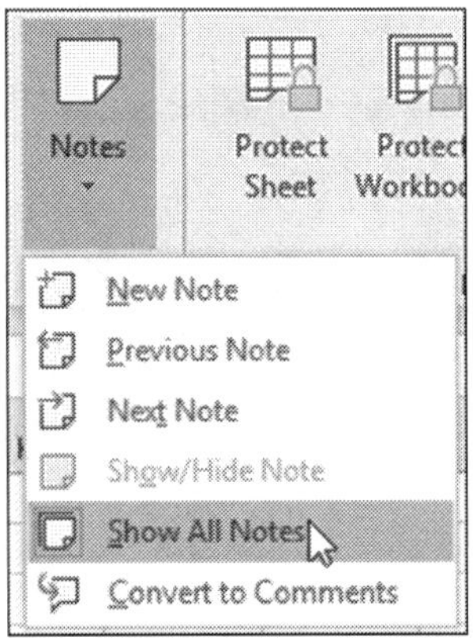

Click: Review→Notes→Show All Notes.

Every note on the worksheet is displayed.

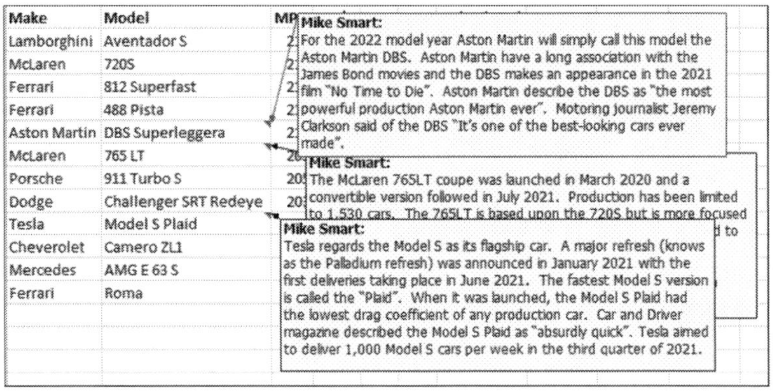

Unfortunately, the notes overlap so you are unable to read them all at the same time. It is possible to view each note by clicking it, as this brings the window to the front, but it isn't very elegant.

4 Move and re-size the notes so that they do not overlap.

Click a note and then hover anywhere on the border *but not on a sizing handle* until you see a four-headed arrow. When you see the four-headed arrow, click and drag to move the note.

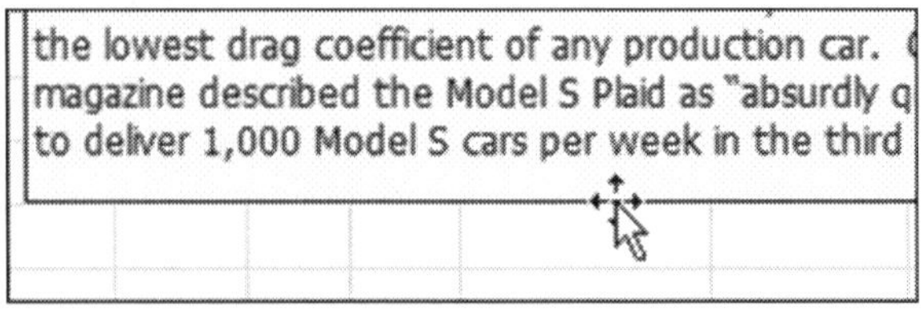

The World's Fastest Cars-10

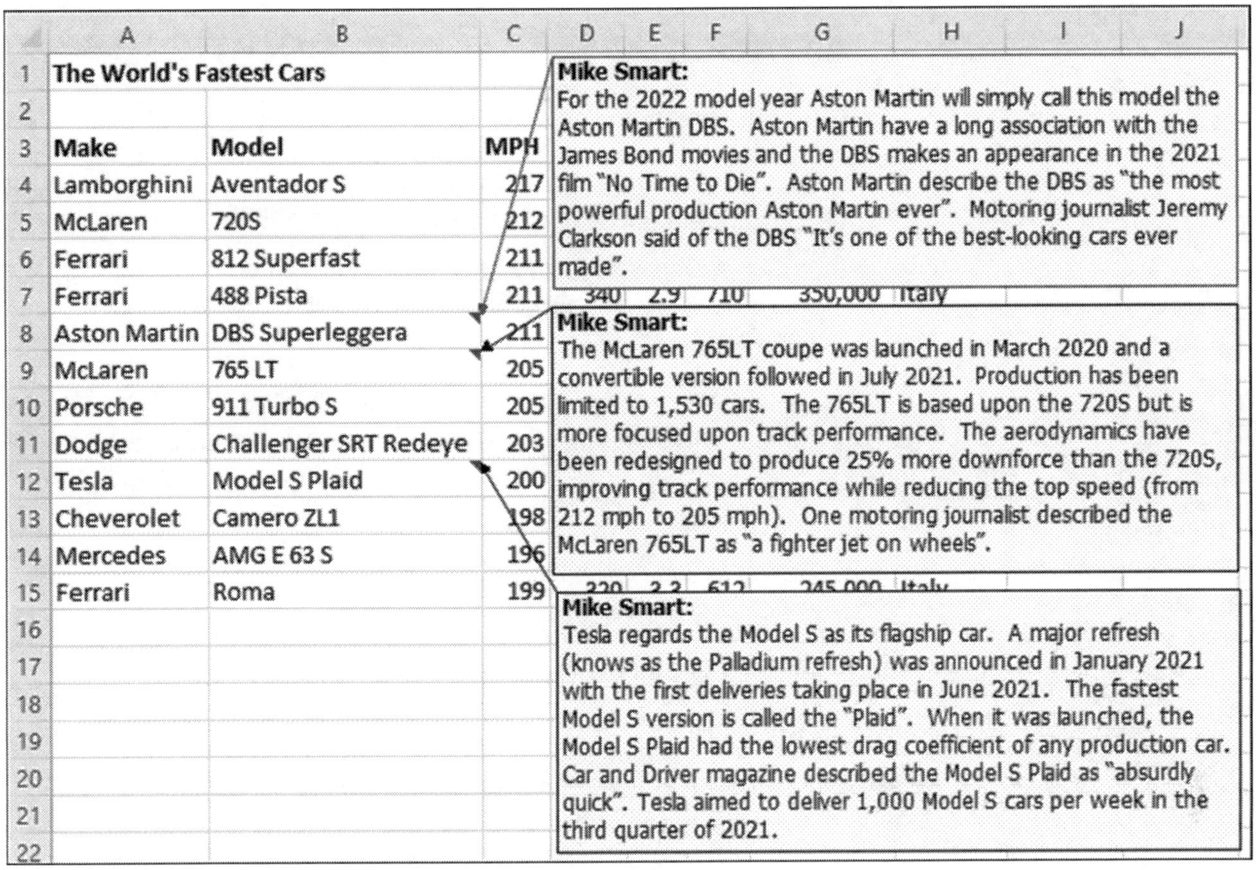

5 Hide all of the notes.

Click: Review→Notes→Show All Notes.

The notes disappear.

6 Make the Aston Martin DBS note display all of the time.

Sometimes you will want to send somebody a worksheet and make sure that an important note is on view when they open it.

Right click cell B8 and choose *Show/Hide Note* from the shortcut menu.

The note remains on display all of the time (even if you are not hovering over the note cell).

7 Hide the Aston Martin DBS note.

Right click cell B8 and choose *Show/Hide Note* from the shortcut menu.

8 Save your work as *The World's Fastest Cars-11*.

Lesson 3-11: Print cell notes

One of the most common note-related questions asked in my Excel classroom courses is: "how can I print a list of notes at the end of a worksheet"? Excel can do this, but the feature is hidden away in the *Page Setup* dialog and missed by most users.

1 Open *The World's Fastest Cars-11* from your sample files folder (if it isn't already open) and select the *World Cars* worksheet.

2 Tell Excel to print notes at the end of the worksheet.

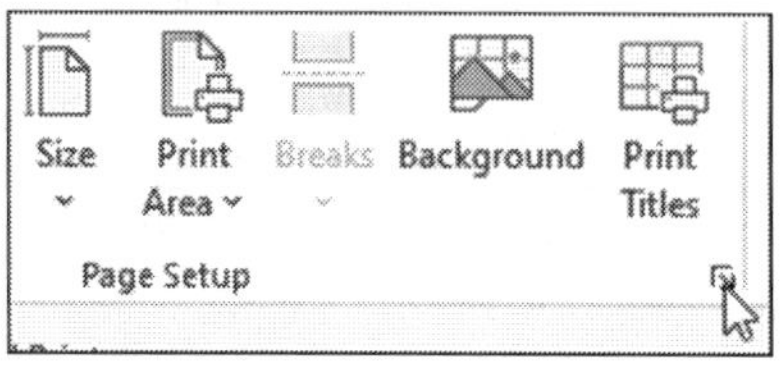

1. Click: Page Layout→Page Setup→Dialog Launcher.

   The *Dialog Launcher* is the small button on the bottom-right corner of the *Page Setup* group.

   The *Page Setup* dialog is displayed.

2. Click the *Sheet* tab.

3. Click the *Comments* drop-down and select: *At end of sheet.*

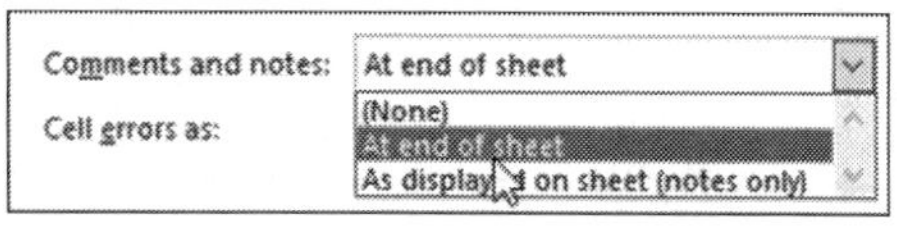

   This drop-down is named *Comments and notes* (rather than *Notes* as you might expect) because the *At end of sheet* option will print both cell comments and cell notes at the end of the worksheet. You'll learn about cell comments later in: *Lesson 3-12: Insert and delete cell comments.*

3 Click the *Print Preview* button to view the notes as they would print.

You can either click the *Print Preview* button on the *Page Setup* dialog or close the dialog and click: File→Print.

Whichever way you choose, the *Backstage* view opens and displays a print preview of the worksheet in the right-hand pane.

Click the *Next Page* button 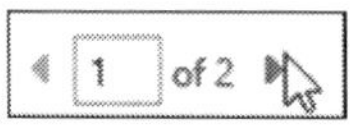 to view Page 2 of the preview. The notes are displayed exactly as they would print.

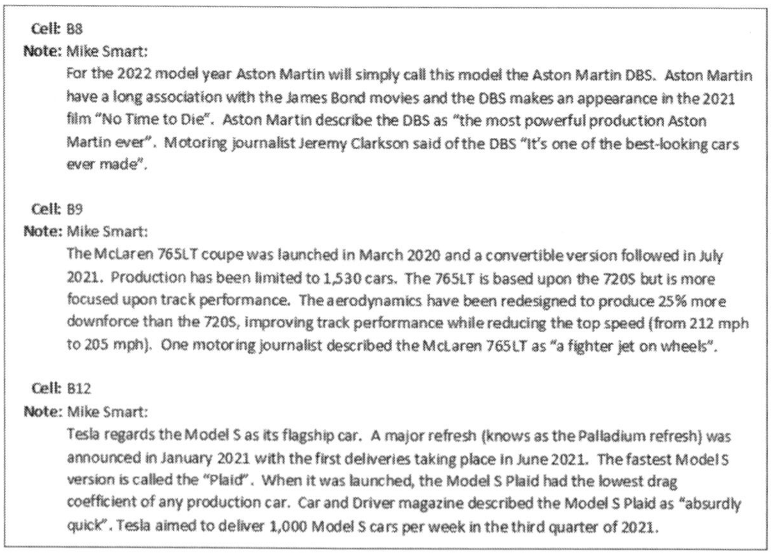

Cell: B8
Note: Mike Smart:
For the 2022 model year Aston Martin will simply call this model the Aston Martin DBS. Aston Martin have a long association with the James Bond movies and the DBS makes an appearance in the 2021 film "No Time to Die". Aston Martin describe the DBS as "the most powerful production Aston Martin ever". Motoring journalist Jeremy Clarkson said of the DBS "It's one of the best-looking cars ever made".

Cell: B9
Note: Mike Smart:
The McLaren 765LT coupe was launched in March 2020 and a convertible version followed in July 2021. Production has been limited to 1,530 cars. The 765LT is based upon the 720S but is more focused upon track performance. The aerodynamics have been redesigned to produce 25% more downforce than the 720S, improving track performance while reducing the top speed (from 212 mph to 205 mph). One motoring journalist described the McLaren 765LT as "a fighter jet on wheels".

Cell: B12
Note: Mike Smart:
Tesla regards the Model S as its flagship car. A major refresh (knows as the Palladium refresh) was announced in January 2021 with the first deliveries taking place in June 2021. The fastest Model S version is called the "Plaid". When it was launched, the Model S Plaid had the lowest drag coefficient of any production car. Car and Driver magazine described the Model S Plaid as "absurdly quick". Tesla aimed to deliver 1,000 Model S cars per week in the third quarter of 2021.

The World's Fastest Cars-11

4 Click the Back button  to return to the worksheet.

5 Make the Tesla note display all of the time.

Right click cell B12 and click: *Show/Hide Note* from the shortcut menu.

6 Move the Tesla note so that it doesn't obscure the data in the worksheet.

You learned how to do this in: *Lesson 3-10: View cell notes*

7 Tell Excel to print notes exactly as they are displayed on the worksheet.

1. Click: Page Layout→Page Setup→Dialog Launcher.

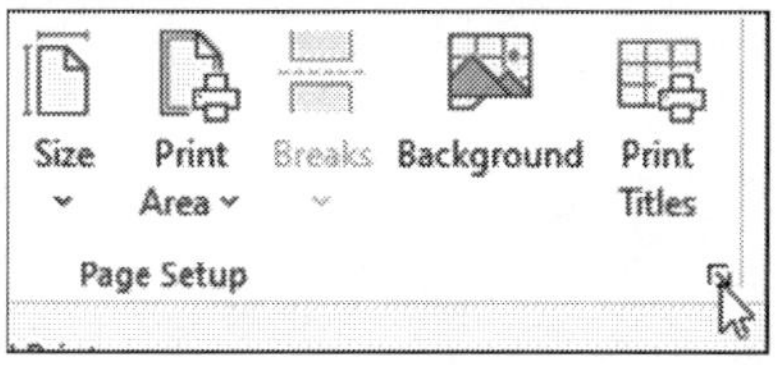

The *Page Setup* dialog is displayed.

2. Click the *Sheet* tab.

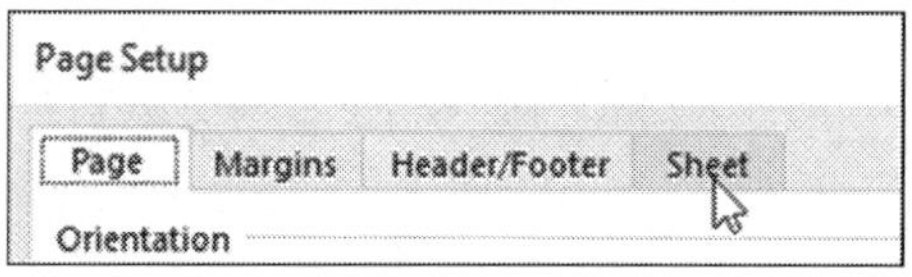

3. Click the *Comments and notes* drop-down and select: *As displayed on sheet (notes only).*

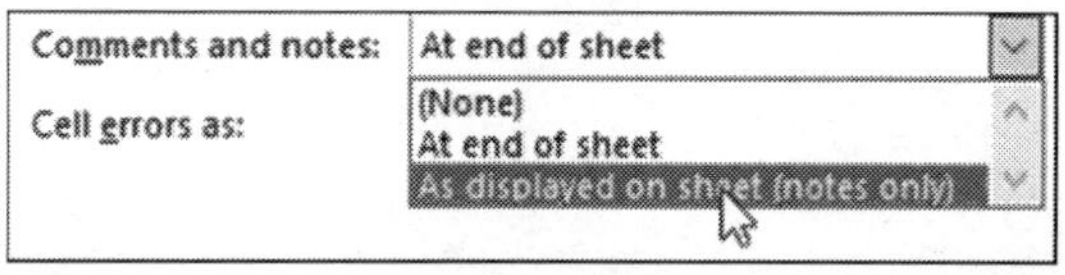

8 Click the *Print Preview* button to view the note as it would print.

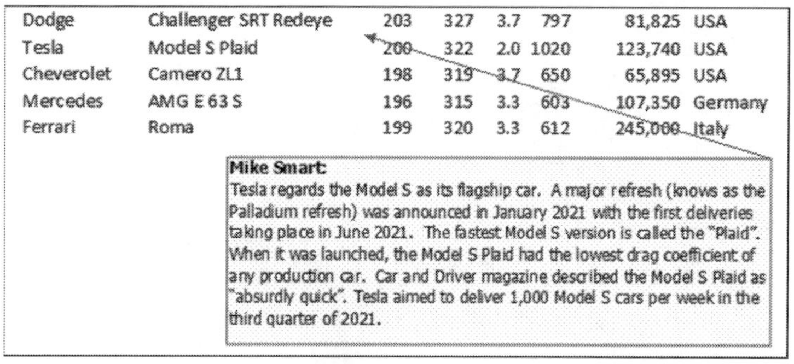

9 Click the *Back* button  on the ribbon to return to the worksheet.

10 Hide the note.

Right click cell B12 and click: Show/*Hide Note* from the shortcut menu.

11 Save your work as: *The World's Fastest Cars-12.*

Lesson 3-12: Insert and delete cell comments

note

Cell notes were formerly known as cell comments

In: *Lesson 3-9: Insert cell notes* you learned about Excel's cell notes feature.

Prior to Excel 2021, cell notes were known as cell comments.

Cell comments are a new feature introduced in Excel 2021. Microsoft decided that the term *Cell Comments* better described the interactive nature of the new feature.

The old *Cell Comments* feature was thus re-named *Cell Notes*.

This can cause confusion if you discuss the *Cell Comments* feature with an Excel 2019 user.

Cell notes

Prior to Excel 2021 Excel only had a *Cell Notes* feature.

You've learned all there is to know about Cell Notes in: *Lesson 3-9: Insert cell notes, Lesson 3-10: View cell notes* and *Lesson 3-11: Print cell notes.*

Here's an example of one of the notes you created:

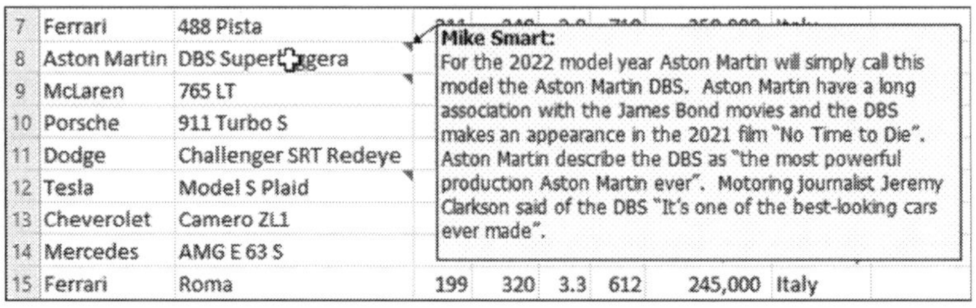

Cell comments

Cell comments are a new Excel 2021 feature.

Cell comments include a reply box. Here's an example of a cell comment:

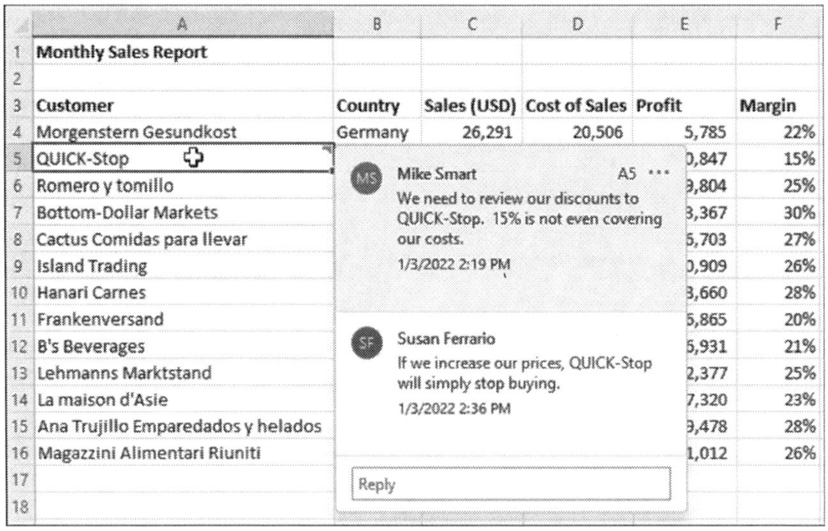

You can see that the comment is more powerful as it enables other users to reply to the comment. A chain of comments that follow in a linear way is referred to as a *thread.*

note

Cell comments can be edited or deleted by anybody – even if they didn't create them

There's a potential problem with cell comments because anybody can edit or delete them.

This means that any user can open the workbook and change a comment that you might have added (making other workbook users think that you made it).

This could cause problems in a corporate environment.

Things you can do with notes that you cannot do with comments.

- Add an image and format text.
- Re-size the note.
- Print notes within the body of the worksheet (you can only print cell comments at the end of the worksheet).

- Remove or change the name at the top of the note.

Things you can do with comments that you cannot do with notes.

- Reply to the comment (creating a threaded comment chain).
- Display comments in a comment task pane alongside the worksheet.

1 Open *Monthly Sales Report* from your sample files folder.

2 Add a comment to cell A16 with the text shown below.

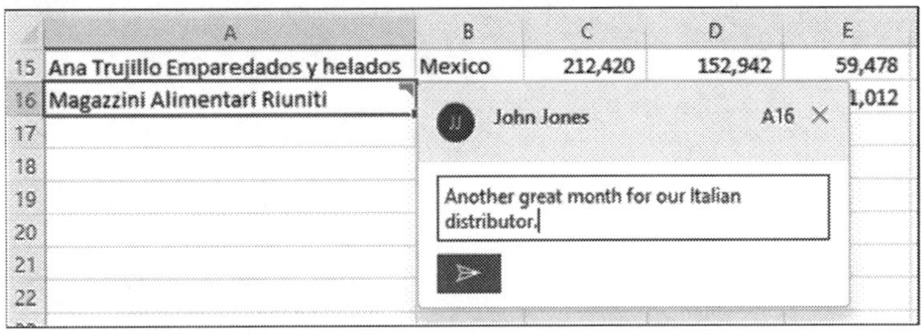

1. Right-Click on cell A16.
2. Click *New Comment* from the shortcut menu.
3. Type: **Another great month for our Italian distributor.** into the text box.
4. Click the *Post* button to save your comment.
5. Click in any other cell to make the comment disappear.

3 View the comment in cell A16.

Notice that a small pink indicator has appeared on the top right corner of cell A16.

Hover the mouse cursor over cell A16 to view the comment.

4 Display all comments in this worksheet in the Comment pane.

Click: Review→Comments→Show Comments.

The Comments pane appears showing all comments in this workbook.

5 Delete the comment in cell A5.

1. Right-click on cell A5.
2. Click *Delete Comment* on the shortcut menu.

You can also delete comments from the ribbon by clicking:

Review→Comments→Delete

6 Save your work as: *Monthly Sales Report-1*.

note

You can print comments at the end of a worksheet in the same way as you do with cell notes

In: *Lesson 3-11: Print cell notes* you learned how to print cell notes both within the body of a worksheet and at the end of a worksheet.

Cell comments can only be printed at the end of the worksheet. This is done in exactly the same way as for cell notes.

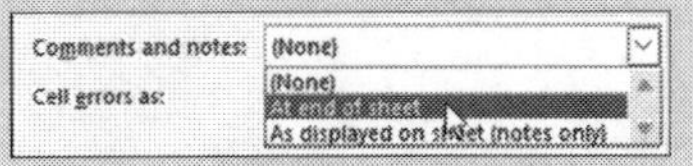

If both notes and comments are present within a worksheet, both comments and notes will be printed out at the end of the worksheet.

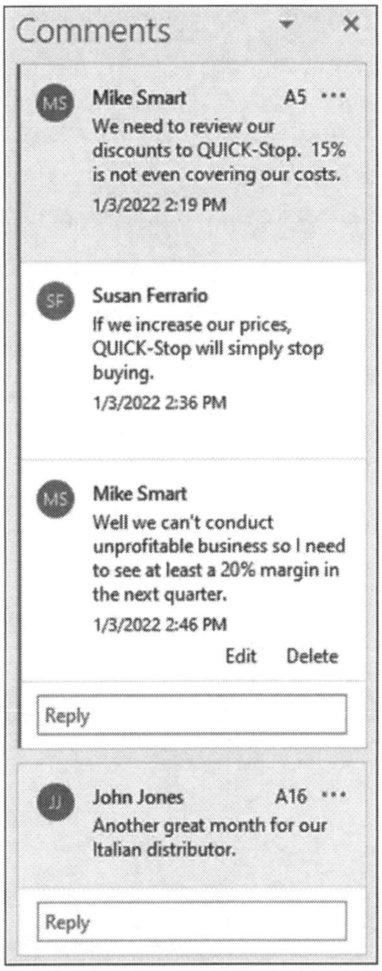

Lesson 3-13: Understand absolute and relative cell references

You've seen how useful Excel's AutoFill is when copying formulas. Most of the time things work perfectly, as you normally want to increment row and column references when you AutoFill down and across.

Sometimes AutoFill can be a little too helpful when it adjusts cell references that you would like to be left alone. This lesson will illustrate the type of worksheet that requires *absolute cell references* as you convert USD (US Dollar) prices to GBP (Great Britain Pounds).

1 Open *The World's Fastest Cars-12* from your sample files folder (if it isn't already open) and select the *World Cars* worksheet.

2 Insert a column to the left of column H.

This skill was covered in: *Lesson 3-1: Insert and delete rows and columns.*

3 Type **Price (GBP)** into cell H3.

4 Type **USD/GBP** into cell G1.

5 Type **0.7428** into cell H1.

This exchange rate will have changed by the time you read this book.

If you want more realism, you can get the current exchange rate from https://xe.com. If you are not in England or America it might be fun to change the exchange rate to match your own currency.

6 If necessary, adjust the number of decimal places in cell H1 to show all four decimal places.

You learned how to do this in: *Lesson 3-5: Use Paste Values and increase/decrease decimal places displayed.*

7 Make the text in cells G1 and H1 bold.

8 Place a formula in cell H4 that will calculate the price of a Lamborghini Aventador S in GBP (Great Britain Pounds).

Formulas were covered in: *Lesson 2-12: Create your own formulas.*

The correct formula is:

=G4*H1

You can now see that the Lamborghini costs £315,706 in Great Britain Pounds.

	G	H	I
1	**USD/GBP**	**0.7428**	
2			
3	**Price (USD)**	**Price (GBP)**	**Country**
4	425,021	315,706	Italy
5	300,000		UK

The World's Fastest Cars-12

9 Consider what will happen if you AutoFill this formula.

AutoFill was covered in: *Lesson 2-15: Use AutoFill to adjust formulas.*

As the formula is AutoFilled downward the number part of each formula will be incremented like this:

	H
1	**0.66519**
2	
3	**Price (GBP)**
4	=G4*H1
5	=G5*H2
6	=G6*H3

Consider cell H5 (the price of the McLaren 720S). The formula in this cell is **=G5*H2**.

AutoFill has done a wonderful job with the formula's reference to cell *G5*. AutoFill has changed the reference from the Lamborghini's price to the McLaren 720S, and that's exactly what you wanted.

But AutoFill has got things wrong with the *H2* reference. The exchange rate is always in cell H1. It never moves.

To express this in Excel terminology: G4 is a **relative reference** (ie you want AutoFill to adjust it) while H1 is an **absolute reference** (ie you want AutoFill to leave it alone).

10 Change the formula in cell H4 to make H1 into an absolute reference.

To make a reference absolute you simply add a dollar sign in front of both the letter and number. Note that this has absolutely nothing to do with the dollar currency, it is simply a way to indicate that a cell reference is absolute.

Click in cell H4 and then edit the formula (shown in the formula bar) so that it now reads:

=G4*$H$1

11 AutoFill the formula in cell H4 to the end of the list.

(AutoFill was covered in: *Lesson 2-15: Use AutoFill to adjust formulas*).

The price of each car is now displayed in both US Dollars and Great Britain Pounds.

Click on each of the GBP prices and observe the formula shown in the formula bar at the top of the screen.

In each cell Excel has adjusted the G4 part of the formula but left the H1 part of the formula alone.

H5 | fx =G5*$H$1

	C	D	E	F	G	H
3	**MPH**	**KM/H**	**0-60**	**BHP**	**Price (USD)**	**Price (GBP)**
4	217	349	2.9	730	425,021	315,706
5	212	341	2.9	710	300,000	222,840

12 Save your work as *The World's Fastest Cars-13.*

tip

A faster way to add those dollar signs

1. Click on the formula bar so that the cursor is touching the cell reference that you want to convert to absolute:

   fx =G4*H1

2. Press the <F4> key on the keyboard. Be careful that you see two dollar signs after pressing the key.

   If you see only one dollar sign it is because you have pressed the key twice and inadvertently created a mixed cell reference.

   You'll learn about mixed cell references later, in: *Lesson 3-14: Understand mixed cell references.*

   If this happens, just keep on pressing the <F4> key until you see the two dollar signs again.

   fx =G5*$H$1

	G	H	I
3	**Price (USD)**	**Price (GBP)**	**Country**
4	425,021	315,706	Italy
5	300,000	222,840	UK
6	350,000	259,980	Italy
7	350,000	259,980	Italy
8	304,995	226,550	UK
9	368,000	273,350	UK

Lesson 3-14: Understand mixed cell references

Before you tackle mixed cell references, I must warn you that this subject is a bit of a brain teaser (see sidebar). The skill is well worth mastering as you'll find it extremely useful in many types of real-world worksheets.

1 Open *International Price List* from your sample files folder.

This worksheet will calculate the price of each car in five different currencies. The exchange rates are shown in row 4.

The real-world exchange rates will have changed by the time you read this book. If you would like more realism, you can obtain the current exchange rates from https://xe.com.

2 Add a formula to cell D6 that will calculate the UK price of a Lamborghini Aventador S.

Formulas were covered in: *Lesson 2-12: Create your own formulas.*

The correct formula is:

=C6*D4

You can see that the Lamborghini costs £315,897.

	C	D	E	F	G	H
3		GBP	EUR	JPY	CAD	CHF
4		0.74325	0.88435	115.302	1.27461	0.91824
5	USA $	UK £	Euros €	Japan ¥	Canada $	Switzerland fr.
6	425,021	315,897				

3 Consider what will happen if you AutoFill this formula.

AutoFill was covered in: *Lesson 2-15: Use AutoFill to adjust formulas.*

As the formula is AutoFilled downward, the number part of each formula is incremented like this:

	C	D
6	425021	=C6*D4
7	300000	=C7*D5
8	350000	=C8*D6

The reference to cell C6 is being correctly adjusted to point to the price of each car in the list. There is a problem with the reference to cell D4 as it should not be adjusted.

You may think that this problem is exactly the same as the one solved in: *Lesson 3-13: Understand absolute and relative cell references.*

Why not simply make D4 into an absolute reference? Like this:

	C	D
3		GBP
4		0.74325
5	USA $	UK £
6	425021	=C6*$D$4

note

Don't worry if you're unable to understand this concept at first

In my "Essential Skills" classroom courses I've found that many students find mixed cell references a very difficult concept to understand.

I never waste a lot of time on this lesson if some students are unable to easily follow the logic.

I'd advise that you take the same approach and don't waste a lot of time on this lesson if you find it difficult to follow.

You won't need to use mixed cell references anywhere else in the *Essential Skills* course and it's a skill that most office workers don't have.

If you do skip this lesson, it's well worth returning to it later, when you've completed the course and have been using Excel for a few months.

By then you will probably have encountered some of the real-world business problems that are more efficiently solved using mixed cell references.

International Price List

This will work just fine for the GBP prices, but think carefully about what will then happen when you AutoFill to the right.

AutoFill knows that when you fill right you ***usually*** want the letter part of each formula incremented like this:

	C	D	E
3		GBP	EUR
4		0.74325	0.88435
5	USA $	UK £	Euros €
6	425021	=C6*$D$4	=D6*$D$4
7	300000	=C7*$D$4	
8	350000	=C8*$D$4	

This will not correctly calculate the Euro price. AutoFill has made two errors:

1. It is still using the GBP exchange rate for the EUR prices because you made D4 an absolute reference.
2. It is referencing the UK price of the Lamborghini instead of the US dollar price because C6 is a relative reference.

Here is how each problem can be solved using mixed cell references:

1. You want the GBP exchange rate to adjust to the EUR exchange rate as the formula is filled to the right. In this case the D part of D4 should be relative but the 4 part should be absolute. This can be denoted by D$4 instead of $D$4.
2. You want the US Dollar price to always be adjusted using the US Dollar Exchange rates in row 4. Therefore, you want the C part of C6 to be absolute. As AutoFill fills downward you need the price to be adjusted to the relevant car so the 6 part of C6 needs to be relative. This can be denoted by $C6 instead of $C$6.

tip

A faster way to add dollar signs to create mixed references

1. Click on the formula bar so that the cursor is touching the cell reference you want to convert to mixed:

   fx =C6*D4

2. Press the **<F4>** key repeatedly on the keyboard.

   Each time you press **<F4>** Excel cycles through all possible absolute and mixed references:

   fx =$C$6*D4

   fx =C$6*D4

   fx =$C6*D4

4 Correct the formula so that it will AutoFill correctly.

Enter the formula **=$C6*D$4** into cell D6.

This will AutoFill correctly like this:

	C	D	E	F
3		GBP	EUR	JPY
4		0.74325	0.88435	115.302
5	USA $	UK £	Euros €	Japan ¥
6	425021	=$C6*D$4	=$C6*E$4	=$C6*F$4
7	300000	=$C7*D$4	=$C7*E$4	=$C7*F$4
8	350000	=$C8*D$4	=$C8*E$4	=$C8*F$4

5 AutoFill across to cell H6.

The correct Lamborghini prices are shown in five currencies.

6 Select cells D6:H6 and AutoFill down to cell H17.

The correct prices are shown for all cars and all currencies.

7 Make the columns wide enough to display the prices.

8 Save your work as *International Price List-1.*

Lesson 3-15: Understand templates and set the default custom template folder

A template is simply a partially completed, normal workbook that contains the starting point for a task that you often need to do. You can put anything into a template that you can put into a regular workbook.

What are sample templates?

A sample template is a template that was created by Microsoft or another third-party. Sample templates aim to give you a starting point to solve common problems with Excel.

Several sample templates are shown on the *New* dialog (the dialog that you see when you first start Excel and click the *New* button), such as a *Household monthly budget* and *Weekly chore schedule.*

There are many thousands more sample templates available online.

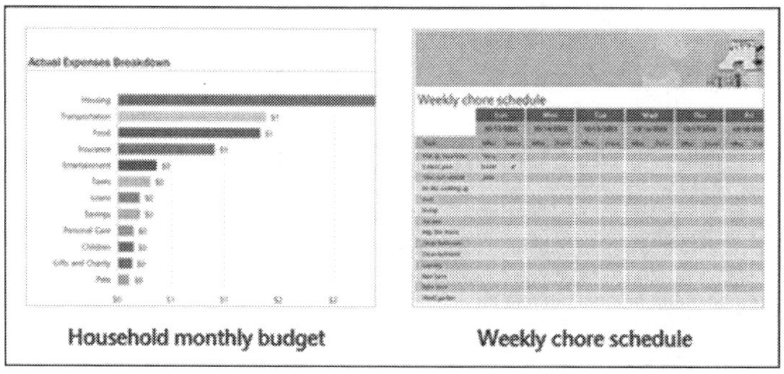

Household monthly budget   Weekly chore schedule

It may seem, at first, as if sample templates are a replacement for having to learn Excel but they are not quite as useful as they first promise to be.

There are three potential problems in using them:

1. Sample templates often appear to provide a solution that is *almost* what you need. You may find that the work involved in converting them to *exactly* what you need takes longer than starting with a blank worksheet.
2. Some templates include very advanced Excel features that non-expert users will find difficult to understand.
3. Some templates include VBA (Visual Basic for Applications) custom program code to extend Excel's normal features. It can be impossible to maintain or customize workbooks containing program code unless you have access to a competent VBA programmer (see sidebar).

What is a custom template?

A custom template is a template that you have created yourself. Because you completely understand how custom templates work, you may find them far more useful than sample templates.

note

Templates and cloud computing

Until you've completed: *Session Eight: Cloud Computing*, you may not completely understand this sidebar as you'd be getting a little ahead of yourself.

In: *Session Eight: Cloud Computing*, you'll learn how you can store your files on a OneDrive so that you can work on the same files from any device (computer, smartphone or pad), at any location.

This way of working is called *Cloud Computing.*

If you do decide to move your files to the cloud, you'll also want your custom templates to reside in the cloud so that they are available on all your devices.

In this case you'd set the default custom template folder to a location in your local synchronized OneDrive folder.

note

VBA code and Excel

If you search the Internet looking for a solution to an Excel problem, it won't be long before you'll find a well-intentioned user suggesting the use of VBA program code.

Most of the problems that users imagine require custom VBA code can be better (and more easily) solved by the correct use of Excel features you've learned about in this book (or will learn about in the *Expert Skills* book in this series).

My advice is to avoid VBA code in your projects. When Excel is being used for its intended purpose (as an analytical tool) there are very few real-world business problems that truly need custom VBA code.

note

How do I create a subfolder?

The concept of folders, subfolders and files is a fundamental Windows skill rather than an Excel skill.

If you do not have basic Windows skills (an understanding of how Windows organizes files) you would get good value from a Windows book to give you the foundation skills you need to use any Windows program.

Here's how you create a new subfolder in Windows 11:

1. Open the *Custom Office Templates* folder.

2. Right-click in a blank area of the screen and then Click: New→Folder from the shortcut menu.

A new folder will appear called *New Folder.*

3. You will now be able to type: **Excel** in order to name the folder.

If this doesn't work for you, right-click the new folder and click the *Rename* icon at the top of the dialog.

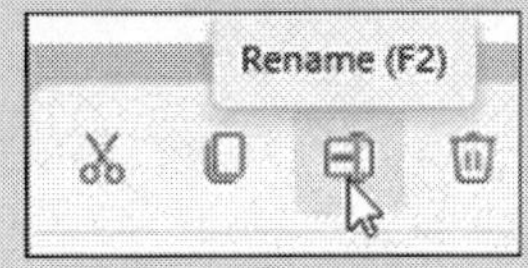

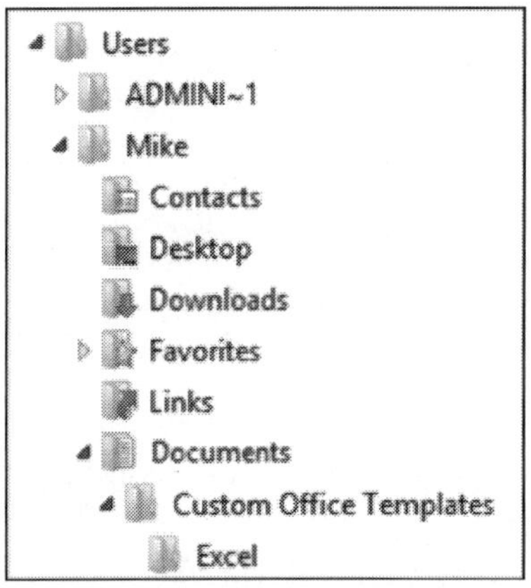

You'll often find yourself making copies of older workbooks that are nearly the same as the one you need. You then edit the workbook by deleting the parts you don't need and adding the parts that you do.

If you find this happening, it's time to make a custom template. You'll learn how to make your first custom template later, in*: Lesson 3-16: Create a template.*

What is the custom template folder?

The custom template folder is where custom templates are stored on your computer. By default, all templates, for all Office applications (such as Excel, Word and PowerPoint), are stored in the same folder. This isn't a great idea as you may create a large number of templates and they will be easier to work with if you organize them. For this reason, it is possible to set a different default custom template location for each Office application.

You're going to organize your templates properly, so you need a folder that will contain only *Excel* custom templates. If you work with Word and PowerPoint, you can use the same technique to create different folders for Word and PowerPoint custom templates.

1 Create a *Custom Office Templates* folder with an *Excel* folder beneath it.

   1. Use *Windows File Explorer* to navigate to the folder:

      C:\Users\[Your Windows Log-in Name]\Documents

   2. Create a sub-folder beneath the *Documents* folder named *Custom Office Templates.* This folder may already exist if custom templates have been created in the past on your computer.

   3. Create a sub-folder beneath the *Custom Office Templates* folder named *Excel.*

      Your folder will look similar to the one shown in the sidebar.

2 Open a new blank workbook.

When you open a blank workbook, you are actually creating a workbook using the *Blank workbook* standard template.

3 Set the default *Custom Office Templates* folder so that it points to the new Excel folder you have just created.

Click: File→Options→Save.

In the *Save Workbooks* section, you'll probably see that the current *Default personal templates folder* is set to a value similar to:

(If the box is blank you may have to type this manually).

Click at the end of the location path and type: **Excel**

4 Click OK and close Excel.

Lesson 3-16: Create a template

1 Make sure that any Excel workbooks are closed and then re-open Excel.

You set a new default template folder in: *Lesson 3-15: Understand templates and set the default custom template folder.*

This new default template location will not come into effect until Excel is closed down and restarted.

2 Open *First Quarter Sales and Bonus* from your sample files folder.

	A	B	C	D	E
1	First quarter sales and bonus				
2					
3	**Sales**				
4					
5	**First Name**	**Last Name**	**Sales**	**Target**	**Over Target Sales**
6	Andrew	Fuller	7,639.30	5,000	2,639.30
7	Anne	Dodsworth	2,979.30	5,000	- 2,020.70
8	Janet	Leverling	29,658.60	5,000	24,658.60
9	Laura	Callahan	19,271.60	5,000	14,271.60
10	Margaret	Peacock	44,795.20	5,000	39,795.20
11	Michael	Suyama	4,109.80	5,000	- 890.20
12	Nancy	Davolio	15,330.10	5,000	10,330.10
13	Robert	King	21,461.60	5,000	16,461.60
14	Steven	Buchanan	2,634.40	5,000	- 2,365.60
15		Total:	**147,879.90**		
16					
17	**Bonus**				
18					
19	**First Name**	**Last Name**	**Salary**	**Bonus**	**Total**
20	Andrew	Fuller	2,500	131.97	2,631.97
21	Anne	Dodsworth	2,000	-	2,000.00
22	Janet	Leverling	2,600	1,232.93	3,832.93
23	Laura	Callahan	2,800	713.58	3,513.58
24	Margaret	Peacock	3,000	1,989.76	4,989.76
25	Michael	Suyama	1,800	-	1,800.00
26	Nancy	Davolio	4,500	516.51	5,016.51
27	Robert	King	2,000	823.08	2,823.08
28	Steven	Buchanan	3,000	-	3,000.00
29		Total:	**24,200**	**5,407.82**	**29,607.82**

This is exactly the type of workbook you'd probably want to convert into a template. Only the data in cells C6:D14 will change each quarter.

Every quarter you could simply open last quarter's workbook, save it with a new name and then delete the old values in cells C6:D14. But you'd have to do that every quarter and then, one day, you might forget the *save it with a new name* step and end up overwriting the old file.

A more efficient solution would be to save a copy of the workbook, with blank values in cells C6:D14, as a template.

First Quarter Sales and Bonus

3 Delete the contents of cells *C6:D14.*

This is the data that changes every quarter. Deleting it will provide an empty template, ready to be populated with each quarter's *Sales* and *Target* figures.

4 Replace the text in cell A1 with the words: **Bonus Calculator**

This is a more generic title that can be used for any quarter.

5 Save your work as: *Bonus Calculator.*

6 Save the workbook again, this time as a template.

1. Click: File→Save As→Browse. 

2. Click the drop-down list arrow labeled *Save as type* at the bottom of the *Save As* dialog.

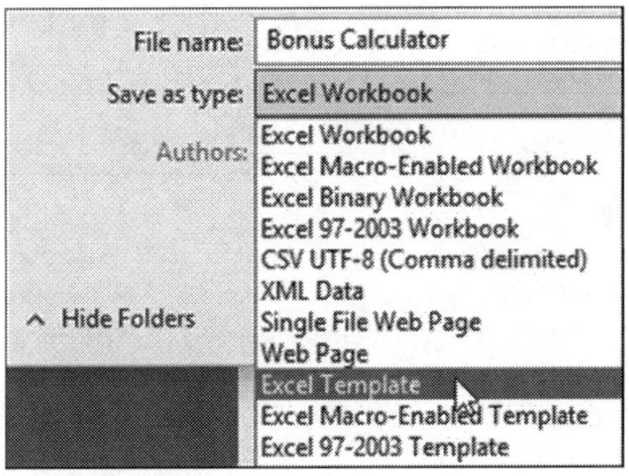

3. The best choice for this workbook is: *Excel Template.*

If this template needed to be used by users with very old versions of Excel, you'd choose *Excel 97-2003* template.

If the workbook contained macros (working with macros is an Expert level skill covered fully in the *Expert Skills* book in this series) you'd need to choose *Excel Macro-Enabled Template.*

4. Click the *Save* button to save the template to the default template folder that you created in: *Lesson 3-15: Understand templates and set the default custom template folder.*

The existing name: *Bonus Calculator* is fine.

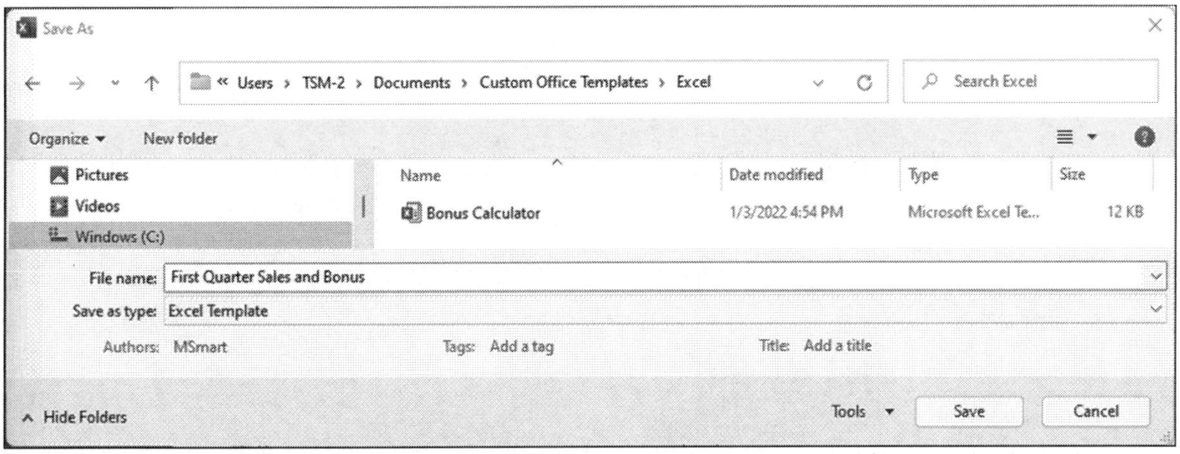

7 Close Excel.

Lesson 3-17: Use a template

1 Open Excel.

2 Click the *New* button on the left-hand menu bar.

3 Display your own custom templates.

Notice that there are two links in the center of the dialog labelled *Office* and *Personal*. The *Personal* templates are your own custom templates.

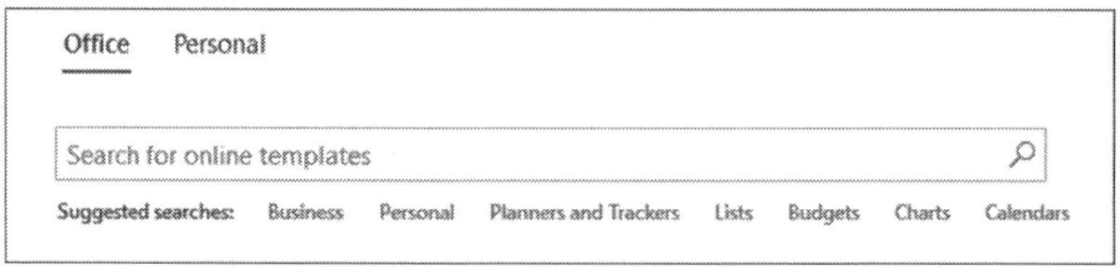

Click the *Personal* link

A dialog appears showing all of the templates in your custom templates folder:

At the moment, the only custom template is the *Bonus Calculator* template that you saved in: *Lesson 3-16: Create a template.*

4 Click the *Bonus Calculator* template.

A new workbook is created from the template.

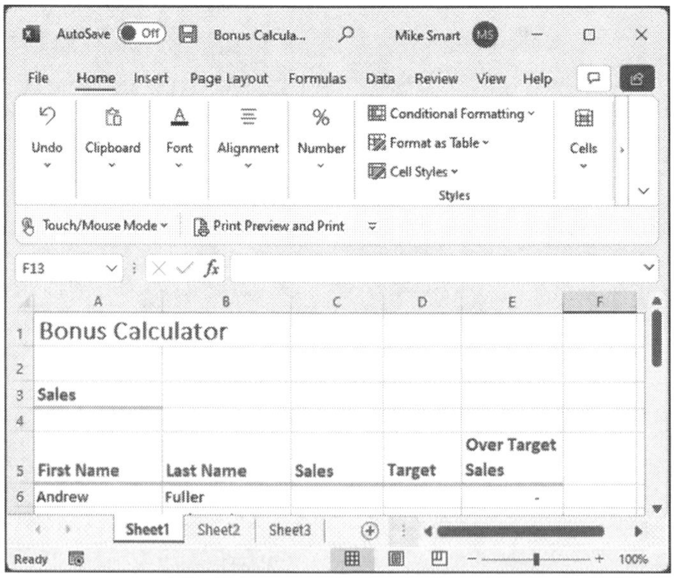

note

How to make your custom template appear at the top of the Office Templates list

Sometimes you may have a template that you use very often.

You may find it tedious to have to click:

File→New→Personal

... every time that you need to use it.

To save time you can *pin* the template. This means that it will appear at the top of the *Office Templates* list.

The template will then be easy to find, and you'll also save a click every time you create a new worksheet based upon it.

To pin a template, click the pin icon at the bottom-right of the template icon:

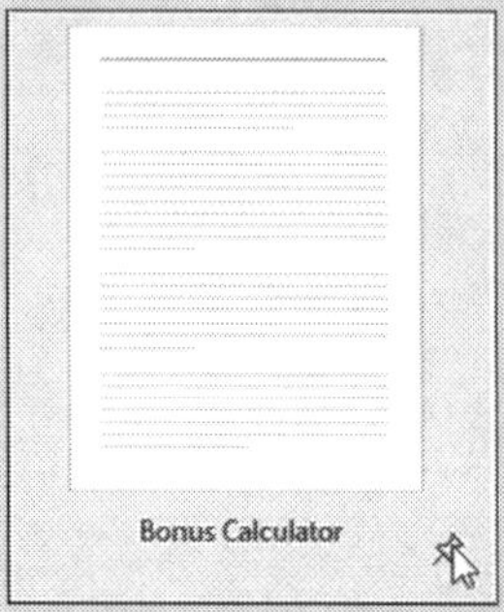

The template will then appear at the top of the *Office Templates* list.

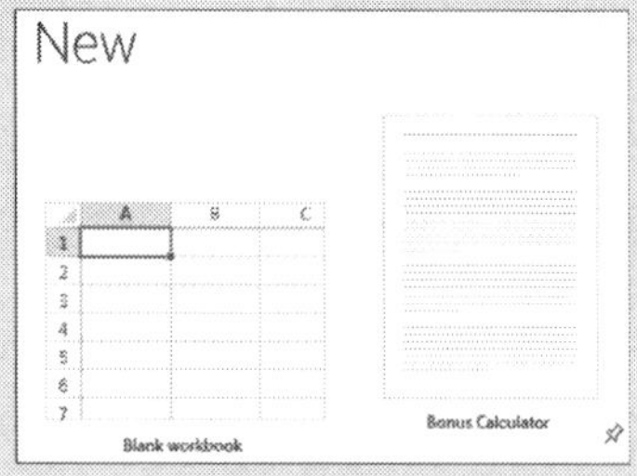

Notice that the workbook has been named *Bonus Calculator1*. You are not looking at the template, but a new workbook created from the template.

5 Use a sample template.

A set of Microsoft sample templates are included with every copy of Excel.

1. Click: File→New.

   The start-up screen is displayed showing a number of sample Excel templates.

2. Click one of Microsoft's sample templates.
3. Click the *Create* button if necessary (for some templates the workbook may be created without any interim dialog).

   A workbook is created from the template.

   Some of Microsoft's sample templates may seem a little overwhelming at the moment but they'll seem far less intimidating by the time you reach the end of this book.

6 Create a workbook from Microsoft's library of online templates.

You'll need to be connected to the Internet to use an online template.

Microsoft have a huge library containing thousands of templates that they add to all the time and make available to you for free.

1. Click: File→New.
2. Type: **Calendar** in the *Search for online templates* box at the top of the screen.
3. Press the **<Enter>** key.

   After a few moments, a huge scrolling list of calendars appears on the screen.

4. Click on any of the calendar templates.
5. Click the *Create* button.

   A workbook (containing a nicely formatted calendar) is created from the template.

note

Don't worry if you can't understand how some of the templates have been constructed

Don't worry if you can't understand how some of the calendar templates work yet.

Many have been constructed using very advanced techniques and some have even had features added using VBA (Visual Basic for Applications) programming code to extend Excel's normal feature set.

For the above reasons, you may find that sample templates are not useful for real-world projects when you need to thoroughly understand how they have been constructed.

Lesson 3-18: Understand Office Add-ins

For many years Excel has supported add-ins. Add-ins allow programmers to create new components that you can add to a workbook. These components can add functionality that isn't present in the standard Excel product.

Excel 2021 supports three types of add-in:

- **Traditional add-ins**: These are installed on your local hard drive and add new functionality to Excel. The *Expert Skills* book in this series comprehensively covers this type of add-in.
- **Task Pane add-ins**. You'll add a Task Pane add-in to a worksheet later, in: *Lesson 3-19: Add an Office Add-In to a workbook.*
- **Content add-ins.** Content add-ins float within the Excel grid (in a similar way to charts, which you will learn about later, in: *Session Five: Charts and Graphics).*

Task Pane add-ins and *Content add-ins* are collectively referred to as *Office add-ins. Office add-ins* can only be accessed from the Microsoft Store (though many are free of charge).

Office add-ins do not require any installation as they are usually hosted on a remote web site (though it is also possible for an IT department to host them on a local network). This means that you normally require an Internet connection in order to use an Office add-in. If you are disconnected from the Internet, the add-in may stop working.

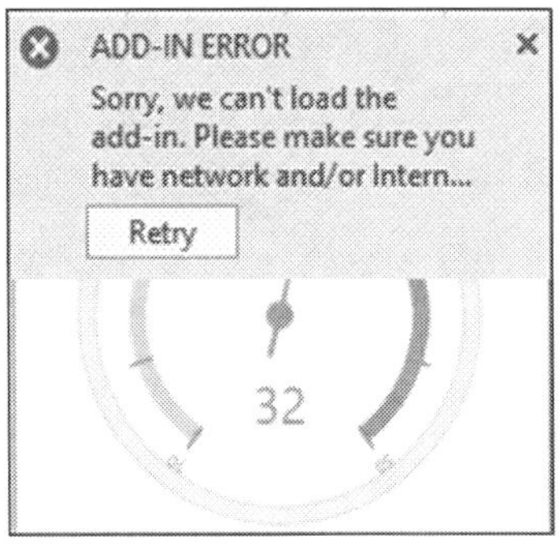

Task Pane add-ins

You are already familiar with the *Clipboard* task pane that you used in: *Lesson 3-7: Use the Multiple Item Clipboard.*

A good example of a task pane add-in is the *Wikipedia* add-in (free at time of writing in Jan 2022). The Wikipedia add-in provides a task pane that can be used to research any subject via the Wikipedia application on the Internet and then enables you to copy and paste data from any Wikipedia article into a worksheet.

In this example, I have used the Wikipedia add-in to research *Record-breaking production vehicles* over the years. I've then copied and pasted the table from the task pane onto my worksheet for further analysis:

note

What are Office add-ins useful for?

Three add-in categories seem to be the most useful:

New Chart types

As you'll discover in: *Session Five: Charts and Graphics,* Excel already has a huge range of chart types. If the built-in chart types do not address a specific business need, it is now possible to pay a programmer to create any chart type that can be described as an *Excel Content add-in.*

The *People Graph* content add-in shown in the lesson is a good example of this.

Interfacing with real-time data

Many users will need to interface with current real-time data (data that is constantly changing). Examples would include exchange rates or share and commodity prices.

There are many add-ins available to provide current currency exchange rates and stock prices.

Interfacing with databases

One of my favourite free content add-ins is the *Bing Maps content add-in.*

This allows you to reference place names (for example *London* or *New York*) and associated data (for example the population of each city) in a worksheet range.

The location is then found in the Bing maps database and displayed as a map embedded within the worksheet. Hotspots on the map can then be clicked to display the associated data.

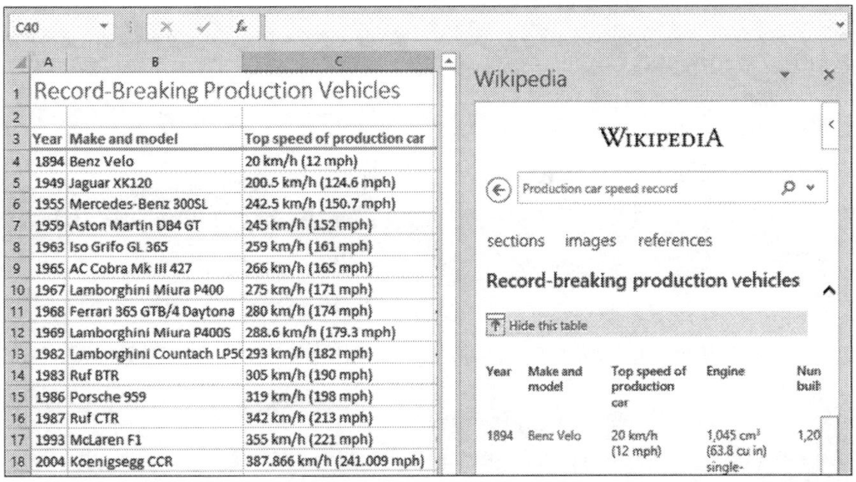

You'll learn how to add a *Task Pane add-in* to a workbook later, in: *Lesson 3-19: Add an Office Add-In to a workbook.*

Content Add-Ins

Content add-ins float within the Excel grid (in a similar way to charts, which you will learn about later, in: *Session Five: Charts and Graphics*).

Content add-ins are useful for adding components to a worksheet. A good example of a content add-in is the *People Graph* add-in. This allows a value to be graphically represented as a row of people icons:

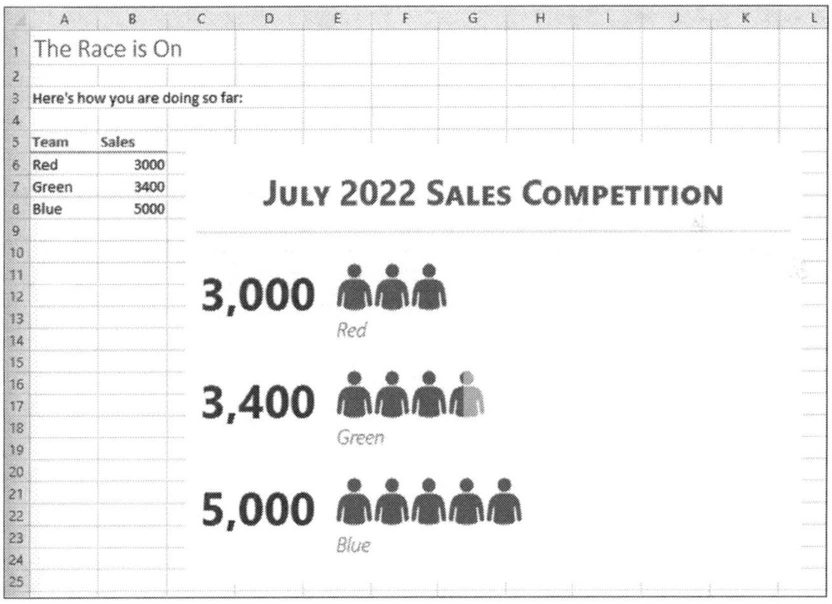

Excel does not provide a ready-to-use People graph type. The above worksheet was created by adding a *People Graph* content add-in to a worksheet.

important

The Internet is constantly changing

After you click:

Insert→Add-ins→Get Add-ins

... you are viewing web pages delivered from Microsoft's web servers.

This allows Microsoft to change their content constantly if they wish to.

It is likely that Microsoft's web store pages will have changed since this book was written.

It is also possible that the *Merriam Webster dictionary* application will have ceased to exist, or will no longer be free, by the time you read this book.

In either case, this lesson should give you enough information to figure out how to navigate Microsoft's site and install a similar add-in.

Lesson 3-19: Add an Office Add-In to a workbook

You will need to be connected to the Internet and logged in to a *Microsoft Account* in order to follow-through with this lesson (You'll learn more about Microsoft accounts in: *Session Eight: Cloud Computing*).

1 Open a new blank workbook.

2 Add the *Merriam Webster dictionary* add-in to the workbook.

1. Click: Insert→Add-ins→Get Add-ins.

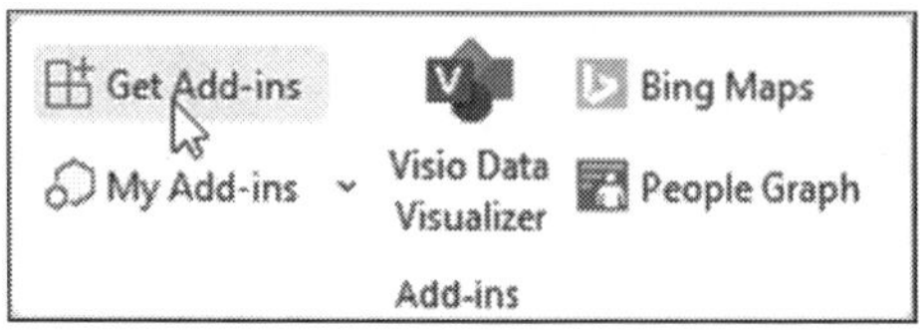

The *Office Add-ins* dialog appears displaying a list of available add-ins.

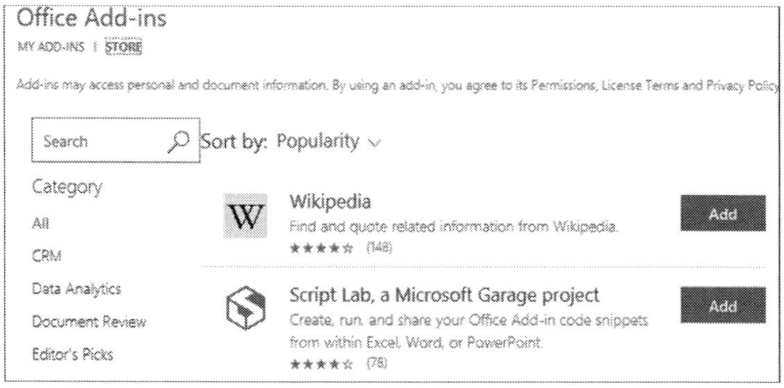

2. Type: **dictionary** into the search box and press the **<Enter>** key.

Several dictionary add-ins are displayed:

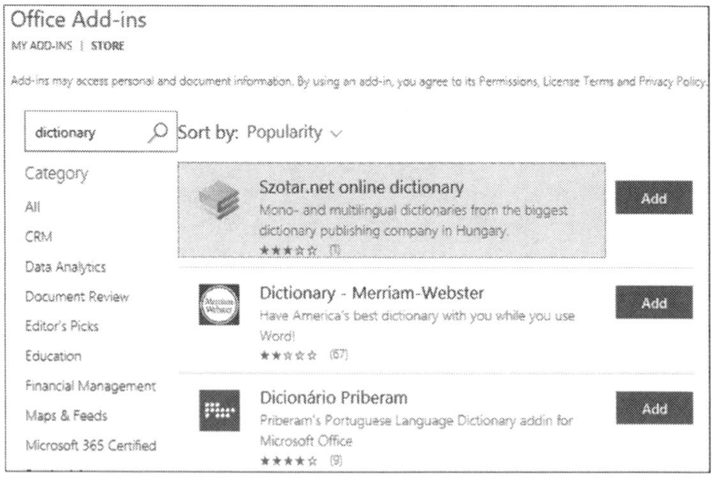

Note that, because this is an online facility, you'll probably see a different list on your screen (see sidebar). The above screen-grab was taken in Jan 2022.

3. Click the *Add* button next to the *Dictionary-Merriam-Webster* add-in (or another free dictionary add-in if this is no longer available).

4. Click the *Continue* button if asked to.

   The *Merriam-Webster Dictionary* task pane appears on the right of your screen.

3 Use the Merriam-Webster Dictionary to research the meaning of the word: **Computer**.

1. Type the word: **Computer** into the search box.
2. Press the **<Enter>** key.

   The dictionary displays its definition:

Lesson 3-20: Freeze columns and rows

1 Open *Sales First Quarter 2022* from your sample files folder.

Notice that it is easy to see which data is in each column when you are at the top of the worksheet and can see the top row:

	A	B	C	D
1	Date	First Name	Last Name	Company Name
2	1-Jan-22	Nancy	Davolio	Eastern Connection
3	1-Jan-22	Nancy	Davolio	Eastern Connection
4	1-Jan-22	Nancy	Davolio	Eastern Connection

But things get confusing when you scroll further down the list:

	A	B	C	D
128	17-Feb-22	Margaret	Peacock	Rancho grande
129	17-Feb-22	Margaret	Peacock	Rancho grande
130	18-Feb-22	Janet	Leverling	Blondel père et fils

It is no longer clear what information is contained in each column because the top row has disappeared.

2 Press **<Ctrl>+<Home>** to quickly move to cell A1.

3 Click: View→Window→Freeze Panes.

A rich menu is displayed:

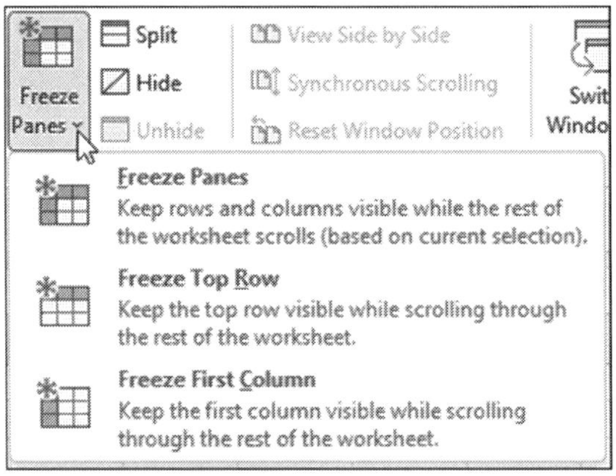

With Excel's rich menus, the meaning of each option is quite clear.

4 Click the *Freeze Top Row* menu item.

A small black line appears beneath the first row.

5 Scroll down the list.

Notice that as you scroll down, the top row now remains in place.

	A	B	C	D
1	Date	First Name	Last Name	Company Name
47	16-Jan-22	Margaret	Peacock	Simons bistro
48	16-Jan-22	Margaret	Peacock	Simons bistro
49	16-Jan-22	Margaret	Peacock	Simons bistro

6 Unfreeze the top row.

note

Another way to freeze the top row would be to convert the range into a table.

Excel automatically freezes column headers in tables.

Working with tables is an Expert level skill covered fully in the *Expert Skills* book in this series.

Sales First Quarter 2022

Click: View→Window→Freeze Panes once more.

The first choice has now changed to *Unfreeze Panes*. Click this menu item to put things back to normal.

7 Freeze the first column.

Do exactly as you did before but this time select *Freeze First Column* from the rich menu.

Notice that the date column is now locked into place. As you scroll to the right, the date remains in the first column.

	A	F	G	H
1	Date	Country	Product Name	Quantity
2	1-Jan-22	UK	Thüringer Rostbratwurst	21
3	1-Jan-22	UK	Steeleye Stout	35

8 Unfreeze the panes.

9 Freeze the first two rows and the left most three columns.

While a simple freezing of the top row or first column will usually be all you need, you may sometimes want to freeze both columns *and* rows.

You may also want to freeze more than one column and/or row.

1. Click in cell D3 to make it the active cell.

   This is your way of telling Excel that you want to freeze all cells above, and to the left of, cell D3.

2. Click: View→Window→Freeze Panes again but, this time, select the first option from the rich menu: *Freeze Panes*.

3. The first two rows and first three columns are frozen.

	A	B	C	F	G
1	Date	First Name	Last Name	Country	Product Name
2	1-Jan-22	Nancy	Davolio	UK	Thüringer Rostbratwurst
18	7-Jan-22	Robert	King	Brazil	Sir Rodney's Scones
19	7-Jan-22	Robert	King	Brazil	Rössle Sauerkraut
20	7-Jan-22	Robert	King	Brazil	Inlagd Sill
21	7-Jan-22	Robert	King	Brazil	Boston Crab Meat

10 Unfreeze the panes.

Lesson 3-21: Split the window into multiple panes

1 Open *Sales First Quarter 2022* from your sample files folder (if it isn't already open).

2 Press **<Ctrl>+<End>** to quickly move to the end of the worksheet (cell J242).

This is quite a long list. Imagine that you need to compare sales for 4th February 2022 to sales for 4th March 2022.

This could involve a lot of scrolling unless you split the window into two panes.

3 Split the window into two horizontal panes.

1. Click in a cell in column A that is positioned around halfway down the screen.

   As you'll see later in this lesson, the active cell determines whether the window will be split horizontally, vertically, or both horizontally and vertically.

   For a horizontal split, the active cell needs to be a cell within column A.

   The position of the active cell also determines where the screen will be split. By positioning it halfway down the screen you will split the screen into two equally sized panes.

2. Click: View→Window→Split.

   The screen is split into two independently scrolling horizontal panes.

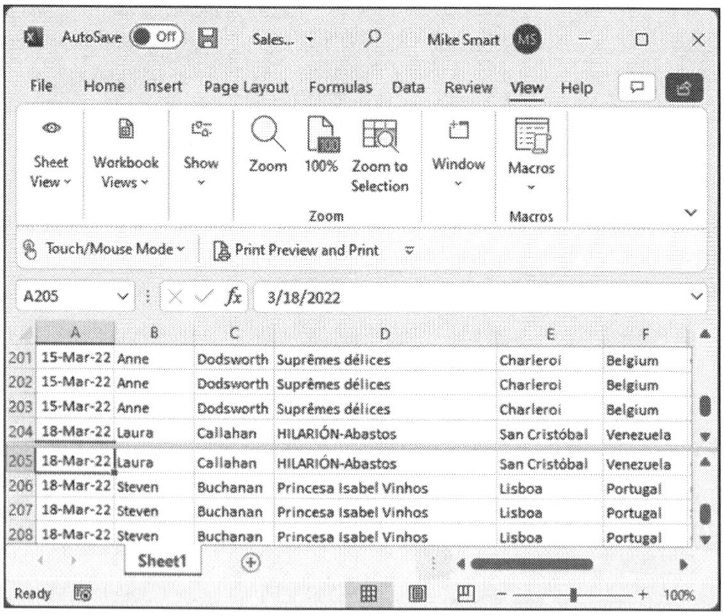

4 Scroll the lower pane so that the first sale on 4th March 2022 is shown on the first line.

Sales First Quarter 2022

5 Scroll the upper pane so that the first sale on 4th February 2022 is shown on the first line.

You will first need to click in the upper pane to make it the active pane.

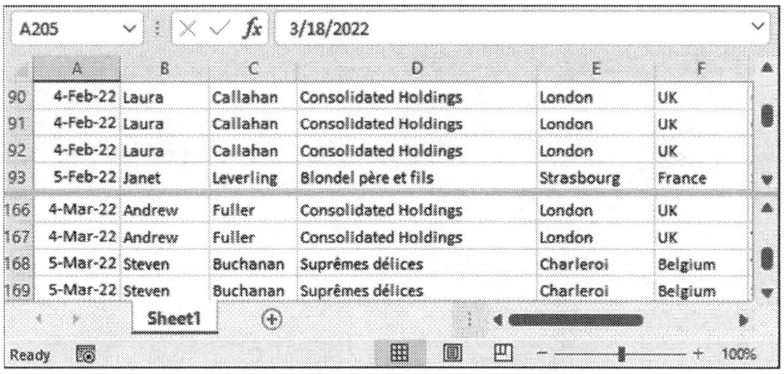

	A	B	C	D	E	F
90	4-Feb-22	Laura	Callahan	Consolidated Holdings	London	UK
91	4-Feb-22	Laura	Callahan	Consolidated Holdings	London	UK
92	4-Feb-22	Laura	Callahan	Consolidated Holdings	London	UK
93	5-Feb-22	Janet	Leverling	Blondel père et fils	Strasbourg	France
166	4-Mar-22	Andrew	Fuller	Consolidated Holdings	London	UK
167	4-Mar-22	Andrew	Fuller	Consolidated Holdings	London	UK
168	5-Mar-22	Steven	Buchanan	Suprêmes délices	Charleroi	Belgium
169	5-Mar-22	Steven	Buchanan	Suprêmes délices	Charleroi	Belgium

6 Remove the split window view.

Click: View→Window→Split.

<u>**OR**</u>

Position the mouse cursor over the split bar and double-click.

7 Split the window into two vertical panes.

1. Click in cell D1.

   If the active cell is in row 1, the screen will be split into two *vertical* panes.

2. Click: View→Window→Split.

   The window is split into two vertical panes

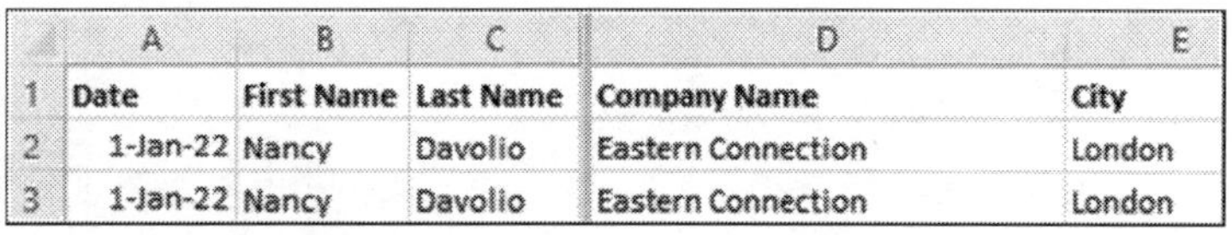

	A	B	C	D	E
1	Date	First Name	Last Name	Company Name	City
2	1-Jan-22	Nancy	Davolio	Eastern Connection	London
3	1-Jan-22	Nancy	Davolio	Eastern Connection	London

8 Move the split bar so that the left pane shows columns A to E.

Click and drag the split bar to its new location:

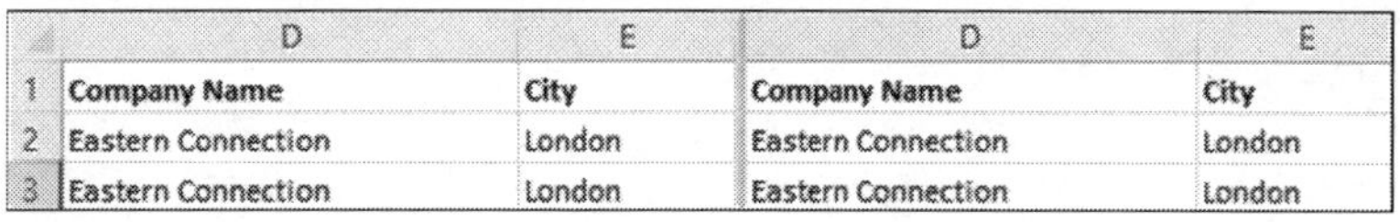

	D	E	D	E
1	Company Name	City	Company Name	City
2	Eastern Connection	London	Eastern Connection	London
3	Eastern Connection	London	Eastern Connection	London

9 Remove the split window view.

10 Split the window into four panes.

If the active cell is not in row 1 or column A, the screen will split into four panes at the cursor position.

1. Click in a cell towards the center of the screen

2. Click: View→Window→Split.

   The screen is split into four windows.

11 Remove the split window view.

Lesson 3-22: Check spelling

anecdote

Fun with dictionaries

I used to tell my students that the Australian English dictionary included such words as G'day, which I thought was a joke.

One day, one of my students checked it out in a coffee break and it's actually true.

Excel shares the same powerful spell checker that is included with Word and other Office applications.

Most European companies have a corporate standard for their spelling, often American English or British English. Excel also includes standard support for eighteen different dialects of English as well as other languages.

While most words are included in Excel's dictionary, you will often be warned that a correct spelling is misspelled. When this is the case, you can add the word to the dictionary so that Excel doesn't keep bothering you about it in the future.

1 Open *Empire Car Sales Stock List* from your sample files folder.

	F	G
5	Colour	Selling points
6	Black	Can accelarate faster than most sports cars.
7	Topaz Blue	One concientous owner from new.
8	Yellow	Acheives nearly 50 miles to the gallon.
9	Silver	Particulaly clean example of this executive coupe.
10	Blue	Reconised as one of the safest cars on the road.
11	Brown	A collector's car strictly for connisseurs.

The *Selling points* column contains many frequently incorrectly spelled words.

You may find it fun to try to identify the spelling errors before you set the Spell Checker loose on the job.

2 Check the spelling for the words in the range F5:G7.

If you select a range of cells before invoking the spell checker, only the selected range will be checked.

1. Select the range: F5:G7
2. Click: Review→Proofing→Spelling to start the spell checker.

   If all of the words are spelled correctly the spell checker does not display. In this case there are errors, so the *Spelling* dialog is displayed.

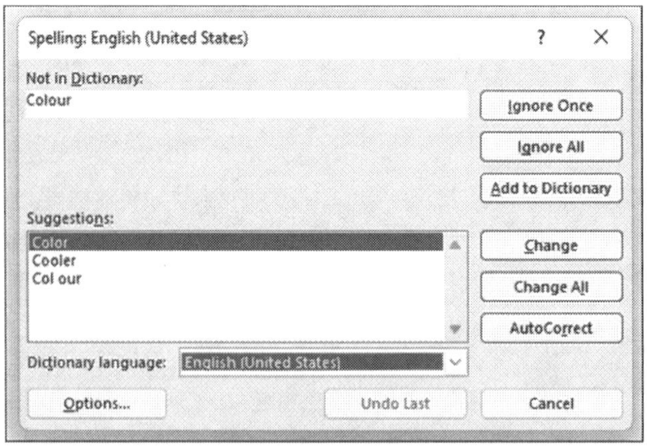

note

Another way to start the spell checker

Press the <F7> key.

Empire Car Sales Stock List

In the example above note that the *Dictionary language* was set to English (United States). The British spelling of the word *colour* does

note

Setting the default language

Click: File→Options→Proofing.

You are then able to set the Excel default dictionary language.

note

Dictionaries for other languages

The English version of Excel includes support for English, French and Spanish.

Microsoft also offer language packs for 35 other languages ranging from Chinese to Ukrainian.

not appear in the American English dictionary because, in America, it is spelled: *color*.

If your dictionary is set to English (United Kingdom) you will not see this error because *colour* is the correct UK English spelling.

See the sidebar if you want to change your dictionary to a different language.

3 Click *Change* to accept Excel's suggested correction.

4 Click *Change* twice more to accept Excel's suggestions for *accelerate* and *conscientious*.

The Spell checker exits and advises that the spell check is complete.

5 Click the OK button to dismiss the dialog.

6 Spell check the single word *Particulaly* in cell G9.

Sometimes you'll type a single word and be unsure that it is correctly spelled. You will want to be able to quickly check the single word.

1. Click cell G9 and then select the word: *Particulaly* in the formula bar at the top of the window.

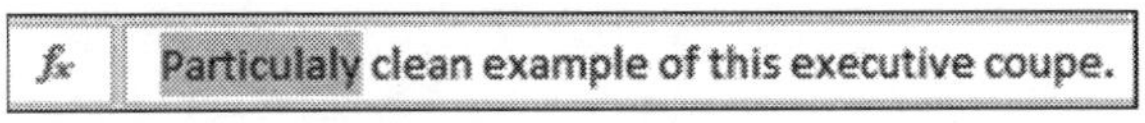

2. Click: Review→Proofing→Spelling to start the Spell Checker.
3. Click the *Change* button to accept the correct spelling.
4. Click the OK button to dismiss the dialog.

7 Spell check the entire worksheet.

1. Click in any cell on the worksheet. When you don't select a range, or a single word, the spell checker checks the entire worksheet.

   If you don't click cell A1, cells to the right and beneath the selected cell are checked first and then Excel asks: *Do you want to continue checking at the beginning of the sheet*?

2. Click: Review→Proofing→Spelling to start the Spell Checker.

8 Click: *Change* to accept each change until you are prompted for MiTo.

MiTo is a real word for a car (a model produced by Alfa Romeo between 2008 and 2018) but it isn't in the Excel dictionary. Perhaps Empire sells a lot of MiTos and don't want to be pulled up by the spell checker every time the word is used.

9 Add MiTo to the dictionary.

Click the *Add to Dictionary* button so that Excel will recognize the word: *MiTo* in the future.

When the spell check has ended, a dialog will display advising you that the spell check is complete. Click the OK button to dismiss the dialog.

10 Save your work as *Empire Car Sales Stock List-1*.

Session 3: Exercise

1 Open *The Best Selling Albums of All Time* from your sample files folder.

2 Insert one row above row 7, type *AC/DC* for the Artist and *Back in Black* for the Album.

3 Use AutoComplete to put the text *Hard Rock* into cell C7 and type *50* for copies sold (millions).

4 Delete rows 11 and 12 to remove the *Eagles* from the list.

5 Insert a formula in cell E6 to calculate how much revenue the album sales would have generated if sold at the Average Album Price shown in cell E3.

Don't forget that the reference to cell E3 will have to be an absolute reference.

6 AutoFill the formula to the end of the list to see the estimated revenue for the top five selling albums.

7 Use AutoSum to add a value for total copies sold and total revenue to cells D11 and E11.

8 Remove the decimal places displayed in cells E6:E11 so that the revenue is rounded to the nearest million.

9 Add a cell note to cell B6 saying "Thriller was Michael Jackson's sixth studio album and was produced with a budget of $750,000."

10 Save your work as *The Best Selling Albums of All Time-1.*

	A	B	C	D	E
1	Best Selling Albums of All Time				
2					US$
3				Average Album Price	14.99
4					
5	Artist	Album	Genre	Copies Sold (millions)	Revenue (Million USD)
6	Michael Jackson	Thriller	Pop/Funk	70	1049
7	AC/DC	Back in Black	Hard Rock	50	750
8	Whitney Houston	The Bodyguard	Pop/R&B	45	675
9	Meat Loaf	Bat Out of Hell	Hard Rock	44	660
10	Pink Floyd	Dark Side of the Moon	Progressive Rock	44	660
11		Total:		253	3792
12					
13					
14					
15					

The Best Selling Albums of All Time

Session 3 Exercise answers

These are the questions that students find the most difficult to answer:

Q 7	Q 5	Q 4	Q 2
1. Click in cell D11. 2. Click: Home→Editing→AutoSum 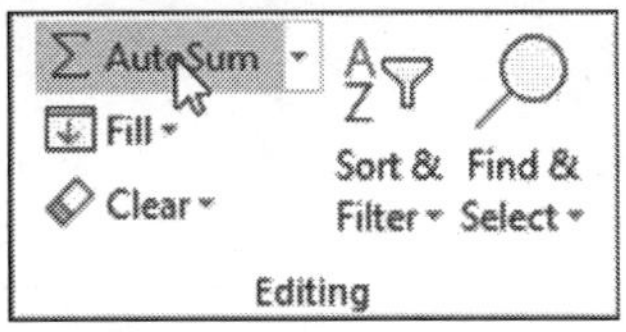 3. Either press the **<Enter>** key or click: Home→Editing→AutoSum one more time. 4. Repeat exactly the same steps in cell E11. This was covered in: *Lesson 2-3: Use AutoSum to quickly calculate totals.*	1. Type the following formula into cell E6: **=D6*$E$3** 2. Press the **<Enter>** key. This was covered in: *Lesson 3-13: Understand absolute and relative cell references.*	1. Click and drag across the row headers for rows 11 and 12 to select both rows. 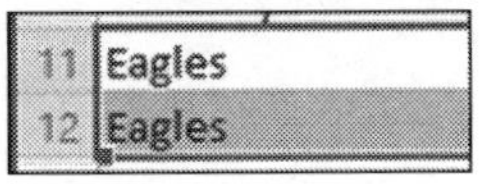 2. Right-click anywhere in the selected area. 3. Click *Delete* from the shortcut menu.  This was covered in: *Lesson 3-1: Insert and delete rows and columns.*	1. Right-click on the row header for row 7.  2. Click *Insert* from the shortcut menu.  This was covered in: *Lesson 3-1: Insert and delete rows and columns.*

If you have difficulty with the other questions, here are the lessons that cover the relevant skill:

1 **Refer to: Lesson 1-9: Open and navigate a workbook.**

3 **Refer to: Lesson 3-2: Use AutoComplete and fill data from adjacent cells.**

6 **Refer to: Lesson 2-15: Use AutoFill to adjust formulas.**

8 **Refer to: Lesson 3-5: Use Paste Values and increase/decrease decimal places displayed.**

9 **Refer to: Lesson 3-9: Insert cell notes.**

10 **Refer to: Lesson 1-10: Save a workbook.**

4

Session Four: Making Your Worksheets Look Professional

It is only shallow people who do not judge by appearances.

Oscar Wilde, writer, poet and playwright (1854 - 1900)

Never under-estimate the importance of presentation. In many areas of life, it is valued more than content. This session will enable you to make your worksheets get noticed.

By the end of this session your worksheets will be visually excellent.

Session Objectives

By the end of this session, you will be able to:

- Format dates
- Understand date serial numbers
- Format numbers using built-in number formats
- Create custom number formats
- Horizontally and vertically align the contents of cells
- Merge cells, wrap text and expand/collapse the formula bar
- Unmerge cells and Center Across Selection
- Understand themes
- Use cell styles and change themes
- Add color and gradient effects to cells
- Add borders and lines
- Create your own custom theme
- Create your own custom cell styles
- Use a master style book to merge styles
- Use simple conditional formatting
- Manage multiple conditional formats using the Rules Manager
- Bring data alive with visualizations
- Create a formula driven conditional format
- Insert a Sparkline into a range of cells
- Apply a common vertical axis and formatting to a Sparkline group
- Apply a date axis to a Sparkline group and format a single Sparkline
- Use the Format Painter
- Rotate text

Lesson 4-1: Format dates

You may notice that I've been very careful to use internationally safe date formats throughout this book.

A classic cause of errors when dealing with international worksheets is the use of a date such as the following:

10/03/2022

This means 3rd *October 2022* in some countries (such as the USA) but *10th March 2022* in others (such as the UK).

If your work may be viewed by an international audience, it is far better to use a date format that cannot possibly cause confusion.

In this lesson, you'll re-format a date into the compact and universally readable format of: *10-Mar-2022*.

1 Open *Sales Week Ended 14th March 2022* from your sample files folder.

Notice the hashes in the date column. This tells you that the column isn't wide enough to display the date.

	A	B	C	D
1	Invoice No	Date	Customer	Country
2	10918	##########	Bottom-Dol	Canada
3	10917	##########	Romero y tc	Spain
4	10926	##########	Ana Trujillo	Mexico

If you're used to calling the hash (#) a **pound sign** or **number sign,** see the sidebar in: *Lesson 2-9: Re-size rows and columns* for an explanation.

2 Auto-resize cells A1:G17 so that their contents are fully visible.

You learned how to do this in: *Lesson 2-9: Re-size rows and columns.*

3 Format the dates in column B so that they display in the format: *10-Mar-2022*

At present the dates are formatted in the *Long Date* format that is appropriate for your region (see sidebar). The screen grab below shows the *Long Date* format for the USA region with the day and month spelled out in full:

	A	B	C
1	Invoic	Date	Customer
2	10918	Thursday, March 10, 2022	Bottom-Dollar Markets
3	10917	Thursday, March 10, 2022	Romero y tomillo
4	10926	Thursday, March 10, 2022	Ana Trujillo Emparedad
5	10929	Friday, March 11, 2022	Frankenversand

You're going to re-format the dates to the more compact form: *10-Mar-2022.*

1. Select cells B2:B17.
2. Right-click anywhere in the selected range and choose *Format Cells…* from the shortcut menu.

   You can also do this from the Ribbon (see sidebar).

note

Why your dates may look different to those in the screen grabs

This book was written using the *English (United States) Region format* settings.

The *Region format* for *English (United States)* dates are:

Short Date

3/10/2022

Long Date

Thursday, March 10, 2022

If you are situated in a different country, your *Short Date* and *Long Date* Region formats may be in a different format that is more appropriate to your location.

While it is possible to change your Region format (in Windows settings) there is no need to do so to work through this book.

Just be aware that some of the screen grabs in this book will be formatted differently to what you see on your screen.

Sales Week Ended 14th March 2022

The *Format Cells* dialog appears.

3. Click the *Number* tab (if it isn't already selected) and then choose *Date* from the *Category* list box.

4. Set the *Locale (location)* to English (United States).

   If your Windows Region Format is not *English (United States)* you will see different data options in the *Type* list. By selecting the *Locale (location)* manually, you will see date formats that are common in the United States.

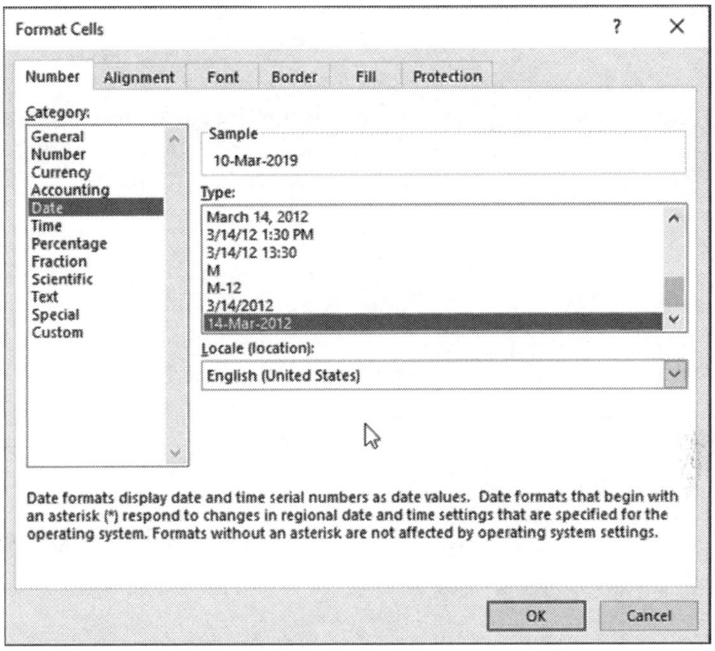

5. Click on one of the list entries in the *Type* list box and then use the **<UpArrow>** and **<DownArrow>** keys to move through the list.

   You can see that as you move through each format a preview is shown in the *Sample* box.

   When you reach the end of the list you should see *10-Mar-2022* in the sample box.

6. Click the OK button.

   The dates in the worksheet are all re-formatted:

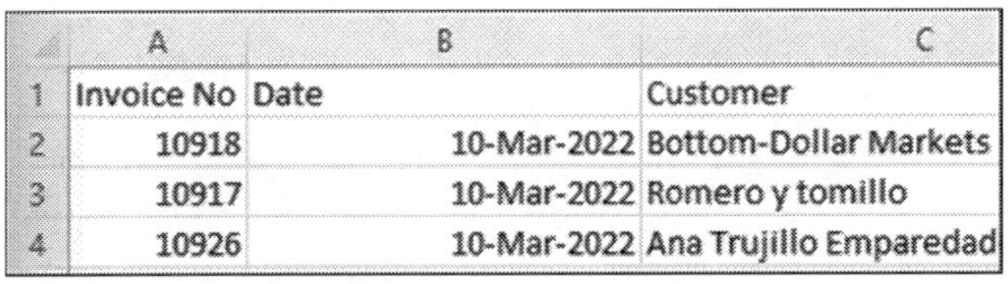

	A	B	C
1	Invoice No	Date	Customer
2	10918	10-Mar-2022	Bottom-Dollar Markets
3	10917	10-Mar-2022	Romero y tomillo
4	10926	10-Mar-2022	Ana Trujillo Emparedad

4 Save your work as *Sales Week Ended 14th March 2022-1.*

note

Launching the Format Cells dialog from the Ribbon

Click:

Home→Number→
Dialog Launcher

The dialog launcher is the small button on the bottom right of the *Number* group.

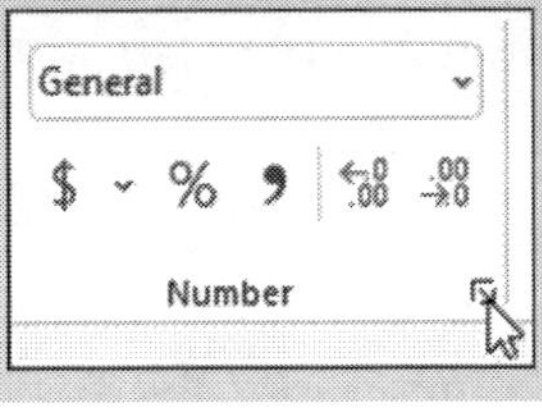

Lesson 4-2: Understand date serial numbers

Excel stores dates in a very clever way. Understanding Excel's date storage system empowers you to use date arithmetic. You can use date arithmetic to compute the difference between two dates (in days) or to shift date ranges by a given time interval.

How Excel stores dates

Dates are stored as simple numbers called *date serial numbers*. The serial number contains the number of days that have elapsed since 1st January 1900 (where 1st January 1900 is 1).

The world began in 1900

An interesting shortcoming of Excel is its inability to easily work with dates before 1900. Excel simply doesn't acknowledge that there were any dates before this time. If you work with older dates you will have to work-around this limitation.

In Excel every time is a date, and every date is a time

You've already realized that 5th January 1900 is stored as the number 5. What would the number 5.5 mean? It would mean midday on 5th January 1900.

It is possible to format a date to show only the date, only the time, or both a time and a date.

When you enter a time into a cell without a date, the time is stored as a number less than one. Excel regards this as having the non-existent date of: 00 January 1900.

When you enter a date into a cell without a time, the time is stored as midnight at the beginning of that day.

1. Create a new blank workbook and put the numbers 1 to 5 in cells A1:A5.

2. Type the formula **=A1** into cell B1 followed by the **<Enter>** key, and then AutoFill the formula to the end of the list.

   AutoFill was covered in: *Lesson 2-14: Use AutoFill for text and numeric series.*

	A	B
1	1	1
2	2	2
3	3	3
4	4	4
5	5	5

3. Apply a date format to column A that will show a four-digit year.

trivia

The Julian and Gregorian calendars

When you work with very old dates you can run into a problem with the Julian and Gregorian calendars.

In 1582 it was noticed that the seasons had drifted by 10 days because the Julian system (named after Julius Caesar who adopted it in 45 BC) had incorrectly miscalculated a year as being 365 ¼ days. A year is actually slightly shorter than this.

Pope Gregory XIII decreed that, in order to put things right, the world had to lose 10 days to make up for all of those extra leap years.

The reformed Gregorian calendar also adopted a new leap year rule to keep things on track in future years.

It took nearly 200 years for everybody to get on board with the Gregorian calendar. The Catholic countries of Spain, Italy and Portugal adopted it at once, but England and parts of America didn't convert until September 14th, 1752.

This means that in Spain the dates October 5th, 1582 to October 14th, 1582 never actually existed. In England it was the dates Sept 3rd, 1752 to September 14th,1752.

The strangest case of all was Sweden who decided to "phase it in gradually" between 1700 and 1740, meaning that their calendar was out of step with the rest of the world for 40 years.

If you work with historical data from this era you have to be very careful indeed.

trivia

The peculiar case of the Excel date bug and Lotus 1-2-3

Here's the Gregorian leap year rule defined by Pope Gregory XIII in 1582:

Every year that is exactly divisible by four is a leap year, except for years that are exactly divisible by 100; the centurial years that are exactly divisible by 400 are still leap years.

This means that the year 1900 wasn't a leap year but 2000 was (causing many millennium software bugs).

Lotus 1-2-3 was a spreadsheet product that was the market leader until Excel overtook it in the early 1990's.

The designers of Lotus 1-2-3 weren't paying enough attention to Pope Gregory's rules. Their DATE function thought that 1900 was a leap year and thus recognised the non-existent date: February 29th 1900.

Because Excel needed to be compatible with Lotus 1-2-3, Microsoft had to replicate the Lotus bug when they designed Excel.

Try entering **29 Feb 1900** into a worksheet and Excel will gladly accept it.

This bug has the effect of introducing a one-day error into any date arithmetic you may do that spans 29th February 1900.

	D
1	1/1/1900
2	1/1/2000
3	36525

This was covered in: *Lesson 4-1: Format dates.*

	A	B
1	1-Jan-1900	1
2	2-Jan-1900	2
3	3-Jan-1900	3
4	4-Jan-1900	4
5	5-Jan-1900	5

This reveals that the whole numbers 1 to 5 represent the dates January 1, 1900 to January 5, 1900.

4 Change the date format in column A again so that it shows both dates and times.

1. Select cells A1:A5.
2. Right-click in a selected cell and select *Format Cells…* from the shortcut menu.
3. Click: *Custom* in the *Category* list.
4. Click in the *Type* box and type the custom format:

   dd mmm yyyy hh:mm
5. Click the OK button (or press the **<Enter>** key).

   Notice that when a date serial number is a whole number, the time is set to midnight (12:00 AM) at the beginning of that day.

	A	B
1	01 Jan 1900 00:00	1
2	02 Jan 1900 00:00	2

5 Change the time in cell A2 to 12:00 PM.

Notice that the number in cell B2 has changed to 2.5 revealing that times are stored by Excel as the decimal part of the date serial number.

	A	B
1	01 Jan 1900 00:00	1
2	02 Jan 1900 12:00	2.5

6 Compute the number of days that occurred between 01/01/1900 and 01/01/2000.

Now that you have a good grasp of Excel's serial numbers, this task is easy.

1. Enter the two dates in cells D1 and D2, one beneath the other.
2. Click in cell D3 to make it the active cell.
3. Click: Home→Number→Comma Style.

   You'll learn more about the comma style later, in: *Lesson 4-3: Format numbers using built-in number formats.* You have told Excel to display a number in cell D3 instead of a date.
4. Subtract one date from the other by entering the formula: **=D2-D1** into cell D3 and press the **<Enter>** key.

   You can see that 36,525 days occurred during the twentieth century (actually 36,524 due to the Lotus bug – see sidebar).

7 Close the workbook without saving.

Lesson 4-3: Format numbers using built-in number formats

Formatting fundamentals

When you format a number, you never change its value. For example, if you format the number:

483.45495

... so that it only displays two decimal places, the number displays like this:

483.45

It is important to realize that the actual value in the cell remains at the old value of 483.45495. All you have done is to change the way in which the value is presented to the user.

1 Open *Sales Week Ended 14th March 2022-1* from your sample files folder.

2 Apply the comma style to column E.

There is an extremely useful quick format button called the *comma style*. This is perfect for formatting monetary values with a single click. The comma style places a comma after thousands and displays exactly two decimal places.

1. Select all of column E.
2. Click: Home→Number→Comma Style.

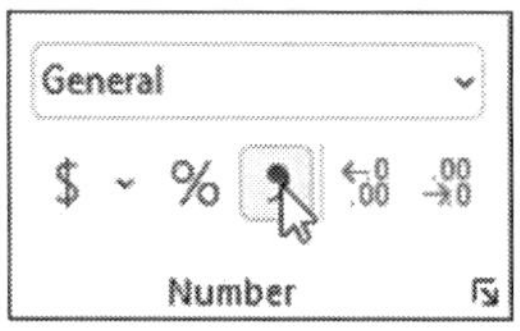

3. Widen column E if necessary, so that it is wide enough to display all of the cell contents.

All of the values in column E now display correctly.

	D	E	F	G
1	Country	Amount	Tax	Total
2	Canada	1,447.50	0.175	1700.8125
3	Spain	365.89	0.175	429.92075

Note that you can also use the *Accounting Number Format* style:

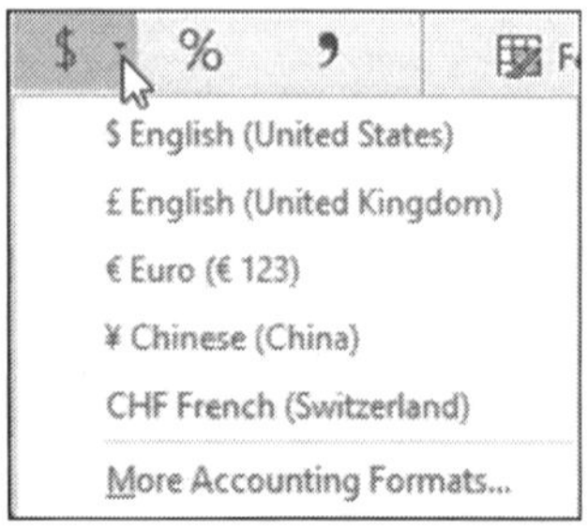

note

The Comma[0] and Currency[0] styles

I've noticed that some Excel users apply the comma style and then remove the decimal places as a quick way to add the thousand separators to whole numbers. This takes them three clicks (comma style|decrease decimal|decrease decimal).

You can save a click with the Comma[0] and Currency[0] styles.

To apply these styles, you'll need to display the *Cell Styles Gallery*.

If you have a very large screen some Cell Styles may already be displayed on the Ribbon.

With a smaller screen you'll have to click:

Click Home→Styles→Cell Styles.

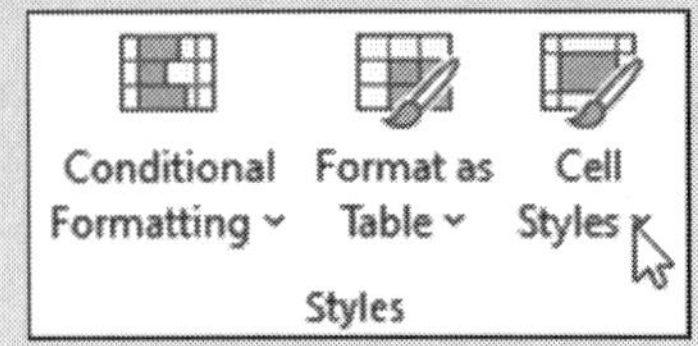

The Cell Styles Gallery is then displayed.

The Cell Styles gallery includes the *Comma[0]* and *Currency[0]* styles:

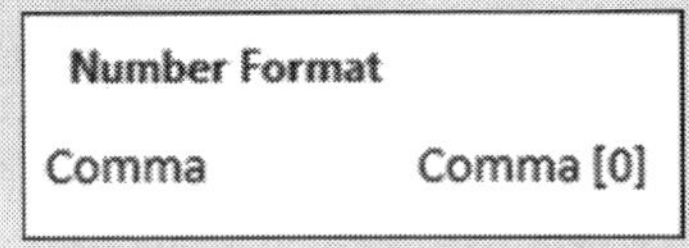

You'll be learning a lot more about cell styles later in this session.

Sales Week Ended 14th March 2022-1

note

Solutions to the "penny rounding" problem

Formatting a floating-point number to two decimal places often results in the *penny rounding problem* when you sum a column of numbers.

There are two solutions to the problem. One is a very good solution, but the other can cause problems.

Best practice

The best solution to the problem is to address it when the column is first calculated.

In this lesson's example worksheet, the formula used to calculate the value in cell G2 is:

=E2*(F2+1)

Excel has a ROUND function that can be used to round the result to two decimal places at the point of calculation.

The new formula would become:

=ROUND(E2*(F2+1),2)

Changing precision

Click:

File→Options→Advanced

In the *When calculating this workbook* group click the *Set precision as displayed* check box.

This alters the default behaviour of Excel so that each value in the worksheet is regarded as being precisely the same as its display value when performing calculations.

Using this option can cause data to become inaccurate as it is a global setting, affecting the entire worksheet (and any other worksheets you may open before turning it off).

Use this feature with extreme caution, or better still, don't use it at all.

This is very similar to the comma style but adds a leading currency symbol and an appropriate number of decimal places.

Try the *Accounting Number Format* style out to see how it works. I've found that the comma style is more appropriate for most of my work, as I'm usually working in one country and one currency, making the currency type obvious.

3 Apply the comma style to column G.

Column G has many decimal places in some cases, as the sales tax calculation results in as many as six decimal places.

Apply the comma style to column G and notice how all of the values are displayed rounded to the nearest two decimal places.

1380.33125 Becomes 1,380.33

879.82825 Becomes 879.83

It is a key concept to realize that the values in the cells have not changed. For example, if you add two cells containing the value 1.4, the result will be 1.4+1.4=2.8. If you then format the cells as whole numbers, you'll see that 1+1=3 as each number is rounded up or down.

See the sidebar for potential solutions to this problem.

4 Apply the percentage style to column F.

The example sales tax rate is 17.5%. When working with percentages, it is useful to enter them so that you can calculate a percentage simply by multiplying by the cell.

Instead of 17.5 (more readable) the values are entered as 0.175 (easier to use in formulas). In order to make percentages both readable and easy to use, Microsoft has created the percentage style. If you type 17.5% into a cell, the actual value within the cell will be 0.175.

1. Select column F.
2. Click: Home→Number→Percent Style.

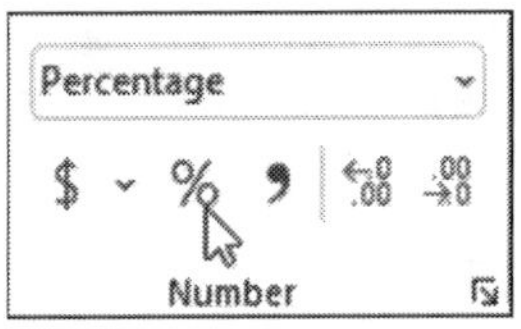

3. Click: Home→Number→Increase Decimal once, to make the values in column F display one decimal place.

	D	E	F	G
1	Country	Amount	Tax	Total
2	Canada	1,447.50	17.5%	1,700.81
3	Spain	365.89	17.5%	429.92

5 Save your work as *Sales Week Ended 14th March 2022-2.*

Lesson 4-4: Create custom number formats

The built-in number formats are very quick and convenient but are also quite limited. Fortunately, it is possible to create your own custom format when none of the built-in styles fit your requirement.

Overview of custom formats

There's plenty of documentation in the help system and on the Internet about the rather cryptic formatting codes provided by Excel. Just about everything is possible once you've got to grips with the basic concepts.

To communicate the custom format to Excel, you must construct a custom format string.

Zeros mean "Display significant zeros". You tell Excel how many you want within the format string. For example, 0.00 means *display at least one leading zero and two decimal places.* The following examples should make things clear:

Custom Format String	Value	Display
0	1234.56	1235
0.0	1234.56 1234.5 .5	1234.6 1234.5 0.5
0.00	1234.56 1234.5 .5	1234.56 1234.50 0.50
00.000	4.56	04.560
0.000	1234.56	1234.560

The hash symbol (#) is mainly used to add comma separators to thousands and millions.

Custom Format String	Value	Display
#	123.4500	123
#.##	123.45 123.50	123.45 123.5
#,#	1234.56	1,236
#,#.##	1234.56 1234.50 12341234.56	1,234.56 1,234.5 12,341,234.56

Because the hash symbol can be used in conjunction with zeros it is also possible to indicate that you want both thousand separators *and* a specific number of leading or trailing zeros.

note

Use the ? custom format string symbol to make number values line up

The question mark inserts a space (when needed) in order to make sure that values that do not display a fixed number of decimal places line up properly.

I must admit that I've never had to use it in a real-world worksheet as I much prefer to pad numbers with trailing zeros.

For example, here's two numbers formatted with the default *General* format:

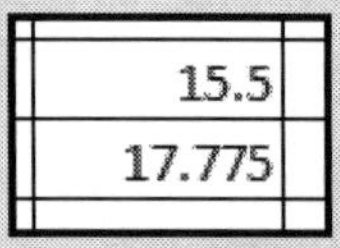

The decimal points don't line up because both numbers are, by default, right aligned.

The custom format:

0.??

Will cause the numbers to round to two decimal places and display as follows:

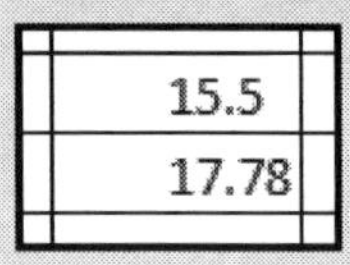

Custom Format String	Value	Display
#,#0.00	12341234.5	12,341,234.50

You can also specify two different format strings separated by a semi colon. The first provides formatting for positive values and the second for negative values. You can also embed colors into number formats.

Here's an example that will show all negative values enclosed in brackets and colored red:

Custom format string	Value	Display
#,#0.00;[Red](#,#0.00)	12341234.5 -12341234.5	12,341,234.50 (12,341,234.50)

1 Open *Sales Week Ended 14th March 2022-2* from your sample files folder (if it isn't already open).

2 Select columns E and G (but not column F).

You learned how to do this in: *Lesson 2-6: Select adjacent and non-adjacent rows and columns.*

3 Apply the default *General* style to column E and G.

1. Select columns E and G (but not F).
2. Click: Home→Number→ Number Format (dropdown list)→General.

The cells revert to Excel's default *General* format (in other words, they are no longer formatted in any special way).

4 Apply the custom format: #,#0.00;[Red](#,#0.00) to every cell in columns E and G.

1. Select columns E and G (but not F).
2. Right click anywhere in column E or G and then select *Format Cells…* from the shortcut menu.
3. Select *Custom* from the category list on the left of the dialog.
4. Type the custom format**: #,#0.00;[Red](#,#0.00)** into the box labelled *Type* and then click the *OK* button.

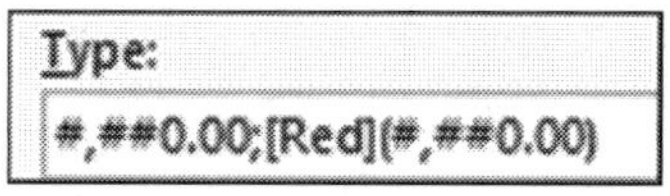

The negative values on the worksheet are now surrounded by brackets and have a font color of red.

Italy	637.49	17.5%	749.05
Italy	(637.49)	17.5%	(749.05)

5 Save your work as *Sales Week Ended 14th March 2022-3.*

note

Custom number formats can also apply a special format to zero values

There are four possible parts to a number format:

Positive format; Negative format; Zero format; Text format. Applying the custom format string:

0.00;-0.00;"Zero";[Blue]

To these cells:

Mike	0	120.119	-345.5744

Would result in:

Mike	Zero	120.12	-345.57

(The text in the left-hand cell is colored blue).

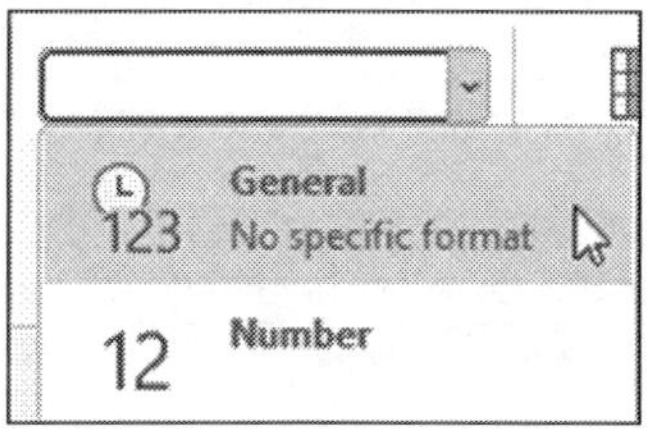

note

Hiding values with the three-semicolon format

You will often want to hide the values in specific cells, even though you want other values in the same column to display.

A common way of doing this is to format the cell with a white foreground color upon a white background. A better solution is to create a custom format consisting of three semicolons:

;;;

Lesson 4-5: Horizontally align the contents of cells

Icon	Description	What it does	Example
General	General (the default)	Aligns numbers and dates to the right and text to the left.	Canada 1,447.50 Spain 365.89
	Align Left	Aligns cell contents left. If the cell contains text and the adjacent cell is empty, text spills to the right.	Bottom-Dollar Markets Bottom-Dollar Markets
		If the cell contains text and the adjacent text isn't empty, text is truncated.	Bottom-Dollar M Canada
	Align Center	Aligns cell contents to the center. If the cell contains text and the adjacent cells are empty, text spills to the left and right.	Bottom-Dollar Markets Bottom-Dollar Markets
		If the cell contains text and the adjacent cells are not empty, text is truncated.	10-Mar-08 om-Dollar Mar Canada
	Align Right	Aligns cell contents to the right. If the cell contains text and the adjacent cell is empty, text spills to the left.	Bottom-Dollar Markets Bottom-Dollar Markets
		If the cell contains text and the adjacent cell isn't empty, text is truncated.	10-Mar-08 om-Dollar Markets C
	Justify	Text lines up to the left and right of the cell (like a newspaper)	to be or not to be, that is the question.
	Distributed	Words are distributed evenly across the cell.	City of London

Sales Week Ended
14th March 2022-3

note

How to access the Justify and Distributed options

The *Justify* and *Distributed* options are not included in the Ribbon's *Alignment* group as most users wouldn't ever find a use for them.

To format a cell (or range of cells) with these options you need to do this:

1. Select the cell or cells you wish to format.

2. Right click on one of the selected cells and click *Format Cells...* on the shortcut menu.

3. Click the *Alignment* tab in the *Format Cells* dialog.

4. Use the *Text alignment* drop down arrows to apply the alignment required.

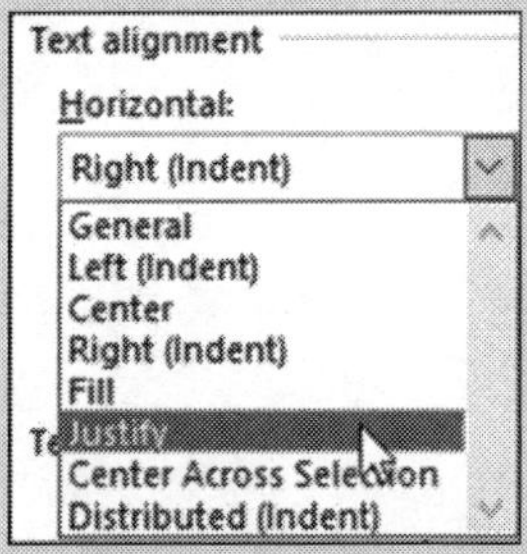

If you find these alignment methods useful you can add *Distribute Text* and *Justify* buttons to the Quick Access Toolbar.

To do this, refer to: *Lesson 1-18: Customize the Quick Access Toolbar and preview the printout.*

The table on the facing page summarizes Excel's different horizontal alignment options.

1 Open *Sales Week Ended 14th March 2022-3* from your sample files folder (if it isn't already open).

2 Notice that the text in row 1 doesn't align with the column contents.

Numerical and date values are, by default, right aligned.

Columns E, F and G contain numerical data, but the text headings of their columns are left aligned.

You can see the problem more clearly if the columns are widened:

E	F	G
Amount	Tax	Total
1,447.50	17.5%	1,700.81
365.89	17.5%	429.92

3 Right-align the column headers for columns E, F and G.

1. Select cells E1:G1.

2. Click: Home→Alignment→Align Right

The column headers now look much better.

E	F	G
Amount	Tax	Total
1,447.50	17.5%	1,700.81
365.89	17.5%	429.92

4 Right-align cell B1.

Column B also has a problem as the dates and column header do not align.

1. Select cell B1.

2. Click: Home→Alignment→Align Right

	A	B	
1	Invoice No	Date	Custo
2	10918	10-Mar-2022	Botto
3	10917	10-Mar-2022	Rome

You will normally align column headers to the right for numeric/date columns, and to the left for text columns.

5 Bold-face row 1.

1. Select row 1.

2. Click: Home→Font→Bold.

	A	B	C
1	**Invoice No**	**Date**	**Customer**
2	10918	10-Mar-2019	Bottom-Dollar Markets

6 Save your work as *Sales Week Ended 14th March 2022-4.*

Lesson 4-6: Merge cells, wrap text and expand/collapse the formula bar

1 Open *Sales Week Ended 14th March 2022-4* from your sample files folder (if it isn't already open).

2 Insert three blank rows above row 1.

This was covered in: *Lesson 3-1: Insert and delete rows and columns.*

3 In cell A1 type: **Sales Week Ended 14th March 2022**

4 Center the title across columns A to G.

The title cell (A1) doesn't look bad, but wouldn't it be nice to center it above the transactions listed beneath? You could simply copy and paste the title text into cell D1 but that wouldn't be perfectly central.

The solution is to merge cells A1:G1 so that they turn into one big cell. It will then be possible to center the text inside the merged cell. Excel provides a handy *Merge and Center* button to do this in one click.

1. Select cells A1:G1.

2. Click: Home→Alignment→Merge & Center.

The title appears at the center of the merged cell.

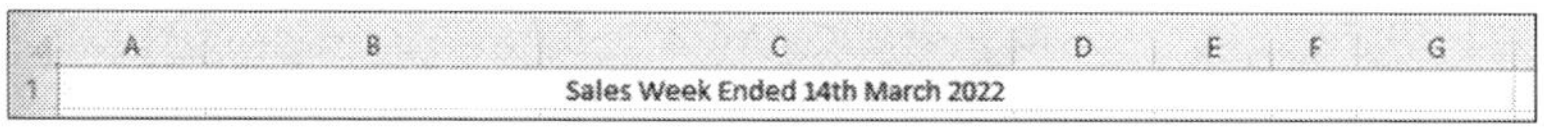

5 View the text in cell A22.

There is a long description in cell A22. You probably can't see all of it on your screen.

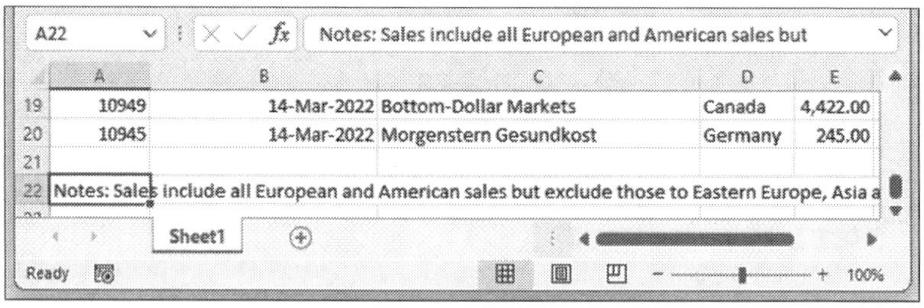

Click cell A22 and then click the *Expand Formula Bar* button. located on the right-hand side of the formula bar.

The text becomes visible in the enlarged formula bar:

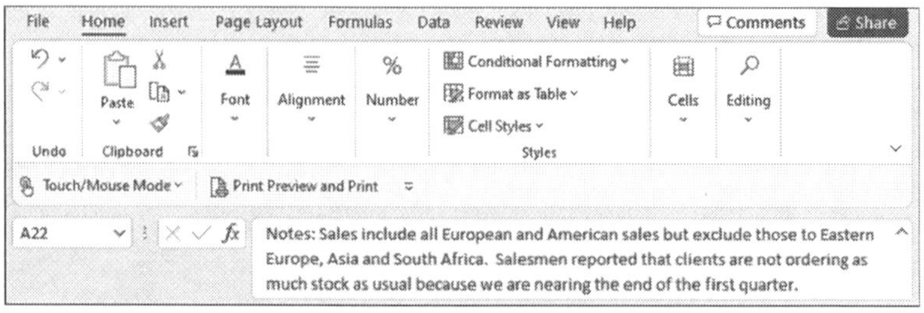

note

The Merge Cells feature taught in this lesson should generally be avoided

Excel has a newer feature called: *Center Across Selection* that does almost the same thing as *Merge Cells.*

You'll learn about the *Center Across Selection* feature later, in: *Lesson 4-7: Unmerge cells and Center Across Selection.*

For new work, it is usually better to use the newer *Center Across Selection* feature in place of *Merge Cells.*

You still need to know how to use *Merge Cells* as you'll find that a huge number of existing workbooks use the *Merge Cells* feature extensively.

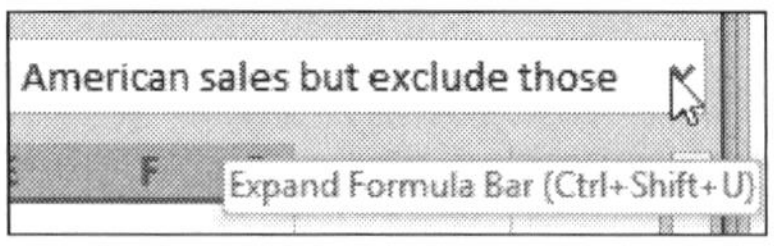

Sales Week Ended 14th March 2022-4

6 Resize the formula bar.

Sometimes there isn't enough space in the expanded formula bar to view all of the text.

If this is the case hover the mouse over the bottom border of the formula bar until you see the double-headed arrow cursor shape.

When the double-headed arrow is visible, click and drag downward or upward to resize the formula bar as required.

7 Collapse the formula bar.

After you have read the text there is no need to keep the formula bar expanded. Click the same button used to expand the formula bar and the bar will collapse.

8 Merge cells A22:G22.

Expanding the formula bar isn't a great solution. It is better to create a box at the bottom of the report to display all of the text.

1. Select cells A22:G22.
2. Click: Home→Alignment→Merge & Center (drop-down).

   A drop-down menu is displayed.

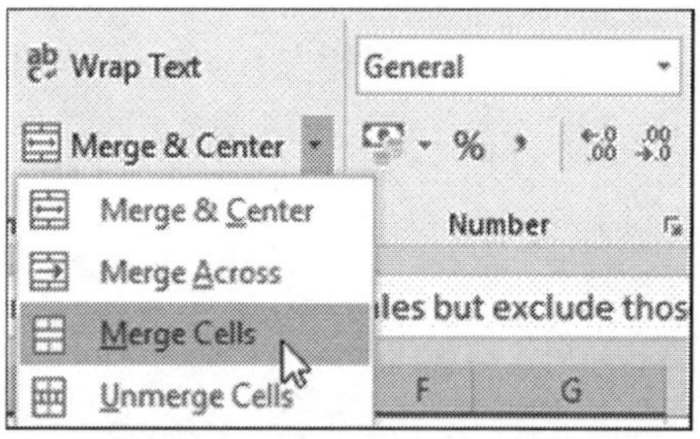

3. Click *Merge Cells* to make all of the selected cells into one large cell. (This is just like *Merge & Center* but without centering).

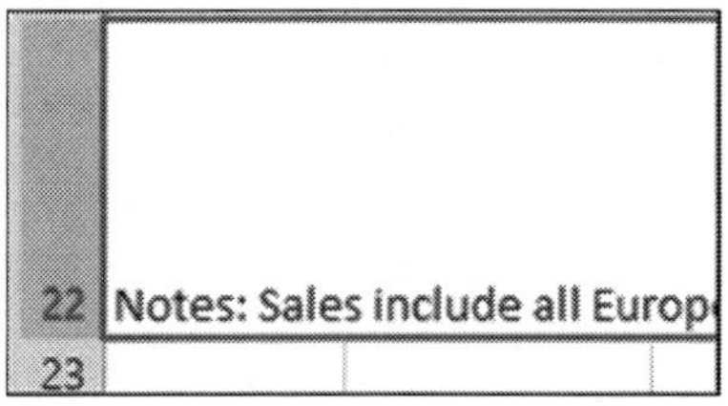

9 Make row 22 deep enough to display all of the text.

This was covered in: *Lesson 2-9: Re-size rows and columns.*

The cell is now deep enough to display the text, but you can still only see one line. This is because the text isn't *wrapping*.

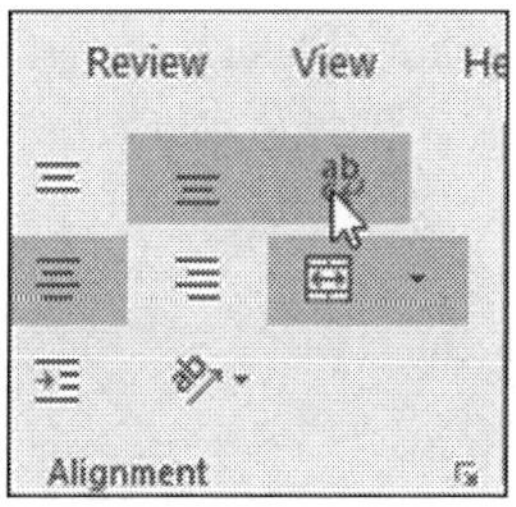

10 Wrap the text within the merged cells.

Click: Home→Alignment→Wrap Text.

The text now displays well, except that it appears at the bottom of the cell. You'll discover how to fix this later, in: *Lesson 4-8: Vertically align the contents of cells.*

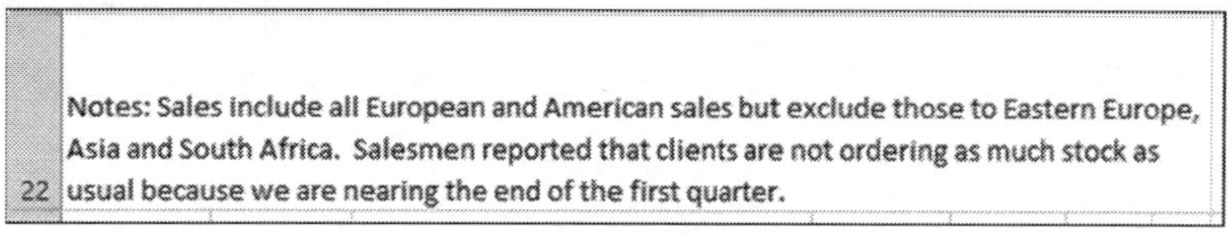

11 Save your work as *Sales Week Ended 14th March 2022-5.*

note

Problems caused by merged cells

1. If you apply a format to a single column, it will not be applied to a merged cell that spans the column.

2. You cannot AutoFill across a merged cell.

3. You cannot select a range within a single column if it contains a merged cell. This is the problem that you encountered at the beginning of this lesson.

4. When working with values it can be unclear which cell a merged value belongs to. This can cause errors when the values in a column that contains a merged cell are totalled.

	A	B
1	Joe	Bill
2		5
3	10	10
4	**15**	**10**

In the example above cells A2:B2 are merged and the merged cell has been right-aligned. The value of 5 is actually in column A, causing the totals in row 4 to seem incorrect.

5. If you copy and paste a merged cell the destination cells will also merge.

6. When you merge cells, only the data in the left-most cell remains. Values in all other cells are discarded.

7. You cannot *Fill Down* a cell if it is part of a merged set of cells.

8. If you progress to the *Expert Skills* book in this series you will learn how to sort data. Any merged cells in a data set will interfere with sort results.

Lesson 4-7: Unmerge cells and Center Across Selection

In: *Lesson 4-6: Merge cells, wrap text and expand/collapse the formula bar,* you learned how to merge cells.

The *Merge Cells* feature is a widely used Excel feature. You'll often encounter merged cells in workbooks that were created by other Excel users. Perhaps after reading this lesson, you will decide not to use the *Merge Cells* feature in your own worksheets.

Unfortunately, the *Merge Cells* feature can cause a number of problems (see sidebar). For this reason, many Excel professionals advise against ever using the *Merge Cells* feature. That's because there is a very similar Excel feature called *Center Across Selection* that doesn't cause any of the problems associated with *Merge Cells.*

Some Excel professionals even advise that existing workbooks containing merged cells should be converted to use *Center Across Selection* instead (but perhaps that is going a little too far).

In this lesson, you will take a workbook that has many merged cells and then unmerge them before achieving the same effect using *Center Across Selection.*

1 Open *Cash and Credit Sales Analysis* from your sample files folder.

	A	B	C	D
1				
2			Total	
3		Analysis Type	Cash	Credit
4		London		
5		Beverages	22,998	30,319
6		Meat/Poultry	63,452	55,030
7		Vegetables	33,351	42,196
8		Paris		
9		Oct	42,972	55,220
10		Nov	34,472	42,216
11		Dec	42,357	51,150
12		New York		
13		UK	53,847	48,230
14		USA	40,040	51,196
15		Canada	25,914	32,215

This workbook has been formatted using Excel's *Merge Cells* feature. You learned how to merge cells in: *Lesson 4-6: Merge cells, wrap text and expand/collapse the formula bar.*

To make the merged cells easier to identify they have been shaded.

You can see that this worksheet has had border lines added to enhance appearance. You'll learn to use border lines to create a very similar worksheet later, in: *Lesson 4-12: Add borders and lines.*

2 Appreciate some of the problems caused by merged cells.

In: *Lesson 2-7: Select non-contiguous cell ranges and view summary information,* you learned that it is simple and convenient to view

note

The Center Across Selection feature cannot be easily added to the Quick Access Toolbar

In: *Lesson 1-18: Customize the Quick Access Toolbar and preview the printout*, you learned that just about every Excel feature can be quickly and easily added to *the Quick Access Toolbar*.

Unfortunately, *Center Across Selection* is one of the very few Excel features that cannot be easily added to the *Quick Access Toolbar* in the normal way.

The *Expert Skills* book in this series provides a full understanding of Excel's *macro* feature and also teaches how to customize the Ribbon.

With this knowledge, it is possible to work-around Excel's usual limitations and add a button to the *Ribbon* or *Quick Access Toolbar* using a different (macro based) technique.

I expect Microsoft to add a Center Across Selection button to the Ribbon in a future Excel release.

the total value of several cells by selecting them with the mouse. The total value of the selected cells is then shown on the status bar at the bottom-right of the screen.

Try to select cells C5:C15 to report the combined cash sales for London, Paris and New York. You will find this impossible to do because of the merged cells in rows 4, 8 and 12.

3 Remove merged cells.

1. Select cell C2. This selects the merged cell range C2:D2.
2. Click: Home→Alignment→Merge & Center.

   The *Merge & Center* button is no longer highlighted and cells C2 and D2 are unmerged.
3. Do the same thing to unmerge cells B4, B8 and B12.

   All worksheet cells are now unmerged. You will now find no difficulty in selecting cells C5:C15.

4 Use Center Across Selection to display text at the center of cells C2:D2.

1. Select cells C2:D2.
2. Right-click anywhere in the selected range and choose *Format Cells…* from the shortcut menu.

   The *Format Cells* dialog appears.
3. Click the *Alignment* tab.
4. Click the drop-down arrow on the side of the *Text alignment→Horizontal* box.
5. Click: *Center Across Selection* from the drop-down list.
6. Click the OK button to dismiss the dialog.

   The text in cells C2:D2 now looks the same as when the two cells were merged. The key difference is that you are now able to individually select cell C2 or D2.

   This may only seem like a small difference, but it avoids all of the problems listed in the facing-page sidebar.

5 Use Center Across Selection to display text at the center of cells B4:D4, B8:D8 and B12:D12.

The worksheet now looks exactly as it did at the beginning of this lesson. The worksheet also no longer contains any merged cells.

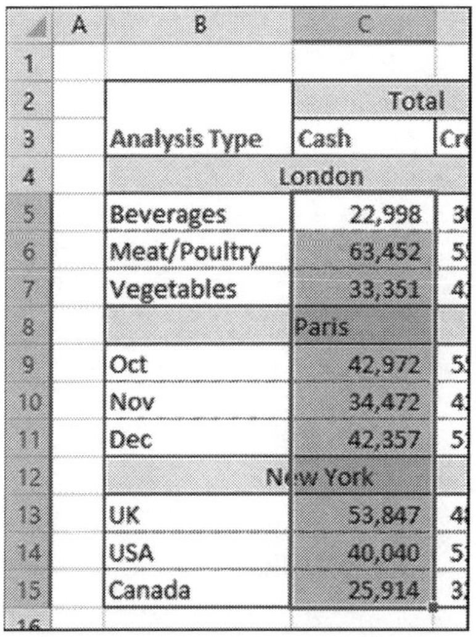

6 Select cells C5:C15 to report the combined cash sales of the London, Paris and New York branches.

This time there is no difficulty selecting the cells and you can read the combined cash sales figure from the status bar (359,403).

7 Save your work as *Cash and Credit Sales Analysis-1.*

Lesson 4-8: Vertically align the contents of cells

This table summarizes Excel's different vertical alignment options.

Icon	Description	What it does	Example
General	General (the default)	Aligns cell contents to the bottom of the cell.	Bottom-Dollar Markets
	Top Align	Aligns cell contents to the top of the cell	Bottom-Dollar Markets
	Middle Align	Aligns cell contents to the middle of the cell.	Bottom-Dollar Markets
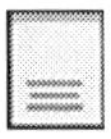	Bottom Align	Aligns cell contents to the bottom of the cell	Bottom-Dollar Markets
No icon	Justify	Lines of text are spread out so that the space between each is equal, the first line is at the top and the last line is at the bottom.	to be or not to be, that is the question.
No Icon	Distributed	The same as Justify!	to be or not to be, that is the question.

1 Open *Sales Week Ended 14th March 2022-5* from your sample files folder (if it isn't already open).

2 Top align the contents of cell A22.

The contents of cell A22 are currently bottom aligned (the default).

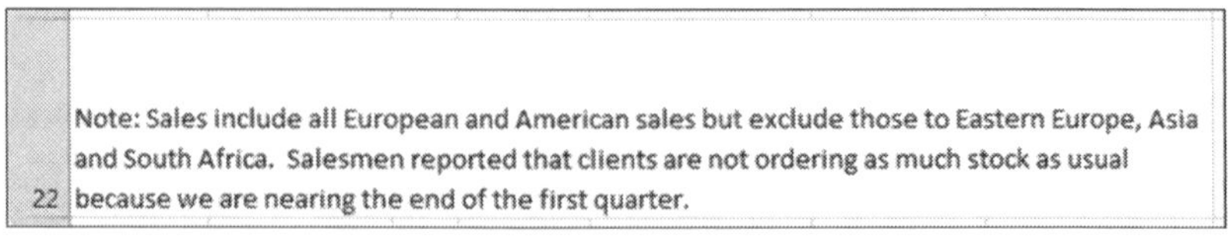

When you place a block of text into a cell in this way, you will typically want it to be top-aligned.

1. Select cell A22.

Sales Week Ended 14th March 2022-5

2. Click: Home→Alignment→Top Align 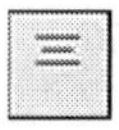 to align the text to the top of the cell.

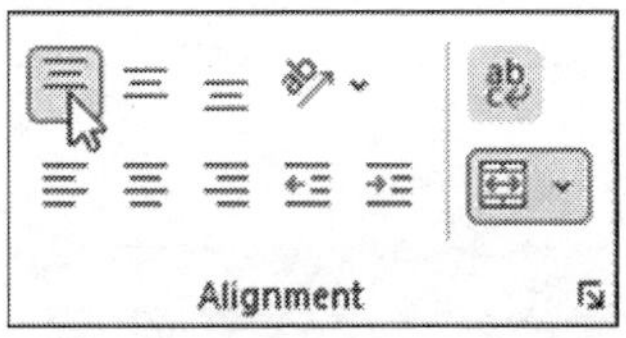

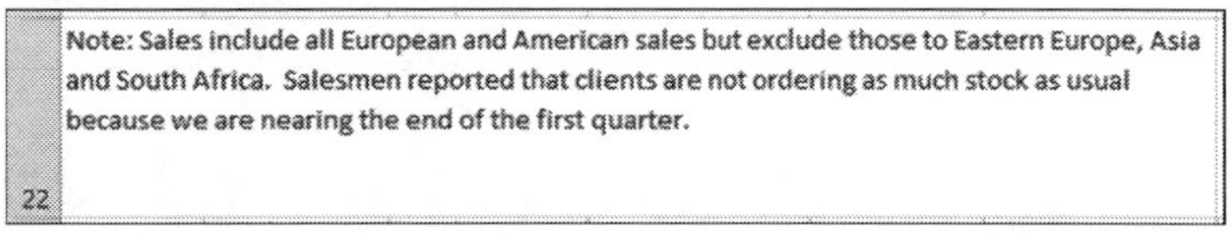

3 Increase the height of row 4 so that it is about twice its present height.

This was covered in: *Lesson 2-9: Re-size rows and columns.*

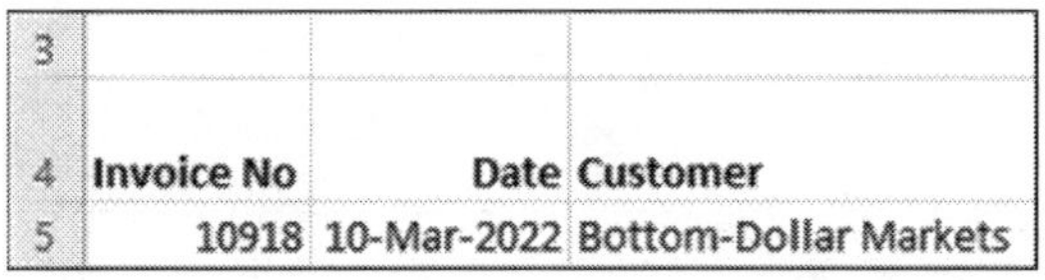

You can see why the default vertical alignment is *bottom align*. This alignment works really well for title rows.

4 Wrap the text in cell A4.

This was covered in: *Lesson 4-6: Merge cells, wrap text and expand/collapse the formula bar.*

5 Split the words *Invoice* and *No* so that they appear on separate lines.

1. Double-click cell A4 to enter Edit mode and then position the cursor to the left of the word *No*.

2. Press **<Alt>+<Enter>**.
3. Press the **<Enter>** key again to exit Edit mode.

   The two words now appear on separate lines.

6 Horizontally right-align the text in cell A4.

This was covered in: *Lesson 4-4: Create custom number formats*

The built-in number formats are very quick and convenient but are also quite limited. Fortunately, it is possible to create your own custom format when none of the built-in styles fit your requirement.

Overview of custom formats

There's plenty of documentation in the help system and on the Internet about the rather cryptic formatting codes provided by Excel. Just about everything is possible once you've got to grips with the basic concepts.

To communicate the custom format to Excel, you must construct a custom format string.

Zeros mean "Display significant zeros". You tell Excel how many you want within the format string. For example, 0.00 means *display at least one leading zero and two decimal places*. The following examples should make things clear:

Custom Format String	Value	Display
0	1234.56	1235
0.0	1234.56 1234.5 .5	1234.6 1234.5 0.5
0.00	1234.56 1234.5 .5	1234.56 1234.50 0.50
00.000	4.56	04.560
0.000	1234.56	1234.560

The hash symbol (#) is mainly used to add comma separators to thousands and millions.

Custom Format String	Value	Display
#	123.4500	123
#.##	123.45 123.50	123.45 123.5
#,#	1234.56	1,236
#,#.##	1234.56 1234.50 12341234.56	1,234.56 1,234.5 12,341,234.56

Because the hash symbol can be used in conjunction with zeros it is also possible to indicate that you want both thousand separators *and* a specific number of leading or trailing zeros.

Custom Format String	Value	Display
#,#0.00	12341234.5	12,341,234.50

You can also specify two different format strings separated by a semi colon. The first provides formatting for positive values and the second for negative values. You can also embed colors into number formats.

Here's an example that will show all negative values enclosed in brackets and colored red:

Custom format string	Value	Display
#,#0.00;[Red](#,#0.00)	12341234.5 -12341234.5	12,341,234.50 (12,341,234.50)

1 Open *Sales Week Ended 14th March 2022-2* from your sample files folder (if it isn't already open).

2 Select columns E and G (but not column F).

You learned how to do this in: *Lesson 2-6: Select adjacent and non-adjacent rows and columns.*

3 Apply the default *General* style to column E and G.

3. Select columns E and G (but not F).
4. Click: Home→Number→
   Number Format (dropdown list)→General.

The cells revert to Excel's default *General* format (in other words, they are no longer formatted in any special way).

4 Apply the custom format: #,#0.00;[Red](#,#0.00) to every cell in columns E and G.

5. Select columns E and G (but not F).
6. Right click anywhere in column E or G and then select *Format Cells…* from the shortcut menu.
7. Select *Custom* from the category list on the left of the dialog.
8. Type the custom format: **#,#0.00;[Red](#,#0.00)** into the box labelled *Type* and then click the *OK* button.

Type:

#,##0.00;[Red](#,##0.00)

The negative values on the worksheet are now surrounded by brackets and have a font color of red.

Italy	637.49	17.5%	749.05
Italy	(637.49)	17.5%	(749.05)

5 Save your work as *Sales Week Ended 14th March 2022-3.*

Lesson 4-5: Horizontally align the contents of cells.

4	Invoice No	Date

7 Automatically resize columns A to G so that each column is just wide enough for the cell contents.

This was covered in: *Lesson 2-9: Re-size rows and columns.*

8 Save your work as *Sales Week Ended 14th March 2022-6.*

Lesson 4-9: Understand themes

A theme is simply a set of fonts, colors and effects that work well together.

Font sets

A font set consists of two complementary fonts that work well as a pair.

A golden rule of typesetting is to never have more than two fonts in a document. Old school typesetters would always use a serif font for the body text (also called the *Normal* text) and a sans-serif font for the titles (just as this book does). See sidebar for the difference between serif and sans-serif fonts.

There's a modern school of thought that suggests that breaking this rule is cool and Microsoft have done just that with their default font set for Excel 2021 (called the *Office* set) by choosing a sans-serif font (Calibri Light) for titles and another sans-serif font (Calibri) for normal text.

You can see all 25 pre-defined font sets by clicking:

Page Layout→Themes→Fonts

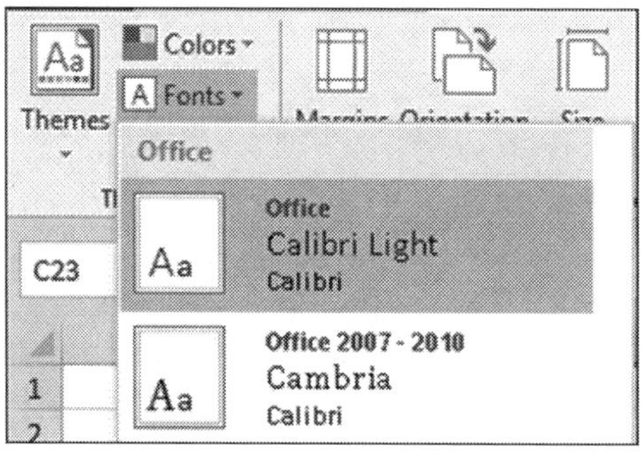

You can also create your own font sets if you don't like any of the pre-defined ones. You'll learn how to do this in: *Lesson 4-13: Create your own custom theme.*

Color sets

If you click: Home→Font→Fill Color (drop down), you will see this dialog:

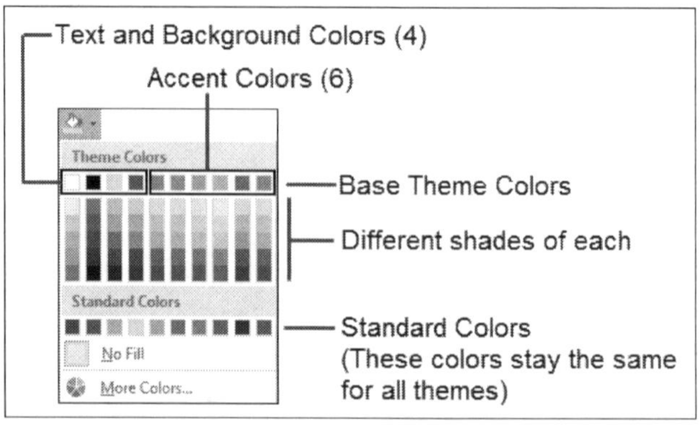

note

What are serifs?

Serifs are the little lines at the edges of text that allow the eye to more easily scan words.

note

Can I change the default theme?

The default theme is simply the theme applied to the *Blank Workbook* template.

If you want to use a different default theme (or change any of the standard Excel options) you will need to create an empty workbook, apply the new theme to it, and then save it as a template (for example: *My Blank Workbook*). You learned how to do this in: *Lesson 3-15: Understand templates and set the default custom template folder.*

If you pin the *My Blank Workbook* template, it will then appear at the top of the list when you open Excel.

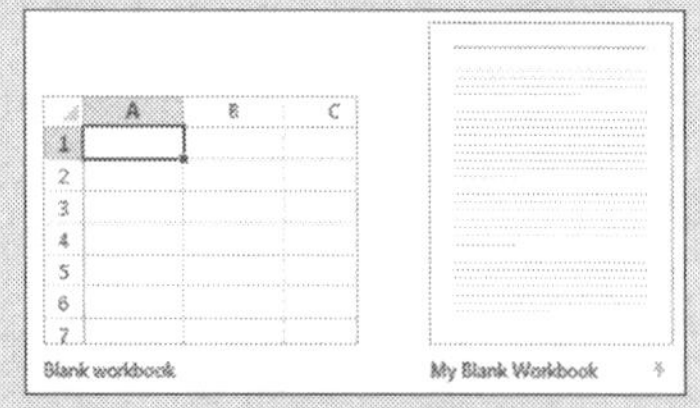

When you create new blank workbooks in future, you can then use your own customized *My Blank Workbook* custom template in place of Microsoft's *Blank Workbook* template.

trivia

Times New Roman is probably the most widely used and successful serif typeface in the world.

This font was commissioned by the British Times newspaper in 1931 and was used to print the Times until 1982 when it was replaced due to incompatibility with faster printing presses. It is still widely used in book publishing.

Times New Roman was the default font in Word for all versions right up to 2007.

Helvetica is probably the most widely used and successful sans-serif font. It was designed in Switzerland in 1957. Windows doesn't include Helvetica but uses *Arial*, a very similar font that most non-experts cannot distinguish from Helvetica.

I used to advise my students that if they stuck to the "killer combination" of Arial/Times New Roman they would never go far wrong, because readers are very used to them and thus find them extremely easy to read.

Microsoft has now changed all of the rules by introducing the Cambria and Calibri fonts.

Just as the Times newspaper designed their font to optimize reading at small type sizes in newspapers, Cambria and Calibri were designed specifically to be easy to read on computer screens using Microsoft's *Clear Type* rendering technology.

Clear Type works particularly well on LCD flat panel displays.

Clear Type has saved me reams of paper because I am able to proofread my books on-screen without causing eye strain. This has saved the lives of many trees.

Color sets are a little more involved than font sets

The ten colors along the top row are the *Theme Colors*. The leftmost four are used for *Text and Background Colors* and the other six are *Accent Colors*. This set of colors has been selected by design professionals to work well together. There are actually twelve theme colors, but you can only see ten of them. The two hidden theme colors are used for hyperlinks.

The *Standard Colors* are best avoided. They are colors that will remain the same no matter what theme is in use. If you use standard colors (or the *More Colors…* option) the worksheet may look odd if the theme needs to be changed in the future. You can see all 23 pre-defined color sets by clicking:

Page Layout→Themes→Colors

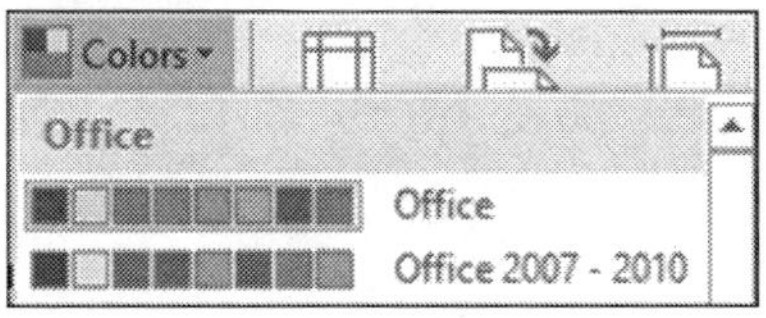

Effects

You'll only notice a change in theme effects if you have graphic elements on your worksheet, such as drawing shapes or chart objects. You'll see this working later in: *Lesson 5-8: Format 3-D elements and add drop shadows.*

Theme effects are applied to the outline and fill of shapes. You can see all 15 pre-defined effect sets by clicking:

Page Layout→Themes→Effects

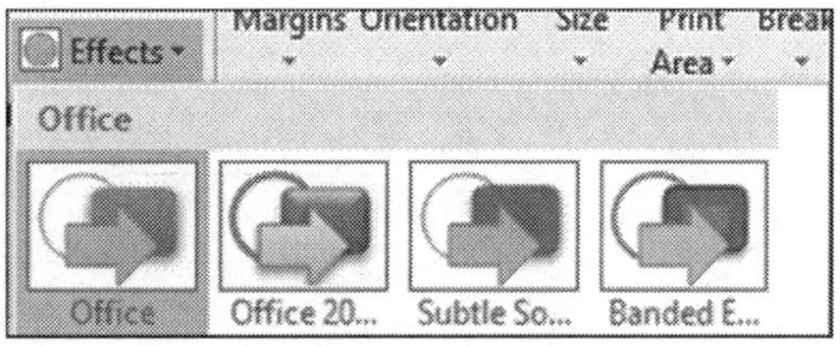

Themes

Themes are simply a group of one *color* set, one *font* set and one *effects* set.

Because Microsoft have consistently named their Colors, Fonts, Effects and Themes, the *Office* theme consists of the *Office* color set, the *Office* font set and the *Office* effects set.

Themes aren't just for Excel

The Themes feature is also included in Word, PowerPoint and Outlook.

Choosing the same theme for your documents, spreadsheets, presentations and Emails can give all of your communications a consistent and professional appearance.

Lesson 4-10: Use cell styles and change themes

In order for themes to work their magic, you must get into the habit of using cell styles to format cells based only upon the options available in the current theme.

For many years, expert Word users have used styles to quickly produce professional documents. Their mortal sin would be to apply a font size or color directly to a document. Professional Excel users should adopt the same discipline.

1 Open *Sales Week Ended 14th March 2022-6* from your sample files folder (if it isn't already open).

2 Apply the *Title* style to cell A1.

Even though cell A1 now encompasses cells A1:G1 it retains the cell reference A1.

A novice user might apply a font and color directly to cell A1 but you're going to do things the professional way and use the *Title* style.

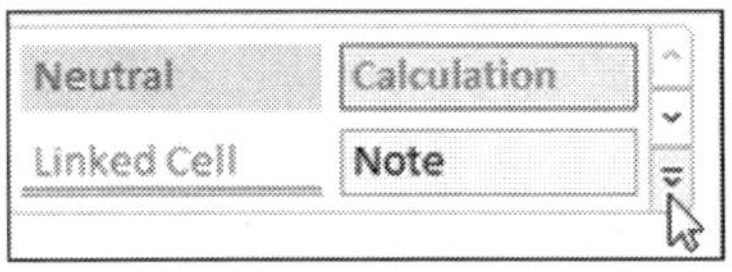

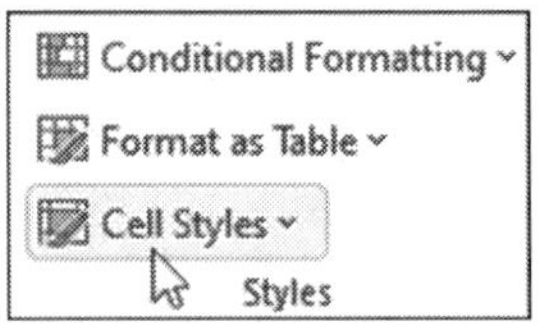

1. Select cell A1.
2. Click: Home→Styles→Cell Styles (gallery)

   Depending on the size of your screen you will see either a *Cell Styles* button or a gallery button (see sidebar for the right place to click).

   The Styles gallery appears.
3. Click *Title* to apply the Title style to cell A1.

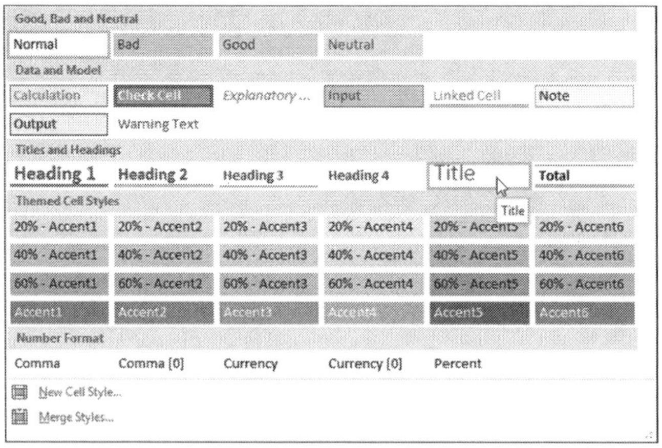

Cell A1 is formatted with the *Title* style.

note

Removing a style from a cell

All cells have the *Normal* style by default. Select a cell or range of cells and click:

Home→Styles→
Cell Styles→Normal

You will then remove the cell style, and all other cell formatting such as bold face or underline, from the cell or range.

3 Apply the *Heading 3* style to cells A4:G4.

1. Select cells A4:G4.
2. Click: Home→Styles→Cell Styles→Heading 3.

4 Apply the *Note* style to cell A22.

1. Select cell A22.
2. Click: Home→Styles→Cell Styles→Note.

Sales Week Ended 14th March 2022-6

note

Microsoft's suggested use for the built-in cell styles

In: *Lesson 4-14: Create your own custom cell styles*, you'll learn how to create your own cell styles.

While you can use the built-in cell styles for any purpose you can see that Microsoft are suggesting the following usage:

Good, Bad and Neutral – to mark particularly good or bad results.

Data and Model – usually used in a worksheet containing formulas to mark cells that require user input or contain formula results.

Titles and Headings – for section titles and column headers.

Themed Cell Styles – to color cells based upon the theme colors.

Number Format – to quickly apply number formats.

Argentina	644.80	17.5%	757.64
UK	220.00	17.5%	258.50
UK	920.60	17.5%	1,081.71
Germany	2,731.87	17.5%	3,209.95
Canada	4,422.00	17.5%	5,195.85
Germany	245.00	17.5%	287.88
			18,137.37

5 Apply the *20% - Accent 1* style to cells A5:D20.

1. Select cells A5:D20
2. Click: Home→Styles→Cell Styles→20% - Accent 1.

6 Apply the *20% - Accent 2* style to cells E5:G20.

1. Select cells E5:G20.
2. Click: Home→Styles→Cell Styles→ 20% - Accent 2.

   The worksheet now looks very different:

	A	B	C	D	E	F	G
1	Sales Week Ended 14th March 2022						
2							
3							
4	Invoice No	Date	Customer	Country	Amount	Tax	Total
5	10918	10-Mar-2022	Bottom-Dollar Markets	Canada	1,447.50	17.5%	1,700.81
6	10917	10-Mar-2022	Romero y tomillo	Spain	365.89	17.5%	429.92
7	10926	10-Mar-2022	Ana Trujillo Emparedados y helados	Mexico	514.40	17.5%	604.42
8	10929	11-Mar-2022	Frankenversand	Germany	1,174.75	17.5%	1,380.33
9	10934	11-Mar-2022	Lehmanns Marktstand	Germany	500.00	17.5%	587.50
10	10939	11-Mar-2022	Magazzini Alimentari Riuniti	Italy	637.49	17.5%	749.05
11	10939	11-Mar-2022	Magazzini Alimentari Riuniti	Italy	(637.49)	17.5%	(749.05)
12	10925	12-Mar-2022	Hanari Carnes	Brazil	475.14	17.5%	558.29
13	10944	12-Mar-2022	Bottom-Dollar Markets	Canada	1,025.32	17.5%	1,204.75
14	10923	12-Mar-2022	La maison d'Asie	France	748.79	17.5%	879.83
15	10937	13-Mar-2022	Cactus Comidas para llevar	Argentina	644.80	17.5%	757.64
16	10947	13-Mar-2022	B's Beverages	UK	220.00	17.5%	258.50
17	10933	13-Mar-2022	Island Trading	UK	920.60	17.5%	1,081.71
18	10938	14-Mar-2022	QUICK-Stop	Germany	2,731.87	17.5%	3,209.95
19	10949	14-Mar-2022	Bottom-Dollar Markets	Canada	4,422.00	17.5%	5,195.85
20	10945	14-Mar-2022	Morgenstern Gesundkost	Germany	245.00	17.5%	287.88
21							
22	Notes: Sales include all European and American sales but exclude those to Eastern Europe, Asia and South Africa. Salesmen reported that clients are not ordering as much stock as usual because we are nearing the end of the first quarter.						

7 Insert a row above row 21.

This was covered in: *Lesson 3-1: Insert and delete rows and columns.*

8 Use AutoSum to place a total in cell G21.

This was covered in: *Lesson 2-3: Use AutoSum to quickly calculate totals.*

9 Apply the *Total* style to cell G21.

1. Select cell G21.
2. Click: Home→Styles→Cell Styles→Total.

10 Re-size column G if necessary, so that it is wide enough to display the total.

The total cell is neatly formatted.

11 Preview your finished work under different themes.

Because you did things the professional way, using styles instead of directly formatting cells, it is now possible to cycle through the themes. You may find one of the other themes more attractive.

1. Click: Page Layout→Themes→Themes.

   The *Themes* gallery appears.

2. Hover over each theme in turn. Notice how the appearance of the worksheet completely changes as each theme's style set is applied.

12 Save your work as *Sales Week Ended 14th March 2022-7.*

Lesson 4-11: Add color and gradient effects to cells

Most of the time solid colors are all you need, but you may want to make a worksheet look more interesting for a PowerPoint presentation, or for publication in a newsletter or a web page.

When you add colors, it is usually best to stay within those of the current theme. This enables you to quickly change the appearance of the worksheet to match that of a PowerPoint presentation or Word document that uses a different theme (see sidebar for an example of this in action).

In this lesson, you'll add a gradient to the sharp transition between the orange totals section and the blue transaction details section of the worksheet.

1 Open *Sales Week Ended 14th March 2022-7* from your sample files folder (if it isn't already open).

2 Check the colors that are currently being used for the transaction and totals section in your worksheet.

1. Click anywhere in the blue area of your worksheet (cells A5:D21).
2. Click the drop-down arrow next to: Home→Font→Fill Color.

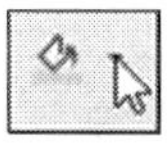

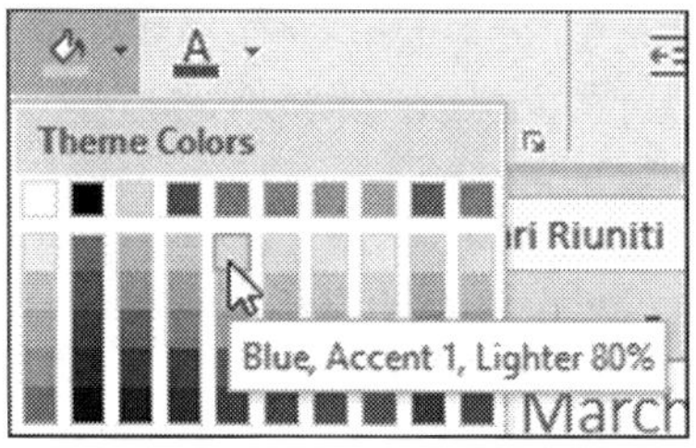

Notice that one color has a small square around it. When you hover over this button you will see that the fill color for the left-hand side of the worksheet is *Blue, Accent 1, Lighter 80%.*

3. Do the same for the orange-colored cells (cells E5:G21). You'll find that they are *Orange, Accent 2, Lighter 80%.*

3 Apply a gradient fill to column D.

1. Select cells D5:D21.
2. Right-click inside the selected range and click *Format Cells…* from the shortcut menu.
3. Click the *Fill* Tab.

note

Why it is a good idea to restrict custom style colors to theme colors

If you restrict your color choice to the 60 *Theme Colors,* you will make your worksheets design-compatible with documents that use other themes.

If you use non-theme colors your worksheets will not seamlessly integrate (from a design point of view) with PowerPoint presentations, Word documents, and other Office documents that use a different theme.

Example

John creates a worksheet using the default *Office* theme.

Mary wants to use this in her PowerPoint presentation that uses the *Circuit* theme. John emails the worksheet to her and then she simply pastes the required cells into her presentation and changes the theme to *Circuit.*

Joe sees the presentation and wants to use the same worksheet in his Word report that uses the *Berlin* theme. Mary emails the presentation to him and then he simply pastes the required slides into his Word document and changes the theme to *Berlin.*

The same worksheet has been used without modification and it blends perfectly into both Joe and Mary's work, because John followed best practice and restricted his color choices to theme colors.

Sales Week Ended 14th March 2022-7

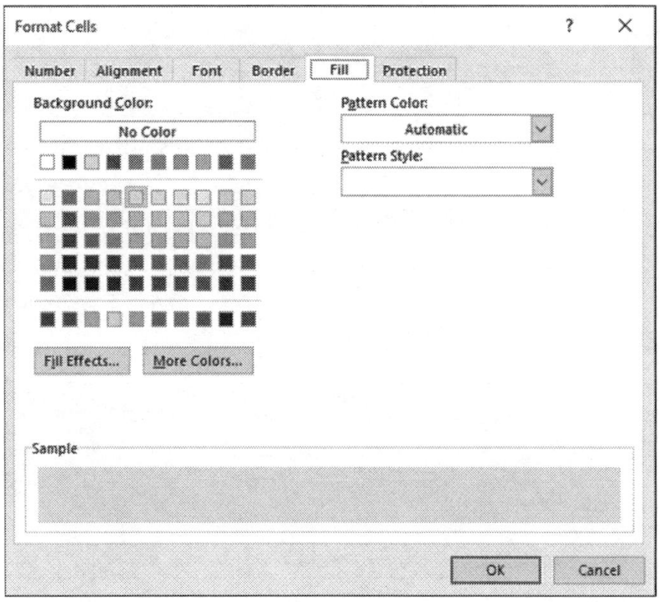

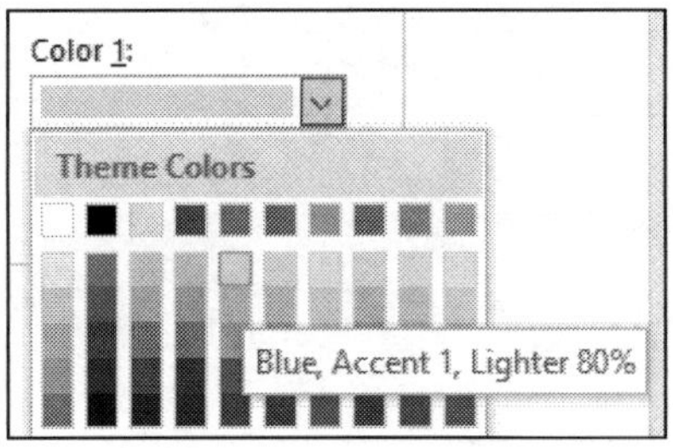

4. Click the *Fill Effects…* button.
5. In the *Colors* frame, choose *Blue, Accent 1, Lighter 80%* for *Color 1*.
6. In the *Colors* frame, choose *Orange, Accent 2, Lighter 80%* for *Color 2*.
7. Select the *Vertical* shading style.
8. Select the top left variant.

Country	Amount
Canada	1,447.50
Spain	365.89
Mexico	514.40
Germany	1,174.75
Germany	500.00
Italy	637.49
Italy	(637.49)
Brazil	475.14
Canada	1,025.32
France	748.79
Argentina	644.80
UK	220.00

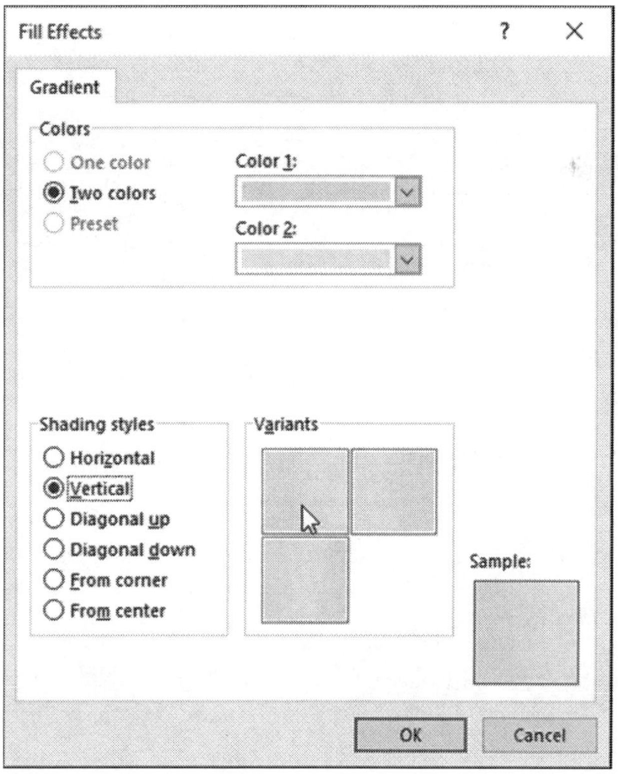

9. Click OK and then OK again.

   A smooth gradient fill has been added to column D.

4 Save your work as *Sales Week Ended 14th March 2022-8.*

Lesson 4-12: Add borders and lines

1 Open *Sales Analysis* from your sample files folder.

You're going to use Excel's powerful *borders and lines* feature to make this worksheet more readable.

Before

	A	B	C	D	E
1					
2			Total		
3		Analysis Type	Cash	Percent	
4		By Category			
5		Beverages	25,326	20%	
6		Meat/Poultry	65,780	52%	
7		Vegetables	35,679	28%	
8		Total	126,785		
9		By Month			
10		Oct	45,300	36%	
11		Nov	36,800	29%	
12		Dec	44,685	35%	
13		Total	126,785		
14		By Country			
15		UK	56,175	44%	
16		USA	42,368	33%	
17		Canada	28,242	22%	
18		Total	126,785		
19					

After

	A	B	C	D	E
1					
2			Total		
3		Analysis Type	Cash	Percent	
4		By Category			
5		Beverages	25,326	20%	
6		Meat/Poultry	65,780	52%	
7		Vegetables	35,679	28%	
8		Total	126,785		
9		By Month			
10		Oct	45,300	36%	
11		Nov	36,800	29%	
12		Dec	44,685	35%	
13		Total	126,785		
14		By Country			
15		UK	56,175	44%	
16		USA	42,368	33%	
17		Canada	28,242	22%	
18		Total	126,785		
19					

2 Add cell styles to rows 2, 3, 4, 9 and 14.

1. Select cells B2:D3.
2. Click: Home→Styles→Cell Styles→40% Accent 6.
3. Select cells B4:D4, B9:D9 and B14:D14.

   This was covered in: *Lesson 2-7: Select non-contiguous cell ranges and view summary information.*
4. Click: Home→Styles→Cell Styles→20% Accent 6.
5. Select cells B2:D3.
6. Click: Home→Styles→Cell Styles→Heading 4.

3 Switch off the worksheet gridlines.

When you are working with borders it is always a good idea to switch off the gridlines so that you can have a better idea of how the worksheet will print.

This feature appears in two different places on the Ribbon. Uncheck either of the following check boxes:

View→Show→Gridlines

OR

Page Layout→Sheet Options→Gridlines→View

4 Add a solid border around the entire range.

note

This worksheet contains a merged cell

In: *Lesson 4-7: Unmerge cells and Center Across Selection*, you learned that some Excel professionals like to avoid merged cells in their worksheets.

In this worksheet cells C2:D2 are merged.

You could unmerge these cells and then center the **Total** text using the **Center Across Selection** feature. If you did this, the appearance of the worksheet would be entirely unchanged.

Sales Analysis

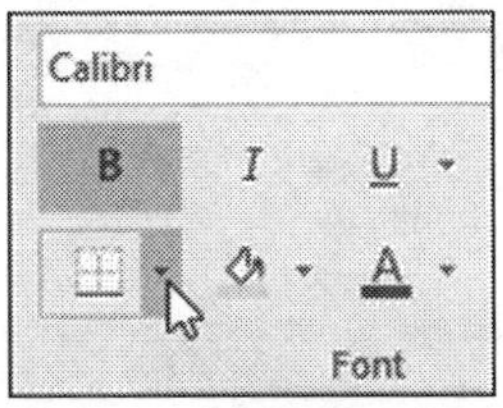

tip

Use the draw border tool to quickly add complex borders

The fastest way to quickly add borders is to simply draw them into place using the *Draw Border* tool.

Click:

Home→Font→
Borders drop-down→
Draw Border

You can then simply draw borders straight onto the grid. There's also an *Erase Border* tool available from the same menu.

note

Changing the border line style or color from the drop-down menu

The ability to change line style and color from the menu means you'll rarely have to resort to using the *Format Cells* dialog for borders.

To change line style or color from the *Borders* drop-down menu, select *Line Color or Line Style.*

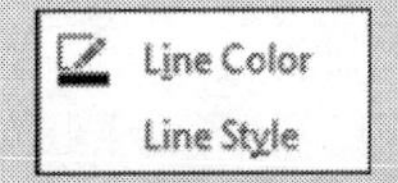

The selected color and/or style will remain active until you close Excel. Next time you open Excel it will have returned to the default.

1. Select cells B2:D18.
2. Click: Home→Font→Borders drop-down→ Outside Borders. 

5 Add solid borders inside cells C2:D3.

1. Select cells C2:D3.
2. Click: Home→Font→Borders drop-down→All Borders.

6 Add top and bottom borders to *By Category*, *By Month* and *By Country*.

1. Select cells B4:D4, B9:D9 and B14:D14.
2. Click: Home→Font→Borders drop-down→ Top and Bottom Border.

7 Add dotted outlines to the borders of cells B5:D8, B10:D13 and B15:D18.

1. Select cells B5:D8, B10:D13 and B15:D18.
2. Right-click any of the selected cells and click *Format Cells…* from the shortcut menu.

   The *Format Cells* dialog appears.
3. Click the *Border* tab of the *Format Cells* dialog.
4. Click the *Dotted Line* style.
5. Click the *Inside* button.

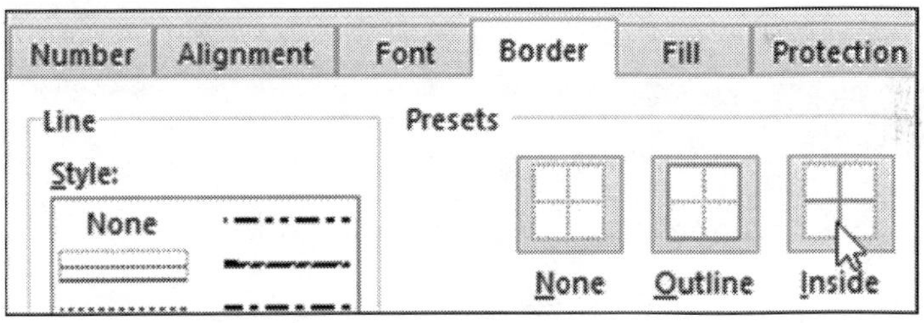

6. Click the OK button.

   Dotted lines are displayed within the cells.

8 Add left and right borders to cells C5:C8, C10:C13 and C15:C18.

1. Select cells C5:C8, C10:C13 and C15:C18.
2. Click: Home→Font→Borders→Left Border.

3. Click: Home→Font→Borders→Right Border.

9 Save your work as *Sales Analysis-1.*

Lesson 4-13: Create your own custom theme

If none of the 30 built-in themes suffice, you can create your own.

Some clients have a defined corporate style and are extremely particular that colors, fonts and other layout items reinforce their corporate identity.

When individuality is important, you need your own custom theme.

1 Open *Sales Week Ended 14th March 2022-8* from your sample files folder.

2 Select a different set of theme colors.

1. Click: Page Layout→Themes→Colors.

   All of the pre-defined sets of colors are displayed (see sidebar). Try hovering your mouse over them one at a time, to see how your worksheet would look if you changed the theme colors.

2. Choose a different set that you think look attractive.

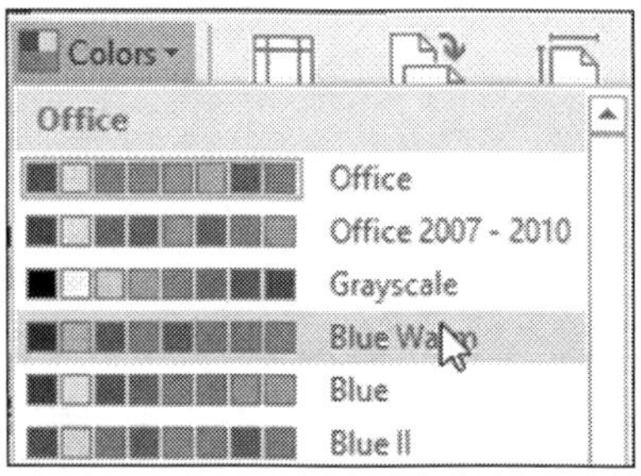

3 Create a custom set of theme colors.

1. Click: Page Layout→Themes→Colors→Customize Colors.

   The *Create New Theme Colors* dialog appears (displaying the color set for the currently selected theme).

2. Click any of the colors on the left of the dialog and select a different color. Notice that, as you do, the *Sample* frame shows a preview of how your theme looks. Let your imagination run wild and create your own custom color theme.

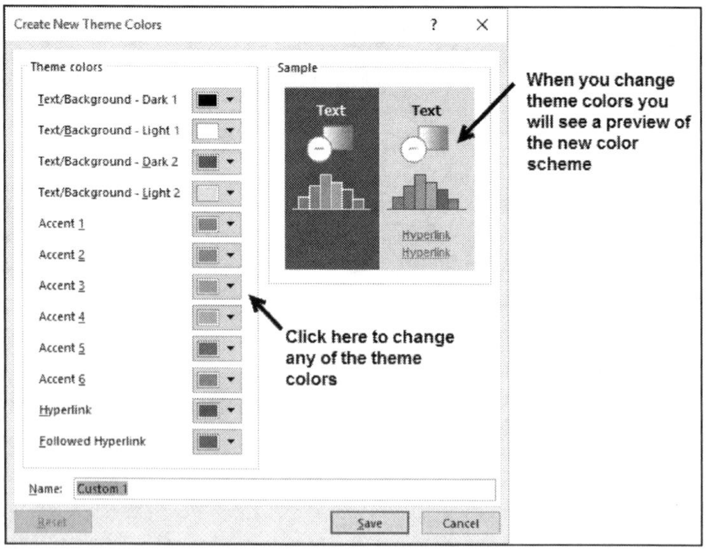

3. Type: **TSM Corporate** into the *Name* box.

4. Click the *Save* button to create your own personalized set of custom colors.

4 Select a different set of fonts.

As discussed in: *Lesson 4-9: Understand themes*, a theme consists of a *color set*, a *font set* and an *effects set*.

note

Can I change the default theme?

If you've adopted a custom theme as your corporate standard, you will probably want to use this when creating new blank workbooks.

To do this, refer to the sidebar in: *Lesson 4-9: Understand themes.*

Sales Week Ended 14th March 2022-8

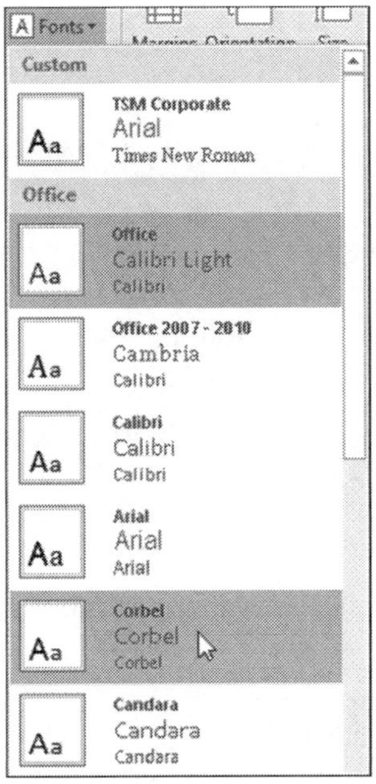

tip

Naming your themes

The built-in themes mostly follow a sensible naming convention.

For example, the *Office* theme has the *Office* font set, the *Office* color set and the *Office* effects set.

In this lesson, you followed the same convention with the *TSM Corporate* theme containing the *TSM Corporate* color set and the *TSM Corporate* font set.

It is good practice to maintain consistent naming across your own custom themes.

A font set consists of two fonts: a heading font and a body font.

1. Click: Page Layout→Themes→Fonts.

   All of the pre-defined sets of fonts are displayed (see sidebar). Try hovering your mouse over them one at a time, to see how your worksheet would look if you changed the theme fonts.

2. Choose a different set that you think look attractive.

5 Create a custom set of theme fonts.

1. Click: Page Layout→Themes→Fonts→Customize Fonts…

   The *Create New Theme Fonts* dialog appears (displaying the font set for the currently selected theme).

2. Select two complementary fonts.
3. Type: **TSM Corporate** into the *Name* box.

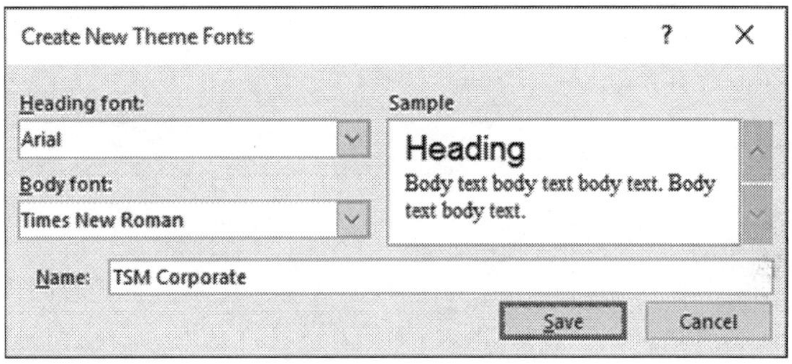

4. Click the *Save* button to create your own personalized set of custom fonts.

6 Select a different set of effects.

Unlike colors and fonts, you can't create a custom set of effects. You have to choose from the pre-defined ones.

Effects change the appearance of drawing objects and you haven't yet covered these (they will make an appearance in: *Lesson 5-8: Format 3-D elements and add drop shadows*).

1. Click: Page Layout→Themes→Effects.
2. Choose a different set of effects.

7 Save the corporate theme.

1. Click: Page Layout→Themes→Themes→Save Current Theme.
2. Enter the name: **TSM Corporate** in the *File Name* text box.
3. Click the *Save* button.

8 Revert to the standard *Office* theme.

1. Click: Page Layout→Themes→Themes.

   Notice that your custom theme is listed at the top in the *Custom* group.

2. Click the *Office* theme to put things back the way they were.

9 Close the workbook without saving.

Lesson 4-14: Create your own custom cell styles

tip

Change the default font (of this workbook) by modifying the Normal style

When you modify a cell style, the change affects every cell that depends upon that style.

For example, suppose you wanted to change the default font of a worksheet to *Times New Roman, 12 point.*

You'd simply modify the *Normal* style's font and then every un-formatted cell in the entire workbook would change to the new default font.

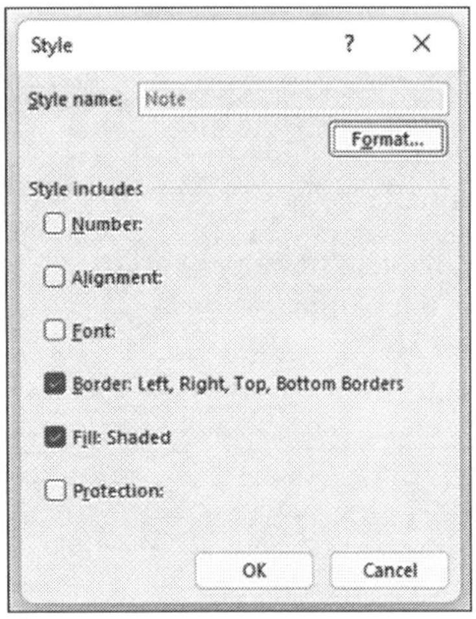

In: *Lesson 4-10: Use cell styles and change themes,* you learned how to use Excel's built-in cell styles. You can also create your own custom styles.

Custom styles are only available in the workbook in which they were originally created. In order to use them in another workbook, you need to use Excel's *merge styles* feature. The *merge styles* feature will be covered later, in: *Lesson 4-15: Use a master style book to merge styles.*

1 Open *Sales Week Ended 14th March 2022-8* from your sample files folder (if it isn't already open).

2 Modify an existing cell style.

Click cell A23 to make it the active cell. This is the cell containing the *Note* text.

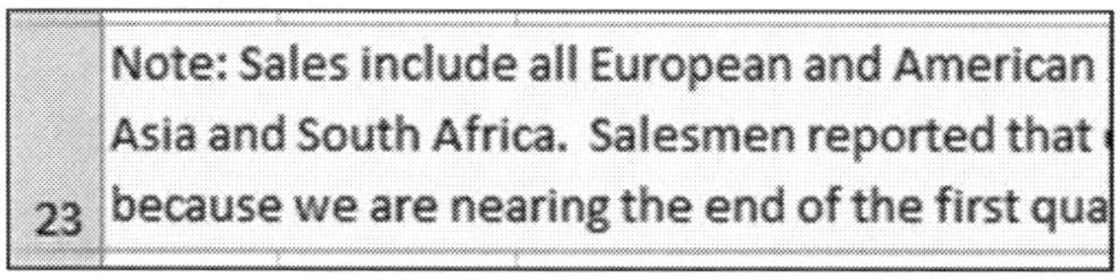

1. Click: Home→Styles→Cell Styles.
2. Right-click the *Note* style and click *Modify* from the shortcut menu.

   The *Style* dialog appears (see sidebar).
3. Click the *Format…* button. The *Format Cells* dialog appears.
4. Click the *Fill* tab and select a light green background color:

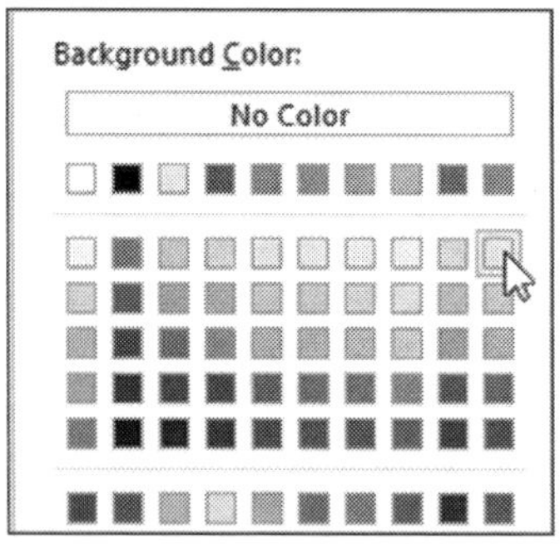

5. Click the OK button and then the OK button once more.
6. If cell A23 isn't green, click: Home→Styles→Cell Styles and click once on the *Note* style.

   Notice that the background color of cell A23 (which has the *Note* style applied to it) has now turned light green.

   You haven't permanently changed the *Office* theme's *Note* style. You've simply changed it for this workbook only. When you open another workbook that uses the *Office* theme, the *Note* style will be light yellow once again.

Sales Week Ended 14th March 2022-8

3 Duplicate the *Note* built-in cell style.

1. Click: Home→Styles→Cell Styles to display the *Cell Styles* gallery.

2. Right-click the *Note* cell style and then click *Duplicate* from the shortcut menu.

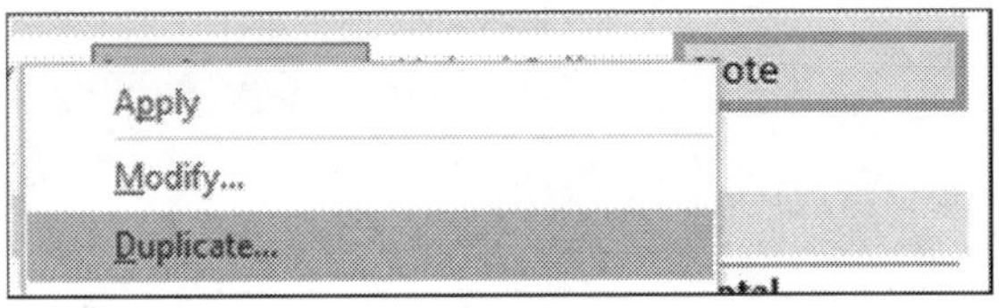

3. The *Style* dialog appears, suggesting the name *Note 2* for your new cell style.

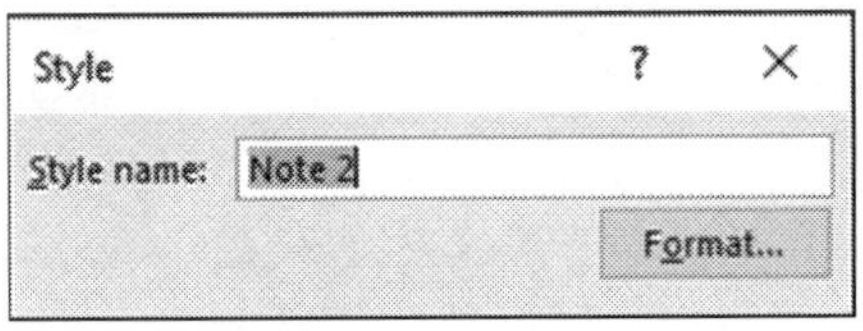

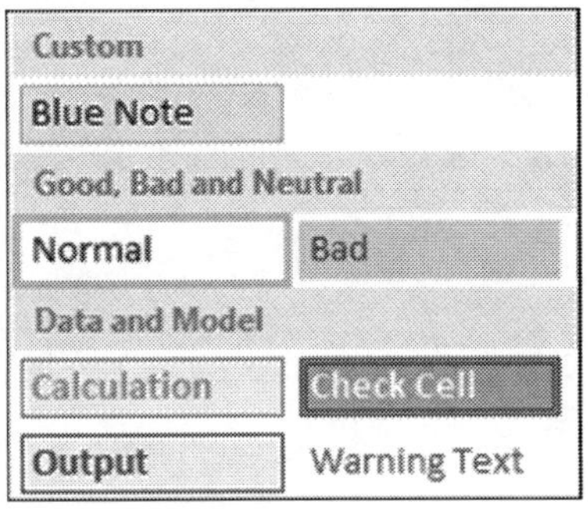

4. Change the style name to **Blue Note** (you're going to change the color in a moment) and click the OK button.

5. Click: Home→Styles→Cell Styles to display the *Cell Styles* gallery once more.

   Notice that the *Blue Note* style is at the top of the gallery in the *Custom* section.

6. Change the background color of the new *Blue Note* style to light blue using the technique learned in: *Step 2 - Modify an existing cell style.*

4 Create a custom cell style *By Example*.

This is the easiest way to create custom cell styles.

1. Select cell A23.

2. Click: Home→Font→Fill Color Drop-down and choose the *Gold, Accent 4, Lighter 80%* theme color.

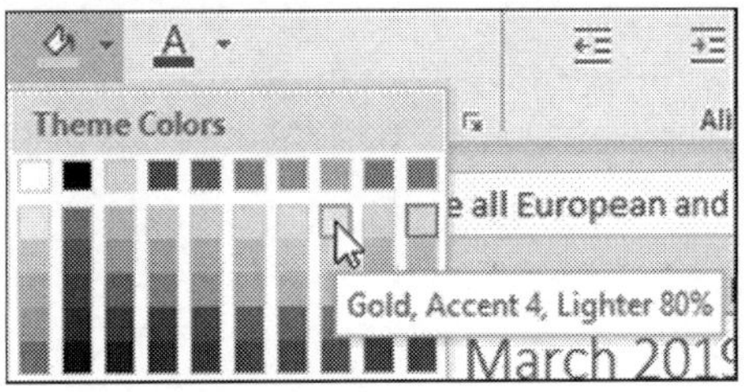

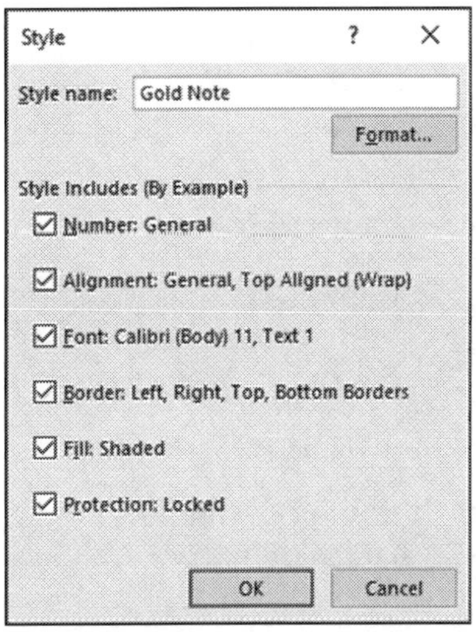

3. Click: Home→Styles→Cell Styles→New Cell Style.

   The *Style* dialog appears but notice the words: *By Example*. This means that the style already contains all of the formatting information for cell A23.

4. Change the style name to **Gold Note** and click the OK button.

5 Save your work as *Sales Week Ended 14th March 2022-9*.

Lesson 4-15: Use a master style book to merge styles

When you create custom styles, they are only available within the workbook in which they were created. Sometimes it is useful to have the same set of custom styles available across multiple workbooks.

In this lesson, you'll cater for the following scenario at Empire Car Sales:

Syd Slater, the owner of Empire Car Sales, knows that you have to keep your stock turning over.

His salesmen are allowed to discount 10% of the sticker price on all cars.

If the car has been on the forecourt for more than two weeks, they are allowed to discount 15%, after three weeks 20%, and after four weeks the car goes back to auction.

Syd's salesmen need to know the maximum discount they can offer, but Syd doesn't want the customers to find this out, so they use a cunning system of color coding on the stock list:

10% Max Discount: Blue

15% Max Discount: Green

20% Max Discount: Orange

The stock list is produced each week in Excel with three custom cell styles, one for each discount.

To avoid having to constantly re-create custom cell styles, they are stored in a master style book called *Empire Styles* which Syd merges with his worksheets so that the three styles are always available.

Empire Car Sales Stock List-1

1. Open a new blank workbook.
2. Create a custom style called: **10% Max Discount** with a background color of *Light Blue*.

   This was covered in: *Lesson 4-14: Create your own custom cell styles.*
3. Create a custom style called: **15% Max Discount** with a background color of *Light Green*.
4. Create a custom style called: **20% Max Discount** with a background color of *Light Orange*.

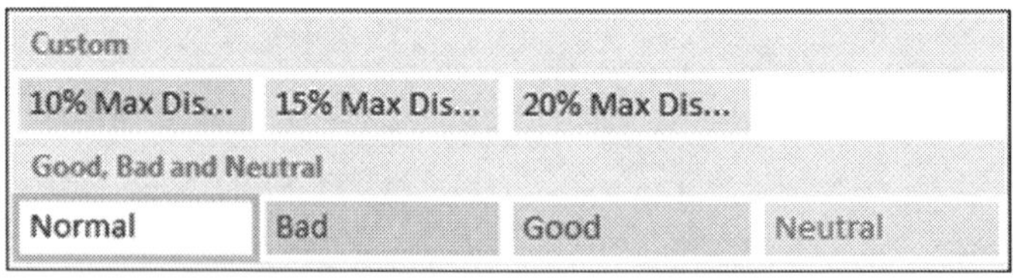

Because you have used theme colors for the custom styles, their color will change if the theme is changed.

For example, if you change the theme to *Slate,* the *10% Max Discount* becomes red, *15%* becomes brown and *20%* becomes tan.

For this reason, you could argue that it would be better to set the colors using the *More Colors* option so that the colors remained the same even if the theme is changed.

For the purposes of this lesson, you will assume that Syd will not change from the *Office* theme and will follow the normal rule of restricting color choice to theme colors. (See the sidebar in: *Lesson 4-11: Add color and gradient effects to cells*, for an explanation of why this is best practice).

5 Save the workbook as *Empire Styles* but don't close it.

6 Open *Empire Car Sales Stock List-1* from your sample files folder.

7 Merge the styles from the *Empire Styles* master style book.

1. Click: Home→Styles→Cell Styles→Merge Styles…
2. The *Merge Styles* dialog appears.

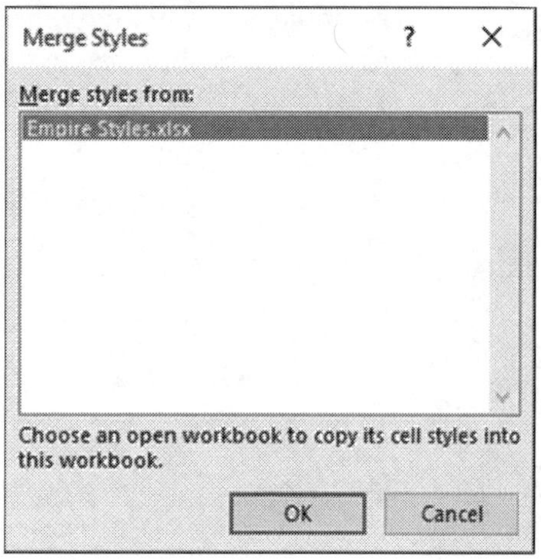

3. Select *Empires Styles.xlsx* and then click the OK button.
4. Click: *Yes* if prompted.

The three custom styles are now available within the current workbook.

8 Apply the 20% style to the Volkswagen and Mercedes.

9 Apply the 15% style to the BMW and Alfa Romeo.

10 Apply the 10% style to the Volvo and Ford.

Syd's salesmen are now ready to start selling.

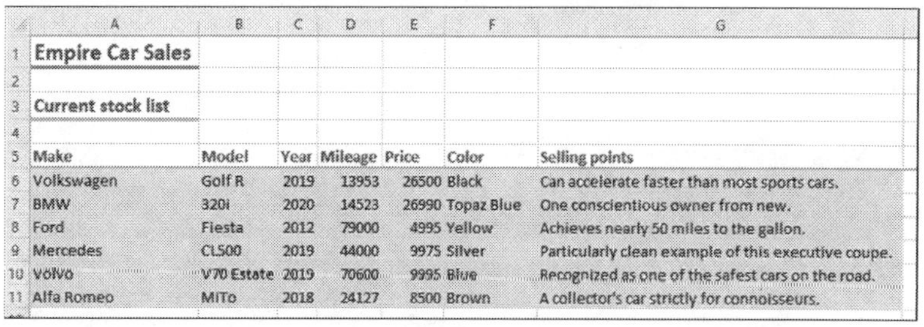

	A	B	C	D	E	F	G
1	Empire Car Sales						
2							
3	Current stock list						
4							
5	Make	Model	Year	Mileage	Price	Color	Selling points
6	Volkswagen	Golf R	2019	13953	26500	Black	Can accelerate faster than most sports cars.
7	BMW	320i	2020	14523	26990	Topaz Blue	One conscientious owner from new.
8	Ford	Fiesta	2012	79000	4995	Yellow	Achieves nearly 50 miles to the gallon.
9	Mercedes	CL500	2019	44000	9975	Silver	Particularly clean example of this executive coupe.
10	Volvo	V70 Estate	2019	70600	9995	Blue	Recognized as one of the safest cars on the road.
11	Alfa Romeo	MiTo	2018	24127	8500	Brown	A collector's car strictly for connoisseurs.

11 Save your work as *Empire Car Sales Stock List-2*.

Lesson 4-16: Use simple conditional formatting

Simple conditional formatting applies a format to a cell based upon the value of the cell. In this lesson, you'll change the cell background color to red if the cell has a value of less than 5,000 and to green if the value is over 30,000.

The same technique learned in this lesson can be used to apply conditional formats based upon text that begins with, ends with, or contains specific characters.

You can also apply conditional formats to cells containing dates. For example, you can highlight dates such as *today, tomorrow, in the last seven days, last week* and *this week.* Conditional formatting will then cause the worksheet to change every time that you open it based upon the current date.

1 Open *Sales Report* from your sample files folder.

2 AutoFit cells A4:A26.

   1. Select cells A4:A26.
   2. Click: Home→Cells→Format→AutoFit Column Width.

3 AutoFit cells D4:D13.

4 Apply the *Comma* style to column B and column E.

   You learned how to do this in: *Lesson 4-3: Format numbers using built-in number formats.*

5 Select cells A3:B3, D3:E3 and D18:E18 and use *center across selection* to place the text in the center.

   You learned how to do this in: *Lesson 4-7: Unmerge cells and Center Across Selection.*

6 Apply the *Title* style to cell A1.

   You learned how to do this in: *Lesson 4-10: Use cell styles.*

7 Apply the *Heading 2* style to cells A3:B3, D3:E3 and D18:E18.

8 Apply the *Heading 3* style to cells A4:B4, D4:E4 and D19:E19.

9 Apply the *Total* style to cells A26:B26, D13:E13 and D26:E26.

   The worksheet is now well formatted and has a professional appearance:

	A	B	C	D	E
1	Sales Report - 6 Months ended March 2022				
2					
3	Sales By Country			Sales by Category	
4	Country	Total Sales		Category	Total Sales
5	Argentina	762.60		Beverages	70,168.10
6	Austria	33,462.58		Condiments	24,938.06

note

You can also apply simple conditional formats using the Quick Analysis button

Whenever you select a range of cells, a *Quick Analysis* button appears just outside the bottom-right corner of the selected range.

24	USA	49,190.99
25	Venezuela	13,189.98
26	Grand Total	266,644.33
27		

When you click the *Quick Analysis* button, the *Quick Analysis* dialog appears.

One of the menu options on this dialog is *Formatting.*

When you click the *Formatting* menu option, one of the options is *Greater Than:*

When you click the *Greater Than* icon you will see the same *Greater Than* dialog that you displayed using the Ribbon in this lesson.

Unfortunately, the *Quick Analysis* button is not as powerful as the Ribbon method used in this lesson.

There is no *Less Than* option, meaning that it would not be possible add the conditional formats described in this lesson using only the *Quick Analysis* feature.

Sales Report

10 Select cells B5:B25.

11 Conditionally format the selected range so that any country with sales below 5,000 has a light red fill with dark red text.

1. Click: Home→Styles→Conditional Formatting→ Highlight Cells Rules→Less Than…

   The *Less Than* dialog appears.

2. Type 5,000 in the left-hand text box and choose *Light Red Fill with Dark Red Text* for the font and fill color.

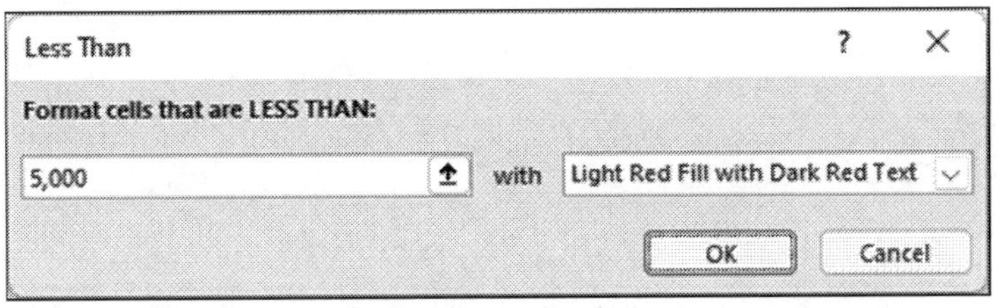

   Notice that when you change the value in the text box, the worksheet adjusts in the background to preview what will happen if this conditional format is applied.

   Note also that there's a *Custom Format...* option (in the drop-down list) which enables you to choose effects such as underlines as well as any color.

3. Click the OK button.

   Cells that have a value of less than 5,000 are now highlighted in red (see sidebar).

3	Sales By Country	
4	Country	Total Sales
5	Argentina	762.60
6	Austria	33,462.58
7	Belgium	6,109.48
8	Brazil	20,524.42
9	Canada	21,306.29
10	Denmark	16,658.80
11	Finland	5,525.00
12	France	26,155.54
13	Germany	28,361.38
14	Ireland	6,157.76
15	Italy	2,585.69
16	Mexico	3,524.30
17	Norway	1,058.40
18	Poland	459.00
19	Portugal	5,584.13

12 Add another conditional format to the same range, so that any country with sales that are greater than 30,000 will have a green fill with dark green text.

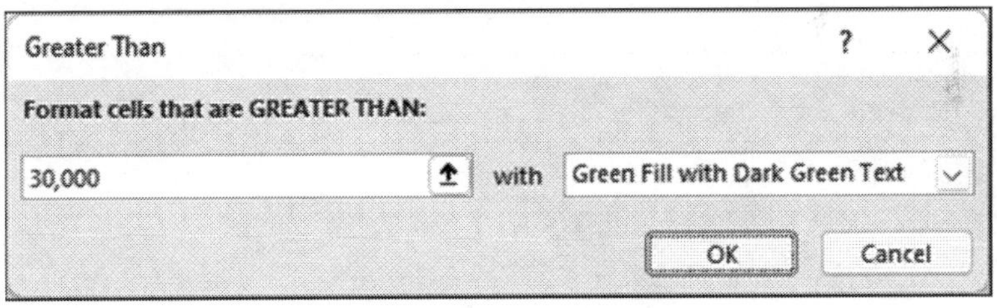

Both conditional formats now display with the two sales values over 30,000 displayed in green.

3	Sales By Country	
4	Country	Total Sales
5	Argentina	762.60
6	Austria	33,462.58
7	Belgium	6,109.48
8	Brazil	20,524.42
9	Canada	21,306.29
10	Denmark	16,658.80
11	Finland	5,525.00
12	France	26,155.54
13	Germany	28,361.38
14	Ireland	6,157.76
15	Italy	2,585.69

13 Remove both conditional formats.

1. Select cells B5:B25.

2. Click: Home→Styles→Conditional Formatting→ Clear Rules→Clear Rules from Selected Cells.

   The conditional formats are removed.

14 Save your work as *Sales Report-1.*

Lesson 4-17: Manage multiple conditional formats using the Rules Manager

The conditional formats applied in the previous lesson depended upon the value of a single cell.

Often you will want a cell to be formatted based upon its relationship to other cells in a range.

In this lesson you'll color the top 25% of sales green, the middle 50% yellow and the bottom 25% red.

This lesson also introduces the *Rules Manager* that allows you to edit conditional format rules and to specify the order in which conditional formats are applied.

1 Open *Sales Report-1* from your sample files folder (if it isn't already open).

2 Select cells B5:B25.

3 Conditionally format the selected range so that any country whose sales are in the top 25% has a green fill with dark green text.

   1. Click: Home→Styles→Conditional Formatting→ Top/Bottom Rules→Top 10%.

      The *Top 10%* dialog appears.

   2. Change the value to 25% and choose *Green fill with Dark Green Text* for the fill.

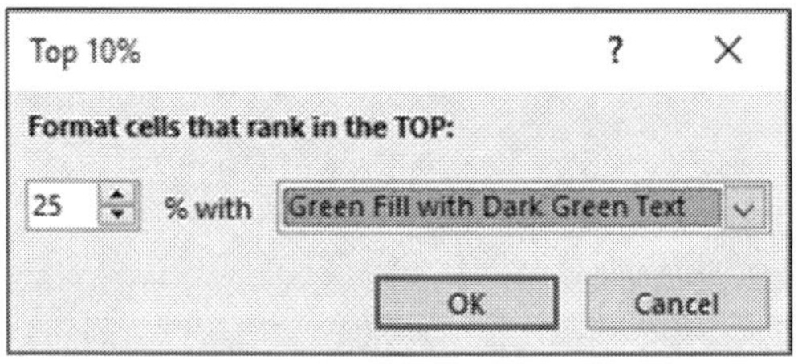

   3. Click the OK button.

4 Conditionally format the selected range so that any country whose sales are in the bottom 25% has a light red fill with dark red text.

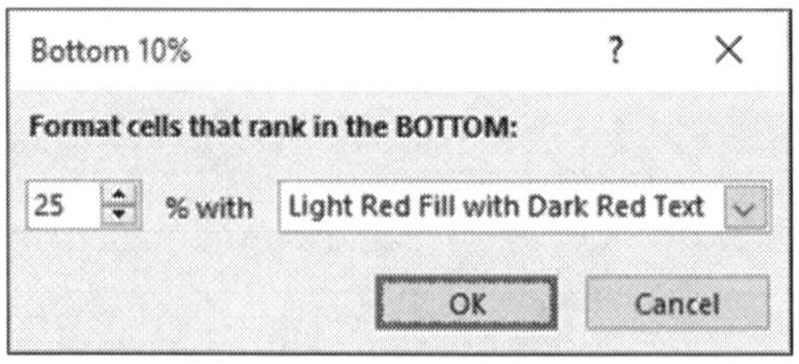

The top and bottom 25% of sales are now highlighted as specified in the two conditional formats.

5 Add another conditional format so that any country with sales greater than zero has a yellow fill with dark yellow text.

3	Sales By Country	
4	Country	Total Sales
5	Argentina	762.60
6	Austria	33,462.58
7	Belgium	6,109.48
8	Brazil	20,524.42
9	Canada	21,306.29
10	Denmark	16,658.80
11	Finland	5,525.00
12	France	26,155.54
13	Germany	28,361.38
14	Ireland	6,157.76
15	Italy	2,585.69

Sales Report-1

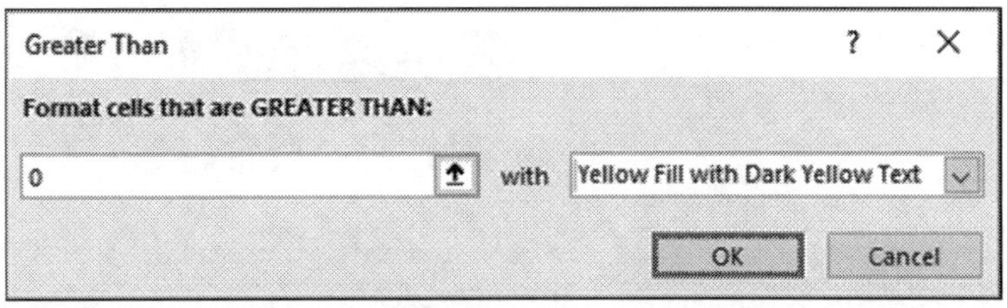

Remember that the specification was to color the middle 50% of sales yellow.

Unfortunately, all sales are now yellow because the yellow cells are over-writing the red and green cells.

6 Use the *Rules Manager* to control the order in which conditional formats are applied.

1. Select cells B5:B25.
2. Click: Home→Styles→Conditional Formatting→ Manage Rules.

   The *Conditional Formatting Rules Manager* dialog is displayed.
3. Click the first rule (the *Cell Value > 0* rule).
4. Use the *Move Down* button  to move the *Cell Value > 0* rule to the bottom of the list (if you don't see the *Move Down* button it is because you haven't selected the rule).

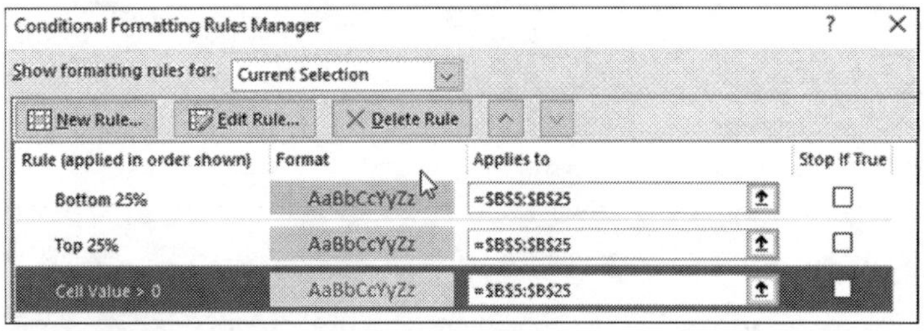

5. Click the OK button.

   The red, green and yellow formatting rules are now applied as required. This works because of the conflict resolution rules (see sidebar).

7 Use the *Rules Manager* to edit the rules so that the top and bottom 30% values are now highlighted.

1. Select cells B5:B25.
2. Click: Home→Styles→Conditional Formatting→ Manage Rules.
3. Select the *Bottom 25%* rule.
4. Click the *Edit Rule...* button  and change the criteria to: *30%*.
5. Edit the *Top 25%* rule in the same way so that it will show the top 30% values.

8 Remove all three conditional formats.

This was covered in: *Lesson 4-16: Use simple conditional formatting.*

note

Conflict resolution rules

In this lesson you applied three different conditional formats to the selected range.

Sometimes there will be a conflict between different conditional formatting rules.

Consider this specification:

- Format every value over 50 as blue, underlined and bold.
- Format every value over 75 as red and italic.

The rules manager has a dilemma with a value of 80. Should it be blue or red, bold, italic, underlined or all three?

To resolve the conflict, rules are applied in the order listed in the *Rules Manager*. Attributes are applied only if an earlier conditional format has not set a conflicting condition.

1. The value is over 50 so apply blue, underlined, bold-face.
2. The value is over 75. Can't format red because the earlier condition has made the cell blue.
3. The value is over 75. Apply italics.

Lesson 4-18: Bring data alive with visualizations

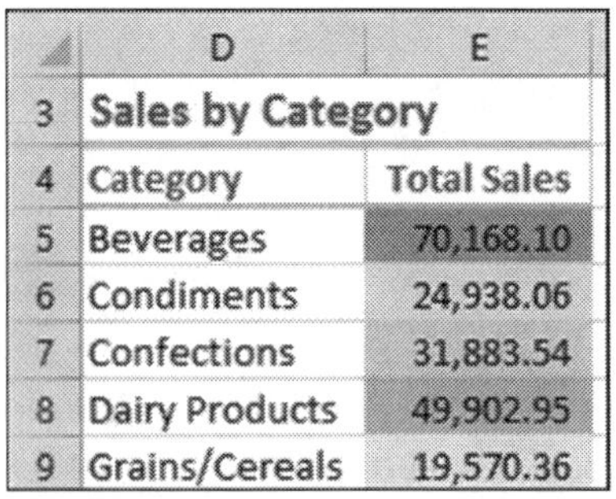

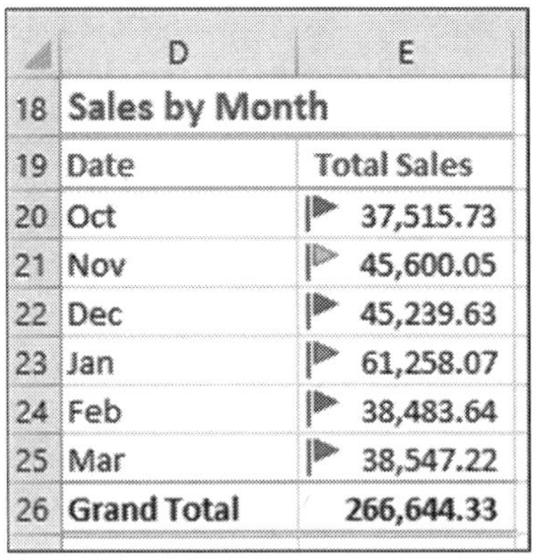

Sales Report-1

Visualizations are a half-way house between raw data and charts. With a few clicks of the mouse, they allow you to express numbers in a visual manner.

1 Open *Sales Report-1* from your sample files folder (if it isn't already open).

2 Add a data bar visualization to the *Sales by Country* figures.

1. Select cells B5:B25.
2. Click: Home→Styles→Conditional Formatting→ Data Bars→Gradient Fill→Red Data Bar.

The visualization is applied (see sidebar).

3 Add a color scale visualization to the *Sales by Category* figures.

1. Select cells E5:E12.
2. Click: Home→Styles→Conditional Formatting→ Color Scales→Green-Yellow Color Scale.

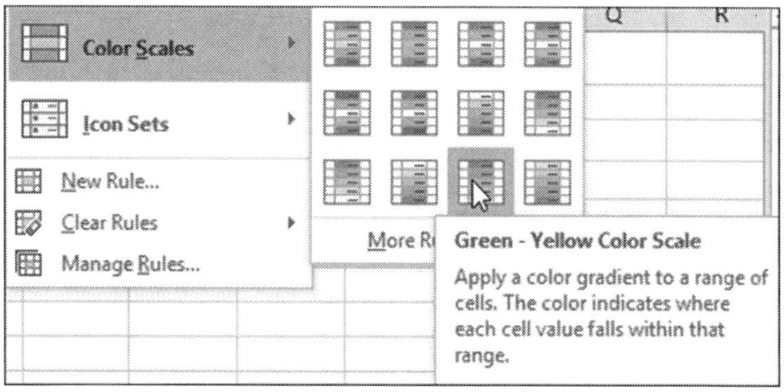

The visualization is applied (see sidebar).

4 Add an icon set visualization to the *Sales by Month* figures.

1. Select cells E20:E25.
2. Click: Home→Styles→Conditional Formatting→Icon Sets→ Indicators→3 Flags.

3. Re-size column E so that it is wide enough to display the values.

The visualization is applied (see sidebar).

When the icon set contains three icons, Excel assigns the relative icons to the top third, middle third, and bottom third of the value range.

You will often need to change these default values.

5 Use the *Rules Manager* to modify the *Sales by Month* visualization so that three green flags are shown.

The *Sales by Month* visualization may discourage your salesforce because only one month is flagged as green, with four months flagged red. You will now adjust the criteria for flag allocation so that three months are shown as green.

1. Select cells E20:E25.
2. Click: Home→Styles→Conditional Formatting→ Manage Rules…

   The *Conditional Formatting Rules Manager* dialog is displayed.
3. Click the *Edit Rule* button. 

4. Change the criteria in the dialog so that values over 45,000 are green, values over 38,000 are yellow and values under 38,000 are red.

   You'll need to set the criteria as follows:

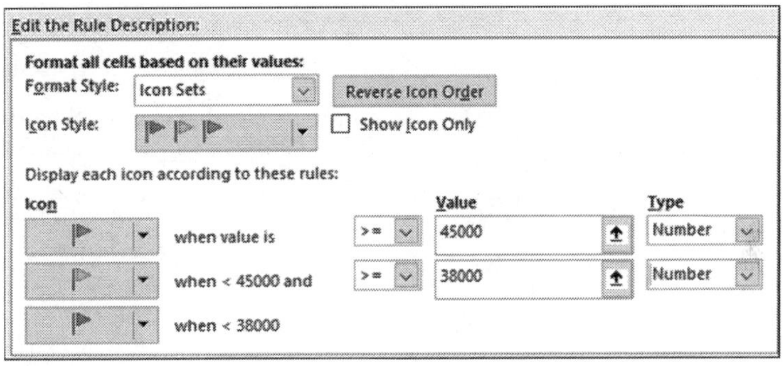

5. Click OK and OK again.

   The flags are now displayed as required, with three green flags (see sidebar).

	D	E
18	**Sales by Month**	
19	Date	Total Sales
20	Oct	37,515.73
21	Nov	45,600.05
22	Dec	45,239.63
23	Jan	61,258.07
24	Feb	38,483.64
25	Mar	38,547.22
26	Grand Total	266,644.33

6 Use the *Rules Manager* to show the visualizations for *Sales by Country* without the underlying data.

1. Select cells B5:B25.
2. Click: Home→Styles→Conditional Formatting→ Manage Rules.

   The *Conditional Formatting Rules Manager* dialog is displayed.
3. Click the *Edit Rule* button. 

4. Check the *Show Bar Only* check box.

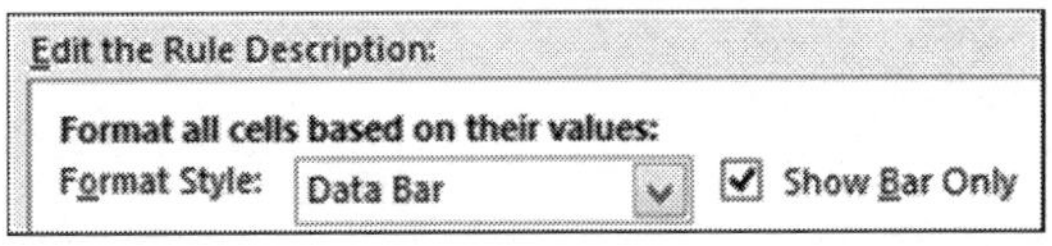

5. Click the OK button on each dialog to close them.

   The bars are now shown without the values.

7 Use the *Rules Manager* to bring back the values for *Sales by Country*.

Follow the same procedure as in the previous step to uncheck the *Show Bar Only* check box.

8 Save your work as *Sales Report-2*.

tip

Use the Show Bar Only feature to create quick charts

To create a "quick chart" for cells E5:E12:

1. Type the formula **=E5** into cell F5.
2. AutoFill cell F5 down to F12.
3. Create a data bar visualization for cells F5:F12 with the *Show Bar Only* option checked.
4. Widen column F to display a "quick chart".

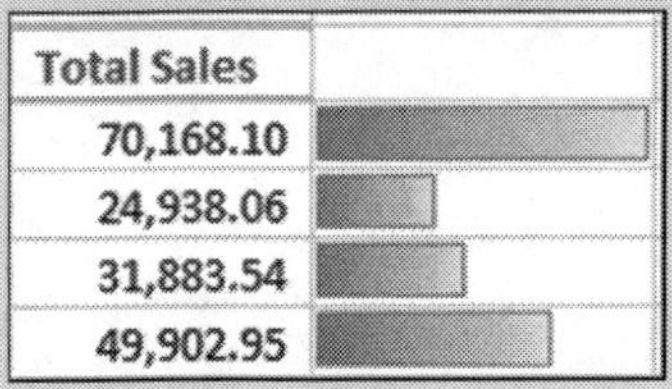

Lesson 4-19: Create a formula driven conditional format

While the built-in conditional format options are very powerful, you will occasionally have a conditional format requirement that is not catered for.

For example, I've lost count of the number of times I have been asked if it is possible to highlight an entire row, rather than a single cell within a row, based upon the value in one of the row's cells.

This lesson will show you how to achieve this using a formula-driven conditional format.

1 Open *Sales Summary First Quarter 2022* from your sample files folder.

Your challenge will be to highlight the entire row when the *Country* column contains the value: *USA*.

2 Apply a conditional format to column C to change the background color to light orange when the cell contains the text: USA.

1. Select column C.
2. Click: Home→Styles→Conditional Formatting→ Highlight Cells Rules→Text That Contains…
3. Type: **USA** in the *Format cells that contain the text* box.
4. Select *Custom Format* as the fill color:

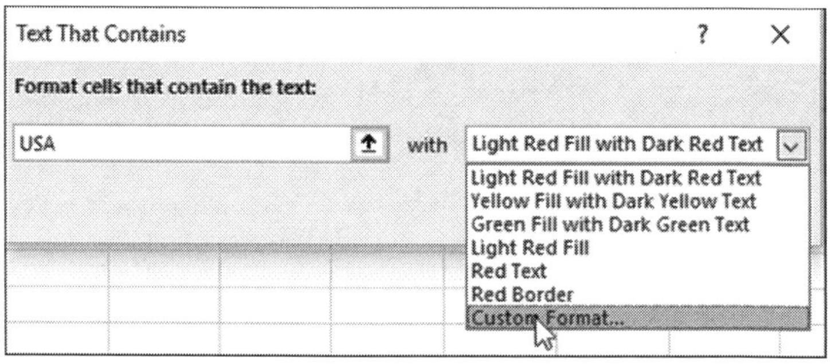

5. Click the *Fill* tab and select a light orange color for the conditional fill.

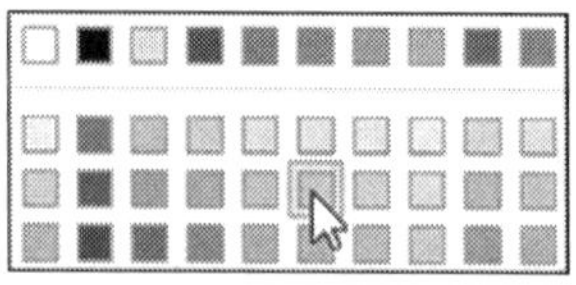

6. Click the OK button once, and then again, to close both dialogs.

Every cell in column C that contains the text *USA* is now shaded light orange.

note

A more expert solution using mixed cell references

In my classroom courses, I always teach this lesson as presented here.

I like to keep things simple by solving the problem using a simple formula.

The reason I do this is that many students find mixed cell references challenging (the subject of: *Lesson 3-14: Understand mixed cell references*).

If you completely understood *Lesson 3-14: Understand mixed cell references*, you might find it interesting to solve this problem in a more efficient way.

You can apply a single mixed cell reference to all four columns in a single operation:

1. Select columns A to D.
2. Click: Home→Styles→ Conditional Formatting→ New Rule…
3. Select: *Use a formula to determine which cells to format.*
4. Type this formula (note the use of a mixed cell reference) into the *Format values where this formula is true* box:

   =$C1="USA"

5. Click the *Format…* button.
6. Click the *Fill* tab and select a light orange color for the conditional fill.
7. Click OK and OK again.

Sales Summary First Quarter 2022

	B	C	D
40	Familia Arquibaldo	Brazil	100.00
41	Hungry Coyote Import Store	USA	62.40
42	Hungry Coyote Import Store	USA	40.00
43	Wartian Herkku	Finland	146.00

3 Apply a formula-driven conditional format to column B so that the same rows are highlighted.

This is a lot more difficult than the simple conditional format applied to column C.

1. Select column B.
2. Click: Home→Styles→Conditional Formatting→New Rule…

   The *New Formatting Rule* dialog appears.
3. Select *Use a formula to determine which cells to format* from the *Select a Rule Type* list.
4. Type the formula **=C1="USA"** into the formula text box.

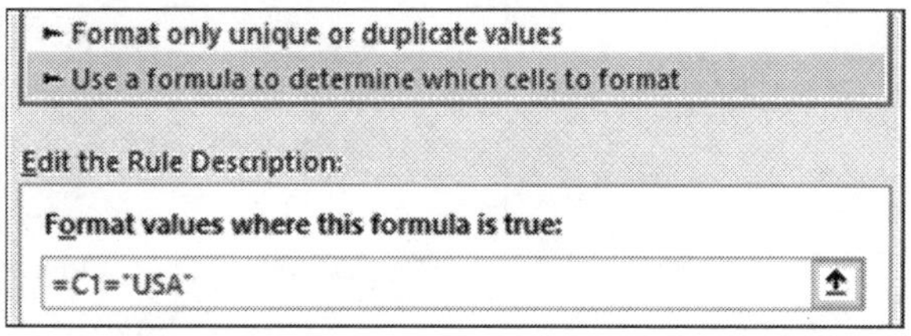

   See sidebar for a discussion of this formula.
5. Click the *Format* button, then the *Fill* tab and apply the same light orange fill color.

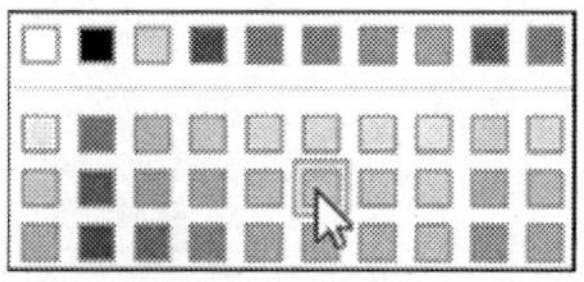

6. Click the OK button once, and then again, to close both dialogs.

   Both columns now have a light orange fill when the country is USA.

	A	B	C	D
40	14-Jan-22	Familia Arquibaldo	Brazil	100.00
41	15-Jan-22	Hungry Coyote Import Store	USA	62.40
42	15-Jan-22	Hungry Coyote Import Store	USA	40.00
43	16-Jan-22	Wartian Herkku	Finland	146.00

4 Apply the same formula-driven conditional format to columns A and D so that the whole row is highlighted.

	A	B	C	D
40	14-Jan-22	Familia Arquibaldo	Brazil	100.00
41	15-Jan-22	Hungry Coyote Import Store	USA	62.40
42	15-Jan-22	Hungry Coyote Import Store	USA	40.00
43	16-Jan-22	Wartian Herkku	Finland	146.00

5 Save your work as *Sales Summary First Quarter 2022-1.*

tip

Why does the formula relate to cell C1?

At first it seems rather odd that you refer to cell C1 in the conditional formatting formula.

C1 is in the title row so how can this be right?

The answer is to be found in Excel's treatment of absolute and relative cell references (originally explained in: *Lesson 3-13: Understand absolute and relative cell references*).

Excel regards the cell reference to be relative to the first row in the selected range.

Since you selected an entire column, row 1 is the reference row used to adjust the formula for every other row within the column.

In other words, Excel will look at cell C2 when applying conditional formatting to row 2, C3 when applying to row 3... and so on.

This is exactly what you want to happen.

Lesson 4-20: Insert a Sparkline into a range of cells

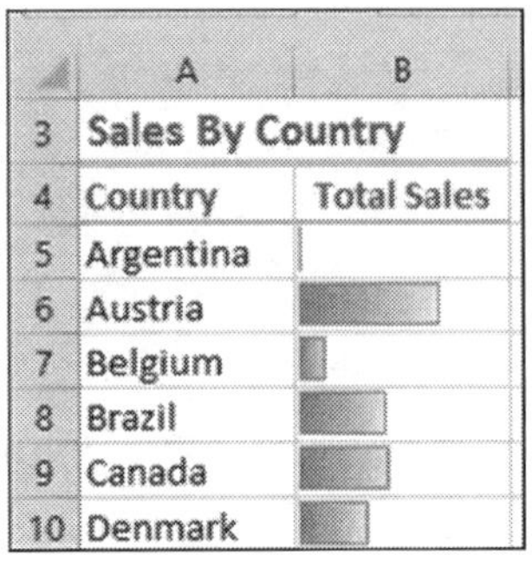

	A	B
3	Sales By Country	
4	Country	Total Sales
5	Argentina	
6	Austria	
7	Belgium	
8	Brazil	
9	Canada	
10	Denmark	

Sparklines solve a very common worksheet problem.

In *Lesson 4-18: Bring data alive with visualizations,* you discovered how visualizations can effectively illustrate the differences between values in a single column of data (see example in sidebar).

In: *Session Five: Charts and Graphics,* you will discover Excel's ability to create fantastic charts of all descriptions. These are especially useful when your data has two dimensions (several columns per row). You'll create this chart:

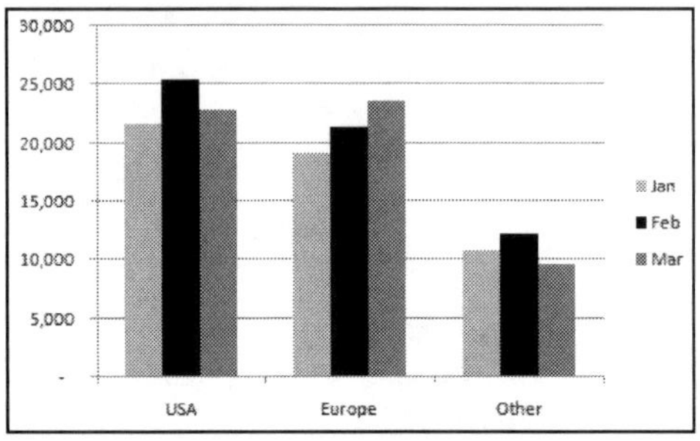

But imagine you had a large number of rows of two-dimensional data to compare. This is the case in the sample worksheet for this lesson, where there are 36 rows (one for each branch), each having six values (Jan-Jun):

	A	B	C	D	E	F	G	H
4	Country	Branch	Jan	Feb	Mar	Apr	May	Jun
5	USA	Chicago	671,185	359,811	745,471	685,637	- 16,562	711,009
6	USA	Dallas	708,157	276,972	227,227	482,136	377,175	198,273

The worksheet contains data for 36 branches and would produce a very confusing chart (with 36 data series, one for each branch):

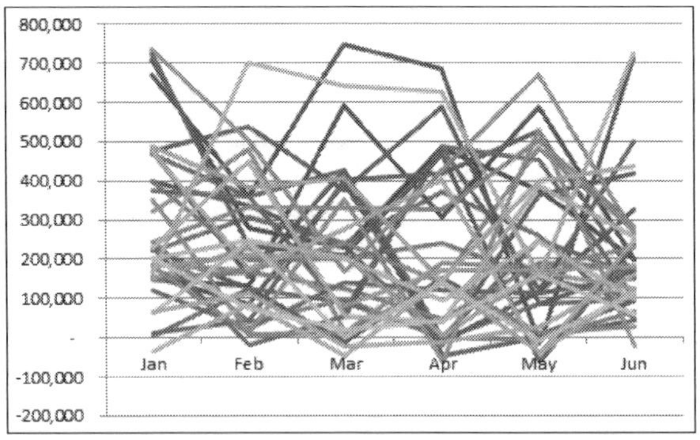

A *Sparkline* is a chart that can be inserted into a single cell, typically charting the values in the cells on the left.

Sparklines provide an elegant way to present users with a visualization of large two-dimensional data sets, even when they contain thousands of rows.

First Half-Year Profit Report

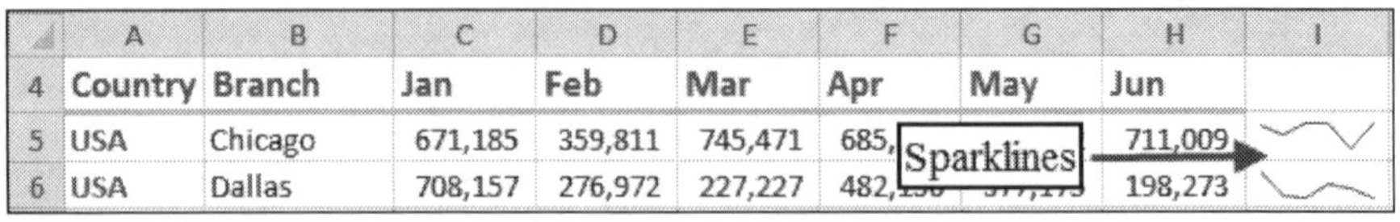

	A	B	C	D	E	F	G	H	I
4	Country	Branch	Jan	Feb	Mar	Apr	May	Jun	
5	USA	Chicago	671,185	359,811	745,471	685,		711,009	
6	USA	Dallas	708,157	276,972	227,227	482,		198,273	

note

You can also add Sparklines using the Quick Analysis button

Whenever you select a range of cells, a *Quick Analysis* button appears just outside the bottom-right corner of the selected range.

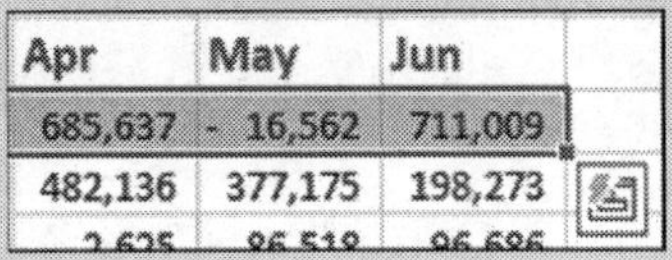

Apr	May	Jun
685,637	- 16,562	711,009
482,136	377,175	198,273

When you click the *Quick Analysis* button, the *Quick Analysis* dialog appears.

One of the menu options on this dialog is *Sparklines.*

It is possible to add *Line, Column* and *Win/Loss* Sparklines using this dialog.

1 Open *First Half-Year Profit Report* from your sample files folder.

2 Create a *Line Sparkline* in cell I5 that charts the data in cells C5:H5.

1. Click in cell I5.
2. Click: Insert→Sparklines→Line. 

   The *Create Sparklines* dialog appears.

3. Click in the *Data Range:* box and then select cells C5:H5.

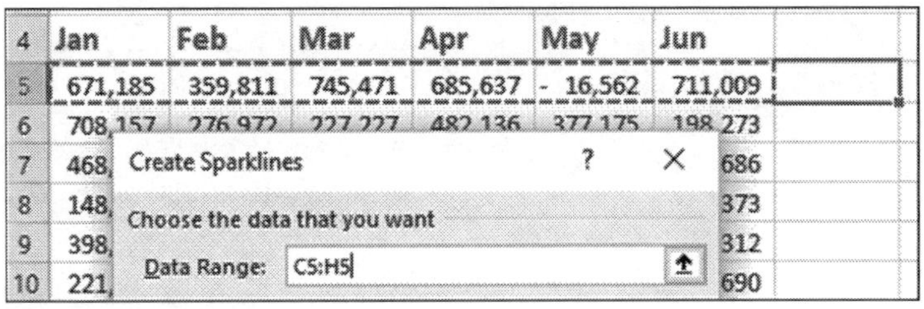

4. Click the OK button.

   A Sparkline appears in cell I5:

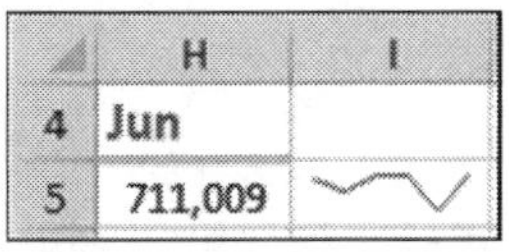

	H	I
4	Jun	
5	711,009	

3 AutoFill the Sparkline to cells I6:I40.

You learned how to do this in: *Lesson 2-14: Use AutoFill for text and numeric series.*

You can now see how Sparklines visualize each branch's performance in a way that is beyond the scope of Visualizations and Charts.

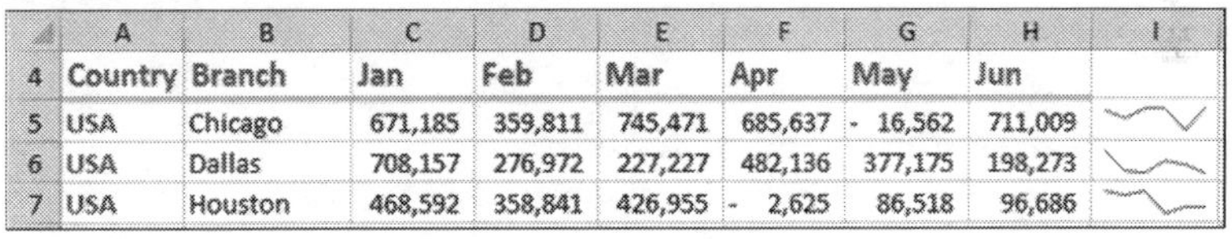

	A	B	C	D	E	F	G	H	I
4	Country	Branch	Jan	Feb	Mar	Apr	May	Jun	
5	USA	Chicago	671,185	359,811	745,471	685,637	- 16,562	711,009	
6	USA	Dallas	708,157	276,972	227,227	482,136	377,175	198,273	
7	USA	Houston	468,592	358,841	426,955	- 2,625	86,518	96,686	

4 Use the same technique to place a *Column Sparkline* in cells J5:J40 that charts the same data range (C5:H5).

5 Use the same technique to place a *Win/Loss Sparkline* in cells K5:K40 that charts the same data range (C5:H5).

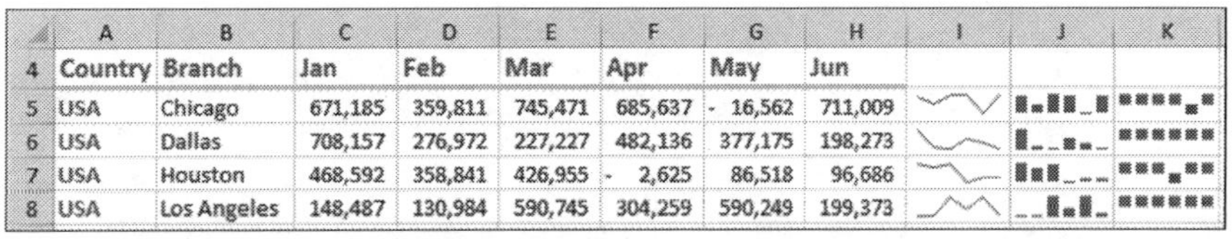

	A	B	C	D	E	F	G	H	I	J	K
4	Country	Branch	Jan	Feb	Mar	Apr	May	Jun			
5	USA	Chicago	671,185	359,811	745,471	685,637	- 16,562	711,009			
6	USA	Dallas	708,157	276,972	227,227	482,136	377,175	198,273			
7	USA	Houston	468,592	358,841	426,955	- 2,625	86,518	96,686			
8	USA	Los Angeles	148,487	130,984	590,745	304,259	590,249	199,373			

The *Column Sparkline* is very similar to the *Line Sparkline* but represents data as a bar chart.

Notice how the *Win/Loss Sparkline* enables you to see at a glance that Chicago and Houston had one loss-making month while Dallas and Los Angeles made a profit every month.

6 Save your work as *First Half Year Profit Report-1.*

important

Win/Loss Sparklines depict zero values with a blank space

In the example data for this lesson, all of the branches have either made a profit or a loss.

If you have a data set with zero values, the Win/Loss Sparkline will show blank spaces in the chart to illustrate zero values.

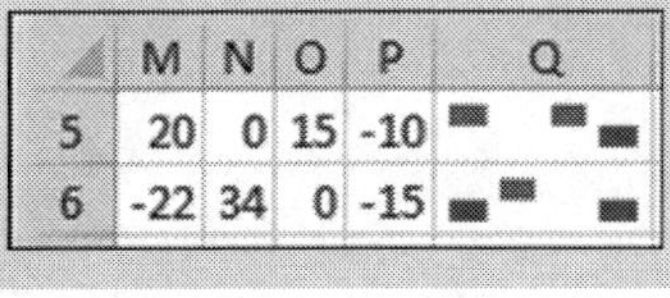

	M	N	O	P	Q
5	20	0	15	-10	
6	-22	34	0	-15	

Lesson 4-21: Apply a common vertical axis and formatting to a Sparkline group

Consider the following column Sparklines:

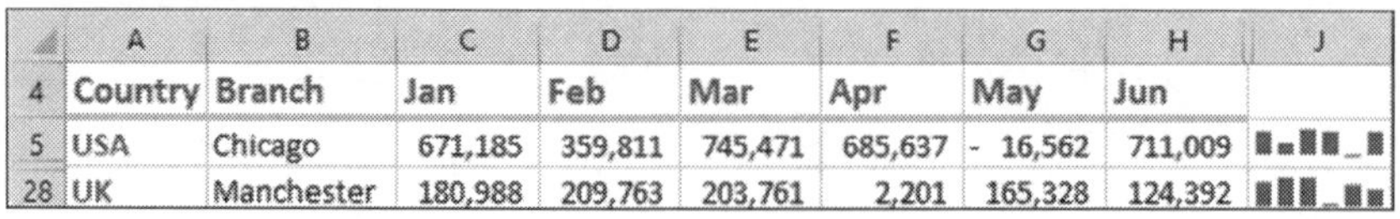

	A	B	C	D	E	F	G	H	J
4	Country	Branch	Jan	Feb	Mar	Apr	May	Jun	
5	USA	Chicago	671,185	359,811	745,471	685,637	- 16,562	711,009	
28	UK	Manchester	180,988	209,763	203,761	2,201	165,328	124,392	

If you only looked at the Sparklines (and not the values) you'd guess that Manchester made more profit in the first three months than Chicago.

A glance at the actual profit values shows that Chicago actually made nearly four times more profit than Manchester.

The *Column* Sparklines are misleading because, by default, Excel only considers each row's values when setting the *Maximum* and *Minimum* values for the bars (also called the *Vertical Axis* values).

In this lesson, you'll change this behavior so that the size of the bars gives a true indication of each branch's profit relative to the other branches in the list.

important

Deleting Sparklines

In this lesson, you deleted two Sparkline groups by deleting the columns that contained them.

Sometimes you will need to delete a Sparkline group without deleting the column that contains them.

To do this:

1. Select the Sparkline group.
2. Click:

   Sparkline→Group→
   Clear→
   Clear Selected Sparkline Groups

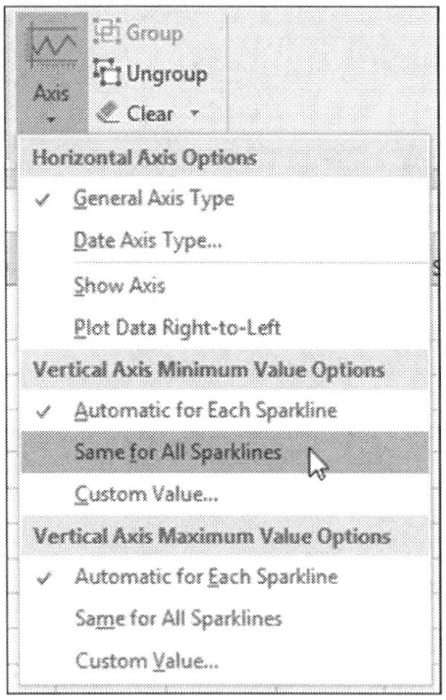

First Half-Year Profit Report-1

1 Open *First Half-Year Profit Report-1* from your sample files folder (if it isn't already open).

2 Delete columns I and K so that only the Column Sparklines remain.

You learned how to do this in: *Lesson 3-1: Insert and delete rows and columns.* Removing the two other Sparklines will help to focus upon the *Column Sparkline.*

3 Set a common Maximum and Minimum value for all Sparklines.

1. Click on any of the Sparklines in column I.

   Notice that a new tab has appeared on the Title bar called *Sparkline.*

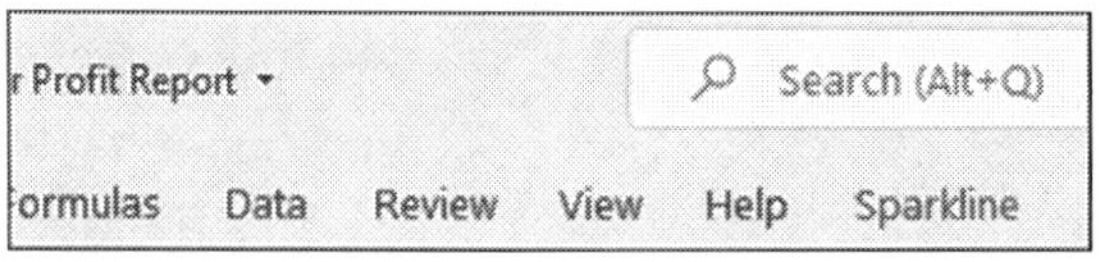

   Notice also that a thin blue line has appeared around all of the Sparklines in column I. This happens because Excel views all of the Sparklines as a *Sparkline Group*. This means that when you use any of the *Sparkline* options available from the Ribbon, the settings will apply to all Sparklines in the group.

2. Click: Sparkline→Group→Axis drop-down→
   Vertical Axis Minimum Value Options→
   Same for All Sparklines.

3. Click: Sparkline→ Axis drop-down→
   Vertical Axis Maximum Value Options→
   Same for All Sparklines.

Notice the change in the Chicago and Manchester Sparklines:

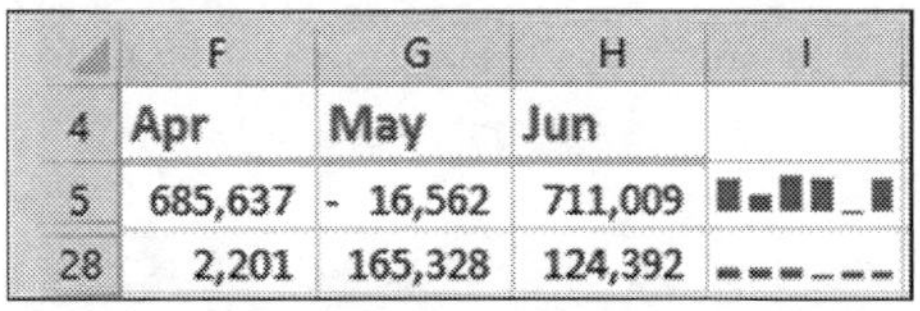

	F	G	H	I
4	Apr	May	Jun	
5	685,637	- 16,562	711,009	
28	2,201	165,328	124,392	

It is now clear, from looking at the bars alone, that in every month (except May) Manchester produced far less profit than Chicago.

4 Explore Sparkline formatting options.

The *Sparkline* tab on the Ribbon provides many ways in which you can change the appearance of a group of Sparklines. Try experimenting with them.

1. Use the *Show* and *Style→Marker Color* options.

   The *Show* check boxes allow you to apply a chosen color to any of the following points on a Sparkline.

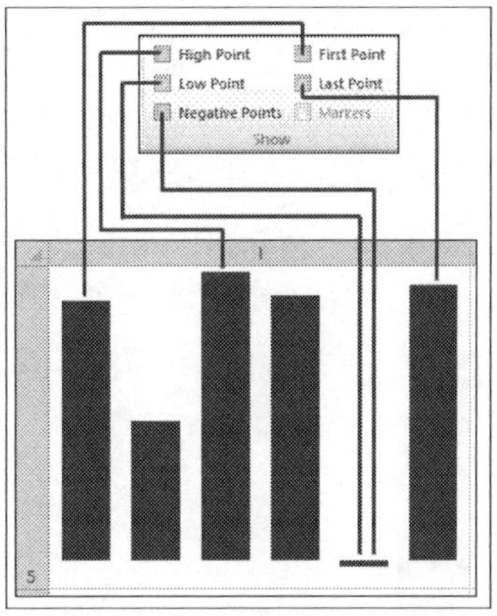

   You can choose a color for each of the points you check from the *Style→Marker Color* drop down.

2. Choose a new *Sparkline Style* from the *Style* gallery.

   Styles allow you to change the color scheme for your Sparkline. Note that the styles use theme colors and will change if you change the current theme. (You learned about themes in: *Lesson 4-9: Understand themes*).

3. Change the *Sparkline Type* to *Line* by clicking:

   Sparkline→Type→Line

4. Add *Markers.*

   Click: Sparkline→Show→Markers.

   When the *Sparkline Type* is *Line,* you are able to select the *Markers* option in the *Show* group. Each data point on the Sparkline is then marked with a dot.

5. Click: Sparkline→Style→Sparkline Color and change the line color.

6. Click: Sparkline→Style→
   Sparkline Color→Weight and change the line thickness.

5 Close *First Half-Year Profit Report-1* without saving.

note

You can change the size of a Sparkline by re-sizing the cell that contains it

In the lessons in this session, the Sparkline cells have been left at their default size for neatness and to keep the worksheet compact.

If you resize a cell that contains a Sparkline it will automatically resize to fill the cell:

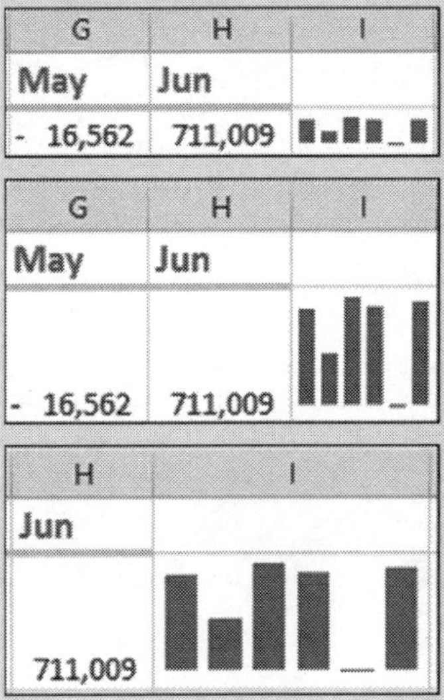

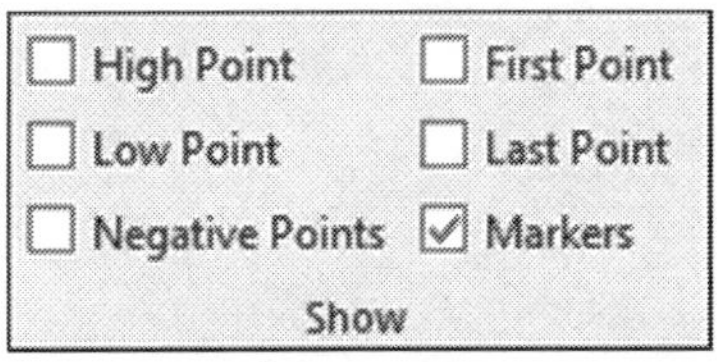

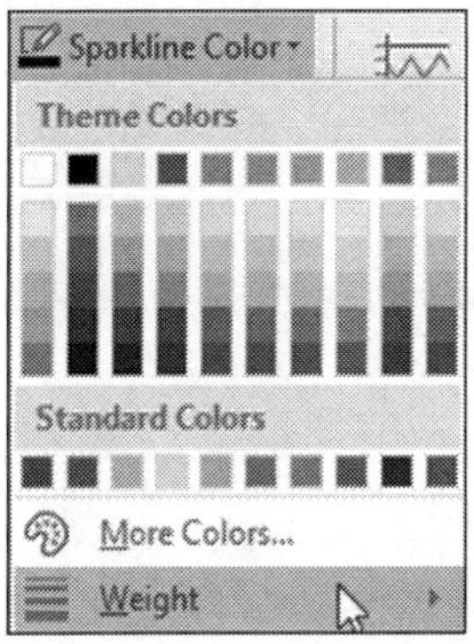

Lesson 4-22: Apply a date axis to a Sparkline group and format a single Sparkline

Sometimes you will encounter data that is attached to dates with uneven time intervals. Here's some of the sample data for this lesson:

	A	B	C	D	E	F	G	H
1	Number of Rings to Answer Phone Survey							
2								
3	Country	Branch	1-Mar-22	3-Mar-22	4-Mar-22	7-Mar-22	8-Mar-22	9-Mar-22
4	USA	Chicago	3	1	1	2	3	2
5	USA	Dallas	2	3	1	3	2	1
6	USA	Houston	10	8	11	7	11	5
7	USA	Los Angeles	1	3	2	3	3	1

This company has a policy that the telephone should be answered within three rings. To make sure the staff are hitting this target, head office phone each branch occasionally and record the number of rings taken to answer. You can see that Chicago, Dallas and Los Angeles are doing well but Houston is performing well below standard.

Head office don't phone every day – only when they have time to do so. This means that they didn't phone at all on 2nd, 5th and 6th March.

By default, a Sparkline will assume that the data is at equal intervals and chart like this:

	A	B	C	D	E	F	G	H	I
3	Country	Branch	1-Mar-22	3-Mar-22	4-Mar-22	7-Mar-22	8-Mar-22	9-Mar-22	
4	USA	Chicago	3	1	1	2	3	2	
5	USA	Dallas	2	3	1	3	2	1	
6	USA	Houston	10	8	11	7	11	5	
7	USA	Los Angeles	1	3	2	3	3	1	

But you'd like the Sparklines to have a common vertical axis and show a gap for the missing dates like this:

	E	F	G	H	I
3	4-Mar-22	7-Mar-22	8-Mar-22	9-Mar-22	
4	1	2	3	2	
5	1	3	2	1	
6	11	7	11	5	
7	2	3	3	1	

1 Open *Phone Survey* from your sample files folder.

2 Insert a Column Sparkline in cell I4 to chart data in cells C4:H4 and AutoFill it down to the end of the range.

You learned how to do this in: *Lesson 4-20: Insert a Sparkline into a range of cells.*

3 Set the *Vertical Axis Minimum Value* and *Vertical Axis Maximum Value* to be the same for all Sparklines.

You learned how to do this in: *Lesson 4-21: Apply a common vertical axis and formatting to a Sparkline group.*

Your worksheet should now look like this:

Phone Survey

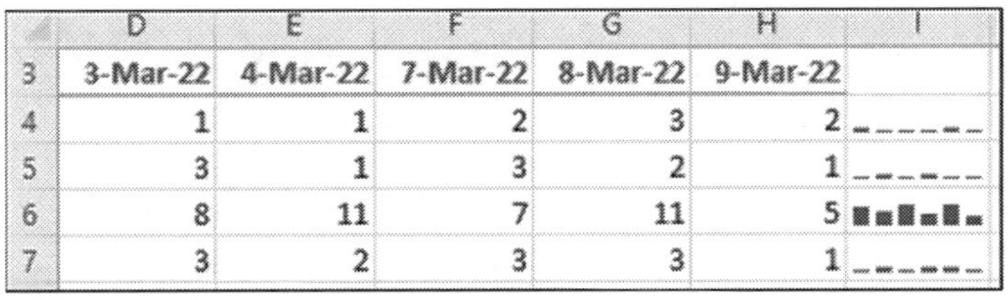

	D	E	F	G	H	I
3	3-Mar-22	4-Mar-22	7-Mar-22	8-Mar-22	9-Mar-22	
4	1	1	2	3	2	
5	3	1	3	2	1	
6	8	11	7	11	5	
7	3	2	3	3	1	

4 Set the *Sparkline Date Range* to C3:H3.

1. Click any Sparkline in column I to select the Sparkline group.
2. Click:

   Sparkline→Group→Axis→Date Axis Type…

   The *Sparkline Date Range* dialog appears.
3. Select cells C3:H3 with the mouse.

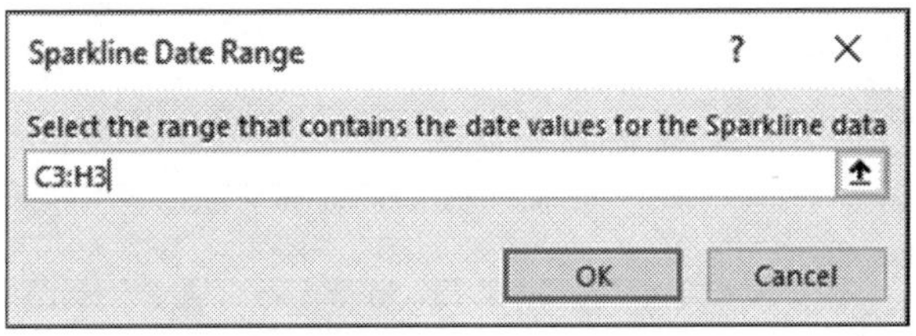

4. Click the OK button.

   The Sparklines are now shown with gaps for the missing dates:

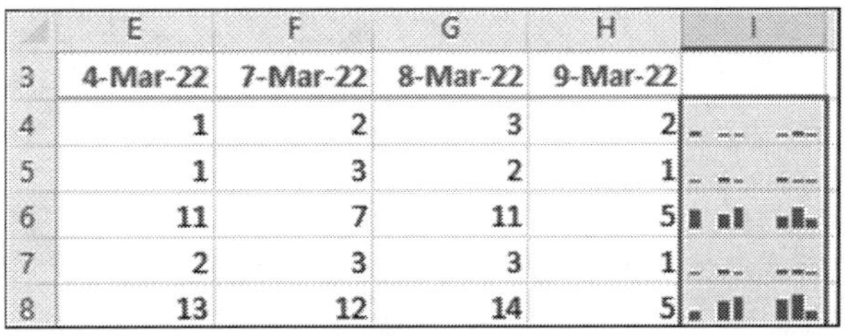

	E	F	G	H	I
3	4-Mar-22	7-Mar-22	8-Mar-22	9-Mar-22	
4	1	2	3	2	
5	1	3	2	1	
6	11	7	11	5	
7	2	3	3	1	
8	13	12	14	5	

5 Format the *Houston* Sparkline (in cell I6) so that all bars are orange.

To format a single Sparkline, it is necessary to *Ungroup* the Sparklines. When Sparklines are ungrouped, it is possible to format them individually.

1. Click in cell I6.
2. Click: Sparkline→Group→Ungroup.
3. Click:

   Sparkline→Style→Sparkline Color→
   Orange Accent 2

   The *Houston* Sparkline is now colored orange, while all other Sparklines remain black.

6 Save your work as *Phone Survey-1*.

note

Options for worksheets that contain Hidden and Empty cells

In:

Lesson 5-15: Chart non-contiguous source data by hiding rows and columns

And:

Lesson 5-17: Deal with empty data points

… you will learn the concept of hidden rows and columns, and also learn how to use Excel's *Hidden and Empty Cell Settings* dialog.

You'll then also be able to use these options when you add a Sparkline to a worksheet that contains empty cells or hidden rows and columns.

The *Hidden and Empty Cell Settings* dialog is available from:

Sparkline→
Sparkline→Edit Data→
Hidden & Empty Cells

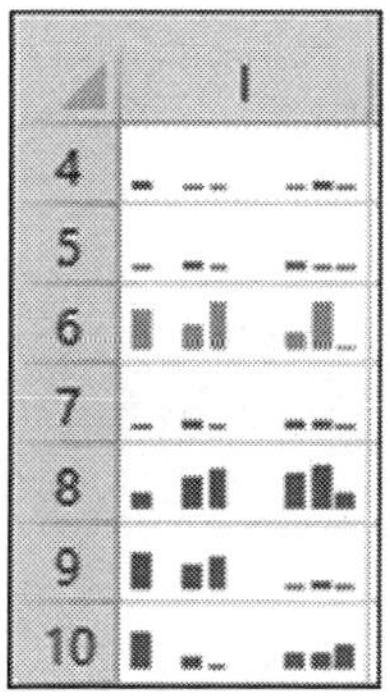

Lesson 4-23: Use the Format Painter

The format painter is one of the most useful tools in Microsoft Office.

You can use the format painter in Excel, PowerPoint, Word and all other Office applications.

I find that at least half of the experienced Excel users who attend my classroom courses have never discovered the format painter. I love it when they gasp in amazement at the enormous amount of time and effort they will save in future when using this tool.

In this lesson, you're going to take a worksheet that is partially formatted and use the format painter to quickly copy formatting information (as opposed to values) from one cell to another.

Sales Report-FP

1 Open *Sales Report-FP* from your sample files folder.

This worksheet has been partially formatted.

	A	B	C	D	E
1	Sales Report				
2					
3	Sales By Country			Sales by Category	
4	Country	Total Sales		Category	Total Sales
5	Argentina	762.6		Beverages	70168.1
6	Austria	33462.58		Condiments	24938.055
7	Belgium	6109.48		Confections	31883.54
8	Brazil	20524.42		Dairy Products	49902.95
9	Canada	21306.29		Grains/Cereals	19570.36
10	Denmark	16658.8		Meat/Poultry	35767.63
11	Finland	5525		Produce	17109.18
12	France	26155.54		Seafood	17304.51
13	Germany	28361.38		Grand Total	266644.325
14	Ireland	6157.755			

2 Apply the comma style to all of the values in column B.

You learned how to do this in: *Lesson 4-3: Format numbers using built-in number formats.*

Values are now formatted with two decimal places and a thousand comma separator.

	A	B
9	Canada	21,306.29
10	Denmark	16,658.80
11	Finland	5,525.00

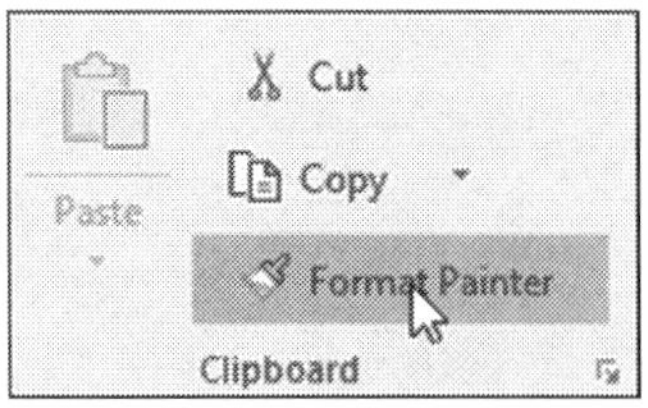

3 Use the format painter to copy formatting from the values in column B to the ranges E5:E13 and E20:E26.

1. Click any value in column B.

2. Click: Home→Clipboard→Format Painter. 

   The cursor shape changes to a paint brush.

note

AutoFill's Paste option is able to match formatting in the same way as the Format Painter

The Format Painter is the fastest and most convenient way to match formatting when you only have to deal with a small range of cells.

Sometimes you'll need to match formatting in very large ranges containing thousands of cells. This would take a long time using the Format Painter but can be quickly achieved using *AutoFill,* or by using *Paste* along with the skills you learned in: *Lesson 2-8: AutoSelect a range of cells.*

AutoFill

AutoFill options were covered in depth in: *Lesson 2-16: Use AutoFill options.* When you AutoFill using a right-click and drag (or AutoFill and then look at the Smart tag options) you'll notice that there's a *Fill Formatting Only* option.

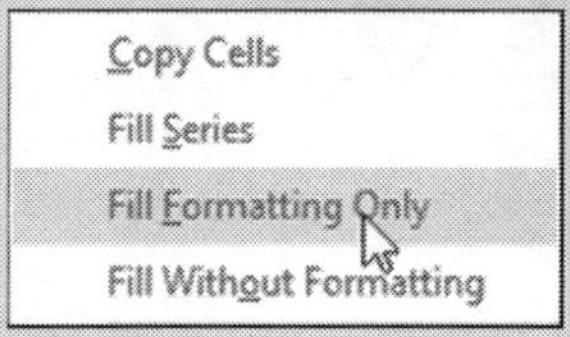

Paste

Copy and Paste were covered in depth in: *Lesson 3-3: Cut, copy and paste.* When you paste there's also a *Formatting* option in the *Paste Options.*

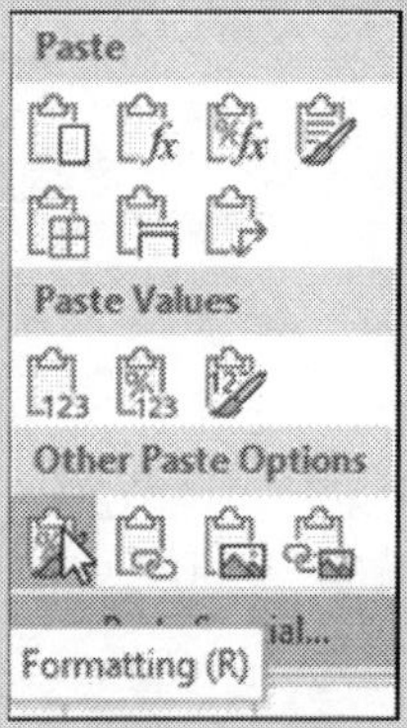

3. Click and drag across cells E5:E13.

   The format of cells E5:E13 changes to match those of the values in column B.

	D	E
4	Category	Total Sales
5	Beverages	70,168.10
6	Condiments	24,938.06

4. Click on any value in column B.
5. Click: Home→Clipboard→Format Painter.
6. Drag across cells E20:E26.

   All values in this worksheet are now formatted with the comma style.

4 Use the format painter to copy formatting from cell A3 to cells D3 and D18.

This time you will use the format painter in a slightly different way. If you double-click the format painter icon Format Painter a *sticky format painter* is enabled. This will stay switched on until you click the format painter icon again to switch it off.

1. Click on cell A3 to make it the active (source) cell.
2. Double-click: Home→Clipboard→Format Painter.

   The cursor shape changes to a paint brush.

3. Click cell D3. The format now matches cell A3 but the cursor remains the same.
4. Click cell D18. The format now matches cell A3 but the cursor remains the same.
5. Click: Home→Clipboard→Format Painter Format Painter to switch off the format painter. The cursor reverts to the normal shape.

5 Copy formatting from cell A4 to cells D4:E4 and D19:E19 using the format painter.

6 Apply the *Total* style to cell B26.

You learned how to do this in: *Lesson 4-10: Use cell styles and change themes.*

7 Copy the total style from cell B26 to cells E13 and E26 using the format painter.

8 Save your work as *Sales Report-FP-1.*

Lesson 4-24: Rotate text

1 Open *Top 20 Films* from your sample files folder.

2 Insert a new column to the left of column A.

You learned how to do this in: *Lesson 3-1: Insert and delete rows and columns.*

3 Cut and paste the contents of cell B1 to cell A1.

You learned how to do this in: *Lesson 3-3: Cut, copy and paste.*

4 Cut and paste the contents of cell B25 to cell A25.

5 Apply the *Title* style to cell A1, the *Heading 2* style to cells A3:E3 and the *Heading 4* style to cell A25.

You learned how to do this in: *Lesson 4-10: Use cell styles and change themes.*

6 Type: **Over 700M** into cell A4, **Over 600M** into cell A8 and **Over 450M** into cell A15.

7 Make column A slightly wider so that all text in the column is visible.

You learned how to do this in: *Lesson 2-9: Re-size rows and columns.*

8 Select cells A4:A7.

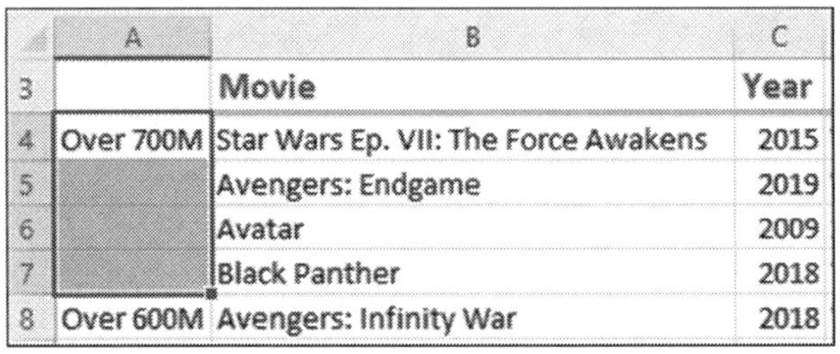

	A	B	C
3		Movie	Year
4	Over 700M	Star Wars Ep. VII: The Force Awakens	2015
5		Avengers: Endgame	2019
6		Avatar	2009
7		Black Panther	2018
8	Over 600M	Avengers: Infinity War	2018

9 Merge the selected cells.

This was covered in: *Lesson 4-6: Merge cells, wrap text and expand/collapse the formula bar.*

10 Rotate the text through ninety degrees.

1. Click: Home→Alignment→Orientation. 
2. Select *Rotate Text Up* from the drop-down list.

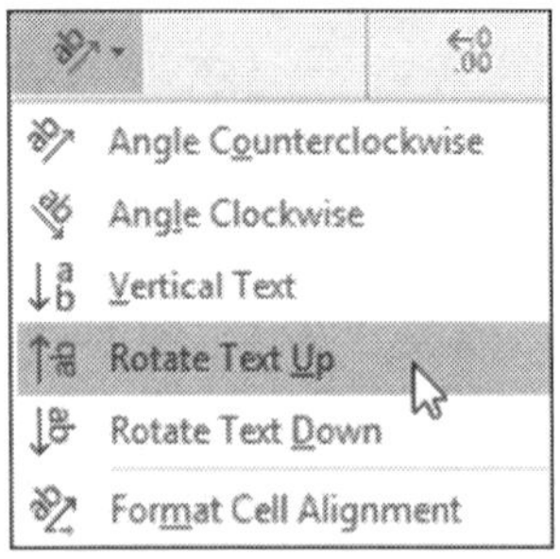

11 Merge and rotate the text up in cells A8:A14 and A15:A23.

Your worksheet should now look like the facing page sidebar.

note

Other ways to rotate text

You can also rotate text using the *Format Cells* dialog, though you'll nearly always find the Ribbon method faster and more convenient.

The *Format Cells* dialog is slightly more powerful as it allows you to rotate text by any angle.

1. Right-click a cell or range and click *Format Cells* from the shortcut menu.
2. Click the *Alignment* tab.
3. In the *Orientation* pane either type in the number of degrees of rotation or click and drag the red marker to set the rotation angle visually.

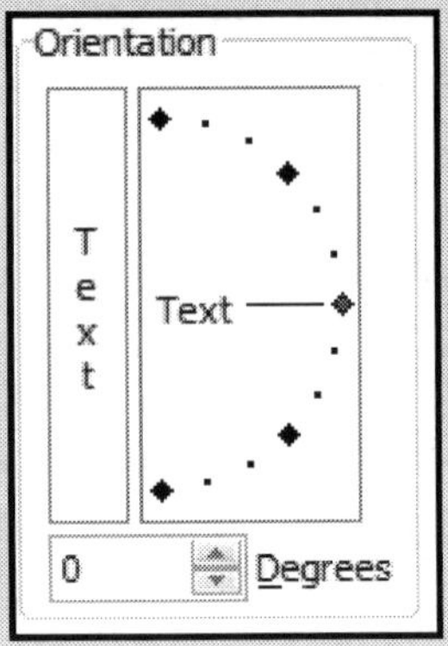

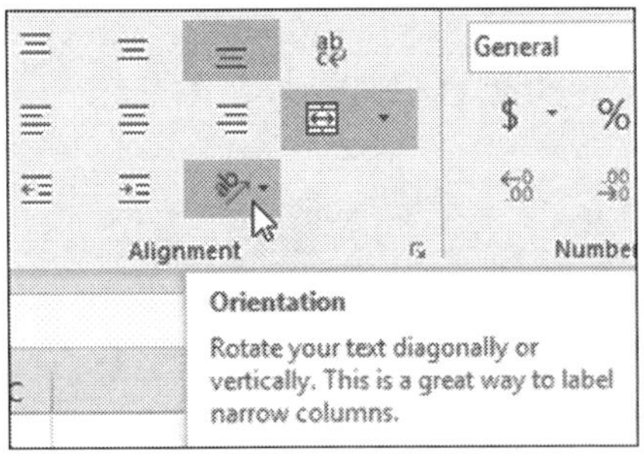

Top 20 Films

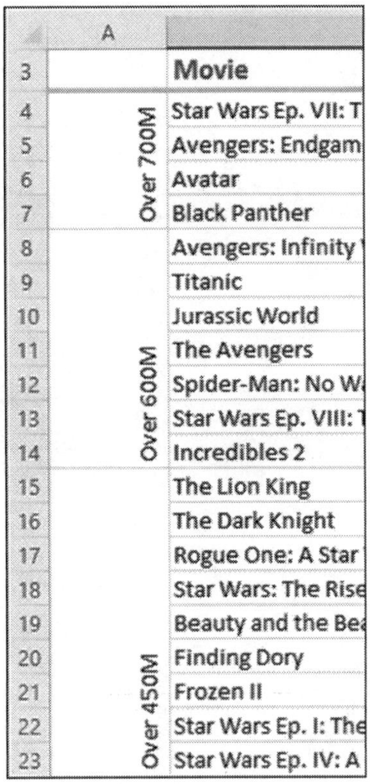

12 Select cells A4:A15 and set the horizontal alignment to *center* and the vertical alignment to *middle*.

You learned how to do this in: *Lesson 4-5: Horizontally align the contents of cells* and *Lesson 4-8: Vertically align the contents of cells.*

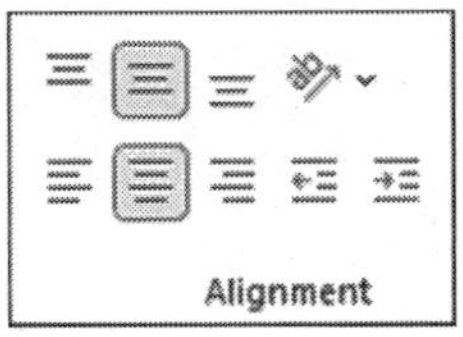

13 Apply the *Heading 4* style to cells A4:A15.

14 AutoFit cells A4:A18 so that they are just wide enough for the text they contain.

You learned how to do this in: *Lesson 2-9: Re-size rows and columns.*

15 Apply the *40% Accent 3* style to cell A4.

You learned how to do this in: *Lesson 4-10: Use cell styles and change themes.*

Note that the cell reference for the old range A4:A8 is now the single cell reference A4.

16 Apply the *40% Accent 6* style to cell A8.

17 Apply the *40% Accent 2* style to cell A15.

18 Re-size row 3 so that it is about three times the normal height.

19 Rotate the text in row 3 by 45 degrees.

1. Select row 3.

2. Click: Home→Alignment→Orientation  → Angle Counterclockwise.

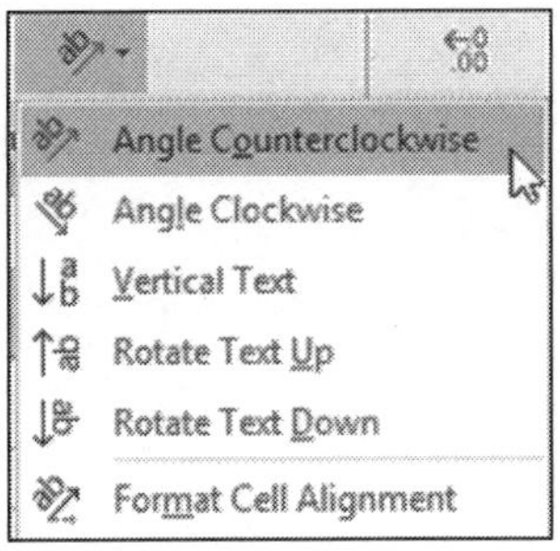

20 Make columns C and E a little wider.

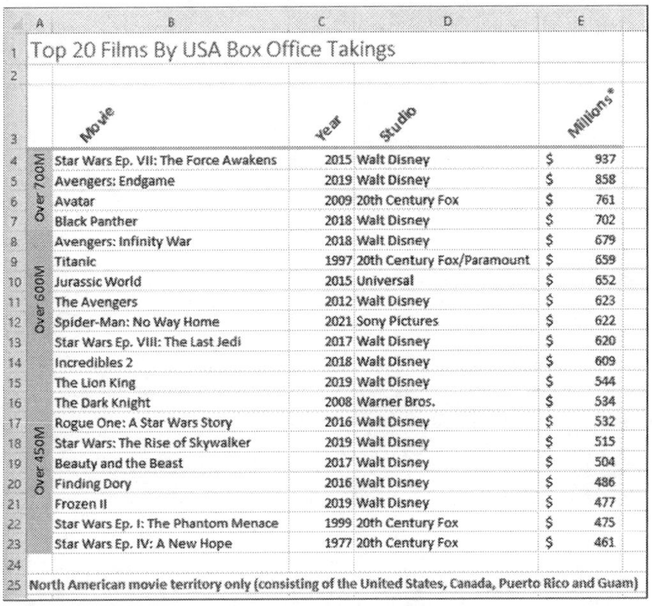

	A	B	C	D	E
1	Top 20 Films By USA Box Office Takings				
2					
3		Movie	Year	Studio	Millions*
4	Over 700M	Star Wars Ep. VII: The Force Awakens	2015	Walt Disney	$ 937
5		Avengers: Endgame	2019	Walt Disney	$ 858
6		Avatar	2009	20th Century Fox	$ 761
7		Black Panther	2018	Walt Disney	$ 702
8	Over 600M	Avengers: Infinity War	2018	Walt Disney	$ 679
9		Titanic	1997	20th Century Fox/Paramount	$ 659
10		Jurassic World	2015	Universal	$ 652
11		The Avengers	2012	Walt Disney	$ 623
12		Spider-Man: No Way Home	2021	Sony Pictures	$ 622
13		Star Wars Ep. VIII: The Last Jedi	2017	Walt Disney	$ 620
14		Incredibles 2	2018	Walt Disney	$ 609
15	Over 450M	The Lion King	2019	Walt Disney	$ 544
16		The Dark Knight	2008	Warner Bros.	$ 534
17		Rogue One: A Star Wars Story	2016	Walt Disney	$ 532
18		Star Wars: The Rise of Skywalker	2019	Walt Disney	$ 515
19		Beauty and the Beast	2017	Walt Disney	$ 504
20		Finding Dory	2016	Walt Disney	$ 486
21		Frozen II	2019	Walt Disney	$ 477
22		Star Wars Ep. I: The Phantom Menace	1999	20th Century Fox	$ 475
23		Star Wars Ep. IV: A New Hope	1977	20th Century Fox	$ 461
24					
25	North American movie territory only (consisting of the United States, Canada, Puerto Rico and Guam)				

21 Save your work as *Top 20 Films-1*.

Session 4: Exercise

1. Open *House Mortgage* from your sample files folder.
2. Merge and center cells B3:J3.
3. Apply the *Title* style to cell A1, the *Heading 1* style to cell B3, the *Heading 3* style to cells A4:J4 and the *Heading 3* style to cells A10:C10.
4. Apply the *Heading 4* style to cells A5:A8 and cells A11:A17.
5. Apply the *Percentage* style to cells B4:J4.
6. Apply the *Comma* style to cells B5:J8.
7. Apply the *Percentage* style to cells B11:C17 and then increase decimals to one place.
8. Type the word *Average* into cell A18 and use the *Format Painter* to match the formatting to that of the cell above (A17).
9. Horizontally right-align the text in cell A18.
10. Use *AutoSum* to place an *Average* function into cells B18 and C18.
11. Place a thin black border beneath cells A17:C17.
12. Change the theme to *Retrospect*.
13. Save your work as *House Mortgage-1*.

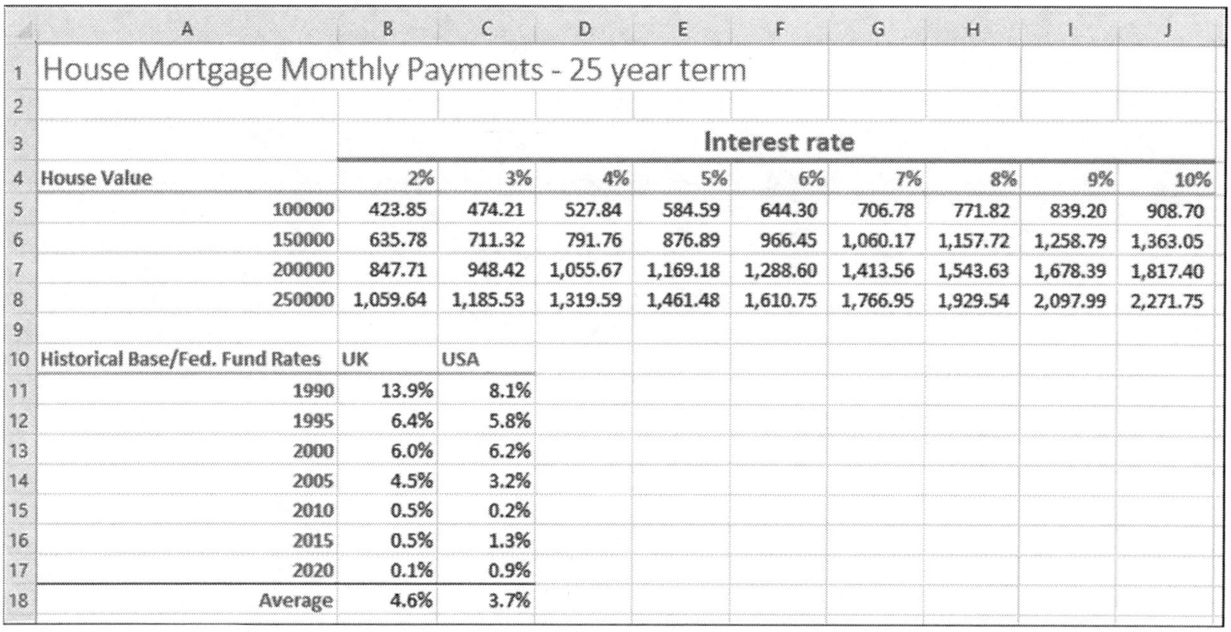

	A	B	C	D	E	F	G	H	I	J
1	House Mortgage Monthly Payments - 25 year term									
2										
3		Interest rate								
4	House Value	2%	3%	4%	5%	6%	7%	8%	9%	10%
5	100000	423.85	474.21	527.84	584.59	644.30	706.78	771.82	839.20	908.70
6	150000	635.78	711.32	791.76	876.89	966.45	1,060.17	1,157.72	1,258.79	1,363.05
7	200000	847.71	948.42	1,055.67	1,169.18	1,288.60	1,413.56	1,543.63	1,678.39	1,817.40
8	250000	1,059.64	1,185.53	1,319.59	1,461.48	1,610.75	1,766.95	1,929.54	2,097.99	2,271.75
9										
10	Historical Base/Fed. Fund Rates	UK	USA							
11	1990	13.9%	8.1%							
12	1995	6.4%	5.8%							
13	2000	6.0%	6.2%							
14	2005	4.5%	3.2%							
15	2010	0.5%	0.2%							
16	2015	0.5%	1.3%							
17	2020	0.1%	0.9%							
18	Average	4.6%	3.7%							

House Mortgage

Session 4: Exercise answers

These are the questions that students find the most difficult to answer:

Q 12	Q 11	Q 10	Q 8
Click Page Layout→ Themes→Themes→ Retrospect. This was covered in: *Lesson 4-10: Use cell styles and change themes.*	1. Select cells A17:C17. 2. Click: Home→Font→ Borders→ Bottom Border. 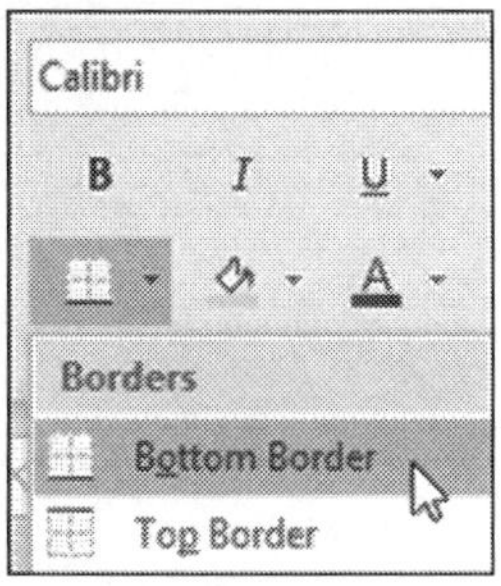 This was covered in: *Lesson 4-12: Add borders and lines.*	1. Select cells B18:C18. 2. Click: Home→Editing→ AutoSum→Average 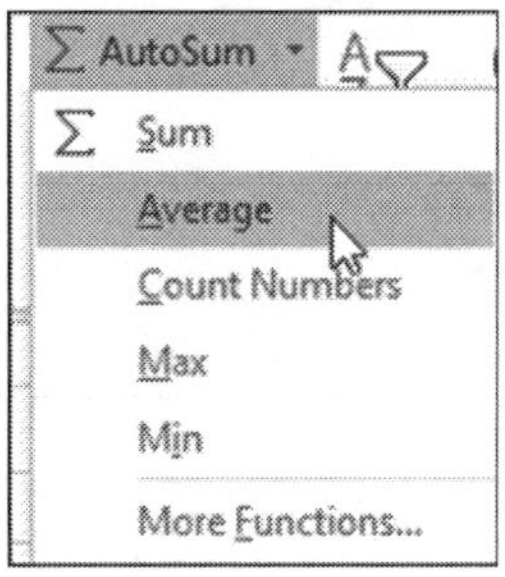 3. Either press the **<Enter>** key or click the AutoSum button again. This was covered in: *Lesson 2-11: Use AutoSum to calculate average and maximum values.*	1. Click in cell A18. 2. Type: **Average**. 3. Click into cell A17, 4. Click: Home→Clipboard→ Format Painter 3. Click in cell A18. This was covered in: *Lesson 4-23: Use the Format Painter.*

If you have difficulty with the other questions, here are the lessons that cover the relevant skills:

1 **Refer to: Lesson 1-9: Open and navigate a workbook**

2 **Refer to: Lesson 4-6: Merge cells, wrap text and expand/collapse the formula bar.**

3 **Refer to: Lesson 4-10: Use cell styles and change themes.**

4 **Refer to: Lesson 4-10: Use cell styles and change themes.**

5,6,7 **Refer to: Lesson 4-3: Format numbers using built-in number formats.**

9 **Refer to: Lesson 4-5: Horizontally align the contents of cells.**

11 **Refer to: Lesson 4-3: Format numbers using built-in number formats.**

13 **Refer to: Lesson 1-10: Save a workbook to a local file.**

5

Session Five: Charts and Graphics

A picture is worth a thousand words.

Frederick R. Barnard in "Printers' Ink", 8th Dec 1921.

In this session, you'll learn to present your data in a chart. You'll also learn some valuable "tricks of the trade" to present your data in the most effective way.

Session Objectives

By the end of this session you will be able to:

- Understand chart types, layouts and styles
- Create a simple chart with two clicks
- Move, re-size, copy and delete a chart
- Create a chart using the Recommended Charts feature
- Add and remove chart elements using Quick Layout
- Apply a pre-defined chart style and color set
- Manually format a chart element
- Format 3-D elements and add drop shadows
- Move, re-size, add, position and delete chart elements
- Apply a chart filter
- Change a chart's source data
- Assign non-contiguous source data to a chart
- Understand data series and categories
- Add data series using the Select Data Source dialog tools
- Chart non-contiguous source data by hiding rows and columns
- Create a chart with numerical axes
- Deal with empty data points and add data labels to a chart
- Highlight specific data points with color and annotations
- Add gridlines and scale axes
- Emphasize data by manipulating pie charts
- Create a chart with two vertical axes
- Create a combination chart containing different chart types
- Work with trend lines and forecast sheets
- Add a gradient fill to a chart background
- Create your own chart templates

Lesson 5-1: Understand chart types, layouts and styles

The Excel designers noted that there are three things that control the design of a chart:

Chart Type

There are many different *types* of chart. The most common are: *Column Charts, Line Charts* and *Pie Charts.*

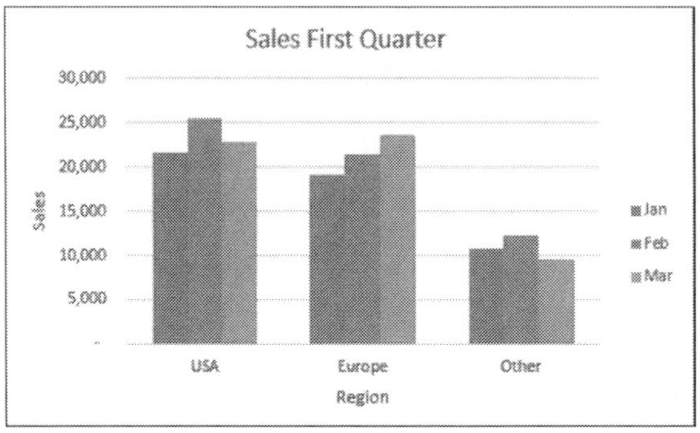

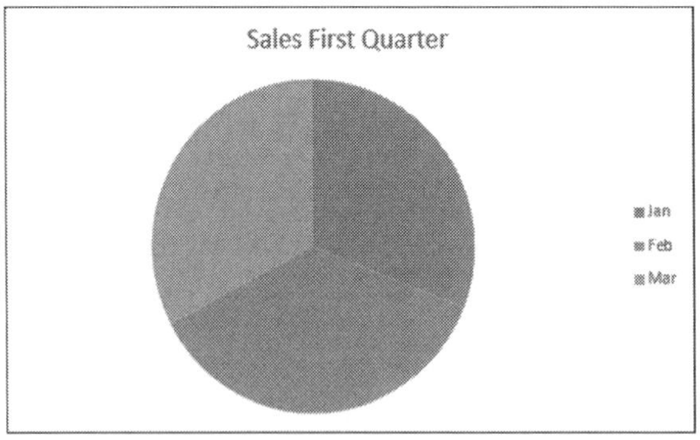

You'll discover how to choose a suitable *Chart Type* in: *Lesson 5-2: Create a simple chart with two clicks.*

Chart Layout

The layout of a chart can be thought of as a list of the *elements* that a chart contains.

Elements are artifacts such as a *Title, Axis Titles or Legend.*

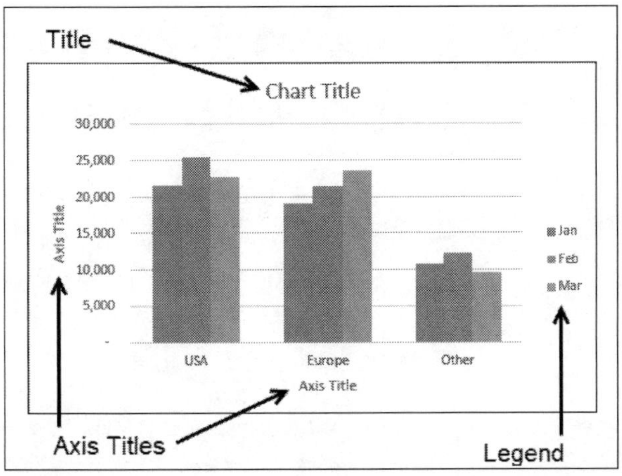

In: *Lesson 5-5: Add and remove chart elements using Quick Layout,* you'll discover how to quickly select a group of common elements for a chart.

Chart Style

The *Chart Style* determines the font, color and positioning of each chart element. Here are two charts that have an identical *Type* and *Layout* but have different styles:

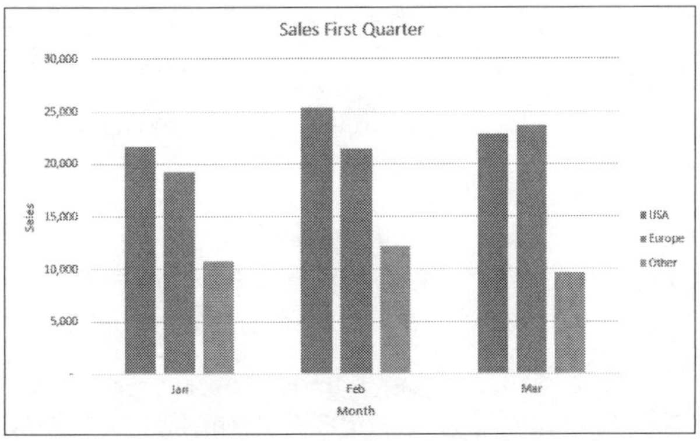

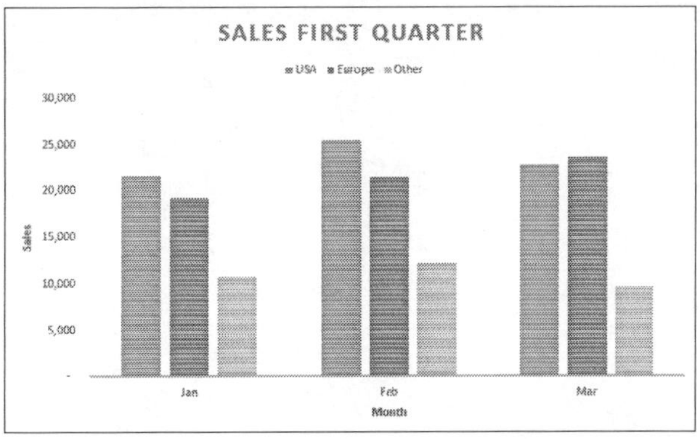

You can see that both charts are of the same type (*Clustered Column*), and that both have the same elements (that include the *Axis Titles, Chart Title* and *Legend* elements).

The differences in appearance (colors, shading of bars, fonts used and position of legend) are collectively referred to as the chart's *Style*.

You'll learn how to change a chart's style in: *Lesson 5-6: Apply a pre-defined chart style and color set.*

Lesson 5-2: Create a simple chart with two clicks

1 Open *World Sales* from your sample files folder.

This is a very simple worksheet containing January, February and March sales data for three regions.

	A	B	C	D
1	Month	USA	Europe	Other
2	Jan	21,600	19,200	10,800
3	Feb	25,400	21,400	12,200
4	Mar	22,800	23,600	9,600

2 Select all of the values and all of the labels (cells A1:D4).

When Excel creates a chart, it needs both values and labels. For this reason, you must always select the labels ***as well as*** the values before you create your chart.

Missing the labels is one of the most common errors in my classroom courses.

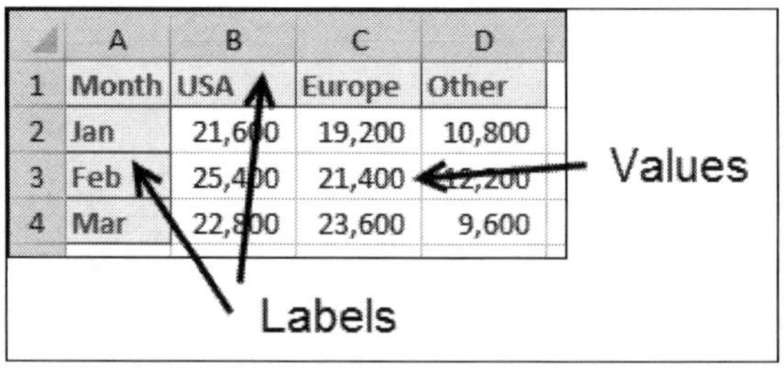

3 Click: Insert→Charts→Insert Column or Bar Chart and hover the mouse pointer over some of the charts in the gallery.

As you hover the mouse cursor over each chart type Excel provides a ScreenTip describing the chart. A preview of how the chart will look is also displayed on the worksheet.

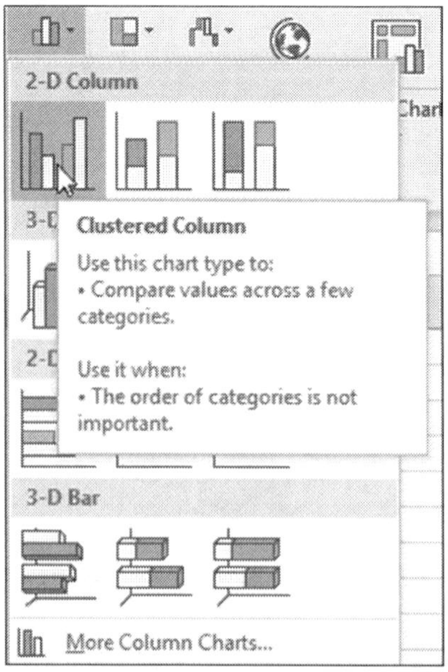

tip

You can create a chart without selecting any data

When your data and labels form a single rectangular range (as is the case in this lesson) you don't need to select the data.

If you simply click anywhere within the range and then click:

Insert→Charts→...

Excel will assume that you want to chart the entire range and will select it for you.

note

Create a chart with the <F11> key

If you click inside a range and then press the **<F11>** key, Excel will instantly create a new chart on a new chart sheet.

A chart sheet is a special type of worksheet that can only contain a chart.

You'll learn more about chart sheets in: *Lesson 5-3: Move, re-size, copy and delete a chart.*

important

Charts are dynamic

If the values underpinning a chart change, the chart will instantly change to represent the new values.

World Sales

note

Changing the chart type of an existing chart

You may create a chart but later decide that you really need a different chart type.

For example, you might create a *bar chart* but later decide you would have preferred a *pie chart* or *line chart*.

To change the type of an existing chart:

1. Right-click on the chart.
2. Click: *Change Chart Type* from the shortcut menu.

note

Create a chart with the Quick Analysis button

Whenever you select a range of cells, a *Quick Analysis* button appears just outside the bottom-right corner of the selected range.

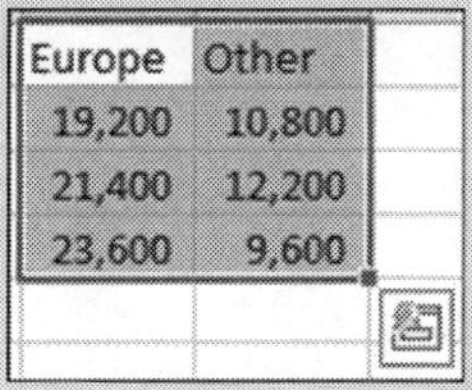

When you click the *Quick Analysis* button, the *Quick Analysis* dialog appears.

One of the menu options on this dialog is *Charts*.

When you click the *Charts* menu option you are presented with a choice of five recommended charts for the range selected. There's also a *More...* button that gives access to the full *Insert Chart* dialog (that you'd see if you clicked: Insert→Charts→Dialog Launcher). This method isn't as versatile as choosing a chart manually (as described in this lesson).

4 Click the left-most 2-D Column chart (the *Clustered Column* chart).

In just two clicks you have created a very presentable chart.

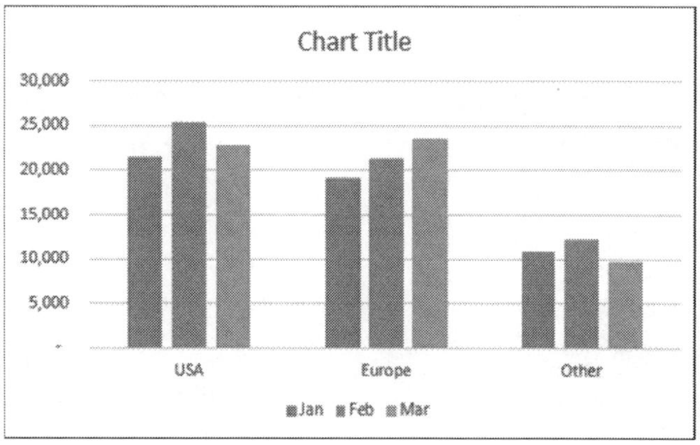

Because you have only specified the chart *Type*, Excel has chosen a default *Layout* and *Style* for you. You'll learn how to change these default choices later in this session.

5 Understand chart activation.

In this example, the worksheet only contains one chart.

It is possible that a worksheet will contain more than once chart.

For this reason, you need to indicate to Excel which chart you want to work on. To do this the chart needs to be *activated.*

To activate a chart, you simply click anywhere inside the chart.

When the chart is activated two things happen:

1. The *Chart Design* Ribbon tab appears:

2. A frame (with sizing handles) and three buttons appear around the chart:

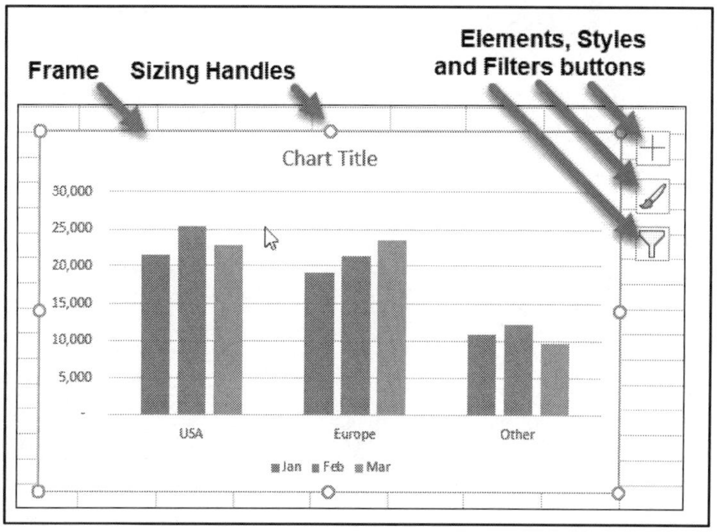

6 Save your work as *World Sales-1.*

Lesson 5-3: Move, re-size, copy and delete a chart

1 Open *World Sales-1* from your sample files folder (if it isn't already open).

2 Move the chart to a different position on screen.

1. Click just inside the border of the chart to activate it.

   When the chart is activated, you will see a frame with corner handles around it.

   Excel also displays the *Chart Design* and *Format* options on the Ribbon.

2. Hover with the mouse cursor just inside the border of the selected chart until you see the four-headed arrow cursor shape.

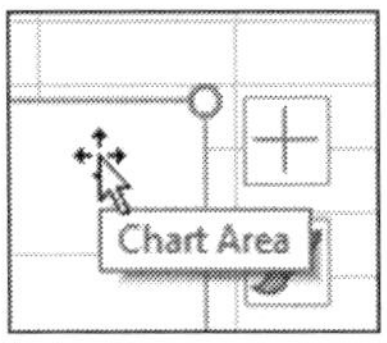

3. Click and drag the chart to the required position.

3 Re-size the chart.

1. Click just inside the border of the chart to activate it.
2. Hover over one of the corner or side sizing handles on the edges of the chart until you see the two-headed arrow cursor shape.

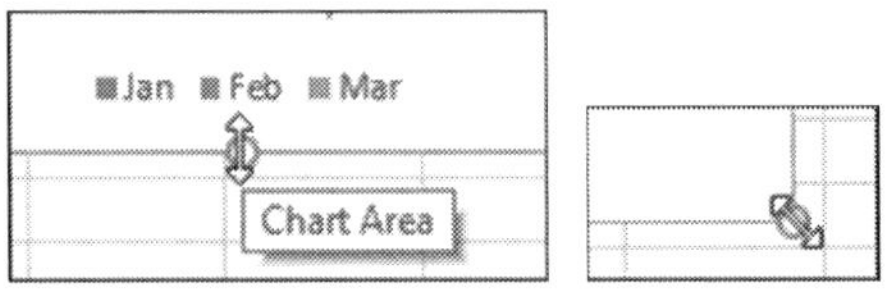

3. When you see the two-headed arrow cursor shape, click and drag to re-size the chart.

   If you hold down the **<Shift>** key as you click-and drag one of the corners of the chart, the perspective will remain constant (the chart will get proportionately wider as it gets taller).

4 Create a duplicate chart using copy and paste.

1. Click just inside the border of the chart to activate it.
2. Right-click on the border of the activated chart (just inside the border works too) and click *Copy* from the shortcut menu.
3. Right-click anywhere on the worksheet and click *Paste*  from the shortcut menu to create the duplicate chart.

tip

Give charts meaningful names to make them easier to find in the *Selection and Visibility* task pane

If you have more than one chart embedded in a worksheet, it is a good idea to give them more meaningful names than the default *Chart1, Chart2* etc.

To rename a chart you need to first activate it and then change the name in the *Name Box* (at the left of the formula bar):

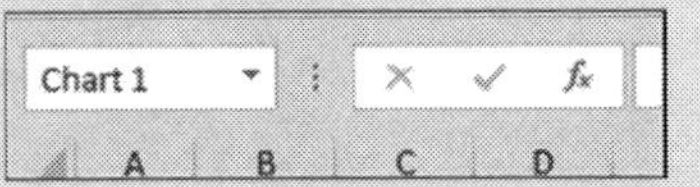

When charts have meaningful names, it is easy to activate them using the *Selection and Visibility* task pane.

To make this task pane appear, first activate the chart and then click:

Format→
Arrange→Selection Pane

The selection task pane will then appear and can be left on screen to quickly activate specific charts.

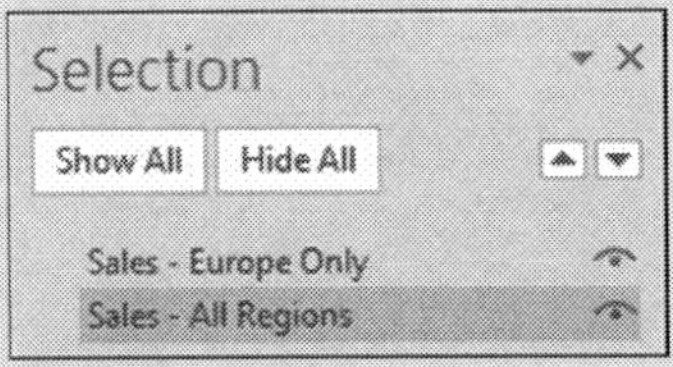

It is also possible to show or hide charts by clicking the eyeball symbol  to the right of the relevant chart.

World Sales-1

note

Another way to copy a chart

1. Hover the mouse cursor over the border of an embedded chart.

   The cursor shape will change to a four-headed arrow.

2. Right-click and drag the chart to a new location.

   When you release the mouse button you will see a prompt asking whether to move or copy the chart to the new location.

3. Click *Copy Here* to copy the chart.

note

Advantages of placing charts on chart sheets

- They are easier to find as you can give each chart sheet a meaningful name.
- They are easier to view as the chart normally takes up the entire screen.
- They are easier to print as you can simply click the chart sheet tab and print. You can also print an embedded chart in isolation but to do so you must first find and activate the chart.

The advantage of embedding charts within worksheets

You are able to print a chart and associated worksheet data on the same page.

If you have no need to print worksheet data alongside your chart, it is usually better to place your charts on chart sheets.

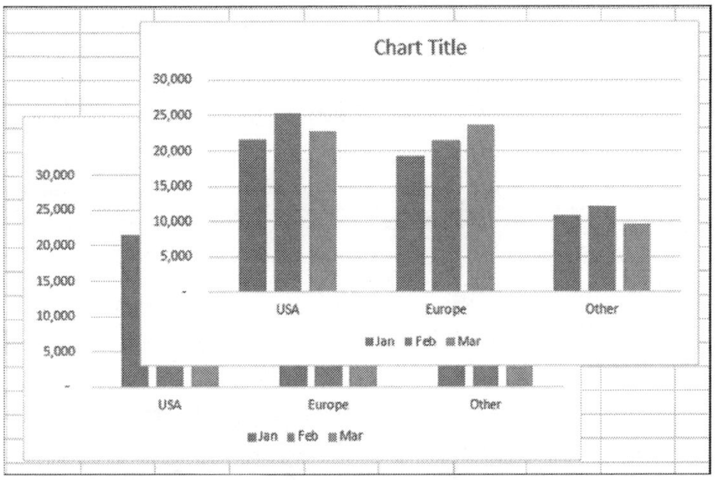

Note that even though the new chart is a duplicate, it is not linked to the original chart in any way. You can freely change any part of either chart and it will never affect the other.

5 Delete one of the charts.

1. Click just inside the border of either of the charts to activate it.
2. Press the **<Delete>** key on the keyboard.

6 Move the chart to its own chart worksheet.

Sometimes it is better to keep charts and data separate by placing a chart in its own *chart worksheet*. A chart worksheet is a special worksheet without any cells that can only contain a single chart.

1. Right-click just inside the border of the chart to activate it and then click *Move Chart...* from the shortcut menu.
2. Click the *New Sheet* option button, name the new sheet *Sales Summary Chart* and click the OK button.

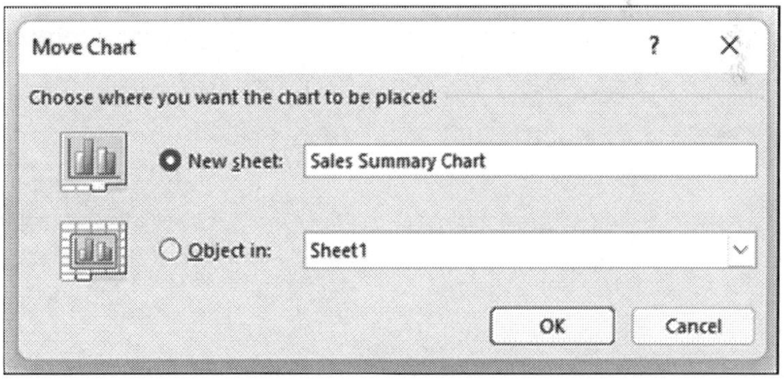

The chart is now displayed within its own dedicated chart worksheet.

7 Move the chart back to its original location.

1. Right-click just inside the border of the chart and click *Move Chart...* from the shortcut menu.
2. Click the *Object in* option button, choose *Sheet1* from the drop-down list and click the OK button.

8 Save your work as *World Sales-2*.

Lesson 5-4: Create a chart using the Recommended Charts feature

Excel is able to intelligently analyze your data and then try to guess which chart type will do the best job of representing it visually.

1 **Open *Hawaii Temperature-1* from your sample files folder.**

This worksheet contains temperature data for Honolulu, Hawaii (one of the nicest year-round climates in the world).

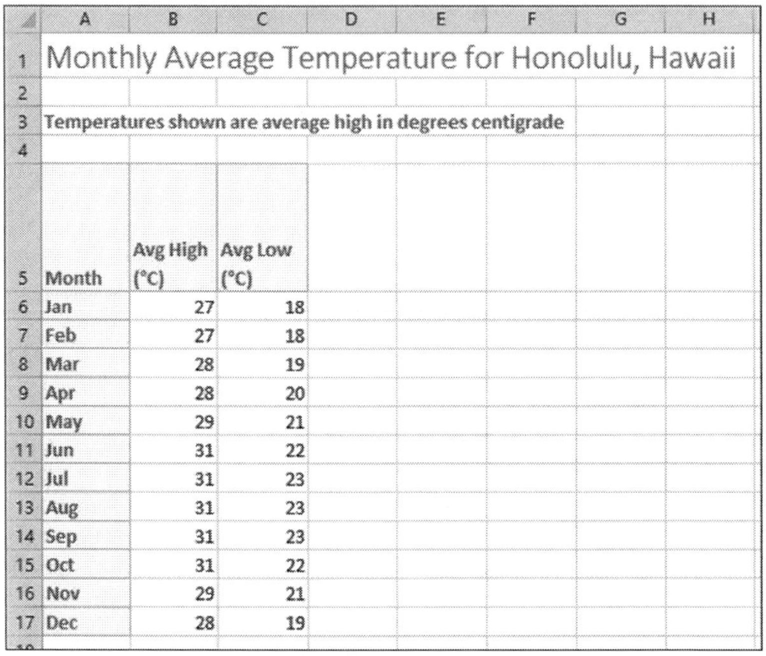

	A	B	C
1	Monthly Average Temperature for Honolulu, Hawaii		
2			
3	Temperatures shown are average high in degrees centigrade		
4			
5	Month	Avg High (°C)	Avg Low (°C)
6	Jan	27	18
7	Feb	27	18
8	Mar	28	19
9	Apr	28	20
10	May	29	21
11	Jun	31	22
12	Jul	31	23
13	Aug	31	23
14	Sep	31	23
15	Oct	31	22
16	Nov	29	21
17	Dec	28	19

2 **Use *Recommended Charts* to select a suitable chart type.**

1. Click anywhere inside the data (in a cell somewhere in the range A5:C17).

   You could also select the range A5:C17, but when you want to chart an entire range, it is only necessary to select a single cell within the range.

2. Click: Insert→Charts→Recommended Charts.

   The *Insert Chart* dialog is displayed with the *Recommended Charts* tab selected.

Hawaii Temperature-1

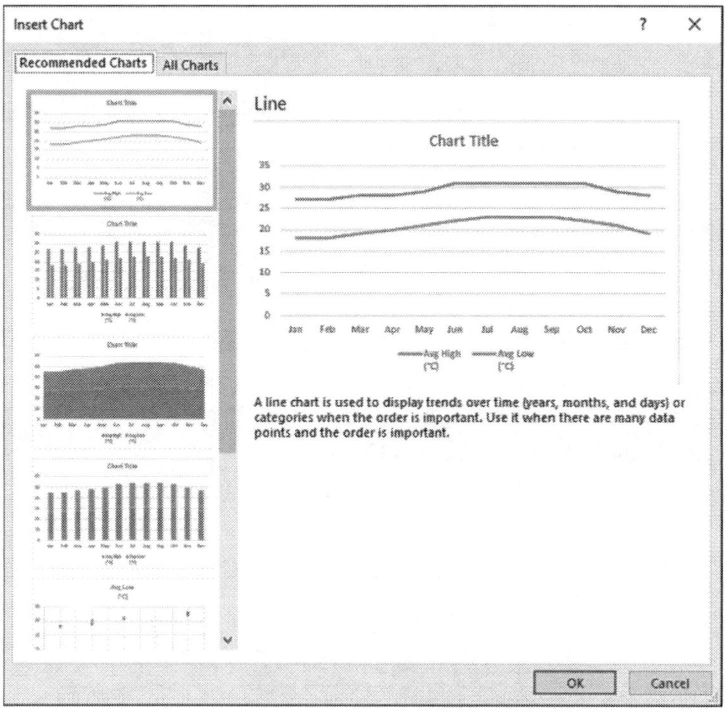

Notice that Excel's first choice for an appropriate chart type is a line chart.

This isn't a bad choice but perhaps Excel's second choice, the *Clustered Column* chart, will work better with this data.

3. Click the *Clustered Column* chart (the second recommended chart in the left-hand list).

   A preview of the clustered column chart is shown in the right-hand pane of the dialog.

4. Click OK to create a *Clustered Column* chart.

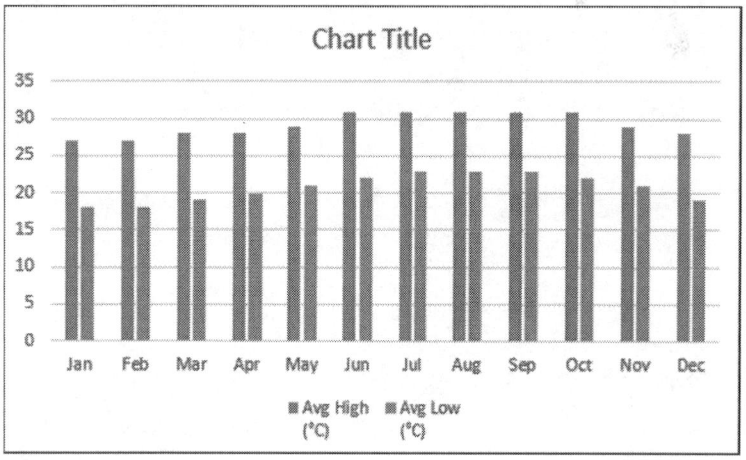

This chart does a very good job of visually representing the temperature range each month in Hawaii.

In: *Lesson 5-5: Add and remove chart elements using Quick Layout,* you'll learn how to change the *Chart Title* element to display appropriate text.

3 Save your work as *Hawaii Temperature-2*.

note

You can also access the Recommended Charts feature using the Quick Analysis button

Whenever you select a range of cells, a *Quick Analysis* button appears just outside the bottom-right corner of the selected range.

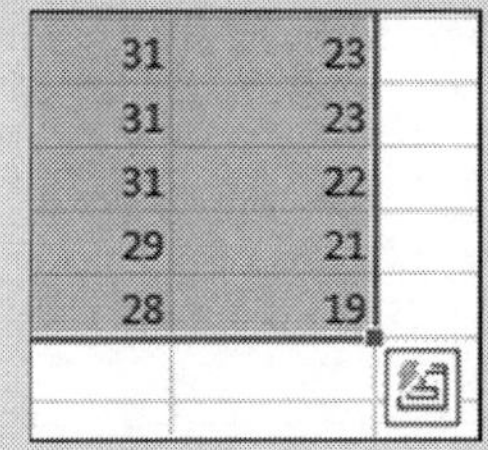

When you click the *Quick Analysis* button, the *Quick Analysis* dialog appears.

One of the menu options on this dialog is *Charts.*

When you click the *Charts* menu option you are presented with a choice of five recommended charts for the range selected.

There's also a *More…* button that opens the more powerful *Insert Chart* dialog used in this lesson:

Lesson 5-5: Add and remove chart elements using Quick Layout

The term *Layout* can be confusing. It is used to describe the *Elements* that a chart contains. For example, here is a simple chart containing only two elements:

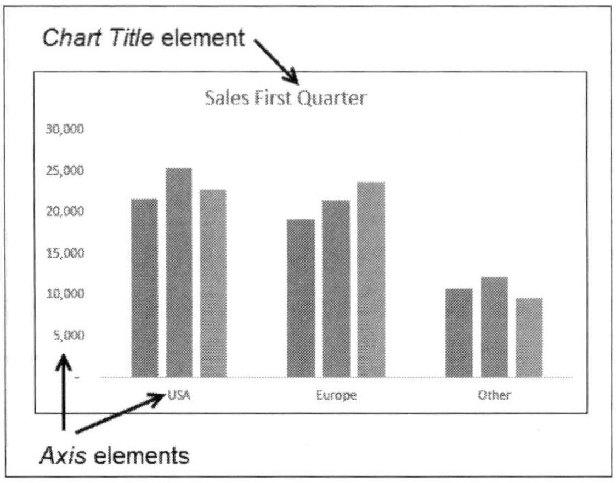

And here's a chart that contains four elements:

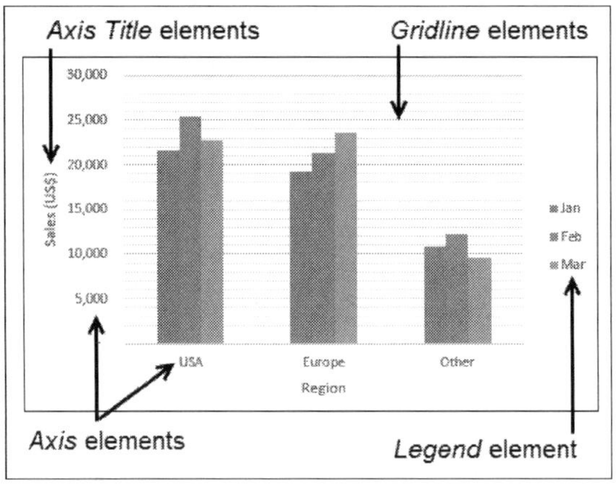

Some layouts also include a *Data Table* element showing the source data for the chart:

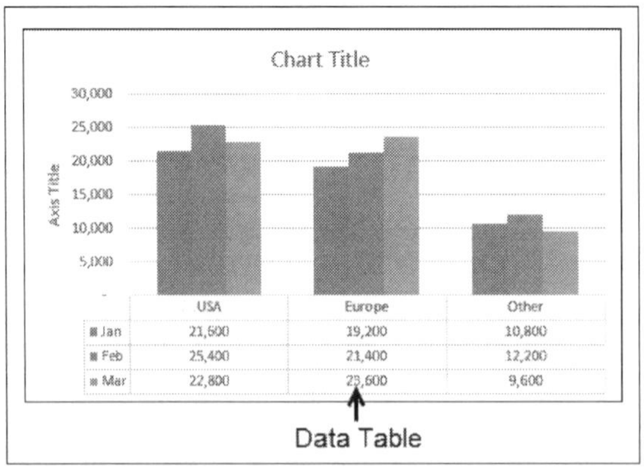

Don't confuse the *layout* (the elements that a chart contains) with the chart *style* (the colors and appearance of the chart elements).

note

More about the horizontal and vertical axes

A chart normally shows category (non-numerical) data along the horizontal axis. The horizontal axis is also sometimes called the X axis.

The vertical axis normally contains numerical data. The vertical axis is also sometimes called the Y axis.

The chart used in this lesson has the non-numerical region categories (USA, Europe and Other) along the horizontal (or X) axis and numerical sales values along the vertical (or Y) axis.

tip

Worksheet cells are more versatile than data tables

If you need to show data alongside an embedded chart, a data table isn't usually the best choice.

Placing an embedded chart adjacent to worksheet cells gives you far more formatting power.

Data tables can be useful when a chart is placed on its own chart sheet and you also need to show values.

World Sales-2

In this lesson, you will use Excel's *Quick Layout* feature to choose from eleven common layouts with a single click.

1 Open *World Sales-2* from your sample files folder (if it isn't already open).

2 Change the *Chart Layout* to: *Layout 9*.

1. Click just inside the border of the chart to activate it.
2. Click: Chart Design→Chart Layouts→Quick Layout.

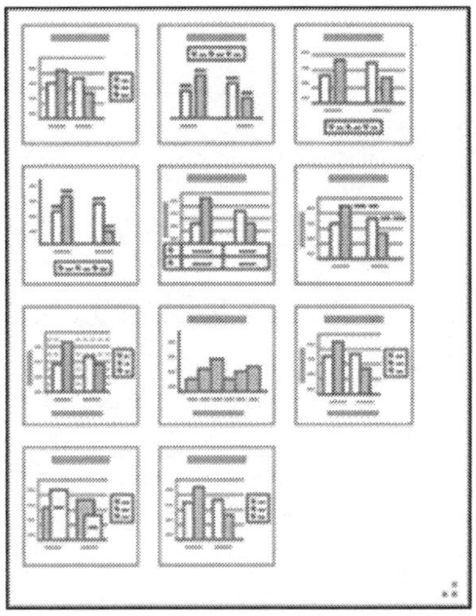

This gallery contains eleven pre-defined chart layouts. Each layout contains a group of elements.

Notice that the chart changes as you hover over each layout so that you can preview how your chart will look if the layout is chosen.

3. Click: *Layout 9*.

This layout includes a *Chart Title* element, a *Legend* element, two *Axis* elements, two *Axis Title* elements and a *Gridlines* element.

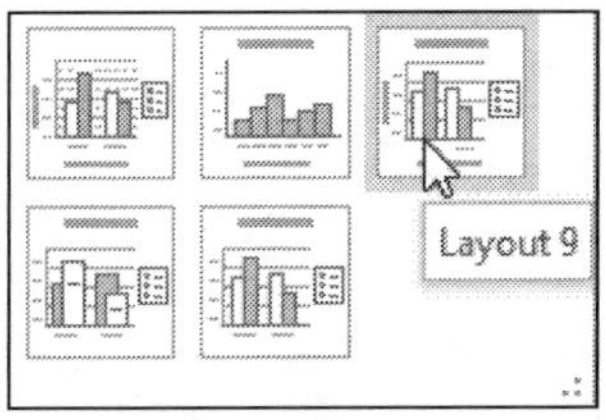

In: *Lesson 5-9: Move, re-size, add, position and delete chart elements*, you'll learn how to add elements one by one. You'll then appreciate how much faster it is to select all five elements with a single click instead of individually adding each one.

3 Click the *Chart Title* element and type: **Sales First Quarter** followed by the **<Enter>** key.

4 Click the *Vertical Axis Title* element and type: **Sales** followed by the **<Enter>** key.

5 Click the *Horizontal Axis Title* element and type: **Region** followed by the **<Enter>** key.

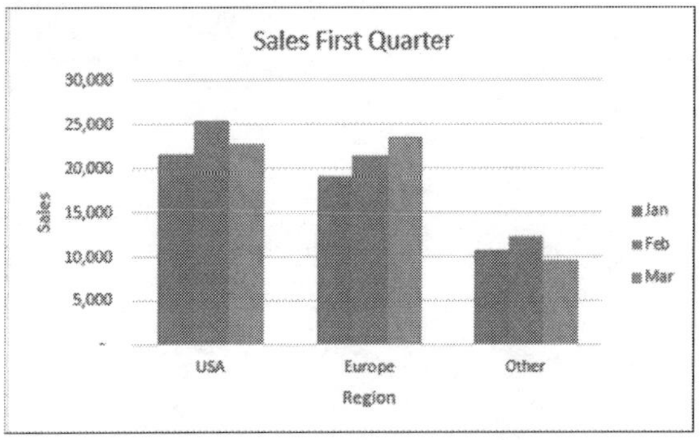

6 Save your work as: *World Sales-3*.

note

Use chart tips to discover chart element names

When you hover the mouse cursor over a selected chart element, the name of the element is displayed in a chart tip.

If this doesn't work on your machine, somebody has switched off the chart tips.

Here's how to switch them back on:

1. Click:

   File→Options→Advanced

2. In the *Chart* section, check the *Show chart element names on hover* check box.

Lesson 5-6: Apply a pre-defined chart style and color set

1 Open *World Sales-3* from your sample files folder (if it isn't already open).

2 Change the chart style.

1. Click just inside the border of the chart to activate it.
2. Click: Chart Design→Chart Styles→ More.

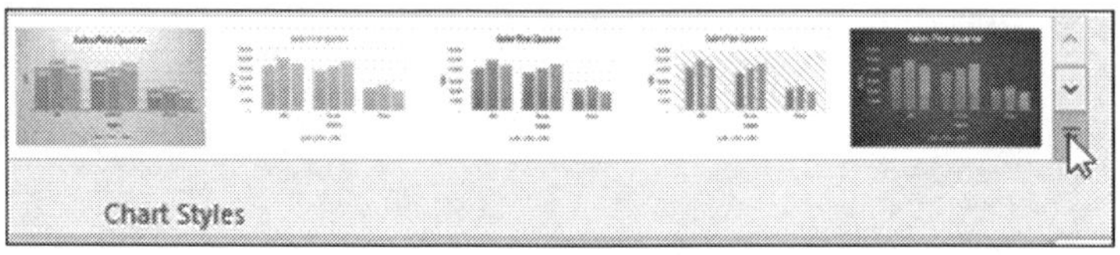

When you click the *More* button you are able to choose a new chart style from 14 pre-defined options. Each chart style uses theme colors, so the chart's appearance will change if you later change the workbook's theme (you learned about themes in: *Lesson 4-9: Understand themes*).

Notice that the chart changes as you hover over each style so that you can preview how your chart will look if the style is chosen.

3. Click a new chart style to change the appearance of your chart.

In the example below, I have chosen *Style 8.*

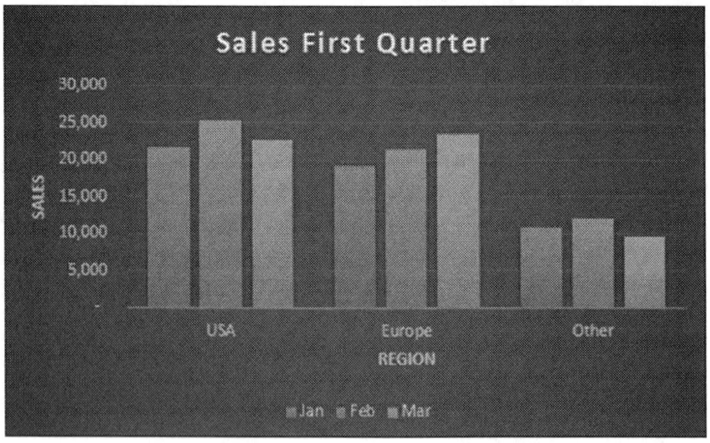

3 Change the chart's color set.

In: *Lesson 4-9: Understand themes,* you learned that every theme has a related color set.

In: *Lesson 4-11: Add color and gradient effects to cells (sidebar)* you learned why it is good practice to restrict colors to theme colors.

Excel provides a quick and convenient way to choose a new set of colors (from the current theme's color set) for your chart.

World Sales-3

note

Another way to change a chart's style or color set

When you activate a chart (by clicking on it), three small icons appear next to the top-right corner:

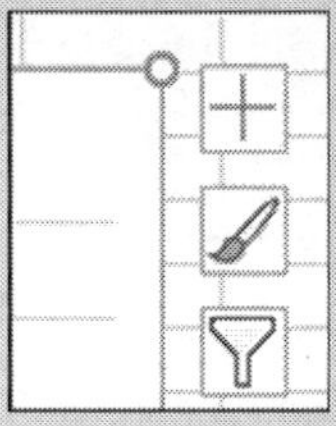

The middle icon provides a different way to select a style or color set.

The other two buttons allow you to select *Chart Elements* and *Chart Filters*.

You'll learn more about Chart Elements later, in: *Lesson 5-9: Move, re-size, add, position and delete chart elements.*

You'll learn about Chart Filters later, in: *Lesson 5-10: Apply a chart filter.*

1. Click just inside the border of the chart to activate it.
2. Click: Chart Design→Chart Styles→Change Colors.

   A set of color palettes (each consisting of six colors) are displayed. All colors belong to the current theme (in this example, the default *Office* theme).

   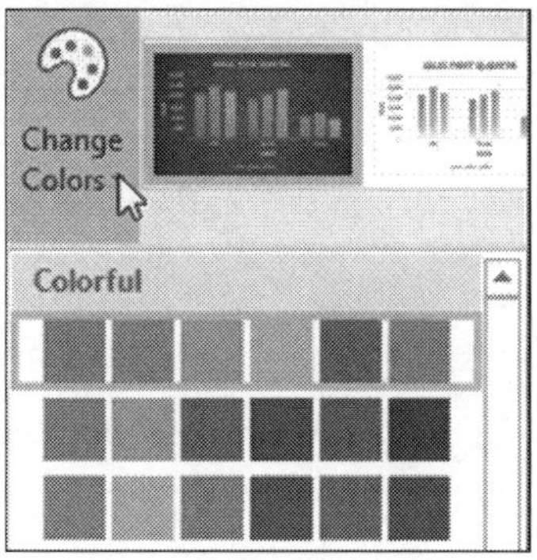

   As you hover the mouse cursor over each palette, the chart changes to preview the effect of choosing the new color set.

3. Click any of the color sets to select one. The new color set is applied to the chart.

   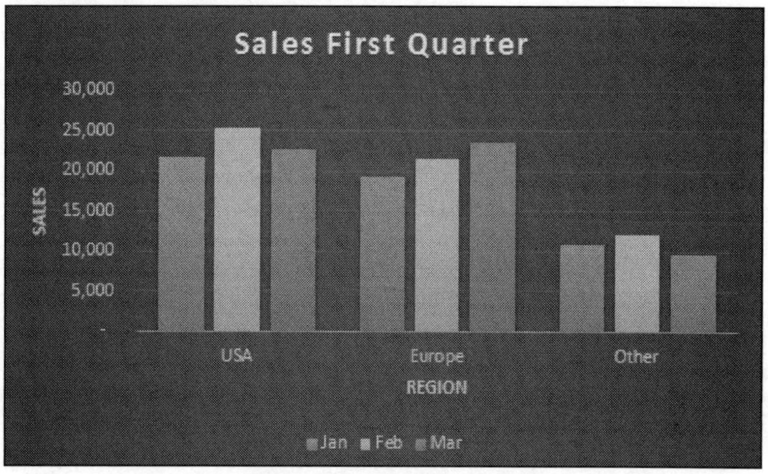

4 Close the workbook without saving.

You want to stay with the original default style, so close this workbook without saving. The chart will then retain the default style.

note

Chart titles can reference and display the contents of a worksheet cell

Normally you will simply type the text that you need directly into the *Chart Title* element.

It is also possible to link the *Chart Title* to a worksheet cell so that it displays whatever text is in the specified cell.

Here's how it is done:

1. Click the *Chart Title* element.
2. Click inside the formula bar.
3. Type: = to start the formula.
4. Click on cell A1 (or the worksheet cell containing the value that you want to be displayed).
5. Press the **<Enter>** key.

   This will add a fully qualified cell reference such as:

   =Sheet1!$A$1

   This is required when you reference a cell from a *Chart Title* element. A simple reference such as:

   =A1

   ...will not work.

   You'll learn more about fully qualified cell references later, in: *Lesson 6-6: Create cross worksheet formulas.*

   The contents of cell A1 are then displayed in the *Chart Title* element and will change whenever the text in cell A1 changes.

World Sales-3

Lesson 5-7: Manually format a chart element

Up until now you've selected a pre-defined chart style and color set from a gallery.

Sometimes you may have a requirement that is not catered for within the selection of pre-defined styles offered by the *Chart Styles* gallery.

In this case you will need to manually format one or more chart elements.

Once you have the hang of how to format one element it becomes easy to work with any other element, because the options are broadly the same.

In this lesson, you'll manually format the *Chart Title* element.

1 Open *World Sales-3* from your sample files folder (if it isn't already open).

2 Click on the *Chart Title* element to select it.

A frame appears to indicate that the element is selected:

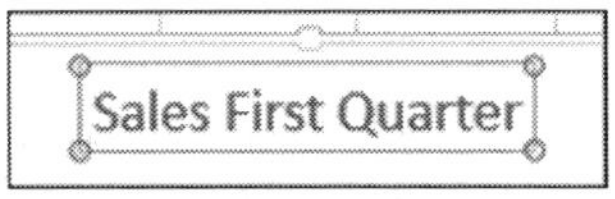

3 Right-click the *Chart Title* element and click *Format Chart Title...* from the shortcut menu.

The *Format Chart Title* task pane appears.

4 Apply a *Blue Accent 1* fill (background color) to the *Chart Title* element.

1. Click the *Fill & Line*  icon in the *Format Chart Title* task pane.
2. Click the *Fill* option to display the fly-out menu.
3. Click the *Solid fill* option button.
4. Click the *Fill Color* icon. 
5. Click the *Blue, Accent 1* fill color.

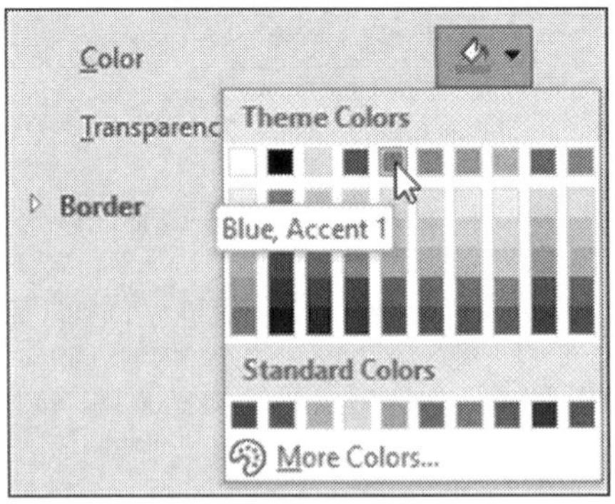

6. Drag the *Transparency* slider to the right to set the transparency to about 80%.

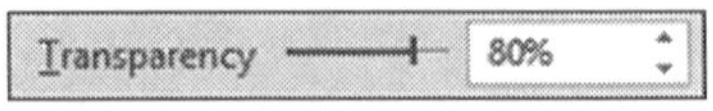

note

Working with the Format Shape task pane

The *Format Chart Title* task pane that you have been working with in this lesson is actually an instance of the more generic *Format Shape* task pane.

The name shown at the top of the *Format Shape* task pane changes depending upon which chart element you are working with.

The *Format Shape* task pane (in common with all other Office task panes) is modeless. You learned about the difference between modal dialogs and modeless task panes in: *Lesson 3-7: Use the Multiple Item Clipboard – sidebar.*

This means that you can go on working and leave the *Format Shape* dialog sitting in the background. Even better, as you select different chart elements, the *Format Shape* task pane will automatically change to show the appropriate settings for the selected element.

This is a huge time saver, especially if you have a large screen (or multiple monitors) enabling you to "park" the task pane on the windows desktop so that it doesn't obscure any part of the worksheet.

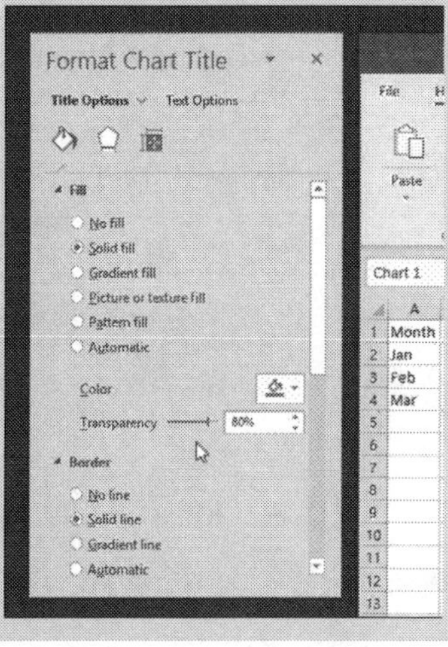

Notice that the background color of the *Chart Title* element becomes lighter as you drag to the transparency slider to the right, and darker as you drag to the left.

5 Apply a 1pt solid black border to the *Chart Title* element.

1. Click the *Fill & Line*  icon in the *Format Chart Title* task pane.
2. Click the *Border* option to display the fly-out menu.
3. In the *Border* section, click the *Solid line* option button.
4. Click the *Color* drop-down arrow and select a solid black color.

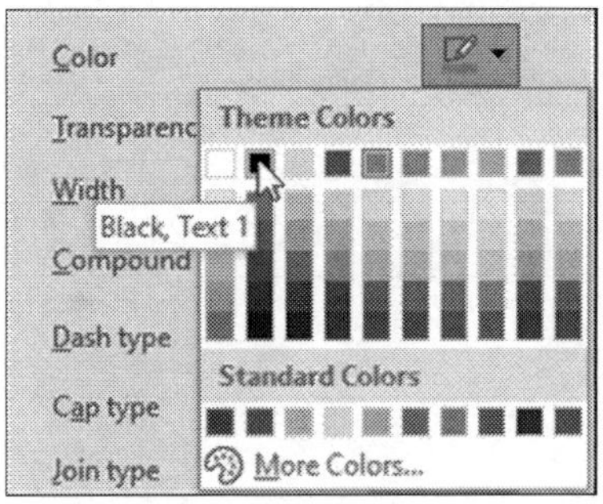

5. In the *Border* section, set the *Width* to: 1pt

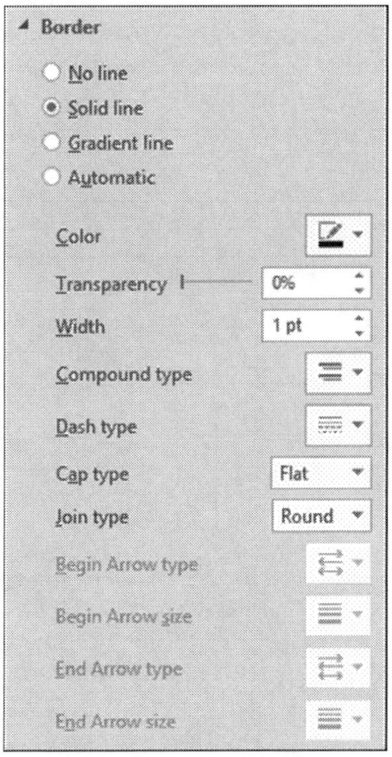

Notice that a solid black border has now been applied to the *Chart Title* element.

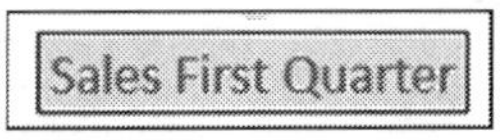

6 Close the *Format Chart Title* task pane.

7 Save your work as *World Sales-4.*

Lesson 5-8: Format 3-D elements and add drop shadows

The use of subtle shadows and 3-D formats will add a professional sheen to your work.

1 Open *World Sales-4* from your sample files folder (if it isn't already open) and click just inside the border of the chart to activate it.

2 Select the *Chart Title* element using the Ribbon.

Click: Format→Current Selection→
Chart Elements drop-down→Chart Title.

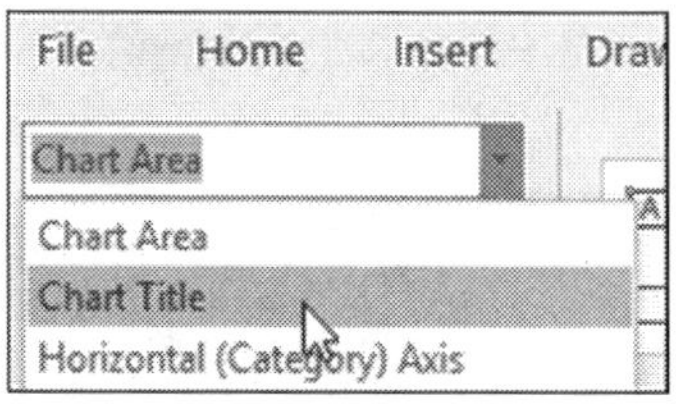

This is an alternative way to select a chart element. The drop-down shows every element in the currently selected chart.

Directly clicking on an element is usually faster but there are some chart elements (such as gridlines) that can sometimes be difficult to select with the mouse.

Here are the elements available in the *Chart Elements* drop-down list for this chart:

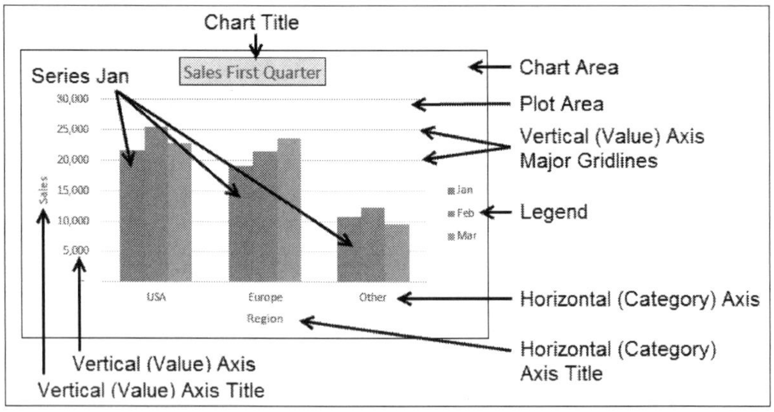

If you do a lot of work with charts it is well worth adding the *Chart Elements* drop-down to the *Quick Access Toolbar* (you learned how to do this in: *Lesson 1-18: Customize the Quick Access Toolbar and preview the printout*).

3 Display the *Format Chart Title* task pane.

Click: Format→Current Selection→Format Selection.

This is an alternative way to bring up the *Format Chart Title* dialog.

4 Apply an *Offset Bottom Right* shadow to the *Chart Title* element.

note

More about data series

A data series is a group of data that is associated with a specific category.

For example, the *Series Jan* data series is a group of values, one for each of the categories *USA*, *Europe* and *Other*.

In this example, there are three data series containing numerical data for each category.

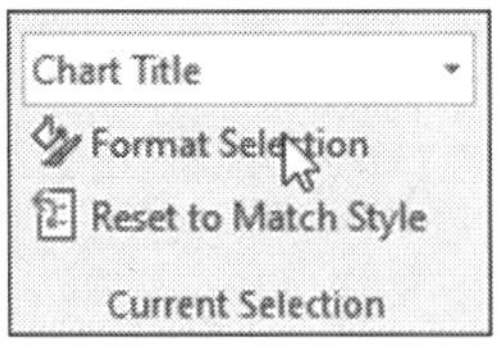

World Sales-4

1. Click the *Effects* icon in the *Format Chart Title* task pane.
2. Select *Shadow* from the four effects options.
3. Click the *Presets* icon.

   While you can create your own shadows using the *Transparency, Size, Blur, Angle* and *Distance* sliders, you'll probably find that the presets will suffice. Presets will also maintain uniformity between different chart elements.

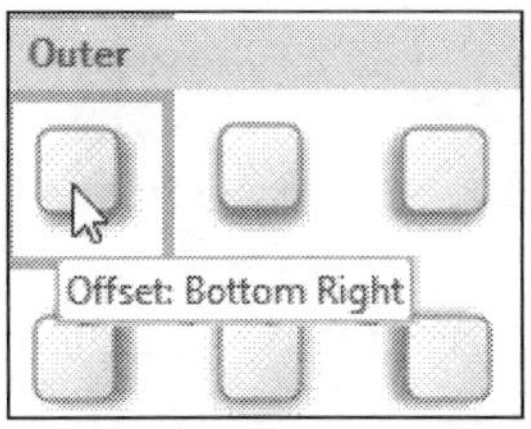

4. Click the *Offset Bottom Right* item in the shadow gallery.

   The effect is applied to the *Chart Title* element.

5 Apply a *Round top bevel* 3D effect to the *Chart Title* element

Bevel effects make an element look like a button.

1. Click the *Effects* icon in the *Format Chart Title* task pane.
2. Select *3-D Format* from the four effects options.
3. Click the *Top Bevel* preset button to display the Top Bevel gallery and choose a *Round* bevel.

   Just like shadows, you'll probably find what you need in the 3-D presets rather than creating your own custom 3-D effects.

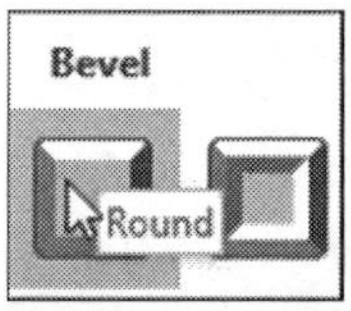

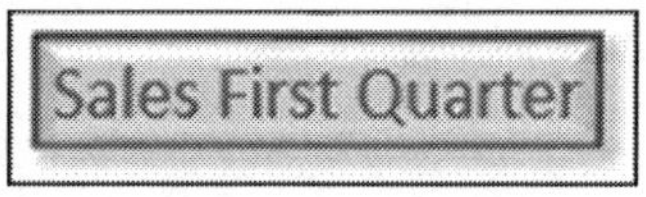

6 Use *Reset to Match Style* to restore the *Chart Title* element to its default state.

You've added a lot of fancy formatting to the *Chart Title* element but haven't really improved the appearance of the element.

Excel provides the *Reset to Match Style* feature to enable you to restore elements back to their original state.

1. Click on the *Chart Title* element to select it.
2. Click: Format→Current Selection→
   Reset to Match Style.

   The *Chart Title* element is restored to its default state.

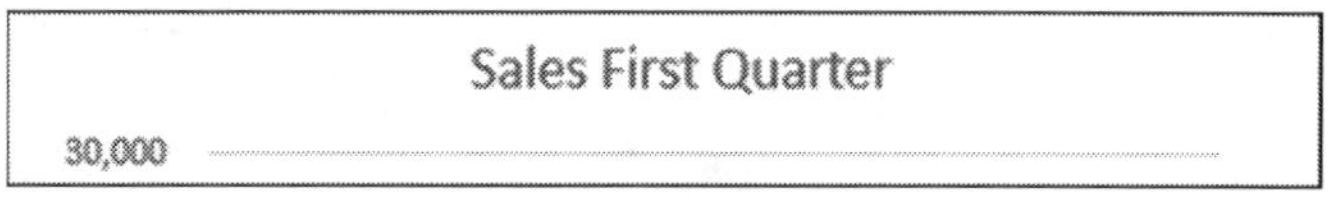

7 Close the *Format Chart Title* task pane.

8 Save your work as *World Sales-5.*

note

The *Chart Elements* button provides the most intuitive and fastest way to select and format an element.

When you select a chart three buttons are displayed to the right of the chart.

The top button is the *Chart Elements* button.

When you click the *Chart Elements* button you will see a checked check box for each element contained within the chart.

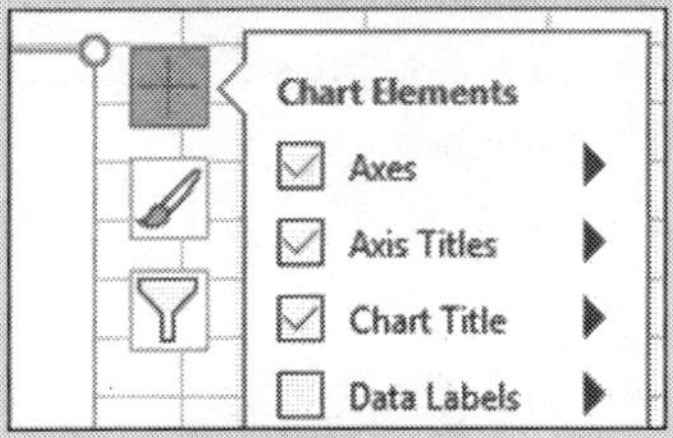

Next to each element is a fly-out menu button.

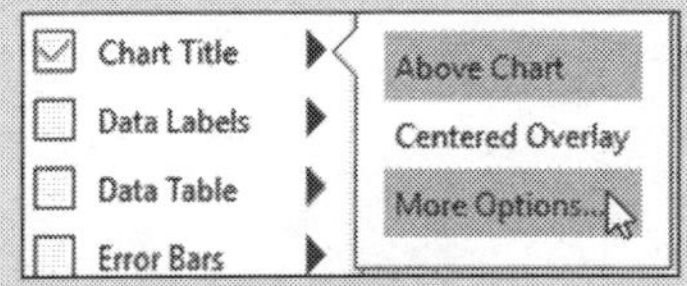

When you click the *More Options…* button the *Format* task pane opens with the chosen element selected.

This is probably the fastest and most intuitive way to select an individual element and open the *Format* task pane.

Lesson 5-9: Move, re-size, add, position and delete chart elements

Several elements such as the *Chart Title*, *Legend* and *Horizontal/Vertical Axis Titles* can be moved by drag and drop.

In this lesson, you'll see how to manually move these elements, and how to automatically restore them to their pixel-perfect locations if you change your mind.

You'll also manually add and remove single chart elements. Once you've got the hang of this, you'll be able to custom design charts for any specific requirement.

1 Open *World Sales-5* from your sample files folder (if it isn't already open).

2 Click and drag the *Chart Title* element to the left-hand side of the chart.

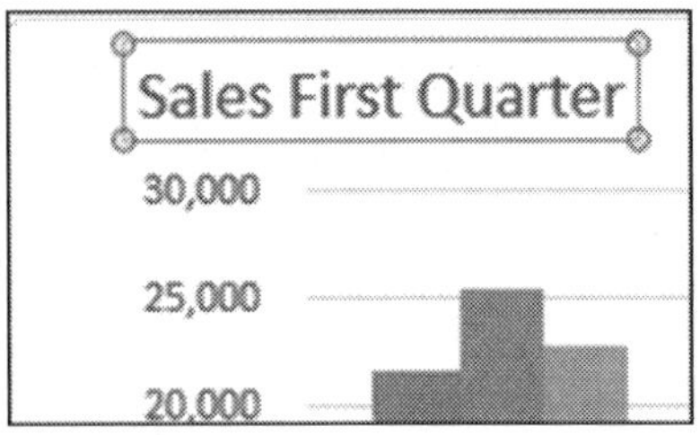

1. Click the *Chart Title* element to select it.
2. Hover the mouse cursor over the border of the *Chart Title* element until you see a four-headed arrow cursor shape.

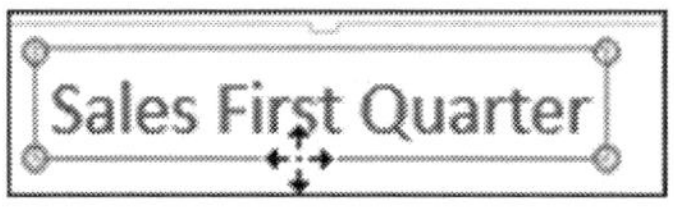

3. When you see the four-headed arrow, click and drag to move the element to the top left corner of the chart.

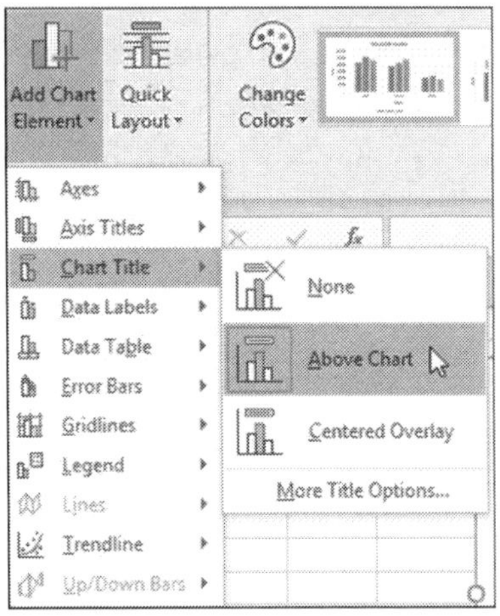

3 Move the *Chart Title* element back so that it is above the center of the chart.

You couldn't position this perfectly using the mouse.

1. Click on the *Chart Title* element to select it.
2. Click: Chart Design→Chart Layouts→ Add Chart Element→Chart Title→Above Chart.

   The *Chart Title* element is restored to the center.

4 Delete the legend.

1. Click the *Legend* element to select it:

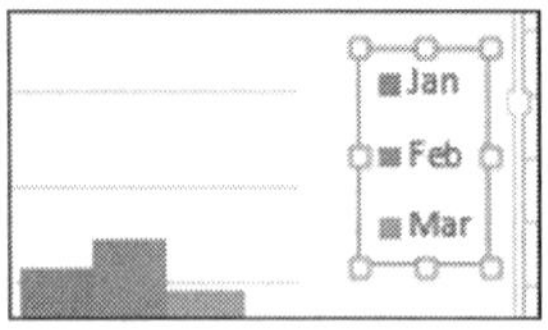

2. Press the **<Delete>** key.

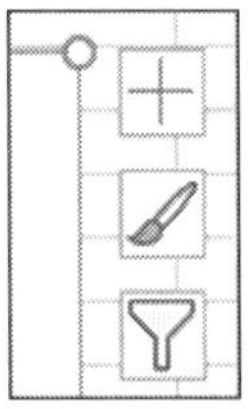

5 Display the legend at the top of the screen.

1. Select the chart.

   Notice that a group of three icons appears outside the top right corner of the chart.

World Sales-5

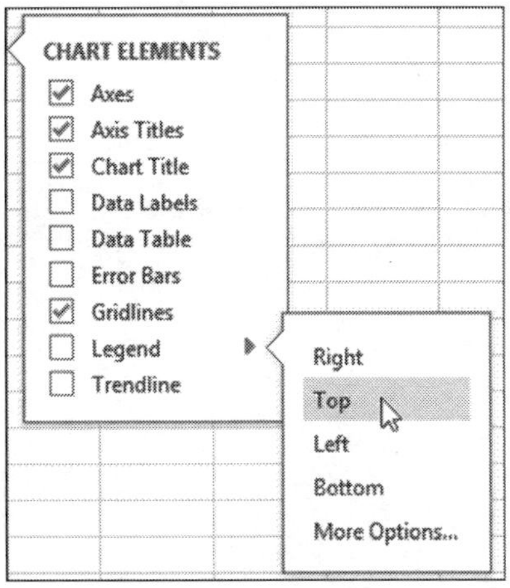

2. Click the *Chart Elements*  icon.

   A list of all elements available for the chart is displayed. This is almost the same as the dialog shown when you clicked the *Add Chart Element* button on the Ribbon earlier in this lesson.

3. Click the arrow button to the right of the word: *Legend* in the list.

   Several options for positioning the legend are shown.

4. Click: *Top*.

   The legend appears at the top of the chart.

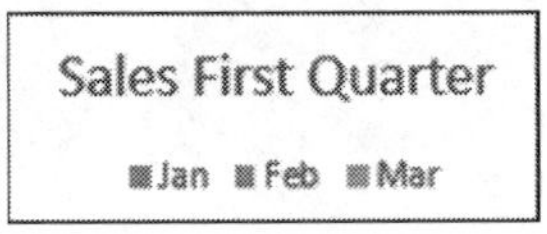

6 Add a thin black border to the *Legend* element.

You learned how to do this in: *Lesson 5-7: Manually format a chart element.*

7 Resize the *Legend* element so that it spans the entire width of the plot area.

1. Click the *Legend* element to select it. Notice the sizing handles on each corner and edge.

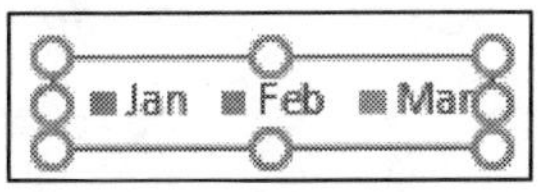

2. Hover over the sizing handle on the right-hand edge of the element. Notice that the cursor shape changes to a two-headed arrow.

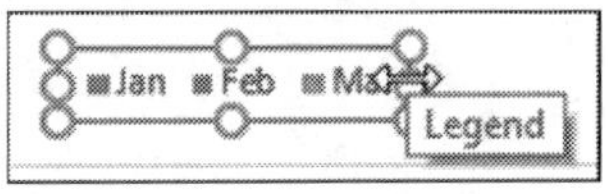

3. When you see the two-headed arrow click and drag to re-size the legend so that it is the same width as the plot area. (You'll have to first re-size the right side and then the left).

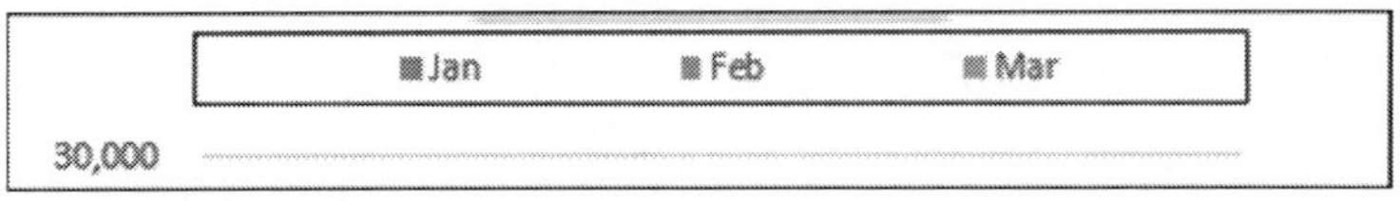

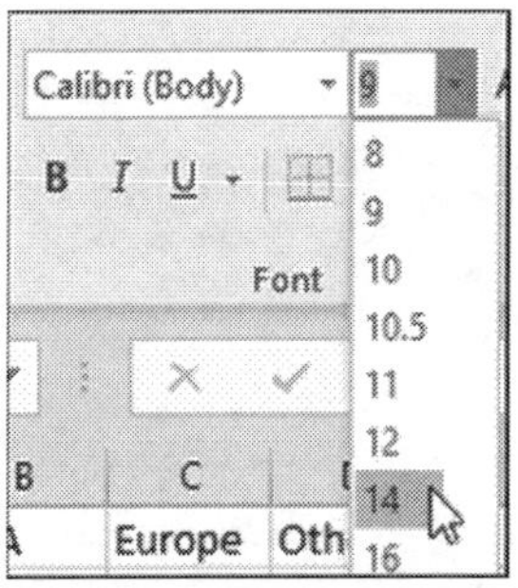

8 Increase the size of the font within the *Legend* element.

1. Click the *Legend* element to select it.
2. Click: Home→Font→Font Size Drop-down.
3. Hover the mouse cursor over each font size and note that *Live Preview* allows you to preview the effect of your choice.
4. Select *14 points* for the new text size.

9 Save your work as *World Sales-6*.

Lesson 5-10: Apply a chart filter

The chart that you have been working with contains three data series and three categories:

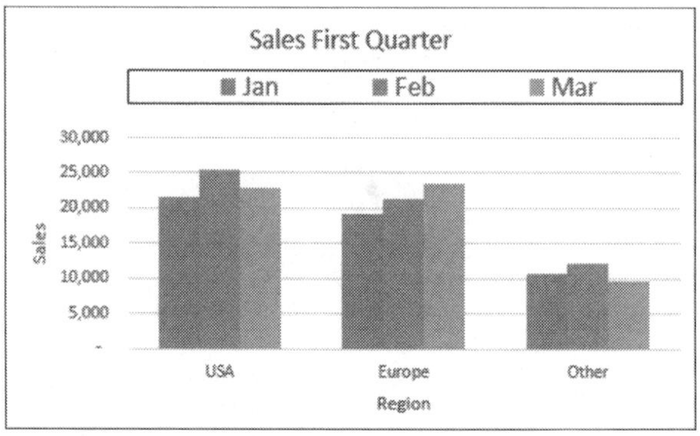

- The *data series* are Jan, Feb and Mar. Each of these data series contain three different values, one for each category.
- The *categories* are USA, Europe and Other.

The *Chart Filters* feature allows you to show or hide any of the data series or categories.

1 Open *World Sales-6* from your sample files folder (if it isn't already open).

2 Apply a *Chart Filter* to only show sales for Jan and Feb.

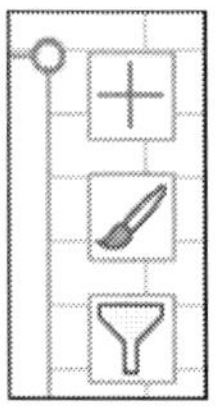

1. Click on the chart to activate it.

   A group of three icons appears outside the top right corner of the chart.

2. Click the *Chart Filters*  icon.

   A list of all the data series and categories used in the chart is displayed (see sidebar).

   Each data series and category have a check box enabling you to hide or show the relevant item.

3. Uncheck the *Mar* check box so that only the *Jan* and *Feb* data series will be shown on the chart.

4. Click the *Apply* button to apply the filter.

   The chart changes so that only *Jan* and *Feb* data is displayed.

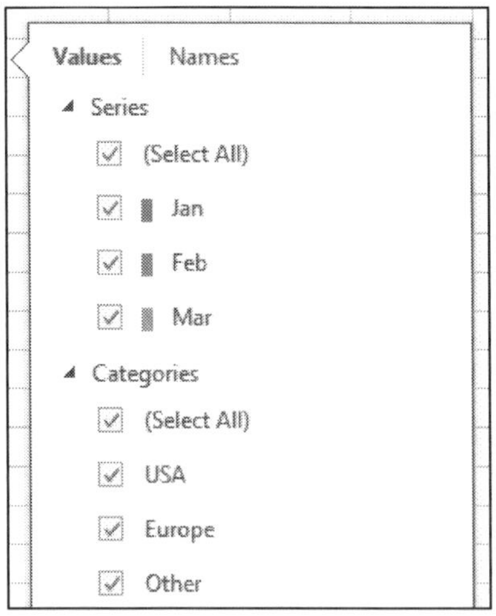

World Sales-6

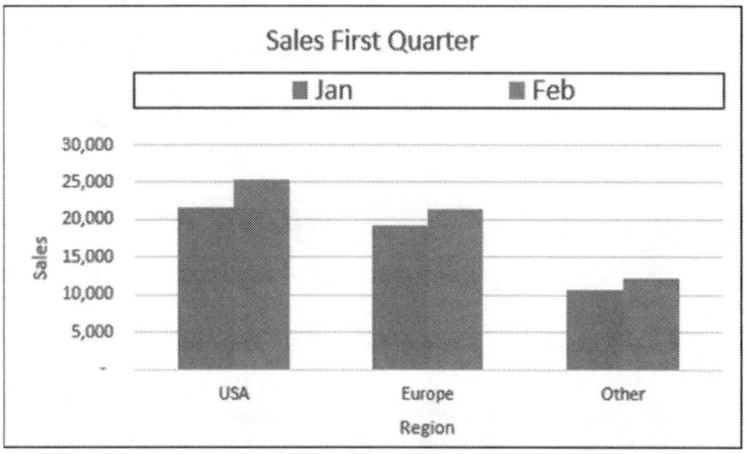

3 Apply *Chart Filters* to show sales for all months, but only in the *USA* and *Europe* categories.

1. Click on the chart to activate it.
2. Click the *Chart Filters*  icon.
3. In the *Series* list check the *(Select All)* check box to select all three months.

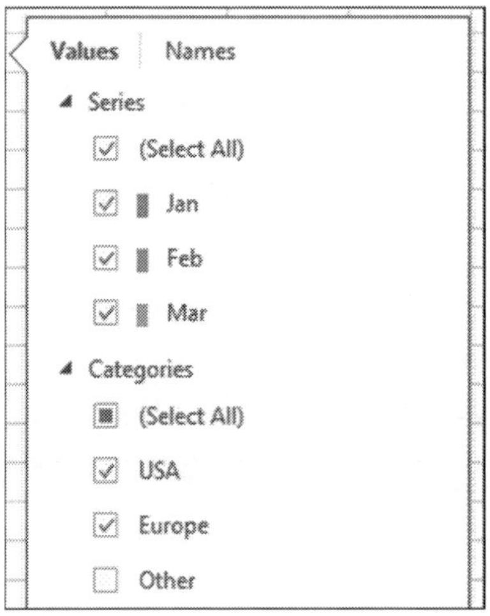

4. In the *Categories* list uncheck the *Other* item so that only the *USA* and *Europe* categories will be shown on the chart.
5. Click the *Apply* button to apply the filter.

   The chart changes so that only *USA* and *Europe* data is displayed for the months *Jan, Feb* and *Mar*.

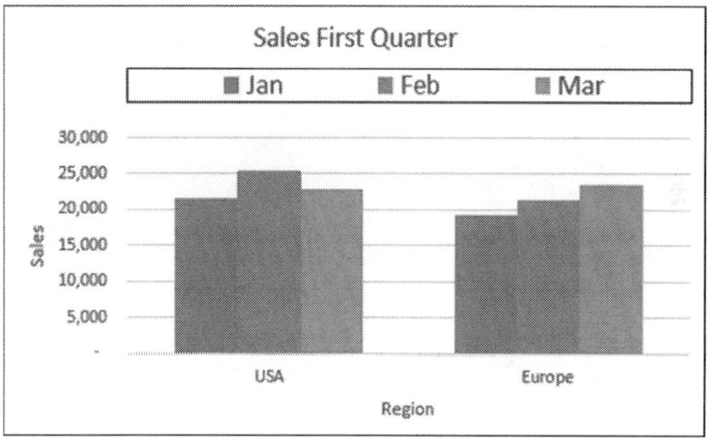

4 Remove all filters so that all data series and categories are displayed.

1. Select the chart.
2. Click the *Chart Filters*  icon.
3. Check the *(Select All)* check box in the *Categories* list to select all three categories.
4. Click the *Apply* button to remove the filter.

Lesson 5-11: Change a chart's source data

You'll often want to chart a small number of columns from a much larger range (that may contain hundreds, or even thousands of columns).

If a range only contains a handful of columns, it may be easier to chart the entire range and then use the *Chart Filters* feature (that you used in: *Lesson 5-10: Apply a chart filter*) to remove the unwanted columns.

When there are a lot of columns, you may find it a lot faster to address the issue in the chart's source data using the technique described in this lesson.

1 Open *World Sales-6* from your sample files folder (if it isn't already open).

note

Another way to display the Select Data Source dialog

You can also bring up the *Select Data Source* dialog from the Ribbon by clicking:

Chart Design→Data→ Select Data

2 Display the *Select Data Source* dialog.

Right-click in the *Plot Area* of the chart and click *Select Data...* from the shortcut menu.

The *Select Data Source* dialog appears.

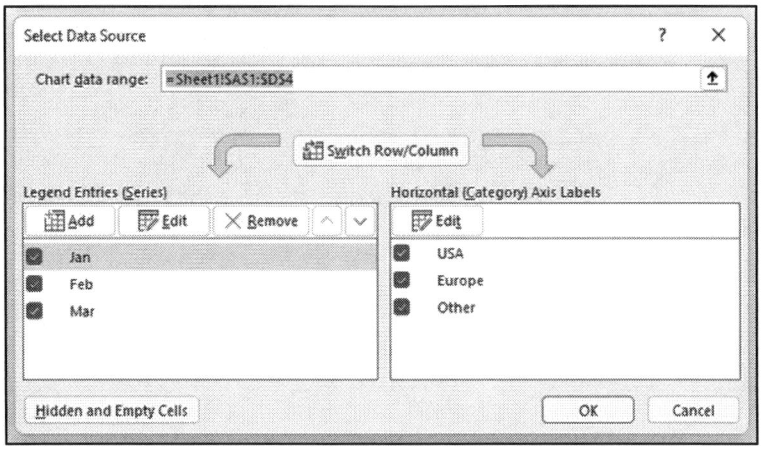

Notice the *Chart data range* shown at the top of the dialog. For the moment, this is all that I want you to concentrate upon.

The range is shown as: *Sheet1!$A$1:$D$4*.

This means the absolute range A1:D4 on the *Sheet1* worksheet.

(You learned about absolute cell references in: *Lesson 3-13: Understand absolute and relative cell references*).

3 Change the *Chart data range* so that only USA sales are charted.

The current range is A1:D4.

	A	B	C	D
1	Month	USA	Europe	Other
2	Jan	21,600	19,200	10,800
3	Feb	25,400	21,400	12,200
4	Mar	22,800	23,600	9,600

World Sales-6

If you change the range to A1:B4 the *Europe* and *Other* regions will be removed.

You could simply type the new reference into the *Chart data range* text box, but it is less error prone if you visually select the data with the mouse.

1. Delete the current contents of the *Chart data range* text box.

2. With the flashing cursor still inside the empty *Chart data range* text box, click and drag with the mouse across cells A1:B4.

   The data range displays in both the *Chart data range* text box and as a marquee on the worksheet.

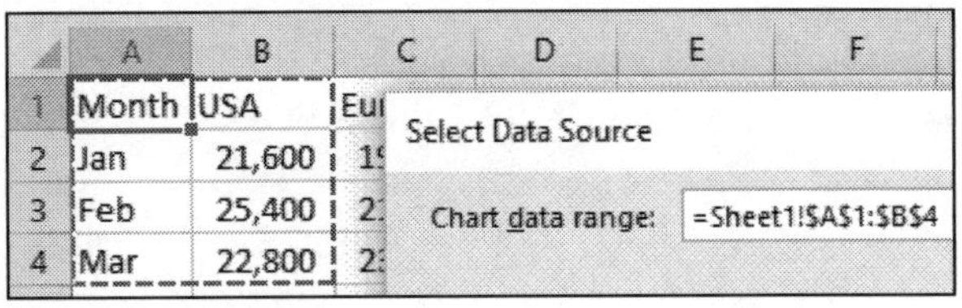

   It is very easy to mess up the data range in the text box. If you get an obscure error message, simply delete all of the contents of the *Chart data range* text box and re-select.

   Notice that, in the background, the chart has changed to reflect the new data range.

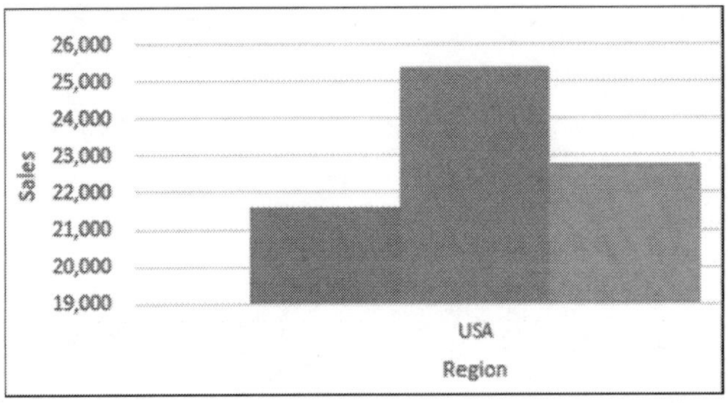

note

The Collapse Dialog button

When you want to visually select data, you'll often find that the dialog is obscuring the data that you need to select.

You could click and drag the dialog out of the way before selecting but there's a better way.

When you click the *Collapse Dialog* button:

...the dialog shrinks to a single line, enabling you to select the data from the worksheet behind the dialog.

Once you've selected the data, click the *Collapse Dialog* button once more to restore the dialog.

4 Change the *Chart data range* to A1:C4 to chart sales for the USA and Europe.

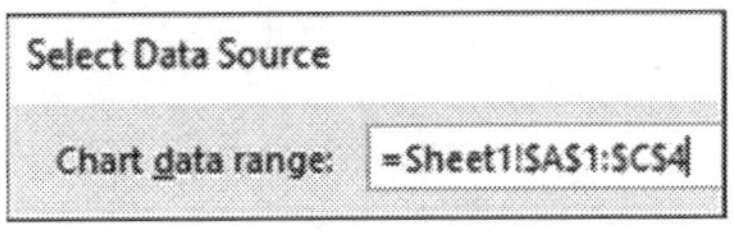

5 Click OK to view the new chart.

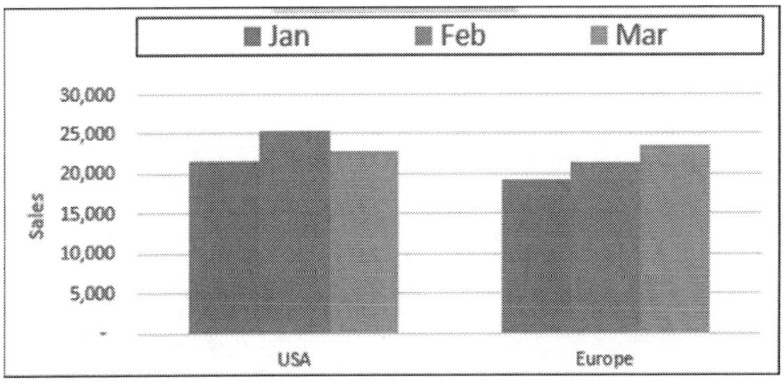

6 Save your work as *World Sales-7.*

Lesson 5-12: Assign non-contiguous source data to a chart

In the previous lesson it was easy to select the source data because it comprised of a single block (we use the word: *contiguous* for this type of range).

In this lesson, you'll take things a little further by selecting data that isn't in a single block (ie non-contiguous data) to show sales for the *USA* and *Other* categories.

1 Open *World Sales-7* from your sample files folder (if it isn't already open).

2 Chart sales for all months in the *USA* and *Other* categories by changing the source data.

1. Right-click in the plot area of the chart and click *Select Data* from the shortcut menu.

   The *Select Data Source* dialog appears.

2. Delete the current contents of the *Chart data range* text box.
3. With the cursor still flashing inside the empty *Chart data range* text box, click and drag with the mouse across cells A1:B4.
4. Release the mouse button.
5. Hold down the **<Ctrl>** key.
6. Select the range D1:D4.
7. Click the OK button.

   Selecting non-contiguous ranges was covered extensively in: *Lesson 2-7: Select non-contiguous cell ranges and view summary information.*

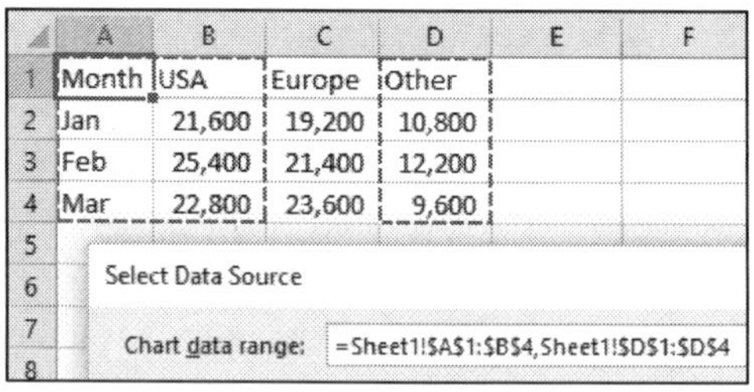

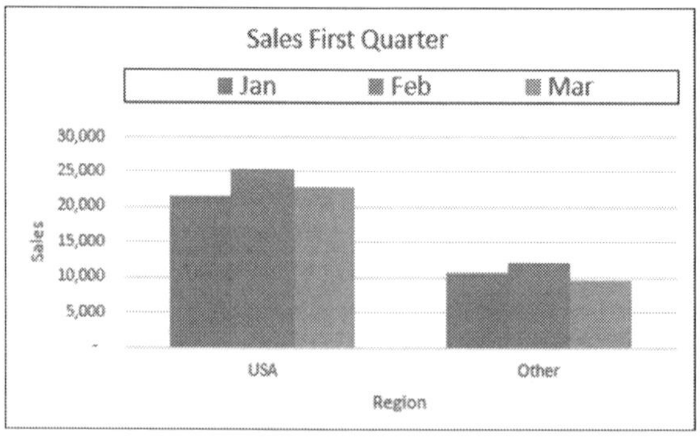

World Sales-7

3 Display the total sales for each month in column E.

Type the word: **Total** into cell E1 and then use AutoSum to place the totals for all regions into cells E2:E4.

You learned how to do this in: *Lesson 2-3: Use AutoSum to quickly calculate totals.*

4 Change the source data so that only the *Total* category is charted.

1. Right-click in the plot area of the chart.
2. Click *Select Data…* from the shortcut menu.
3. Delete the current contents of the *Chart data range* text box.
4. With the mouse cursor still flashing inside the empty *Chart data range* text box, click and drag with the mouse across cells A1:A4 and then release the mouse button.
5. Hold down the **<Ctrl>** key.
6. Select cells E1:E4.

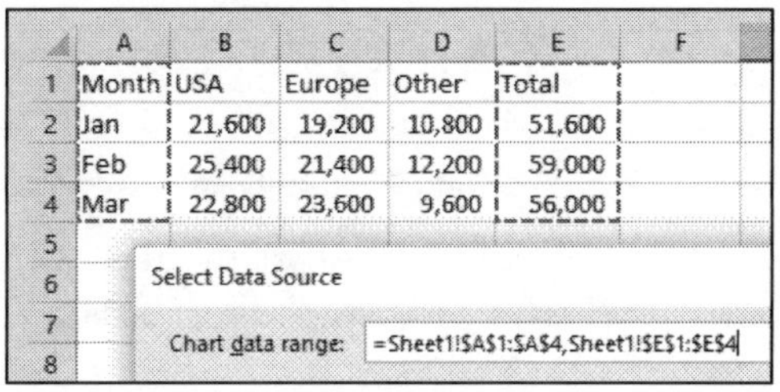

	A	B	C	D	E	F
1	Month	USA	Europe	Other	Total	
2	Jan	21,600	19,200	10,800	51,600	
3	Feb	25,400	21,400	12,200	59,000	
4	Mar	22,800	23,600	9,600	56,000	
5						
6						
7						
8						

7. Click OK to close the *Select Data Source* dialog.

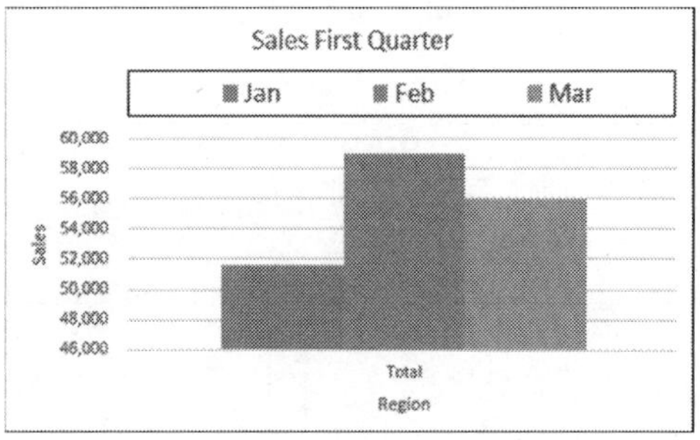

5 Change the source data so that sales for *USA*, *Europe* and *Other* regions are shown (but not the total).

1. Right-click in the plot area of the chart and click *Select Data* from the shortcut menu.
2. Select cells A1:D4.
3. Click OK to close the *Select Data Source* dialog.

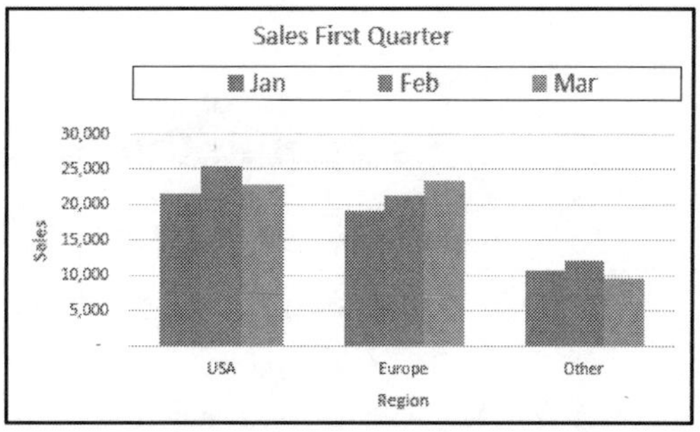

6 Save your work as *World Sales-8.*

Lesson 5-13: Understand Data Series and Categories

In order to use the *Select Data Source* dialog in a more advanced way, you will need to understand how Excel automatically divides a range of data into *data series* and *categories.*

Data series and categories

Here is the data you have been working with for most of this session:

	A	B	C	D	
1	Month	USA	Europe	Other	← Category
2	Jan	21,600	19,200	10,800	← Series 1 (Jan)
3	Feb	25,400	21,400	12,200	← Series 2 (Feb)
4	Mar	22,800	23,600	9,600	← Series 3 (Mar)

Excel interprets this data as having three data series (Jan, Feb and Mar).

In this example, each data series has three values. For example, the *Jan* data series has the three values 21,600, 19,200 and 10,800.

The values are plotted along the left-hand vertical axis (sometimes referred to as the Y axis).

Each of the values in a data series is associated with a *Category*. This is simply a label that identifies each value in the series. For example, the *Jan* series value of 19,200 belongs to the *Europe* category.

The category is shown along the bottom horizontal axis (sometimes referred to as the X axis).

Showing this on the chart makes things clearer:

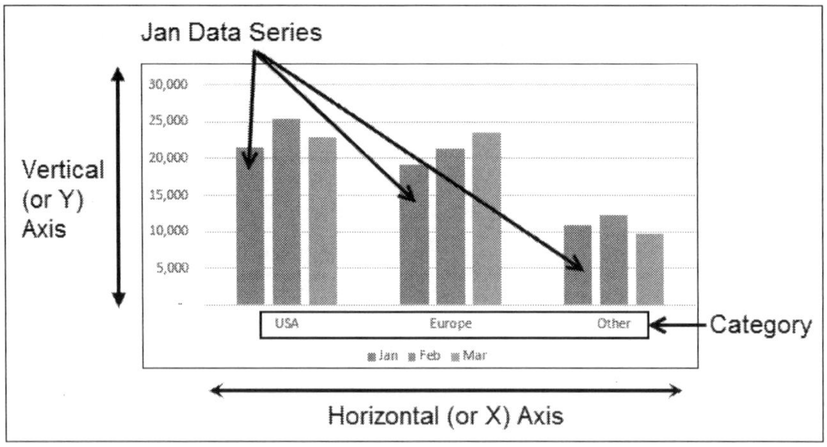

Swapping the rows and columns

It is also possible to take a different view of the same data.

The old *data series* become *categories*, and the old *categories* become *data series*.

World Sales-8

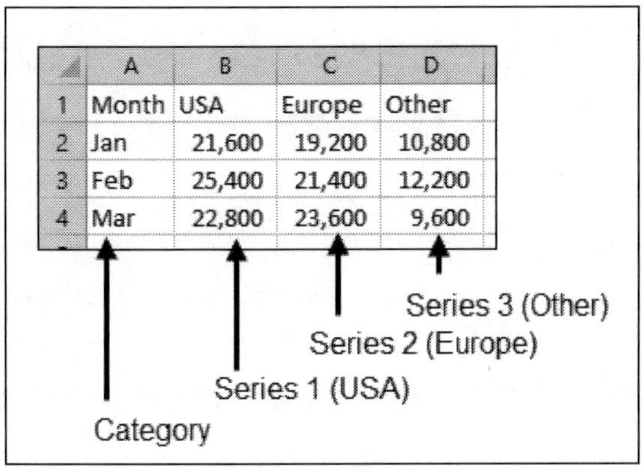

When the data is viewed in this way a different chart will result.

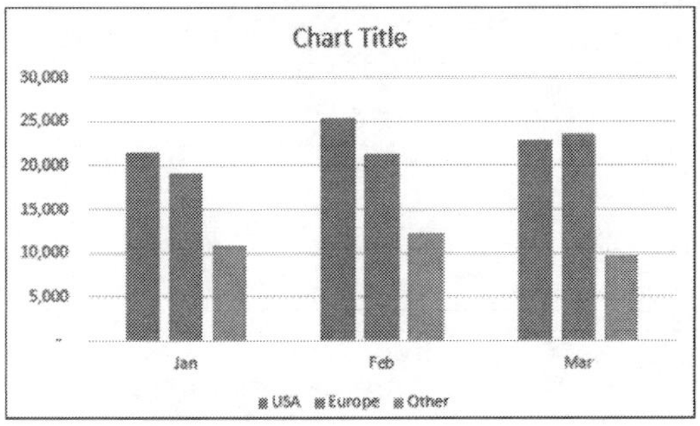

1 Open *World Sales-8* from your sample files folder (if it isn't already open).

At present Excel regards months as data series, and regions as categories:

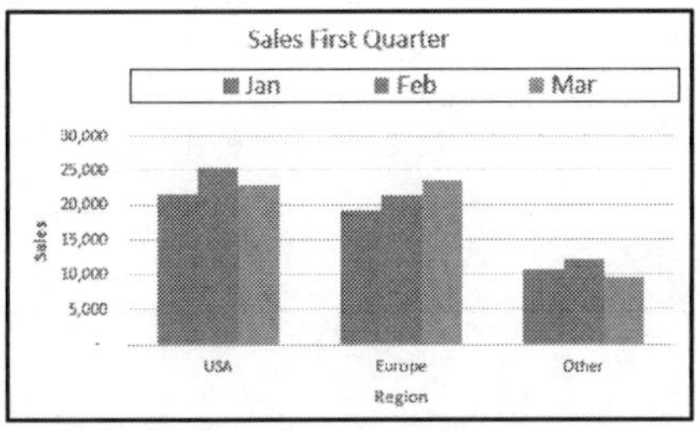

2 Switch the rows and columns so that the X axis shows months instead of regions.

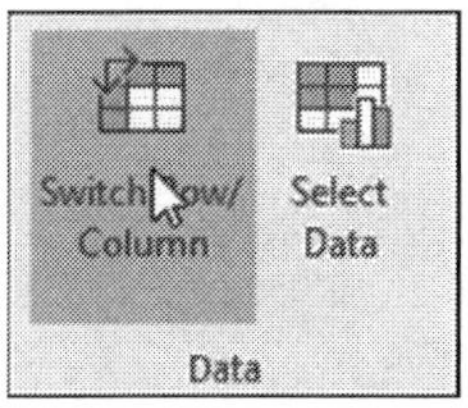

1. Click just inside the border of the chart to select it.
2. Click: Chart Design→Data→Switch Row/Column.
3. If necessary, re-size the legend box so that all three series are visible.

   Excel now regards the regions as data series, and the months as categories.

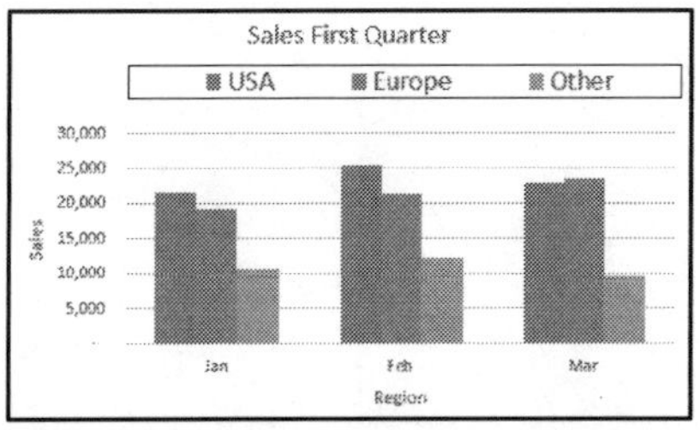

3 Save your work as *World Sales-9*.

Lesson 5-14: Add data series using the Select Data Source dialog tools

note

An alternative method for selecting source data

The *Select Data Source* dialog is by far the best way to set and modify source data for charts.

An alternative (and less intuitive) way is to copy a data range, activate the chart, and then click:

Home→Clipboard→Paste→Paste Special...

A *Paste Special* dialog is then displayed that is specifically designed for charts:

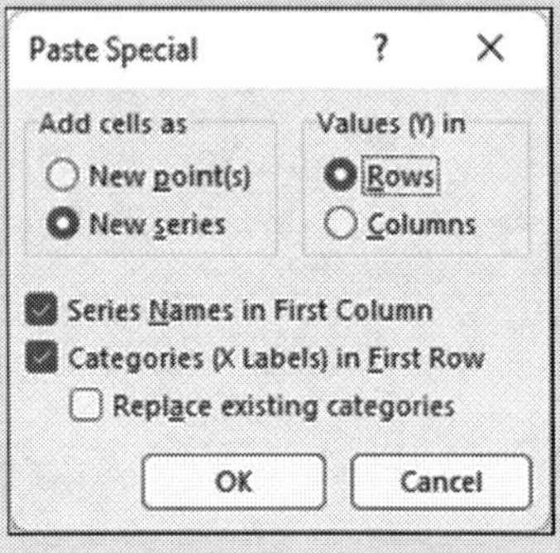

World Sales-9

1 Open *World Sales-9* from your sample files folder (if it isn't already open).

2 Display the *Select Data Source* dialog.

Right-click in the *Plot Area* of the chart and click *Select Data...* from the shortcut menu.

The *Select Data Source* dialog appears.

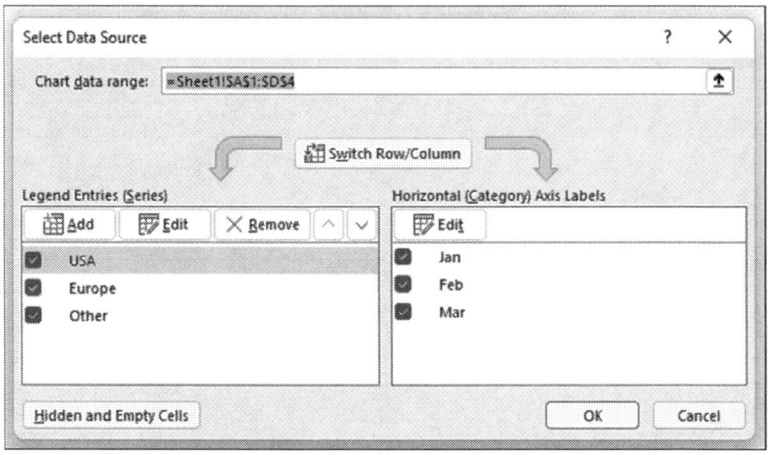

Notice that there are check boxes next to each series and category.

You can check and uncheck these boxes to apply a chart filter (a different way to do the same thing that you did in: *Lesson 5-10: Apply a chart filter*).

3 Add a *Total* data series.

Click the *Add* button in the *Legend Entries (Series)* pane.

1. Type: **Total** for the series name.
2. Delete any text currently appearing in the *Series values* text box.
3. Select the range E2:E4 for the *Series values*.

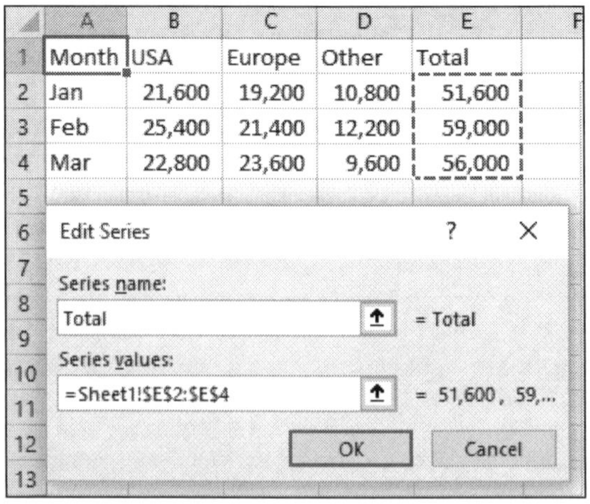

4. Click OK.

   The series is added to the dialog.

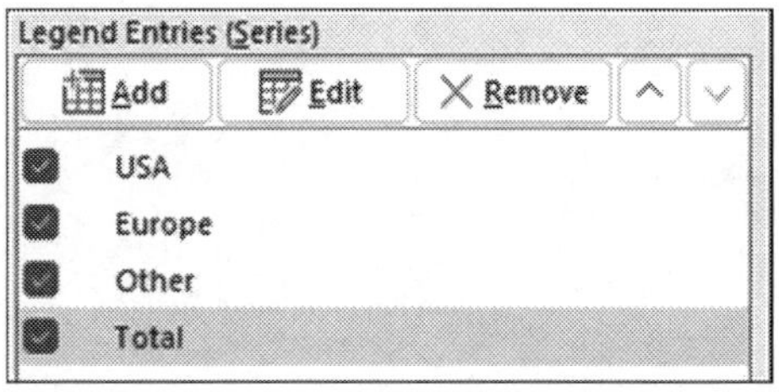

   The series also appears on the chart.

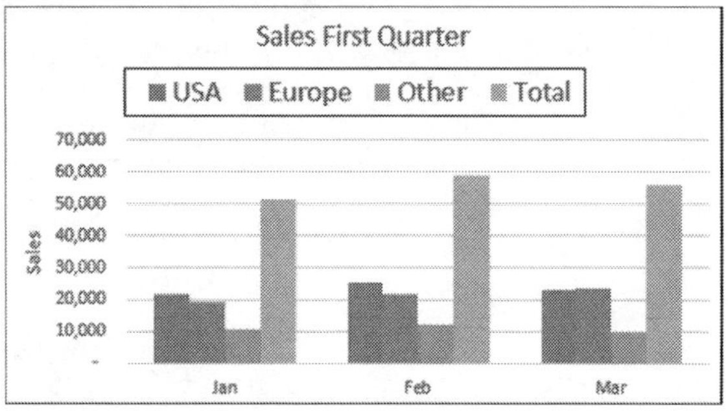

4 Delete the *Total* data series.

1. Display the *Select Data Source* dialog (if it isn't already open).
2. Click the *Total* data series in the *Legend Entries (Series)* list to select it.
3. Click the Remove button. 

   The series is removed from both the dialog and the chart.

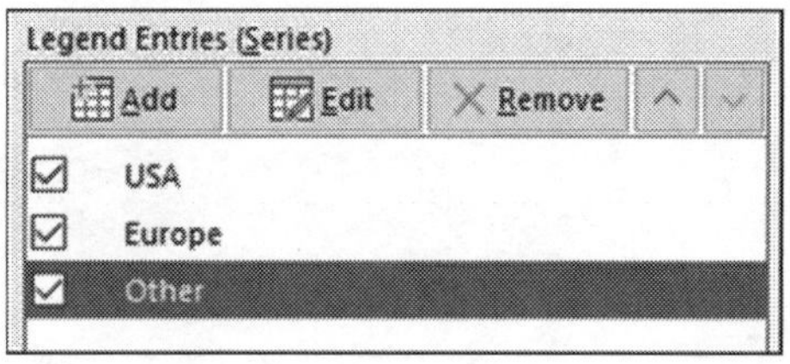

5 Switch the rows and columns so that the X axis shows regions instead of months.

You learned how to do this using the Ribbon in: *Lesson 5-13: Understand Data Series and Categories.*

You can do the same thing by clicking the *Switch Row/Column* button on the *Select Data Source* dialog.

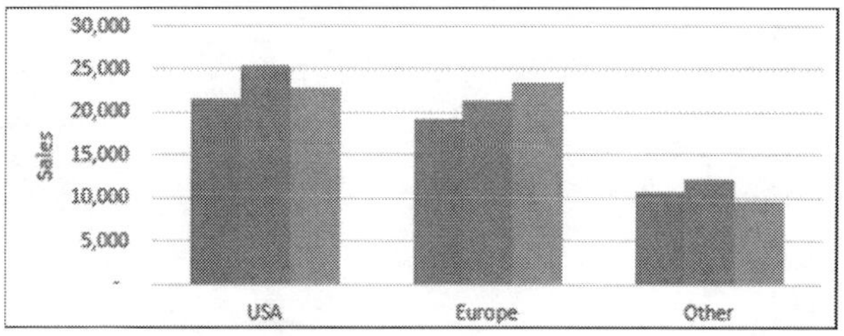

6 Click the OK button to close the *Select Data Source* dialog.

7 Save your work as *World Sales-10.*

Lesson 5-15: Chart non-contiguous source data by hiding rows and columns

In this lesson, you'll look at an alternative method of charting a non-contiguous range simply by hiding the data elements that you don't want to chart.

Excel allows you to hide rows and columns in a worksheet by effectively setting their width to zero. The default behavior of charts is to ignore these hidden rows and columns.

It is also possible to override this default behavior and instruct Excel to chart hidden rows and columns.

1 Open *World Sales-10* from your sample files folder (if it isn't already open).

2 Remove the *Europe* series from the chart by hiding column C.

1. Right-click on the column header button at the top of column C. 

2. Click *Hide* from the shortcut menu.

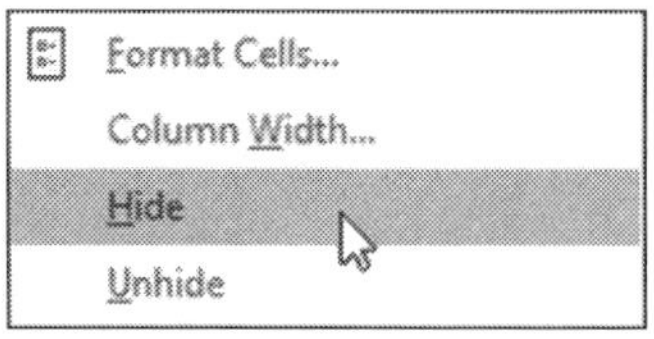

The *European* sales data is no longer shown on the chart.

3 Remove the *February* data from the chart by hiding row 3.

1. Right-click on the row header button to the left of row 3. 

2. Click *Hide* from the shortcut menu.

February data is no longer shown on the chart.

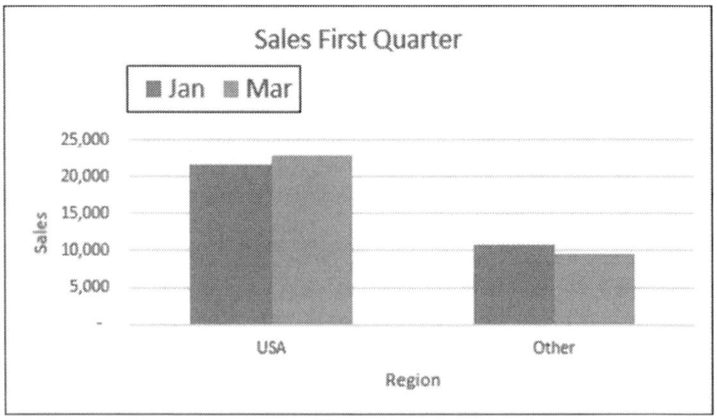

4 Display the hidden data in the chart.

Excel allows you to chart hidden data if you want to.

World Sales-10

1. Right-click in the plot area of the chart and click *Select Data…* from the shortcut menu.

   The *Select Data Source* dialog appears.

2. Click the *Hidden and Empty Cells* button on the bottom left corner of the dialog.

   The *Hidden and Empty Cell Settings* dialog appears.

3. Check the *Show data in hidden rows and columns* check box.

   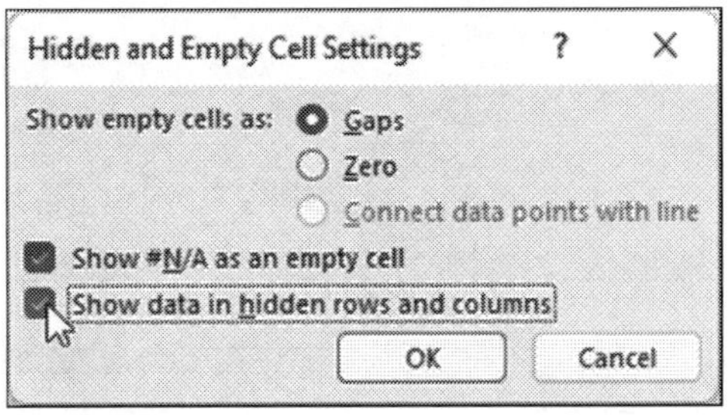

4. Click the OK button twice to dismiss the dialogs.

   The previously hidden chart data re-appears.

   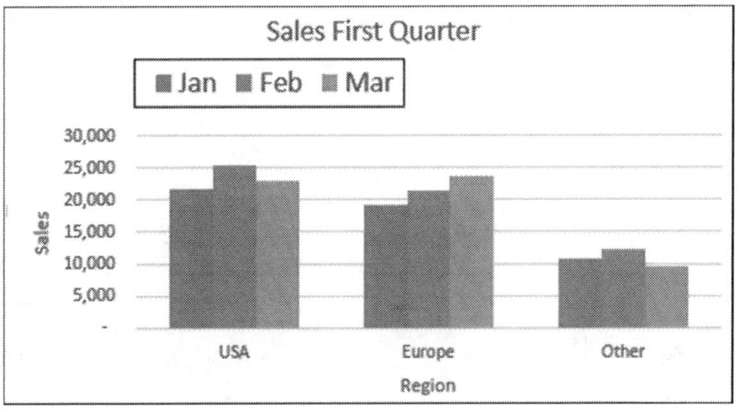

5 Unhide the hidden rows and columns.

1. Click any cell in the worksheet to de-activate the chart.
2. Click the *Select All* button at the top left corner of the worksheet to select every cell.

   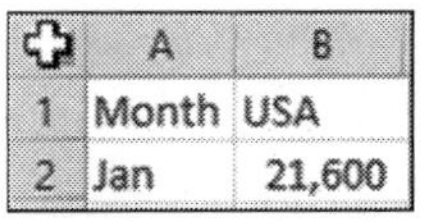

3. Click: Home→Cells→Format→Hide & Unhide→Unhide Rows.
4. Click: Home→Cells→Format→Hide & Unhide→
   Unhide Columns.

6 Save your work as *World Sales-11.*

note

The Hidden and Empty Cell Settings dialog can also be used with Sparklines

If you select a Sparkline group and click:

Sparkline Tools→Design→Sparkline→Edit Data→Hidden & Empty Cells

… you will see the same *Hidden and Empty Cell Settings* dialog that is used in this lesson to deal with hidden rows and columns in charts.

You can use it in exactly the same way to deal with hidden rows and columns in Sparkline source data.

You learned how to create Sparkline groups in: *Lesson 4-20: Insert a Sparkline into a range of cells.*

Lesson 5-16: Create a chart with numerical axes

Sometimes Excel gets a little confused when it attempts to automatically generate a chart.

Problems usually occur when you need to plot numerical information along the horizontal axis. Excel sees the numerical labels and assumes that they are a series.

In this lesson, you'll use such a worksheet to confuse Excel and then fix things up manually using the *Select Data Source* dialog.

1 Open *Annual Sales Summary* from your sample files folder.

2 Display the range as a clustered column chart.

1. Click on any single cell inside the range.

   Note that it isn't necessary to select the range when you want to chart all of it.

   If you simply click any cell inside the range, Excel will automatically select the entire range for the chart's source data.

2. Click: Insert→Charts→Insert Column or Bar Chart→ 2D Column→Clustered Column.

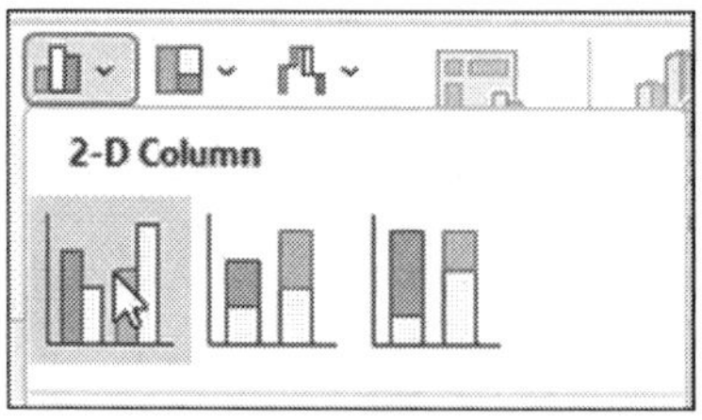

The range is displayed as a chart, but there's a problem. Excel has assumed that the numbers in the *Year* column are a data series.

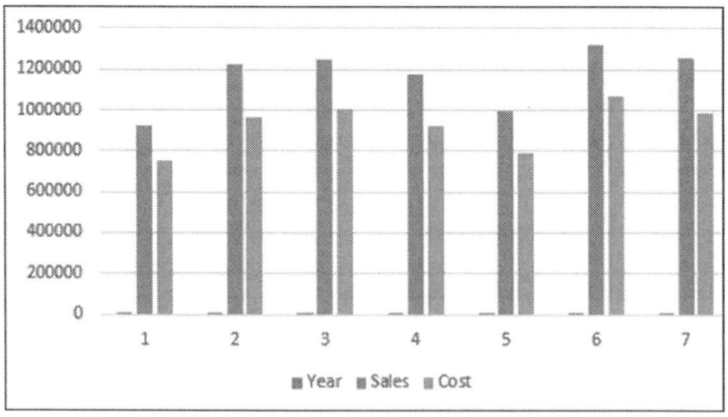

Note that the numbers for the *Year* data are so small in relation to the *Sales* and *Cost* data that you can hardly see their bars in the bar chart. The bars are there, but they are so short that they are almost invisible.

Annual Sales Summary

3 Right-click just inside the plot area of the chart and click *Select Data…* from the shortcut menu.

note

You can usually sidestep the problem described in this lesson using Recommended Charts

When Excel provides several Recommended Chart options it usually includes one that will solve the problem described in this lesson.

If you click inside the data and then click:

Insert→Recommended Charts

... you'll see that all of the recommended charts have intelligently guessed that the numbers in the *Year* column are category axis labels.

The *Select Data Source* dialog is displayed.

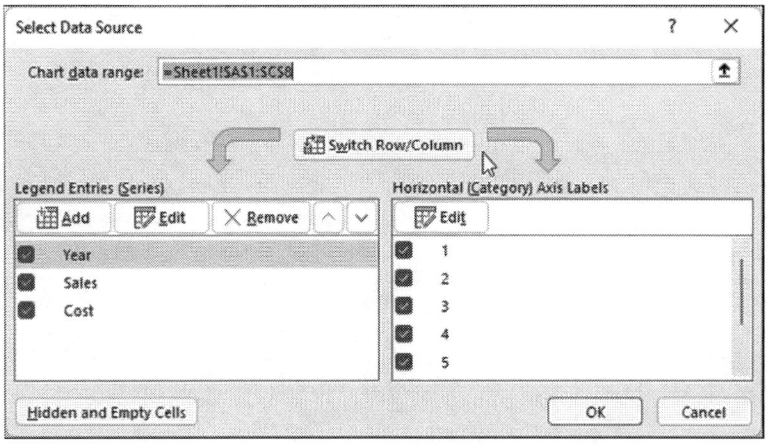

The problem is immediately apparent. Excel has wrongly identified the *Year* as series data rather than as category axis labels.

4 Remove the *Year* data series and add the *Year* data as *Horizontal (Category) Axis Labels*.

1. Click *Year* in the left-hand pane of the dialog and then click the Remove button. 

2. Click the *Edit* button 

 at the top of the right-hand pane.

3. Select cells A2:A8 for the *Axis label range* (the year data but not the column header).

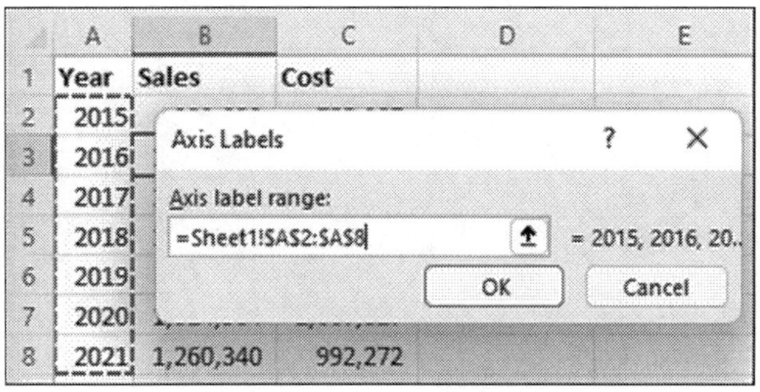

4. Click the OK button twice to close both dialogs.

   The chart now displays correctly.

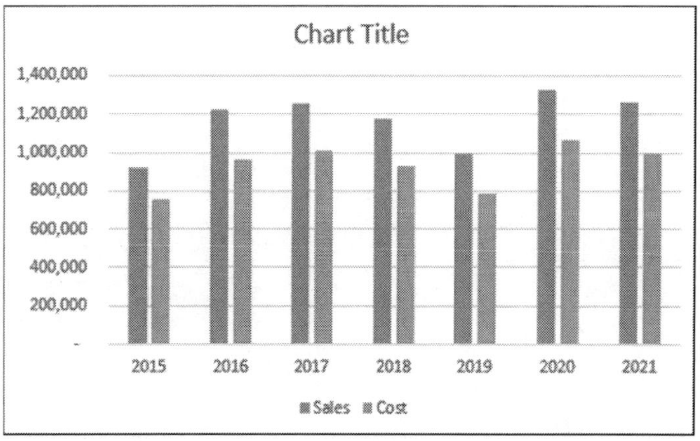

5 Save your work as *Annual Sales Summary-1*.

Lesson 5-17: Deal with empty data points

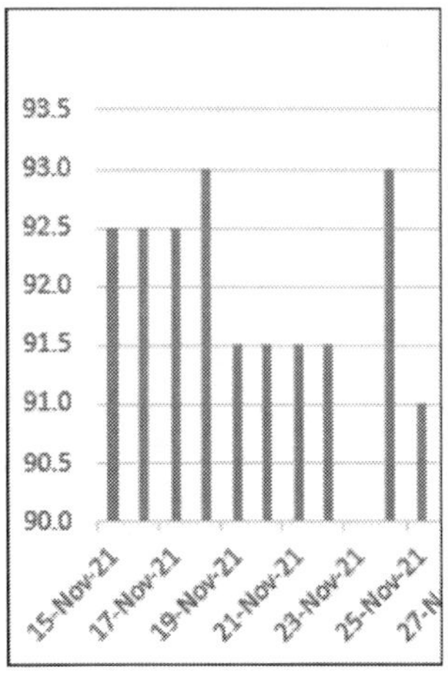

	A	B
1	Date	Weight
2	15-Nov-21	92.5
3	16-Nov-21	92.5
4	17-Nov-21	92.5
5	18-Nov-21	93.0
6	19-Nov-21	91.5
7	20-Nov-21	91.5
8	21-Nov-21	91.5
9	22-Nov-21	91.5
10	23-Nov-21	
11	24-Nov-21	93.0
12	25-Nov-21	91.0
13	26-Nov-21	91.0
14	27-Nov-21	91.0
15	28-Nov-21	92.0
16	29-Nov-21	
17	30-Nov-21	
18	1-Dec-21	91.5

Weight 2018

Sometimes you'll only have partial data for a series.

In the worksheet used for this lesson I'll share a secret with you. I weigh myself every day and keep a chart on my bathroom wall to make sure that I'm staying at a healthy weight.

Sometimes I'm away travelling and can't weigh in as usual. When I get back, I need to fill in the gaps.

If I used a column chart, there would be no problem (see sidebar) as the missing days would have missing columns.

But I use a line chart for my weight, and I'd like the chart to draw a line connecting the last data point recorded before I went away with the first recorded upon my return. Unfortunately, Excel doesn't do this by default and will leave gaps for the missing data points:

1 Open *Weight 2021* from your sample files folder.

This is a simple worksheet showing my weight in kilograms for each date in November 2021. Notice that there are missing days when I was away from home.

2 Display the range as a *Line with Markers* chart.

1. Click on any of the date values within the range.
2. Click: Insert→Charts→Insert Line or Area Chart→Line with Markers.

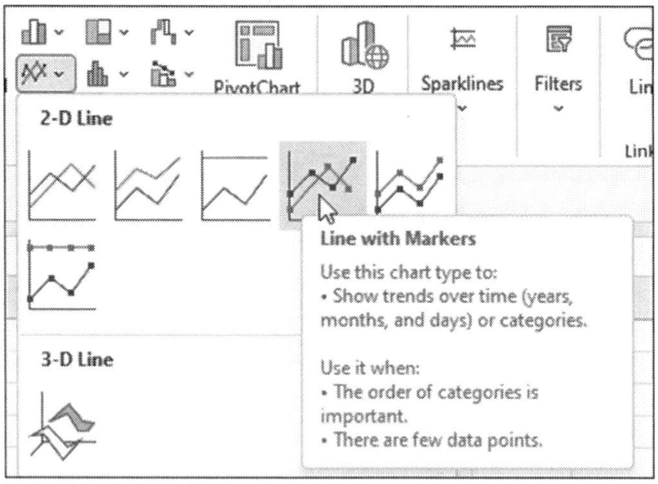

The chart displays, but there are gaps for the missing entries.

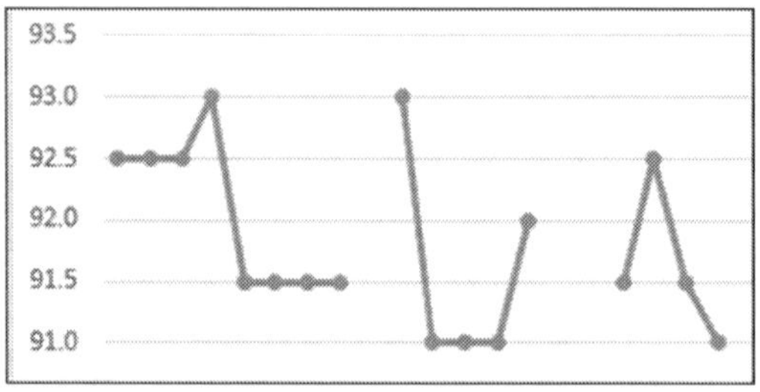

3 Tell Excel to connect the gaps in the chart with a line.

1. Right-click just inside the plot area of the chart and click *Select Data* from the shortcut menu.

   The *Select Data Source* dialog is displayed.

2. Click the *Hidden and Empty Cells* button at the bottom left corner of the dialog.

   The *Hidden and Empty Cells* dialog appears.

3. Click the *Connect data points with line* option button.

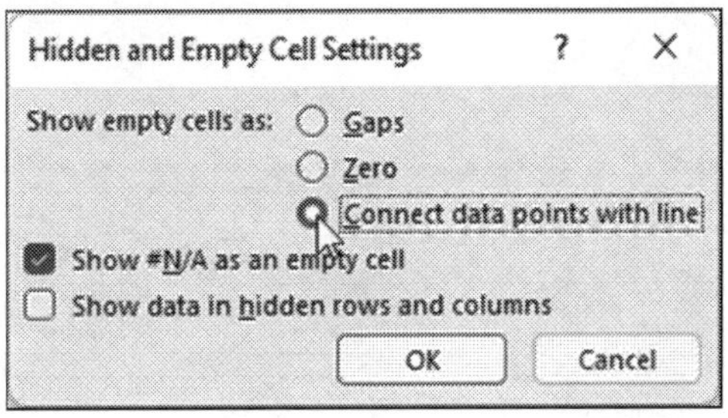

   Note the checkbox: *Show #N/A as an empty cell.* #N/A is an error value that Excel displays when a value is not available to a function or formula. Excel's normal behavior when encountering #N/A values is to *Connect data points with line* (even if you select *Gaps* or *Zero*).

   The *Show #N/A as an empty cell* option enables you to tell Excel to treat any #N/A errors in the same way it would treat an empty cell. This means that Excel will respect your choice (*Gaps, Zero* or *Connect data points with line*).

4. Click the OK button and OK again to dismiss both dialogs

   All data points are now connected with a line.

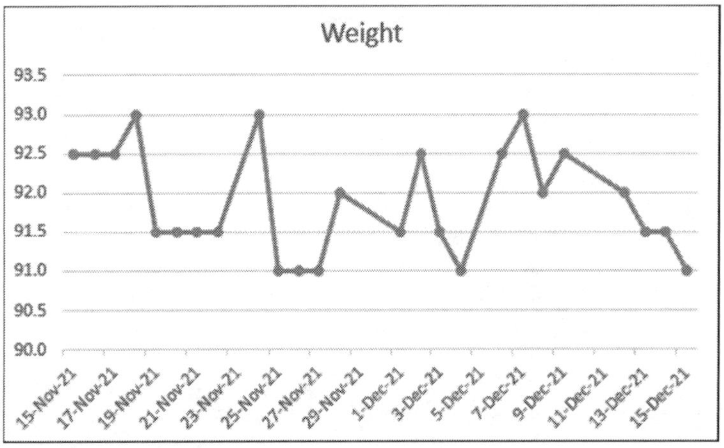

4 Save your work as *Weight 2021-1.*

note

The Hidden and Empty Cell Settings dialog can also be used with Sparklines

If you select a Sparkline group and click:

Sparkline Tools→Design→ Sparkline→Edit Data→ Hidden & Empty Cells

... you will see the same *Hidden and Empty Cell Settings* dialog that is used in this lesson to deal with empty data points in charts.

You can use it in exactly the same way to deal with empty data points in Sparklines.

You learned how to create Sparkline groups in: *Lesson 4-20: Insert a Sparkline into a range of cells.*

Lesson 5-18: Add data labels to a chart

It is possible to approximate the values that are displayed in a chart by looking at the vertical axis.

Sometimes you will need to convey the precise values that are being charted. There are three ways of doing this:

- Embed the chart in the worksheet containing the source data so that the user can see both the chart and data.
- Add data labels to each point on the chart.
- Add a *Data Table* chart element to the bottom of the chart.

1 Open *Annual Sales Summary-1* from your sample files folder.

2 Change the chart's source data so that only sales (not costs) for 2018 to 2021 are charted.

1. Activate the chart by clicking just inside the chart's border.
2. Click the *Chart Filters* icon  that appears outside the top-right corner of the chart.
3. Uncheck the Cost series.
4. Uncheck 2015, 2016 and 2017.

   The Filter should now look like this:

   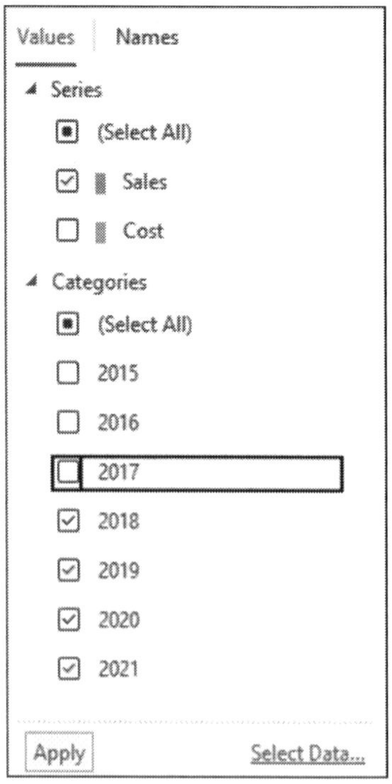

5. Click the *Apply* button.

   The chart should now look like this.

tip

Data labels can be moved and formatted just like any other element

When preparing a chart for a PowerPoint presentation, the data labels are often too small to be visible at the back of the room so you may wish to increase the font size.

You may also want to fine-tune the positioning of data labels.

Re-positioning data labels

1. Click on a data label to select the entire series.

2. Hover the mouse cursor over any data label until you see the four-headed cursor arrow shape.

3. Click and drag the data label to move it to a new position.

Change the data label font or font size

1. Click on a data label to select the entire series.

2. Click: Home→Font→Font Size

OR

Right-click a data label and then click *Font…* from the shortcut menu.

Format data labels

Right-click a data and then click *Format Data Labels…* from the shortcut menu.

Annual Sales Summary-1

tip

How to format a single data label

If you need to work with a single data label, click once on a data label to select the data label series and then a second time to select the individual label you want to work with.

tip

Changing the label shape

Right-click a data label to select the entire series and then click *Change Data Label Shapes* from the shortcut menu.

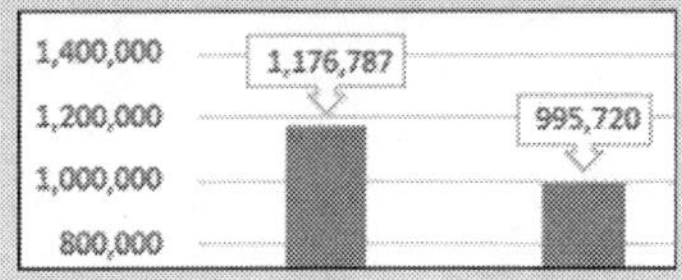

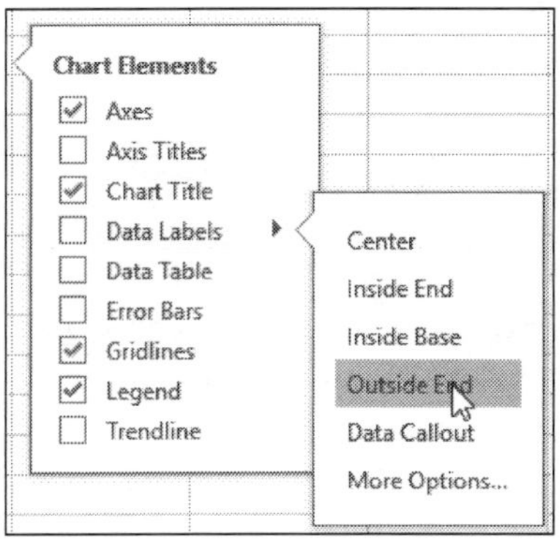

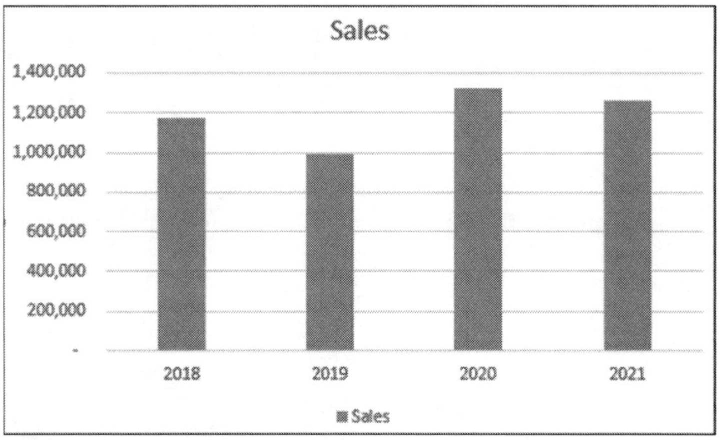

6. Click the OK button to close the dialog.

3 Add data label elements outside the end of each bar.

1. Activate the chart by clicking just inside the chart's border.
2. Click the *Chart Elements* icon that appears outside the top-right corner of the chart.
3. Click: Data Labels→Outside End.

   Data labels are now shown outside the end of each bar:

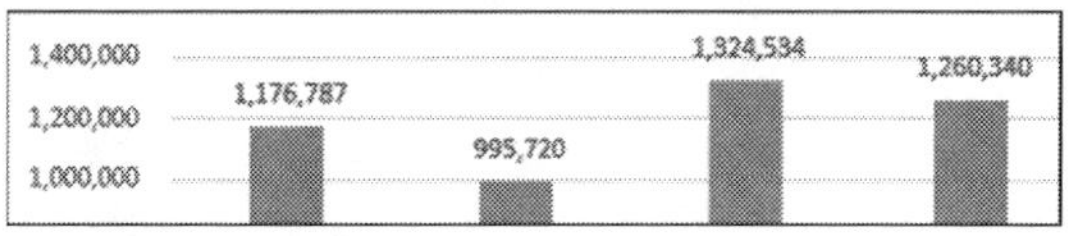

4 Switch off the data labels.

1. Activate the chart by clicking just inside the chart's border.
2. Click the *Chart Elements* icon that appears outside the top-right corner of the chart.
3. Uncheck the *Data Labels* check box.

5 Add a *Data Table* element to the bottom of the chart.

1. Activate the chart by clicking just inside the chart's border.
2. Click the *Chart Elements* icon that appears outside the top-right corner of the chart.
3. Check the *Data Table* check box.

   A table is displayed below the chart:

	2018	2019	2020	2021
Sales	1,176,787	995,720	1,324,534	1,260,340

6 Save your work as *Annual Sales Summary-2.*

Lesson 5-19: Add data labels from a range

In: *Lesson 5-18: Add data labels to a chart*, you added data labels to a column chart to show the precise value represented by each column.

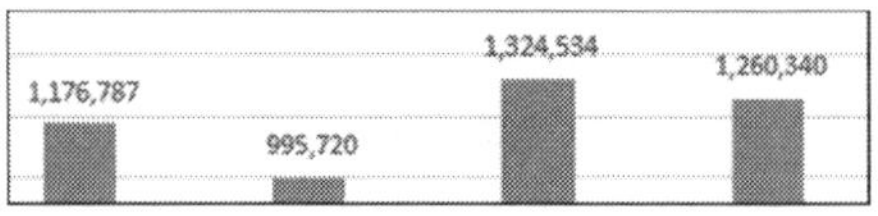

This is the most common use for data labels.

Data labels can also display any other type of information.

The values to be used for the data labels are placed in a range on the worksheet. It is then possible to specify this range as the source for the data labels to be displayed.

In this lesson, you'll use a column chart to show the actual mark achieved in an examination. Data labels will then be added to show the grade that corresponds to each mark:

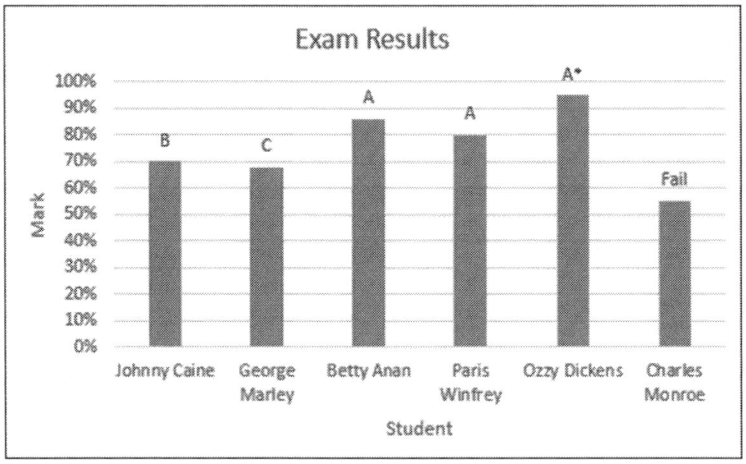

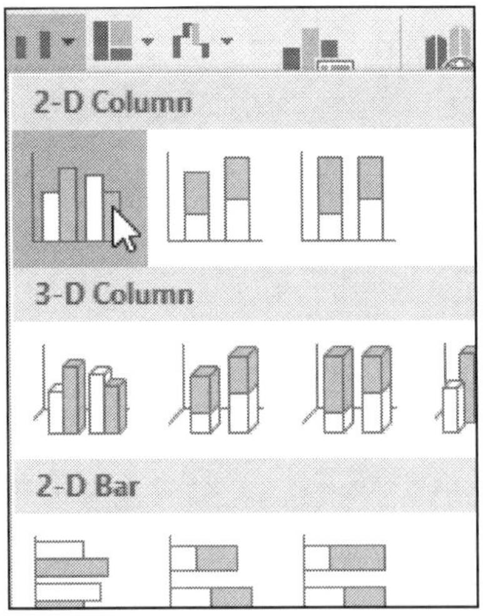

You can see how this adds value to the chart. It is easy to see at a glance that although Betty Annan and Paris Winfrey both achieved a grade A pass, Betty actually had a higher mark.

1 Open *Exam Results-1* from your sample files folder.

2 Create a column chart showing the student's name and percentage mark.

1. Select the range A3:B9.
2. Click: Insert→Charts→Insert Column or Bar Chart→ 2D Column→Clustered Column.

3 Add *Axis Title* elements to the chart.

You learned how to do this in: *Lesson 5-9: Move, re-size, add, position and delete chart elements.*

4 Change the *Vertical Axis Title* text to: **Mark**, the *Horizontal Axis Title* text to: **Student** and the *Chart Title* text to: **Exam Results**.

Exam Results-1

You learned how to do this in: *Lesson 5-5: Add and remove chart elements using Quick Layout.*

5 Add data labels to show the student grade above each bar.

1. Click anywhere on the chart to activate it.

2. Click the *Chart Elements* icon  that appears just outside the top right-hand corner of the chart.

3. Click the fly out menu button to the right of *Data Labels.*

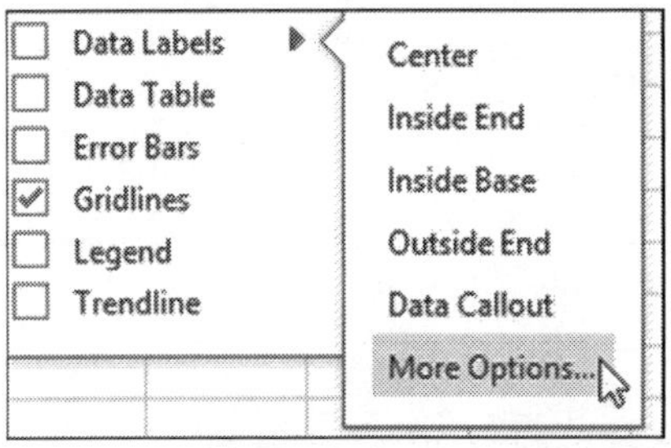

4. Click: *More Options…* from the fly out menu.

   The *Format Data Labels* task pane appears.

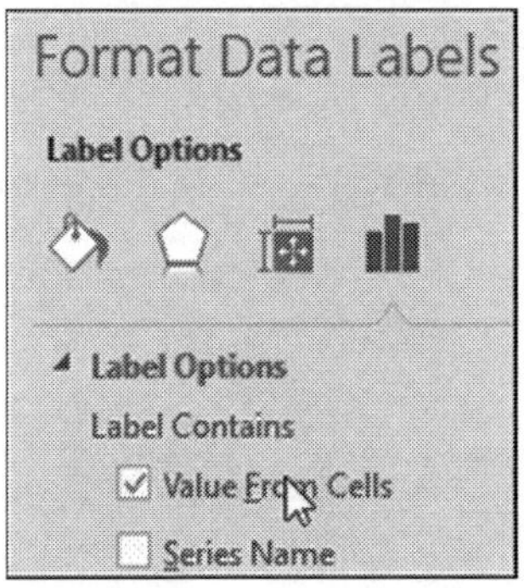

5. Click the *Label Options* icon. 

6. Click the fly out menu button to the left of *Label Options.*

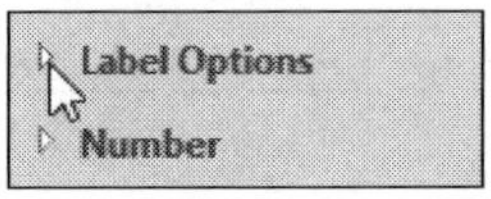

7. In the *Label Contains* list, uncheck any checked check boxes and then check *Value From Cells.*

   The *Data Label Range* dialog appears.

8. Click inside the *Select Data Label Range* text box.

9. Select cells C4:C9 with the mouse.

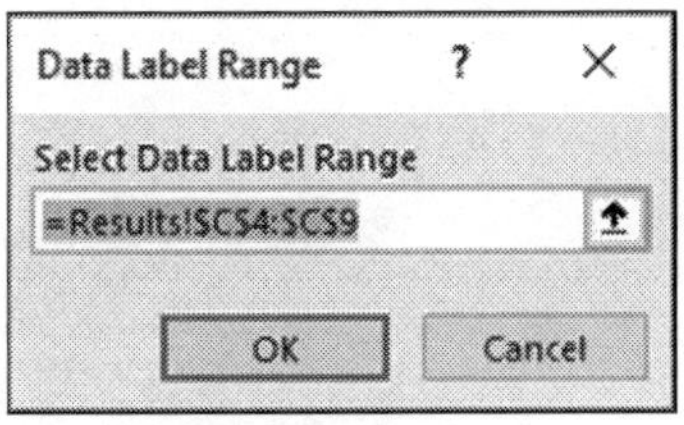

10. Click the OK button.

    Your chart should now look like this:

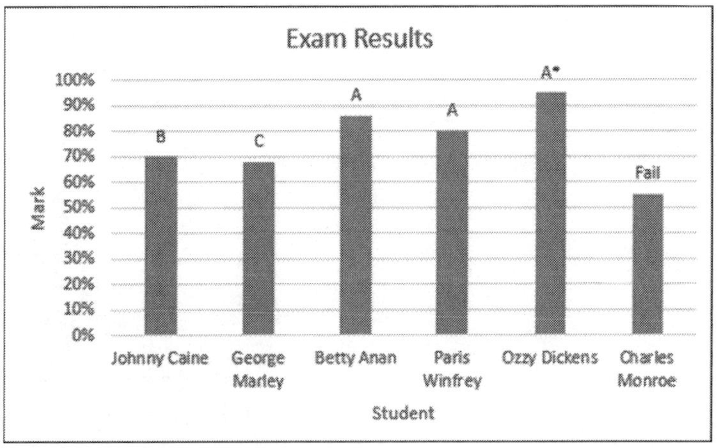

6 Save your work as *Exam Results-2.*

tip

Text boxes are more flexible than the built-in Chart Title elements

This lesson shows you how to add a Text Box to a chart.

Elements such as *Chart Title* and *Horizontal (Category) Axis Title* appear to have sizing handles but you cannot, in fact, re-size them. The only way to make them wider is to type in more text or change the font.

Text boxes have no such restrictions. For this reason, you may sometimes find that it is preferable to substitute a text box for a *Chart Title* element.

note

A different way to format a data point

In the context of this lesson's chart a data point is a single bar in the chart.

1. Click on a data point once to select the entire data series.

2. Click on the data point once more to select a single data point.

3. Right-click on the single selected data point and click *Format Data Point…* from the shortcut menu.

The *Format Data Point* task pane appears offering many formatting options.

Annual Sales Summary-2

Lesson 5-20: Highlight specific data points with color and annotations

A single value within a data series is often referred to as a *data point.*

Sometimes you will want to emphasize a specific data point in a series. For example, you may want to color a single column differently to its neighbors to emphasize some special attribute of the data point.

Color alone cannot always convey why the data point is special. You will normally want to also add a text box to the chart to explain the reason for its different color.

In this lesson, you'll imagine that the company is a hotel, and that 2019 was the centenary year in a competing resort, leading to an expectation of decreased sales. To mark this, you'll color the 2019 bar blue and add an annotation saying *Centenary Year* to the bar.

1 Open *Annual Sales Summary-2* from your sample files folder (if it isn't already open).

2 Change the color of the 2019 bar to blue.

1. Click the 2019 bar once. Notice that the entire data series is selected.
2. Click the 2020 bar once more. This time only the 2019 bar is selected.
3. Click: Format→Shape Styles→ Shape Fill→Blue, Accent 5.

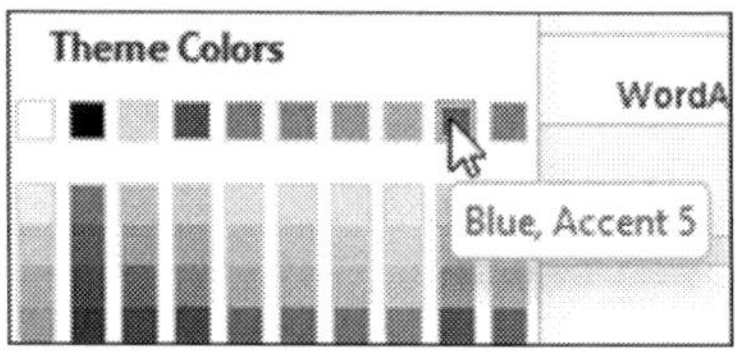

4. The 2019 bar is now colored blue. The legend has also changed to give a further visual prompt that the blue bar relates to 2019.

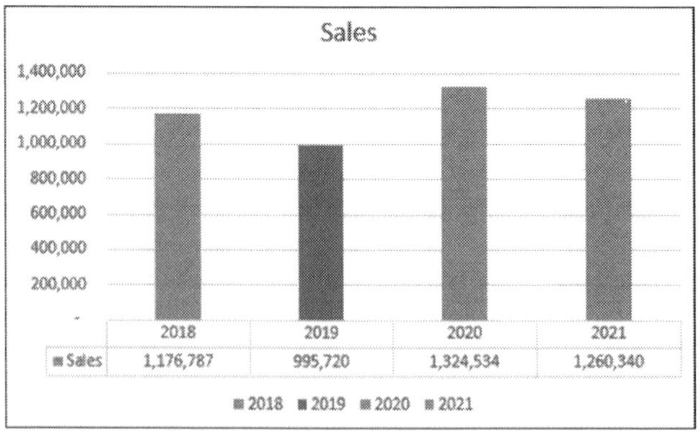

3 Add a text box above, and to the right of, the 2019 bar containing the text: **Centenary Year**.

1. Click just inside the border of the chart to activate it.

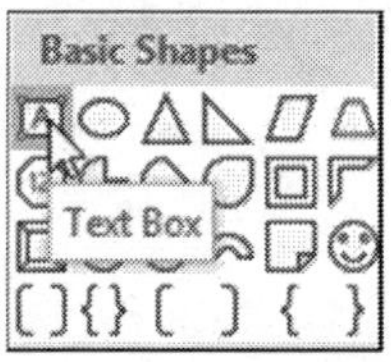

2. Click: Format→Insert Shapes→ More→Basic Shapes→Text Box.

3. Click on the chart, above the blue 2019 bar, and type **Centenary,** then press the **<Enter>** key and then type **Year.**

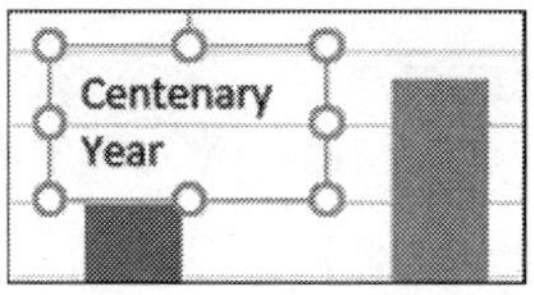

4 Add a border and fill to the text box.

Click the text box to select it and then click:

Shape Format→Shape Styles→
More→Subtle Effect – Blue, Accent 1

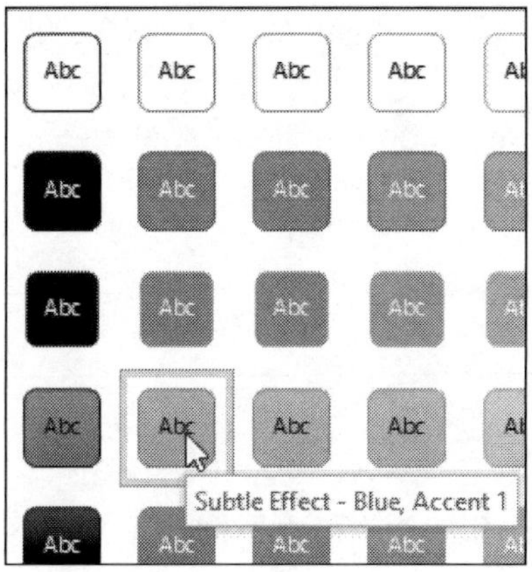

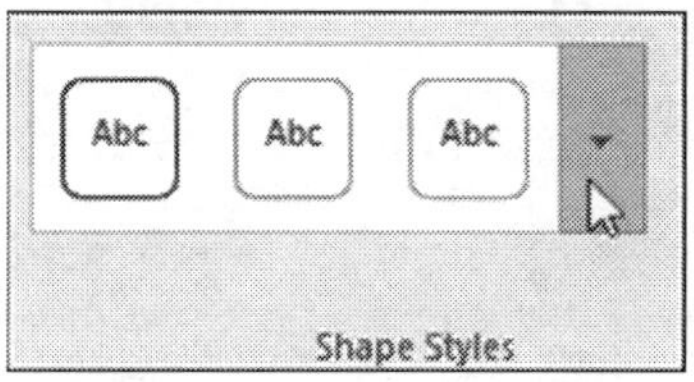

This effect is the second on row four (see sidebar).

5 Resize the text box.

Click the text box once to select it and then drag the sizing handles to resize the text box so that the text fills the box.

6 Move the text box.

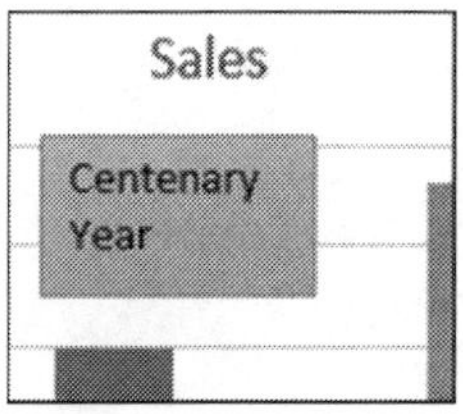

Click the text box once to select it and then hover over any part of the border that is not a sizing handle. You will see the four-headed arrow cursor shape (see sidebar). When you see the four-headed arrow, click and drag to move the text box to an ideal position.

7 Add an arrow pointing from the text box to the blue 2019 bar.

1. Click the chart to activate it. (Make sure that you click just inside the border of the chart and not on the text box. The *Format* tab will not be displayed on the Ribbon when the text box is selected).

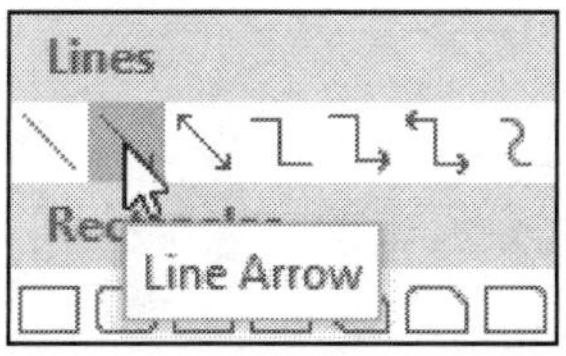

2. Click: →Format→Insert Shapes→ More→Lines→Line Arrow. (see sidebar).

3. Click and drag to draw an arrow pointing from the text box to the blue bar.

4. With the arrow selected, click: Shape Format→ Shape Styles→More.

5. Choose an attractive style for the arrow.

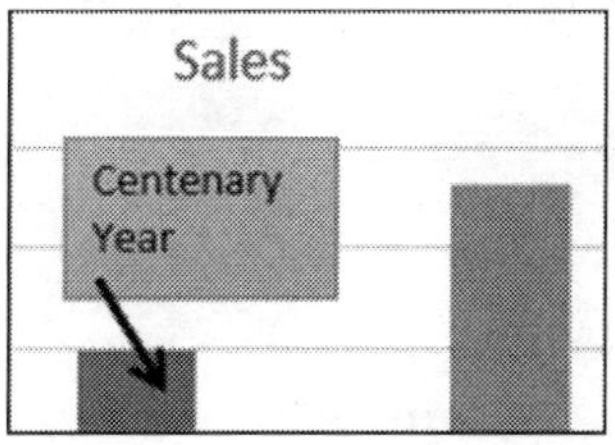

8 Save your work as *Annual Sales Summary-3.*

Lesson 5-21: Add gridlines and scale axes

In this lesson, you'll manipulate the vertical axis of a sales chart to give two entirely different views of a company's sales. Each chart emphasizes one of the following true statements.

- It is true that sales are increasing every month.
- It is true that sales are almost completely flat.

You'll see how you can manipulate a column chart to visually convey each of these "truths" to an audience. After this session, you'll never look at a chart again without paying close attention to the vertical axis.

1 Open *Sales First Quarter* from your sample files folder.

	A	B
1	**Month**	**Sales**
2	Jan	80,010
3	Feb	80,040
4	Mar	80,080

This worksheet shows sales that are almost completely flat. Sales increased by 0.04% in February and by 0.05% in March.

A twentieth of a percent increase isn't really anything at all.

2 Create a chart that illustrates flat sales.

Imagine you are the sales director of the company and need to have a pep talk with your salespeople.

You want to show them a chart that demonstrates the lack of sales growth in order to motivate them to do better in April.

1. Click inside the data range.
2. Click: Insert→Charts→Insert Column or Bar Chart→ 2-D Column→Clustered Column.

The following chart is automatically generated:

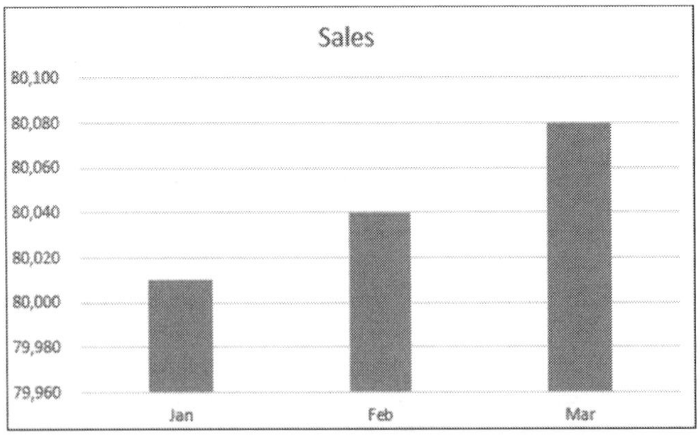

This isn't the chart you want. In this chart sales growth looks impressive (although it isn't really). The chart isn't as honest as it should be because the vertical axis begins at 79,960. You're looking at the tips of columns that are very long.

Sales First Quarter

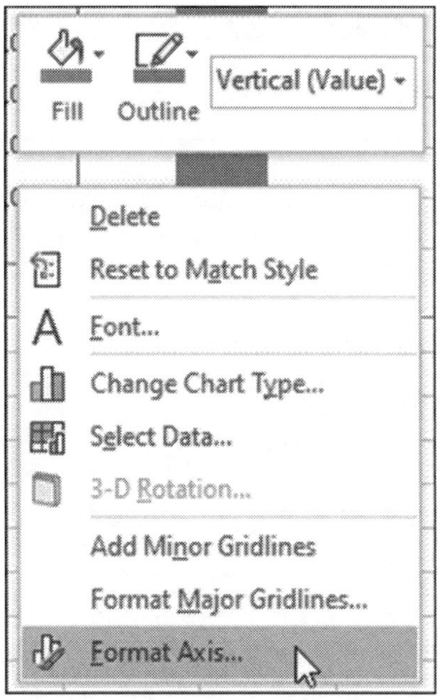

To fix things up you need a more honest vertical axis (one that begins at zero).

3. Right-click on the vertical axis and select *Format Axis...* from the shortcut menu.

   The *Format Axis* task pane appears.

4. Change the *Minimum* value to zero and press the **<Enter>** key.

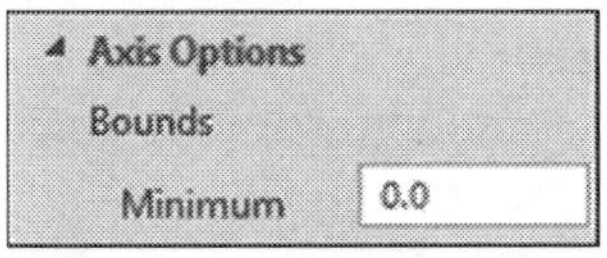

The chart now depicts a more honest representation of flat sales growth.

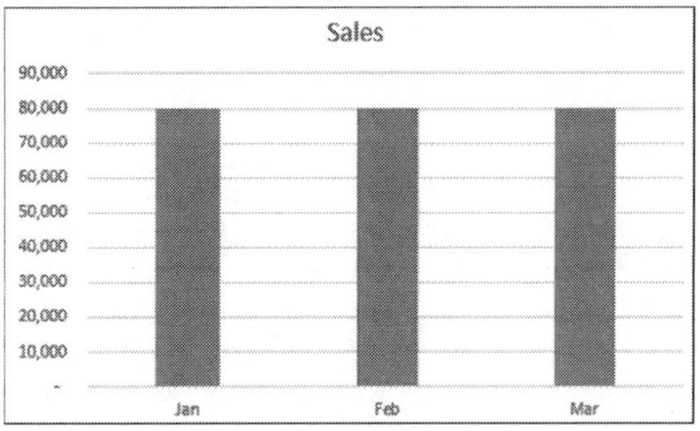

Look at the task pane and notice how Excel has automatically managed the other settings. *Major units* for gridlines (the interval between numbers on the vertical axis) have now changed to 10,000.

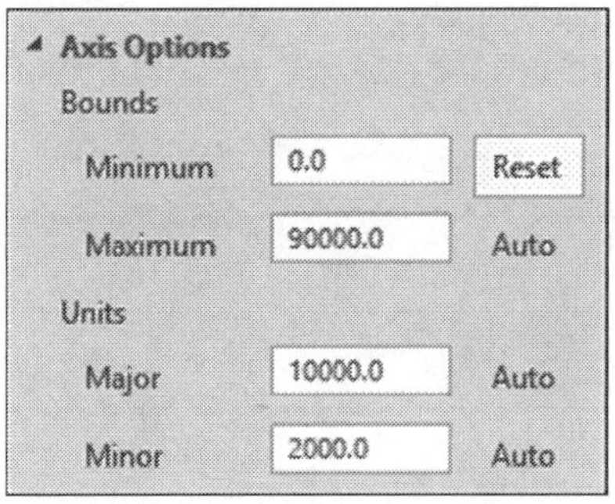

5. Change the *Minor Units* gridline value to 5000 (without a comma as Excel has a problem with commas in this task pane). You will enable the display of minor gridline elements in a moment and will see one minor gridline between each major gridline.

tip

Use gridlines sparingly

Too many gridlines can make a chart difficult to read.

This lesson's chart looks cluttered with minor gridlines and might even look cleaner without any gridlines.

When you do use gridlines, always choose a light color to focus attention upon foreground elements.

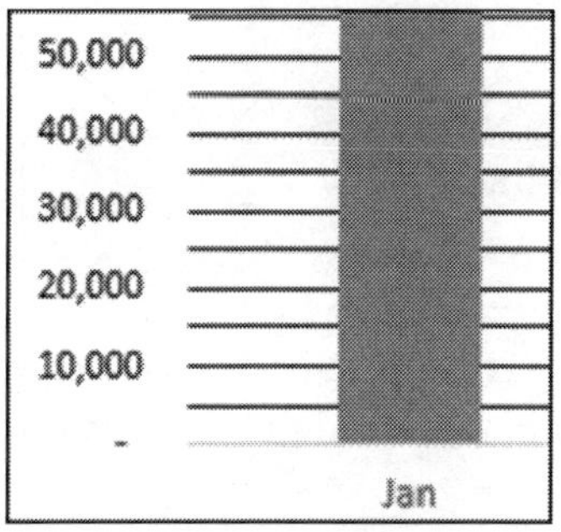

3 Add minor horizontal gridlines to the chart.

1. Activate the chart by clicking just inside the chart's border.
2. Click the *Chart Elements* icon  outside the top right of the chart.
3. Click: Gridlines→Primary Minor Horizontal.

Minor gridlines are now displayed on the chart (see sidebar).

4 Save your work as *Sales First Quarter-1*.

Lesson 5-22: Emphasize data by manipulating pie charts

In the last lesson, you saw how a column chart could visually reinforce different characteristics of the same data.

Pie charts also offer several techniques to present data in a way that will best convey your objectives. Designers of pie charts often use the presentation methods described in this lesson to make one value in a series seem bigger or smaller in relation to its neighbors.

1 Open *Competitor Analysis* from your sample files folder (if it isn't already open).

	A	B	C
1	**Splendid Supplies Competitor Analysis**		
2			
3	**Competitor**	**Annual Sales (Millions)**	**Market Share**
4	Cheapo discount stores	22.2	28%
5	Budget supplies	16.3	21%
6	Lo Cost warehouse	24.5	31%
7	Splendid Supplies	16.2	20%

Splendid Supplies have compiled this worksheet to monitor the activity of their three competitors. Splendid aren't doing so well. In fact, they have the lowest market share of the four.

There's a big investor meeting coming up and Splendid would like to make their market share seem a little more impressive.

2 Create a 3-D pie chart for the range A3:B7.

1. Select the range A3:B7.
2. Click: Insert→Charts→Insert Pie or Doughnut Chart→3-D Pie (see sidebar).

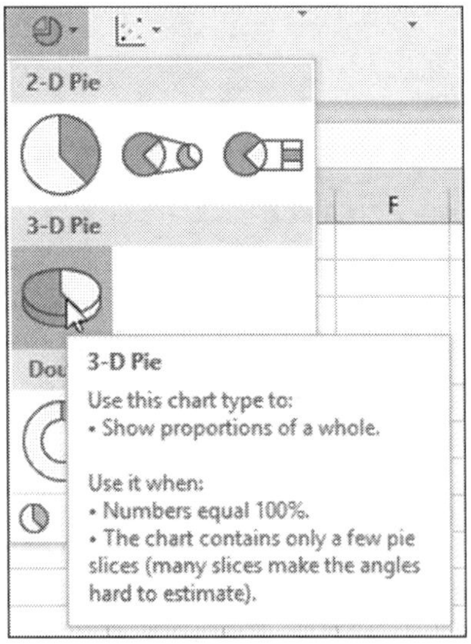

A pie chart is displayed, illustrating the market share of the four companies.

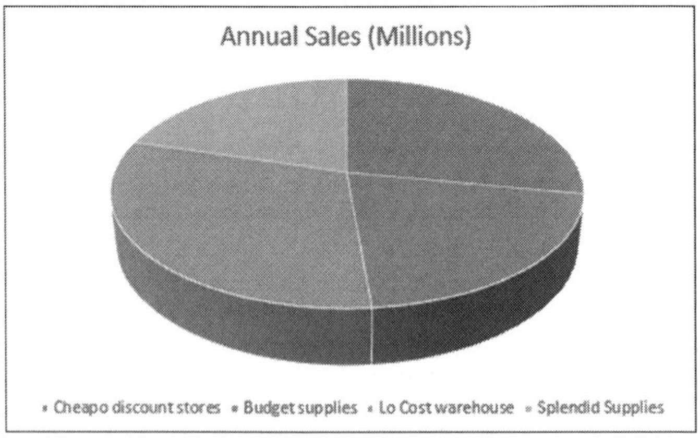

Splendid Supplies don't look very impressive on this chart. You can use a simple presentational technique to make things seem a little better.

Competitor Analysis

3 Rotate the pie chart so that Splendid Supplies sales are at the front.

Because of the perspective of a 3-D pie, the slice at the front always seems the biggest (especially if you keep the perspective angle high).

1. Right-click in the plot area of the pie chart. To do this you'll need to click just outside one of the pie chart's slices.
2. Click *Format Plot Area* from the shortcut menu. If you don't see *Format Plot Area* in the shortcut menu it is because you have right clicked in the wrong place. In this case try again, making sure that you click just outside one of the pie chart's slices.

   The *Format Plot Area* task pane appears.
3. Click the *Effects* icon  at the top of the task pane.
4. In the *3-D rotation* section, click the *X Rotation* spin button until the Splendid Supplies (yellow) slice is at the front of the pie chart (about 220 degrees).

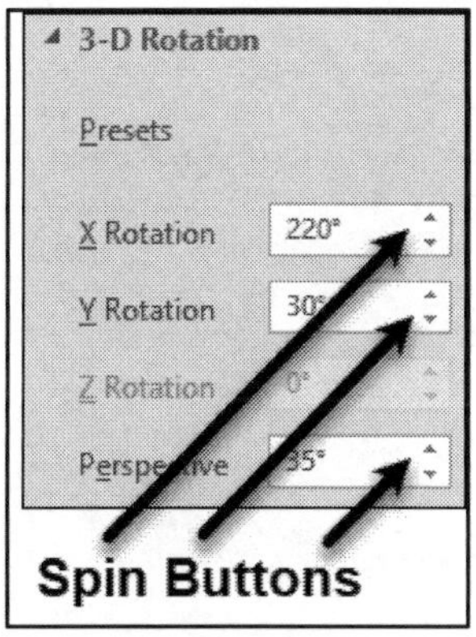

4 Change the pie chart's perspective to emphasize Splendid Supplies' sales.

In the 3-D rotation section, click the *Perspective* spin button to make the Splendid Supplies sales seem as large as possible. I found that a setting of 35 degrees worked well.

5 Pull the Splendid Supplies slice slightly out of the pie.

A very common pie chart presentational technique is to pull the slice that you want to emphasize away from the pie chart. This slice then appears to be larger in relation to the other slices.

1. Click just inside the chart border to activate the chart.
2. Click one of the slices on the chart once to select the entire pie.
3. Click the Splendid Supplies slice once to select it.
4. Click and drag the slice slightly out of the pie.

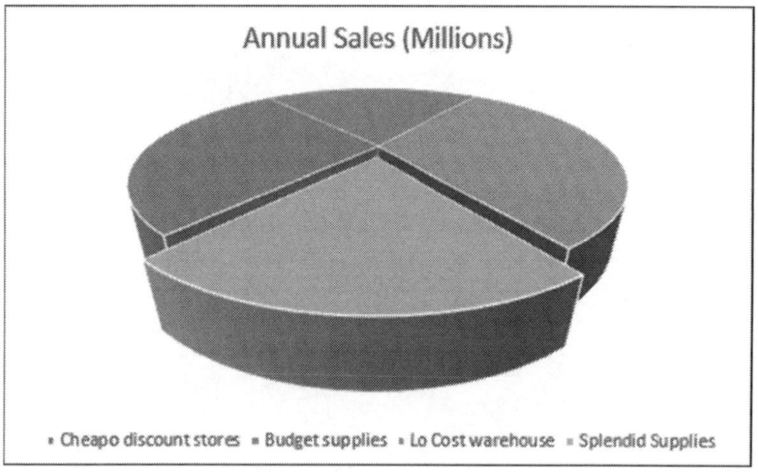

You'd never guess now that Splendid Supplies actually have the lowest market share.

6 Save your work as *Competitor Analysis-1.*

Lesson 5-23: Create a chart with two vertical axes

Sometimes you'll have two data series that are very different in magnitude, but you still want to show them on the same chart.

The examples used in this lesson are *UK Average House Prices* and *Bank Base Rates*. Economists widely believe that when interest rates come down, house and commodity prices go up. Since 2008 many world governments have used low interest rates as a tool to attempt to support asset prices. To test whether this theory has succeeded, you will create a chart showing UK bank base rates and average house prices for the twenty years up to 2021.

During the twenty-year period, house prices ranged from 148,658 to 214,158 while base rates fluctuated between 0.25% and 5.25%. You need two different vertical axes to make this chart work.

1 Open *UK House Prices* from your sample files folder.

2 Create a default *Line with Markers* chart from the range.

1. Click anywhere within the data.
2. Click: Insert→Charts→Insert Line or Area Chart→2-D Line→ Line with Markers.

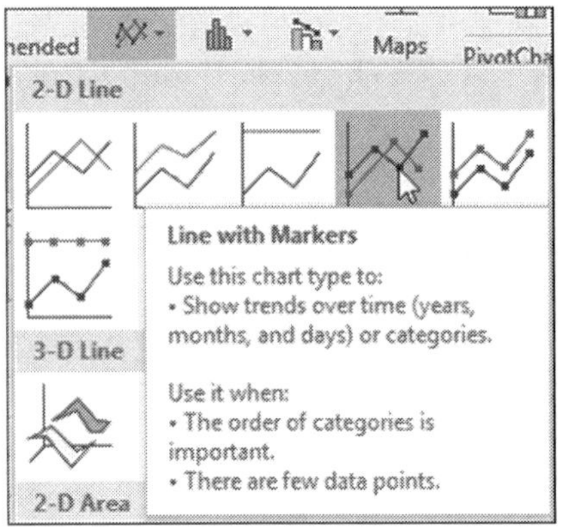

The default chart is displayed.

3 Remove the *Year* data series and show the years 2002 to 2021 along the *Horizontal Axis.*

You learned how to do this in: *Lesson 5-16: Create a chart with numerical axes.*

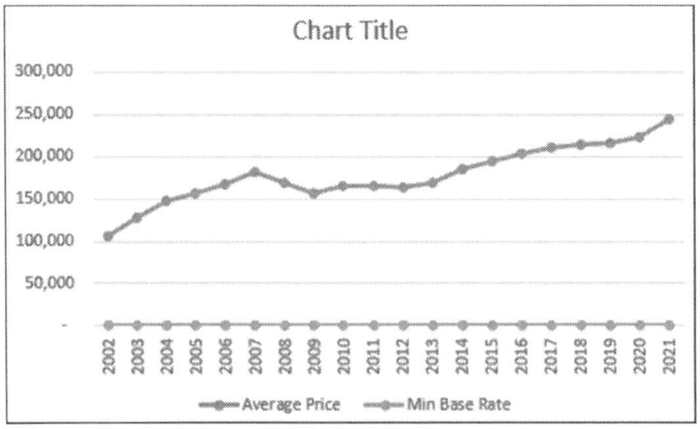

UK House Prices

4 Select the *Min Base Rate* series.

Because the *Min Base Rate* series is in almost the same place as the horizontal axis, this can be difficult to do with the mouse (though it is possible).

You may find it easier to select the chart and then click:

Format→Current Selection→
Chart Elements drop down→Series "Min Base Rate"

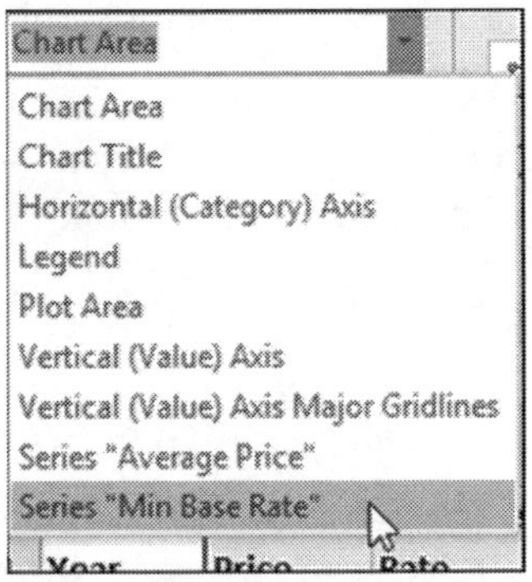

5 Move the *Min Base Rate* series to a secondary axis.

1. With the *Min Base Rate* series selected, click:

   Format→Current Selection→Format Selection

   The *Format Data Series* task pane is displayed.

2. Click the *Series Options* icon. 

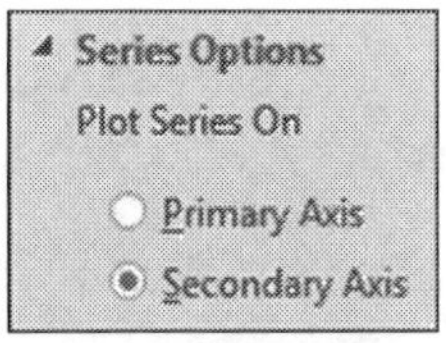

3. Click the *Secondary Axis* option button.

   The chart is displayed with two vertical axes and Excel even auto-scales the new axis for you.

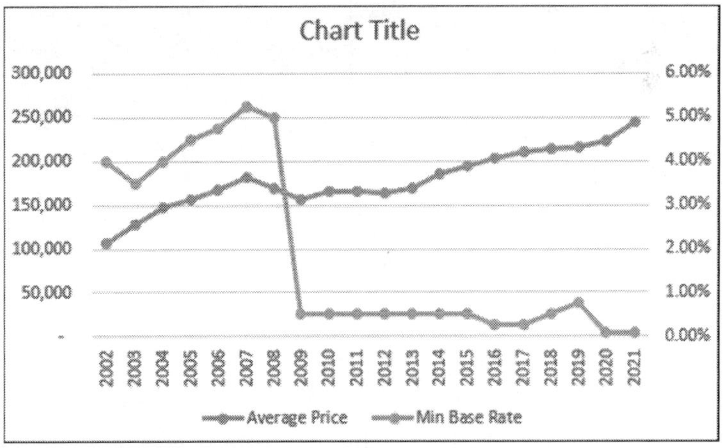

It is now easy to see at a glance that the UK government appears to have succeeded in their objective as the fall in house prices from 2007 to 2009 appears to have been reversed by the fall in interest rates.

6 Save your work as UK House Prices-1.

note

The secondary axis always appears on top of the primary axis

You can see in the example chart that when the *Min Base Rate* series (the gray line) crosses the *Average Price* series (the orange line), the gray line is on top.

You can change the stacking order of the plot lines by attaching the plot line you need to be on top to the secondary axis (and the other series to the primary axis).

Lesson 5-24: Create a combination chart containing different chart types

Excel allows you to allocate a different chart type to each data series. This opens up many interesting possibilities such as superimposing a *Clustered Column* chart on top of an *Area* chart.

In this lesson, you'll chart the Hawaii climate as a combination Clustered Column/Area chart with clustered columns for high/low temperature and an area chart for rainfall.

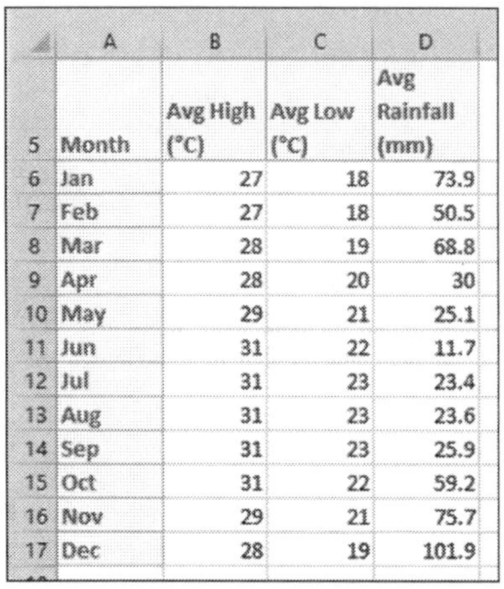

	A	B	C	D
5	Month	Avg High (°C)	Avg Low (°C)	Avg Rainfall (mm)
6	Jan	27	18	73.9
7	Feb	27	18	50.5
8	Mar	28	19	68.8
9	Apr	28	20	30
10	May	29	21	25.1
11	Jun	31	22	11.7
12	Jul	31	23	23.4
13	Aug	31	23	23.6
14	Sep	31	23	25.9
15	Oct	31	22	59.2
16	Nov	29	21	75.7
17	Dec	28	19	101.9

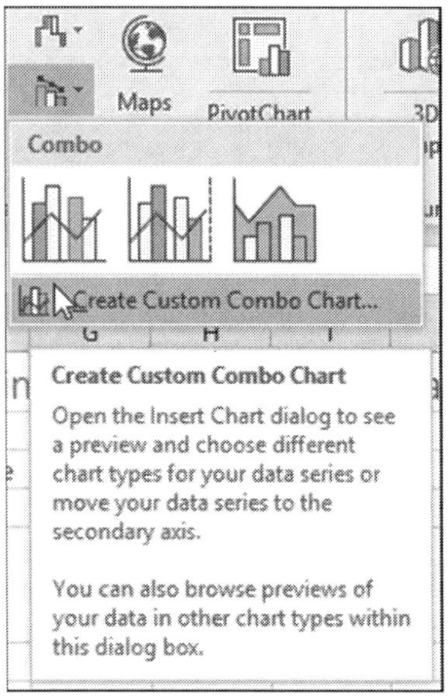

1 Open *Hawaii Climate-1* from your sample files folder.

This workbook documents the temperature range and rainfall in Hawaii for each month of the year.

2 Create a combination chart showing temperature as a *clustered column* chart type and rainfall as an *area* chart type.

1. Click in any cell within the range.

   Because you want to chart the entire data range, there's no need to select the range of cells.

2. Click: Insert→Charts→Insert Combo Chart→ Create Custom Combo Chart…

   The *Insert Chart* dialog appears with the *Combo* chart type chosen in the left-hand menu bar.

3. Set the chart types to *Clustered Column* for both *Temperature* series and to *Area* for the *Avg Rainfall (mm)* series.

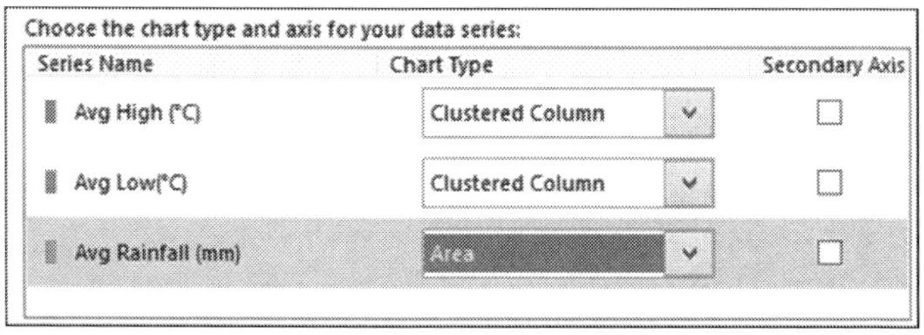

4. Click the OK button.

   The combination chart is created:

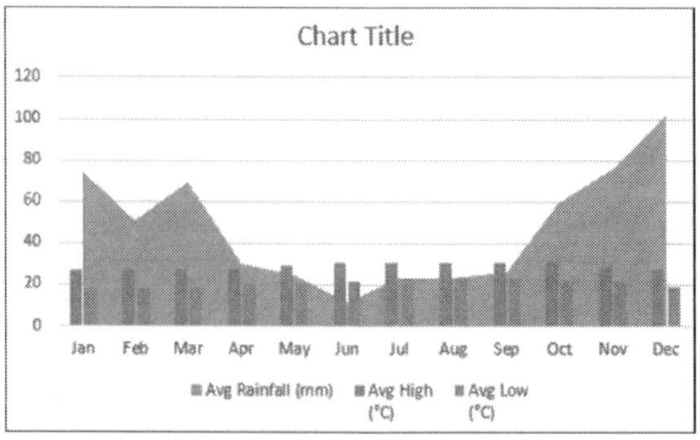

Hawaii Climate-1

The chart isn't bad, but it can be improved. Because there is only one axis, the rainfall's *Area* chart type dominates the chart.

Adding a second vertical axis will solve this problem.

3 Add a secondary axis for rainfall.

You could do this using the technique learned in: *Lesson 5-23: Create a chart with two vertical axes.*

Instead, you'll use a different technique by recalling the *Insert Chart* dialog (this time it will be called *Change Chart Type*).

1. Right click anywhere in a blank area of the chart and click: *Change Chart Type…* from the shortcut menu.

   The *Change Chart Type* dialog appears.

2. Click the *Secondary Axis* check box next to *Avg Rainfall (mm).*

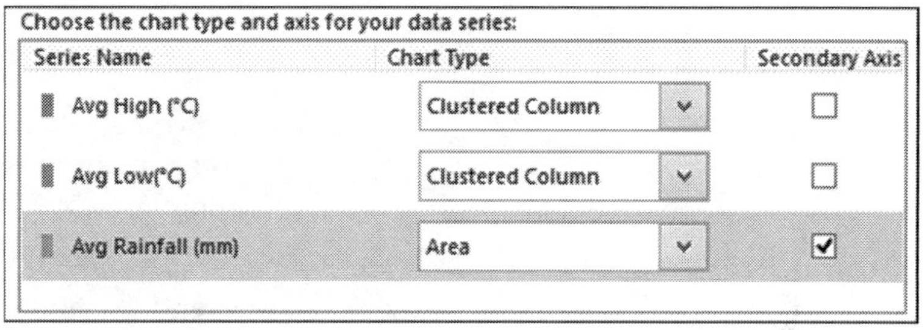

3. Click OK.

   The chart now looks a lot better with two axes (one for temperature and one for rainfall).

4 Add *Axis Title* elements and give them (along with the *Chart Title* element) appropriate names.

You learned how to do this in: *Lesson 5-9: Move, re-size, add, position and delete chart elements* and *Lesson 5-5: Add and remove chart elements using Quick Layout.*

The chart now looks professional:

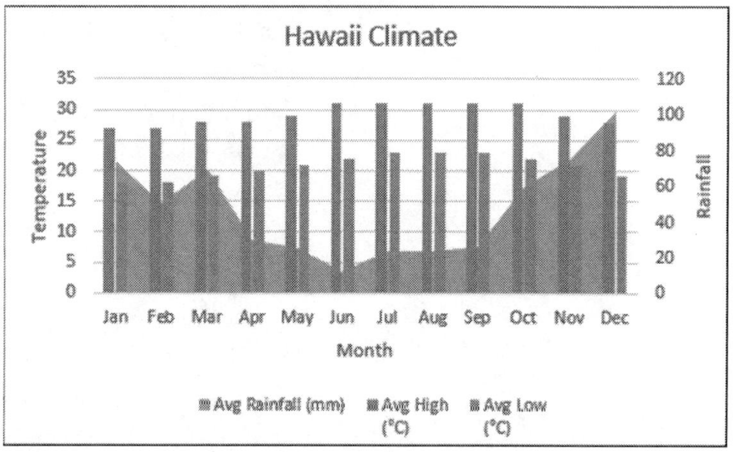

5 Save your work as *Hawaii Climate-2.*

Lesson 5-25: Add a trend line

It is impossible to demonstrate empirically that a cause produces an effect. Just because the sun has risen every day since the beginning of the Earth does not mean that it will rise again tomorrow. However; it is impossible to go about one's life without assuming such connections, and the best that we can do is to maintain an open mind and never presume that we know any laws of causality for certain.

David Hume (1711-1776),
Scottish philosopher, economist, and historian.
From "An Enquiry Concerning Human Understanding".

Trend analysis applies the science of mathematics to the art of fortune telling.

If a value has been increasing for a long time, trend analysis would suggest that it will go on increasing. Some would say that the reverse is true, but Excel remains healthily optimistic that it is possible to predict the future from the past.

Excel provides several different types of trend analysis. You're going to use a linear trend line and a two-period moving average to decide whether it is a good idea to buy a house in 2022.

1 Open *UK House Prices-1* from your sample files folder (if it isn't already open).

2 Remove the *Min Base Rate* data series from the chart.

1. Click on the *Min Base Rate* data series plot line to select the series.
2. Press the **<Delete>** key on the keyboard.

3 Format the Vertical Axis so that it plots values between 100,000 and 275,000.

You learned how to do this in: *Lesson 5-21: Add gridlines and scale axes.*

4 Add a linear trend line element to forecast where property prices will be in the year 2027.

1. Activate the chart by clicking just inside the chart's border.
2. Click the *Chart Elements* icon  outside the top right of the chart.
3. Click: Trendline→More Options…

   The *Format Trendline* task pane appears.
4. Click the *Trendline Options* icon. 
5. Make sure that the *Linear* trendline type is selected (this is the default).
6. As 2027 is 6 periods after 2021, enter 6 in the *Forecast Forward* text box and then press the **<Enter>** key.

UK House Prices-1

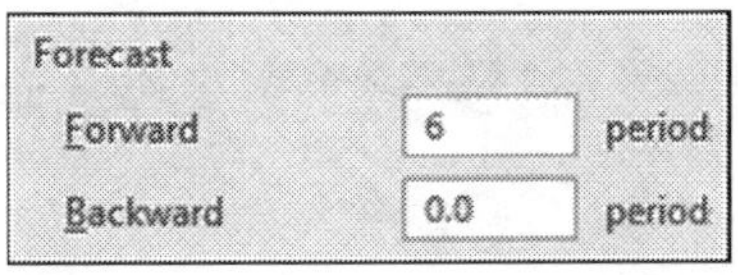

7. Select the chart and then click and drag one of the right-hand sizing handles to make the chart wider.

   Notice the trend line shown on the chart.

   Excel isn't very confident that your new house will be a great investment and predicts that it will only grow in value by around 1.0% per year during the next six years (although David Hume would have advised you that Excel may well be wrong).

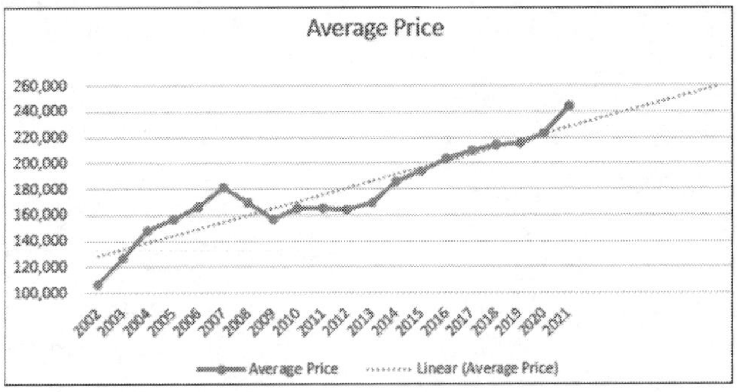

trivia

In the 2008 edition of this book, Excel got it right

In this same lesson in "Learn Excel 2007 Essential Skills" (published in 2008) Excel advised that a fall in house prices was imminent and that you should sell.

On this occasion Excel got it right and correctly forecast the top of the market.

It will be interesting in future years to see how well Excel has read the market this time.

5 Remove the trend line.

1. Click on the trendline to select it.
2. Press the **<Delete>** key on the keyboard.

6 Add a two-period moving average.

Moving averages are one of the most loved instruments of speculators who predict the future values of shares, currencies and commodities based entirely upon charts. The theory is that when the price crosses beneath the moving average it is time to sell.

1. Activate the chart.
2. Click the *Chart Elements* icon ⊞ outside the top right of the chart.
3. Click: Trendline→Two Period Moving Average.

   This time the analysis shows that you should have sold in 2008 and then re-purchased in 2010. Between 2010 and 2021 the two-period moving average recommended a hold.

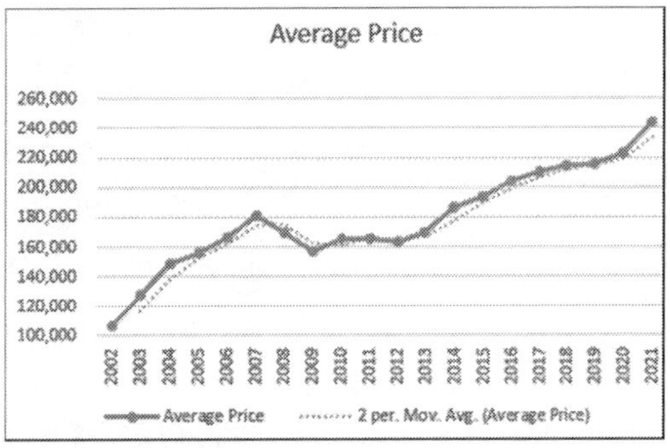

7 Save your work as *UK House Prices-2*.

Lesson 5-26: Add a forecast sheet

> 'Tis impossible to be sure of anything but Death and Taxes.
>
> ***Christopher Bullock, from: The Cobler of Preston (1716)***

Excel includes a very sophisticated *Forecast Sheet* feature to predict the future more reliably. The new forecast sheets can be used to predict the likely movement of trending data such as currencies, stocks, bonds and commodity prices. Just like the weather forecast, Excel's new forecast sheets allow you to add a confidence factor. Excel can even forecast the future with a 99.9% chance of being correct (at least, this is Excel's bold claim).

This lesson uses the New York average monthly temperature for each month until Dec 2021. You're going to use Excel's *Forecast Sheet* feature to predict what the average New York monthly temperature will be in January, February and March 2022.

1 Open *Weather Forecast* from your sample files folder (if it isn't already open).

This workbook contains the average monthly temperature recorded in New York's Central Park for the ten years up until Dec 2021. There's also a simple chart to give a visual representation of the data:

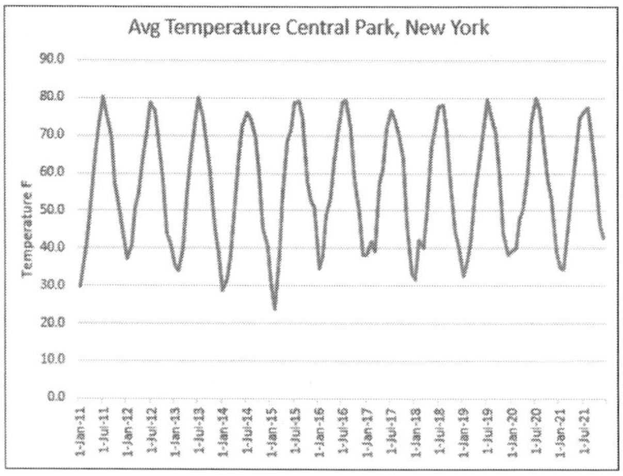

You can see that the temperature data is cyclical. You wouldn't be able to predict the average January 2022 temperature with a trend line as a trend line is not sophisticated enough to allow for the cyclical nature of the seasons.

2 Create a forecast sheet that will predict the average monthly temperature for January, February and March 2022.

1. Select cells A4:B136.

   A quick way to do this is to place the cursor anywhere in the range and then press the **<Ctrl>+<A>** keys on the keyboard.

2. Click: Data→Forecast→Forecast Sheet.

note

Excel's forecast sheets make use of five functions

The forecast feature was added to Excel in 2016 and, at the same time, five new functions were added to support the new feature.

Excel automatically creates these functions for you when you create a *Forecast Sheet.*

You can see the use of two of these functions on this lesson's forecast sheet:

FORECAST.ETS
FORECAST.ETS.CONFINT

The functions are quite easy to understand as their parameters simply mirror those shown on the *Create Forecast Worksheet* dialog.

In reality, you'll probably never use these functions directly as it is far simpler to use the *Forecast Sheet* feature described in this lesson to create them automatically.

The other three forecasting functions are:

FORECAST.ETS.SEASONALTY
FORECAST.LINEAR
FORECAST.ETS.STAT

Weather Forecast

The *Create Forecast Worksheet* dialog appears.

3. Set the *Forecast End date* to 31st March 2022.
4. Click the *Options* button at the bottom left of the dialog.
5. Set the *Confidence Interval* to 95%.

   The *Confidence Interval* will probably already be set to 95% as this is the default value. This will result in a prediction that Excel is 95% confident will be correct.

   Notice the *Seasonality* setting. You can see that Excel has correctly identified a seasonal trend that occurs every 12 months.

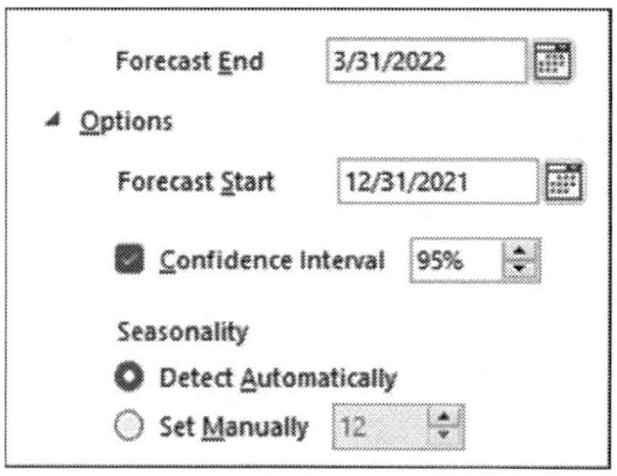

   Notice also that there are two icons at the top right of the dialog that enable you to select a *Line* or *Column* chart type. You'll probably find that the line type works best for most forecasts.

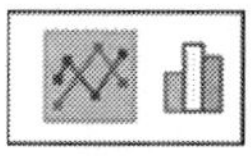

6. Click the *Create* button.
7. Click the OK button to dismiss the advisory dialog if it appears.

   Excel inserts a new worksheet containing a forecast chart along with the data used to create the chart. The data is presented in an Excel table (see sidebar for more about tables).

   You can see that Excel has provided both a forecast and the margins of error Excel needs to be 95% sure that the forecast is correct.

   If you scroll to the end of the table you'll see that the chart is advising you:

   In March 2022, the average temperature is forecast to be 44.1 F. There is a 95% probability that the average temperature will be no lower than 37.5F and no higher than 50.6F.

   By the time you read this book you may even be able to confirm that Excel was right (when this lesson was prepared the latest data available was for Dec 2021).

   If you had set the *Confidence* setting to more than 95%, Excel would have forecast a wider temperature range to allow for a higher margin of error.

3 Save your work as *Weather Forecast-1.*

note

About Excel tables

Microsoft could easily have used a normal Excel range to present the data in the Forecast Sheet. Instead, they have chosen to use an Excel table.

The data in the table is used as the source data for the forecast chart.

Tables are an expert-level feature and are covered in depth in the *Expert Skills* book in this series. Tables make some expert-level functions and features easier to use as they have many advanced features.

Forecast sheets don't use any of the advanced features supported by tables. Simply regard the table that supports the forecast chart as a rather colourful range.

You don't need to learn anything about Excel tables to use the *Forecast Sheet* feature.

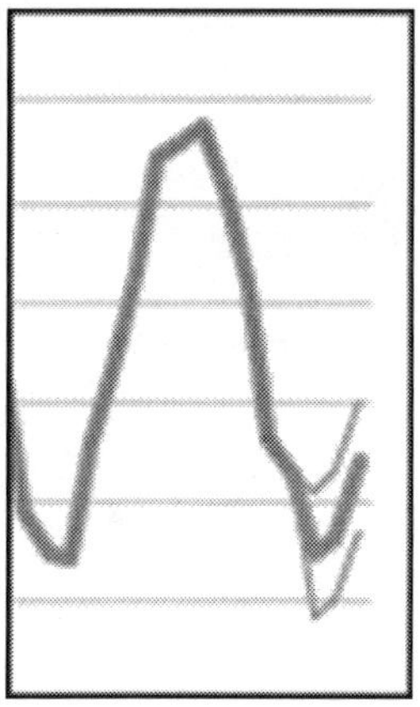

Lesson 5-27: Add a gradient fill to a chart background

When you prepare a chart for a PowerPoint presentation, or for inclusion in a high-quality color publication, you want the chart to look professional and interesting. A *Gradient* background fill will put the finishing touch to your chart so that it looks like it was produced by a professional graphic artist.

1 Open *World Sales* from your sample files folder.

2 Create a *Clustered Column* chart from the entire range.

1. Click anywhere in the range.

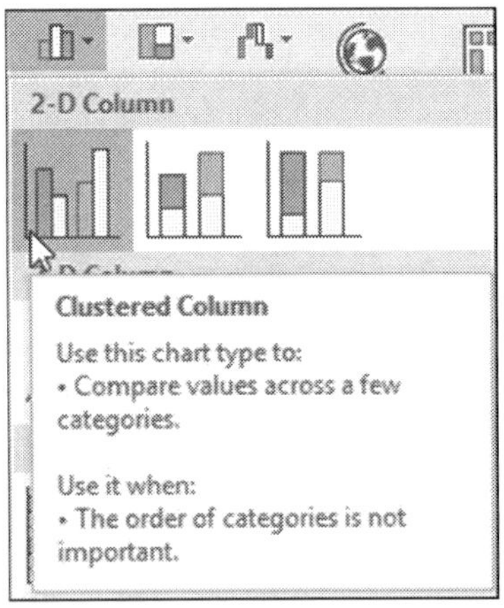

2. Click: Insert→Charts→Insert Column or Bar Chart→ 2-D Column→Clustered Column.

The chart is created:

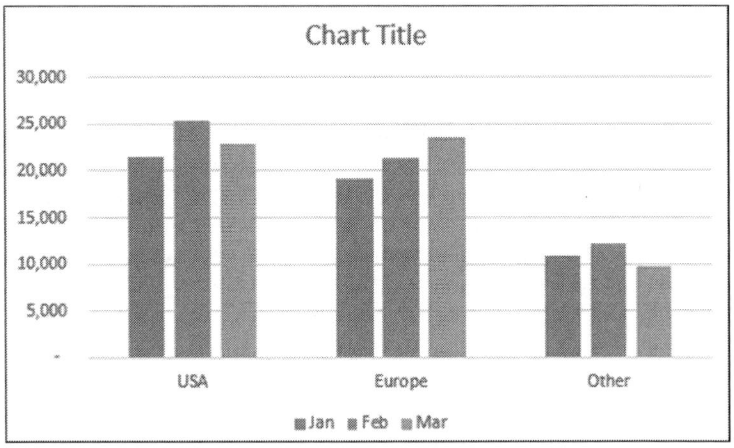

3 Switch Rows/Columns to transpose the *Legend* and *Regions*.

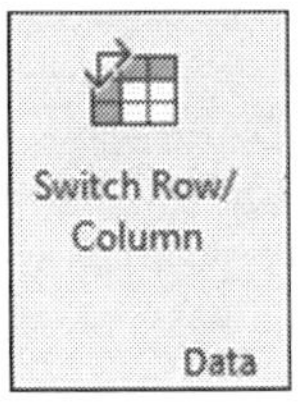

You learned how to do this in: *Lesson 5-13: Understand Data Series and Categories.*

The regions are now listed in the legend and the months are shown along the horizontal axis.

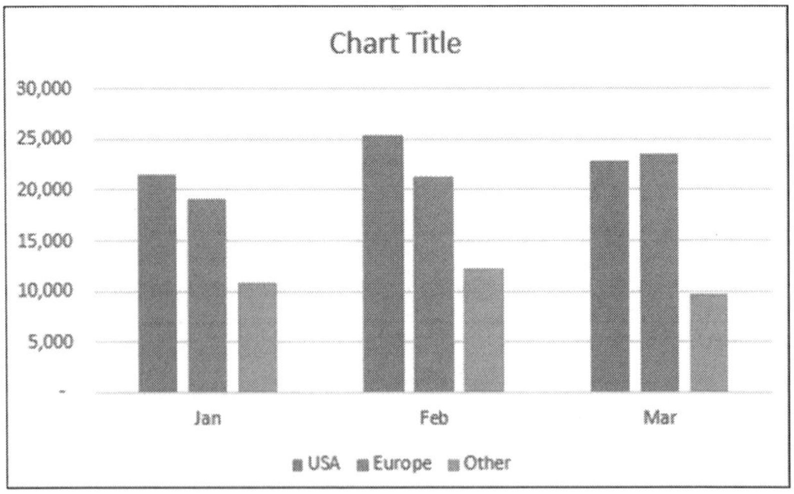

World Sales

4 Add a gradient fill to the chart background.

1. Right-click on the *Chart Area* element (just inside the border of the chart).
2. Click *Format Chart Area* from the shortcut menu.

   The *Format Chart Area* task pane appears.
3. Click the *Fill & Line* icon. 
4. Click the *Fill* menu item.
5. Click the *Gradient Fill* option button.

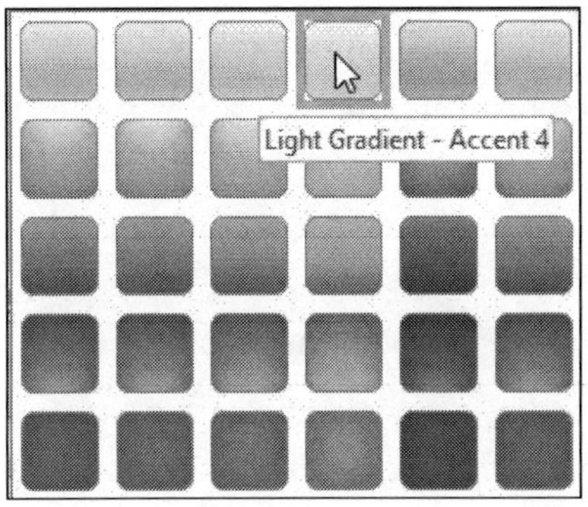

6. Choose one of the preset gradients (I chose *Light Gradient – Accent 4*).
7. Explore the *Type/Direction/Angle/Transparency* and other settings until you are happy with the fill.
8. Click the *Close* button to close the *Format Chart Area* task pane.

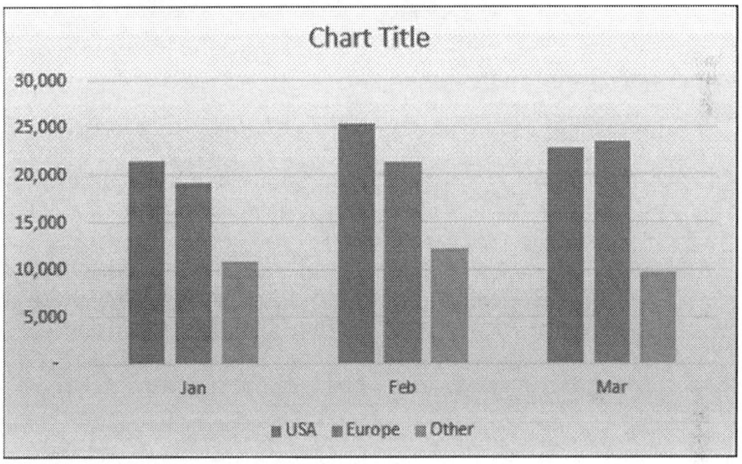

5 Save your work as *Gradient Fill*.

Lesson 5-28: Create your own chart templates

note

You can also change chart text font sizes with the mini toolbar

When you want to change attributes such as font type and size for a single piece of text (such as the Chart Title) it is quicker to use the mini toolbar.

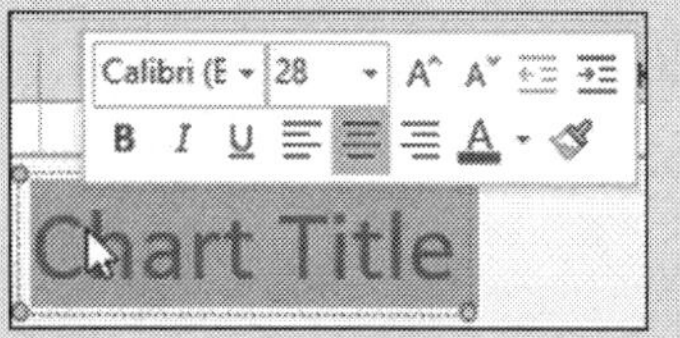

The mini toolbar pops up when you first select text within an element.

Gradient Fill

If you use charts a lot you may find yourself applying the same fonts, fills, layouts and other attributes repeatedly. If you find this happening, it is time to create a chart template.

Chart Templates can be used just like the built-in chart types. You can use templates to create a unique, personal, or corporate chart style that will enable you to produce consistently styled work.

In this lesson, you'll develop a useful chart template with larger fonts to enable them to be more readable when incorporated into a PowerPoint presentation. You can then use this template in future for any chart that is destined to be used in a presentation.

1 Open *Gradient Fill* from your sample files folder (if it isn't already open).

2 Increase the font size of the *Chart Title* element to 28 Points.

1. Select the *Chart Title* element.
2. Click: Home→Font→Font Size Drop-Down→28 Points.

3 Increase the font size of the *Vertical (Value) Axis*, *Horizontal (Category) Axis* and *Legend* elements to 14 points.

Select each element in turn and set the font size in the same way as in the previous step.

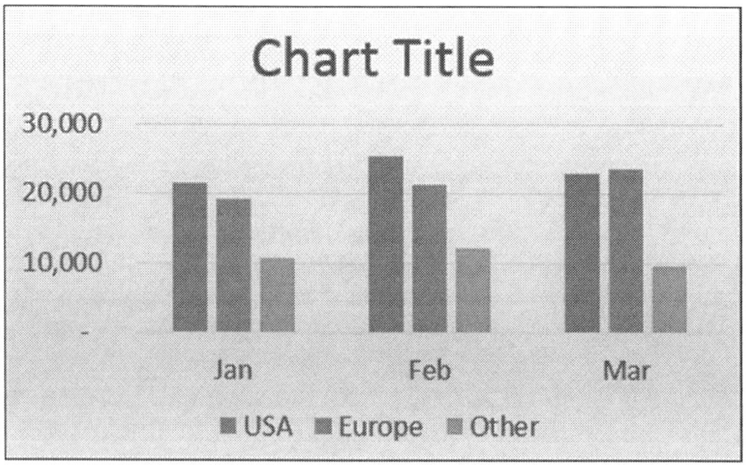

The chart now has labels that will be readable by viewers at the back of the room when projected onto a screen.

4 Save the chart design as a template.

1. Right-click in the *Chart Area* (just inside the border of the chart).
2. Select *Save as Template…* from the shortcut menu.
3. Type **PowerPoint Clustered Column with Title and Gradient Fill** as the *File Name*.
4. Click the *Save* button.

5 Delete the chart.

Click once, just inside the border of the chart, to select it and then press the **<Delete>** key.

6 Create a new chart from the template.

1. Click anywhere inside the data range A1:D4.
2. Click: Insert→Charts→Recommended Charts.

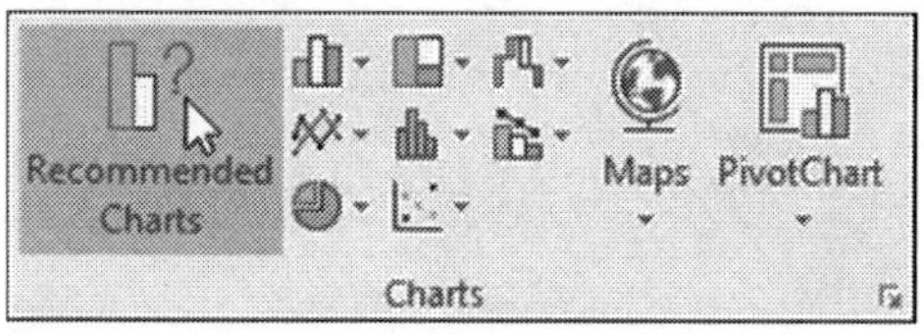

The *Insert Chart* dialog is displayed.

3. Click the *All Charts* tab at the top of the *Insert Chart* dialog.
4. Click the *Templates* category on the left of the dialog.

A single icon is displayed on the right-hand side of the dialog, showing a preview of the template that you just saved:

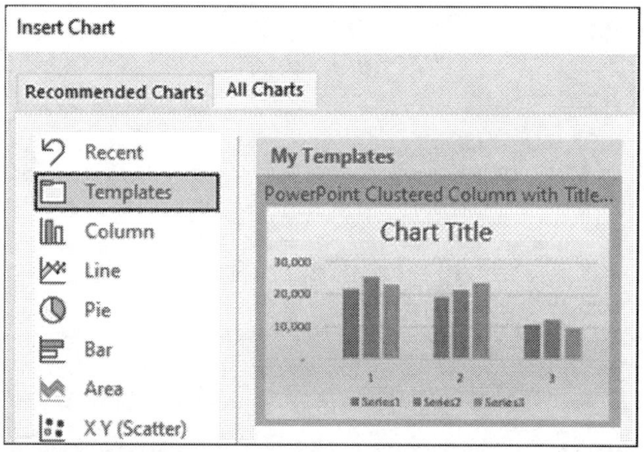

Notice that when you hover the mouse cursor over the icon a larger preview is shown.

5. Either double-click the template icon, or click it once to select, and then click the OK button.

A chart is displayed with all of the attributes defined in your template.

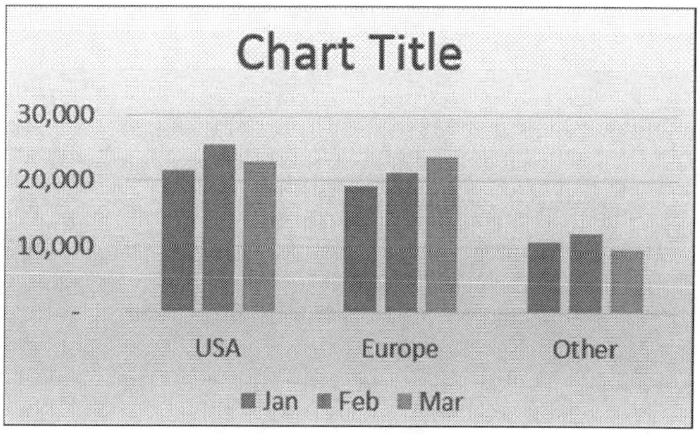

7 Save your work as *PowerPoint Template.*

Session 5: Exercise

1 **Open *Exercise 5* from your sample files folder.**

2 **Click any cell in the range A3:F8.**

3 **Click: Insert→Charts→Insert Column or Bar Chart→2-D Column→Clustered Column.**

The chart will look strange at first as there are many errors to correct.

4 **Switch rows and columns so that the European country names are shown in the *Legend*.**

5 **Use the *Select Data Source* dialog to remove the *Year* series and place the years along the *Horizontal (Category) Axis*.**

6 **Change the scale of the vertical axis so that it has a *Minimum* value of 15 and a *Maximum* value of 50.**

7 **Format the *Legend* so that a solid line black border appears around it.**

8 **Apply a *Chart Filter* so that sales are only shown for the UK, Spain and Italy.**

9 **Increase the font size of the legend to 12 points.**

10 **Change the *Chart Title* text to: *European Sales*.**

11 **Add a gradient fill to the *Chart Area* element using the *Light Gradient – Accent 5* preset.**

12 **Save your work as *Exercise 5-1*.**

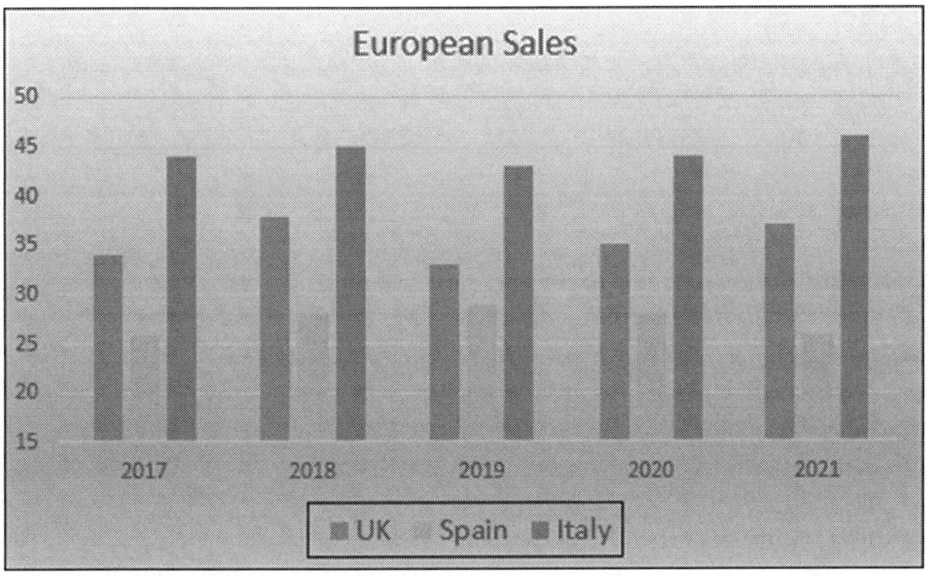

Exercise 5

Session 5: Exercise answers

These are the questions that students find the most difficult to answer:

Q 11	Q 8	Q 6	Q 5
1. Right-click just inside the border of the chart and click *Format Chart Area…* from the shortcut menu. 2. Choose the *Fill & Line* icon  in the *Format Chart Area* task pane. 3. Click the *Fill* menu item. 4. Click the *Gradient Fill* option button. 5. Select the *Light Gradient – Accent 5* preset gradient. This was covered in: *Lesson 5-27: Add a gradient fill to a chart background.*	1. Click just inside the border of the chart to select it. 2. Click the *Chart Filters* icon  at the top right of the chart. 3. Uncheck the *France* and *Germany* check boxes. 4. Click the *Apply* button. This was covered in: *Lesson 5-10: Apply a chart filter.*	1. Click the vertical axis to select it. 2. Right-click the vertical axis and click *Format Axis…* from the shortcut menu. 3. Click the *Axis Options* icon  in the *Format Axis* task pane. 4. Type the value **15** in the *Minimum* text box and press the **<Enter>** key. 5. Make sure that **50** is shown in the *Maximum* value text box. This was covered in: *Lesson 5-21: Add gridlines and scale axes.*	1. Right-click just inside the border of the chart and click *Select Data…* from the shortcut menu. 2. Click the *Year* item in the *Legend Entries (Series)* list and then click the *Remove* button. 3. Click the *Edit* button on top of the *Horizontal (Category) Axis Labels list.* 4. Select cells A4:A8. 5. Click the OK button on each dialog. This was covered in: *Lesson 5-16: Create a chart with numerical axes.*

If you have difficulty with the other questions, here are the lessons that cover the relevant skills:

1 **Refer to: Lesson 1-9: Open and navigate a workbook.**

2 **Refer to: Lesson 1-9: Open and navigate a workbook.**

3 **Refer to:** ***Lesson 5-2: Create a simple chart with two clicks.***

4 **Refer to:** ***Lesson 5-13: Understand Data Series and Categories.***

7 **Refer to:** ***Lesson 5-7: Manually format a chart element.***

9 **Refer to:** ***Lesson 5-7: Manually format a chart element.***

10 **Refer to:** ***Lesson 5-5: Add and remove chart elements using Quick Layout.***

12 **Refer to:** ***Lesson 1-10: Save a workbook.***

6

Session Six: Working with Multiple Worksheets and Workbooks

There are no big problems; there are just a lot of little problems.

Henry Ford (1863-1947)
American industrialist and pioneer of assembly-line production

Henry Ford knew that big problems are really just a lot of little problems bundled together.

Often you will find that a worksheet is getting over-complicated and difficult to work with. This session will give you the skills needed to quickly break one very complex worksheet into many smaller and easier to manage worksheets.

This session will also show you how to view different parts of large worksheets at the same time and how to create cross-worksheet formulas that summarize data from several different worksheets.

Session Objectives

By the end of this session, you will be able to:

- View the same workbook in different windows
- View two windows side by side and perform synchronous scrolling
- Duplicate worksheets within a workbook
- Move and copy worksheets from one workbook to another
- Hide and unhide a worksheet
- Create cross worksheet formulas
- Understand worksheet groups
- Use find and replace

Lesson 6-1: View the same workbook in different windows

Excel allows you to view the same worksheet in two separate worksheet windows. This is useful when you need to compare different areas of the same worksheet.

1 Close any Excel workbooks that are currently open.

2 Open *Sales First Quarter 2022* from your sample files folder.

This workbook has only one worksheet containing 242 rows of data.

3 Open a new window to see February 2022 and January 2022 sales at the same time.

Click: View→Window→New Window.

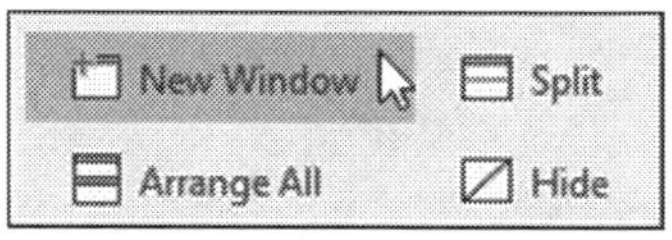

Nothing seems to have happened, except that the Title bar now reads: *Sales First Quarter 2022 - 2 - Excel*

Two views of the same workbook are now open at the same time but, because they are both maximized, you can only view one at a time which isn't very useful.

4 View both windows at the same time.

Click: View→Window→Arrange All.

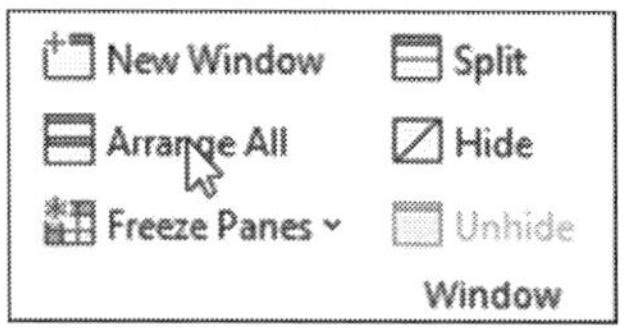

The *Arrange Windows* dialog appears.

5 Select the *Horizontal* option and then click the OK button.

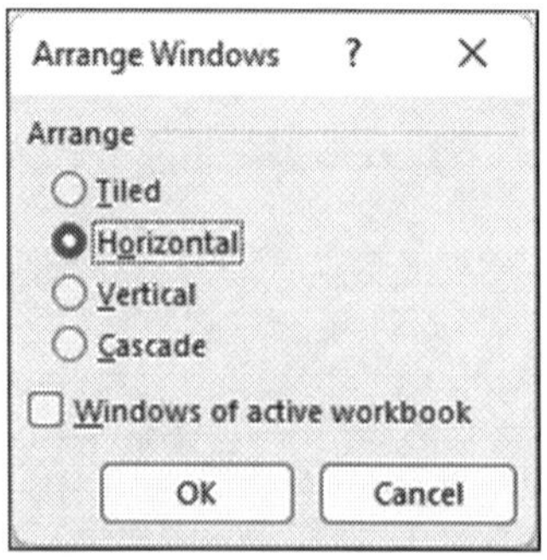

Both worksheets are displayed on your monitor, one below the other. You are able to freely scroll to any position in either window.

Sales First Quarter 2022

You will now appreciate the importance of closing any open workbooks in step 1. If you had several workbooks open, you would now be viewing all of them in multiple windows.

In the screen grab below, I've scrolled the bottom window down to see February sales:

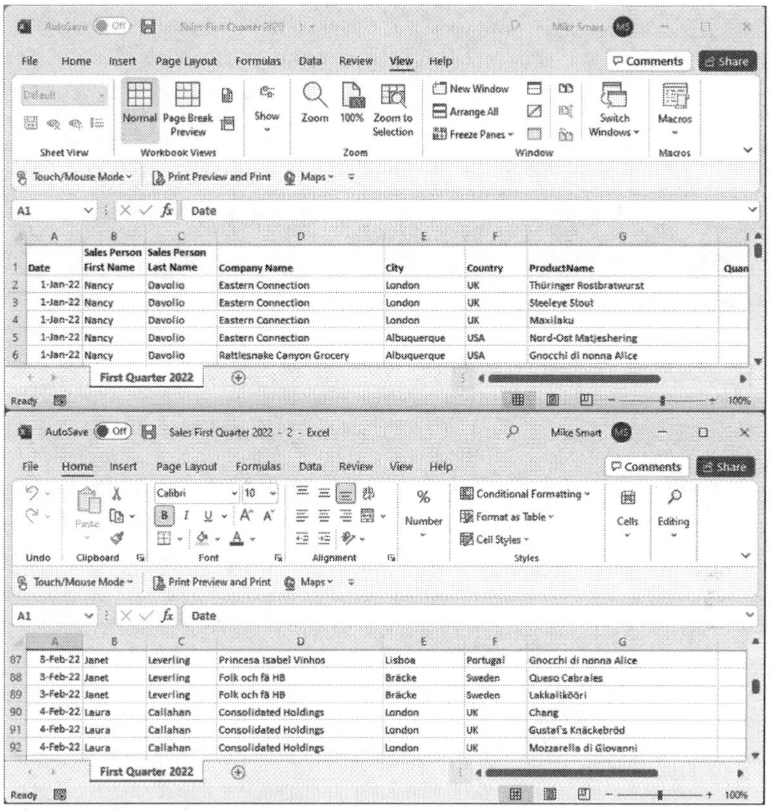

It's important to realize that you are not looking at two different worksheets, but two different views of the same worksheet.

If you change a value in one of the views, you'll immediately see the changed value in the other.

Click in the *Sales First Quarter 2022 - 2* window. Notice how the title text is no longer grayed out, indicating that this is now the active window.

6 Close the *Sales First Quarter 2022 - 2* window and maximize the *Sales First Quarter 2022 - 1* worksheet.

1. Click the *Close* button in the top right-hand corner of the worksheet.

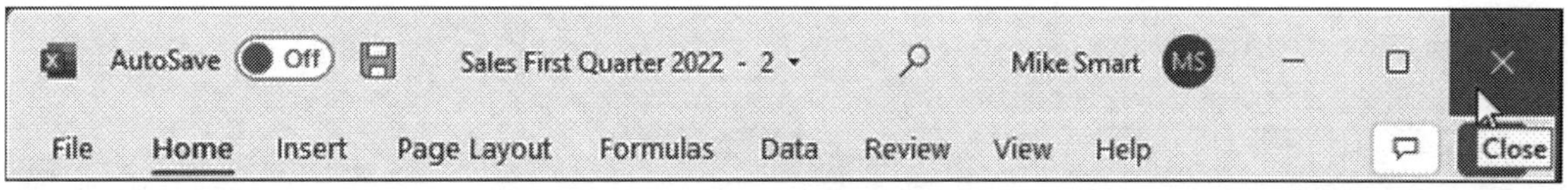

2. Click the *Maximize* button in the top right-hand corner of the *Sales First Quarter 2022 - 1* worksheet.

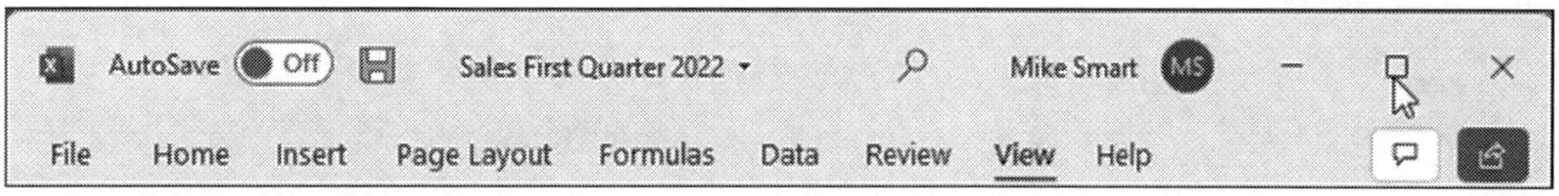

Lesson 6-2: View two windows side by side and perform synchronous scrolling

When only two workbooks are open, the *Arrange All* method covered in the previous lesson will work just fine.

It is more likely that you will have many workbooks (or views of the same workbook) open and will want to see two specific workbooks on screen at the same time.

You may sometimes be given a workbook that somebody else has changed and need to identify what has been altered. You'll use Excel's synchronous scrolling feature to make this task easier.

1 Close any Excel workbooks that are currently open.

2 Open *Exercise 6* from your sample files folder.

3 Open *Sales First Quarter 2022 Revised* from your sample files folder.

4 Open *Sales First Quarter 2022* from your sample files folder.

Three workbooks are now open but only the last workbook opened: *Sales First Quarter 2022* is visible on screen.

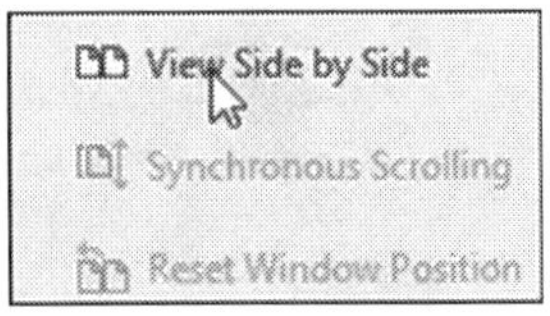

5 Click: View→Window→View Side by Side.

The *Compare Side by Side* dialog is displayed.

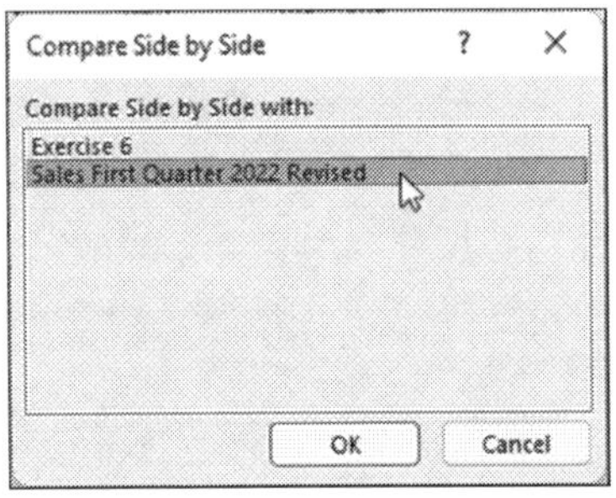

6 Select *Sales First Quarter 2022 Revised* as the workbook that you want to view with the current workbook and then click the *OK* button.

The workbooks should display one above the other.

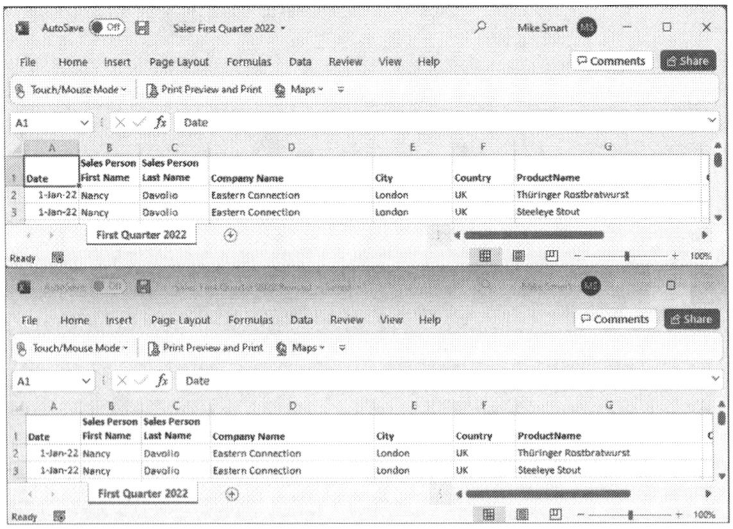

If you don't see this, click:

View→Window→Reset Window Position.

This is often needed when the workbooks have been moved or re-sized.

Notice that when you use the scroll bars to move up and down the list (scroll) in one window, the other window scrolls at the same time. This is called *synchronous scrolling*.

7 Unlock the windows so that they no longer scroll together.

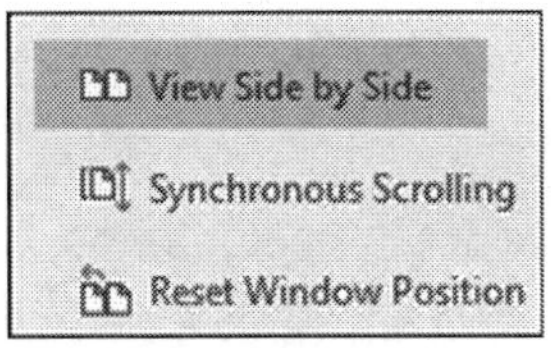

1. Click: View→Window→Synchronous Scrolling to switch synchronous scrolling off. You are now able to freely scroll each window independently.
2. Scroll each window to the top (so that row 1 is at the top of each window).

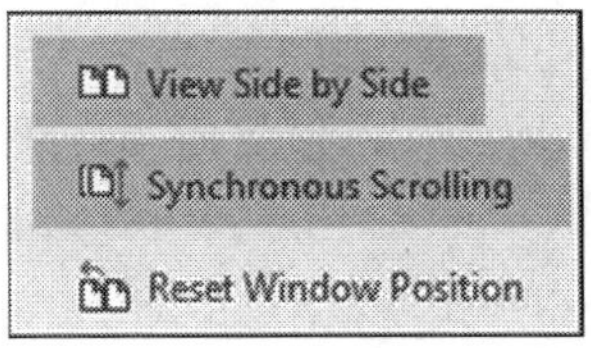

3. Click: View→Window→Synchronous Scrolling to switch synchronous scrolling back on so that both windows automatically scroll together.

8 Identify differences between the two workbooks.

Scroll down so that you can see row 77. Notice that row 78 has gone out of synchronization because one of the 29-Jan-22 sales to Hungry Owl has been deleted from the *Revised* workbook.

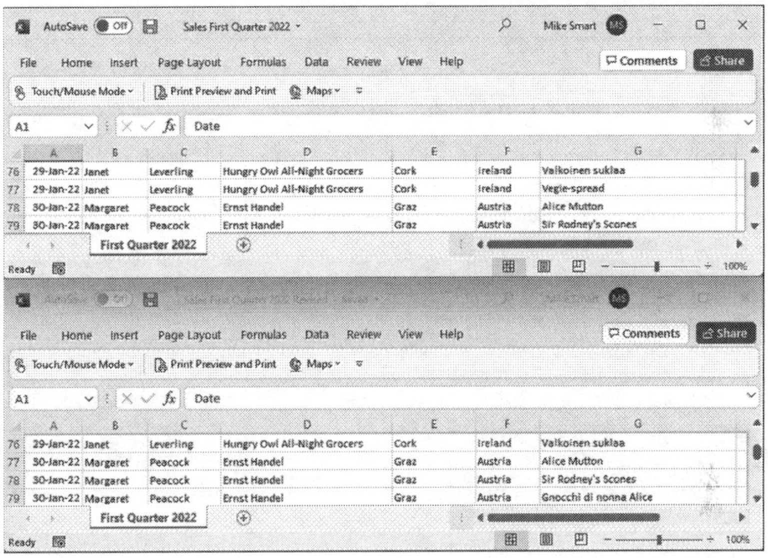

9 Re-synchronize the windows.

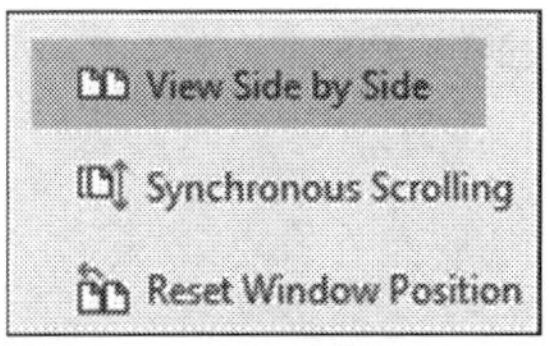

1. Click: View→Window→Synchronous Scrolling to switch Synchronous Scrolling off.
2. Scroll so that the first transaction on 30th Jan 2022 is on the first row in both windows.

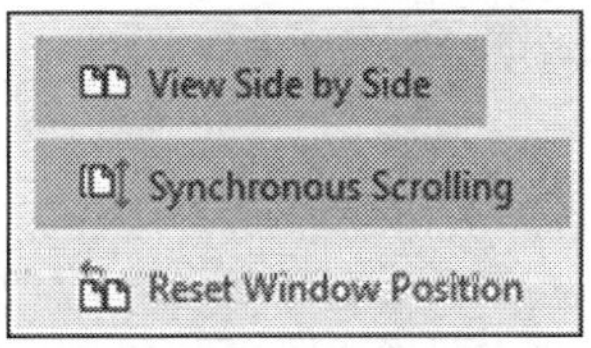

3. Click: View→Window→Synchronous Scrolling to switch Synchronous Scrolling back on.

10 Close all open workbooks without saving.

Lesson 6-3: Duplicate worksheets within a workbook

In this lesson you're going to disassemble a large worksheet and make it into three smaller worksheets.

You'll often find that data is easier to work with if you divide it into logically separated sections.

1 Open *Sales First Quarter 2022* from your sample files folder.

This workbook shows all sales completed in January, February and March 2022. Your task will be to split them into separate months.

2 Create a new worksheet and name the worksheet: **January**

You learned how to do this in *Lesson 1-13: View, move, add, rename, delete and navigate worksheet tabs.*

3 Select every cell in the *First Quarter 2022* worksheet.

1. Click the *First Quarter 2022* worksheet tab.

   There's a special button at the top left corner of every worksheet called the *Select All* button.

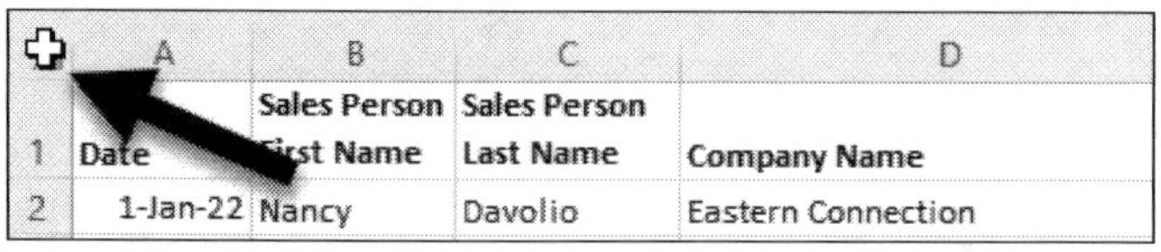

2. Click the *Select All* button to select every cell in the worksheet.

4 Copy all selected cells.

The easiest way to do this is to right-click within the selected range and then click *Copy* from the shortcut menu.

5 Paste the copied cells into the *January* worksheet beginning at cell A1.

Click the *January* tab, right-click in cell A1 and select *Paste* from the shortcut menu.

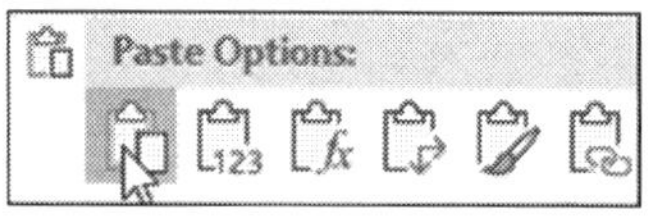

6 Create another copy of the worksheet using *Move or Copy*.

Excel provides a simpler way to duplicate a worksheet.

1. Right-click the *First Quarter 2022* worksheet tab and choose *Move or Copy…* from the shortcut menu.

   The *Move or Copy* dialog appears.

2. Select *(move to end)* in the *Before sheet* list.
3. Check the *Create a copy* check box.
4. Click the *OK* button.

note

Other ways to select all cells

Select All is a very common requirement and it is well worth remembering the keyboard shortcut:

<Ctrl>+<A>

It's a shortcut I use every day.

If the active cell is inside a range this keyboard shortcut will select every cell within the range (rather than every cell within the worksheet).

If you press **<Ctrl>+<A>** a second time, the selection will then expand to include every cell within the worksheet.

Sales First Quarter 2022

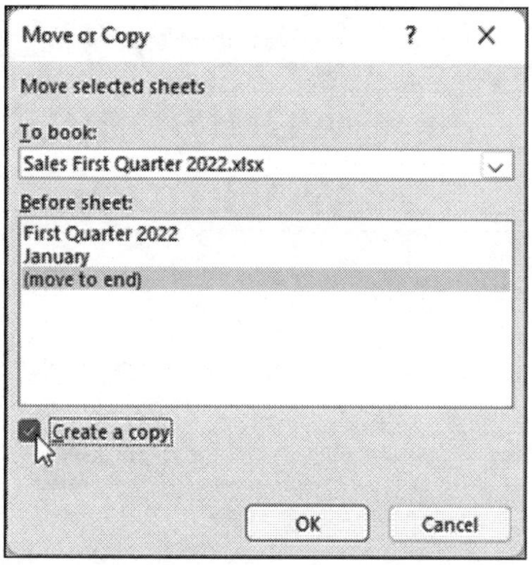

Notice that Excel has named the new worksheet: *First Quarter 2022 (2).*

7 Change the name of the new worksheet to: **February**

This skill was covered in *Lesson 1-13: View, move, add, rename, delete and navigate worksheet tabs.*

8 Create another copy of the worksheet using *drag and drop*.

There's an even quicker way to create a duplicate worksheet.

1. Click once on the *First Quarter 2022* tab to select it.

2. Hold down the **<Ctrl>** key and drag slightly to the right.

   The cursor changes shape to a page with a plus sign:

3. Drag more to the right until you see a black insertion arrow to the right of the *February* tab.

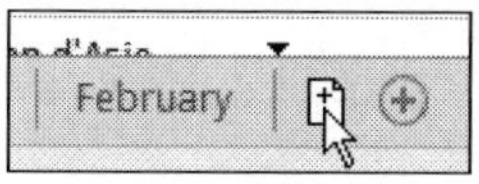

   When you release the mouse button another copy of the worksheet is created.

9 Change the name of the new worksheet to: **March**

10 Remove rows from the January, February and March workbooks so that only the named month's transactions remain.

You learned how to do this in: *Lesson 3-1: Insert and delete rows and columns.*

11 Save your work as *Sales First Quarter 2022-1*.

Lesson 6-4: Move and copy worksheets from one workbook to another

In *Lesson 6-3: Duplicate worksheets within a workbook*, you worked with a single workbook.

It is also possible to move and copy worksheets between different workbooks using a similar technique.

1 Close any workbooks that are currently open.

2 Open *Sales First Quarter 2022-1* from your sample files folder (if it isn't already open).

3 Open *First Quarter Sales and Bonus* from your sample files folder.

4 Arrange the windows *Horizontally*.

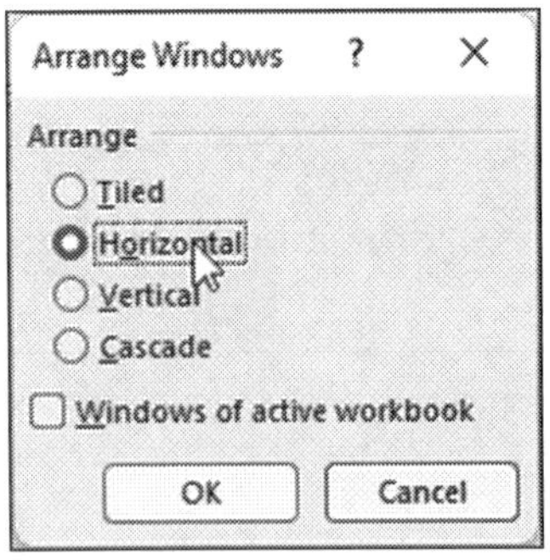

1. Click: View→Window→Arrange All→Horizontal.
2. Click: OK.

The two workbooks are now shown together.

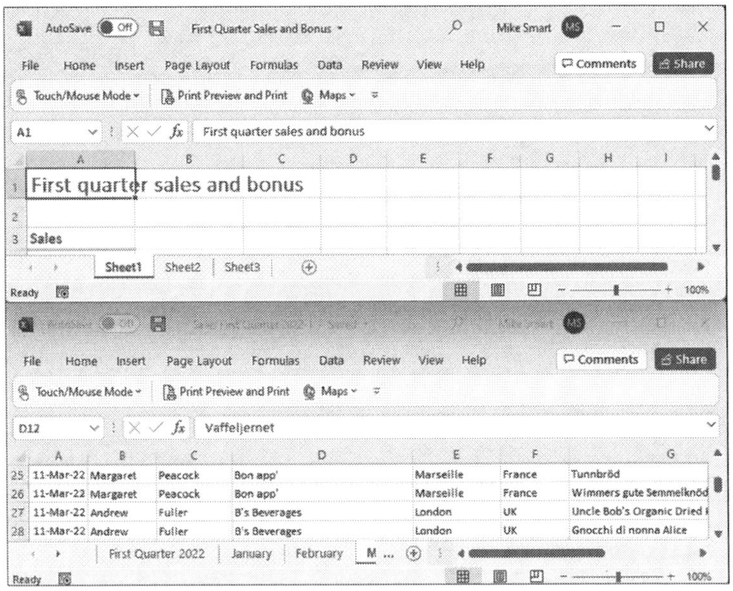

5 Rename *Sheet1* in the *First Quarter Sales and Bonus* workbook to: **Bonus**

You learned how to do this in: *Lesson 1-13: View, move, add, rename, delete and navigate worksheet tabs.*

First Quarter Sales and Bonus

6 Hold down the **<Ctrl>** key and drag and drop the *Bonus* sheet from the *First Quarter Sales and Bonus* workbook to the *Sales First Quarter 2022-1* workbook.

Sales First Quarter 2022-1

A copy of the *Bonus* worksheet is created in the *Sales First Quarter 2022-1* workbook.

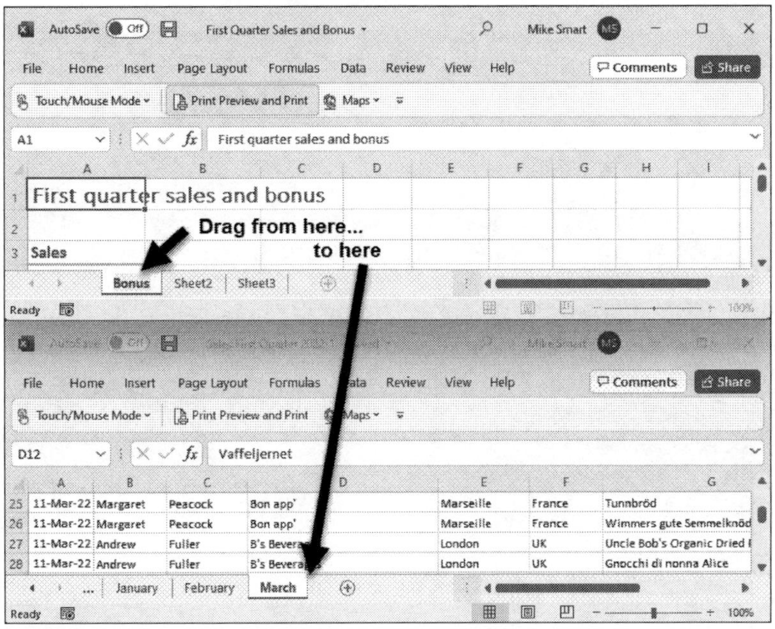

7 Drag and drop the *Sheet3* worksheet from the *First Quarter Sales and Bonus* workbook to the *Sales First Quarter 2022-1* workbook.

You will have to click the *First Quarter Sales and Bonus* workbook once to activate it before you can drag and drop the sheet tab.

This time, because you didn't hold the **<Ctrl>** key down, the worksheet is moved rather than copied.

8 Change the name of the moved worksheet to: **Summary**

You learned how to do this in: *Lesson 1-13: View, move, add, rename, delete and navigate worksheet tabs.*

9 If necessary, move the worksheet tabs in the *Sales First Quarter 2022-1* workbook so that they appear in the following order:

You learned how to do this in: *Lesson 1-13: View, move, add, rename, delete and navigate worksheet tabs.*

10 Maximize the *Sales First Quarter 2022-1* workbook window.

You learned how to do this in: *Lesson 1-7: Maximize, minimize, re-size, move and close the Excel window.*

11 Close the *First Quarter Sales and Bonus* worksheet without saving.

12 Save your work as *Sales First Quarter 2022-2*.

Lesson 6-5: Hide and unhide a worksheet

Sometimes you'll want to prevent users from viewing and changing one or more worksheets.

In this case you will want to *Hide* the worksheet.

A hidden worksheet becomes invisible to the user but is still there. You can bring back hidden worksheets by *Unhiding* them.

important

Don't rely on hidden worksheets for security

There is no password associated with hiding and unhiding a worksheet. A knowledgeable user can easily unhide any hidden worksheets.

It is possible to password-protect the structure before distributing a workbook. When this is done it isn't possible to unhide and view the hidden worksheet unless you know the password.

This topic is fully covered in the *Expert Skills* book in this series, in which a whole session is dedicated to security.

1 Open *Sales First Quarter 2022-2* from your sample files folder (if it isn't already open).

In this workbook you may not want viewers to see the *First Quarter 2022* worksheet as the information is already contained in the *January/February/March* worksheets.

You might also want to hide the *Bonus* worksheet as it contains confidential information. Note that you should not rely upon hidden worksheets to secure confidential information (see sidebar).

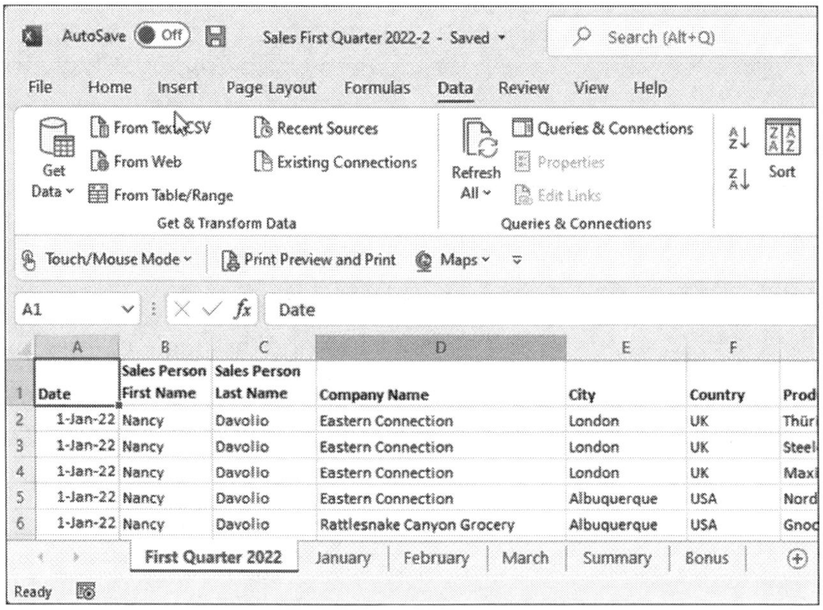

2 Select the *First Quarter 2022* and *Bonus* worksheets.

1. Click on the *First Quarter 2022* worksheet tab.
2. Hold down the **<Ctrl>** key.
3. Click on the *Bonus* worksheet tab.

Both worksheet tabs should now be highlighted:

3 Hide the *First Quarter 2022* and *Bonus* worksheets.

The easiest way to do this is to right click on either of the selected tabs and then click *Hide* from the shortcut menu.

The worksheets vanish.

Sales First Quarter 2022-2

note

Hiding and unhiding a worksheet using the Ribbon

The right-click method is far faster than using the Ribbon but here's how it can be done:

To *Hide* a worksheet

Click:

Home→Cells→Format→
Hide & Unhide→Hide Sheet

To *Unhide* a worksheet

Click:

Home→Cells→Format→
Hide & Unhide→Unhide Sheet

Then select the sheet that you want to hide/unhide from the dialog and click the OK button.

It's also possible to do this less efficiently from the Ribbon (see sidebar).

4 Unhide the *Bonus* worksheet.

Excel will never allow you to hide all of the worksheets, so this method of unhiding sheets will always work.

1. Right-click on any of the visible worksheet tabs.
2. Click *Unhide* from the shortcut menu.

   The *Unhide* dialog is displayed:

3. Click *Bonus* and then click the OK button.

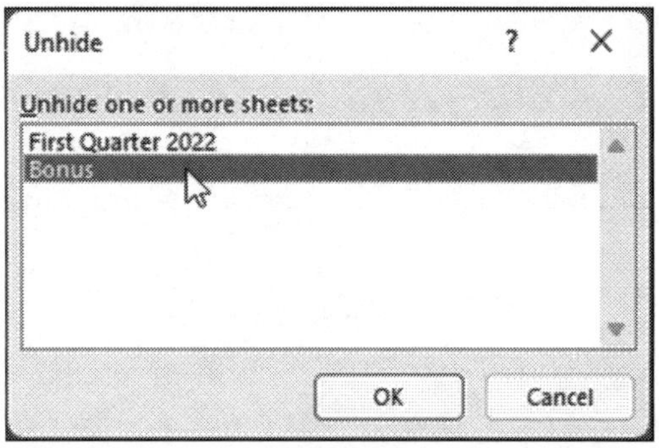

You can also unhide the worksheets less efficiently by using the Ribbon (see sidebar).

5 Save your work as Sales First Quarter 2022-3.

Lesson 6-6: Create cross worksheet formulas

You'll often want to summarize information from multiple worksheets within a workbook.

This can be done by simply prefixing the cell reference with the worksheet name followed by an exclamation mark.

1 Open *Sales First Quarter 2022-3* from your sample files folder (if it isn't already open).

2 Select the *January* tab and scroll to the bottom of the range.

3 Type the word **Total:** into the first empty cell in column G (cell G87).

4 Right-align cell G87.

You learned how to do this in: *Lesson 4-4: Create custom number formats*

The built-in number formats are very quick and convenient but are also quite limited. Fortunately, it is possible to create your own custom format when none of the built-in styles fit your requirement.

Overview of custom formats

There's plenty of documentation in the help system and on the Internet about the rather cryptic formatting codes provided by Excel. Just about everything is possible once you've got to grips with the basic concepts.

To communicate the custom format to Excel, you must construct a custom format string.

Zeros mean "Display significant zeros". You tell Excel how many you want within the format string. For example, 0.00 means *display at least one leading zero and two decimal places*. The following examples should make things clear:

Custom Format String	Value	Display
0	1234.56	1235
0.0	1234.56 1234.5 .5	1234.6 1234.5 0.5
0.00	1234.56 1234.5 .5	1234.56 1234.50 0.50
00.000	4.56	04.560
0.000	1234.56	1234.560

The hash symbol (#) is mainly used to add comma separators to thousands and millions.

Custom Format String	Value	Display
#	123.4500	123
#.##	123.45 123.50	123.45 123.5
#,#	1234.56	1,236
#,#.##	1234.56 1234.50 12341234.56	1,234.56 1,234.5 12,341,234.56

Because the hash symbol can be used in conjunction with zeros it is also possible to indicate that you want both thousand separators *and* a specific number of leading or trailing zeros.

Custom Format String	Value	Display
#,#0.00	12341234.5	12,341,234.50

You can also specify two different format strings separated by a semi colon. The first provides formatting for positive values and the second for negative values. You can also embed colors into number formats.

Here's an example that will show all negative values enclosed in brackets and colored red:

Custom format string	Value	Display
#,#0.00;[Red](#,#0.00)	12341234.5 -12341234.5	12,341,234.50 (12,341,234.50)

1 Open *Sales Week Ended 14th March 2022-2* from your sample files folder (if it isn't already open).

2 Select columns E and G (but not column F).

You learned how to do this in: *Lesson 2-6: Select adjacent and non-adjacent rows and columns.*

3 Apply the default *General* style to column E and G.

5. Select columns E and G (but not F).
6. Click: Home→Number→
   Number Format (dropdown list)→General.

The cells revert to Excel's default *General* format (in other words, they are no longer formatted in any special way).

4 Apply the custom format: #,#0.00;[Red](#,#0.00) to every cell in columns E and G.

9. Select columns E and G (but not F).
10. Right click anywhere in column E or G and then select *Format Cells…* from the shortcut menu.

11. Select *Custom* from the category list on the left of the dialog.

12. Type the custom format: **#,#0.00;[Red](#,#0.00)** into the box labelled *Type* and then click the *OK* button.

Type:
#,##0.00;[Red](#,##0.00)

The negative values on the worksheet are now surrounded by brackets and have a font color of red.

Italy	637.49	17.5%	749.05
Italy	(637.49)	17.5%	(749.05)

5 Save your work as *Sales Week Ended 14th March 2022-3.*

Lesson 4-5: Horizontally align the contents of cells.

5 Bold-face all of row 87.

You learned how to do this in: *Lesson 1-19: Use the Mini Toolbar, Key Tips and keyboard shortcuts.*

6 Use AutoSum to add totals to columns H and J.

You learned how to do this in: *Lesson 2-3: Use AutoSum to quickly calculate totals.*

	G	H	I	J
85	Gumbär Gummibärchen	10	24.90	249.00
86	Tourtière	40	5.90	236.00
87	**Total:**	**2,401**		**66,692.80**

7 Add similar totals to the *February* and *March* worksheets.

8 Select the *Summary* tab.

9 Type the text: **First Quarter Summary** into cell A1 and apply the *Title* cell style.

You learned how to do this in: *Lesson 4-10: Use cell styles and change themes.*

	A	B	C	D
1	First Quarter Summary			

10 Type **Month**, **Units** and **Price** into cells A3, B3 and C3.

11 Type **Jan** into cell A4 and then AutoFill down two cells to add Feb and Mar.

You learned how to do this in: *Lesson 2-14: Use AutoFill for text and numeric series.*

12 Apply the *Heading 2* style to cells A3:C3.

Sales First Quarter 2022-3

13 Apply the *Heading 4* style to cells A4:A6.

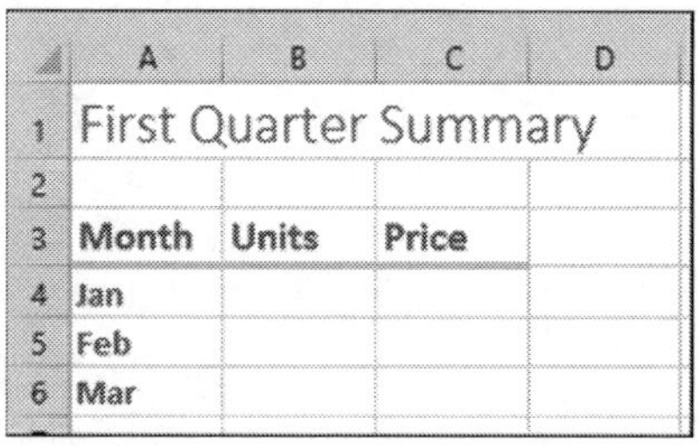

14 Add a formula to cell B4 to display the total units sold in January.

1. Click in cell B4.
2. Press the equals key on your keyboard **(=)** to begin a formula.
3. Click on the *January* tab. 

4. Scroll to the bottom of the screen using the scroll bars, arrow keys or mouse wheel being careful not to click on any cell.
5. Click on cell H87 (the cell with the total units in it).
6. Press the **<Enter>** key on the keyboard.

The total is shown on the *Summary* sheet.

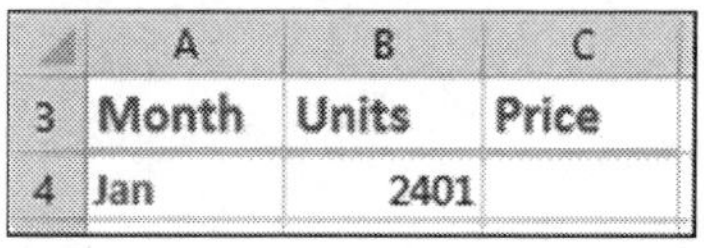

important

You must use quotation marks if a worksheet name contains spaces

The example worksheet names used in this session do not contain any spaces.

If you had a worksheet called *January Sales* you would have to construct your formula like this:

='January Sales'!K22

Because worksheet names with spaces are more difficult to work with, many Excel users prefer to name their sheets without spaces by capitalizing the first letter of every word.

Example:

JanuarySales
EuropeIncludingSouthAfrica

15 Use the same technique to add summary totals for **Units** and **Price** for all three months.

16 Apply the comma style to all of the values in column C.

You learned how to do this in: *Lesson 4-3: Format numbers using built-in number formats.*

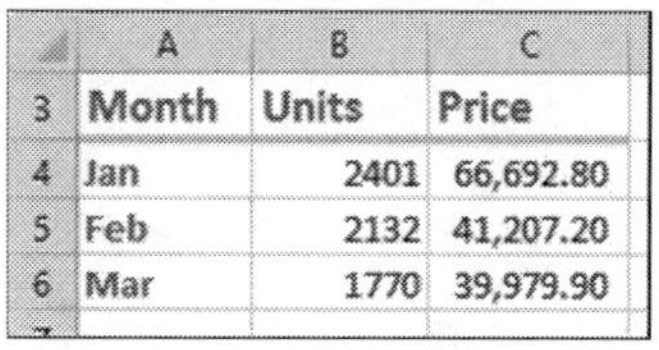

17 Examine the formulas that Excel has created.

Click in cell B4 and then look at the formula bar at the top of the screen. Note that the formula is:

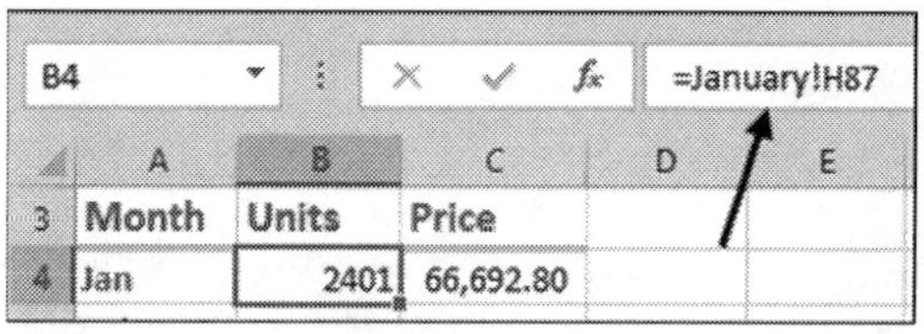

The formula is simply the worksheet name, followed by an exclamation mark, followed by the cell reference.

Note the important sidebar information regarding worksheet names that contain spaces.

18 Save your work as *Sales First Quarter 2022-4*.

Lesson 6-7: Understand worksheet groups

A very interesting (and little known) feature of Excel is its ability to group worksheets into a three-dimensional array of worksheet cells.

When worksheets are grouped, it is possible to perform a single operation upon all of the worksheets in the group. This can be very useful when you need to:

- Print out all of the worksheets in the group.
- Enter data into the same cell for all worksheets in the group.
- Apply formatting to the same cell or range for all worksheets in the group.

1 Open *Widget Supplies Price List* from your sample files folder.

The formatting of this workbook leaves a lot to be desired. It consists of three worksheets all showing similar information but lacking any style.

	A	B	C	D	E	F	G
1	Price List						
2	Prices Effe	20th March 2022					
3	When calculating prices the following exchange rates will be used						
4							
5		USD	GBP	EUR	JPY		
6	USD	1	1.35468	1.13029	0.00863		
7							
8	Descriptic	Dollars	Pounds	Euros	Yen		
9	Standard \	3.75	2.768181	3.317733	434.5307		
10	Premium	5.5	4.059999	4.866008	637.3117		
11	De-luxe g	7.95	5.868545	7.033593	921.2051		

You're going to use the magic of grouping to format all three worksheets at the same time.

note

Selecting non-contiguous worksheets

Non-contiguous simply means *not next to each other.*

When the worksheet tabs aren't next to each other, hold down the **<Ctrl>** key and click each in turn. If you make a mistake, you can **<Ctrl>+<Click>** a second time to de-select one tab.

You can also use a combination of **<Shift>+<Click>** and **<Ctrl>+<Click>** when some of the tabs are next to each other and others are not.

2 Select all three worksheets to create a worksheet group.

1. Click the *Widgets* worksheet tab.
2. Hold down the **<Shift>** key and click the *Sprockets* worksheet tab.

All three tabs now have a white background to show that they are selected.

Something else has also happened. The title bar at the top of the screen now indicates that the worksheets form a worksheet group.

Widget Supplies Price List

3 Apply formatting to the *Sprockets* worksheet to make it look attractive.

When you have grouped every worksheet in a workbook, you have a little problem. You can't switch between worksheets and still keep the group selected. As soon as you click a selected sheet the other two are de-selected.

To work-around this you'll have to insert a new blank worksheet. The sheet's only purpose is to allow you to switch between sheets in the selected group.

1. Add a worksheet called *Dummy*.
2. Select the *Widgets, Grommets* and *Sprockets* group as before.

3. Click on the *Sprockets* tab. The group remains selected and the *Sprockets* worksheet is now active.

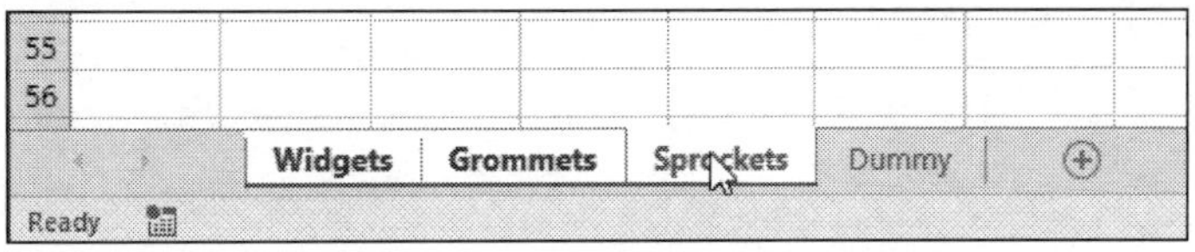

4. Apply the comma style to the range B9:E11. You learned how to do this in: *Lesson 4-3: Format numbers using built-in number formats.*
5. Adjust the widths of all columns so that they fully display their contents. You learned how to do this in: *Lesson 2-9: Re-size rows and columns.*
6. Apply the *Title* style to cell A1, the *Heading 4* style to cells A2, A6 and A9:A11 and the *Heading 3* style to cells B5:E5 and A8:E8. You learned how to do this in: *Lesson 4-10: Use cell styles and change themes.*
7. Adjust the height of rows 2, 3 and 4 to tidy the top part of the price list.
8. Click on the *Widgets* and *Grommets* tabs in turn. Notice how the formatting has been applied to the entire worksheet group.

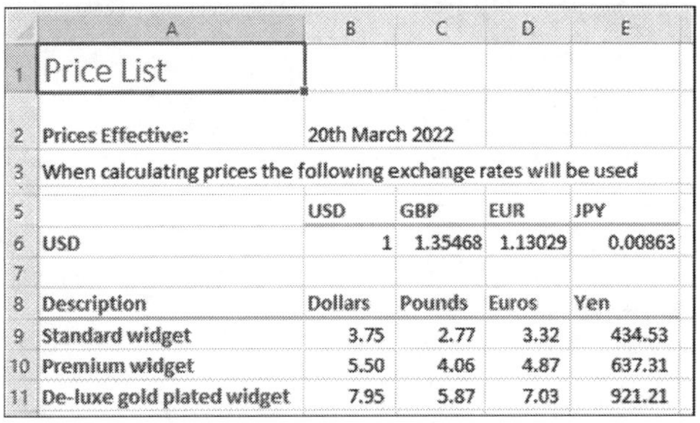

	A	B	C	D	E
1	Price List				
2	Prices Effective:	20th March 2022			
3	When calculating prices the following exchange rates will be used				
5		USD	GBP	EUR	JPY
6	USD	1	1.35468	1.13029	0.00863
7					
8	Description	Dollars	Pounds	Euros	Yen
9	Standard widget	3.75	2.77	3.32	434.53
10	Premium widget	5.50	4.06	4.87	637.31
11	De-luxe gold plated widget	7.95	5.87	7.03	921.21

4 With the group still selected, change some exchange rates and the *Prices Effective* date.

Notice that you have updated the exchange rates for all three price lists at the same time. This would be regularly needed as exchange rates fluctuate. When a group of worksheets are selected, any change made to one worksheet is also made to all of the others.

5 Save your work as *Widget Supplies Price List-1*.

Lesson 6-8: Use find and replace

note

Other ways to display the Find and Replace dialog

Find

Use the **<Ctrl>+<F>** keyboard shortcut.

Replace

Use the **<Ctrl>+<H>** keyboard shortcut.

Excel's *Find and Replace* tool is amazingly powerful. There are several special features that can massively shorten many common tasks. This lesson will explore *Find and Replace* special features and suggest useful ways in which they can be used to solve real-world problems.

1 Open *Sales First Quarter 2022-4* from your sample files folder (if it isn't already open).

2 Use *Find and Replace* to change the text *Davolio* to *O'Reilly* throughout the workbook.

Nancy Davolio has married Sean O'Reilly and now wants the worksheet to refer to her new married name. She's made a request for you to change her name throughout this workbook.

1. Click: Home→Editing→Find & Select→Replace.

   The *Find and Replace* dialog is displayed.

2. Click the *Replace* tab.
3. Type **Davolio** in the *Find what:* text box and **O'Reilly** in the *Replace with:* text box.
4. Click the *Options>>* button. 

5. Select the *Within→Workbook* option.

   You don't want to only look in the current worksheet, but in all of the worksheets in this workbook.

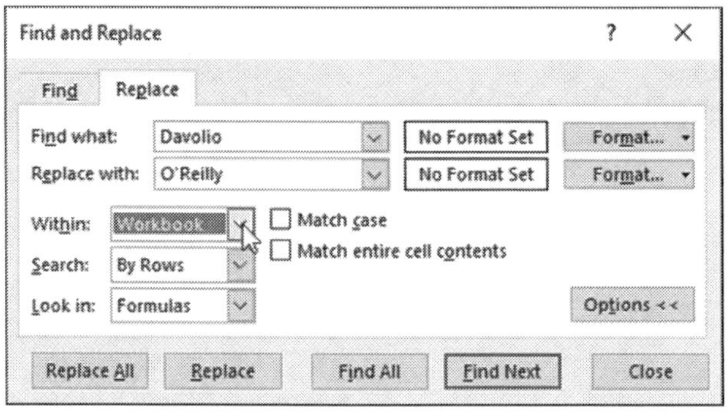

note

Searching only part of a worksheet

If you only select a single cell, *Find and Replace* will search the entire worksheet.

If you select a range of cells, *Find and Replace* will only search within that range.

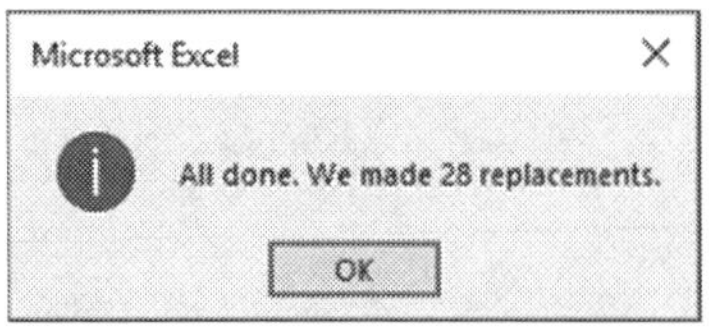

6. Click the *Find Next* button. The first instance of *Davolio* is found on the worksheet.
7. Click the *Replace* button to replace just this one instance. The cursor moves to the next instance found.
8. Click *Replace All* to replace all remaining instances of *Davolio* with *O'Reilly*. Excel prompts that it has made 28 replacements.
9. Click the *OK* and *Close* buttons to close both dialogs.
10. Examine the worksheets. Notice that Nancy's last name has now changed in every worksheet.

Sales First Quarter 2022-4

3 Apply the *Good* style to cell G21 on the *January* worksheet.

note

Wildcard searches

Sometimes you will only have a partial idea of what you need to find.

In this case you can use the wildcard characters – the asterisk (*) and the question mark (?).

The asterisk means that any number of wildcard letters can occur between the letters.

The question mark means that one wildcard letter can occur for each question mark.

It is easiest to show how wildcards work with a few examples:

C*g Finds **Containing**
Finds **Citing**
Finds **Changing**

S??d Finds **Said**
Finds **Sand**
Finds **Seed**
Doesn't Find **Sound**
Doesn't Find **Surround**
Doesn't Find **Sad**

important

The *Look in:* option

Searches are normally done on the contents of the formula bar.

This works well for text entries but can cause problems when searching for values.

Imagine that you want to search for all cells containing the value 25. If you search the formula, you will also find cells with formulas such as **=25*A1** while missing cells with formulas such as **=5*5**.

In this case you'd select *Look in: Values* to find all cells displaying the value 25.

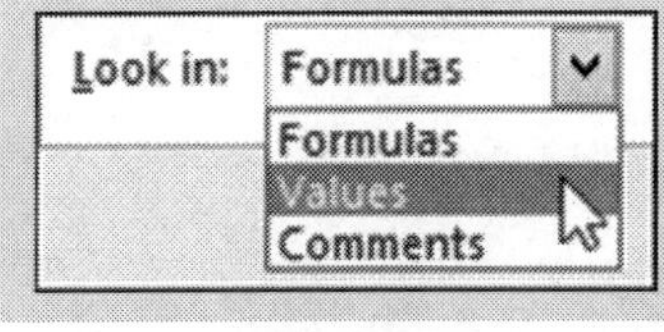

Click cell G21 to select it and then click:

Home→Styles→Cell Styles→Good

The *Good* cell style has a light green background and dark green text.

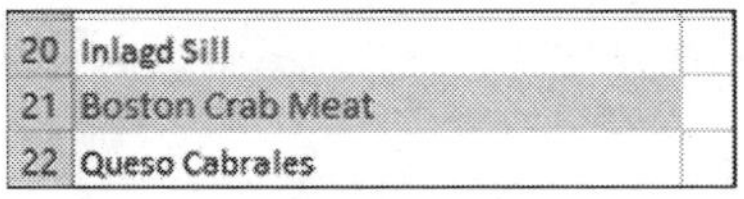

4 Apply the same style to every other mention of *Boston Crab Meat* in the workbook.

1. With cell G21 still visible on the workbook click:

   Home→Editing→Find & Select→Replace…

2. Click the *Replace* tab if necessary.
3. Type **Boston Crab Meat** in the *Find what:* text box.
4. Delete the current contents of the *Replace with* box.
5. Click the *Format* button drop-down arrow alongside *Replace with:* and select *Choose Format From Cell…* from the drop-down menu.

   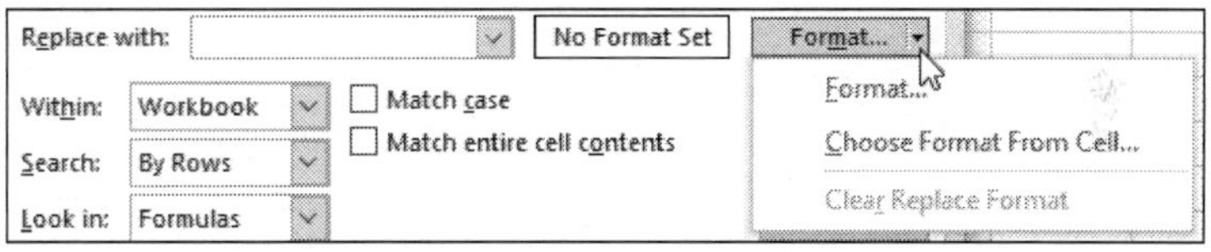

   It is really important that you click the lower of the two *Format* buttons. If you get it wrong click: Format→Clear Replace Format, to start again.

   The cursor shape changes to an eye-dropper.

6. Click on cell G21.

   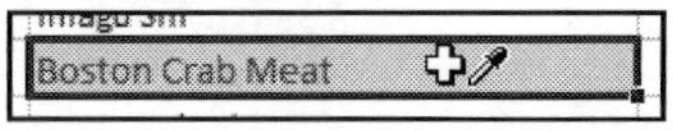

   The same format now appears in the *Replace with:* format text box on the *Find and Replace* dialog

   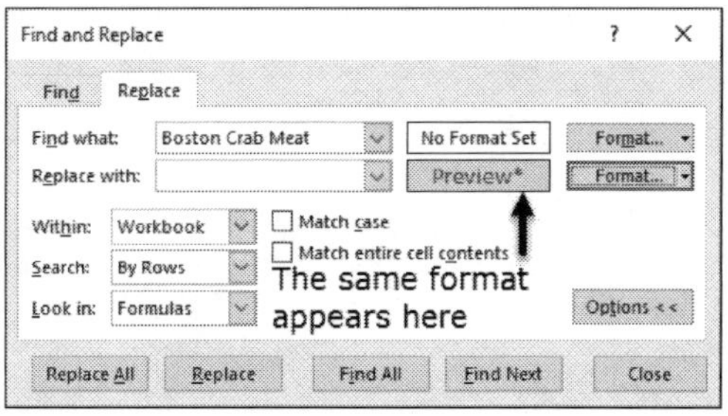

7. Click *Replace All* to re-format all instances of *Boston Crab Meat* to the *Good* cell style.

   Excel advises that it has changed the format of seven cells.

8. Click the *OK* and *Close* buttons to close both dialogs.
9. Examine all of the worksheets and notice that every cell containing the text *Boston Crab Meat* has now turned green.

5 Save your work as *Sales First Quarter 2022-5.*

Session 6: Exercise

1 Close any workbooks that are open.

2 Open *Exercise 6* from your sample files folder.

3 View two copies of the worksheet in different windows stacked horizontally.

4 Scroll one of the windows so that the first USA sale is visible in the first row.

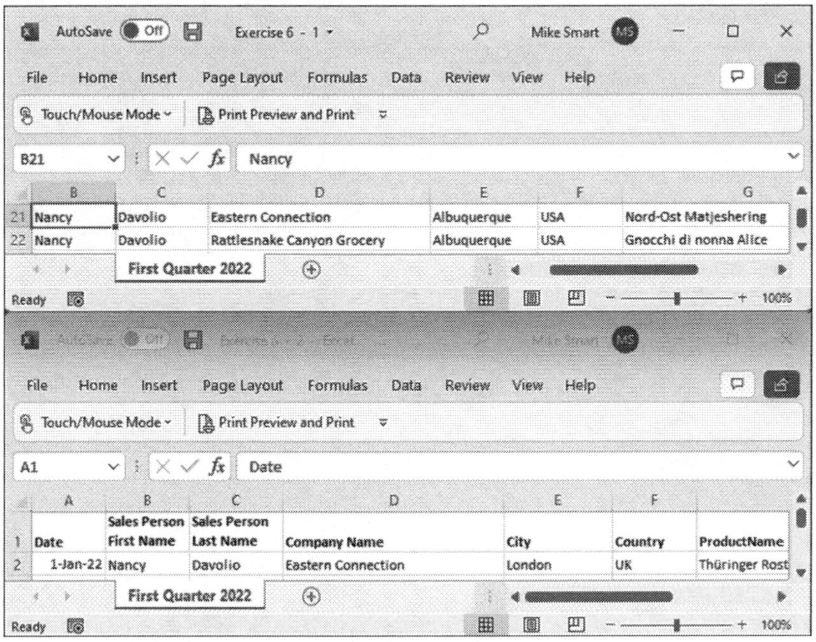

5 Close the *Exercise 6 - 2* window and maximize the *Exercise 6-1* window.

6 Make two duplicate copies of the *First Quarter 2022* worksheet and name them *USA* and *UK*.

7 Delete all of the non-USA rows from the USA worksheet and all of the non-UK rows from the UK worksheet.

8 Hide the *First Quarter 2022* worksheet tab.

9 Use AutoSum to create totals at the bottom of columns H and J (*Quantity* and *Total*) for both the *USA* and *UK* worksheets.

10 Add a new worksheet and name it: Summary

11 Complete the summary sheet as illustrated below using cross-worksheet formulas to calculate the totals.

	A	B	C	D
1	USA and UK Sales Summary			
2				
3	Country	Units	Sales	
4	USA	913	26,572.20	
5	UK	379	7,299.40	
6	**Total**	**1292**	**33,871.60**	

Exercise 6

12 Save your work as *Exercise 6-End.*

Session 6: Exercise answers

These are the questions that students find the most difficult to answer:

Q 11	Q 8	Q 6	Q 3 and 4
In the example the following styles were used: A1 Title A3:C3 Heading 2 A4:A5 Heading 4 A6:C6 Total 1. Click cell B4 and type an equals sign into it (=). 2. Click the *USA* tab. 3. Use the scroll bars to make the total cell (cell H27) visible, being careful not to click on any of the cells within the worksheet. 4. Click cell H27 and then press the **<Enter>** key. This was covered in: *Lesson 6-6: Create cross worksheet formulas.*	1. Right-click the *First Quarter 2022* worksheet tab. 2. Click *Hide* from the shortcut menu. This was covered in: *Lesson 6-5: Hide and unhide a worksheet.*	1. Click on the *First Quarter 2022* worksheet tab to select it. 2. Hold down the **<Ctrl>** key. 3. Click and drag the *First Quarter 2022* worksheet tab to the right. 4. Double-click the duplicated worksheet's tab and type the tab's new name. This was covered in: *Lesson 6-3: Duplicate worksheets within a workbook.*	1. Click: View→Window→ New Window 2. Click: View→Window→ Arrange All 3. Click the *Horizontal* option in the *Arrange Windows* dialog. 4. Click the OK button. 5. Scroll one of the windows to the first USA sale (row 21). This was covered in: *Lesson 6-1: View the same workbook in different windows.*

If you have difficulty with the other questions, here are the lessons that cover the relevant skills:

1 **Refer to: Lesson 1-7: Maximize, minimize, re-size, move and close the Excel window.**

2 **Refer to: Lesson 1-9: Open and navigate a workbook.**

5 **Refer to: Lesson 6-1: View the same workbook in different windows.**

7 **Refer to: Lesson 3-1: Insert and delete rows and columns.**

9 **Refer to: Lesson 2-3: Use AutoSum to quickly calculate totals.**

10 **Refer to: Lesson 1-13: View, move, add, rename, delete and navigate worksheet tabs.**

12 **Refer to: Lesson 1-10: Save a workbook.**

7

Session Seven: Printing Your Work

> The greatest misfortune that ever befell man was the invention of printing.
>
> ***Benjamin Disraeli, British Prime Minister and Novelist (1804-1881).***

As the world of commerce moves nearer to the paperless office, printing will become less important.

In the last few years, screen and rendering technology have improved to the extent that I now prefer to read on-screen rather than from paper.

Apple now claim that their "retina" display has such a high pixel density that the human eye is unable to detect pixelation at a typical viewing distance. This suggests that there is no longer any quality advantage in printing on paper.

Perhaps the world is not far away from a time when all communication will be done electronically, but in today's world, paper printed documents are still used in many areas of business.

Excel has a range of tools that will allow you to present your work as polished and professional printed reports. This session will give you all the skills you need to control every aspect of printing your work on paper.

Session Objectives

By the end of this session, you will be able to:

- Print Preview and change paper orientation
- Use Page Layout view to adjust margins
- Use Page Setup to set margins more precisely and center the worksheet
- Set paper size and scale
- Insert, delete and preview page breaks
- Adjust page breaks using Page Break Preview
- Add auto-headers and auto-footers and set the starting page number
- Add custom headers and footers
- Specify different headers and footers for the first, odd and even pages
- Print only part of a worksheet
- Add row and column data labels and gridlines to printed output
- Print several selected worksheets and change the page order
- Suppress error messages in printouts

Lesson 7-1: Print Preview and change paper orientation

1 Open *Sales Report* from your sample files folder.

Make sure that you open the Session 7 *Sales Report* file as there's also a sample file of the same name in an earlier session.

2 *Print Preview* the worksheet to see how it will look on paper.

1. Click: File→Print.

   Backstage Print View appears, showing a preview of the printed page in the right-hand pane.

2. Click the *Next Page* and *Previous Page* buttons to page through the document.

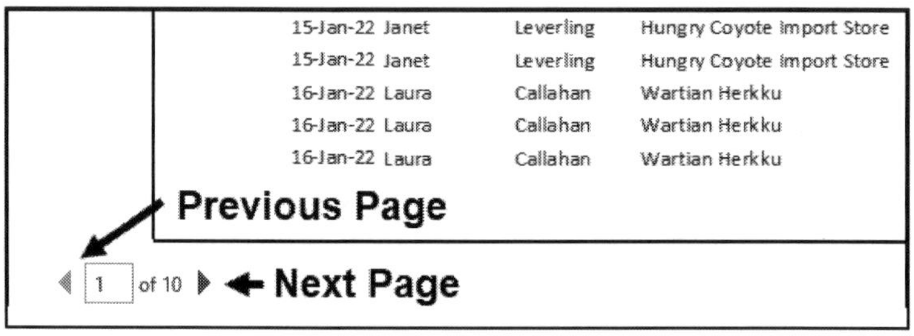

Notice that the paper isn't wide enough to show all of the columns. Excel tries to help out by printing the left-most columns across the first five or six pages followed by the right-most columns on the next five or six pages.

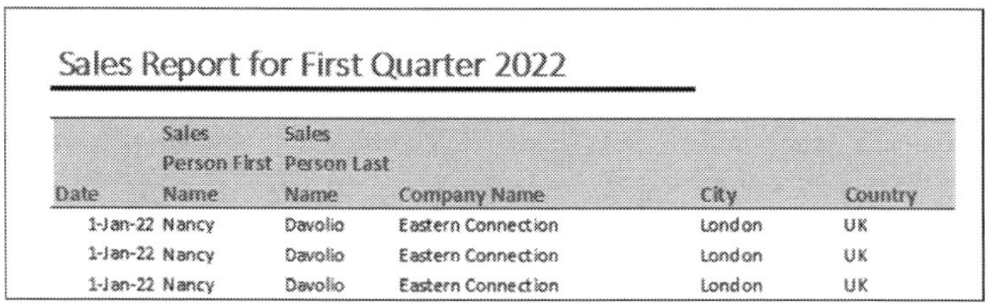

Sales Report for First Quarter 2022

Date	Sales Person First Name	Sales Person Last Name	Company Name	City	Country
1-Jan-22	Nancy	Davolio	Eastern Connection	London	UK
1-Jan-22	Nancy	Davolio	Eastern Connection	London	UK
1-Jan-22	Nancy	Davolio	Eastern Connection	London	UK

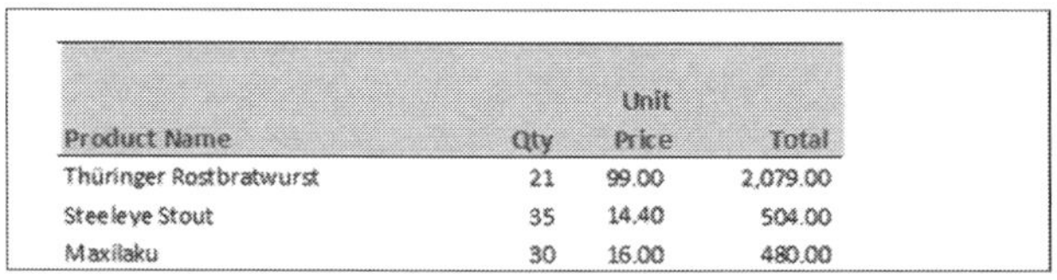

Product Name	Qty	Unit Price	Total
Thüringer Rostbratwurst	21	99.00	2,079.00
Steeleye Stout	35	14.40	504.00
Maxilaku	30	16.00	480.00

You would have to take the two pages, cut them with scissors, and tape them together in order to see all of the rows and columns.

3 Change the paper orientation to *Landscape* in order to print more columns on each sheet of paper.

Click the drop-down arrow next to *Portrait Orientation* in the center pane of the *Backstage Print View* and then click on *Landscape Orientation*.

tip

Add a print preview button to the Quick Access toolbar

I use the *Backstage Print View* so often that I like to display it with a single click (instead of two). To do this I always add the *Print Preview and Print* button to the Quick Access Toolbar.

I recommend that this button is a "must have" for the Quick Access Toolbar.

You learned how to add this button to the Quick Access Toolbar in:
Lesson 1-18: Customize the Quick Access Toolbar and preview the printout.

Sales Report

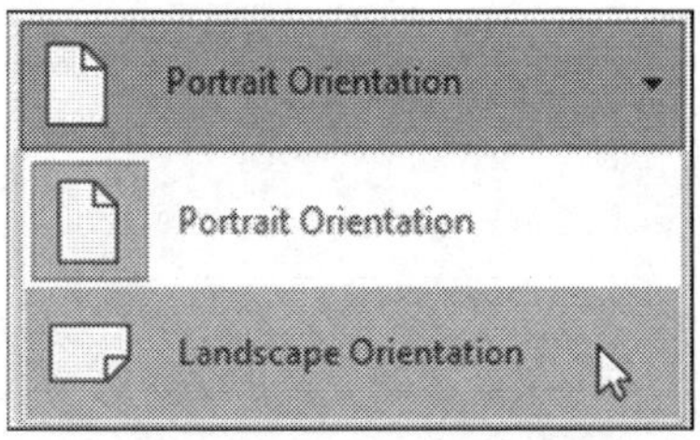

In *Landscape* orientation the paper is printed as if it had been put into the printer sideways.

The printout is very nearly there now, but there is still a problem with the last column which prints out all on its own.

Sales Report for First Quarter 2022

Date	Sales Person First Name	Sales Person Last Name	Company Name	City	Country	Product Name	Qty	Unit Price	Total
1-Jan-22	Nancy	Davolio	Eastern Connection	London	UK	Thüringer Rostbratwurst	21	99.00	2,079.00
1-Jan-22	Nancy	Davolio	Eastern Connection	London	UK	Steeleye Stout	35	14.40	504.00
1-Jan-22	Nancy	Davolio	Eastern Connection	London	UK	Maxilaku	30	16.00	480.00

You'll discover a solution to this problem later in: *Lesson 7-2: Use Page Layout view to adjust margins.*

4 Print a copy of the worksheet.

If you'd like to save the forests (and save the cost of sixteen sheets of paper), you may wish to skip this step.

Click the *Print* button.

Even if you didn't actually print the worksheet, I'm sure you will believe that the printout would not have been very good. You'd be back to the scissors and tape if you wanted the pages to show that missing last column.

The printout would have been in *Landscape* orientation because you've told Excel to do that.

5 Save your work as *Sales Report-1*.

important

If you are in North America or Canada, you may see a slightly different printout

If you are in North America or Canada, your printer will probably contain Letter size paper.

The sample file has been set up for A4 size paper.

You'll still be able to complete all lessons in this session, but you may find that screen grabs and any hard copy printed is slightly different to that shown in the book.

International differences in paper sizes will be discussed in depth in the sidebar: "A4 and Letter Paper Size" in: *Lesson 7-4: Set paper size and scale.*

Lesson 7-2: Use Page Layout view to adjust margins

You discovered how to change between Excel's three "views" in: *Lesson 1-20: Understand views.*

Page Layout view is a bit like *Print Preview* as you can see just how your page prints. The big difference is that, unlike *Print Preview,* you can edit a worksheet in this view. You can also set up many page layout features including margins, headers, footers and page numbering.

You'll be exploring all of this view's features in coming lessons. This lesson will focus upon changing the page margins (the blank areas at the top, bottom, left and right of the printout).

1 Open *Sales Report-1* from your sample files folder (if it isn't already open).

2 Display *Page Layout* view.

The fastest way to do this is to click the *Page Layout* button on the status bar at the bottom right of the screen.

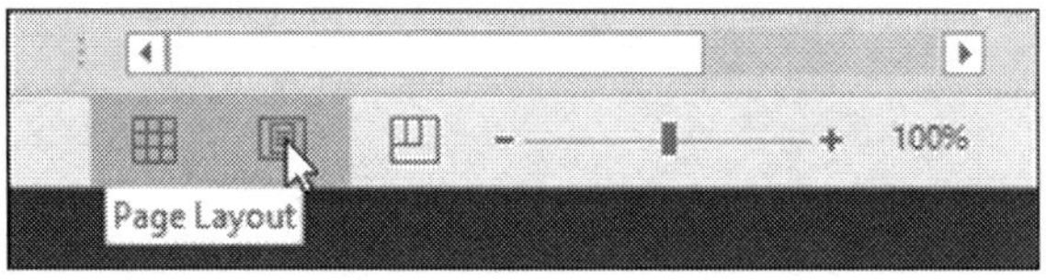

You can also do this from the Ribbon by clicking:

View→Workbook Views→Page Layout

Page layout view shows almost exactly how the worksheet will print.

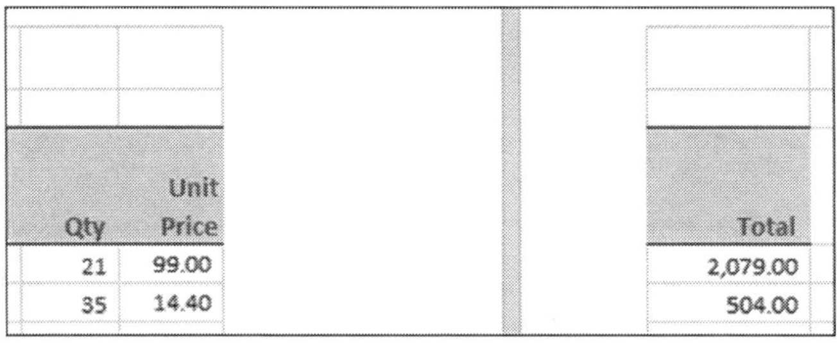

The missing *Total* column problem is immediately obvious.

3 Make sure that the rulers are visible.

Unless you've turned them off, you'll see a ruler at the top and left of the page that contains the active cell.

Click cell A1, to make it the active cell, and look for the rulers.

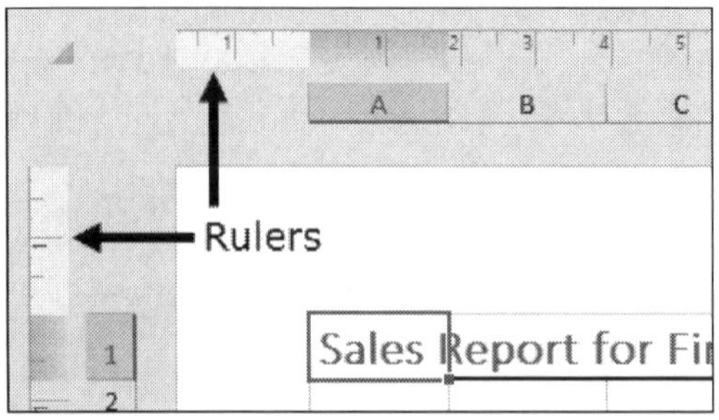

Sales Report-1

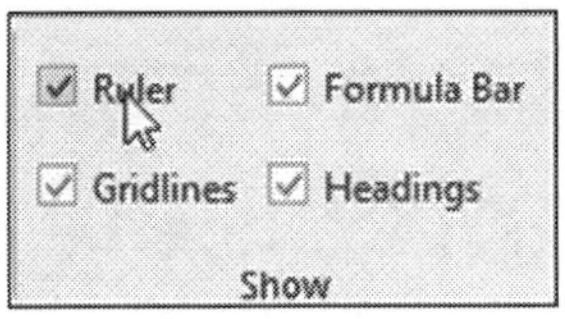

If you don't see the rulers, switch them on by clicking:

View→Show→Ruler

4 Set the ruler units to centimeters.

Many regions (called locales in earlier Windows versions) display ruler units in centimeters by default but some display ruler units in inches. The examples in this session assume that your ruler units are set to centimeters.

1. Click: File→Options→Advanced→Display→Ruler units.
2. Select *Centimeters* from the *Ruler units* drop-down list.
3. Click the OK button.

5 Adjust the left margin using the rulers.

1. Select column A.

   Notice how a portion of the ruler above column A is shaded green. This gives you a visual indication of where the margin begins.

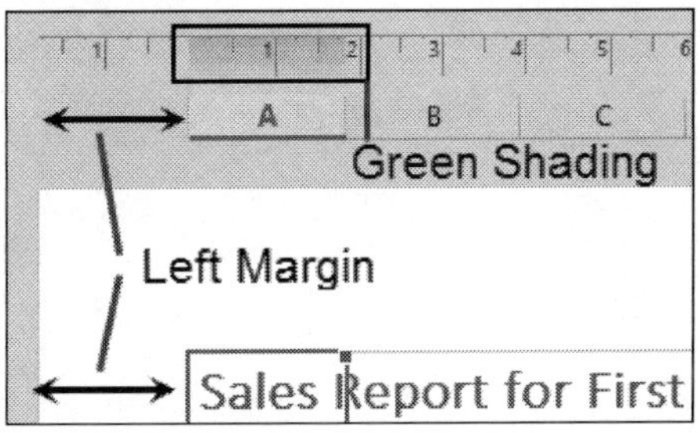

2. Hover the mouse cursor over the left-hand side of the ruler's green shaded section.

   The cursor shape changes to a double headed arrow and the current left-hand margin size is displayed.

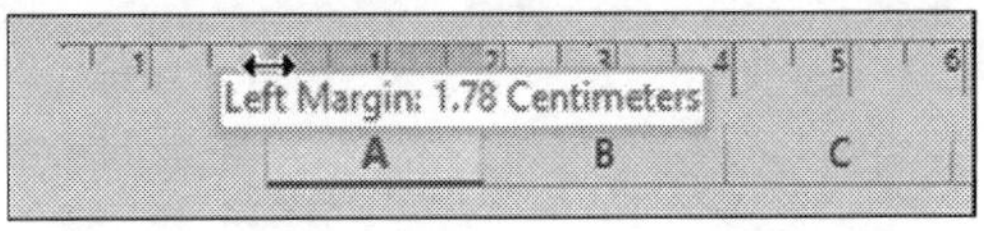

3. When you see the double-headed arrow, click and drag to the left to reduce the margin to about one centimeter. You'll probably find it impossible to set exactly 1.0 centimeters with this method and will have to settle for 1.01.

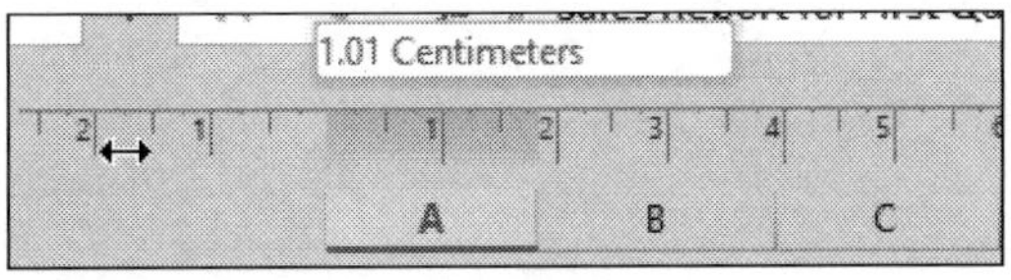

   All of the columns now fit onto one page.

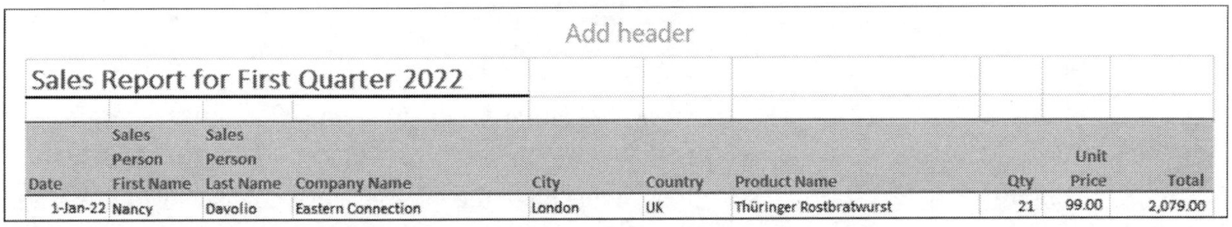
Add header

Sales Report for First Quarter 2022

Date	Sales Person First Name	Sales Person Last Name	Company Name	City	Country	Product Name	Qty	Unit Price	Total
1-Jan-22	Nancy	Davolio	Eastern Connection	London	UK	Thüringer Rostbratwurst	21	99.00	2,079.00

6 Save your work as *Sales Report-2.*

note

Can I change the default margin settings?

You can set the default margins, and any other Excel default setting, by incorporating the margin settings into a replacement *Blank Workbook* template.

The technique of using a replacement *Blank Workbook* template to change default settings is discussed in: *Lesson 4-9: Understand themes (sidebar).*

Lesson 7-3: Use Page Setup to set margins more precisely and center the worksheet

In the last lesson you adjusted the left margin using the horizontal ruler, and that's often the best way. It is quick and easy, and you can immediately see the results of the change on the printed output.

Sometimes you will want the pages in your report to have precise margins. This would be the case when you were going to insert the report into another report (perhaps prepared in Word) and you need the margins to be consistent throughout the publication.

Another common requirement is the need to center the report on the printed page.

1 Open *Sales Report-2* from your sample files folder (if it isn't already open).

2 Display *Page Layout* view (if you aren't already in it).

You learned how to do this in: *Lesson 7-2: Use Page Layout view to adjust margins.*

3 Set margins to the *Narrow* preset.

1. Click: Page Layout→Page Setup→Margins.

   A rich menu appears, showing three preset margin setups along with the last custom margins applied.

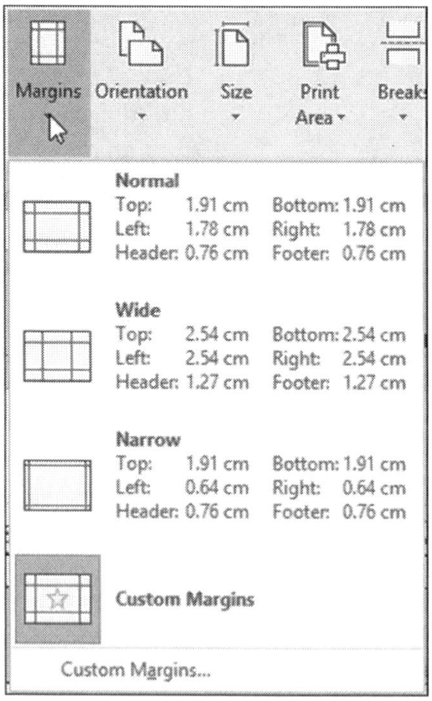

2. Click the *Narrow* option to apply left and right margins of 0.64cm.

   Notice that all of the margins have now changed to the *Narrow* specification.

note

If your margins display in inches instead of centimeters

Refer to: *Lesson 7-2: Use Page Layout view to adjust margins.*

During this lesson you should have set your ruler units to display in centimeters.

Sales Report-2

4 Set a custom left and right margin of exactly one centimeter.

Imagine that this report will be bound within another that uses margins of one centimeter.

Since there's no suitable preset, you'll have to apply the margins manually using the *Custom Margins* options.

1. Click:

   Page Layout→Page Setup→Margins→Custom Margins…

   The *Page Setup* dialog appears with the *Margins* tab selected.

2. Type directly into the text boxes, or use the spin buttons, to set the left and right margins to exactly one centimeter.

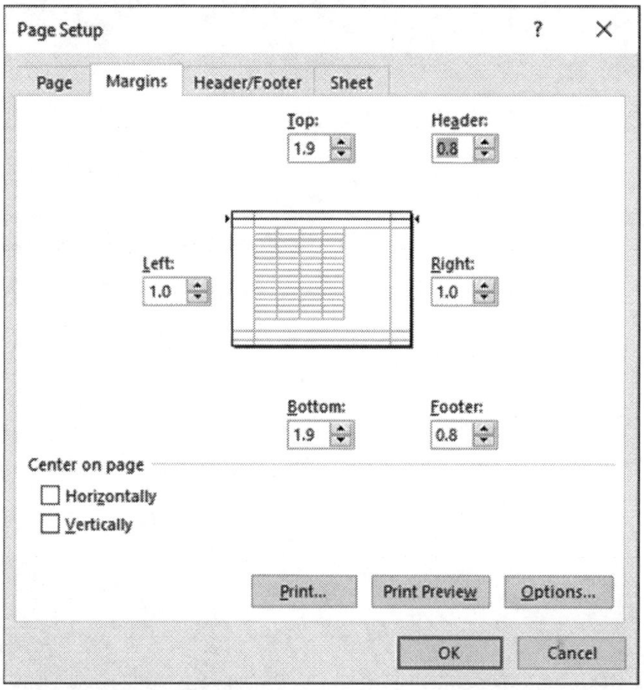

3. Click the OK button.

5 Horizontally center the printout on the page.

The page would look better centered.

1. Bring up the *Page Setup* dialog again by clicking:

   Page Layout→Page Setup→Margins→Custom Margins…

2. Check the *Center on page Horizontally* check box.

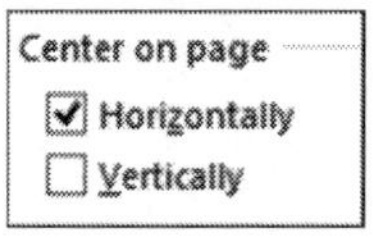

3. Click the OK button.

   The page is now perfectly centered, both on the screen and on any hard copy printed.

6 Save your work as *Sales Report-3.*

Lesson 7-4: Set paper size and scale

Imagine that *Landscape* orientation isn't an option for you.

You need *Portrait* orientation and you simply must print all of the columns on each page.

There's only two ways you can achieve this.

1. Buy some bigger paper. As long as your printer can accept it, you will have a larger area upon which to print.
2. Print everything in a smaller font.

The second option often works well (provided that you have good eyesight).

You'll be relieved to know that you don't have to manually re-format every font on the page. You can automatically scale the existing fonts to fit.

1 Open *Sales Report-3* from your sample files folder (if it isn't already open).

2 Display *Page Layout* view (if you aren't already in it).

This was covered in: *Lesson 7-2: Use Page Layout view to adjust margins.*

3 Change the paper orientation back to *Portrait.*

Click: Page Layout→Page Setup→Orientation→Portrait.

Notice that the columns no longer fit upon one sheet of paper.

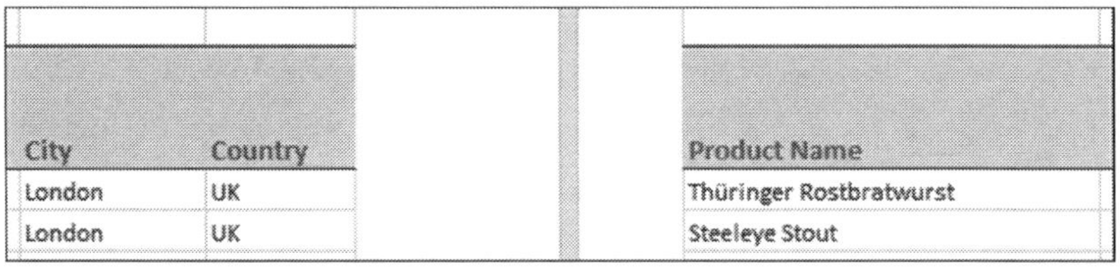

4 If possible, change the paper size to A3.

You will not see an A3 paper option if there are no printer drivers installed on your machine that support A3 (see sidebar).

Click: Page Layout→Page Setup→Size→A3.

In the USA and Canada, the nearest equivalent of A3 is ANSI B 17X11 (see sidebar on the facing page for more on this). For the purposes of this lesson, you should still set the size to A3 if you are able to.

That works fine. All columns now fit across one sheet of A3 paper.

But what if you don't have an A3 printer, or if the report has to fit on a sheet of A4 (or Letter sized) paper?

5 Change the paper size to A4 (or Letter) sized.

In every country in the world except the USA and Canada the normal business paper size is A4 (see facing page sidebar).

important

The paper sizes that are available depend upon the printer drivers installed on your machine

Excel sensibly restricts your choice of paper sizes to those that are supported by your printer(s).

If you do not have a printer driver installed that supports A3 paper, you will not see A3 in the list when you click:

Page Layout→Page Setup→Size

Sales Report-3

trivia

A4 and Letter paper size

A long time ago everybody used different sizes of paper until the Germans produced a DIN standard (Din 476) in 1922.

So good was their DIN standard (that defined the familiar A0, A1, A2, A3, A4… A8 sizes) that it was gradually adopted by every country in the world except the United States and Canada. It is also the official United Nations document format.

As DIN 476 was now a world standard, it was ratified in 1975 as ISO 216.

The genius behind the guiding principle of ISO 216 was the German scientist George Lichtenburg (1742-1799). George noticed that if a sheet of paper with an aspect ratio of the square root of two was folded in half, each half would also have the same aspect ratio.

The wonderful thing about this system is that paper merchants only need to stock one size of paper (A0) to be able to cut A1, A2, A3, A4...A8 without any waste. It also means that a document designed in any A size will perfectly scale to all other sizes in the series.

A0 has an area of 1 square meter. Fold it in half and you have A1. Fold that in half for A2, then in half again for A3 and so on.

The USA and Canada are the only major countries that use a different system.

In 1995 the American National Standards Institute defined a series of paper sizes based upon 8.5"X11" *Letter sized* paper. Unlike the ISO standard, the arbitrary size means that the series has alternating aspect ratios for other derivative sizes.

The ANSI A size (8.5X11) is the nearest to ISO A4 and the ANSI B size (17X11) is nearest to A3.

In the USA and Canada, the slightly narrower and longer Letter size (or ANSI A) is the most common.

Click: Page Layout→Page Setup→Size→A4.

6 Make the report fit on a sheet of A4 (or Letter size) paper by scaling.

Click the Page Layout→Scale to Fit→Scale spin button. Each time you reduce the percentage, the worksheet shrinks until it fits the page at about 70%.

Bear in mind that, even though it fits the page, the information on the page may not be very easy to read at such a small type size.

7 Make the report fit perfectly between the page margins.

Click: Page Layout→Scale to Fit→Width→1 page.

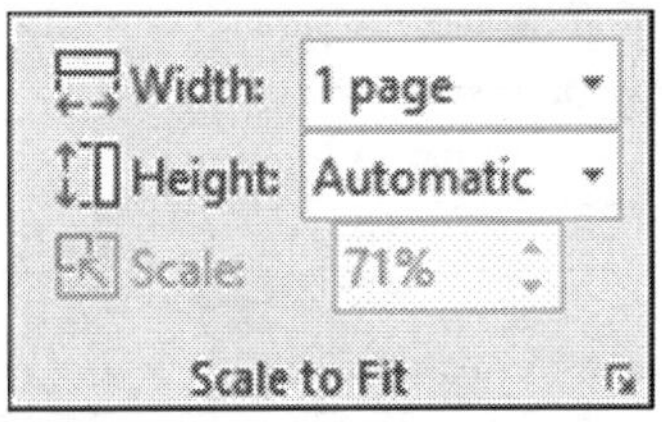

The content now perfectly fits between the page margins. This looks better and avoids the need to center the printout on the page.

8 Save your work as *Sales Report-4.*

Lesson 7-5: Insert, delete and preview page breaks

After you've either printed a worksheet (or entered *Page Layout* view or *Page Break Preview* and then returned to *Normal* view), you will see thin dotted lines indicating where the page will break.

Sometimes you need to take control of page breaks. This lesson will show you how.

1 Open *Sales Analysis Chart* from your sample file folder.

Note that no page breaks are shown. This is because the worksheet has never been printed or previewed.

2 Use the *Backstage Print* view to Print Preview the worksheet.

Click: File→Print.

The *Print Preview* reveals that the printout will cut the pie chart in half:

9-Oct-21	Germany	Dairy Products	1,112.00	USA
10-Oct-21	Spain	Condiments	422.40	Venezuela
10-Oct-21	Spain	Grains/Cereals	249.60	Grand Total
10-Oct-21	Spain	Beverages	310.00	
11-Oct-21	Sweden	Beverages	304.00	
11-Oct-21	Sweden	Dairy Products	672.00	
11-Oct-21	Sweden	Seafood	579.60	

You need to solve this problem by inserting a vertical page break.

3 Return to *Normal* view and notice that page breaks are now shown as dotted lines.

Click the *Back Button* at the top left of *Backstage View* to return to *Normal* view and notice the dotted lines showing the vertical and horizontal page breaks.

If you don't see any dotted lines, somebody may have disabled them. See the sidebar for instructions on how to switch them back on.

Vertical Break

	C	D	E	F
26	Beverages	310.00		
27	Beverages	304.00		
28	Dairy Products	672.00		

It is immediately clear where the problem lies. The vertical break needs to occur at the left of column E to solve the problem.

4 Insert a vertical page break to the left of column E.

1. Click in cell E1. It is important to choose row 1, otherwise both a horizontal and vertical page break would be inserted.
2. Click: Page Layout→Page Setup→Breaks→Insert Page Break.

note

If you don't see the dotted line page breaks, somebody has switched them off

By default, automatic page breaks are shown as dotted lines in *Normal* view. Manually inserted page breaks are shown as solid lines.

Like so many features in Excel, Microsoft has given users the ability to switch this feature off, though I can't imagine why anybody would want to.

If you don't see the dotted lines, somebody has done just that on your machine.

To bring the dotted lines back click:

File→Options→
Advanced→
Display options for this worksheet→Show page breaks

This check box needs to be checked in order to display page breaks in *Normal* view.

Sales Analysis Chart

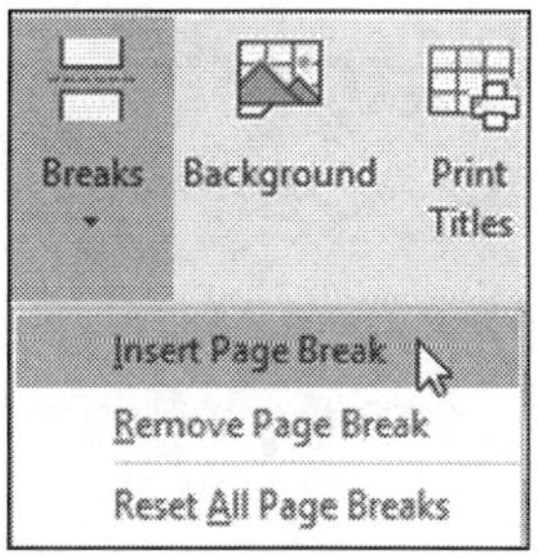

A solid line appears to the left of the active cell to show the new position of the vertical page break. When you see a solid line (rather than a dotted line) you know that the break was manually inserted (rather than automatically added by Excel).

5 Confirm that the worksheet will now print correctly.

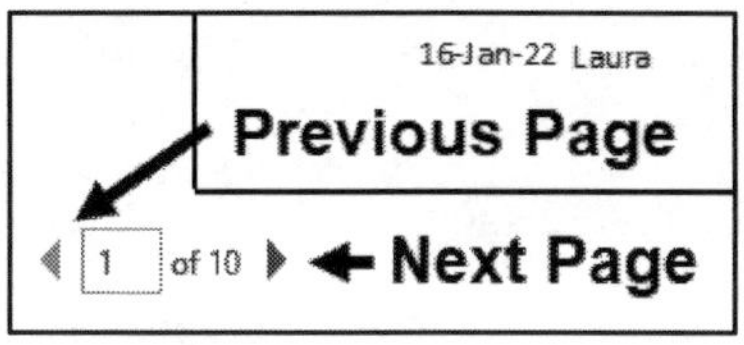

1. Click: File→Print. A preview is displayed showing how the worksheet will print.
2. Use the *Next Page* button to move to the last page that will print.
3. Click the *Back Button*  at the top left of *Backstage View* to return to *Normal* view.

note

You can type a page number directly into the page box to quickly move the preview to any page

In this lesson you clicked the *Next Page* button ten times to move from page one to page eleven.

You could also have done this by typing the number **11** into the page box and then pressing the **<Enter>** key.

6 Insert a horizontal page break above row 78.

Row 78 displays the first sale for November 2021.

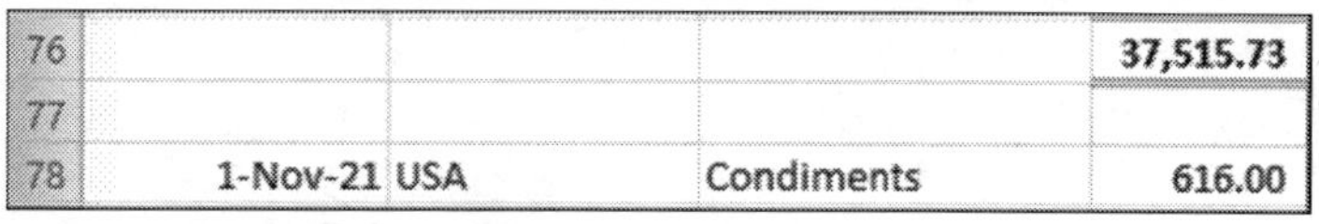

For presentational reasons you want November's sales to begin on a new page, so you need to insert a page break above row 78.

1. Click in cell A78. It's important to click in column A, otherwise both a horizontal and vertical page break would be inserted to the left of, and above the active cell.
2. Click: Page Layout→Page Setup→Breaks→Insert Page Break.

   A solid line appears above the active cell (row 78) to show the position of the new (manually inserted) horizontal page break.

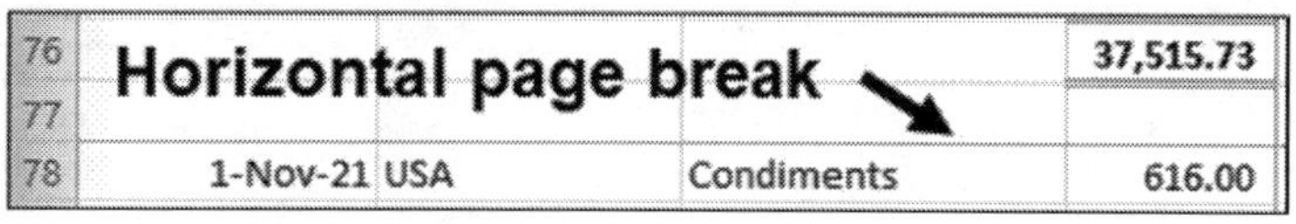

7 Confirm that the worksheet will now print correctly.

Print Preview the worksheet or view the page in *Page Layout* view.

The page now breaks at row 77 and a new page begins for row 78.

8 Remove the horizontal page break above row 78.

1. Click anywhere in row 78 except cell E78. If you were to select cell E78 you would remove both the horizontal and vertical page breaks.
2. Click: Page Layout→Page Setup→Breaks→ Remove Page Break.

   The solid line disappears, indicating that the page will no longer break before row 78.

9 Save your work as *Sales Analysis Chart-1*.

note

Your pages may break in a different place to the screen grabs shown in this lesson

In: *Lesson 7-4: Set paper size and scale (sidebar),* you learned that the two most widely used paper sizes are *Letter* sized (used in the USA and Canada) and *A4* (used in the rest of the world).

The screen grabs in this lesson were done using a computer that had A4 paper set as the default paper size for the default printer.

If your default printer uses *Letter Size* paper by default, you'll see the page breaks in a slightly different place.

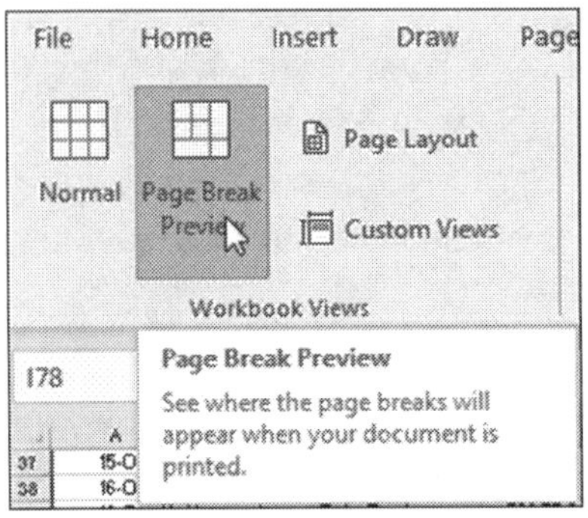

Sales Analysis Charts-1

Lesson 7-6: Adjust page breaks using Page Break Preview

In the last lesson you learned how to adjust page breaks in *Normal* view. Many users also like to adjust page breaks in *Page Layout* view.

Microsoft recommends that you don't use either. There's a purpose-built view just to handle page breaks called *Page Break Preview* view.

I tie my tongue in knots during my classes just trying to say *Page Break Preview view.*

This view allows you to click and drag page breaks (something that you can't do with the other views).

1 Open *Sales Analysis Chart-1* from your sample file folder (if it isn't already open).

2 Display *Page Break Preview* view.

Click the *Page Break Preview* button at the bottom right of the screen.

You can also select this view from the Ribbon by clicking:

View→Workbook Views→Page Break Preview

Just like *Normal View, Page Break Preview* allows you to see which breaks are manual and which are automatic. Breaks shown as solid lines were manually inserted. Breaks shown as dotted lines were automatically inserted by Excel.

	A	B	C	D	E
48	21-Oct-21	France	Confections	100.00	
49	22-Oct-21	Ireland	Beverages	85.12	
50	22-Oct-21	Ireland	Dairy Products	200.00	
51	22-Oct-21	Ireland	Dairy Products	122.88	

Notice that your manually inserted vertical break (to the left of column E) is shown as a solid line while Excel's automatic page break (after row 49) is shown as a dotted line.

3 Move the automatic break from between rows 99 and 100 to between rows 77 and 78.

1. Move the mouse cursor over the dotted blue line between rows 99 and 100 until you see the double-headed arrow cursor shape.

99	12-Nov-21	Portugal	Meat/Poultry	100.30
100	13-Nov-21	Austria	Dairy Products	161.28

2. When you see the double-headed arrow, click and drag to move the page break up the page so that the line is between rows 77 and 78.

When you release the mouse button, the page break is shown as a solid blue line.

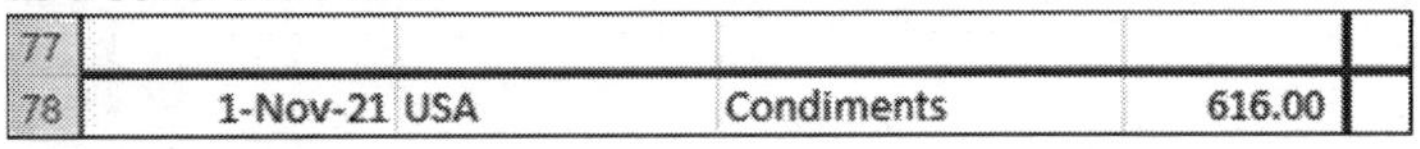

4 Automatically scale the sheet so that all of November's sales fit on one sheet.

An interesting feature of *Page Break Preview* is its ability to scale a page to fit the paper. You did this manually in: *Lesson 7-4: Set paper size and scale.* The process is far more intuitive in this view.

1. Scroll to row 127.

   Notice that there is an automatic page break between rows 127 and 128.

2. Drag this page break to a new position between rows 145 and 146.

   Excel hasn't inserted another automatic break anywhere in Page 3 even though Page 3 is now a lot longer than it was before. The only way that Excel can possibly print Page 3 is by automatically scaling it down to fit the page.

3. Click: File→Print to Print Preview the worksheet. Notice that the fonts for the entire report have been reduced. Excel cannot scale a single page in isolation; it scales all pages to keep the font size of all report pages consistent.

4. Click the *Back Button*  at the top left of *Backstage View* to return to *Page Break Preview* view.

tip

In Page Break Preview you can enter page breaks using a right-click

It is usually quicker to add page breaks by using the shortcut menu – the menu that appears when you right-click a cell.

1. Right-click the cell that you want the page break to appear above, or to the left of.
2. Click *Insert Page Break* from the shortcut menu.

5 Remove all manually applied page breaks.

Excel's automatic scaling system means that it is easy to lose track of what is happening. Sometimes you want to set everything back to the way it used to be and start again.

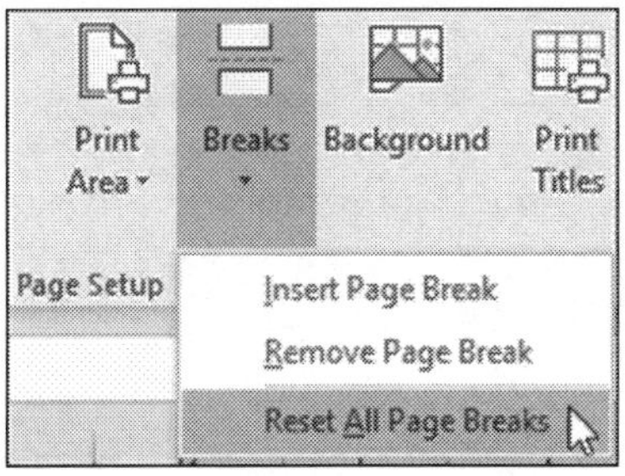

Click: Page Layout→Page Setup→Breaks→Reset All Page Breaks.

All solid lines disappear and Excel's automatic page breaks (shown as dotted lines) reappear.

6 Save your work as *Sales Analysis Chart-2.*

Lesson 7-7: Add auto-headers and auto-footers and set the starting page number

Headers and footers are displayed at the top and bottom of each printed page.

If you are printing a long report, it is very useful to add page numbers. Other items commonly added to page headers and footers include:

- A title.
- The date and time that the report was printed.
- The report author's name.
- The name of the Excel file that was used to generate the report.
- The full path to the Excel file.
- A company logo.
- Copyright notices.
- A distribution list or the security level of the document (for example you may want to include the word: *Confidential*).

1 Open *Sales Report-4* from your sample files folder.

2 Display *Page Layout* view (if you aren't already in it).

You learned how to do this in: *Lesson 7-2: Use Page Layout view to adjust margins.*

3 Scroll to the top of the worksheet.

4 Click in the page header area at the top of the screen.

The page header area contains the text: *Add header*.

When you click in this area a new Ribbon tab appears.

You will use the *Header & Footer* Ribbon tab to access Excel's *Auto Header and Footer* feature.

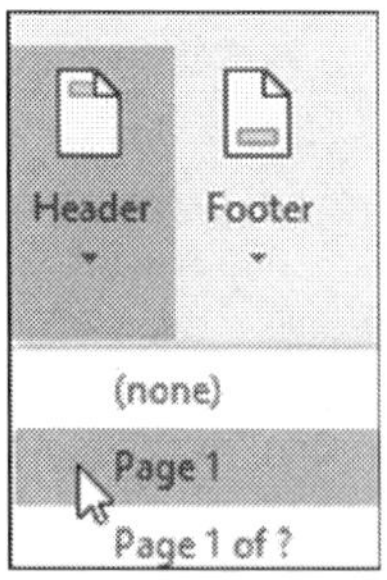

Sales Report-4

5 Add an Auto Header that will display page numbers at the top of each page in the format: *Page 1*.

When you click in the header area you are able to access the *Header & Footer* Ribbon tab.

1. Click:

   Header & Footer→Header & Footer→Header

2. Choose the option *Page 1* (see sidebar). Page numbers are now shown at the top of each page (you may need to scroll up and down the page to see the page number update).

6 **Add an Auto-Footer to show the filename at the bottom of the page.**

1. Click in the *Add footer* area at the bottom of any page.

2. Click:

   Header & Footer→Hader & Footer→Footer

3. Choose the *Sales Report-4* item from the drop-down list (see sidebar).

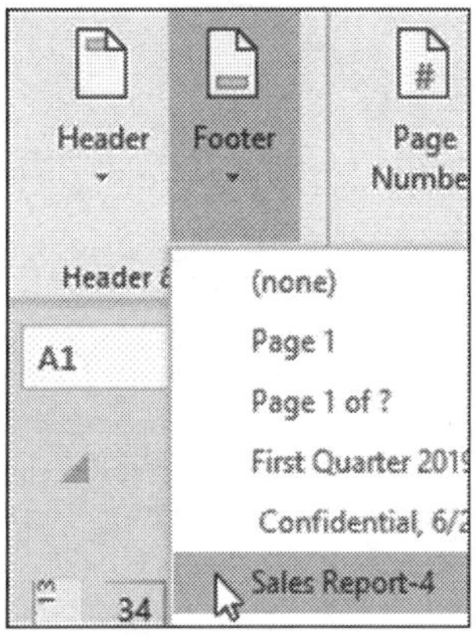

   The filename is now shown at the bottom of every page in the report (you may need to scroll up and down the page to see the footer update).

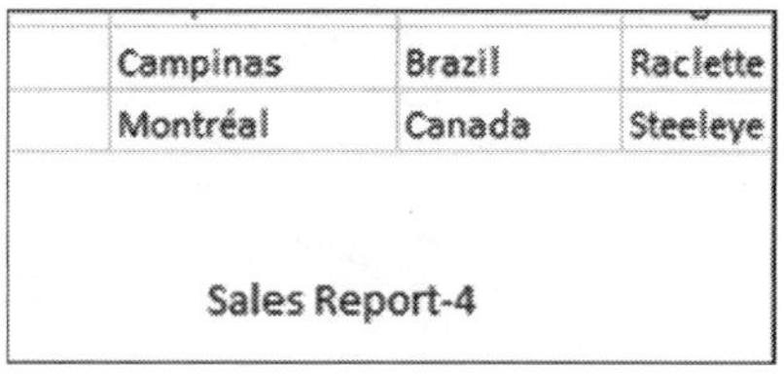

7 **Change the page numbering so that numbering begins at page ten.**

It is very common to print an Excel report and then collate it into another report (perhaps produced using Word). If the pages were to be inserted after page nine you would want Excel to begin numbering at page ten.

1. Click: Page Layout→Page Setup→Dialog Launcher.

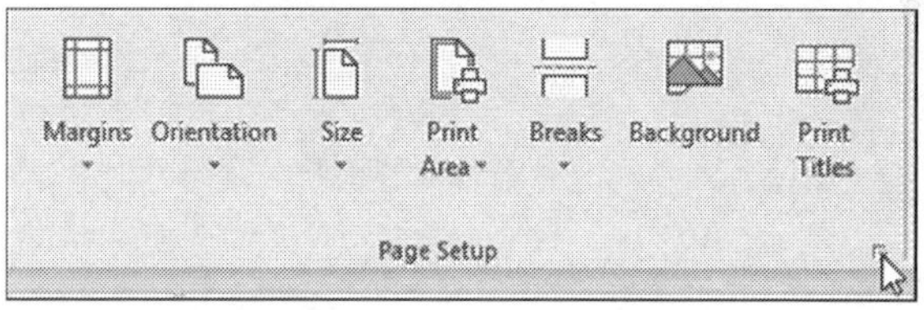

2. Click the *Page* tab and type the number 10 into the *First page number* text box.

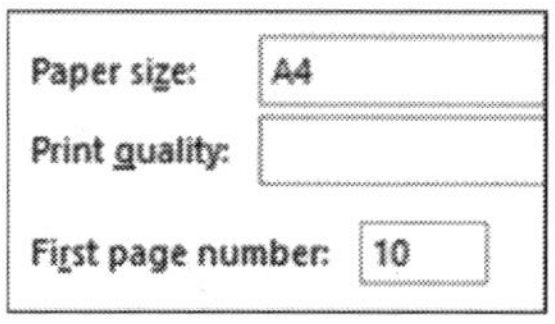

   Click the OK button. Page numbering now begins at Page 10.

8 **Save your work as *Sales Report-5*.**

note

You can edit a header and footer on any page

It doesn't matter which page you add your header and footer to.

You can add or edit header and footer information on any page, and it will then automatically apply to every other page.

Later in this session (in: *Lesson 7-9: Specify different headers and footers for the first, odd and even pages*) you'll explore a technique that will allow you to have multiple headers and footers in a single worksheet.

Lesson 7-8: Add custom headers and footers

Auto-headers and footers provide a quick and convenient method when your needs are simple. Custom headers allow you to combine your own text with report fields (such as page numbers). You are also able to add text to three different sections in the header and footer areas (Left, Right and Center).

1 Open *Sales Report-5* from your sample files folder (if it isn't already open).

2 Display *Page Layout* view (if you aren't already in it).

This was covered in: *Lesson 7-2: Use Page Layout view to adjust margins.*

3 Click in the *Page Header* area.

Notice that when you click the *Page Header* area the contents change from *Page 10* to *Page &[Page].*

The Ampersand (&) is called an *escape character*. It tells Excel that whatever text follows is a field rather than literal text. The field *&[Page]* tells Excel to insert the current page number.

4 Change the page header to: *The Gourmet Food Company.*

Click in the center of the header area (where you currently see the page number) and type: **The Gourmet Food Company**

5 Place the date and time in the left-hand part of the page header.

There's no Auto-header for date and time. In this case you'll have to create your own custom header field.

1. Click in the **left-hand** section of the header area.

2. Type the text **Printed on:** followed by a space.
3. Click: Header & Footer→Header & Footer Elements→Current Date.

4. Type a space followed by **at:** and then another space.
5. Click: Header & Footer→Header & Footer Elements→Current Time.

The left-hand section of the header bar now contains the following text:

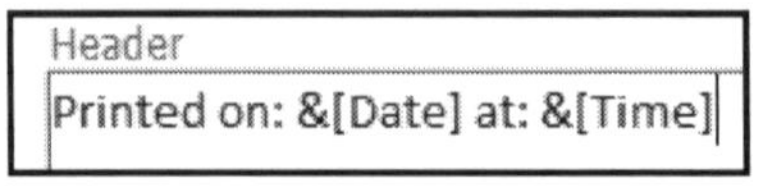

note

How to include an ampersand in a header or footer

In the header and footer area, the ampersand (&) denotes the beginning of a field.

Sometimes you will need to put an ampersand into header text. For example, your company might be called:

Marks & Spencer

To do this you need to incorporate a double ampersand into the header to tell Excel to print the ampersand. You would need to type:

Marks && Spencer

note

Headers and footers may have multiple lines

You can make your header and footer information span as many lines as you need. Press the **<Enter>** key when you want to move to a new line.

If you use many lines, it may be necessary to adjust the top margin as the header can sometimes overlap the worksheet.

Sales Report-5

When you click away from the header section the date and time are displayed. The date is displayed in a format dictated by the region format of your operating system (called the locale in previous Windows versions). In this example it is the date: Jan 7, 2022 displayed in USA format (month/day/year):

Printed on: 1/7/2022 at: 3:37 PM

6 Place the page number on the right-hand side of the page header.

There is an *Auto Header* for this purpose, but you can't use it. Auto headers may only be used in the center section of the header. You'll have to make your own using the *Header & Foot er Elements* just as you did for the date and time.

1. Click in the right-hand part of the page header and type **Page:** followed by a space (the space won't appear on screen but don't worry, it is there).
2. Click: Header & Footer→ Header & Footer Elements→Page Number.

   The right-hand section of the header bar now contains the following text:

   Page: &[Page]

   When you click away from the header section, the current page number is displayed:

   Page: 10

Printed on: 1/7/2022 at: 3:40 PM	The Gourmet Food Company	Page: 10

7 Apply an attractive format to the page header section.

1. Click the left-hand section of the header. The text is automatically selected.

   Header
   Printed on: &[Date] at &[Time]

2. Click: Home→Font→Font and set the font face to *Calibri Light 10 Point Bold*. Note that, following good design practice, this is one of the two theme fonts (see sidebar).
3. Click: Home→Font→Font Color and set the color to the *Blue-Gray, Text 2* theme color.
4. Apply the same format to the right-hand section of the header.
5. Format the center section of the header as *Calibri Light, 28 point, Blue-Gray, Text 2*.

Printed on: 1/7/2022 at: 3:43 PM	The Gourmet Food Company	Page: 10

8 Save your work as *Sales Report-6.*

note

Adding a graphical header

Sometimes you will need a page header that requires more sophisticated formatting than Excel is capable of. The solution is to create the header as a graphic using a program such as Adobe Photoshop.

When the graphic has been prepared click:

Header & Footer→
Header & Footer Elements→
Picture

You are then able to insert the graphic into the header.

When a graphic appears in the header a new *Format Picture* button appears in the *Header & Footer Elements* group.

note

Good design practice

It is always a good idea to restrict your font choice to one of the two provided by the current theme.

The reasons for this are discussed in *Lesson 4-11: Add color and gradient effects to cells* (sidebar).

Lesson 7-9: Specify different headers and footers for the first, odd and even pages

If you look at the pages in this book, you'll notice that there's a different header and footer for odd and even pages. The first page of each session is also different.

If the sample worksheet needed to be inserted into a publication similar to this book, you'd need to specify three different headers and footers, one for odd pages, one for even pages, and one for the first page.

1 *Open Sales Report-6* from your sample files folder (if it isn't already open).

2 Display *Normal* view.

Click the *Normal* view button at the bottom right of the screen.

3 Insert five blank rows above row 1.

You learned how to do this in: *Lesson 3-1: Insert and delete rows and columns.*

4 Insert a manual page break above row 6.

You learned how to do this in: *Lesson 7-5: Insert, delete and preview page breaks.*

A solid line appears above row 6.

5 Merge and center cells A2:J2 and enter the text: **Sales Report Jan-Mar 2022** into the merged cell.

You learned how to do this in: *Lesson 4-6: Merge cells, wrap text and expand/collapse the formula bar.*

6 Apply the *Title* style to the newly added text.

You learned how to do this in: *Lesson 4-10: Use cell styles and change themes.*

7 Merge and center cells A3:J3 and enter the text: **Private & Confidential**

8 Apply the *Heading 4* style to the newly added text.

9 Apply a fill color of *Blue, Accent1, Lighter 80%* to cells A2:A3.

Sales Report-6

10 Resize row 1 so that it is about 200 pixels deep.

11 *Print Preview* the worksheet.

Click: File→Print.

You can see that you've created a cover sheet for the report. It doesn't look bad, but the header and footer are spoiling things. You need to suppress the header and footer from the cover sheet.

12 Remove the header and footer from the first (cover) page.

1. Click the *Back Button* at the top left of *Backstage View* to return to *Normal* view.
2. Change the view to *Page Layout* view.
3. Click in the *Header* area of any page.
4. Click: Header & Footer→ Options→Different First Page.

   The header and footer information vanish from the cover page.

13 Set a different odd and even page header and footer.

1. Click in any *Header* area.
2. Click Header & Footer→ Options→Different Odd & Even Pages.

   The header and footer information vanishes from odd pages but remains on even pages.

14 Remove all header and footer information.

You're going to replace the existing page header and footer, so delete the contents of all header and footer sections.

15 Add odd and even page footers so that the page number appears on the right of all odd pages and on the left of all even pages.

If you look at the footer of this book, you will see that the page numbers are arranged in this manner.

1. Click in the footer area of any of the pages except the first page.
2. Insert a page number into the odd and even page footer area.

   You learned how to do this in: *Lesson 7-8: Add custom headers and footers.*

   Notice that when you click in the footer area, Excel indicates which footer you are editing (odd or even).

Results in→

   You may wonder why Excel thinks that even pages are odd, and odd pages are even, see the sidebar for an explanation.

While a cover page is useful in all reports, different odd and even page footers (or headers) will only improve the presentation of reports that will be printed on both sides of the paper and then bound.

16 Save your work as *Sales Report-7.*

Important

Page numbering confusion

You have set this workbook to begin its page numbering at page 10 (an even page).

As far as Excel is concerned the "real" starting page number is page one (an odd page).

This can cause a little confusion as you will find:

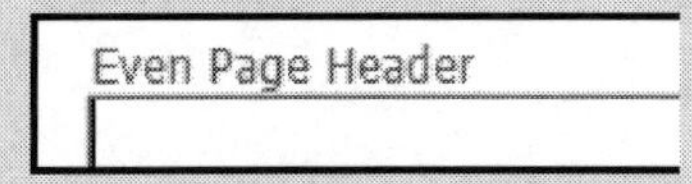

... at the top of the second page in this report even though it has a page number of eleven and is thus an odd page.

Excel uses the "real" page numbers when it labels the page header and footer areas.

Lesson 7-10: Print only part of a worksheet

Sometimes you will want to print a selection of cells from a worksheet.

Excel provides two ways to do this. The first method is applicable when the requirement is a one-off. In other words, the next time you print, the entire worksheet will be printed in the usual way.

The second method involves setting a print area. If you then save the worksheet, the defined print area will remain until you clear the print area.

In this lesson you'll explore both methods.

1 Open *Sales Report-7* from your sample files folder (if it isn't already open).

2 Display *Normal* view.

Click the *Normal* view button at the bottom right of the screen.

Imagine that you need to print a listing for all of January's sales.

3 Select all of the transactions for January 2022 (cells A8:J93).

4 Print only the selected cells.

1. Click: File→Print.

   The *Backstage Print* view is displayed showing many print settings along with a print preview.

   Notice the first option in the *Settings* list currently shows:

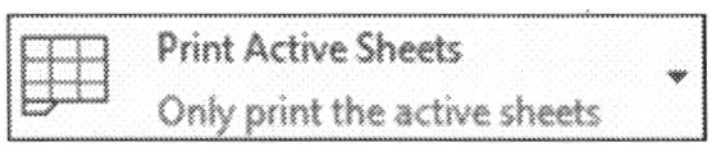

2. Click the drop-down arrow and select *Print Selection* from the drop-down list:

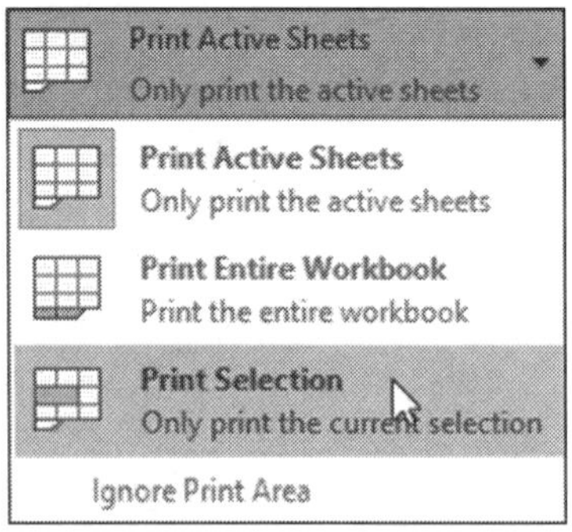

   Notice that only January transactions (cells A8:J93) are now displayed in the right-hand *Print Preview* window.

   If you were to click the *Print* button at this stage only January sales would be printed.

5 Save, close and re-open the workbook and then enter *Backstage Print* view.

note

Print areas do not have to be contiguous

You may want to print several different sections from your worksheet.

Simply select the non-contiguous (non-adjacent) ranges (covered in: *Lesson 2-7: Select non-contiguous cell ranges and view summary information*) and then use either of the techniques discussed in this lesson to print the selected cells.

trivia

Origins of the term: "One-off"

Many years ago, I studied engineering and spent part of my time discovering the joys of lathes, milling machines, grinders and all of the other paraphernalia found in machine shops.

Sometimes I would wander around the factory where the lathe operators would sit next to their machines – usually reading a book.

They would have a specification drawing next to them with something like "600 Off" written on it. This would mean that they would make 600 parts to the defined specification.

A *One-off* would be quite unusual as it would be expensive to set-up the lathe to produce just one part.

The term "one-off" is now commonly used in the UK to describe something that happens, or is made, only once.

Sales Report-7

1. Save and close *Sales Report-7.*
2. Re-open *Sales Report-7.*
3. Click: File→Print to return to *Backstage Print* view.

   Notice that the print settings have reverted to *Print Active Sheets.*

   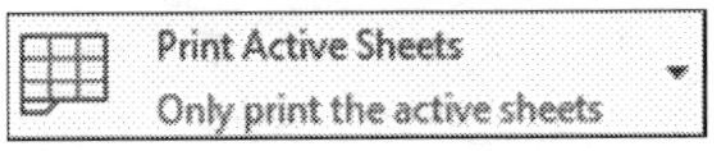

   In other words, the instruction to only print the selected cells is lost when the workbook is closed (even if it is saved first).

   But consider the case of a worksheet where you will only ever want to print a selected range. In this case you'd like the print settings to be saved with the workbook.

6 Set the print area to Jan 2022 transactions (A8:J93).

1. Click the *Back Button*  at the top left of *Backstage View* to return to *Normal* View.
2. Select cells A8:J93.
3. Click: Page Layout→Page Setup→Print Area→Set Print Area.

   When you set the print area it remains set even if you close and re-open a workbook.
4. Click: File→Print to return to *Backstage Print* view.

   Notice that only January sales are shown in the preview in the right pane of the window.

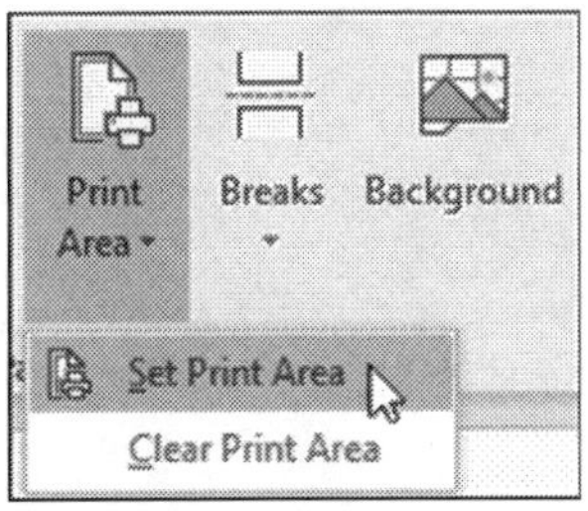

> **note**
>
> **The print area is implemented using a named range**
>
> Excel has a feature called "named ranges". The definition and use of named ranges are expert-level skills covered in the next book in this series: *Learn Excel 2021 Expert Skills with The Smart Method.*
>
> When you set a print area, Excel simply creates a sheet-level named range called *Print Area* for the currently active worksheet. Each worksheet can have its own print area.
>
> If you do progress to become an Excel Expert, it is possible to define this named range manually and to use it in formulas.

7 Save, close and re-open the workbook and then enter *Backstage Print* view.

1. Save and close *Sales Report-7.*
2. Re-open *Sales Report-7.*
3. Click: File→Print to return to *Backstage Print* view.

   Notice that only January sales are still shown in the preview in the right pane of the window, proving that the print area was saved with the workbook

8 Clear the print area.

1. Click the *Back Button*  at the top left of *Backstage View* to return to *Normal* View.
2. Click: Page Layout→Page Setup→Print Area→
   Clear Print Area.

9 Print preview to prove that the full worksheet will be printed in future.

Click: File→Print to enter *Backstage Print* view.

Notice that the cover sheet, along with all sales, are now shown in the preview in the right pane of the window.

10 Save *Sales-Report 7.*

Lesson 7-11: Add row and column data labels and gridlines to printed output

1 Open *Sales Report-7* from your sample files folder (if it isn't already open).

2 View the worksheet in *Page Layout* view.

There's a slight problem with this worksheet. The first page is easy to understand as it has a column header row to indicate which data is in each column (such as *Date, City* and *Company Name*):

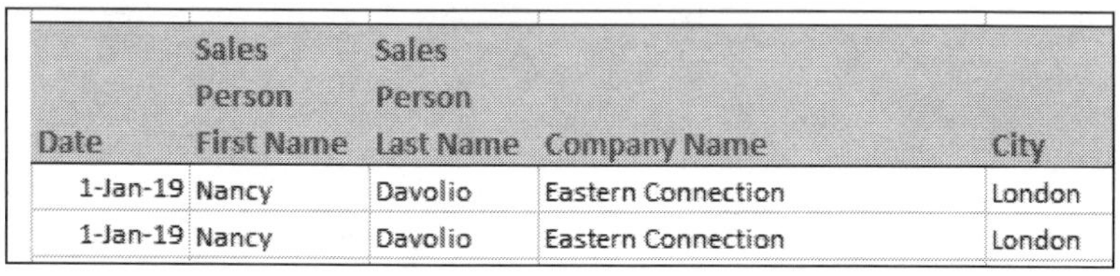

Date	Sales Person First Name	Sales Person Last Name	Company Name	City
1-Jan-19	Nancy	Davolio	Eastern Connection	London
1-Jan-19	Nancy	Davolio	Eastern Connection	London

The second page isn't so easy to understand because the column header row is missing:

23-Jan-19	Robert	King	Mère Paillarde	Montréal
23-Jan-19	Robert	King	Mère Paillarde	Montréal
24-Jan-19	Michael	Suyama	La maison d'Asie	Toulouse

3 Add column headings to each printed page.

1. Make sure that row 8 is visible on screen.

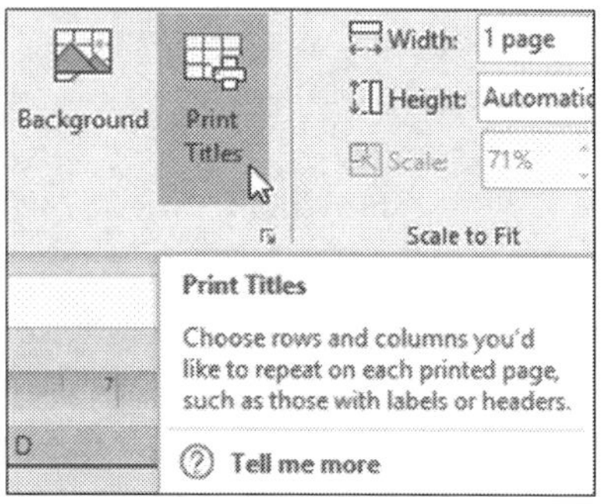

2. Click: Page Layout→Page Setup→Print Titles.

   The *Page Setup* dialog is displayed with the *Sheet* tab selected.

3. Click inside the *Rows to repeat at top* text box.
4. Select all of row 8 by clicking anywhere in row 8.

   The row reference appears in the dialog.

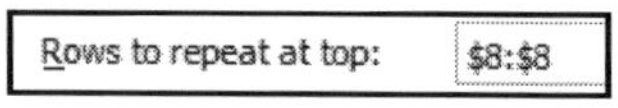

   The dollar signs denote an absolute reference. You learned about absolute references in: *Lesson 3-13: Understand absolute and relative cell references.*

5. Click the OK button

   Notice that the column headings now appear for every page in the printout.

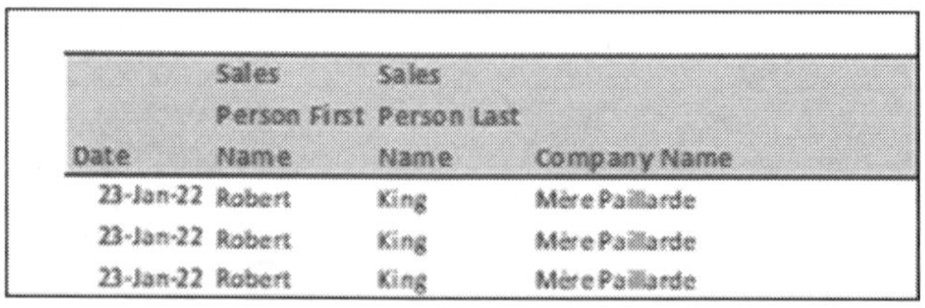

Date	Sales Person First Name	Sales Person Last Name	Company Name
23-Jan-22	Robert	King	Mère Paillarde
23-Jan-22	Robert	King	Mère Paillarde
23-Jan-22	Robert	King	Mère Paillarde

4 Add gridlines to the printout.

Sometimes it is difficult for the eye to track across printed lines. For this type of report, it is useful to print gridlines onto the printed page in a similar way to the ones displayed on the worksheet.

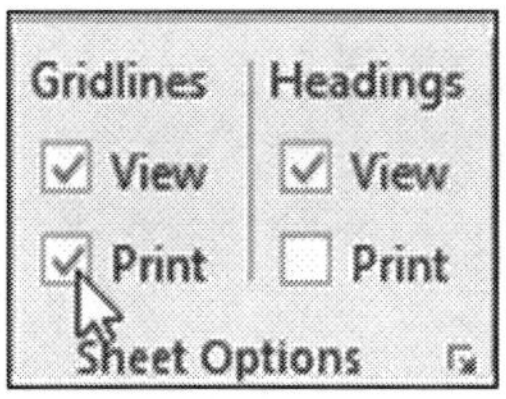

Click: Page Layout→Sheet Options→Gridlines→Print.

5 Print Preview the worksheet.

Click: File→Print to enter *Backstage Print* view.

The *Print Preview* in the right-hand pane shows that gridlines will be printed upon each page:

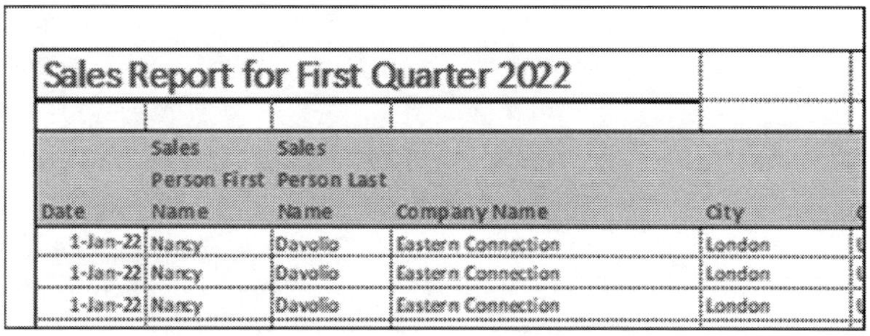

6 Add row and column headings to the printout.

You may want to send a printed worksheet to a colleague and then discuss it on the telephone. It might be useful to be able to ask: "what do you think of the value in cell H11?" This isn't possible because row and column headers are not normally shown on the printed page.

1. Click the *Back Button*  at the top left of *Backstage View* to return to *Page Layout View.*

2. Click: Page Layout→Sheet Options→Headings→Print.

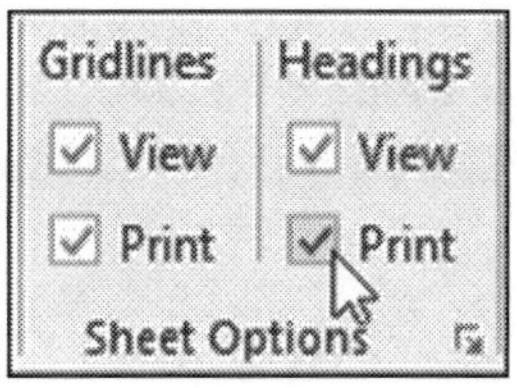

7 *Print Preview* the worksheet.

Click: File→Print to enter *Backstage Print* view.

The *Print Preview* in the right-hand pane shows that row and column headers will be printed upon each page:

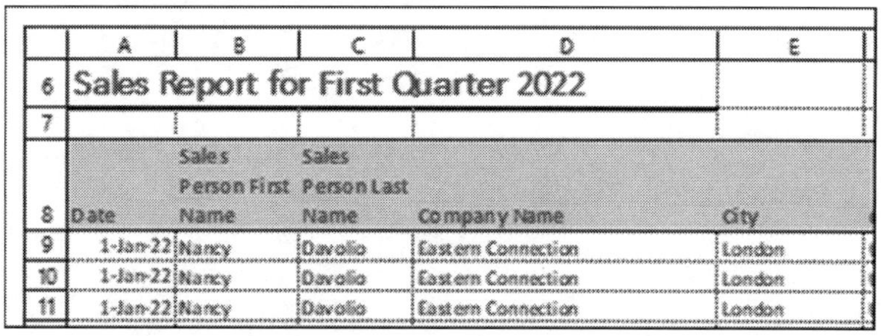

8 Remove the gridlines and column headers from the printout.

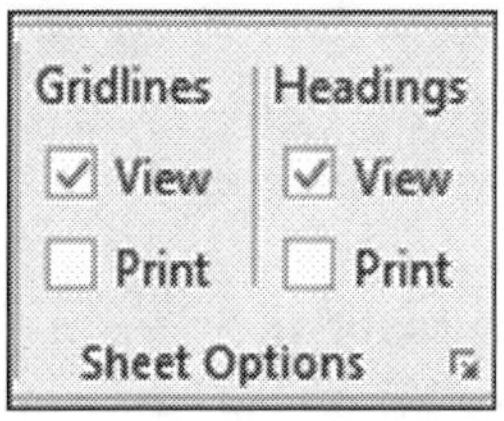

1. Click the *Back Button*  at the top left of *Backstage View* to return to *Page Layout* View.

2. Clear the two check boxes that were ticked in the previous steps (see sidebar).

9 Save your work as *Sales Report-8*.

Lesson 7-12: Print several selected worksheets and change the page order

1 Open *Palace Hotel Bar Activity* from your sample files folder.

2 Print Preview the worksheet.

1. Click: File→Print to enter *Backstage Print* view.
2. Use the *Next Page* button  at the bottom left of the *Print Preview* window 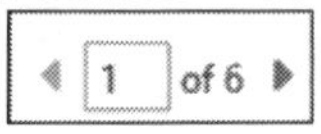

to view each page in the report.

   Notice that the worksheet prints downward first (listing all activity between 11:00 AM and 3:00 PM for all days).

   When it reaches the bottom of the list it moves across to print all activity between 4:00 PM and 9:00 PM and so on.

3 Change the view to *Page Break Preview*.

1. Click the *Back Button*  at the top left of *Backstage View* to return to *Normal View.*
2. Click the *Page Break Preview* button at the bottom right of the screen.

In this view it is easy to see the page order by looking at the watermarks on each page (the watermarks are the transparent large gray text saying *Page 1, Page* 2 etc).

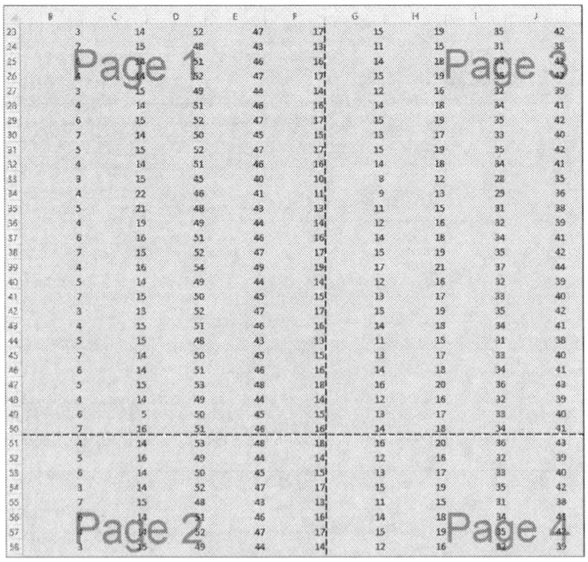

But what if you don't want to print in this order? Perhaps you would like to first print all activity for all times. In other words, you want the above display to make the existing *Page 3* into *Page* 2.

Palace Hotel Bar Activity

4 Change the print order to *Over, then down*.

1. Click: Page Layout→Page Setup→Dialog Launcher.

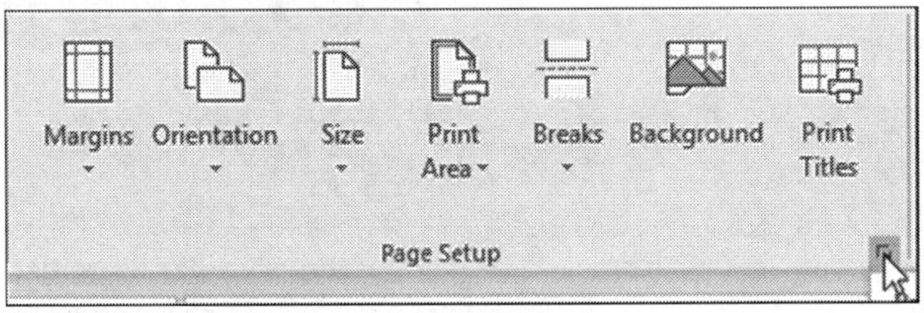

2. Click the *Sheet* tab.

3. Click the *Over, then down* option button.

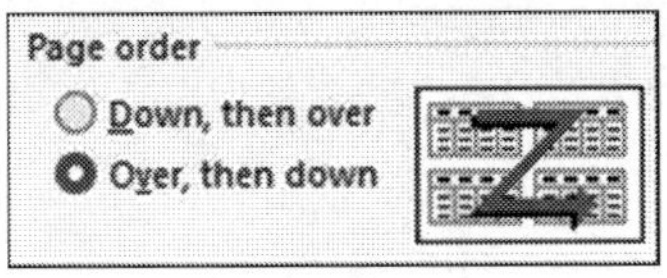

4. Click the OK button.

   It can be seen from the page break preview that the page order has now changed.

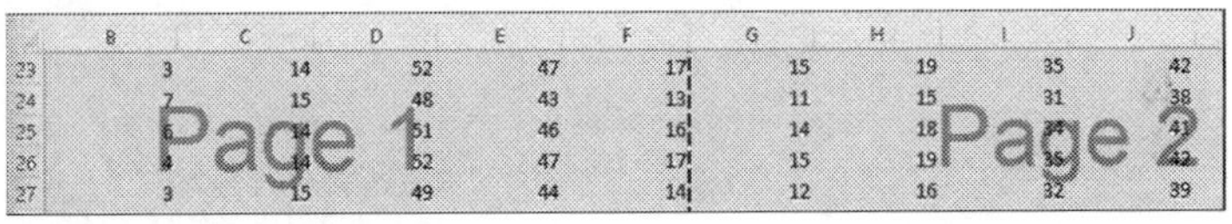

5 Print the headcount for *Jul-Aug* and *Nov-Dec* in one printout.

You can print several worksheets at the same time, and they needn't be adjacent.

1. Click the *Jul-Aug* tab.

2. Hold down the **<Ctrl>** key and click the *Nov-Dec* tab.

   Both tabs are now colored white

3. Click: File→Print.

   The *Backstage Print* view is displayed.

   Note that when more than one worksheet is selected, the first item in the *Settings* list has the *Print Active Sheets* option selected.

4. Click the *Next Page* button at the bottom left of the print preview to confirm that the contents of the *Jul-Aug* and *Nov-Dec* worksheets would have been printed.

5. Click the *Back Button*  at the top left of *Backstage View* to return to *Page Break Preview*.

6 Save your work as *Palace Hotel Bar Activity-1*.

Lesson 7-13: Suppress error messages in printouts

Excel has several built-in error messages such as the divide by zero error:

#DIV/0!

Sometimes you're quite happy to have these errors appear in a worksheet. For example, divide by zero errors could be quite normal when there is incomplete data.

Even though the errors are fine in the worksheet, you may not want them to appear in your printed output.

1 Open *Average Revenue per Sale* from your sample files folder.

2 View the worksheet in *Normal* view.

	A	B	C	D	E
1	Average Revenue Per Sale				
2					
3	**First Name**	**Last Name**	**Sales**	**Units**	**Average Revenue per Sale**
4	Andrew	Fuller	7,639.30	15	509.29
5	Anne	Dodsworth	-	-	#DIV/0!
6	Janet	Leverling	29,658.60	60	494.31
7	Laura	Callahan	19,271.60	40	481.79
8	Margaret	Peacock	44,795.20	90	497.72
9	Michael	Suyama	4,109.80	8	513.73
10	Nancy	Davolio	-	-	#DIV/0!
11	Robert	King	21,461.60	43	499.11
12	Steven	Buchanan	2,634.40	5	526.88
13		Total:	**129,570.50**	**261.00**	

This is an example of a worksheet with errors. In actual fact, you are simply waiting for Anne Dodsworth and Nancy Davolio to send you their sales figures, so the errors shown in cells E5 and E10 aren't really errors.

Divide by zero errors occur when you attempt to divide any number by zero.

You want to print out this interim report but replace the ugly #DIV/0 errors with a blank space on the printed page.

3 Replace errors with a blank space in printed output.

1. Click: Page Layout→Page Setup→Dialog launcher.

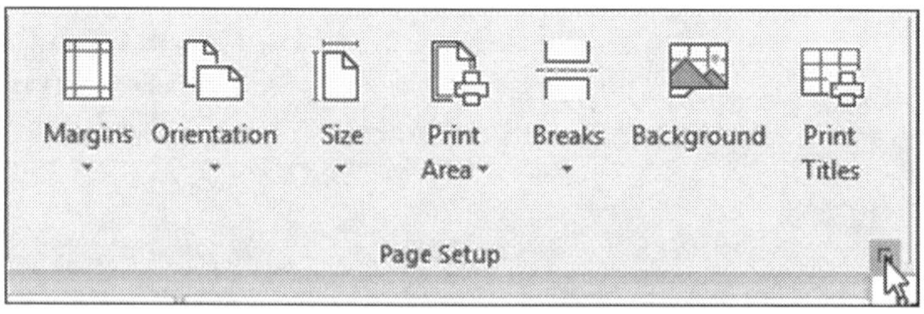

Average Revenue per Sale

The *Page Setup* dialog appears.

2. Click the *Sheet* tab.
3. Click the *Cell errors as* dropdown list and then click *<blank>*.

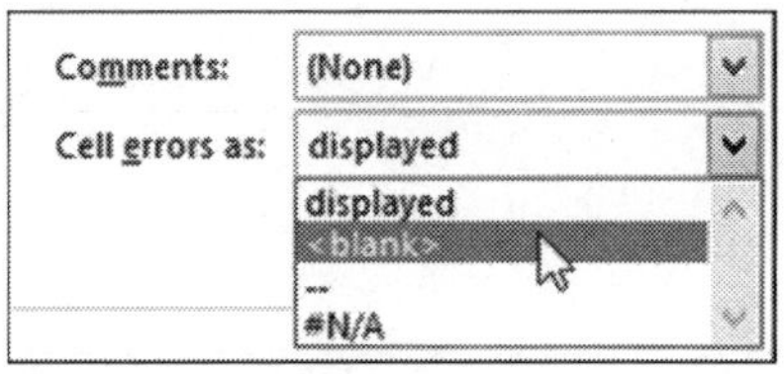

4. Click the OK button.

4 *Print Preview* the worksheet.

1. Click: File→Print to open *Backstage Print* view.

   The errors are no longer printed. Blank spaces are substituted for the divide by zero errors.

Average Revenue Per Sale

First Name	Last Name	Sales	Units	Average Revenue per Sale
Andrew	Fuller	7,639.30	15	509.29
Anne	Dodsworth	-	-	
Janet	Leverling	29,658.60	60	494.31
Laura	Callahan	19,271.60	40	481.79
Margaret	Peacock	44,795.20	90	497.72
Michael	Suyama	4,109.80	8	513.73
Nancy	Davolio	-	-	
Robert	King	21,461.60	43	499.11
Steven	Buchanan	2,634.40	5	526.88
	Total:	129,570.50	261.00	

2. Click the *Back Button* at the top left of *Backstage View* to return to *Normal View*.

5 Save your work as *Average Revenue per Sale-1*.

Session 7: Exercise

1 Open *Exercise 7* from your sample files folder.

2 Change to *Page Layout* view.

3 Change the left margin to about 1.0 cm using the click and drag method.

4 Click: Page Layout→Page Setup→Margins and use the *Custom Margins…* option to set top and bottom margins to precisely 2.0 cm and the left and right margins to precisely 1.0 cm.

5 Horizontally center the printout on the page.

6 Change the page orientation to landscape.

7 Change the view to *Page Break Preview*.

8 Insert a horizontal page break between rows 27 and 28.

9 Move the page break so that it now occurs between row 24 and 25.

10 Change to *Page Layout* view.

11 Add an auto-header to match the following:

Page 1 of 3

12 Make the data labels in row 1 repeat on every page.

13 Set the print area to A1:J12 and then *Print Preview* to prove that only these cells would be printed.

14 Clear the print area.

15 Add gridlines to the printout.

16 *Print Preview* to prove that gridlines would be printed.

Page 2 of 4

Date	Sales Person First Name	Sales Person Last Name	Company Name	City	Country
8-Jan-22	Laura	Callahan	Folies gourmandes	Lille	France
8-Jan-22	Laura	Callahan	Folies gourmandes	Lille	France
8-Jan-22	Laura	Callahan	Folies gourmandes	Lille	France

17 Save your work as *Exercise 7-End*.

Exercise 7

Session 7: Exercise answers

These are the questions that students find the most difficult to answer:

Q 13	Q 12	Q 8	Q 5
1. Select cells A1:J12. 2. Click: Page Layout→ Page Setup→ Print Area→ Set Print Area 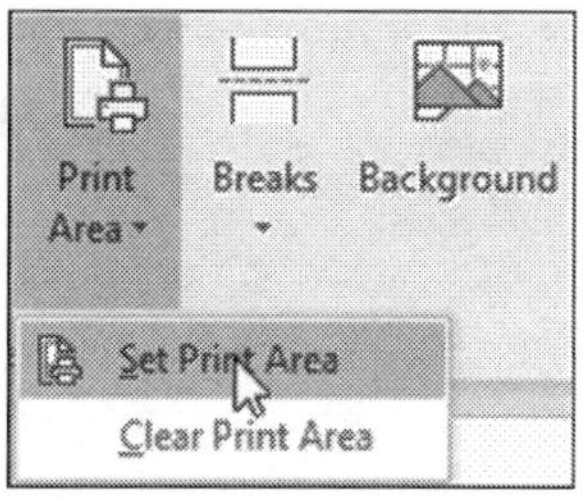 This was covered in: *Lesson 7-10: Print only part of a worksheet.*	1. Click: Page Layout→ Page Setup→Print Titles 2. Click in the *Rows to repeat at top* text box. 3. Either click in row 1 with the mouse or type 1:1 into the box. This was covered in: *Lesson 7-11: Add row and column data labels and gridlines to printed output.*	1. Click in cell A28. 2. Click: Page Layout→ Page Setup→ Breaks→ Insert Page Break This was covered in: *Lesson 7-5: Insert, delete and preview page breaks.*	1. Click: Page Layout→ Page Setup→ Dialog launcher.  2. Click the *Margins* tab. 3. Check the *Center on page Horizontally* check box. This was covered in: *Lesson 7-3: Use Page Setup to set margins more precisely and center the worksheet.*

If you have difficulty with the other questions, here are the lessons that cover the relevant skills:

1 **Lesson 1-9: Open and navigate a workbook.**

2,3 **Lesson 7-2: Use Page Layout view to adjust margins.**

4 **Lesson 7-3: Use Page Setup to set margins more precisely and center the worksheet.**

6 **Lesson 7-1: Print Preview and change paper orientation.**

7 **Lesson 7-6: Adjust page breaks using Page Break Preview.**

9 **Lesson 7-6: Adjust page breaks using Page Break Preview.**

10 **Lesson 7-2: Use Page Layout view to adjust margins.**

11 **Lesson 7-7: Add auto-headers and auto-footers and set the starting page number.**

14 **Lesson 7-10: Print only part of a worksheet.**

15 **Lesson 7-11: Add row and column data labels and gridlines to printed output.**

16 **Lesson 7-1: Print Preview and change paper orientation.**

17 **Lesson 1-10: Save a workbook.**

8

Session Eight: Cloud Computing

Cloud is about how you do computing, not where you do computing.

Paul Maritz, Computer Scientist and Software Executive

In this session you will learn how *Excel for Windows, Excel for the web, Office Mobile* and *OneDrive* work together to enable you to access Excel, and all your files, on any modern device, anywhere.

Cloud computing is one of the most rapidly evolving areas of Information Technology today. This session will show you how to make the most of this exciting new way of working.

Session Objectives

By the end of this session, you will be able to:

- Understand cloud computing
- Save a workbook to a OneDrive
- Open a workbook from a OneDrive
- Understand Office versions
- Understand Excel for the web
- Open a workbook using Excel for the web
- Share a link to a workbook
- Understand OneDrive AutoSave and Version History
- Edit a workbook simultaneously with other users using Excel for the web

Lesson 8-1: Understand cloud computing

First to mind when asked what 'the cloud' is, a majority respond it's either an actual cloud, the sky, or something related to weather.

Citrix Cloud Survey Guide (August 2012)

Cloud computing simply means the use of Internet-hosted files and applications

When you access Internet hosted applications such as Facebook, Twitter, Zoom, Skype, Google Search, or Amazon using a web browser you are experiencing cloud computing (the Internet is often referred to as "the cloud").

You can access modern cloud applications, without installing any software, by typing a simple URL into any modern web browser. True cloud applications will run on any device with a modern browser (including the iPad, PC, Apple Mac and nearly all tablets and smartphones).

Cloud applications (hosted in a web browser) often have rich functionality that rivals traditional desktop applications. This ability became possible with the 2014 release of HTML 5 (the markup language used by modern web browsers).

It is easy to envisage a future where you will never have to install an application onto your computer. You'll simply visit the application's URL and start using it immediately. Instead of saving files to your local hard drive, you'll save them to the cloud. Microsoft's "hard drive in the cloud" product is called *OneDrive*. (You'll learn to use a OneDrive later, in: *Lesson 8-2: Save a workbook to a OneDrive*).

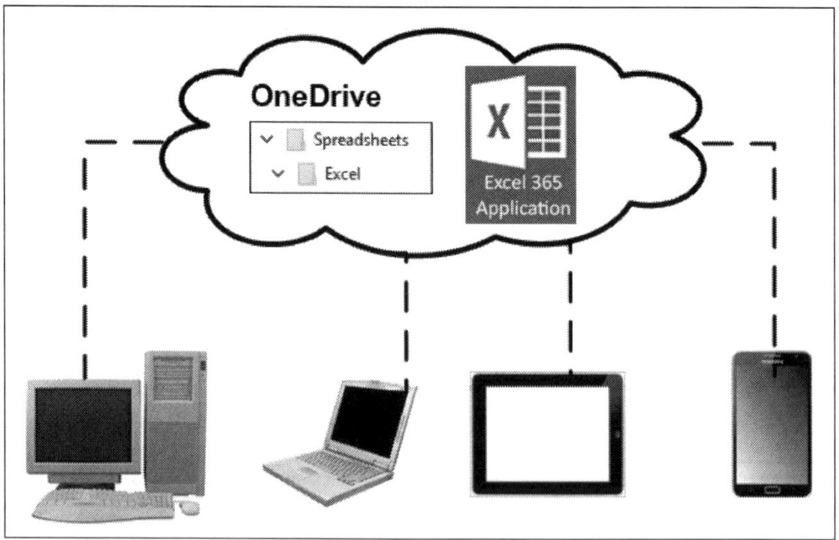

In the case of Microsoft Office, it is already possible to use a special limited-feature cloud version of Office (called *Office on the web*). You'll

note

Cloud computing and thin clients

Office on the web is a true cloud application. It was designed to be used without any software installation, on any device that supports a modern web browser.

The term "cloud computing" (in its modern context) was first used in 2006 (by the Google CEO Eric Schmidt).

There is a much older concept in the IT world called *thin client computing*.

Thin client computing allows traditional applications (written for desktop computers) to be deployed, unmodified, as cloud applications.

In the thin client model, the user doesn't use a web browser but installs a special thin client application.

The user then starts the thin client application and can effectively operate a computer located in the cloud by remote control. The user's computer sends keystrokes to the cloud computer. The cloud computer then returns a copy of the screen display back to the user.

Microsoft's *Remote Desktop Services (RDS)* and products from *Citrix Systems* are the most widely used thin client solutions.

The huge advantage of thin client implementations is that a company can continue to use the old desktop applications that they are used to.

Thin clients are very simple applications compared to sophisticated modern web browsers.

Browsers make better use of Internet bandwidth and usually provide a better user experience than thin client solutions.

learn about Office on the web later, in: *Lesson 8-5: Understand Excel for the web.*

Office on the web requires no installation and will run in any modern web browser. When you use *Office on the web*, you'll typically also store your files to the cloud (usually in a Microsoft OneDrive).

Advantages of cloud computing

Cloud computing promises many advantages over traditional IT implementations:

- Users can work anywhere using any device. They can continue their work while at the office, at home or on the road and will always have full access to their files.
- Companies will not need a dedicated IT department as support can be outsourced to technicians working at a remote data center.
- The responsibility for backups can be delegated to the data center. This reduces the possibility of data loss after hardware failure.
- Businesses will not need to concern themselves with keeping software and anti-virus measures up to date.
- Access to software will usually be purchased on a subscription basis. When a given piece of software isn't needed any more, the company can simply unsubscribe. This concept is often referred to as: *Software as a Service* (SaaS).
- Computers that only access cloud applications are inexpensive as they do not need powerful processors or large amounts of memory.
- If there is a major disaster (such as a fire or flood) the company's data remains safe and business can resume a lot faster.
- In the 2020/2022 Coronavirus health emergency companies that used cloud computing were able to instantly enable their workers to work from home.

anecdote

Latency

A long time ago (in the mid 1990's) I was involved in a very early implementation of a cloud project. It was so long ago that the term "cloud computing" wouldn't be invented for another ten years.

The multi-million-dollar project involved connecting a network of computers in Europe and Africa to a common database located in the United Kingdom.

We decided that a thin client solution (see facing page sidebar) was the most appropriate way to cater for the business requirement.

Testing went wonderfully well in European countries but when the software was rolled out to Africa there was a little problem.

The network link was routed via satellite. More specifically, a geostationary satellite located 22,236 miles above the Earth's surface (to achieve geostationary orbit).

The speed of light is approximately 186,000 miles per second. Unfortunately, this wasn't fast enough to prevent an infuriating lag between African users pressing a key and the corresponding letter appearing upon the screen.

This problem is referred to as *latency*. Geostationary satellites have a latency of around 600 milliseconds.

In late 2021 a new type of low-cost satellite link (called Starlink) became available to both home users and businesses.

Starlink is a US$10 billion project that aims to reduce latency by using 42,000 small satellites orbiting as low as 210 miles above the earth' surface.

The Starlink service can provide latency of below 20 milliseconds.

Lesson 8-2: Save a workbook to a OneDrive

To complete this lesson, you will need a OneDrive account. A free 5Gb OneDrive account was automatically created when you installed Office 2021.

A OneDrive can be visualized as a "hard drive in the sky". Saving a workbook to a OneDrive means you'll be able to access it from any device, anywhere in the world.

The files are usually stored on one of Microsoft's servers (accessed via the Internet). Some corporate users may prefer to store their OneDrive files on their own servers for security reasons (see sidebar facing page).

1 Open *Smartphone Sales* from your sample files folder.

2 Sign into your OneDrive account.

1. Click the *File* button  at the top-left of the screen.

2. Click: *Save As*  in the left-hand list.

3. Click *OneDrive* in the *Save As* menu.

You may be prompted to sign into your OneDrive account if you are not already logged in.

There may also be a *sign-up* link that will enable you to create a *Microsoft Account* if you don't already have one.

The right-hand side of the screen now gives you the ability to save the file to your OneDrive.

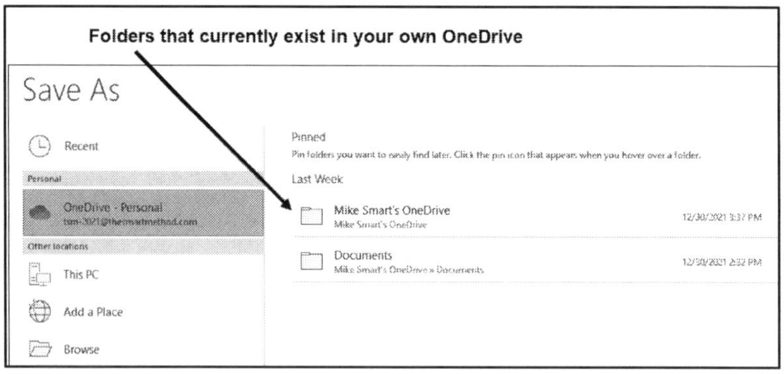

You may see different OneDrive folders as Microsoft change the default OneDrive folders from time to time.

When this book was written (in Jan 2022) the OneDrive had two folders by default called: *[Your Name]'s OneDrive* and *Documents.*

3 Save the workbook to your OneDrive in a folder called: **Documents\Excel\Practice**

1. Click the *Documents* folder icon.

note

OneDrive subscription types

Visit: https://OneDrive.com for current pricing and availability of all Microsoft OneDrive plans.

In Oct 2021 the following plans were available:

Free Account

The free OneDrive account does not have as many features as paid-for accounts and is limited to 5Gb of storage.

A free account is created when you install Office 2021.

OneDrive Standalone 100Gb

In January 2022 this plan cost $1.99 US/month and was available to Office 2021 users.

Office 365 Subscriber

The only way to expand storage beyond 100Gb is to subscribe to Office 365 (the subscription version of Microsoft Office).

As an Office 365 subscriber you will have One Terabyte (1,024 Gigabytes) of storage included as part of the Office 365 package.

OneDrive expanded storage for Office 365 subscribers

Office 365 subscribers can add up to an additional 1Tb to their OneDrive for a monthly subscription. In January 2022 you could add another 1Tb (making 2Tb in total) for an additional $9.99/month.

OneDrive for Business

OneDrive for Business provides more sophisticated file sharing within an organization.

OneDrive for Business is often deployed as a *Microsoft SharePoint* component (see facing page sidebar).

Smartphone Sales

note

OneDrive security concerns

When you store a file on your local hard drive, you can be reasonably sure that nobody else can access the contents (provided that they cannot gain access to your computer).

When you upload a file to a Microsoft OneDrive server you may worry that the file contents are vulnerable to theft.

Because a very reliable encryption method called SSL (Secure Sockets Layer) is used to transport files to and from the OneDrive, there isn't any realistic possibility of your file being intercepted when travelling to and from the Microsoft Servers.

Some users may worry that if Microsoft's servers are compromised your files might be accessed by others.

There are three potential solutions for users who have security concerns:

1. Encrypt your files before saving them to the OneDrive.

The *Expert Skills* book in this series comprehensively covers encryption of security-sensitive Excel files.

2. Host your own private OneDrive using *Microsoft SharePoint* along with the *OneDrive for Business* SharePoint component.

Once installed, *OneDrive for Business* can be used to store and access files on corporate servers in a similar way as you do on Microsoft's own OneDrive servers.

3. Use a competitive cloud provider that offers end-to-end file encryption. This type of encryption does not allow the cloud provider to have access to your auto-encrypted files.

A *Save As* dialog appears showing the contents of your OneDrive *Documents* folder (a local OneDrive folder is a standard feature of Windows 10 and Windows 11).

If you haven't used your OneDrive before the folder will be empty.

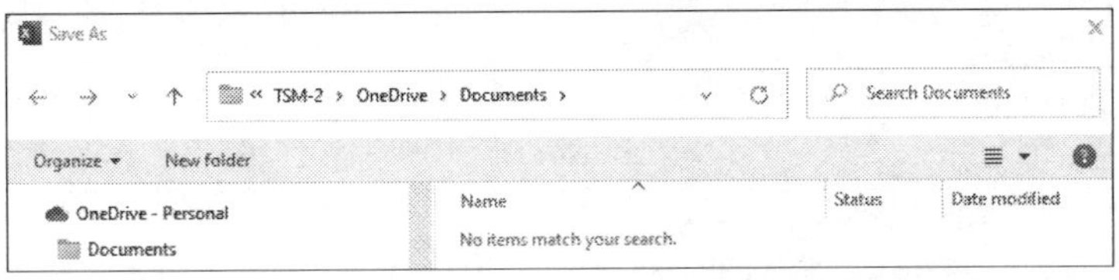

OneDrive folders are special because anything you save into them will be copied (via the Internet) to a matching *OneDrive* folder on a Microsoft server at one of Microsoft's data centers. With larger files, or with a slow Internet connection the synchronization process may take some time.

In *Lesson 1-12: Pin a workbook and understand file organization,* you learned why it is a good idea to place your Excel files into a separate folder within your local *Documents* folder. You will also create an *Excel* folder beneath the *Documents* folder on your OneDrive.

2. Right-click in the empty *Documents* folder and click: New→Folder from the shortcut menu.

3. Type **Excel** as the name of the new folder and press the **<Enter>** key.

4. Create a new OneDrive subfolder inside the newly created *Excel* folder and name it: **Practice**

5. Click: *Save* to save the *Smartphone Sales* workbook into the new *OneDrive\Documents\Excel\Practice* folder.

   The workbook is saved, and you are returned to the main Excel screen. (A help dialog may be displayed at this point).

   Files opened from a OneDrive are automatically saved as you work.

   You can disable this feature using the switch at the top left of your screen (shown above). You'll learn more about this feature later, in: *Lesson 8-8: Understand OneDrive AutoSave and Version History.*

4 Close Excel.

note

OneDrive alternatives

Excel 365 integrates OneDrive features into the *Save As* dialog.

There are similar rival services to OneDrive.

The biggest competitors are Dropbox, Google Drive, Apple iCloud and Amazon Drive.

Lesson 8-3: Open a workbook from a OneDrive

Once a workbook has been saved to a OneDrive it can be opened from absolutely anywhere, provided you are connected to the Internet.

In: *Lesson 8-6: Open a workbook using Excel for the web*, you'll discover that you can also open a workbook from any device that has a web browser (even if Excel 2021 is not installed on the device). This includes smartphones and tablets such as the iPad.

In this lesson you'll consider the scenario where you have a Windows PC at your office, and another Windows PC at home.

You want to be able to view and edit the same workbook on both computers.

1 Open Excel.

The start-up screen is displayed.

2 Open the *Smartphone Sales* sample file from your OneDrive.

Click: *Open* on the left-hand menu bar.

1. Click: *OneDrive - Personal* in the *Open* menu.

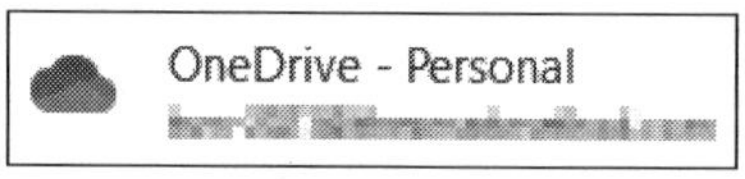

If you haven't already signed into your OneDrive account, you may now be prompted for an e-mail address and password.

You can now see your OneDrive folders on the right-hand side of the screen. You may see different folders in your own OneDrive.

2. Click the *Documents* folder.

You can now see the Excel sub-folder.

3. Click the *Excel* folder.

You can now see the *Practice* sub-folder.

4. Click the *Practice* folder.

You should see the previously saved *Smartphone Sales* file in the folder:

Smartphone Sales

note

Some of the advantages of using a OneDrive instead of a local drive

1. You can access your workbooks from any Internet connected device, anywhere in the world.

This means that you can work with your tablet device, smartphone or laptop when travelling, without having to copy files between devices.

2. You can share files with other users without having to e-mail the files to them.

You do this by sending a hyperlink to the other user rather than the file itself.

You'll discover more about this later, in: *Lesson 8-7: Share a link to a workbook.*

3. You can collaborate more easily with other users by giving certain users the right to edit your files.

4. You can allow users who do not have Excel installed upon their device to view, or even edit, your workbook.

You'll discover more about this later, in: *Lesson 8-5: Understand Excel for* the web.

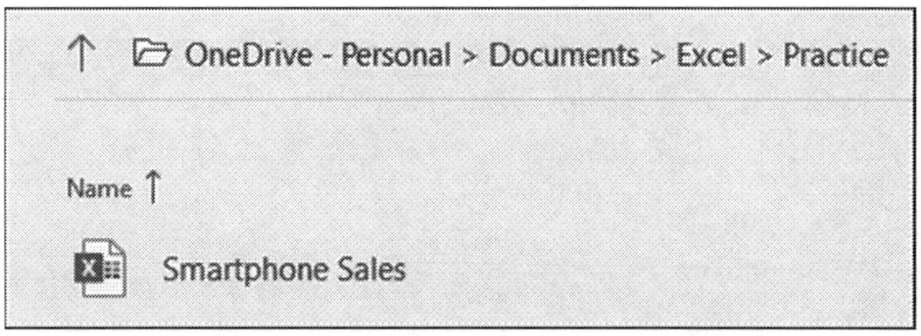

5. Click on the *Smartphone Sales* file to open it.
6. The *Smartphone Sales* workbook opens from the OneDrive:

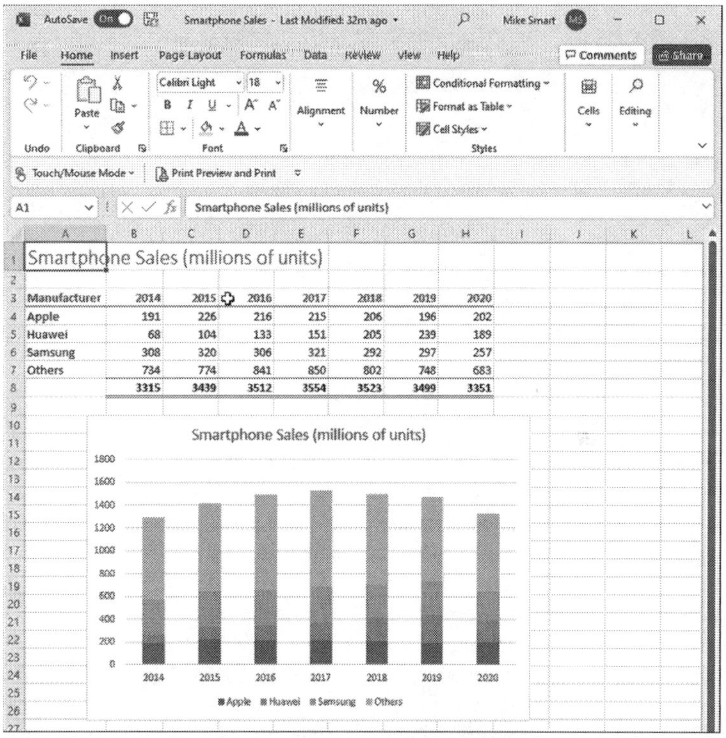

You can now use this technique to open the same workbook using any computer, anywhere in the world.

Later, in: *Lesson 8-6: Open a workbook using Excel for the web,* you'll learn how to open any workbook stored on your OneDrive from any device using only a web browser (even if Excel is not installed upon the device).

3 Close Excel.

Lesson 8-4: Understand Office versions

Office 365 and 2021 for Windows

This is the full (and most powerful) version of Office that only runs on the Windows 10 or 11 operating system (including *Windows 10 or 11 for ARM – see sidebar*).

Office 2021 will never have any new features added to it during its lifetime while Office 365 is improved with new features often added each month.

Office 365 and 2021 for Mac

Microsoft produce a version of Office that runs on the Apple *macOS* operating system (used on Apple desktop and laptop computers).

The *Excel 2021 for Mac* and *Excel 365 for Mac* versions have a reduced feature set compared to the Windows versions of Excel.

We've produced a different version of our 2019 books that are suitable for Apple Mac users but do not currently have plans to publish any more Excel for Mac books.

Learn Excel 2019 Essential Skills for Mac with The Smart Method
ISBN: 978-1-909253-32-2

The Office app

The Office app was launched in February 2020 and combines Word, Excel and PowerPoint into a single app. The app is aimed at mobile phone users rather than devices with larger screens.

The app runs on both the Android and iOS operating systems (meaning most mobile phones and tablet devices).

The mobile version of Excel has limited features and is most useful to perform minor edits to workbooks created with the full desktop version.

The Office app is free for personal use but you will need an Office 365 subscription to unlock a small number of premium features. If you don't have an Office 365 subscription you will not be able to edit documents on devices with a screen size greater than 10.1 inches.

At time of writing, (in Jan 2022) it was also possible to download individual mobile versions of Excel, Word and PowerPoint. These versions share the same codebase as the Office app.

It seems likely that the Office app will eventually replace the individual standalone mobile apps.

Excel for the web is far more powerful than the Excel version included in the Office Mobile app and will usually be a better choice if offline access isn't important to you.

note

Windows 11 for ARM

Tablet computers and smartphones need to have a long battery life, slim profile and light weight.

This means that they mostly use processors that support a more limited instruction set than desktop computers called ARM.

Windows 11 for ARM can run on most modern ARM devices.

At time of writing (in Jan 2022) Windows 11 for ARM (and thus the full version of Microsoft Office) was available on many ultralight PC's including the HP Elite Folio, Lenovo Flex 5G, Acer Spin 7, Surface Pro X and Samsung Galaxy Book Go.

While there is no technical barrier to installing the Windows 11 for ARM operating system on a mobile phone it is unlikely that you'll ever see a Windows phone manufacturer offer this option.

Windows 11 is designed for use on desktop and tablet computers rather than small screen devices.

Excel for the web

Excel for the web (previously called Excel Online) is part of the *Office on the web* suite.

This free (for personal use) web version does not have all of the features found in the desktop version, but is surprisingly feature-rich and is continuously improved and upgraded.

Excel for the web is designed to be used on larger devices (such as tablet and desktop computers) and is a true cloud application providing many advantages over traditional applications (see sidebar).

This application is also useful when sharing documents with users that do not have Excel installed on their device.

Excel for the web will be discussed in depth in: *Lesson 8-5: Understand Excel for the web.*

Office version availability (at Jan 2022)

Device	Office 365/2021 for Windows	Office 365/2021 for Mac	Office Mobile	Office on the web
Windows 10/11 PC or tablet computer	X			X
Apple Mac		X		X
Apple iPad			X	X
Apple iPhone			X	X
Android Tablet			X	X
Android Phone			X	X

Note that Office Mobile does not support all Android devices.

note

Office on the web supported web browsers

Office on the web explicitly supports the latest versions of the Chrome, Firefox, Safari and Microsoft Edge.

Browser technology is one of the fastest-moving areas of Information Technology. For this reason, it is vital that you use the latest version of your browser. Most browsers will update themselves automatically unless you specifically switch off automatic updates.

note

Advantages of cloud applications

Operating system independence

Cloud applications don't care what operating system your device is using as they run inside a web browser.

Almost every modern smartphone, tablet computer, laptop computer and personal computer has at least one of the supported browsers available.

No installation required

Because cloud applications reside on an Internet server (usually referred to as "in the cloud") no software installation is needed.

Always up to date

Cloud applications are always up to date because you are always accessing the latest version published in the cloud.

The main disadvantage of cloud applications is that you must be connected to the Internet to use them.

Lesson 8-5: Understand Excel for the web

Excel 2021 and 365 for Windows desktop applications

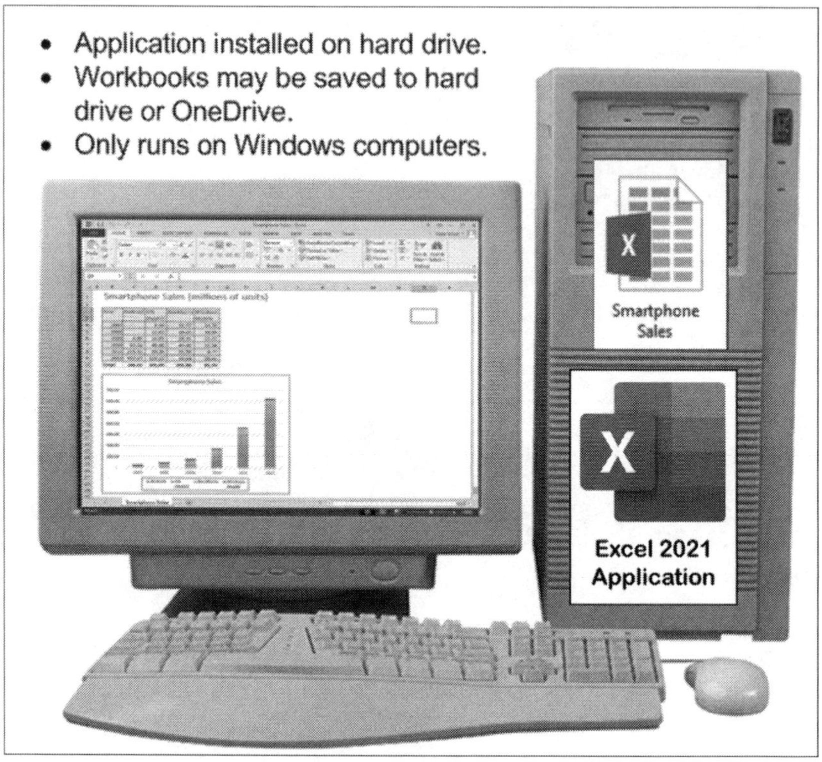

The *Excel 2021 for Windows* and *Excel 365 for Windows* desktop applications are conventional locally installed applications.

- You need to purchase a license to use the desktop applications.
- You need to install the desktop application software onto your computer before you can use it.
- The desktop applications will only run on a computer using the Windows 10 or 11 operating system.
- Workbooks may be saved to (and opened from) either the local hard drive or a OneDrive.

Excel 365 and 2021 for Mac desktop applications

The *Excel 365 for Mac* and *Excel 2021 for Mac* desktop applications run on the *macOS* (previously called *Apple OS X*) operating system found on Apple desktop and laptop computers.

Excel 365 for Mac and *Excel 2021 for Mac* have reduced feature sets compared to the more powerful Windows versions of Excel.

Excel for the web

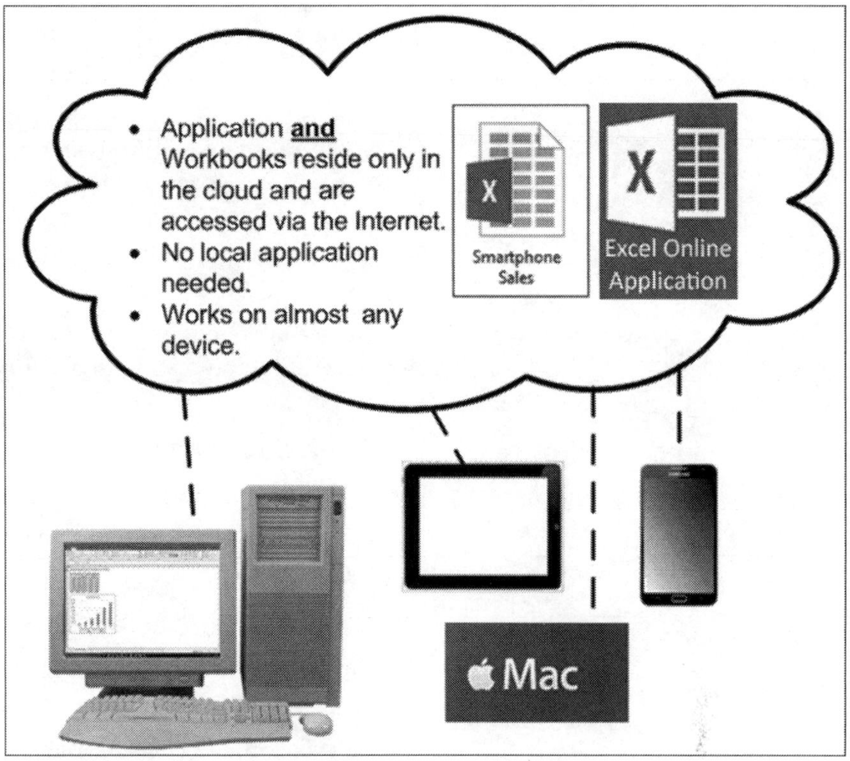

Excel for the web is a cloud application that runs inside a web browser. This means:

- You don't need to purchase a license to use Excel for the web.
- You don't need to install any software to use Excel for the web.
- Because a cloud app doesn't directly communicate with the operating system, Excel for the web will run on any device that has a supported web browser. This includes the Windows PC, Apple Mac, iPad and almost all recent tablet and smartphone devices.
- Excel for the web has fewer features than the desktop versions (Excel 2021 and Excel 365).

Excel for the web makes it possible to share a workbook with just about anybody

If you e-mail a copy of a workbook to another user (as an attachment), you have to assume that the recipient has a Windows computer with a compatible version of Excel installed.

When you send a user a link to a workbook stored on your OneDrive it will open using *Excel for the web*. You can then be confident that the user will almost certainly be able to open the workbook. You'll learn how to share links that open using Excel for the web later, in: *Lesson 8-7: Share a link to a workbook.*

The recipient of a link can have any type of device (such as a Windows PC, Windows Surface tablet, Apple Mac, iPad tablet, Android tablet, Chromebook or even a Smartphone) and does not have to have a copy of Excel installed.

Lesson 8-6: Open a workbook using Excel for the web

Now that you have saved a workbook to your OneDrive, you can use *Excel for the web* to open it from any device that has a supported web browser (see facing page sidebar). This includes most recent smartphones, tablet devices and personal computers. Even if the device does not have Excel installed, you will be able to view and edit the workbook using the free *Excel for the web* cloud application.

If you have a tablet computer (such as an iPad), or recent smartphone, you might find it interesting to use this device (rather than your Windows PC) for this lesson.

1 Open *Smartphone Sales* from a web browser using Excel for the web.

1. Open a web browser on your PC (or ideally using another device).
2. Enter the url: **https://OneDrive.com**
3. If necessary, click the *Sign in* link and enter your Microsoft Account username and password to log in.
4. Click the *Documents* folder. (If you are using a smartphone or tablet computer, see sidebar for the touchscreen gesture that simulates a left click).
5. Click the *Excel* folder. You created this folder in: *Lesson 8-1: Understand cloud computing.*
6. Click the *Practice* folder.

   You will now see the *Smartphone Sales* workbook that you saved in: *Lesson 8-1: Understand cloud computing.*

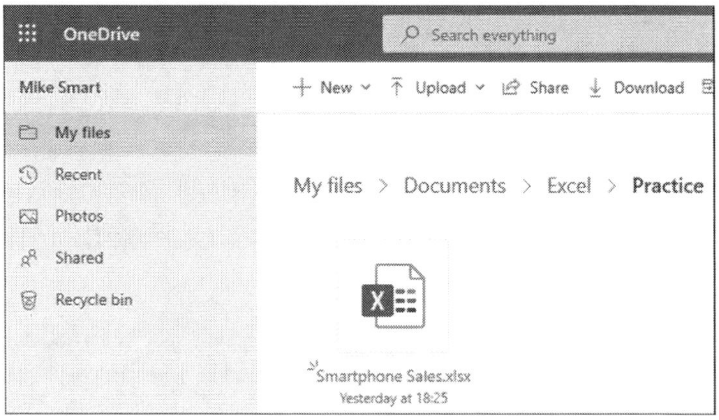

7. Hover the mouse cursor over *Smartphone Sales.*

   The icon changes and includes a white circle to allow selection.
8. Click on the white circle

   The white circle now contains a tick to show that this workbook is selected.

   Click *Open* on the top menu and then *Open in Excel Online* from the drop-down list.

note

Touchscreen gestures

Touchscreen devices (such as tablet computers and smartphones) do not usually have a mouse.

When using a touchscreen, you can use the following gestures to work with Excel for the web:

Left click: Tap the touchscreen.

Right click: Touch and hold your finger on the touchscreen.

Scroll: Touch a blank area of the workbook and slide your finger in the direction you wish to scroll in.

Zoom in: Touch two points on the touchscreen and then move your fingers away from each other. (This is normally done with the thumb and forefinger).

Zoom out: Touch two points on the touchscreen and then move your fingers towards each other.

Select text: Tap on the text to place the insertion point. If it is in the wrong place, tap again to move it. Drag the circular handles (called *grippers*) to select.

Smartphone Sales

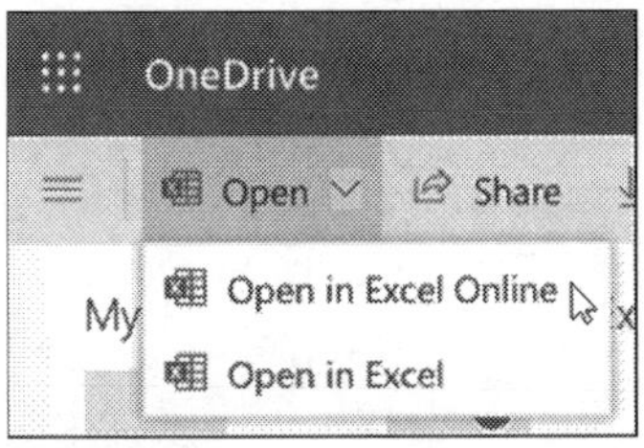

Note that when this lesson was written (in Jan 2022) *Excel for the web* was still showing its old name (Excel Online). By the time you read this book it may have been updated to *Excel for the web* (see sidebar).

In a real-world situation you'd usually select *Open in Excel* (if it was available) because Excel has more features and is faster than Excel for the web. For the purposes of this lesson, you have opened the file using *Excel for the web* so that you can share the experience of a user who does not have Excel installed on their device.

The *Smartphone Sales* workbook opens in *Excel for the web*.

2 Show the full Ribbon.

Click the downward pointing chevron on the bottom-right of the Ribbon. This is the *Switch Ribbons* button.

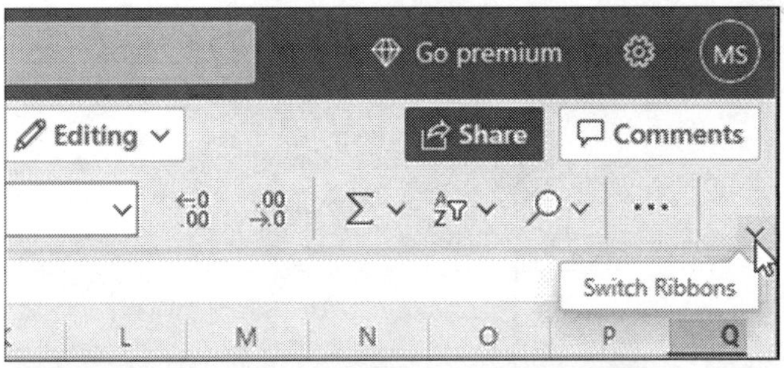

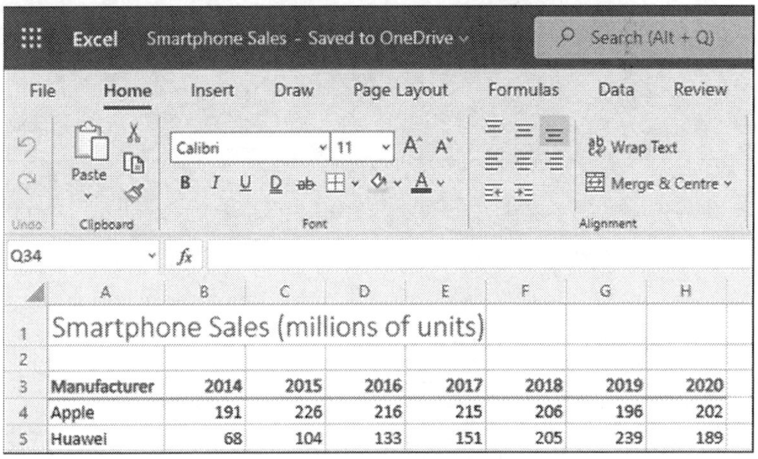

Excel for the web looks very much like the desktop Excel application. Many (but not all) of Excel's features are now available from the Ribbon.

3 Close your web browser.

note

Excel for the web used to be called *Excel Online*

In July 2019 Microsoft announced that they were changing the name of *Excel Online* to *Excel for the web.*

Microsoft sometimes also use other names when referring to *Excel for the web* including:

- Excel on the web
- Excel on Office.com
- Excel in a browser

note

Supported web browsers

Excel for the web is only supported by recent versions of the four most commonly used browsers: Microsoft Edge, Chrome, Safari and Firefox.

Almost all recent devices (such as the Windows PC, Apple Mac, iPad, Android tablet, Microsoft Surface and most smartphones) can run at least one of the supported browsers.

Microsoft Edge is always the best browser to use if it is available. If not, use the latest version of Chrome, Firefox or Safari.

If you find that *Excel for the web* does not work correctly with one of the supported browsers, try again using a different supported browser.

note

OneDrive for Business offers more sophisticated security

If you see a different sharing dialog you may be using *OneDrive for Business.*

The standard OneDrive product only supports the concept of a *public link.* The links you share work just like an e-mail attachment. Any user who has the link can forward it or share it with others.

OneDrive for Business supports the concept of a private link. This enables you to share files with one or more named users.

If you save a file to a *Personal OneDrive* and then try to share the file, you will see the dialogs discussed in this lesson.

If you save a file to *OneDrive for Business* and then try to share the file, you will see this dialog:

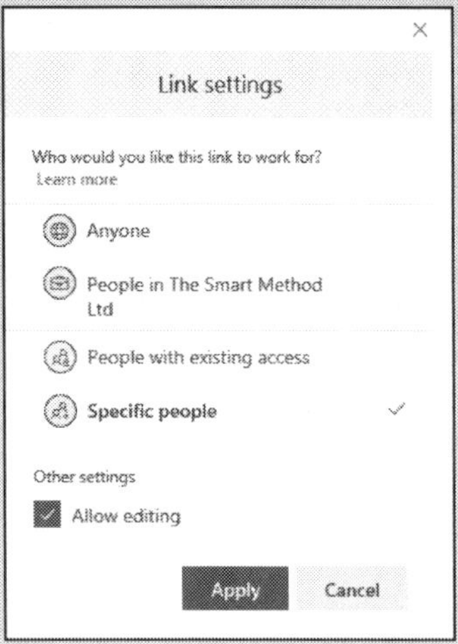

You are then able to send a link that will only work for a specified user (identified by e-mail address). The user must have a Microsoft account.

When *OneDrive for Business* is hosted as a SharePoint component, administrators may choose to only allow link sharing with users within their own organization.

Smartphone Sales

Lesson 8-7: Share a link to a workbook

When your workbooks are stored on a OneDrive, it is possible to share them without sending a physical copy of the file to the recipients. This is done by distributing a simple hyperlink to the recipient.

There are two types of sharing link:

View-only Link: This gives read-only access to anybody that has the link. The user does not have to log in to OneDrive and can open the workbook on any device, even if Excel is not installed. This is usually the only type of link that is appropriate for a Facebook page, Twitter tweet, blog or web page.

Edit Link: This gives read-write access to anybody that has the link. This is the type of link you will need to use for online collaboration (when a group of users can all edit the same worksheet at the same time).

You'll use this type of link later, in: *Lesson 8-8: Understand OneDrive AutoSave and Version History.* Edit links can be more safely shared using OneDrive for Business (see sidebar).

1 Open Excel.

The start-up screen is displayed.

2 Open the *Smartphone Sales* sample file from your OneDrive.

This is the file that you saved in: *Lesson 8-2: Save a workbook to a OneDrive.*

3 Create a link that will enable any user with the link to open (but not change) the workbook.

1. Click the *Share* button at the top right of the screen.

The *Send Link* task pane appears (see sidebar if a different dialog appears).

2. The box at the top of the dialog will show one of the two messages shown below:

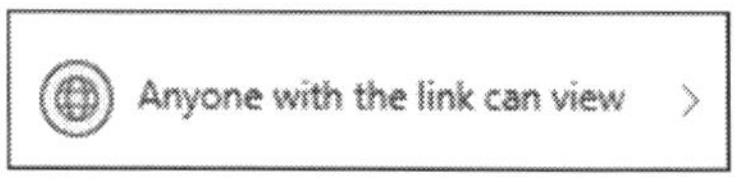

A *View-only link* allows anyone with the link to view the workbook (but they cannot change it in any way).

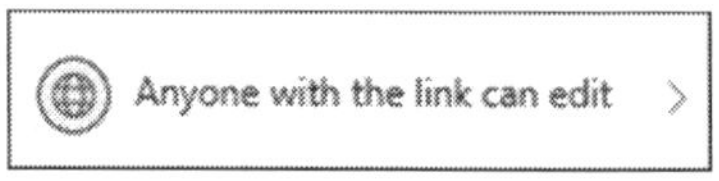

An *Edit link* allows anyone with the link to both view and edit the workbook. You should be very careful about who you share this type of link with.

All links work just like an e-mail attachment. Any user who has the link can forward it or share it with others. OneDrive for Business offers a more secure type of link sharing (see facing page sidebar).

3. Copy a *view-only link* to the clipboard.

   If you see the "Anyone with a link can edit" button you need to click on the button and clear the *Allow Editing* check box:

   .. and then click the *Apply* button

4. Click the *Copy Link* button.

4 Test the link.

1. Open a web browser.
2. Put your browser into *Incognito Mode* (Google Chrome) or open a *Private Window* (Firefox, Edge). If you can't figure out how to do this consult your browser's documentation.

   When in Incognito/Private mode your browser will not be able to establish that you are logged in to OneDrive, enabling you to test the link as if you were an anonymous user.

   You need to do this because while you are logged in to your OneDrive you will always have full access to your own files. This means that even though the link is read-only (a view link) you would still be able to edit the file as if it were an edit link.
3. Paste the link (that you previously copied) into the address bar of the web browser and press then **<Enter>** key.

   The workbook opens in *Excel for the web.*
4. Try to type a value into one of the worksheet cells.

   Notice the warning at the top of the window:

   This is displayed because you created a view link that does not allow the recipient to edit the workbook. Note that the user is still able to save (and then edit or further share) a local read/write copy of your workbook.

   Later, in: *Lesson 8-9: Edit a workbook simultaneously with other users using Excel for the web*, you'll create and use an edit link.

5 Close Excel for the web.

note

How to set an expiration date or password for a OneDrive link

Users of social media often forget that anything written online can be potentially found many years in the future.

For this reason, many users set an expiry date or password for OneDrive links.

Here's how it is done:

1. Click the *Share* button at the top right of the Excel screen.

2. Click on the first button:

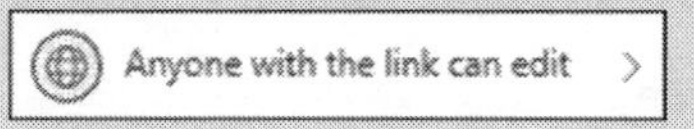

You can now see three options for the link:

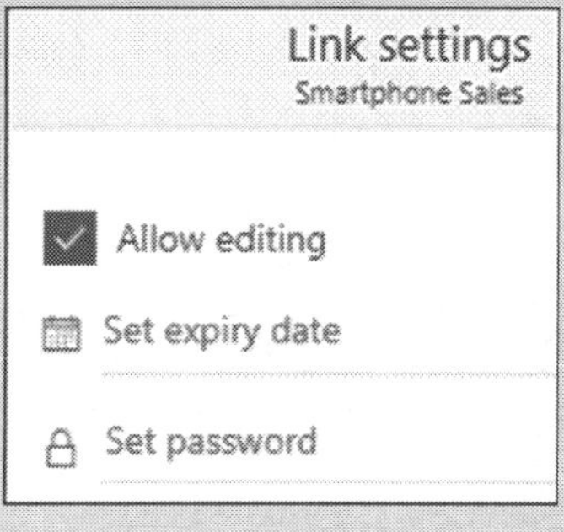

Lesson 8-8: Understand OneDrive AutoSave and Version History

note

How to switch AutoSave off by default

AutoSave will be switched on by default for any file that resides upon a OneDrive.

If you would like to change this default (to off) proceed as follows:

1. Click: File→Options→Save.

2. In the *Save Workbooks* group, clear the check box from the option:

AutoSave OneDrive and SharePoint Online files by default on Excel.

You'll need to restart Excel for this change to take effect.

AutoSave

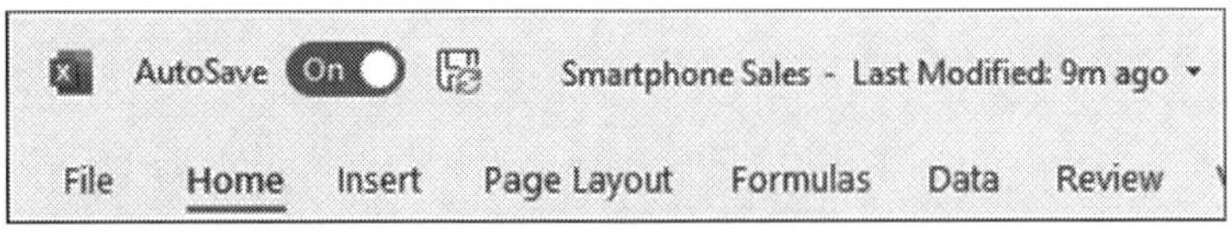

The AutoSave feature is only enabled when a file is stored on a OneDrive.

Any changes you make to a document are automatically saved every few seconds, meaning that (when working with a OneDrive) there's no need to save your work.

When working with AutoSave switched on (the default) the save option is removed from the *File* menu bar (as it is no longer required). Instead, you'll see a *Save a Copy* option (enabling you to save a local copy of your OneDrive file).

If you'd prefer to work with OneDrive as if it were a traditional disk drive (where you have control of when your work is saved) you can use the AutoSave switch shown above to switch this feature off.

Version History

The *Undo* feature discussed in: *Lesson 3-8: Use Undo and Redo* allows you to undo recent changes.

Version History goes a lot further than this, allowing you to revert to any previous version of the workbook. This is a different (and far more powerful) feature than the *Versions* feature that you used in: *Lesson 1-15: Use the Versions feature to recover an earlier version of a workbook.*

You can display the *Version History* task pane by clicking:

File→Info→Version History.

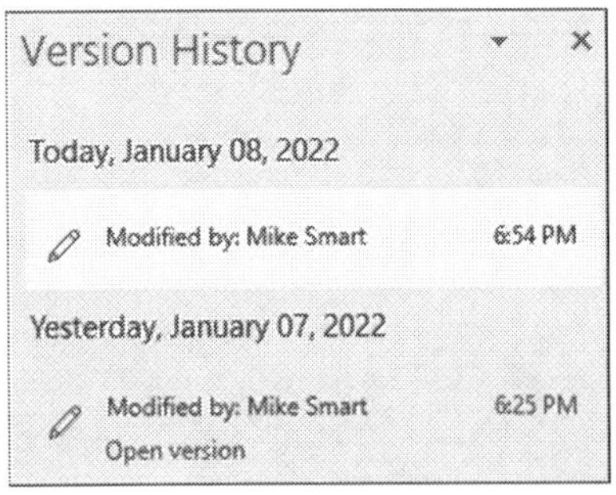

When you do this, you are returned to the workbook with the *Version History* task pane enabled. An example of a file's version history is shown in the sidebar. Note that you are able to identify the person who made each change to the workbook.

You can click upon any previous version of a file to make this version into the current version of the file.

How long are old versions kept for?

If you are using the standard version of OneDrive the version history is retained for 30 days and then automatically deleted. It isn't possible to change this setting.

If your organization uses the *OneDrive for Business* component deployed within SharePoint, your administrator can set the amount of time that older versions are kept before deletion to any duration required.

important

All browsers are not equal

Excel Online officially supports Microsoft's own Edge browser along with the Chrome, Safari and Firefox browsers.

You can always expect Excel Online to work perfectly with the *Microsoft Edge* browser. That's because Microsoft have full control over updates to their own browser and will test Excel Online with each browser (and Excel) update before release.

Users often report glitches with other browsers after they are updated (and browsers are usually updated very frequently).

For this reason, always use Excel Online with the Microsoft Edge browser if it is available.

If you use a different supported browser and it does not work, try using a different supported browser (they are all free to download).

For example, if you run into a problem with Firefox, try again using Chrome or Safari.

Lesson 8-9: Edit a workbook simultaneously with other users using Excel for the web

When working with Excel for the web you never have to save

In: *Lesson 8-8: Understand OneDrive AutoSave and Version History* you learned that *Excel for the web* automatically saves every few seconds meaning that (when working with a OneDrive) there's no need to save your work.

This feature provides an unexpected benefit.

If several users are all working with the same workbook (and the workbook is stored on a OneDrive with AutoSave enabled), any change made (by any user) will magically, and almost instantly, appear on every other user's screen.

This provides a completely new (and better) way of collaborating with other users.

1 Open the *Smartphone Sales* sample file from your OneDrive using Excel (not Excel for the web).

This is the file that you saved in: *Lesson 8-1: Understand cloud computing.*

2 Make sure that AutoSave is switched on.

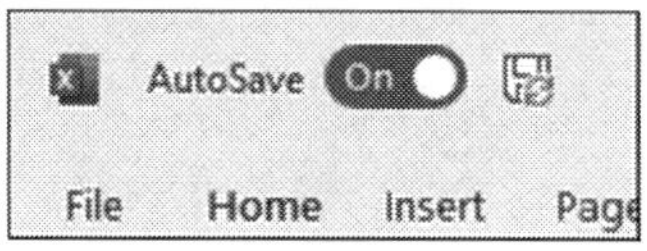

The AutoSave button should be visible at the top left of your screen. AutoSave is switched on by default (if you have switched it off the collaboration feature will not work).

3 Create a public *Edit* link and copy it.

You learned how to do this in: *Lesson 8-7: Share a link to a workbook.* Make sure that you create an *Edit link* rather than a *View-only* link.

Any user of an edit link will be able to both view and edit the workbook via Excel for the web.

4 Open a web browser in incognito or private mode.

Put your browser into Incognito Mode (Google Chrome) or open a Private Window (Firefox, Edge). If you can't figure out how to do this consult your browser's documentation.

When in Incognito/Private mode your browser will not be able to establish that you are logged in to OneDrive, enabling you to test the link as if you were a different user.

5 Use the *Edit Link* to open *Smartphone* Sales in your web browser.

Paste the edit link into the web browser's address bar and press the **<Enter>** key.

The workbook opens using *Excel for the web.*

6 Click: Viewing→Editing.

By default, Excel for the web will open the file in *Viewing* (read only) mode. You need to change this to *Editing* mode in order to make changes.

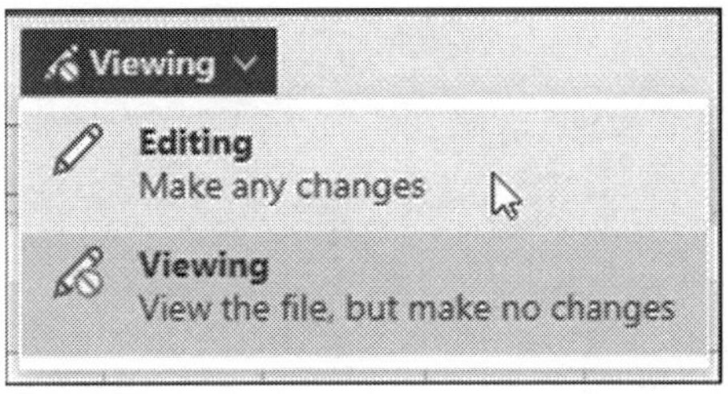

Excel may now prompt you to enter your Microsoft Account name and password. If it does you may have to close your browser (and any other browser windows that are open) and then re-open your brower.

7 Arrange the Excel and web browser windows side-by-side on your screen.

You have now simulated two users (who could be thousands of miles away from each other) viewing the same workbook simultaneously.

Any changes made to the workbook by either user will almost instantly appear on the screen of the other user.

8 Make a change to the workbook in one of the windows.

Notice that the change appears (almost instantly) in the other window's screen.

Perhaps many users will be collaborating in real-time. Note that, in this scenario, any user who is not viewing the workbook in *Edit* mode will not see any changes made by other users unless they refresh the browser window.

9 Close the web browser.

There is no need to save the workbook. Your changes were automatically saved to the OneDrive as you made them.

note

The cell comment feature is useful when you are collaborating with other users

In: *Lesson 3-12: Insert and delete cell comments,* you learned how to use the new cell comment feature.

Cell comments can be interactively edited when collaborating with other users opening many interesting possibilities.

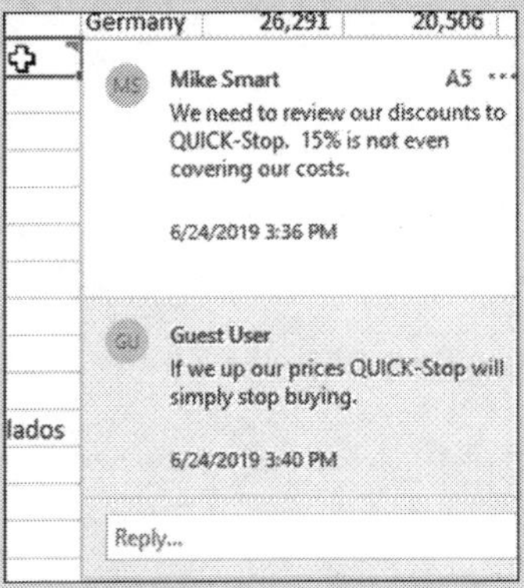

OneDrive for business has a new @mentions feature

To use the new @mentions feature your workbook must be stored on SharePoint or OneDrive for Business and you must have desktop Outlook installed on your computer.

If our configuration is as above, you are able type @ into a comment and then begin typing the recipient's name. You are then prompted with a list of your contacts.

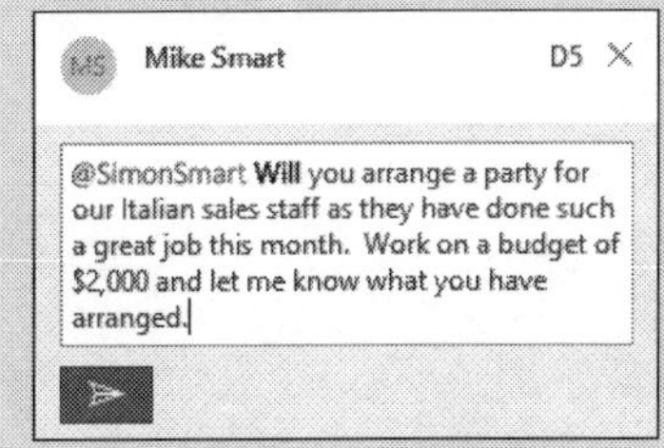

Excel will then automatically send them an e-mail with a sharing link (that will open the workbook using Excel Online).

Session 8: Exercise

1 **Open *Broadband Speeds* from your sample files folder.**

2 **Create a new sub-folder in your OneDrive documents folder called: Exercise 8**

3 **Save the *Broadband Speeds* workbook into the */Documents/Exercise 8* folder of your OneDrive.**

4 **Create a *View Link* and an *Edit Link* for the *Broadband Speeds* workbook.**

If you have a slow Internet connection, you may have to wait a few seconds until synchronization completes before you are able to do this.

5 **Close Excel 2021.**

6 **Use the *Edit Link* to open the *Broadband Speeds* workbook using *Excel for the web.***

7 **Enable editing within Excel for the web.**

8 **Change the *Average Speed (Mbs)* for *Thailand* (cell B11) to: 299.00 and press the <Enter> key.**

9 **Close the web browser.**

10 **Open the desktop Excel 2021 application.**

11 **Open *Broadband Speeds* from your OneDrive.**

Note that the average speed for Thailand is now 299.00 Mbs.

12 **Change the *Average Speed (Mbs)* for *Thailand back* to: 223.69.**

13 **Close Excel.**

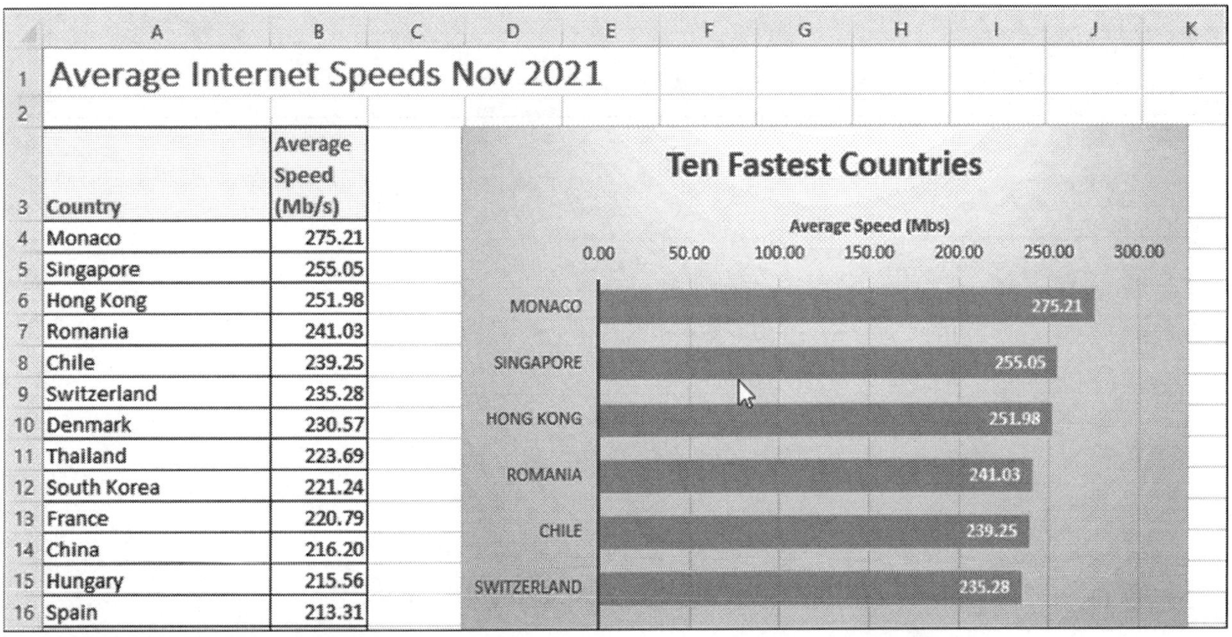

Broadband Speeds

Session 8: Exercise answers

These are the questions that students find the most difficult to answer:

Q 7	Q 4	Q 2
1. Click the *Viewing* button on the *Excel for the web* ribbon. 2. Select *Editing* from the drop-down list. 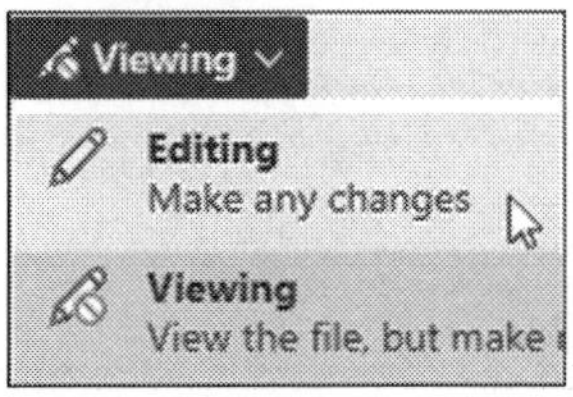 This was covered in: *Lesson 8-9: Edit a workbook simultaneously with other users using Excel for the web.*	1. Click the *Share* button at the top right of the screen.  The *Share* dialog appears. 2. Click: *Copy link* at the bottom of the dialog. 3. Click the *Share* button at the top-right of the screen again. 4. Click the *Anyone with a link can edit* button. 5. Uncheck the *Allow editing* check box and click *Apply.* 6. Click: *Copy link* at the bottom of the dialog. This was covered in: *Lesson 8-7: Share a link to a workbook.*	1. Click: File→Save As. 2. Click: *OneDrive* in the *Save As* menu. 3. Click on the *Documents* folder. 4. Right-click in a blank area inside the *Documents* folder and select: *New Folder* from the shortcut menu. 5. Type: **Exercise 8** as the name of the new folder. This was covered in: *Lesson 8-2: Save a workbook to a OneDrive.*

If you have difficulty with the other questions, here are the lessons that cover the relevant skills:

1,10	**Lesson 1-9: Open and navigate a workbook.**
3	**Lesson 8-2: Save a workbook to a OneDrive**
5	**Lesson 1-1: Start Excel and open a new blank workbook.**
6	**Lesson 8-8: Understand OneDrive AutoSave and Version History.**
8,9	**Lesson 8-8: Understand OneDrive AutoSave and Version History.**
11	**Lesson 8-3: Open a workbook from a OneDrive.**
12	**Lesson 2-1: Enter text and numbers into a worksheet.**
13	**Lesson 1-7: Maximize, minimize, re-size, move and close the Excel window.**

Index

G

H

I

J

K

L

M

N

O

P

Q

R

T

U

V

W

X

Z

Moving to the next level

The next book in the series (Expert Skills) covers only the most advanced Excel features

The Expert Skills book teaches Excel to an extremely high level of competence that is very rarely found in the workplace (even amongst top professionals).

At Expert level your skills will be greater and broader than almost all other Excel users and you will understand (and be able to use) absolutely every Excel feature. You'll have a complete mastery of skills that are often even a mystery to Excel power users.

This book will be available during **February 2022** as both a paper printed book and e-book.

The full course outline for the *Expert Skills* book can be viewed on the https://thesmartmethod.com web site.

Use your new Excel skills to teach your own classroom courses

If you've worked through this book carefully you will now have excellent Excel skills and if you progress to the *Expert Skills* book in the series, you'll be a true Excel expert. There is a huge demand, everywhere in the world, for Excel training at all levels. The skills you have learned in this book will enable you to teach an introductory Excel course (providing all of the skills needed by most office workers).

This book is available for all Excel versions in common use (Excel 2013, 2016, 2019, 2021 and 365 for Windows along with Excel 2016 & 2019 for Apple Mac). You can use the books as courseware during your classes and then give each student a copy of the book to take home as reference material when the course is over.

Windows Perpetual Titles

978-1-909253-52-0

978-1-909253-51-3

978-1-909253-35-3

978-1-909253-34-6

978-1-909253-09-4

978-1-909253-08-7

978-1-909253-16-2

978-1-909253-15-5

Mac Titles

978-1-909253-32-2

978-1-909253-33-9

978-1-909253-21-6

978-1-909253-22-3

Office 365 Titles

978-1-909253-47-6

978-1-909253-48-3

A new edition of the Excel 365 book is published whenever there are significant Excel 365 feature updates.

You can quote the ISBN numbers shown above to any book retailer or wholesaler. All major distributors (in every country of the world) have our books in stock for immediate delivery.

Place a direct order for 5+ books for wholesale prices and free delivery worldwide

To place a publisher-direct order you only need to order five books or more (of the same title). To view wholesale prices, go to this web page: https://thesmartmethod.com/wholesale-printed-books

Made in the USA
Monee, IL
08 November 2026

67816237R00210